STATE AND SOCIETY IN CHINA

STATE AND SOCIETY IN CHINA

Japanese Perspectives on
Ming-Qing Social and Economic History

Edited by
Linda Grove and Christian Daniels

UNIVERSITY OF TOKYO PRESS

The translation and publication of this volume were supported by a grant-in-aid from the Ministry of Education, Science and Culture.

© 1984 UNIVERSITY OF TOKYO PRESS
ISBN 4-13-026042-1 (UTP 26422)
ISBN 0-86008-356-X

Printed in Japan

CONTENTS

Preface vii

Introduction 3
The Formation of the Early Chinese Cotton Industry
    Nishijima Sadao 17
Rural Handicraft in Jiangnan in the Sixteenth and Seventeeth
    Centuries
    Tanaka Masatoshi 79
Large Landownership in the Jiangnan Delta Region
    During the Late Ming-Early Qing Period
    Oyama Masaaki 101
Popular Uprisings, Rent Resistance, and
    Bondservant Rebellions in the Late Ming
    Tanaka Masatoshi 165
The Other Side of Rent and Tax Resistance Struggles:
    Ideology and the Road to Rebellion
    Kobayashi Kazumi 215
Rural Control in the Ming Dynasty
    Tsurumi Naohiro 245
Reforms in the Service Levy System in the
    Fifteenth and Sixteenth Centuries
    Yamane Yukio 279
An Introduction to the *Shandong jinghui lu*
    Iwami Hiroshi 311
The Origins and Structure of Gentry Rule
    Shigeta Atsushi 335
Foreign Trade Finance in China, 1810–50
    Hamashita Takeshi 387

Reign Periods of the Ming and Qing Periods 437
Measure Equivalents 437

v

Glossary 439
Bibliography 453
Index 485

Maps following p. x and on p. 180.

PREFACE

The last few years have seen a mini-boom in the publication of works in English on Ming-Qing history and society. A careful reading of the arguments and footnotes of much of that work reveals the large intellectual debts that many scholars owe to the Japanese professors and colleagues with whom they have studied. Through the books and articles of such younger western scholars, some of the analytical approaches of Japanese historians have been presented indirectly to a foreign audience. The work of a few Japanese scholars has also been translated into English, but with a few rare exceptions the translations have either appeared in little-known journals or been so hastily done as to be almost incomprehensible to the English reader.

We believe that the outstanding accomplishments of Japanese scholars in the field of Ming-Qing history can contribute a great deal to the creation of a more solidly founded and broadly based interpretation of Chinese society. In general, the strengths of Japanese scholarship lie in fields in which the Western—and particularly the American—tradition is weakest, i.e., social and economic history. For this reason we believe that the essays translated here will be of particular interest to a non-Japanese audience. Many of the issues discussed in these essays have also been the subject of great controversy among historians of Europe. Those interested in comparative history should also find here much information that can help to establish the basis for fuller comparison of development in China and Europe.

Given the wealth of material available, selection of the articles for translation was difficult. Anyone familiar with Japanese Ming-Qing studies could probably come up with a separate list of articles equally worthy of translation. In making our selections we tried to follow a set of guidelines that included the enduring nature of the contribution and its role in setting the parameters for later theoretical and empirical discussion. We also tried to include scholars whose work has not yet appeared in English. This last consideration led us to exclude the work of a number of outstanding scholars whose work has already been translated elsewhere.

With the exception of the essay by Iwami Hiroshi, all of the selections are drawn from authors who are part of what is often called the "Tokyo school." We made this choice, partly because our own contacts have been with members of the "Tokyo school," and partly because their work has been largely neglected in the West. This neglect may be partly the result of the strong attraction that life in Kyoto, the old Japanese capital, holds for many foreign scholars. Until quite recently, most foreign graduate students and research scholars chose life in Kyoto over Tokyo, and as a result there seems to be a much greater familiarity with the work of such "Kyoto school" scholars as Miyazaki Ichisada and Shimada Kenji. In addition, many of the Kyoto scholars are more interested in contemporary Western social science theory than in Marxism and political economy, and as a result their approaches are often quite close to those of Western scholars.

In making our selection, we first consulted with a group of senior Japanese scholars, each of whom provided a list of articles that he thought had been most important in shaping Japanese understanding of the Ming-Qing period. There was a suprisingly high degree of general agreement among our Japanese advisors with regard to the most important works in the field. In the end, our tendency has been to translate the "classics," and as a result most of the articles selected were originally published in the 1950s and 1960s. We wish we had the time and energy to translate the work of a number of other scholars and hope that this publication encourages other people more energetic than we to produce other volumes.

Once the selections had been made, the next task was finding a group of translators. Almost all of those who have contributed to this project are younger foreign scholars who have spent some time studying in Japan; many have studied with the scholars whose work they have translated. We faced many problems in the translation of the articles presented here. Anyone familiar with Japanese academic style is well aware of the often dense nature of the conceptualization and prose. Added to that is the frequent use of concepts from the Marxist historiographical tradition, a language that is second nature to almost all Japanese academics, whether of Marxist or non-Marxist persuasion. Further problems come from the fact that almost all of our selections are liberally filled with citations from traditional Chinese sources in sometimes quite difficult classical Chinese.

We have tried to make the translations read like essays written in English. This has sometimes meant the rearranging of sentences and paragraphs to follow what is logical progression in English. At the same time, we have tried, as much as possible, to preserve the richness and complexity of the orginal argument.

The Marxist concepts that are frequently encountered in the essays are an integral part of our authors' understanding of Ming-Qing society, and we have made no attempt to remove such terms. On the contrary, we urge our readers to take those concepts seriously, and to see to what extent they offer new ways of looking at Chinese society. We believe that these essays will show that far from being a simple-minded and rigid framework, Marxist concepts are often used in a flexible way to shed new light on issues. Furthermore there is at the same time a great deal of disagreement about the application and use of those terms. The reader is not being presented with a cut-and-dried system borrowed from European models, but rather with attempts to develop new ways of interpreting changes in Ming-Qing China.

In translation of Chinese sources, especially those in which the meaning is in dispute, we have followed the reading of the citations used by the Japanese author of the essay. When there is major dispute over the meaning of a certain passage, we have appended notes suggesting the different interpretations.

All of the translations have been checked against the Japanese originals, either by the original author or by Usui Sachiko, a fellow at the Tōyō Bunko.

The other major difference between the translations and the originals involves the method of citation. Since Japanese articles are printed using Chinese characters, most authors quote directly from Chinese sources, presenting the evidence which allows the reader to make his own reading of the cited passages. As a result of this method, citations are usually given only to chapter (*juan*) in a source, a chapter often being 40 or 50 pages in length. Since it is impossible in an English book to provide all of the citations in the original Chinese, we have done everything possible to make it easier for the English reader to check the translations against Chinese texts. All notes have been checked against the original Chinese texts and exact citations to pages have been provided. We offer our thanks to the translators who have each individually spent long hours in this task.

The debts we have accumulated in working on this volume are numerous and the small appreciation we can offer quite inadequate. At the top of our list are thanks to the Japanese authors who have been unstintingly generous with their time in consultation over the translations. Professors Saeki Yūichi (Ochanomizu Women's University) and Tanaka Masatoshi (Shinshū University) have given generously of their time to discuss the outlines of the postwar Japanese development of Chinese studies. Any number of Japanese colleagues have aided us by explaining obscure passages in both Chinese and Japanese: our thanks here go particularly to Kishimoto-Nakayama Mio and Usui Sachiko.

Editing work has been a truly collective effort and each of the articles has been rewritten several times. Timothy Brook has been our expert on the translation of Chinese titles; he also worked out the standardized method for translation of Ming administrative subdivisions that we have used throughout, and compiled the bibliography. Cynthia Brokaw, who has an unusually sensitive ear for problems in English grammar and meaning, has made invaluable contributions to the improvement of the English style of the essays; she also compiled the glossary.

Our special thanks to Frank Baldwin and Kano Tsutomu of the Asia Foundation's Translation Service Center in Tokyo, two of the most skilled professional translators of social science material from Japanese to English. They have offered much useful advice, and if we had listened more carefully to them we might have abandoned the project before we started. While their advice has not saved us from all errors, it certainly helped us to avoid many problems. The Translation Service Center also arranged for the translations of the articles by Kobayashi Kazumi and Hamashita Takeshi. Finally we would like to acknowledge the financial assistance that this project has received from the Japanese Ministry of Education, Science and Culture as part of its program for grants-in-aid for both the translation and publication of scientific research results.

While we have done everything possible to be certain that the essays are both accurate and readable, any problems that still remain are the responsibility of the editors.

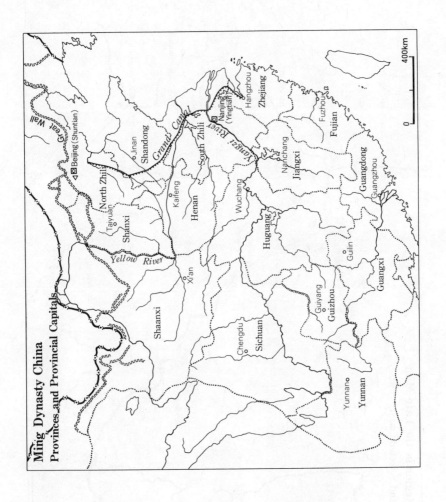

Ming Dynasty China
Provinces and Provincial Capitals

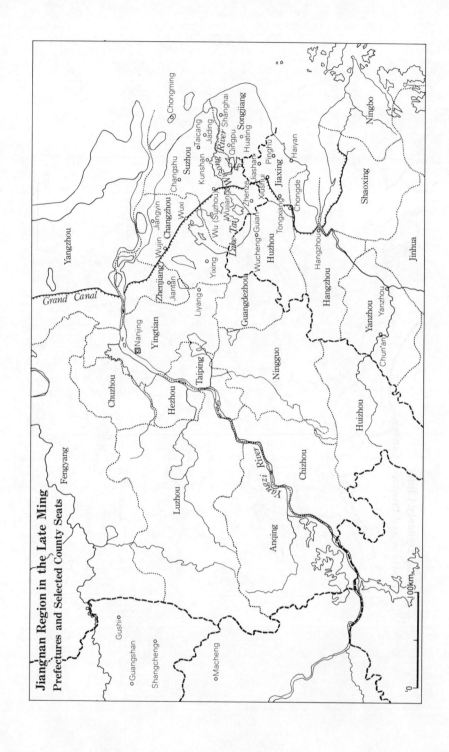

Jiangnan Region in the Late Ming
Prefectures and Selected County Seats

STATE AND SOCIETY IN CHINA

INTRODUCTION

The study of Ming-Qing social history is primarily a postwar phenomenon in Japan. The huge strides that have been made in this relatively new field are the result of the coming together of three factors: a solid grounding in the earlier textual criticism tradition, a serious concern for conceptualization, and an encouraging and collegial sense of academic community that has given rise to a number of supporting institutions. The coincidence of these three factors has given energy to Chinese studies in Japan.

Any foreign scholar who has spent even a short time at a Japanese university has undoubtedly been immediately struck by the time given to training in reading the basic sources. Particularly for the scholar who comes from an American graduate situation where most of the stress is on "ideas" and interpretation, the Japanese approach may seem unnecessarily slow and painstaking. And yet it is the very nature of that training in the reading of original sources which has given Japanese Ming-Qing studies such strength. That training has then been put to work exploiting the rich collections of materials on Chinese history held by many Japanese libraries.

Solid training in the use of original sources is directly reflected in the essays in this volume. For example, one finds in the work of Oyama Masaaki on Ming-Qing landholding a survey of what are believed to be almost all extant, non-archival sources on the problem. Much work has also been done in the field of local history. Such studies, which are particularly well developed for the Jiangnan region, reflect a very lively sense of the nature of local communities and of regional differentiation.[1]

The careful attention given to the gathering and weighing of evidence stands in direct contradiction to certain common assumptions about Japanese scholarship held by many Western scholars. It has often been argued that the use of Marxist historiographical concepts has distorted their interpretation of the reality of Chinese history. While there is a strong interest in theory among Japanese China specialists,

3

theory must be substantiated by empirical research. Sloppy research or careless reading of sources receives sharp criticism. This is facilitated by that fact that most Japanese studies include the Chinese texts in the original, allowing readers to make their own interpretation of the relevant sources.

While the close attention to sources has been one of the strengths of Japanese scholarship, it has on occasion led to too exclusive an emphasis on empirical knowledge. Not all scholars have been able to achieve that happy blending of facts and theory, and a comprehensive bibliography would reveal dozens of articles that have got lost in the pursuit of the facts without sufficient concern for interpretation.

The best of Japanese scholarship on Ming-Qing history, however, has developed in response to major interpretative questions, an orientation that Japanese refer to as *mondai ishiki* (critical perception of problems). What distinguishes this concern for "the big questions" from similar practices in the Western academic world is the stronger sense of collective endeavor in the definition of questions and the search for answers.

A number of organizations have played a major role in shaping the collective concerns among Japanese historians. The single most important organization in the postwar period has been the Rekishigaku kenkyūkai (The Historical Science Society of Japan). The society was founded in 1932 by a group of younger scholars who split off from the then authoritative academic historical association, Shigakkai. The Shigakkai had been founded by scholars of Asian, European, and Japanese history at Tokyo Imperial University in the late nineteenth century.

From the beginning, the new society supported two iconoclastic approaches: a historiographical approach based on universal, primarily Marxist, methodology, and an attempt to transcend the individual university factions. Reorganized after the war, the society has played a decisive role in shaping the interpretative questions for the Japanese historical community.

World War II left Japan in ruins, and there was much reflection and serious thinking done on the question of where Japan had gone wrong. Historians of China were certainly no exception. They turned a critical eye to prewar studies, were skeptical of many prewar theories and assumptions and saw the immediate need to revise prewar research methods. Young researchers were brimming over with enthusiasm for new approaches and ideas. The success of the 1949 Chinese revolution gave further encouragement to Japanese historians of China. It was in this milieu that the Rekishigaku kenkyūkai served as a forum of opinion which worked out the central themes that have dominated Japanese historical research for the last three decades.

Beginning with its first postwar national meeting, the Rekishigaku kenkyūkai has set an annual comprehensive theme for debate at national meetings. At the first postwar meeting (1946), the theme was "Basic historical laws in world history" and involved a reconsideration of the applicability of such universal historical patterns as those suggested by Marx to both Chinese and Japanese history. Subsequent themes have included such questions as state power, stages of development, the relationship of nationalism to internationalism, the question of national culture, and the role of popular culture.

At the annual meetings, panel discussions are organized chronologically rather than by area specialty, an alignment encouraging discussions among specialists in different fields. As a result of this organizational structure, at least through the early 1960s there was very close interaction between historians of China and historians of Japan and Europe, with much cross-fertilization of ideas. Many of the interpretative questions developed by Ming-Qing historians have been directly related to the debates set by the annual themes of the Rekishigaku kenkyūkai.

In addition to such national organizations as the Rekishigaku kenkyukai, other smaller groups have also played a part in shaping the collegial relations among China scholars. Beginning with the junior or senior year in college, most academic training is centered around seminars led by individual senior professors. On the graduate level, new students are incorporated into seminars where they receive training not only from the professor but also from other more senior graduate students.

Graduate students usually spend five years in graduate school, two years in the M.A. course and three years in the doctorate course. To partially fulfill the requirements of each course students are required to obtain a prescribed number of credits by attending different seminars. In these seminars all participants take turns in either reading and translating a Chinese source, or in presenting reports on specific topics. Though students may participate in various seminars, they usually devote most energy to the ones closest to their own thesis topics. The professor supervises the seminar carefully, correcting any translation mistakes and factual errors, but all participants are free to contribute to the discussion. In fact in some cases senior graduate students are more familiar with the sources and problems under consideration than the professor, so they are assigned the task of leading the discussion. This type of seminar system has built very close ties among scholars who have studied with a common professor, with the normal expectation that such former students would at least share some common perceptions.

Such seminars have been supplemented by research groups which are organized around a specific theme and which normally cut across university boundaries. Any individual may belong to a number of research groups, each of which would normally meet at least once a month. Some research groups are set up to implement a given publication project, while others bring together those who share long-term common research interests.

Such research groups and seminars, by maintaining close ties between graduate students and more senior faculty, ensure a certain continuity in research interests. They offer a forum for on-going research and a path of communications about developments in the field. The sense of community so created is particularly important in sustaining productive professional activity by people who, at least in America, might otherwise "leave the field." With the current shortage of academic appointments, many younger scholars find themselves teaching in high schools or holding down nonacademic jobs. The system of research groups works to sustain interest and helps to break down some of the elitism of the major universities, at the same time increasing the number of productive scholars. The collective volumes that are often produced by such research groups are a further important bonus of the system.

No discussion of the major factors that have influenced postwar China studies would be complete without some mention of Marxist historiography. It has had a major influence in shaping the vocabulary and conceptualization of most Japanese historians. While there was a time in the past when Japanese historians could be divided between "Marxists" and "academics" (i.e., non-Marxists), that division is now almost meaningless. Even such supposed bastions of "academic" historiography as the *Shigaku zasshi* now draws much of its material from authors who use a Marxist vocabulary.

It is important to note, however, that for most historians Marxism is primarily a methodological approach, a set of analytical concepts that can be used in empirical studies. Just as most Western social historians will immediately connect the notion of "bureaucratization" with the whole associated frame of reference provided by Max Weber's interpretation of modernization, most Japanese historians will automatically make similar connections when using common Marxist concepts.

For the Western reader who may be more familiar with Weberian or Parsonian vocabulary than with the Marxist, the use of such language may be disconcerting. In the translations we have attempted to

achieve a style that should be self-explanatory without a deep understanding of Marxist methodology, but obviously some understanding
will bring out the richer implications of what are often quite complex
interpretations.

Themes in Ming-Qing history

Many Western historians of China describe their specialties by dynasty,
and there are a number of associations organized around such interests.
In those cases where Ming-Qing is taken as a single field, it is usually
seen as simply an alternative definition of the late imperial state. The
Japanese use of Ming-Qing differs from this definition. In the postwar
period, Japanese historians have spent much time working out an
appropriate periodization scheme for Chinese history.[2] The most
generally accepted periodization scheme is based on changes in the
socio-economic system, and generally follows the patterns suggested
by Marx.

According to this periodization scheme, the origins of Chinese
feudal society can be traced to the late Tang-early Song, when the
older, aristocrat-dominated society and economy broke down. Feudal
society developed slowly, reaching a major transition stage in the late
Ming-early Qing. While there is considerable dispute about the
interpretation of that Ming-Qing transitional stage, there is common
agreement that in economic terms the period represents a major shift
in development. It is largely for that reason that Japanese scholars
first began their intensive study of the Ming-Qing period.

The essays in this volume fall into six major thematic divisions,
themes which we believe reflect the major areas of Japanese research
on the Ming-Qing period. Here we would like to provide a brief survey
of those themes and how they interrelate.

Rural handicraft industries

Almost from the very beginning of their advance into Asia in the late
nineteenth century the Japanese attempted to justify imperialism as
a modernizing force that would rescue more backward Asian societies
and set them on the road to development.[3] Many of these efforts
assumed that Asian societies were stagnant, caught in economic and

political structures that without outside assistance were unlikely to develop on their own. In the prewar and wartime period one of the most influential academic proponents of such theories in Japan was the prominent Kyoto University professor, Naitō Konan.[4] While Naitō was the chief Japanese proponent of such views, he followed a long European tradition that included many of the French *philosophes*. Marx's discussions of the Asiatic mode of production and the work of such later scholars as Wittfogel with his theory of hydraulic society also had a major impact.[5]

In the postwar period, Japanese historians of China took the critique of the Asian stagnation theory as their first major task. The successful overthrow of the semifeudal, semi-colonial Chinese state in the revolution of 1949 spurred them on in these efforts. One of the most effective ways to counter the stagnation theory was to demonstrate through empirical research the occurrence of indigenous development in the Chinese economy. This approach stood in sharp contrast to the methodology of most of the stagnation theorists who had based their assumptions on sweeping theories of the Chinese social structure, providing little solid empirical evidence as support.[6]

The empirical base for the criticism of the Asian stagnation theory was laid first by the work of Nishijima Sadao on the Ming cotton textile industry. His work was among the first to single out the late Ming and early Qing period as the chief subject for the study of Chinese indigenous economic development and was followed by a large number of studies of handicraft in the Ming-Qing period.[7] Studies were also made of urban handicraft industries as well as rural ones. The first two essays in this volume, by Nishijima Sadao and Tanaka Masatoshi, are generally recognized as among the most influential in the field.

Land relations

While study of the rural handicraft industries opened new areas of knowledge and successfully countered the Asian stagnation theory, it also left certain questions unanswered. Among the most important was the relationship of the emerging handicraft industries to the overall system of land tenure. In the rural industries, most of the producers were peasants who most commonly continued farming while engaging in handicraft industries. A deeper understanding of the land tenure system and the relations between landlords, tenants, and owner-cultivators was essential.

Beginning in the late 1950s more effort was devoted to the exploration of the land tenure system and the interpretation of the nature of production and control relations among the various parties. Local gazetteers and various prose and poetry collections were searched for the data they reveal on land systems and rural social relations. The most comprehensive survey of such materials is provided by Oyama Masaaki whose essay on large landholding is translated in this volume. Oyama is the proponent of a controversial theory which argues that the late Ming-early Qing period marks the beginning of the Chinese feudal age. He is convinced that the slave-like nature of dependency ties between landlords and tenants up to that time logically meant that earlier Chinese society had to be seen as a slave society.

The more common view is to argue that the late Ming marks a further development in the Chinese feudal system, with what had formerly been more dependent relations, becoming less so. Much of the argument centers around economic relations, with the assumption that the tenant who can, with only minimal landlord assistance, continue production is much more likely to be socially and politically independent than is the tenant who has to rely on the landlord for tools, seed, and financial assistance.

The broader questions of dependence have led to the study of forms of land rent and the development of technological capacity.[8] The late Muramatsu Yūji devoted the last part of his life to the study of landlord management in the Qing.[9] His pioneering studies have stimulated much research on the land system during the Taiping and post-Taiping rebellion period.

Given the nature of the sources and the fact that the landlord system was highly developed in central and south China, most work has concentrated on the Jiangnan region. Kataoka Shibako, and more recently Adachi Keiji, have done some work on land relations in the north, but much more work on regional variations is still required before a comprehensive picture of Ming-Qing land relations can be fully constructed.[10]

Popular rebellions

The role of popular struggles in Ming-Qing history has inspired much lively debate among Japanese scholars and elicited hundreds of articles on anti-rent, anti-tax, and religiously inspired revolts, as well as a number of studies on urban uprisings. Interest in such popular struggles has been inspired by several factors. For some scholars, including two of the pathbreakers in this field, Tanaka Masatoshi and Saeki Yūichi, research on popular struggles was the natural outgrowth of their earlier work on handicraft industries. Their study of handicraft industry had clearly demonstrated the possibility for indigenous development in China.[11]

The problem, however, was to determine how such economic development had created new socio-political conditions. Historians such as Tanaka, Saeki, and Oyama treated the anti-rent and anti-tax movements as class struggles because they reasoned that without such struggles economic development could not become a political reality. As a result, a great deal of attention was paid to peasant struggles and other forms of protest by producers. The article by Tanaka Masatoshi on popular rebellions translated here is representative of this mode of analysis. By the early 1970s this concept of class struggle had come under attack from the generation of younger scholars who had participated in the student struggles that swept through Japanese universities during the late 1960s. These younger scholars were very critical of the simple formula that attributed the cause of rebellions and social protest solely to economic factors. While recognizing the importance of economic factors they demanded that more attention be given to religious, psychological, and cultural factors. Thus to the younger generation the older generation's labeling of anti-rent movements as class struggles was a misnomer; to them anti-rent movements because they only aimed at improving living conditions have to be interpreted as purely economic struggles. Kobayashi Kazumi's article translated in this volume is a good example of this line of thought.

Many of the scholars who studied the popular rebellions of the Ming-Qing were also interested in the revolutionary phenomena of the twentieth century; in looking at the past, they sought continuities between traditional rebellions and the modern revolution. Still others were influenced by events within Japan. The nationwide popular struggle against the renewal of the Japan–U.S. Security Treaty in 1960 focused the attention of historians on the role of popular struggle in history. The Rekishigaku kenkyūkai took up a number of themes associated with popular struggles and further stimulated research and debate. In 1976 Yamane Yukio edited a bibliography on peasant rebellions which listed all work in Chinese and Japanese to that date, and it provides a general survey of the materials available.[12] Since that time a number of younger scholars have also entered the field, and the study of popular rebellions remains one of the major themes in Ming-Qing studies.[13]

Taxation and institutional reform

Institutional history has long been a strength of Japanese Sinology. Among Western historians the recent stress on the role of finance and administration in state-building and state consolidation has also revived interest in institutional studies.[14] The consolidation of the tax base and tax collection are crucial to the success of any political system. At the same time, changes in taxation policy and methods are directly connected to other changes in the economic and social base of the state. The inclusion of three essays on Ming-Qing administration and taxation in this book should provide an introduction to the vast literature in Japanese on these problems.

In the case of Ming-Qing history, interest has focused on two topics: the *lijia* system as a unit for taxation and social organization, and the major tax reforms of the mid and late Ming which are usually grouped together as the Single Whip reform. These reforms radically altered the tax system by initiating a shift away from labor taxes collected in kind toward taxes linked to the land. The political implications of this shift—which were not to be fully apparent until the Qing—brought a dramatic change in the relationship between the state and landlords.[15]

Studies of the Ming *lijia* lead into controversial territory. It is now generally agreed that the *lijia* was more than merely a tax collection unit and that its organization in the early Ming represented an attempt by the central state to reorganize and then freeze village society in such a way as to be most beneficial to the state; of secondary importance were the social guarantees offered to small-scale owner peasants. As Tsurumi's study of the *lijia* clearly shows, the attempt was thwarted at the outset, and by the end of the Ming the system was in shambles, with small-scale ownership dwarfed by the large-scale gentry landowners who had gradually gathered estates and political power throughout the Ming.

Studies of the *lijia* are controversial, not only for what they suggest about the pattern of landownership, but also because they have been used to focus attention on the problem of community (*kyōdōtai*). The concept of community has been used in various ways by different Japanese scholars, and there has been a heated debate over the extent to which community organizations existed in Chinese villages at all. On the basis of village surveys done in North China in the twentieth century, it has been argued that the absence of clear village boundaries and clear definitions of village membership suggests the absence of any kind of communal ties.[16]

Nishijima Sadao has taken a major role in the critique of the above position, stating that if peasants cannot achieve reproduction without certain communal-style organizations, then such organizations must be present in China even if the form they take is strikingly different from those of Europe. Much research has been done on the form such communal obligations take, with two of Nishijima's students, Hamashima Atsutoshi and Kawakatsu Mamoru, devoting their efforts to the examination of such institutions as village water control systems. Tanigawa Michio, a leading expert on Chinese history from the third to seventh centuries, tends to look for evidence of community organizations in moral stipulations. Kobayashi Kazumi also urges that more attention be paid to the psychological and spiritual structure of certain communal groups, rather than to strictly economic factors.[17] Those who stress the economic side of community relations tend to regard such factors as a negative force: they believe that landlords manipulated communal rights and obligations, thus strengthening their hold over village society. Others like Tanigawa and Kobayashi have a more positive evaluation and see such communal ties as the basis for solidarity in popular struggles.

The interpretation of the *lijia* has been at the center of many of the debates over community in Ming rural society. The essay by Tsurumi, included in this volume, provides what is now the generally accepted interpretation of this phenomenon. The controversy, however, is far from settled, and debate at academic meetings on this subject continues.[18]

The often heated debates over the character and implications of the *lijia* system and the Single Whip reforms are predicated on a solid and detailed knowledge of the intricate workings of the Ming-Qing tax system. That solid base of knowledge has been built up through a painstaking search for and analysis of sources on fiscal administration. The essays by Yamane Yukio and Iwami Hiroshi included in this volume clearly show the kind of results that can be achieved in the best textual criticism tradition. The two articles, taken together, give a clear picture of the important Single Whip reforms which radically altered the state's fiscal policy and tax collection methods. The social implications of the shifts in taxation and fiscal policy continue to be a major field of research interest.

The gentry

Western scholars have often noted the amazingly small size of the Ming-Qing bureaucracy when measured against the administrative tasks it faced. The work of the Chinese scholar Chang Chung-li and others has demonstrated the role played in administration by such informal power groups as the gentry.[19] The exact nature of the gentry has been a topic of much debate in the West as well as in Japan. Dennis Twitchett in a very perceptive review has catalogued the major theories, dividing them roughly between those that argued that the gentry were a social class (i.e., their position derived from their economic status and therefore they were in some sense a natural elite) and those that argued the gentry were a subdivision of the bureaucracy (i.e., gentry status was derived from examination degree, a form of conferred status, and thus the gentry were an appendage of the bureaucracy).[20]

Debates in Japan have also centered on the nature and role of the gentry and particularly on the creation in the late Ming of a new form of landownership that can be defined as gentry landownership. The long article by Shigeta Atsushi begins with a lengthy critique of prewar Japanese theories of the gentry. For a summary of more recent arguments including a critique of Shigeta's own work, readers may want to look at the excellent review articles by Mori Masao.[21]

Although such phrases as gentry-style landownership have now become fixed as part of the scholarly vocabulary among Ming-Qing scholars, there is still a great need for more empirical study to supplement the theoretical conceptualizations. We note particularly the work of Yamane Yukio, who has in recent years been combing through classical texts to see how contemporary Chinese used the word gentry (xiangshen) and, in a more recent work, has examined the composition of the gentry in Henan.[22]

China and world capitalism

A general criticism of Chinese historical research in Japan during the 1970s is that it failed to critically build upon the work of the 1950s. While progress was made in some of the fields introduced above others were neglected. One characteristic feature of research in the 1970s was the opening up of new subjects of study such as financial and price history. It is in this context that the final theme of China's relationship to world capitalism is of interest. In terms of the Japanese chronology of Chinese history this theme belongs to the modern period which begins after the Opium War. There are two reasons we have included it in this volume. First, it provides a means of understanding how the traditional Qing economy was incorporated into the world economy from the early nineteenth century on. Second, it is one of the most recently developed fields of historical research in Japan, yet almost unknown by Western scholars.

This is also one of the only fields in Ming-Qing history in which many of the basic sources are written in European languages. Both Western and Japanese scholars have been interested in the history of China's foreign relations and the impact of imperialism in China. The work we introduce here is, however, in many ways strikingly different from both the work done in Japan in the past and from the research of Western scholars. Taken together with the study of price history, it represents what we believe will be one of the major areas of Japanese scholarly accomplishment in the 1980s.

Although Hamashita Takeshi, who has been the pioneer in this new field, began with a very different theoretical background, his work does share certain common perceptions with that of world systems theorists like Immanuel Wallerstein. Hamashita argues that nineteenth-century Chinese economy must be placed in the larger world context if one is to understand its full dimensions. He has focused on finance as the method to explore the intricacies of the total system. Although both the theory and the methodology involved are quite difficult, the fuller picture presented of both Qing China and of the world economy make Hamashita's work particularly rewarding.

Notes

[1] For such studies on the Qing, see the bibliography compiled by Tanaka Masatoshi in *Hatten tojōkoku kenkyū*. Other local studies of particular interest include Kawakatsu Mamoru, *Chūgoku hōken kokka no shihai kōzō*; Hamashima Atsutoshi, "The Organization of Water Control in the Kiangnan Delta in the Ming Period" and his recent book, *Mindai Kōnan nōson shakai no kenkyū*; and Usui Sachiko, "Taihei tengoku zen, Soshūfu-Shōkōfu ni okeru fuzei mondai." *Acta Asiatica*, no. 38 (1980) was a special issue on Ming social and economic history edited by Yamane Yukio.

[2] See the various articles collected in Suzuki Shun and Nishijima Sadao, *Chūgokushi no jidai kubun*. This volume was a collective effort published following the first visit of a delegation of historians from the People's Republic of China. Of particular use here are the bibliography of articles on periodization and the long essays by

Tanaka Masatoshi on sprouts of capitalism and Saeki Yūichi on commodity production. See also, Linda Grove and Joseph Esherick, "From Feudalism to Capitalism: Japanese scholarship on the transformation of Chinese rural society."

[3] See the work of Asada Kyōji on the development of Japanese theories of colonialism: "Nihon shokuminshi kenkyū no kadai to hōhō," "Nihon shokuminshi kenkyū no genkyō to mondaiten," and "Nihon teikokushugi to shokuminchi mondai." For the links between Japanese imperialism and prewar Asian studies, see Goi Naohiro, *Kindai Nihon to Tōyō shigaku.*

[4] For more on Naitō Konan see Joshua Fogel, "Prewar Japanese studies of Republican China."

[5] See Shiozawa Kimio, *Ajiateki seisan yōshikiron.*

[6] See Tanaka Masatoshi, "Ajia shakai teitairon hihan no hōhōronteki hansei."

[7] See the bibliography attached to Saeki Yūichi, "Nihon no Min-Shin jidai kenkyū ni okeru shōhin seisan hyōka o megutte."

[8] Yasuno Shōzō, "Minmatsu Shinsho Yōsukō chūryūiki no dai tochi shoyū ni kansuru ichi kōsatsu"; Suzuki Tomoo, *Kindai Chūgoku no jinushisei*; Adachi Keiji, "Min-Shin jidai no shōhin seisan to jinushisei kenkyū o megutte"; and Adachi Keiji, "Minmatsu Shinsho no ichi nōgyō keiei—*Shinshi nōsho* no saihyōka."

[9] Muramatsu Yūji, "A Documentary Study of Chinese Landlordism in the Late Ch'ing and Early Republican Kiangnan"; idem, *Kindai Kōnan no sosan.*

[10] Kataoka Shibako, "Minmatsu Shinsho no Kahoku ni okeru nōka keiei"; and Adachi Keiji, "Shindai Kahoku no nōgyō keiei to shakai kōzō."

[11] Saeki Yūichi, "Mindai zenpanki no kiko"; Saeki Yūichi and Tanaka Masatoshi, "Juroku-Jūnana seiki no Chūgoku nōson seishi kinuorigyō"; and Tanaka Masatoshi, *Chūgoku kindai keizaishi kenkyū josetsu.*

[12] Yamane Yukio, *Chūgoku nōmin kigi bunken mokuroku.*

[13] Mori Masao, *Nuhen to kōsō—Minmatsu Shinsho o chūshin to suru Kachū-Kanan no chiiki shakai ni okeru minshū no teikō undō*; and Fuma Susumu, "Minmatsu to toshi kaikaku to Kōshū minpen."

[14] See, for example, Charles Tilly, *The Formation of National States in Western Europe.*

[15] See Grove and Esherick, "From Feudalism to Capitalism" for a fuller explanation of this shift.

[16] Hatada Takashi, *Chūgoku sonraku to kyōdōtai riron.*

[17] Tanigawa Michio, *Chūgoku chūsei shakai to kyōdōtai*; and Kobayashi Kazumi, "Kyōdōtai no rekishiteki igi o megutte."

[18] The Rekishi Gakkai (Historical Science Society), the descendant of the former Ōtsuka Shigakkai which had been founded by graduates of the Tokyo University of Education, has devoted several annual meetings to debates over community. Tsurumi Naohiro and Oyama Masaaki both presented papers at the 1977 annual meeting. They are included in *Shichō*, no. 4 (1979).

[19] Chang Chung-li, *The Chinese Gentry.*

[20] Dennis Twitchett, "A Critique of Some Recent Studies of Modern Chinese Social-Economic History."

[21] Mori Masao, "The Gentry in the Ming Period—An Outline of the Relations between the *Shih-ta-fu* and Local Society"; "Nihon no Min-Shin jidaishi kenkyū ni okeru kyōshinron ni tsuite."

[22] Yamane Yukio, "Kananshō Shōjōken no shinshisō no sonzai keitai."

THE FORMATION OF
THE EARLY CHINESE COTTON INDUSTRY

NISHIJIMA SADAO

This essay by Nishijima Sadao was the center piece of four articles
on the development of the Chinese cotton industry that the author
published from 1947 to 1949. Nishijima's pathbreaking effort
marks the real beginning of serious study of Ming-Qing social and
economic history in Japan. This essay is of more than simply historiographical interest. Although the first draft was written in
1942 as part of the author's graduation thesis, it is still worth reading as the most thorough treatment of the late Ming rural cotton
industry.

Nishijima's encyclopedic command of the sources and his bold
analytical argument have a freshness that belies the years since its
publication. The critiques and counter-critiques of Nishijima's
work were the real starting point of the lively and contentious
study of Ming-Qing economic history in Japan. In the 1966 collection of Nishijima's articles on Chinese economic history (*Chūgoku
keizaishi kenkyū*), the author included an appendix surveying the
debates that followed the publication of his original articles.

Nishijima's interest in the cotton industry was stimulated by
his own critical approach to the theory of Asian stagnation, which
had been supported by a number of prewar Japanese Sinologists.
That theory argued that Asian societies (specifically China) had
been caught in stagnant social and economic structures which had
the potential to continue indefinitely. It was only the impact of
outside forces (Western and Japanese imperialism) which could
rescue China from its stagnant state, initiating development along
modern lines. This stagnation theory, while serving as a justification for imperialism, also carried an interpretation of Asian society which saw Chinese history as basically unchanging.

This essay was first published in *Orientalica*, vol. 2, 1949. The translation follows the
revised version, "Chūgoku shoki mengyō no keisei to sono kōzō" [中國初期棉業の
形成とその構造], in *Chūgoku keizaishi kenkyū* [中國經濟史研究] (Tokyo: Tokyo
Daigaku Shuppankai, 1966), pp. 805–72. Translation by Linda Grove.

17

Nishijima's study of the late Ming cotton industry demonstrated that Chinese society was far from stagnant by tracing the indigenous development of a widespread rural industry which had stimulated important changes in production and marketing structures. At the same time, Nishijima was careful to argue that while the seventeenth-century cotton industry was evidence of the possibility of indigenous economic development within China, it should not be mistaken for capitalism. On this point, his analysis stands in sharp contrast to the later work of a number of Chinese scholars who were to argue for the genesis ("sprouts") of capitalism in the late Ming. Nishijima, in fact, believed that certain societal and structural factors blocked the possibilities for modern (capitalist-style) development. This part of Nishijima's analysis was strongly influenced by the work of Ōtsuka Hisao, a leading Japanese economic historian who produced a number of outstanding works in European and comparative economic history.

Many questions were left unanswered by Nishijima's study of the cotton industry, and other scholars, stimulated by the questions he raised, began to explore other possibilities. Nishijima had argued that the chief causative factor in the development of the cotton industry was the excessively heavy tax demands imposed by the state on the Jiangnan region. Handicraft developed as a supplement to family income under the pressure of such taxes. Later scholars have questioned Nishijima's formulation, arguing that more attention should be given to rent than to tax. This controversy stimulated study of land relations in the Ming and Qing, a subject which in turn has become one of the cornerstones of Japanese study on the social and economic history of that period.

In later years, Nishijima turned away from the study of Ming-Qing social and economic history and devoted his efforts to the study of early Chinese history. His main concern has been to explore relations between economic history and political structures, particularly the role of the autocratic state. Nishijima Sadao retired from his position at University of Tokyo in 1980 but continues an active teaching and research career as professor at Niigata University.

*   *   *

This essay will examine the early cotton industry as one example of Chinese industry in the period before the establishment of modern industrial forms. I have chosen the cotton industry for several reasons.

First, the cotton industry developed in China's most advanced economic region, the Yangzi delta. Unlike the imperially sponsored industries which produced luxury goods for the court, it was a new industry directly linked to the consumption demands of the ordinary people all over the country. It thus provided a direct reflection of the social and economic conditions of that age. Second, from the eighteenth century on, the cotton industry played an important role in foreign trade and directly confronted the modern cotton industries of the advanced European nations. Thus a study of the cotton industry will also allow us to raise important questions with regard to world history.

Cotton was not originally native to China. Accounts from the ancient period show that cotton was not planted, nor were cotton textiles produced in China, although imported cotton from foreign countries was offered as tribute.[1] In China itself, cotton was first planted and cotton textiles first produced in Lingnan Province during the Tang dynasty. Gradually cotton moved north, arriving in the Yangzi delta region in the late Song-early Yuan period. At about the same time, cotton seeds which had been transmitted via Central Asia were first planted in the Shaanxi area. During the Yuan dynasty, cotton cultivation thus spread from Guangdong and Fujian to the lower Yangzi region, the Huai River basin, Sichuan and the Shaanxi area.[2] By the Ming period cotton cultivation was common all over the country as we see from the fact that cotton textiles and raw cotton had been included as part of the tax assessments. In order to provide uniforms for the military forces assigned to the northern defense garrisons, the provinces of Shandong, North Zhili, Shanxi, Henan, and Shaanxi were annually required to submit a total of between one and two million bolts of cotton cloth and up to one million *jin* of cotton. At the same time the provinces of South Zhili, Jiangxi, Huguang, and Sichuan were also required to submit cotton textiles as taxes in kind. All of this indicates that cotton production had spread over a very wide area.[3]

If we examine the geographical distribution of the cotton industry we find that cotton cultivation in the several northern provinces was well developed and output quite high, although spinning and weaving were not very well developed. It is difficult to identify commodity production of cotton cloth in those areas before the mid-Ming. In contrast, in spite of the high level of development of spinning and weaving technology in the several southern provinces, output of raw cotton was quite low. The boundary line between these two regions fell just at the line of the Yangzi River, and it was in Songjiang prefecture, which was located along that boundary line, that the early cotton industry developed.[4]

Songjiang prefecture was located in the center of China's most advanced economic region, the Yangzi delta. It was said of that prefecture that "the cotton garments of Songjiang clothe the whole empire."[5] This phrase echoes a similar saying of the Han period with regard to Shandong silks, which reputedly provided "the official hats, belts, gowns, and shoes for the whole empire." Songjiang was famous not only for the quantity of its textile output, but also for its quality. The 1534 *Nan ji zhi* (South Zhili gazetteer) claims that "the quality of the cotton cloth is finer than brocade."[6] Any study of the Chinese cotton industry thus must begin with a study of the Songjiang area.

Since some place names have changed over time, we need first to clarify the area we are referring to as Songjiang. During the Ming dynasty, Songjiang prefecture had three subordinate counties: Huating, Shanghai, and Qingpu.[7] Later growth brought further administrative change. Our discussion of Songjiang includes the modern counties of Songjiang, Nanhui, and Fengxian and the city of Shanghai, plus the neighboring three Suzhou prefecture counties of Jiading, Kunshan, and Taicang, as well as Haiyan county to the south, which was later attached to Jiaxing prefecture (Zhejiang).

The major question this essay addresses is why the cotton industry developed only in the Songjiang area. We know that cotton cultivation had started earlier in Guangdong and Fujian and at approximately the same time in Shaanxi, and yet their cotton industries remained undeveloped. Our initial aim is to describe the process of development of the Songjiang cotton industry. First, we need to examine the structure of the cotton industry, particularly the relationship between the cotton industry and the supply and demand for raw cotton and cotton cloth in north China as well as in the interior regions of central and south China. Since I have written extensively on this subject elsewhere, the evidence demonstrating Songjiang's central role will not be presented here.[8] We will rather turn immediately to the origins of the Songjiang cotton industry.

Cotton cultivation and technology in Songjiang

Songjiang prefecture is located at the eastern edge of the lower Yangzi delta in the center of the Jiangnan cultural region. A brief review of the administrative history of the area will provide some background for our discussion. Huating county was established in 751 as a county administratively subordinate to Suzhou. During the Song dynasty, the area was part of Xiuzhou, which was under the Liangzhe circuit. In 1119 a Maritime Trade Office was established in Huating on the site that was to be the location of the Songjiang prefectural offices during the Ming. At that time Songjiang was a very prosperous seaport. As sea trade with the south developed, one of the results was the transmission of cotton cultivation from Fujian and Guangdong.[9]

Although we believe that cotton cultivation began in Jiangnan in the Southern Song period, it is difficult to find concrete evidence supporting this belief. For example, the following lines from a poem by the Southern Song poet Xie Fangde clearly suggest that cotton cultivation in Jiangnan was still not common:

> Why has Heaven been so generous to Fujian
> As to give them a good plant like cotton?
> The soil there is not suitable for mulberry
> And so sericulture is very difficult.
> But if they harvest a thousand cotton plants
> Then the rich need not worry about want.
> If the people of Jiangnan also planted it,
> They too would be rich. . . .
> Heaven's bounty is shared equally,
> But just as no one animal has both horns and tusks
> So the benefits derived from cotton
> Have not been given to the people of Jiangnan.[10]

A Qing-dynasty essayist, Zhao Yi, cited this poem and commented, "This source shows that in the late Song the advantages of cotton were known in Fujian, but it had not yet spread to Jiangnan."[11] From this, and from a variety of other sources, it seems that cotton cultivation was not brought to Jiangnan until the early Yuan.[12]

Spinning and weaving technology as well as cotton cultivation was eventually imported as a result of the maritime contacts with the south. The clearest evidence for this is the legend of the Taoist nun Huang which has already been studied by both Fujita Toyohachi and Hirth.[13] The Yuan writer, Tao Zongyi, gives the following version of the legend:

> In Fujian and Liangguang there are many who plant cotton, and then spin and weave it into cloth. They call it *jibei* (lucky cowry). There is a place 50 *li* east of Songjiang prefectural city called Wunijing. The land there is quite barren and does not sustain the people. Therefore, they sought new crops which would provide support.

They discovered cotton and began to plant it. At first they did not have the foot treadle gin or the cotton bow. They hand-separated the seeds and used narrow slips of bamboo to brush and clean it. This work was very trying. Early in this dynasty an old woman, the Taoist nun Huang, who came from Yazhou, taught them how to make the tools for ginning, spinning, and weaving. There were special methods for arranging the threads according to the colors, dyeing, and sizing. They then wove the cotton into mats, covers and hand-kerchiefs and, smiling broadly, designed and wove patterns of branches and phoenixes and checkerboardlike designs. After they had received instruction, they competed in its production, selling their output in other districts, thus enriching their families. After a while, the old woman died. All were bereaved, and they joined together to give her a funeral. They built a shrine and annually honored her there. The shrine was destroyed after thirty years. A local native, Zhao Yuxuan, rebuilt the shrine, and again it was destroyed. There was no one to rebuild it. Time has passed, and there are few today who know the name of the Taoist nun Huang.[14]

There is another account of the legend in a poem entitled "The Shrine to the Taoist Nun Huang," by the Yuan writer Wang Feng. Wang's prose poem says:

The Taoist nun Huang was from Wujing [Wunijing] in Songjiang.
When she was young she lived in Yazhou.
During the Yuanzhen era (1295–96) she came by sea.
She spun and wove the cotton quilts of Yazhou
And never tired of teaching the women of other families.
Before long, the name of Wujing was known everywhere.
More than a thousand families were supporting themselves in this way.
After she died, a rural elder Zhao Rugui
Set up a shrine and made sacrifices to honor her.
The small shrine was later destroyed in a military raid.
In 1362 Zhang Shouzhong moved the shrine to a vacant plot of ancestral land and reestablished the sacrifices.[15]

If we put these two accounts of the legend together, we find that the town of Wunijing in Songjiang prefecture was an area with very barren soil and as a result the residents were very poor. When the techniques for cotton cultivation were transmitted from Fujian and Guangdong, many took it up. At first their technological level was very low, and they lacked both the treadle wheel for spinning and the cotton bow. The Taoist nun Huang, who was originally from Wunijing, had gone to Yazhou on Hainan island and returned in 1295 or 1296, bringing back the more sophisticated tools for ginning, spinning, and weaving that were then used in the Hainan area. As a result there was a rapid improvement in the textile technology of the region; local people began to produce high-quality cotton cloth and sold it in other districts. The people of Wunijing prospered. After the death of the Taoist nun Huang they set up a shrine and carried out sacrifices there.[16]

While Songjiang's role as an entrepôt in the maritime trade with the Southern Seas played an important part in the introduction of cotton cultivation and the cotton textile industry, not all of the technology involved was imported from the south. Much was also modeled on the technology used in the Jiangnan silk industry. For example, we find in Song Yingxing's seventeenth-century technological manual *Tiangong kaiwu* (The creations of nature and man) the statement: "The patterns used for figure-weaving of cotton fabrics are 'cloud,' 'twill,' 'elephant eye,' etc. These patterns are modeled after those used in the weaving of silk fabrics by the drawloom."[17] The drawloom referred to here is the *kongyinji* (empty pulling loom). The illustration given in *Tiangong kaiwu* shows it to be a very complex loom that was used for weaving high-quality silk fabrics like brocade. Suzhou prefecture, neighboring Songjiang, was a famous silk textile center, and we can assume that the drawloom was used there. Further, every list of the cotton textiles produced in Songjiang includes twill weaves, evidence that the cotton looms in Songjiang were using the drawloom technology from neighboring areas. Thus two factors contributed to the beginning of the cotton textile industry in Songjiang: the importation of textile technology from the south and the adaptation of silk textile technology that had already reached a high level in China in ancient times.[18]

In summary, we can see that Songjiang prefecture had both a guaranteed supply of raw materials and the necessary technology required for the development of the cotton textile industry, and thus compared with other areas, it stood in an advantageous position.

Songjiang economic development

While the cultivation of cotton and the presence of textile technology were important prerequisites, they only created the possibility for the development of the cotton industry. We now need to search for other factors that helped to turn those possibilities into reality. Such a search naturally leads to an examination of the economic environment of the Songjiang region from the late Song on.

The early Qing scholar Gu Yanwu noted that "there were heavy taxes in the two prefectures of Suzhou and Songjiang."[19] This statement is simply a repetition of the well-known fact that from the late Song on the prefectures of Zhexi paid heavier taxes than any other region in China. A report dated to the 21st day of the second lunar month of 1510 describes the situation in Songjiang:

The Song county of Huating covered the same area as present-day Songjiang prefecture. In the Shaoxi period (1190–94) the autumn crop was only 112,300 *shi*. In the Jingding period (1260–64), Jia Sidao bought commoners' land and made it into government land. The tax return on the fields was 158,200 *shi*. In the late Song the tax assessment of private and government fields together was 422,800 *shi*. In measuring it a round *dou* measure was used. In the early Yuan the land tax was much lighter than in the late Song. During the Dade period (1297–1307) the fields of Zhu Qing and Zhang Huan were confiscated, and later during the Zhiyuan period (1335–40) the lands of Zhu Guozhen, Guan Ming, and others. The prefecture's tax assessment had grown to 800,000 *shi*. Before the end of the Yuan, Zhang Shicheng further combined various tax assessments including the *yufu*, military fields (*ying*), sandy reclamation fields, official fields (*zhi*), monastery fields, and relay station (*zhanyi*) fees. From the Hongwu period (1368–98) on, the prefecture's total land tax assessment has been more than 1,300,000 *shi*. The taxes on government land are too heavy, and the people have no way to survive. The emperor, sympathizing with the difficulties of the people and heeding the sounds of their distress, reduced the tax assessment on government land by 20 to 30 percent, but Songjiang's tax quota was only reduced to 1,029,000 *shi*. In looking over the historical records of the past there is no other case of taxes as heavy as these.[20]

To summarize the data here, we see that in the Shaoxi period of the Southern Song the tax quota for Songjiang prefecture was only a little over 110,000 *shi*; in the Jingding period Jia Sidao bought up private holdings and turned them into government lands. It was at this time that what was formerly private rent was first incorporated as part of the tax quota. As the land held by the government increased following similar conversions, the tax quota rose, reaching 800,000 *shi* during the Yuan dynasty and climbing to more than 1,300,000 *shi* by the early Ming.

Xu Jie, a native of Huating county, made the following comments on the tax problem during the Jiajing era (1522–66):

> In the western regions of Songjiang the land tax is 3 to 5 *dou* per *mu*, and the rent in that area is 1.3 to 1.5 *shi* per *mu*. There are some places like the market town of Jinzezhen where it reaches 1.7 to 1.8 *shi* per *mu*. In the western regions of the prefecture fields that have a tax of 5 *dou* and a rent of 1.3 *shi* are classified in the lowest rank. In the eastern regions of the prefecture, tax is .5 to 1 *dou* per *mu* and the rent is 5 to 7 *dou* per *mu*. There are some who pay their rent in cotton or beans, for example, those who live in the 14th and 15th townships (*bao*). The fields on which a tax of .5 *dou* and a rent of 7 *dou* are paid are the superior fields in the eastern regions.[21]

From this passage we see that the tax rates in Songjiang prefecture in the Ming varied from 3 to 5 *dou* in the western regions to .5 to 1 *dou* in the eastern areas. How do these rates compare with national standards? An essay included in *Ming shi* (Standard history of the Ming) reports that "at first the Emperor Taizu fixed the land tax quota for all government land and private land in the empire. The tax on all government land was set at .53 *dou* per *mu* and at .2 *dou* per *mu* on private land."[22] Another source tells us that "beginning with the reign of Ming Taizu the rate for collection of land rent throughout the empire was .3 to .5 *dou* per *mu* but there were some who paid .03 to .05 *dou* per *mu*."[23]

If we compare these rates with those of Songjiang, we can see that the latter were obviously much heavier. These excessively heavy taxes greatly increased the burdens on the tenants, as is demonstrated in Xu Jie's statement that in the western regions of the prefecture rent had reached 1.3 to 1.8 *shi* per *mu* and that in the eastern areas it stood at .5 to .7 *shi* per *mu*.

The great gap in both tax and rent rates between the eastern and western sections of the prefecture was the result of quite different conditions in the two areas. This variation was largely the result of differences in environment, but these factors had in turn given rise to different forms of agrarian management. One contemporary account describes these natural variations:

> In many places there are differences between fertile and barren lands, but there is no place where the extremes between good and bad equal

those in Songjiang. In the eastern and western districts there is not merely a difference between barren and fertile soil. In the west the land is low-lying and the water is level, making it easy to use water wheels. A husband and wife working together can cultivate 25 *mu*, and those who work very hard can cultivate as much as 30 *mu*. The land is fertile and the harvest great. Disregarding those who harvest as much as 3 *shi* per *mu*, let us only speak of those who harvest 2.5 *shi* per *mu*. Each year they will bring in 70 to 80 *shi* of rice. Therefore they often pay 1.6 to 1.7 *shi* per *mu* in rent. In the eastern areas the land is high with many banks and terraces. The use of water wheels is quite restricted and is really no different from those areas where water has to be drawn from wells. The water is often insufficient, and the sprouts dry up and die. Whenever there is a drought, the sound of the water wheels can be heard unceasingly throughout the night. Even if a husband and wife expend all of their energy in cultivation, they can still till only 5 *mu*. In years when there is a bumper harvest, they may bring in 1.5 *shi* per *mu*. Therefore those whose rent is high pay 8 *dou* and those whose rent is low may pay only 4 to 5 *dou* of yellow beans. Even if he works diligently throughout the year, after he pays his rent a peasant will only have enough rice for two or three months. They must look to the maturing of the spring wheat crop to provide the income for future cultivation. Throughout the summer they drink weak wheat gruel. Day and night they peddle the water wheels until the soles of their feet are calloused. This is different from the situation in the west.[24]

This passage describes the land in the western districts of Songjiang prefecture as low, level, and fertile, and thus quite suitable for paddy fields, while that in the east was higher and difficult to irrigate. We will put aside, for the moment, consideration of the western sections of the prefecture and turn our attention to the eastern districts. Tenant management in this region was conditioned by the hard labor required to irrigate the fields. Even when working to exhaustion, a husband and wife together could cultivate no more than 5 *mu*. On a 5-*mu* unit, the harvest might be 1.5 *shi* per *mu* or a total annual return of 7.5 *shi*. If we subtract a rent of 7 *dou* per *mu* or a total of 3.5 *shi*, the real income is only 4 *shi*. Since a Ming dynasty *shi* is equal to a contemporary Japanese measure of 5.8 to 5.9 *tō*,[25] an income of this amount, even if we take into account the additional wheat crop, could not provide even a low level of subsistence. In other words, the tax increases from the late Song on had resulted in extreme impoverishment for the tenants who made up most of Songjiang's peasant population,[26] particularly for the tenants in the eastern districts who could not meet their subsistence needs if they produced only rice.[27]

The trend toward fragmentation in the scale of the peasant economic unit which we see reflected here was not, of course, peculiar to Songjiang prefecture, but was rather a general phenomenon common to the other Zhexi prefectures subject to heavy taxation. However, in these other prefectures, handicraft activities formed a regular supplement to the peasant family's income. For example, silk textiles were produced in Suzhou and Hangzhou, ramie cloth was produced in Changzhou and Zhenjiang, and sericulture and the production of raw silk were well developed in Huzhou and Jiaxing. The development of such sideline industries as a supplement to the family economy allowed peasant families to retain some small surplus even after the payment of land taxes. In contrast, the situation in Songjiang was quite different, as we can see from the following description:

Mulberry: Songjiang prefecture does not put much effort into sericulture, and there is little planting of mulberry. During the Yuan dynasty, Prefect Wang Zhihe had an illustrated explanation on mulberry cultivation printed and encouraged the people to plant it. For a while it grew like forests, and he was referred to as Prefect Forest. Qian Qingyu planted a thousand mulberry trees at Panlong-tang. The Provincial Censor Zhou Bowen referred to them as the "brocade mound." Xu Xuanhu urged the people in the coastal areas to practice sericulture, and he himself planted several hundred mulberry trees in his family garden. Nevertheless, it was difficult to promote these customs, and sericulture did not develop. The trade in raw silk was all in other districts.[28]

As this text shows, although there was much promotion of mulberry cultivation and sericulture, it never really caught on in Songjiang prefecture, and as a result a rural silk textile industry never developed.[29]

As for flax and ramie, we find no mention of them in the 1504 *Shanghai xianzhi* (Shanghai county gazetteer) and only the following note in the 1521 *Huating xianzhi* (Huating county gazetteer): "In recent years none of the following have been produced: ramie, *huangcao* cloth, flax cloth, and Jinshan cloth."[30] Clearly by the Zhengde period (1506–21) these textiles had disappeared. According to this record, the production of ramie and flax-style textiles did not develop into a full-scale rural handicraft industry but rather disappeared as the production of cotton cloth developed. It would seem that for Songjiang prefecture sericulture was not advantageous and the production of

ramie and flax were only slightly so. Neither sideline was profitable
enough to meet the heavy tax demands. If things had continued to
develop in the way that they then seemed to be headed, there was a
danger of a complete collapse in the agrarian economy.

The escape from this impending crisis was provided by the development of the cotton handicraft industry, which had its start about the
same time as the first increases in the land tax. The Songjiang cotton
industry functioned in the same way as the various rural sideline
industries in the other Zhexi prefectures—that is, as a supplement that
allowed for the payment of heavy taxes. It was the coming together
of the technological preconditions (i.e., cotton cultivation and weaving
technology) with strong economic necessity that spurred the development of the Songjiang cotton industry.

Songjiang's superiority in cotton textile production was already
recognized by the Yuan period, as we can see from a reference that
notes with regard to cotton, "the Songjiang area is good [at its pro-
duction]."[31] From the legend of the Taoist nun Huang we know that
by this time the people of Wunijing were already trading their cotton
textiles in other areas, and by the Ming dynasty cotton was so well
established that it was included in the tax assessment quotas as we
can see from the following Board of Revenue memorial:

[The Board of Revenue memorializes:] In rewarding the military
a great quantity of cotton cloth is needed. We request that you order
the four prefectures of Zhexi to include 300,000 bolts of cotton cloth
in the fall tax assessment. [The Emperor comments:] Songjiang is a
cotton-cloth producing area. Therefore order that prefecture to
forward this tax. This will also be convenient for the people there.
Any remaining tax due should be paid in rice as before.[32]

This change in the tax assessment is mentioned in many sources of the
day. In addition, a number of literary sources refer to the shift in
production. For example, Gu Yu, a resident of Shanghai, included
the following poem in a collection published in 1588: "On the plains
they plant much cotton / And the weavers have ceased working in
ramie. / Since the officials are rigorous in their tax collections /
Many in the town are selling cotton yarn."[33] This passage agrees with
our earlier data that the production of ramie cloth had been supplanted
by cotton spinning and weaving, and clearly shows that cotton spinning
and weaving had been adopted as a sideline industry for the purpose
of meeting tax demands. The last line of the poem tells us that local
producers were selling their yarn for cash. It would seem most likely

that they used the cash thus obtained to purchase rice which was then turned over to the state in payment of taxes. I am assuming here that the assessments like that of 1370 for 300,000 bolts of cloth were of a temporary nature and that most taxes were still paid in rice.

During the first part of the Ming dynasty new tax payment methods were gradually developed. The 1512 *Songjiang fuzhi* (Songjiang prefectural gazetteer) describes the development beginning with the reform by Provincial Governor Zhou Chen:

In 1433 the Governor of South Zhili, Zhou Chen, memorialized with regard to converting the tax quotas and surcharges. During the Hongwu and Yongle reigns [1368–1424] the local tax quota was high and undelivered grain was accumulating. (For example, in 1429, 439,000 *shi* should have been delivered to the capital, but in fact only 66,000 *shi* were actually sent.) For every *shi* of tax grain, surcharges equaling one *shi* were added on, bringing the leveling grain assessment (*pingmi*) to a total of 2 *shi*—and even this was insufficient to meet the expenses of transport. Zhou Chen suggested that if the new system were implemented, the previous evil practices would disappear and within two years all taxes would be paid in full. His plan was as follows:

Surtaxes [omitted]

Tax conversion statute

"Gold Floral Silver" of 1.1 taels of silver will be equal to 4.4 to 4.6 *shi* of rice. For every tael, a transport and meltage charge of .008 tael will be added.

One bolt of wide, white "three shuttle cloth" will be equal to from 2 to 2.4/2.5 *shi* of rice. For each bolt of cloth, a transport and boat fee of .20 to .26 *shi* of rice will be added. Each bolt of cloth should be 4 *zhang* long and 2.5 *chi* wide. According to the old standards it should weigh 3 *jin*. Those who are presenting it must bring it for inspection. In his memorial Zhou Chen suggested that if the cloth was deficient in weight then a longer or wider length of cloth could be collected. Red yarn was to be woven into both ends of each bolt of cloth to prevent thieves from cutting off the ends.

At present we are still following this plan. A bolt of wide white cotton cloth should be equal to .99 to 1.0 *shi* of rice, and for each bolt a transport and shipping surcharge of .10 to .12 *shi* will be added.

Since the taxes on government land were very heavy, this was a method for equalizing them (commonly called *qingji*).

One *shi* of white glutinous rice should be equal to 1.2 *shi* of regular white rice.

The above assessments were lighter on privately owned land, and this was a way of equalizing the tax.[34]

On the basis of this proposal submitted by the governor of South Zhili in 1433 a new tax collection method which allowed for the collection in kind of cotton cloth and silver was implemented. On the government lands that had unusually high tax rates, this tax was collected at a specified conversion rate in either "three shuttle cloth" or wide white cotton cloth. From this time on, the cotton cloth produced in Songjiang became a permanent part of the tax assessment. There is no question that this shift in the taxation system indirectly encouraged the development of the Songjiang cotton textile industry. Historical sources record a great leap in cotton production at this time. We find further support for this assertion in a tax relief proposal written by the prefect of Donghai, Zhang Bi: "Although cotton cloth is a famous product of Songjiang, in the past not so much was produced. Therefore it was not part of the tax quota. In the last twenty or thirty years many of the people of Songjiang have come to depend on weaving for their livelihood, and cotton cloth is included as part of the regular land tax."[35] Zhang Bi was active during the Chenghua era (1465–87) and thus his "last twenty or thirty years" would refer to the reigns of Xuande and Zhengtong (1426–49). This evidence further confirms our supposition that the development of the cotton industry was closely related to the inclusion of cotton cloth as a permanent part of the tax assessments.

At the same time that cotton was first included on a permanent basis in the Songjiang tax quota, a similar process was taking place in neighboring cotton-producing counties. As an example, we can cite the 1605 edition of the *Jiading xianzhi* (Jiading county gazetteer):

His Honor (Zhou Chen) saw that the soil of Jiading was of poor quality and the people impoverished, and yet the taxes were the same as those of neighboring counties. This was a pitiful situation since the land produced cotton and the people customarily produced cloth. He memorialized and it was ordered that the tax should include 200,000 bolts of "official cloth" (*guanbu*), with each bolt substituting for one *shi* of rice. This was put into effect the next year. . . when they allocated the quota and 15,000 [of the 200,000] bolts to Taicang. Late in the Zhengde era, an inspector shifted some of the quota, and 10,000 bolts were assigned to Yixing and 46,000 bolts to Kunshan.[36]

It was the same governor of South Zhili, Zhou Chen who initiated tax reforms in these neighboring areas, so it is likely that the cotton industries there began to develop in ways very similar to the industry in Songjiang.

We have traced the process by which Songjiang peasant households, pressed by heavy tax obligations, undertook cotton textile production to help meet such tax demands. Cotton textile production thus first developed as a supplement to household income. As time passed and output increased, the quality of such representative fabrics as "three shuttle cloth" also improved. The character of the developing cotton industry also began to change. Cotton cloth was no longer produced just to meet tax demands but was sold on a more general market, and as the commercial trade in cotton grew, eventually a nationwide market was formed.[37] Eventually the production of cotton cloth, which had originally been directly linked to taxation, developed into pure commodity production. In examining this shift we must consider the connections to the spread of silver exchange in the Jiangnan region and the development of commercial activities which accompanied this monetization of the economy. A further factor is the general unification of tax collection methods in the Single Whip reform. In the new tax collection methods, the old tax captains (liang-zhang) were replaced by wholesale merchants who took responsibility for the collection of cotton cloth taxes: "1486, Songjiang Prefect Fan Ying memorializes: excluding the portion of the grain tax that has for a long time been delivered in kind, the remainder should be converted and collected in silver. . . this should reduce infringements by the tax captains. The cloth wholesalers will replace the tax [captains][38] as those responsible for forwarding cloth, and when there are deficits they should use their private stocks to fulfill the quota."[39]

This suggests a new stage in the process which had begun during the Xuande reign (1426–35), when Zhou Chen had allowed the substitution of cotton for payment in rice. In this new stage we find the substitution of cash payment for payment in cotton cloth. When Fan Ying suggested this change in 1486, his proposals followed the general trend toward conversion of payments in kind to payment in silver that is collectively known as the Single Whip reform. His proposal, however, also suggests that there had been significant changes in the Songjiang region. The role given to cotton textile merchants clearly shows the expansion of the cotton exchange market and the merchants' active role in it. It also suggests that while part of the cotton forwarded as tax came from the cloth directly turned over in kind by the producers, some of it also probably had passed through the market in its commodity form. This in turn was made possible by the fact that Songjiang cotton production was no longer conducted solely for the purpose of tax payment, but had shifted into the commodity production stage. A late-Qing gazetteer for Huating county gives a summary of the developments in the tax system:

> Songjiang and other prefectures were ordered to pay 60 percent of the tax that had been collected in wide, white cotton cloth in kind, and the remaining 40 percent of the tax should be converted to payment in silver. We are not certain when the tax on "three shuttle cloth" was first converted to cash payment. . . . A 1620 regulation stated that each bolt of three shuttle cloth was to be converted at a rate of 6.1 *qian* per bolt, while the conversion rate for white cotton cloth was 3 *qian* per bolt. Those who had previously been required to pay in kind could now present cash, according to the conversion rate, to the tax-paying households. This system was established during the Jiajing reign period. At first the rice tax was converted to payment in cotton, and then payment in cotton was again converted to payment in silver. So those who had once paid in rice now all must pay in silver.[40]

In 1504, 40 percent of the wide white cotton cloth quota was converted to silver, and by 1620 both white cotton cloth and three shuttle cloth had been converted to silver. This statement shows that at tax-paying time, the cotton textile producing Songjiang peasants who had formerly paid their taxes in cotton cloth would now pay in silver an amount equal to the value of the cloth. This silver was given to those designated as tax-remitting households,[41] who were then responsible for tax collection. The tax-paying households would then use the silver to purchase the cotton cloth which they turned over to the government.

This system was the result of the tax reform initiated in 1443 by Zhou Chen. Songjiang cotton production had developed as a rural sideline industry in response to increases in taxes from the Song on and the resulting fragmentation in the scale of the peasant family economy which had made it unable to meet basic subsistence needs. Cotton textile production, which was originally seen as a way of meeting tax assessments, was quickly drawn into the network created by the spread of the monetary economy in the Jiangnan region from the mid-Ming on. This led to the expansion of the commercial market, and cotton textile production increasingly took on the character of full-scale commodity production. This stage of full-scale commodity production represents the final form of the early Chinese cotton industry.

To this point, our attention has been centered on the development of the cotton industry. It is also important to recognize the limits of this early cotton industry. The economic functions of cotton production are convincingly described in a late-Ming agricultural handbook written by the famous Shanghai Christian convert, Xu Guangqi. Xu says:

During the Shaoxing era [1131–62] of the Song the tax quota for Songjiang was 180,000 *shi*. Now it is 970,000 *shi* of leveling grain. In making the calculations it is necessary to add on the surcharges for wastage fees and transport fees, which were originally part of the service levy. These bring the total to ten times the Song assessment.[It is often said that] the land is extensive, but it does not exceed 100 *li* north-south or east-west. Nor is the income from agriculture more than that of other prefectures and counties. This total of one million taels in tax assessments has been in existence for three hundred years. The people all depend on the shuttle and the loom. This situation is not peculiar to Songjiang. The same applies to the cloth and silk floss produced in Suzhou, Hangzhou, Changzhou, and Zhenjiang, and to the silk produced in Jiaxing and Huzhou. All depend on women's skills. [By relying on them] it is possible to pay all of the above taxes and also provide for daily livelihood. If they had to rely on the income from the land, there would be no way to manage.[42]

This passage describes the situation in Songjiang from the late Song on, when tax increases were accompanied by agrarian distress and the income from the cotton industry was used to make up deficits. In this situation the economic role of cotton production was an important part of the rural economic structure. The cotton industry was thus developing on the base of a greatly weakened rural society. To draw an analogy it is as if the cotton industry was the fetus developing within the womb of a thin and weakened mother. Where normally the mother would provide nourishment to the child, in this case the child was fated to nourish the mother. As a result, there was no way for the child to separate and become independent. Thus because of the limitations of the agrarian economic structure of Songjiang, the early cotton industry was blocked from achieving a more modern character.

Regional distribution of cotton cultivation

In analyzing the structure of the early cotton industry we can divide it into two major sections, the production of raw materials (cotton cultivation) and the processing of the finished textiles. In this section we will examine the first of these, paying specific attention to the structure of management and its relationship to the overall agrarian order.

Cotton was generally grown on higher-lying fields in the areas close to the sea.[43] In Songjiang this corresponded to the eastern parts of the prefecture, the region stretching from Shanghai county to the borders of Jiading and Taicang counties in Suzhou prefecture. Xu Guangqi verifies this, commenting: "In the areas around Suzhou, cotton is planted, particularly in our Haishang and Lianquan, and the profits are very high."[44] In this passage, "Haishang" refers to Shanghai county[45] and Lianquan is another name for Lianjitang in Jiading county.[46] The late Ming-early Qing poet Wu Weiye from Plum Village (Meicun) in Taicang, wrote in the preface to his poem "Cotton" that cotton was planted "from Shanghai and Lianquan [Jiading]—all the way to Taicang, / The hills and ridges and the high fields are very suitable for this."[47]

Why did cotton cultivation spread in this region? We have already noted that in the eastern parts of Songjiang the land was elevated and irrigation was inconvenient. Even the most diligent efforts brought only small rewards. In the areas close to the sea, the soil was alkaline and thus unsuited to paddy rice. Cotton, however, grows well on high-lying fields and also does quite well in alkaline soils.[48] A sub-prefect, Sun Gongying, discussed these conditions in an essay on the problems of heavy taxation:

> In the areas near the sea, the people fear the clouds and rain at dawn and dusk, and in the areas far from the sea, they fear the difficulties of arranging water, wheels. Therefore, neither is suitable for the cultivation of paddy rice. Under these conditions it is better to plant cotton or beans. Even in planting cotton and beans, they still cannot avoid dependence on weather conditions. If there are no wind and rain storms, there will be a bountiful harvest. If the harvest is plentiful, they can buy rice to pay taxes and still have some left over.[49]

From this quotation we see that, barring natural disasters, there was greater profit in growing cotton or beans. Using the profits the people purchased rice to meet tax obligations and still had some surplus left over.[50] The source cited above states that such high-lying fields were suitable for either cotton or beans, but Xu Guangqi suggests that cotton was the more common option. He gives the following reason: "In the higher fields bordering the sea to the southeast of our native area. . . in these areas they do not dare to grow paddy rice. If they plant cotton and there is a long drought, then parasitic insects will appear. If they plant beans, the profits are lower."[51] On these higher-lying fields, cotton, whose only shortcoming was dependence on the weather, was the only crop that was economically superior to rice. To summarize, the development of cotton cultivation in this area was the result of natural conditions that were unsuitable for rice yet suitable for cotton, and cf the superior profit level of cotton.

In this region, the fields planted in cotton were referred to as *miantian* or *huatian*.[52] Since neither of these terms was part of the official, legal vocabulary used in land registration, it is impossible to get statistics on the percentage of the cultivated land planted in cotton. However, we do find the following information in Xu Guangqi's handbook: "In Shanghai there is a total of two million *mu* of land, including government land, privately owned land, military colony land, and salt household land. More than half is planted in cotton, that is, more than one million *mu*."[53] Shanghai county was in the eastern part of Songjiang prefecture. Xu tells us that more than half the land was planted in cotton; the rest was probably used for paddy rice. In an early-Qing source, the poem mentioned earlier by Wu from Plum Village, we find: "In the border area where Jiading, Taicang, and Shanghai counties come together, 30 percent of the land is in rice and 70 percent is in cotton."[54] This suggests that in areas of higher elevation the division between cotton and rice was 70/30, but we must remember that Jiading county had the highest percentage of its arable land in cotton of any county in the Ming. The 1605 Jiading gazetteer includes a report on tax payments for 1583 which notes: "Jiading county is surrounded on three sides by the sea. At the higher elevations, the soil is depleted, and the lower lying areas are sandy. Irrigation is difficult, and the use of well sweeps is often impossible. Although in the registration it may still be listed as paddy land, in fact it is used exclusively for cotton."[55] Thus because of the difficulties of irrigation, well over half of the land was planted in cotton. Let us compare this report with the results of an investigation by the county magistrate Zhu Tingyi [1546–1600]:

Total arable land	1,298,617 *mu**
Forested and waste land	130,190 *mu*
Planted in rice and grain	131,160 *mu*
Planted in cotton and beans	1,037,250 *mu*

*Numbers have been rounded off to the closest *mu*.[56]

According to these figures, land planted in cotton and beans comprises a little less than 80 percent of the total. If we subtract the forest and wasteland which was probably not cultivable, then it comprises 89 percent of the total arable land. If we consider the fact that profits from beans were low and the fact (cited later) that beans and cotton were often interplanted, then it seems clear that we will not be far off if we assume that most of the land said to be planted in cotton and beans was in fact planted in cotton. Therefore, we can see that just a little under 90 percent of the land in Jiading county was planted in cotton.

From the above we can determine that the percentage of arable land under cotton cultivation stood at just over 50 percent for Shanghai county and just under 90 percent in Jiading. Such extensive planting of cotton helped to supply the raw materials for the flourishing Songjiang cotton textile industry. In addition, raw materials were brought in from North China (to which cotton cultivation had been introduced in the late Ming), and there were also large-scale imports of raw materials from the Fujian and Guangdong areas.

Such wide-scale cultivation of cotton obviously played a role in influencing the agrarian structure. We now want to turn to the question of the impact of cotton cultivation on the overall agrarian structure. In doing so, we will investigate the managerial structure of cotton cultivation.

Management of cotton cultivation

The increasing sophistication of cotton growing technology is evident in the very detailed data that is provided in Xu Guangqi's agricultural handbook. Let us begin with his discussion of the different varieties of cotton:

There are many varieties of cotton grown in China. *Jianghua* variety comes from central Chu. The fiber content is not high and 20 *jin* of unginned cotton yields 5 *jin* of cotton fiber that is very strong. The *beihua* variety comes from Zhili and Shandong; it is soft and fine and suitable for spinning and weaving. Its fiber content is quite low, 20 *jin* of unginned cotton giving 4 to 5 *jin* of fiber. *Zhehua* comes from Yuyao and is suitable for spinning and weaving. The fiber content is quite high, with a return of 7 *jin* of fiber from 20 *jin* of unginned cotton. The cotton planted in the Suzhou area generally is similar to these varieties, but there are also some varieties that are slightly different. One is called *huangdirang*. Its stalks are yellow, and it is about the size of corn, with a high fiber content. Another variety is called *qinghe*. It is green is color with a fiber that is finer than other varieties, and it has a high fiber content. Another variety is called *heihe* (black stalk). It also has a very fine fiber. The plant's stalk is black in color, and the fiber content is high. Another variety is called *kuandayi*; its stalk is white and "floating," and it has a high fiber content. All of these yield 9 *jin* of fiber for every 20 *jin* of unginned cotton. *Huangdirang* is quite strong and its fiber is softer and finer, making it suitable for spinning and weaving. Therefore it is planted. There is one variety called *zihua*; its surface is smooth, and it has a large stalk. It has a low fiber content, yielding 4 *jin* of fiber for every 20 of unginned cotton. Its cloth is used for making clothes that are rather thick and elegant. In the market the cloth that is dyed before sale is not as good as that which is undyed; therefore the *zihua* variety is planted.[57]

This source records the different varieties of cotton grown at that time, their quality, and the percentage of ginned cotton that can be obtained. According to this, the three chief varieties growing in this region were *jianghua*, *beihua*, and *zhehua*, but there were other varieties as well. During the Qing there are records of other varieties including *tiegengdayi* (iron stalk), *huanghedayi* (yellow stalk), *jiaoqihuang*, *xiaomaihuanghua*, and *pudong qinggeng*.[58] This precise knowledge of the different varieties of cotton and their special characteristics seems to be the result of the fact that cotton was being produced as a commodity (i.e., for market sale).

Cultivation technology, including crop rotation patterns, double-cropping, and interplanting, had also developed. With regard to crop rotation, Xu Guangqi says that on the higher elevation fields where it was possible to cultivate either cotton or rice, if cotton was grown for two successive years, rice should be planted in the third year. If this was not done, he warned, insects would appear.[59] A Qing edition of one of the local gazetteers notes, "If you plant rice this year, then next year, you should plant cotton or beans. This is called turning over the field."[60] This form of crop rotation was limited to fields where it was possible to grow rice. In places like Jiading where lack of irrigation had led to the planting of almost 90 percent of the land in cotton, the situation was quite different. A 1594 stele inscription written by Wang Yijue states:

In the past, people regarded water control as an important government responsibility. Therefore for two hundred years it was maintained without collapse. During the Zhengde and Jiajing reigns there were still those who maintained this commitment. But in recent years 80 to 90 percent of the irrigation channels have fallen into disuse and only narrow creeks remain. This is because people have linked their fate to cotton cultivation. One of the characteristics of cotton is that it does not require flooded fields. In Jiading it can be grown for ten years straight without rotation and with continuing good harvests.[61]

In areas like Jiading it was thus possible to have almost full-time cotton farming with no crop rotation.

As for double-cropping in conjunction with cotton cultivation, Xu Guangqi advises that double-cropping will lower the fertility of the land and should be avoided. In those cases where it cannot be avoided, a second crop of either barley or highland barley could be grown, provided a generous amount of fertilizer was used. But double-cropping of cotton with crops with a late harvest date like wheat should absolutely be avoided. The 1744 *Zhenyang xianzhi* (Zhenyang county gazetteer) states: "The people in this county are very busy working at cotton and don't plant wheat. They only plant it on the banks and borders between the fields. This is done to preserve the land's fertility and because the harvest season for wheat is too late. Those who plant wheat on all their land are planning to plant rice."[62] Behind this statement is the assumption that cotton and wheat could not be double-cropped. Chu Hua's *Mumian pu* (Treatise on cotton) offers further evidence: "Those who plant cotton plant barley as a second crop. In the summer they harvest the barley and in the autumn, the cotton. This is known as barley mixed with cotton."[63] This double-cropping of cotton with barley is a reflection of the basic intensive, garden-style nature of Chinese agriculture.

In the case of interplanting, the cotton seed was planted in early to mid-April. There was thus a short overlap between the two crops. With regard to interplanting, Xu Guangqi warned that the planting of beans on the field banks would damage the cotton harvest and should be avoided. In spite of this warning, beans, sesame, or imported barley were usually interplanted.[64]

It is clear from this cropping pattern that even though cotton production in this region had begun as a form of commodity production, it had not yet been able to separate itself from the traditional multicrop intensive style of Chinese agriculture and had not yet developed into modern monoculture. The 1673 *Jiading xianzhi* (Jiading county gazetteer) offers further support for this conclusion: "Tenants today plant beans in the inter-rows between the cotton plants. If the cotton crop should fail, they still have the beans to meet the rent payment."[65] The cropping pattern described here represents one of the passive methods of self-preservation adopted by cotton-growing peasants and is an indication of the overall fragility of agrarian commodity production when under the control of merchant capital. It is also important to note that although there had been some structural changes in agriculture (i.e., the development of commodity production), the rent relationship that linked landlord and tenant still continued to exist.

We will not go into other aspects of the technology of cotton farming —that is, irrigation, use of fertilizers,[66] planting, and cultivating—since the details can be found in any of the agricultural manuals (*nongshu*) of this period.[67]

Following the harvest, cotton was dried on top of a reed screen, bundled up in packages made of bulrushes, and sold.[68] The major question here is whether the cotton that was sold by the peasants was ginned or unginned cotton. If we cannot clarify this problem, then we will not know whether the cotton-ginning process should be included as part of the peasant economy or not, and it will be difficult to calculate the profit rates for cotton cultivation. This problem is also linked to consideration of the question of why cotton cultivation was largely restricted to the eastern section of Songjiang prefecture and did not spread to the western regions of the prefecture. In answering this question we should also come to a better understanding of the limits of cotton cultivation within the peasant economy.

Chu Hua's *Mumian pu* (Treatise on cotton) provides some data that will help answer this question. He first notes that "most of the people selling cotton in the county come from the two areas of Chongming and Haimen. The people there pound the cotton to get out the seeds which they sell in various places. The cotton fiber is stiff and strong but not suitable for spinning and weaving." Thus in at least the two areas mentioned here, Chongming and Haimen, the ginning is done by local people. Further on in the same book we find, "In the second and third months people from Fujian and Guangdong bring sugar candy for sale. In the fall they buy ginned cotton (*huayi*)—not cloth—and then return home." *Huayi* here refers to ginned cotton, as we see from another passage in Chu Hua's book describing the cotton gin: "The cotton gin is called the *liche*. . . . The cotton is pressed between two rollers which are moved by the hands and feet, forcing the seeds to fall out and putting out seedless cotton. The cotton that emerges piles up like banks of clouds and is called ginned cotton (*huayi*)."[69] From this we know that the cotton that appeared on the market had already been ginned. However, it is still not clear whether the ginning was done by the cotton producers themselves since we do not know whether the "local people" refers to peasants. Further, this reference is to a kind of low-grade cotton that was not suitable for spinning and weaving. In addition, we cannot be certain whether the ginned cotton that appeared in its commodity form on the market was being directly sold by peas-

Table 1. Rice and cotton prices late Ming-early Qing

	Rice Prices			Cotton Prices					
Year/Month	1 *shi*	1.5 *shi*	2.5 *shi*	100 *jin*	80 *jin*	28 *jin*	A	B	C
pre-1628				1.6–1.7	1.28–1.36	.44–.47			
1628				4–5	3.2–4	1.12–.4			
1632	1.0[a]	1.5	2.5						
1642	5.0[b]	7.5	12.5	.5–.6	.4–.48	.175	X	X	X
1647	4.0	6.0	10.0						
1649	1.2[c]	1.8	3.0	3.4–3.5	2.7–2.8	.95–.98	O	X	X
1650/2	1.0[d]	1.5	2.5						
1650/9	2.0[e]	3.0	5.0	5.0	4.0	1.4	O	X	X
1651/2	3.0[f]	4.5	7.5						
1651/3	3.5	5.25	8.75	9.0	7.2	2.52	O	X	X
1651/4	4.0	6.0	10.0						
1651/6	4.8–4.9	7.2–7.35	12–12.23						
1651/7	2.0[g]	3.0	5.0						
1652/summer	4.0[h]	6.0	10.0						
1652/fall	2.5–2.6	3.75–3.9	6.25–6.5						
1657/2	0.8	1.2	2.0	2.5	2.0	0.7	O	X	O
1659/3	2.0	3.0	5.0	4.5	3.6	1.26	O	X	X
1661/10	1.5[i]	2.25	3.75	2.0	1.6	0.56	X	X	X
1661/11	1.8[j]	2.7	4.5						
1662/1	1.9[k]	2.85	4.75	3.0	2.4	0.84	X	X	X
1662/7	1.2[l]	1.8	3.0	2.0	1.6	0.56	X	X	X
1670/6	1.3[m]	1.95	3.25						
1670/8	0.9[n]	1.35	2.25	1.7–1.8	1.36–1.44	.47–.5	O	X	X
1670/9	0.8[o]	1.2	2.0	2.5	2.0	0.7	O	X	O
1670/10	0.9[p]	1.35	2.25	3.0	2.4	0.84	O	X	O
1670/late 10	1.3	1.95	3.25	4.0	3.2	1.12	O	X	X
1671/fall	1.1	1.65	2.75	3.0	2.4	0.84	O	X	X
1673/fall	0.63[q]	0.94	1.57						
1674				1.9[r]	1.52	0.53			
1677/summer				2.6–2.7[s]	2.08–2.16	.72–.75			
1678	0.73[t]	1.09	1.82						
1679/spring	1.4–1.5	2–2.25	3.5–3.75						
1679/8	2.0[u]	3.0	5.0	1.5–1.6	1.2–1.6	.42–.47	X	X	X
1680/summer	2.0[v]	3.0	5.0	3.0	2.4	0.48	X	X	X
1681/summer				3.5–3.6	2.8–2.88	0.98–1.008			
1682/5	0.85[w]	1.275	2.125	4.1[x]	3.28	1.14	O	X	O
1682/winter	0.56[y]	0.84	1.4						
1684/fall-winter	0.9[z]	1.35	2.25	1.3–1.4[aa]	1.04–1.12	.36–.39	X	X	X

All prices are given in silver taels; years have been converted to the Western calendar, but months refer to lunar calendar months.

a. price is quite high so people are suffering
b. later in the year, average of 2–3
c. bumper harvest
d. price of polished rice
e. price of new rice; glutinous rice, 1.8, and polished rice, 2.5

ants or whether there were intermediaries involved in the process. Therefore, solely on the basis of the above source we cannot determine whether the peasants were doing the ginning themselves.

In examining this question let us turn to the *Yueshi bian*, written by a man from Shanghai, Ye Mengzhu. This book includes detailed data on changes in rice and cotton prices in Shanghai in the early Qing. On the basis of the comparison between these prices we will attempt to determine whether the prices given are for ginned or unginned cotton and on the basis of that decision, whether the ginning was done by the peasants themselves or by others. After figuring out what was involved in peasant management of cotton cultivation, we will then attempt to calculate income and profit ratios. Table 1 provides the basic data from the *Yueshi bian*.[70]

Before we can reach any conclusions, it is important to discuss the estimates involved. First we will turn to an estimate of output per *mu*. One Qianlong-era source, the [*Yuti*] *Mianhua tu* (Cotton manual bearing the emperor's poems), offers the following estimates: "The cotton

---

f. price of polished rice
g. new unhusked rice
h. price of polished rice
i. price of polished rice; new rice, 1.3
j. price of new rice
k. coarse rice; polished rice, 2.1
l. price of early rice; glutinous rice, 1.3–1.4
m. price of polished rice; earlier in the year 0.5–0.6 a *shi*
n. new rice
o. glutinous rice, 0.7
p. glutinous rice, 0.8
q. new rice
r. best quality of cotton
s. best quality up to 3.0; accumulated cotton stocks from earlier years all sold, rich merchants making huge profits
t. new rice
u. earliest new rice, 1.7
v. polished rice
w. polished rice
x. superior-quality white cotton
y. new chaff rice
z. polished rice
aa. superior white cotton

In column A, an O means that the value of 80 *jin* of cotton was higher than that of 1.5 *shi* of rice; an X indicates that it was lower.

In column B an O indicates that the value of 28 *jin* of cotton was higher than 1.5 *shi* of rice; an X indicates that it was lower.

In column C with cotton output at 80 *jin* and rice at 2.5 *shi* per *mu*, an O indicates that cotton was more profitable; an X that rice was more profitable.

still attached to the stem is called unginned cotton (*zihua*), and after the seeds are removed it is called ginned cotton (*ranghua*). The superior quality of ginned cotton is known as *jinghua*. . . . If there is a bumper harvest, the yield per *mu* will be 120 *jin* of unginned cotton; if the harvest is average, the yield will be 80 to 90 *jin* of unginned cotton. For every *jin* of cotton, you will get one-third of a *jin* of ginned cotton."[71] This source reflects the conditions in the northern provinces, particularly North Zhili. For the conditions in the area around Songjiang, we can turn to a 1511 report by the governor, Zhang Feng, which comments on the eastern areas of Songjiang: "On the lower-grade fields in the area near the sea, the cotton yield will not exceed 50 to 60 *jin*."[72] Xu Guangqi notes in his chapter on cotton: "For Shandong and Zhejiang cotton growers, a harvest of 200 to 300 *jin* per *mu* is considered normal. The people of Yuyao and Haiyin know that if they exert all of their energy in cultivating cotton they also can harvest 200 to 300 *jin* per *mu*. . . . When the people from these areas hear of our dense planting and small harvests, they laugh at us."[73] Xu thus suggests that the low harvests of Songjiang in comparison with other areas may be due to too dense cultivation. He continues, "If there is a return of 30 *jin* per *mu* it is sufficient to meet the land tax quota, and 50 *jin* per *mu* will meet the labor service obligation."

From this we can see that it must have been possible to raise the harvest from 30 to 50 *jin* per *mu*, but there is no question that the Songjiang harvest fell way behind the 200 to 300 *jin* harvests of other areas. If we look at contemporary output figures, native cotton yields approximately 100 *jin* per *mu*.[74] Since the source cited above suggests a yield of 50 to 60 *jin* on lower grade fields, it would seem appropriate to assume an average yield of approximately 80 *jin* per *mu*. This is a little less than the figure given in the *Mianhua tu*. This may be an underestimate, but when we use this in calculations in conjunction with the price figures given in Table 1 we must remember that the prices given are market prices. The price received by the direct producers would have been lower, and thus if this is an underestimate of output, it will help to compensate for this difference. Therefore we will use an estimate of output of 80 *jin* per *mu* of unginned cotton in our calculations.

Turning to the prices given in Table 1, we can see that if we figure an output of 80 *jin* of unginned cotton per *mu*, and if we assume that the quoted price is for unginned cotton, then the calculation in the table of the price for 80 *jin* gives us the value of output per *mu*. If, however, we assume that the quoted price is for ginned cotton, and if we calculate the ratio of unginned to ginned cotton at the 20/7 rate cited earlier for the *zhehua* variety, then the calculation in the chart for the price of 28 *jin* in fact represents the expected income from one *mu* of land. In order to see if these estimates are accurate, let us compare the results with the quoted rice prices. Sources that we have already cited noted that the average rice harvest in the eastern districts of the prefecture was 1.5 *shi* per *mu* and in the west 2.5 *shi* / *mu*. Our two calculations thus represent the cash value of the rice crop per *mu* in these two regions of Songjiang prefecture. In the column labeled A, an O means that the value of 80 *jin* of cotton was higher than that of 1.5 *shi* of rice, an X indicates that it was lower. In column B an O indicates that the value of 28 *jin* of cotton was higher than 1.5 *shi* of rice, and an X indicates that it was lower.

Since our sources earlier indicated that in the eastern regions of the prefecture cotton cultivation was more profitable than rice, and if we assume that the prices given in the *Yueshi bian* are for ginned cotton, then column B should be a line of O's. However, in fact, we find a solid line of X's. This suggests that cotton was less profitable than rice, and thus contradicts our earlier sources. Therefore, we must conclude that the prices quoted are not for ginned cotton. What happens if we assume that the price was for unginned cotton? If this is correct, then column A should be primarily O's. A check shows eleven O's and seven X's.

Before we discount this figure, we should stop for a moment to consider whether there were any unusual conditions that might have effected the prices. If we do so, we first realize that the year 1638 should be disregarded as an exception. As a result of warfare, market conditions were very confused: the price of rice, a food commodity, escalated while the cotton market was closed and the cotton price fell sharply. The prices quoted for 1661/10 and 1662/1 simply represent seasonal price changes during a single year for both cotton and rice, and only one should be taken into account in the calculation. If we follow the price changes for that year we find that the 1661/10 price is for old polished rice, and new rice for the same month stood at 1.5, in 1661/11 at 1.8, and in the following 1662/1 at 1.9. In a corresponding time period cotton prices showed the following change: 1661/10, 2.0 and in 1662/11, 3.0, or a 50-percent jump in price. If the output should rise just a little above 80 *jin* per *mu*, then the X would become an O. For 1662/7 the difference in income per *mu* for cotton and early rice is very slight. The 1679/8 and 1680/summer prices also belong to one crop year and should be considered together. As we can see, the 100-percent rise in the price of cotton in the latter half of the year left little differential in income per *mu*. The price for 1684/fall-winter is given for polished rice; if we had the price for unhusked rice, it would be lower than that quoted, leaving only a very small difference in profit per *mu* when compared with cotton.

In summary, we can see that of the total of 7 X's two represent seasonal price fluctuations and should not be considered, leaving five X years. The price given for 1642 can be accounted for by very extraordinary circumstances. In the cases of the four remaining examples, the differences in profit are all very small. Turning to the O years, even if we combine all of the quotations for 1662, we are still left with eight examples in which it can be demonstrated that cotton production was economically superior to rice.

From this evidence it is also clear that the prices quoted in the *Yueshi bian* are for unginned cotton. Since the cotton brought to the market was unginned cotton, the ginning process was not part of the work of cotton-growing peasants. The peasants managed the process only as far as picking and drying the cotton. We can find further support for this judgment in an early-Qing Songjiang gazetteer which says: "Cotton is measured by the boll. Superior-quality cotton weighs at least 8 *li* a boll; cotton that weighs less is inferior. The country people divide it according to its size."[75] If the peasants were selling ginned cotton, it would no longer be possible to separate and judge the size of individual bolls of cotton.

Now that we have verified our calculations, we can move on to an estimate of the profit rates for cotton cultivation. We can get an estimate of gross income by multiplying the price of unginned cotton (the 80-*jin* line) by the total area planted in cotton.

If we were to assume that cotton cultivation was only carried out in the western districts, and if we were to compare the profits from cotton with those from rice, what would the results be? Turning again to Table 1, we want to look at column C. If we assume that cotton output per *mu* stands at 80 *jin* and rice output per *mu* at 2.5 *shi*, then column C gives us a comparison of their prices. Looking at column C we find four cases where cotton is more profitable and fourteen cases where rice is more profitable. If we eliminate those entries that simply represent seasonal price changes within a single year, we have a total of thirteen cases with three O's and ten X's.

What does this tell us? It clearly shows that the profits from cotton cultivation do not equal those of rice cultivation in fertile regions like western Songjiang prefecture, and it thus makes clear the reason why cotton cultivation developed in the eastern section of the prefecture and in areas that shared similar conditions. In spite of the fact that cotton cultivation was a profitable business which supplied essential raw materials to the textile industry, it still had to compete with other crops, particularly rice, and was only grown in those areas where it would bring in a higher profit. One important factor here is the fact that the market for raw materials for the Songjiang cotton textile industry was not monopolized by just this one region. As the national market developed, cotton from other regions was imported to help supply the Songjiang textile industry.[76]

While it is not difficult to imagine that for the impoverished peasants of eastern Songjiang prefecture cultivation of the more profitable cotton as a commodity did improve their finances, it is important to note the significant role played by merchant capital in this development. Such merchant capital controlled cotton cultivation, and the profits that resulted from price fluctuations or from a bumper harvest did not necessarily go to the direct producers. Most of the profits flowed into the pockets of the cotton merchants. For example, our chart shows a huge jump in the cotton price for 1677 with the price of one bale (100 *jin*) standing at 2.6 to 2.7 taels of silver, with higher quality cotton selling for as much as three taels/bale. But our source notes, "The cotton stocks from previous years were all sold. The rich merchants made huge profits." Those who had capital, that is, the cotton merchants, would buy up cotton when the price was low and would store it in anticipation of a price rise, making large profits at a later date. Further evidence for this can be found in the statistics on cotton prices for 1642. In spite of the war conditions which led to the fall of the Ming and the rise of the Qing, the price of cotton only fell by five to six *qian*/bale. This can only be the result of a merchant withdrawal from the market in response to the military strife.

It was not only the merchants who were drawing off the profits of cotton-producing peasants. The system of landownership, which remained much as before, also contributed to the drain: "In the eastern districts. . . there are those who pay their rent in cotton or beans; for example in the 14th and 15th townships."[77] From this we see that even in agricultural areas specializing in commodity production the tenants were still paying rent to their landlords in kind. In the local dialect this practice was called "cotton rent" (*huazu*).[78] Since this custom was not limited to eastern Songjiang, it would seem that large quantities of cotton accumulated in the hands of landlords who collected it as rent in kind. As a result the profits from its sale as a commodity would not go to the producers but would rather flow into the pockets of the large landholders.

The above evidence illustrates the qualitative changes in the agrarian structure brought about by the introduction of cotton cultivation. However, these changes did not result in economic independence for the direct producers. Rather, they became dependent on merchant capital; at the same time the large landowners were able to use the changing structure to reap additional profits.

Structure of the Songjiang textile industry

Textile technology

Technology played a major role in determining the structure of the cotton textile industry. Our considreation of the technological aspects of the production process will look at the machines available and at the pattern of their distribution among different kinds of management units.

The cotton sold by the direct producers was unginned cotton. The first stage in its processing was ginning, which separated the cotton fiber from the seeds. The cotton gin passed through several stages of development and was called by different names in different periods. It first appears under its modern name (*yache*) in the 1765 [*Yuti*] *Mianhua tu*. The improvements in this machine stand in contrast to the history of agricultural implements in China, most of which changed very little.[79]

After ginning, the cotton was well dried and then disentangled with a cotton bow. The cotton, after bowing, was referred to as "processed cotton" (*shu huayi*) in the *Mumian pu* or as "ginned cotton" in the [*Yuti*] *Mianhua tu*. There are many similar differences in terminology which seem to reflect regional variations in usage.

The next stage in the process involved drawing out the roving. The processed cotton was wrapped around a thin bamboo stick; the stick was then removed, leaving a cylindrical-shaped bundle that was hollow in the middle. This bundle was called a roving, which was spun by being held in one hand while an end was drawn out and fastened to the spinning wheel. Keeping pace with the turning wheel, the yarn was wound around a bamboo spindle. This finished yarn was called *miansha* according to the *Mumian pu* or *miansui* according to Xu Guangqi's handbook. In the north spinning was called *fangxian*, while in the Suzhou and Songjiang area it was referred to as *fangsha*. The process involved using the foot peddle to rotate the wheel while using the hands to feed in three to five rovings. The *Nanhui xianzhi* (Nanhui county gazetteer) gives the following description of the spinning wheel "Among the women who spin and weave, those of Pudong (eastern Zhejiang) work the hardest. They use a spinning wheel which can simultaneously spin two rovings into yarn. There is another spinning wheel called the treadle wheel which is foot propelled and which can spin three strands at once. There are many treadle wheels in the Pudong area."[80] From this we know that in the eastern areas of Shanghai county—the area that in the Qing became Nanhui county—this three spindle treadle wheel was commonly used.[81] There is further data in Xu Guangqi's handbook: "The spinning wheel that can handle three strands is now used in the Suzhou area. There are also some that can spin four, and in Le'an in Jiangxi there are those that can spin five strands."[82]

The next stage in the process is to warp the yarn so that it is ready for the loom. The *Mumian pu* describes the process as follows:

> In order to turn the cotton yarn into finished warps, in the past they used a machine called the *boche*. This machine had only one rod winding around on a square bamboo frame. You could not process very many spindles a day. Later they began to use a new kind of machine which resembled a chair. Eight spindles could be placed on top, and there was a handle for unwinding them. They separated and spread the yarn, completing the warp. It was much more convenient than the machine used before. The one that is described here with its cross-frame could be operated by one person, with one additional person needed to keep the yarn in order when it was transported. After a number of changes we arrive at the machine which is in use now, called the *jingche* (warp wheel).[83]

The next stage in the process, sizing, is discussed in Xu Guangqi's handbook:

> In the south there are two methods for sizing. One is to form the yarn first into skeins and pass them through the starch pots. Then they were placed on the *boche* to form spools which were used on the *jingche* to produce warp. In the Wu dialect this was called "starching yarn." The other way is to first use the warp wheel to align the thread and then to pass the warp through the starch. Bamboo is used to make a frame which pulls the thread taut. A bamboo comb is used to apply the starch, and it is dried on the frame. This in the Wu dialect is called "painting the yarn." In the south, the best cloth is all processed in this manner.[84]

There is another description in the *Mumian pu*:

> After the warp is produced, it has to be starched. Starch must be fine, like white, high-quality flour. When it is mixed, it should not

be too hot. It should not be too old; if it is, it may cause the thread
to darken in color. But the starch also cannot be too fresh, or it will
not stiffen the thread. The yarn should be left in the pot for a night,
then hung up early in the morning before the dew has dried. Or on
a cloudy but not rainy day, a bamboo frame can be set up in a wide
open space, with both ends tied with a thick rope. Use a bamboo
comb to comb the yarn. After it has dried on the frame, the yarn should
be separated with bamboo slats and rolled up, ready for the loom.
Best-quality yarn produced in this fashion is called "carded yarn."
Sometimes this is rolled up like a cake and sold. It is called a "cloth
warp set." If it is too dry, it will have many broken ends. If it is
too moist, it will mildew and blacken. There is also a method in
which the cotton yarn is made into twist and then passed through
liquid starch. It is called *jiangsha* and is of the lowest quality.[85]

The processes described above of warping and sizing were used to
prepare the warp. It was not necessary to size the woof. The thread
that had been sized was then ready for the loom. A waist or low-warp
loom was used for weaving ordinary cloth, and a pattern or drawloom
was used for weaving high-quality patterned fabrics. In some cases,
the yarn was dyed before weaving, and in other cases the finished
fabric would be dyed. The dyeing process is also described in the
Mumian pu:

Dyeing work: Indigo workshops dye fabrics sky blue, light blue,
and moonlight blue. Red workshops (*hongfang*) dye fabrics bright
red and pink. Bleaching workshops (*piaofang*) bleach yellowish
fabrics to make them white. There are also miscellaneous color
workshops which dye fabrics yellow, green-black, purple, steel
grey, charcoal grey, blood tooth, etc. There is also a process called
"resist dyeing." Lime is used to make a mortar which is brushed on the
cloth through a stencil. The cloth can then be dyed any color. When
the lime is extracted, a white pattern appears. One other method is
to use woodblocks carved with designs of flowers, people, or animals.
Multicolor dyes can be placed on the woodblock, which is then
pressed down on the fabric. Wherever it is placed, the patterns will
appear. This process is called "cloth printing."[86]

From this passage we see that there were different kinds of dyeing
shops, each with its own special techniques, including resist dyeing
and cloth printing.[87]

Types of cloth

In the previous section we have taken a brief look at technology in the textile industry, and now we will turn to the product that technology produced. Cotton cloth types were divided into categories according to the raw materials used, the type of weave, the color and finish, the size and shape, and the place of production. The 1631 *Songjiang fuzhi* comments, "As for cotton cloth . . . every village and market town has its own varieties and names; the list is inexhaustible."[88] In our own day, the samples of fabrics no longer exist, and it is almost impossible to sort out all the names one finds in the local gazetteers. In some cases a single kind of cloth will have different names in different villages and market towns; in other cases fabrics will be cited as subdivisions of a common type even though they are different; and in still other cases names that come from the type of the weave are confused with names that come from the place of origin. Let us start with a list from local gazetteers.

The 1512 prefectural gazetteer for Songjiang in a section on cloth lists 15 different types. Of these, the following seem to be cotton fabrics: (1) *sansha* cotton, (2) *fan* cloth, (3) *jiansi* cloth and (4) *yaoban* cloth. While each of these seems to represent a type, there are still a number of subdivisions for each category, as is evident from the following discussion.[89]

Sansha cloth. According to this gazetteer, this fabric was first produced during the Yuan dynasty in the area of Shagang and Chedun. Originally it had a width of a little more than three *chi* and was thin and fine like poplin. Later on, it declined in quality, and the width became narrower. In general this category included high-quality plain white cloth, including one variety called "fine cloth" (*xibu*) which was produced in the East Gate area of Songjiang prefectural city. This variety of cloth was also called "wide Ding cloth" and was famous over a large area. According to one source, it took its name from a Ding family who had once lived near Twin Temple Bridge outside the East Gate of the prefectural city. The Ding family wove unusually fine cloth, and that is how it was said to have gotten its name.[90] It was also called "flying-flower cloth" (*feihuabu*). The 1512 gazetteer also notes that the fabric that Governor Zhou Chen had listed as convertible for more than 2 *shi* of grain seems to have corresponded to this category. Sometimes this cloth was called "red yarn official cloth" (*hongsha guanbu*) since red borders were woven into both ends to prevent people from cheating on their taxes by shortening the bolts. This *sansha* cotton cloth also seems to be the same as the three shuttle cloth (*sansuobu*) that we have mentioned earlier. This latter was equivalent in tax conversions to more than 2 *shi* of rice and had a value of about two times that of ordinary white cloth. We find further information on its exchange value from an incident reported in the *Da Ming huidian*. According to that source, when a military official in Beijing went to exchange the three shuttle cloth that he had been given in salary payment, one bolt of three shuttle cloth could be exchanged for one bolt of silk.[91] We find similar data for 1480 in the Veritable Records of Emperor Xianzong of the Ming dynasty, where the conversion rate between official grain rations and cloth is given. It states that ordinary cotton cloth was worth .30 to .40 taels per bolt, but that the finest three shuttle cloth was worth two taels per bolt.[92] This clearly shows that three shuttle cloth was a luxury item. In the 1494 *Shuyuan zaji* there is a note that reads, "If you ask people what kind of clothes they value tailors will tell you that the best undergarments are all made of three shuttle cloth from Songjiang."[93] Another source tells us, "In Ming times, all the imperial undergarments were made of Songjiang three shuttle cloth."[94] In the 1630 Songjiang prefectural gazetteer, where we find a list of the kinds of cotton cloth that were to be sent as tax payment, we find such names as three-thread fine cloth, two-thread fine cloth, improved-weave yellow-thread three-strand cloth, and two-strand cloth. All of these seem to be mentioned in contrast to rough or unbleached white cloth, and all are probably different kinds of the luxury three shuttle cloth.[95] The same gazetteer also mentions *qiudun* cloth and *youdun*[96] cloth. The former was cotton cloth that was a little more than 3 *chi* wide; the latter was thick and quite expensive, but not really suitable for clothing, so that the number of people producing it was quite small. Both of these were probably also varieties of three shuttle cloth. Given the close similarity in pronunciation of *qiu* and *you*, it is possible that the two may be the same thing. In this same source we also find mention of a fine cotton gauze (*saimianchou*), which is mentioned together with flying-flower cloth as being of highest quality. Also mentioned are *zhihuarong* cloth and eyebrow-weave (*meizhi*) cloth.

Fan cloth. The 1512 Songjiang prefectural gazetteer in a note describes *fan* cloth as coming from Wunijing and goes on to mention the legend of the Taoist nun Huang.[97] From this we might imagine that *fan* cloth used the southern technology brought in by the nun Huang. However, the same source tells us that "later, *sansha* cloth developed further as elephant eye, damask pattern, cloud cluster, knee garment, and breast and back. All were produced here." *Sansha* patterned cotton fabrics were influenced by the technology employed for weaving *fan* cloth, and thus it is important to note the technology exchange. It is still unclear what the differences in the two kinds of cloth were. Our earlier source continues:

During the Chenghua era there was a kind of cloth that local natives presented to the wealthy and high ranking. When the court heard of this, it ordered the prefectural commissioner to produce it in ocher yellow, crimson red, and pure purple. They wove the patterns of phoenixes, the north star, and unicorns. Those who worked in the offices conspired together, and in the end the cost of producing one bolt was 100 taels of silver. The Xiaozong emperor knew of the expense before he came to the throne, and when he came to the throne, immediately prohibited it. When he inspected the imperial household budget, he saw the price and said, "One bolt of this cloth costs as much as ten bolts of patterned damask." To the end of his life, he prohibited its use. And so the production of this cloth was ended.[98]

There is a similar report in the 1524 Shanghai county gazetteer: "According to the Guo prefectural gazetteer, Qian Yuanpu, a board president from Huating, regularly used crimson-red cloth to make ceremonial garments for attending court. The eunuchs saw it and, finding it pleasing, talked about the cloth in the emperor's presence. From then on the Imperial Textile Workshops annually produced crimson-red cloth."[99] From this reference we can see that during the Chenghua era the Imperial Textile Workshops in Songjiang did produce high-quality cotton fabrics like crimson-red cloth. In the 1512 gazetteer there is a further reference to the case of Song Duan, who served as magistrate of Huating during the Chenghua era. He presented a bolt of cloud-pattern cloth to his teacher Li Chun, who was a vice minister. Li Chun, citing an ancient precedent, refused the gift.[100] The Veritable Records of the Xiaozong emperor recorded the death of Li Chun and, in reciting the record of his accomplishments, described the cloth in question as red-cloud cloth.[101]

All of the above references to crimson-red cloth, cloud cloth, and red-cloud cloth put them in the category of *fan* cloth. Taking into consideration the special characteristics of all the fabrics described, all seem to be colored, patterned weaves. We can also include in this category twills (*xiawenbu*), checkered cloth (*qihuabu*), and "victory flower" cloth (*shenghuabu*), which are listed in the 1605 Jiading county gazetteer, and the twill and square-pattern cloth and Korean cloth, which are mentioned in the *Mumian pu*.[102] With reference to the twills we find in the 1605 Jiading gazetteer a reference that says that superior examples which had a value of one tael were soft and finely woven and appeared to be something like velvet.[103] According to a Qing gazetteer from the same county, such twills were a special product of Loutangzhen (market town).[104]

In the *Mumian pu* we find a reference which says that among the fabrics produced in Sanlintang in Shanghai county were "those with a texture like twill, those with a square victory pattern called *zhengwen*, and those with a brocade-like pattern, which were called Korean."[105] In other words, these three types were distinguished by the pattern of their weaves. A Qing gazetteer for Nanhui county mentions a square pattern and a twill; the former may have been a variety of *zhengwen* cloth. With reference to checked cloth we find the following description in the 1605 Jiading gazetteer, "Checked cloth is made of blue and white placed together to look like a chessboard. It is used for making handkerchiefs and covers."[106] This patterned fabric which was woven of a mixture of blue and white thread was probably quite similar to modern checked fabrics; it was produced in the market town of Antingzhen in Jiading county.[107] We find a further reference to a similar kind of checked cloth which was produced in Chongming county and was made of blue and white or purple and white thread; it was locally called *jianbu*.[108]

Blends (*jiansibu*). This category included fabrics that used silk thread for the warp and cotton thread for the weft; it was also referred to as *sibu* and was easy to dye.[109] Another variety was called *morongbu*, which was a kind of cloud cloth that used silk yarn blended with cotton as the weft. The cloth was produced in many varieties using silk-weaving techniques similar to those used to produce damasks.[110] There were several other types of blends. One kind used a pre-dyed cotton yarn for the warp and wool thread for the weft. After weaving, it was clipped producing a napped fabric that was several feet wide. Another variety produced in the market town of Xiashazhen in Shanghai county used a mixture of silk floss and cotton.[111] Finally an early-Qing source refers to a blend called *jingbu* which used ramie as the warp and cotton as as the weft.[112]

Dyed Fabrics (*yaobanbu*). This category includes printed cotton fabrics. First produced in the area of Qinglong and Zhonggu, it later spread and was widely produced in the prefectural city and its suburbs.[113] The 1379 Suzhou prefectural gazetteer noted that it was produced in Jiading county by a resist-dyeing process in which the pattern portions remained white while the surrounding areas were dyed with indigo.[114] This seems to be identical to the process we have described earlier. A more detailed description given in the 1506 Suzhou gazetteer said: *"Yaobanbu* is produced in Jiading county and in Antingzhen. It was first produced by a Gui family during the Jiatai era (1201–4) of the Song dynasty. A mortar made of ash is rubbed into the cloth, and then it is dyed blue. After it dries, the mortar is removed, and both the blue and white appear. There are various patterns with towers and pavilions, human figures, flowers and birds, and poems. It is used for canopies, curtains, quilts, and handkerchiefs."[115] This source places the origins of this dyeing method in the Song, and we do find further evidence in a Song gazetteer from Kunshan county.[116] That source uses the name *yaobanbu*, but that does not mean that cotton textiles were being produced and dyed during the Song period. Rather in the early period, the same dyeing method was used to finish ramie fabric. Since the *yaoban* dyeing method is mentioned in the cotton sections of two late-Ming gazetteers, it seems safe to assume that this process was used on cotton textiles from the Ming on.[117] In the 1633 edition of the gazetteer for Songjiang we find the following comment: *"Yaobanbu* is commonly called *jiaohuabu*. It is now produced everywhere."[118] There are several similar references in other late-sixteenth and early-seventeenth century gazeteers.[119] There was one other kind of cloth that seems to fit in this same category. The 1631 Songjiang gazetteer describes it in the following way: "There is also a fabric called *mobu*. First the thread is tightened and then dyed. It looks just like the rubbed brocade produced on Suzhou looms."[120] Thus it seems to be another dyed fabric, but it was not produced by the same process as regular *yaobanbu*. There was one further kind of dyed cotton cloth which was called *fenqing shengbu*.[121]

The four categories of cloth described so far included only high-quality cotton textiles which were produced with special weaving and dyeing techniques. In addition to these high-quality fabrics there were the more common products which were collectively called "coarse cloth" (*cubu*). Chen Jiru's "Regulations for cotton taxes," which were included in the 1631 gazetteer for Songjiang, listed a cotton-cloth tax quota for Huating county that included 16,185 bolts of fine cloth and 48,535 bolts of coarse cloth.[122] The former had a conversion rate of 6.1 *qian* per bolt, while the latter had a conversion rate of 3 *qian* per bolt. The ratio between the two is similar to that given by Zhou Chen for bleached three shuttle cloth and bleached cotton cloth. It seems safe to assume that this coarse cloth was bleached cotton fabric which was white in color and of a plain weave. In our inquiry into the types of cloth, let us then finally turn to such coarse cloth.

Coarse Cloth (*cubu*). The 1793 gazetteer for Nanhui county gives the following description: "Cloth is made from cotton. One kind is sheeting (*koubu*), which is commonly called "small cloth" (*xiaobu*). It is also sometimes called middle loom. There is another kind called "standard cloth," commonly called "large cloth" (*dabu*), which is wider than small cloth. *Pingxiao* is 16 *chi* in length, and *taoduan* is 20 *chi* in length. A third variety is *xibu* (thin cloth). It is 3 or 4 inches wider than large cloth and comes in two varieties, *dankou* and *shuangkou*.[123] A gazetteer from the same period for Jinshan county provides a slightly different division: "There are two kinds of small cloth: brushed warp (*shuajing*) and beat starch (*paijiang*). Brushed warp is particularly fine. Wide cloth is called *xibu*. It has several other names including *danchuang* and *shuangkou*."[124] The distinction here is made according to sizing method, while wide cloth and *xibu* seem to be the same thing. The account continues: "Other varieties include purple cotton, twill, scraped floss, and warp cloth. Not as many people produce these as produce small and wide cloth."

The production levels of the four high-quality varieties were quite low in comparison with small and wide cloth, which were woven in every household. Production of coarse cloth dominated the Songjiang cotton textile industry. The rural textile industry was built on the coarse cloth base, and it was coarse cloth, particularly standard cloth and middle loom, that was traded in a nationwide market in the late Ming and early Qing.[125] In the 1631 gazetteer for Songjiang there is further mention of *fangkuobu*, improved cloth, and standard-inch cloth.[126] The first was a variety of wide cloth; the second, as I have explained elsewhere, was another name for middle loom, and the last seems to be related to standard cloth.

Finally, in the 1744 gazetteer for Zhenyang county we find the following note: "Thick, heavy, long, wide cloth is called "large cloth." Smaller cloth that is 2 to 4 feet in width is called *qianwujing*." The large cloth here seems to be the same as that of Nanhui county, while *qianwujing* seems to have been a kind of small cloth produced in a place called Qianwujing. Other varieties of coarse cloth included *zhujibu* and *zihuabu* (purple cotton cloth). The latter was made from purple cotton which gave it a light reddish-brown hue. It was quite popular and had a market price that was double the standard varieties.[127]

Textile management

In this section we want to consider the forms of rural textile management and the internal organizational structure of each form. Textile management in the Songjiang region can be roughly divided into two types. In one type the whole production process was incorporated in one management unit; in the other form there was a division of labor between two or more management units. An example of this first type of management can be seen in the poem "Weaving Song" by the Ming poet Dong Xianliang:

He tends his cotton in the garden in the morning,
In the evening makes his cloth upon the loom.
His wife weaves with ever-moving fingers,
His women spin with never-ceasing wheels.
It is the humid and unhealthy season
When they finish the last of the cotton from their garden.
Prices go up and up if merchants come to buy;
So if the warp's plentiful a lack of weft brings grief.
They therefore buy raw cotton and spin it night after night.[128]

This poem describes a backword form of management in which the whole process, from cotton cultivation through weaving the finished product, takes place within one peasant household. A survey of the cotton textile industry shows that this form was less common, and that the second form of management, involving a division of labor, dominated Songjiang production. Even in the case described in the "Weaving Song," the production unit is no longer isolated, since the poem points to the activities of cotton merchants outside the production unit. Thus the forces that would ultimately lead to a division of labor were already beginning to impinge upon the individual, small peasant management unit.

Why did such a division of labor appear? The chief factor was the character of the peasant management unit. Such units were made up of poor peasants who lacked working capital and thus found it necessary to repeat over and over the small-scale production process in as short a time as possible. This seems to have been the dominant form of management within the Songjiang cotton textile industry. A section in the 1512 Songjiang prefectural gazetteer describes this second form of management: "The textile industry is not limited to the rural villages, but is also seen in the city. Old rural women enter the market at dawn carrying yarn and, after trading it for raw cotton, return home. The next morning they again leave home carrying yarn. There is not a moment for rest. The weavers finish a bolt a day, and there are some who stay awake all night. After the harvest when the peasant households have paid their taxes and repaid interest, they find that before the end of the year their cupboards are empty. They rely on the textile industry for their own food and clothing."[129,130] From this description we know that at least raw cotton and cotton yarn appeared in the market in their commodity forms. Thus there was clearly already a division of labor in the production process; that is, some individual production units had come to specialize in spinning raw cotton into yarn (producing rovings and spinning).

One point, however, is still unclear. We discovered earlier that the cotton sold by peasant producers was unginned cotton. Were the old women buying unginned cotton? If they were, it indicates that the old women either ginned it themselves at home, or received it from another separate production unit that specialized in ginning cotton. A lack of sources makes it difficult to give a hard and fast answer to this question. We have seen earlier that cotton buyers from Fujian and Guangdong bought ginned cotton in this area. This would suggest that the unginned cotton sold by the peasant producers was bought and ginned, and then resold on the market a second time. It thus seems to me that a separate and distinct ginning unit must have existed and that the cotton that the old women bought was ginned cotton which was making its second appearance in the market.

This division of labor between ginning and spinning took place at a very early date. The two processes were already distinct by the Hongwu era, as we see from the line in the poem by Gu Yu cited earlier, "Many in the town are selling cotton yarn." By that time cotton yarn had appeared as a commodity in the market.

Textile production was not limited only to rural villages but was also going on in the cities. There is evidence for this in the opening statement from the 1512 Songjiang gazetteer cited earlier and in the following statement from Xu Guangqi's handbook: "In the south, many of those who have moved to the cities spin outside their dwellings in the morning and evening."[131] This custom of spinning outside in the morning and evening was also common in the rural villages; during the early morning and the evening hours, humidity was higher and thus conditions for spinning were better. We can find further support for this in the biography of a virtuous woman of the Kangxi era [1662–1722], which notes, "The people in the village engage in the cotton industry. They almost all work outside the home. The woman engaged in spinning for ten years. She didn't change her life at all."[132]

As spinning became a separate unit in the division of labor, it spread beyond the borders of Songjiang prefecture, where weaving technology was well developed, into the neighboring areas where weaving technology was not developed. This spread is described in a 1517 gazetteer: "[In this area the people] weave silk damask, but in weaving coarse cloth they do not equal Songjiang. Therefore, those who spin cotton into yarn do not weave it but sell it for cash."[133] Thus in Jinshan wei (later Jinshan county) only cotton spinning had developed. The finished yarn was then sold to the weaving areas. There is a further reference in a late-Ming gazetteer for Haiyan county:

In this area there is little cotton cultivation, but cotton spinning and weaving are commonly carried out in most households. This is not only common in rural areas, but also in the city. Many merchants regularly bring in cotton that they have purchased in neighboring areas, and our peasants spin and weave, producing either yarn or cloth. They come to the market at dawn and, after buying cotton, return home and use it to spin and weave. The next morning they bring the finished product to exchange. There is not a moment for rest. The spinners can produce 4 to 5 ounces of yarn a day, and the weavers can produce a bolt of cloth a day. Working at night, they burn the oil lamps. At midnight, the men and women have still not gone to bed. After the harvest when the peasant households have paid their taxes and repaid interest, they find that before the end of the year their cupboards are empty. They rely on the textile industry for their own food and clothing.[134]

Although major sections of this source are identical to the section we have already quoted from the 1512 Songjiang prefectural gazetteer, and were undoubtedly quoted from it, it does add some new information. This new data would seem to reflect special characteristics of Haiyan county that were not seen in Songjiang. Since Haiyan county failed to produce enough cotton to supply its own spinning wheels, raw cotton had to be brought in from neighboring areas, probably Songjiang prefecture. There was also a division in management between those who spun and those who wove. We know from other sources that the spinning industry in Haiyan produced yarn as a raw material to supply not only the local weaving industry but also the Songjiang weaving industry. For example, one contemporary merchant's handbook gives the following evidence on water transport between Songjiang and Jiaxing: "Those who have no luggage and want to go from Jiaxing to Songjiang do not need to rent small boats. They can board small boats at Dongpengkou for Jiashan county. Or they can board a cotton yarn boat[135] for Songjiang. There is no need to take a large boat."[136]

The above data clearly show that spinning had been established as an

independent process in the division of labor, and that this development
was not limited to the rural villages and towns of Songjiang prefecture,
but had also spread to neighboring Haiyan county in Zhejiang. Next we
want to turn to weaving and examine the form of management involved
in that part of the production process.

As a result of the excessively heavy tax demands which had stimulated
the development of the Songjiang textile industry, weaving was a
common occupation in most rural households. This situation created the conditons that led to Zhou Chen's conversion of the cotton tax
to payment in silver. As we see from the statements cited earlier from
the Songjiang gazetteer, income from the land was only sufficient to pay
taxes and repay interest on loans. The income to pay for food and clothing came from the textile industry. Weaving thus developed as a
sideline industry within the peasant household.

Although rural weaving was the dominant form of management,
weaving was not restricted to the rural areas of Songjiang; this fact is
illustrated by the following statement in the 1512 Songjiang prefectural
gazetteer: "Textile production was not limited to the rural areas, but
also took place in the cities."[137] In the cities there were many professional weavers. We find evidence for this in a statement from a 1631
source: "There are now in the city weaving households that weave official cloth."[138] This is clear evidence that there were professional urban
weavers who produced the official cloth that was sent to the central
government as part of the tax quota.

Geographically, we can divide weaving between rural areas and cities, the former involving production as a supplementary activity in rural households, while the latter was characterized by specialized production by professional weaving households. This pattern of division was
not only one of geographical location and management type; we can
also make some general—if not hard and fast—distinctions in the type
of cloth produced. In general, the rural industry was weaving fabrics
that fell in the general category of coarse cloth. For example, the 1735
Nanhui county gazetteer notes that "the cloth produced in the Zhoupu
area is standard cloth, while in Xinchang, Xiasha, and other rural villages and market towns they produce sheeting, which is also called middle loom."[139] All of these fall within the category of coarse cloth. A 1752
gazetteer for Jinshan county comments, "More households are producing small cloth and broad cloth than are producing purple cotton cloth,
twills, brushed nap cloth, and silk floss cloth."[140]

In contrast, those designated as professional urban weavers were producing official cloth and such high-quality cotton textiles as three shuttle cloth. The *Yueshi bian* notes, "Three qualities of cotton cloth are

produced in our county. They are the flying flower (*feihua*), *youdun*, and eyebrow weave (*meizhi*) of Songjiang."[141] Thus high-quality goods were among the products of Songjiang city. In general, production of high-quality cotton textiles was probably a special characteristic of the urban weaving industry.

Although there were single units that managed all stages of the textile production process, the dominant form of textile management in this region was one in which there was a division of labor with separate management units handling ginning, spinning, and weaving. While we cannot fully define the form of management in the ginning process, we do know that spinning took place not only in both rural and urban areas, but also in such neighboring areas as Jinshan wei[142] and Haiyan, and that weaving can be divided between a rural form (or peasant sideline industry) and an urban (or professional) form. Next we want to examine the structure and character of each of these three separate units in the division of labor. However, due to the limitation of sources, this discussion will focus on the weaving industry alone.

First, in looking at rural weaving we want to consider the question of labor supply. In many of the gazetteers from this region there are accounts in the section of biographies of good or virtuous women, of frugal women who were able to support their families by spinning and weaving. One example can be found in Dong Hongdu's "Complaint of a Weaving Wife":

Hungry, she still weaves.
Numbed with cold, she still weaves
Shuttle after shuttle after shuttle.
The days are short, the weather chill.
Each length hard to finish.
The rich take their rent,
The clerk the land tax,
Knocking repeatedly with urgent insistence.
Her husband wants to urge her on,
But has no heart to do so.
He says nothing,
But stands beside the loom.
Fate has not treated her well.
The ten years since she came as a bride have passed
And already her bridal clothes are frayed.
A hundred patches on her trousers,
Morning and evening she works without ceasing.
Inch by inch she weaves the floss

But none will she wear.
Her husband longs to be rich and wealthy
But if he should make it
Will he forget his companion of the bitter days?
The more she tries to get it done
The more her strength fails her.
She turns away, choking down tears,
And consoles herself that their neighbors are poorer
—and lonelier.
For they sold their loom
And next had to sell their son.[143]

Like the "Weaving Song" of Dong Xianliang cited earlier and the "Prose Poem on Cotton Cloth" by Xu Xianzhong, which we will refer to later, this ode poetically describes weaving in this region. All of the weavers mentioned are women. All of the poems describe weaving as a rural sideline developed to help pay rent and taxes. Their description of the labor employed in weaving is a concrete illustration of the proverbial saying that comes down from ancient times that "men till and women weave." Thus in the case of weaving as a rural supplement, labor for weaving was supplied by the female members of the household while the men were engaged in agriculture work. Both pooled their earnings to meet household expenses.

Next we want to examine the marketing arrangements for selling the cotton cloth produced by peasant women. Since I have already written extensively elsewhere about the cotton cloth market, we will not discuss it here.[144] The marketing arrangements for the rural cloth produced in such peasant sideline industry are described in a prose poem written by Xu Xianzhong, a native of Huating county who was active during the Jiajing era:

The woman works bitterly
Disregarding her chapped hands.
Her hungry husband takes the bolt
And sets out on the long journey.
Carrying it, he enters the market.
Fearing that the cloth's quality is not good enough
He describes it in terms of jewels and powder.
Clutching it close to ward off the cold wind
And tapping shoulders to gain attention,
He shouts for them to buy his cloth,
Thinking of the money he will gain,

He treats each buyer as politely as if he were his father.
When the cloth is finally sold,
It is like the lifting of a heavy burden.
Sitting for a moment to catch his beath,
He turns to go as the sun rises.[145]

The Ming law codes provided strict regulations with regard to cloth selection: "Silk cloth. Those who sell silk with imperfections or cloth that is thin, short, or narrow will get 50 blows. Their goods will be confiscated."[146] Thus the sale of silk goods that were not up to standard was forbidden, and there were cases where merchants refused to buy coarse or badly woven goods with low commercial value. It is not difficult to imagine that what is described here might be an inspection system associated with a putting-out system. However, if that were the case, the producer would have to be subservient to the merchant; other evidence suggests that that was not the case. For example, an essay by Qin Shan comments, "They gamble their lives on yarn. Two out of three days they are hungry. When they bring their cloth to market, its price is as low as dirt. This is the work of the 'death merchants.'"[147] From this we can see that the cloth buyers, the cotton cloth wholesalers, were cursed as death merchants. The peasant producers had been forced by a lack of capital to specialize in only one part of the production process. Strong merchant capital had then moved into the exchange process between the different units of the division of labor and exercised control over them.

As we can see from the prose poem quoted earlier, the textile producers took their cotton cloth to the market where they sold it for cash. The buyers were merchants, and their relationship with the producers started at this point of market exchange. There is still no evidence to verify the existence of a putting-out system—that is, an organizational system centered in the operations of merchant capital which would loan out either the tools of production or raw materials, thus incorporating textile production by rural households into a unified and organized system. At the end of "Complaint of a Weaving Wife" we learn that an impoverished neighbor had sold her loom. This clearly indicates that the producers owned their own looms. With regard to raw materials (yarn), the question is less clear. We earlier quoted a description of the situation in which old women went to markets early in the morning to sell cotton yarn and get new supplies of cotton, repeating the process day after day. While we might hypothesize that this production took place within a putting-out system, it is not clear whether the merchants who handled raw cotton and those who took in the finished yarn were the same people. Nor is it clear whether the money the old women received was the sale price of the yarn or whether it was wages. Thus there is simply not enough evidence to determine whether this rural sideline style of management was incorporated within a putting-out system.

However, what we have shown so far does raise a question of whether the form and organization of textile production by impoverished small peasants was not different from that of the upper layers of rural society, the rich peasants and landlords. A description by Xu Xianzhong suggests the possibility that rich peasants were hiring women and carrying on large-scale management. Xu says, "In Songjiang middle peasants and below daily weave small cloth which provides for their livelihood. Even if we say that the great households do not themselves work, they do supervise women workers, so we cannot say that they are not working."[148] It is not clear whether the women involved were free laborers. Other evidence is found in an epitaph for a woman identified simply as the mother of a man named Wu: "She came from an old lineage in Qingpu, Jiading county. . . . Her family employed women who worked diligently as women textile laborers, and she continued to work with them. Then her husband died. After this, she often ate only vegetables and refused to wear silk garments and cosmetics. Even in the bitterest winter cold, she led the bondservant women in spinning."[149] Another similar epitaph for a woman of the Yang family provides more information:

> The Lady née Yang was ennobled with a fourth-class honor. She was the wife of Governor General Zhang Xuye. The Yang family came from Wujili. . . . After the Governor General retired and returned home, he spent his days leisurely in writing poetry and drinking, studying, and teaching the Confucian classics to the children. He never inquired about family affairs. His lady, in contrast, worked diligently, leading the bondservant women in spinning. Even though she was of high rank, she wore the same *jingbu* cloth garments as the commoners. She educated her family in the ways of frugality.[150]

Both of these epitaphs describe the use of bondservant labor for spinning. The kind of large-scale operation described by Xu Xianzhong is not a manufacturing form which used women and children as hired labor but is rather a special form that had appeared when the self-sufficient family form was surrounded by impoverished peasant families engaging in sideline industry. It was a form of upper-class home industry that incorporated the use of slave-style bondservant labor. This upper-class management form did not play an important role in the overall textile industry. Although this upper-class form did exist, the dominant mode of management was still production by impoverished peasants. It is important to note that while income from textile output was an important supplement to peasant budgets, it had not supplanted income from landownership.

In summary, what we have described so far is a form of management in which rural weaving was a supplement to peasant household income. Labor power was supplied by the female members of the family. The family itself owned the raw materials, the tools for production, and the work place, and the finished product was sold for cash. This was a form of handicraft organization, and its basic character was as a function of the peasant family economy. It had not established itself as an independent industry, nor even as a form independent of landownership. This kind of handicraft organization is quite different from both the manufacturing and the putting-out systems of factory-style handicraft production in which a merchant entrepreneur was able to organize the collection and distribution of the output of various producers under his own control.

What about the forms of organization in the urban textile industry? A 1524 gazetteer for Shanghai county gives the following description: "There is work both inside and outside the house. In peasant families, women will assist in agriculture work. In the market towns and cities, men also are well acquainted with weaving."[151] Thus while labor was supplied by women in the rural, household-sideline style of industry, in the professional weaving done in the cities labor was supplied by both men and women.

Next we want to look at the scale of production in the urban textile industry in the Shanghai area. Alvaro Semedo,[152] a Portuguese Jesuit missionary, wrote a report in 1621 that included information on the cotton industry in Shanghai and Jiading:

That part which is towards the West, is the most rich, and maketh so much Cotton-wool, that those of the Country affirme, that there is only in the towne of *Xanuchi* and the precinct thereof, which is large, 200000 Loomes for this stuffe; so that from that place only the King draweth 150000 crownes yearly.

In one house there useth to be many of them for they are narrow, as the stuffe is. Almost all the women are employed in this work.[153]

Since Semedo lived in Shanghai, it seems fair to assume that this account reflects his own personal observations. Although he certainly traveled outside the city walls of Shanghai, there is no reason to assume that this description only deals with rural industry. Rather, it seems certain to include the urban textile industry. Semedo claims that there were 200,000 looms in Shanghai city and its administrative area. A 1622 report gives a total of 81,960 households in Shanghai city and county.[154] Even if we assume that rural textile production had spread to every household and that each household had one or two looms, we still must assume a fairly high concentration of looms in the city itself in order to reach this 200,000-loom total. If we assume that Semedo's report is accurate, then we must conclude that there was a concentration of loom ownership in the urban areas. Although Semedo had no accurate statistics for his total and was only quoting common estimates, there is no reason to disregard the part of his report on the number of looms with in a single establishment.

There is an additional question about Semedo's statement that almost all the work is done by women. This does not seem to refer to the use of labor in the urban textile industry. If we add our earlier data on the existence of professional weaving households and the existence of male laborers to the data on the concentration of looms from Semedo's report, we get a fairly good picture of the general alignment. There is still a great deal of uncertainty as to whether this urban textile industry relied only on the labor power of family members. We note that in the silk textile industry in nearby Suzhou city there was a labor market for artisans in the Kangxi period.[155] It is tempting to suppose that a similar labor market existed in the Songjiang cotton industry. To date we have not been able to find any documentary evidence to confirm this hypothesis.

Let us turn now to an examination of the urban textile industry which was based on the work of professional weavers. Zhang Youxuan, from Huating provides the following description:

According to the old regulations, there were four tax-transmitting households. They were required to transmit 16,185 bolts of shuttle cloth and 48,935 bolts of cotton cloth. . . . Now among the weaving households in the cities there are those who specialize in weaving official cloth. In inspection, the cloth is divided into two types—two-thread and three-thread, with a fixed price per bolt of 3.8 to 4.0 qian. If the price of each bolt were to be raised by two fen, then the weaving households would not complain but would take responsibility for producing it. After the weaving households have been designated, the responsibility can be divided among the heads of lijia administrative units (lipai), each of whom will be ordered to purchase 20 to 30 bolts of cloth for transmission in tax payment. This will count as the payment of their tax assessments and conversions to silver. One or two months before the transfer is due, the silver can be given directly to the weaving households, with the amounts being officially recorded. The *lijia* heads will then not be required to pay other taxes. One or two months later the weaving households will be strictly held to the deadline for turning over the cloth. This is different from the current practice in that responsibility stops with the weaving household. No longer will the *lijia* heads be subject to excessive exactions. This is not too severe, and the *lijia* heads should not complain.[156]

This was a proposal for reform of the cloth transmission system which was part of the oppressive service levy obligation in this region. The reform included the following proposals: (1) In order to stabilize the economic conditions of the urban professional weavers who produced the cotton cloth that was part of the tax quota, the purchase price of two-thread and three-thread fine cloth was to be raised by two *fen* per bolt. (2) In order to reform the existing system, the large households responsible for tax transmission were to receive silver from the officials who then would use it to purchase the cotton cloth for the quota from wholesale merchants. In its place, a system would be created in which *lijia* captains (*lizhang*) and heads of *jia* ten-family units would collect the silver received in payment of converted taxes and directly purchase cloth from the professional weavers. Responsibility for meeting quality standards would rest with the professional weaving households. From this we can see that the cotton cloth transmitted as part of the tax quota was in fact produced by urban professional weavers. As for the quota amounts of 16,185 bolts of shuttle cloth and 48,935 bolts of plain cotton cloth, we find further evidence in the 1630 Songjiang prefectural gazetteer: "In Huating county four households are named as tax-transmitting households each year. They are responsible for transmitting 16,185 bolts of fine cloth and 48,935 bolts of coarse cloth."[157] From this it is clear that the quota is only for the one county of Huating. We can assume that the professional weavers in Songjiang prefectural city (where the Huating county government also had its headquarters) were producing a total of 65,140 bolts of the two qualities of cloth for tax payment in the late Ming.

If we assume that the major part of the total output was produced by the urban weaving households, then this tells us something about their character: the urban professional weavers monopolized the production of tax-quota cloth and were able to maintain production on the basis of that guaranteed market. In the late Ming responsibility for purchasing tax-quota cloth lay with the tax-transmitting households. As a result professional weavers could avoid becoming dependent on the capital of wholesale merchants. The professional weavers were also not endangered by changes in market prices. From the description of the reform program which provided for direct purchase from the professional weavers, we can see that there were no putting-out style merchant capital organizations that could control professional weavers. The professional weavers formed their own independent management units. In spite of this, the professional weavers were really working on commission—that is, producing for government purchase—and were thus outside the bounds of commodity production or market sale.

An important factor here is the source of the government funds that paid for the purchase of the professional weavers' finished output. Such funds came from the silver collected in the countryside as a result of the conversion of the cotton tax to silver. To review briefly the history of the conversion process: first taxes payable in grain had been converted to payment in cotton cloth. Then from the mid-Ming on, the development of commodity production in rural villages had led to the conversion of the cloth payment into an approximately equal amount of silver. The silver thus collected was then used by the tax-remitting households to purchase cotton cloth from the professional weavers. The position of the professional weavers was thus guaranteed by their monopoly of the production of tax-quota cloth. This monopoly allowed them to carry out independent, professional production. This independent position was not created by the professional weavers themselves, nor by the government which provided the orders that insured their continued operation, but rather by the existence and spread of commodity production in the rural weaving industry.

This is an important consideration in any comparison of the development of the late Ming-Songjiang cotton textile industry with that of the textile industries of other areas or countries. The existence of a system of professional weaving in itself did not give a progressive character to the rural weaving industry. Rural weaving was limited by its original purpose. It had started as a way to meet heavy tax demands, and even when it moved into the commodity production stage, it was bound by the requirements of the land system and heavy taxation. Given the important role of production of official cloth in the urban textile sector, it is not an exaggeration to argue that the professional weaving households who monopolized its production controlled the whole Songjiang weaving industry to a large degree.

Production of tax quota cloth was not restricted to Songjiang city; other counties had similar arrangements as we can see from this 1631 account: "There are three tax-remitting households in Shanghai county.

They have a quota of 10,620 bolts of fine cloth and 32,109 bolts of coarse cloth. There is one tax-remitting household in Qingpu county. It has a quota of 6,195 bolts of fine cloth and 18,730 bolts of coarse cloth."[158] Shanghai thus had a total quota of more than 40,000 bolts of cloth, and Qingpu county more than 20,000. To the extent that the tax-transmitting households used a method similar to that employed in Songjiang for obtaining the tax-quota cloth, we can expect that the character of the professional weaving households in these two cities was also similar.

This urban, professional weaving industry enlarged its base to keep pace with the rural weaving industry. The urban industry may appear to have been an independent, specialized form of management, but it did not in fact have the potential to become the core of the region's textile industry. As a result, the early cotton industry could not become independent of its rural village base. In looking at the evidence that shows that high-quality cotton cloth was almost exclusively produced by the urban textile industry, we must remember that it was the coarse cotton cloth produced by rural weavers which came to dominate the nationwide consumers market. We also must remember that the urban textile industry was able to grow as a result of the support in the form of silver which was extracted from the rural textile industry and which was then used to pay for the compulsory production of specific qualities and standards of tax-quota cloth. Such cloth was produced in the cities because of the superior technical skills of city artisans.

Urban professional weaving, with its use of male labor, the concentration of looms within a single establishment, and the production of high-quality fabrics, may also appear to have been a small-scale manufacturing form. However, to see it as such is to ignore the basic nature of the industry, which was still closely linked to the exploitative land system. A more comprehensive examination shows that the urban weaving industry was merely an adjunct to the rural weaving industry.[159]

The basic structure of the Songjiang textile industry still found its center in the rural weaving industry. This rural weaving industry was carried on as part of the peasant family economy. It developed out of the needs of impoverished peasants operating within an exploitative land system. Both the larger-scale production of the wealthy households who made use of bondservant labor and the urban professional weaving industry developed as adjuncts to the rural weaving system. Any discussion of the forms of premodern Chinese rural industry must take into consideration the special characteristics of this cotton textile industry.

Conclusion

The Songjiang cotton textile industry developed in response to heavy land taxation. The intervention of merchant capital led to the development of handicraft-style commodity production and distribution through an interregional market.[160] However, the cotton industry was ultimately not able to free itself from the demands of the land system. It continued to develop as an integral part of the peasant economy and provided a supplement to family income. As the cotton industry developed, the agrarian structure in some areas shifted from rice farming to cotton farming. However, the profits from such commodity production of raw cotton did not stay in the hands of cotton-producing peasants, for the peasants were victims of expropriation by merchant capitalists and landowners. This inability to escape from the land system also played a major part in determining the form of management in the textile industry. Given this context, the character of the early textile industry, and the intervention of merchant capital, the rural cotton textile industry developed to a remarkable level. The urban weaving industry developed as a derivative of this rural industry, with the determining role being played by the rural textile sector.

The establishment of the early cotton industry as a form of rural industry meant that it had a very different character from the so-called Asian form, in which agriculture and industry are integrated within a single community (kyōdōtai) unit. The development of the cotton industry in response to internal developments in the domestic economy rather than to external foreign pressures also directly challenges assumptions about the "stagnant" nature of Chinese society.

These internal developments began as early as the Song dynasty, with the growth of the Jiangnan rice-growing areas, which then led to an expansion of the forces of production. Accompanying that economic development was a strengthening of the power of the centralized, authoritarian state. A number of factors, working together, gave rise to the cotton industry as a new rural industry in the Jiangnan region. Among those factors were the penetration of merchant capital into rural villages and the formation of an interregional market. These in turn were shaped by the special characteristics of the Chinese land system. Naturally the nature of the early cotton industry was influenced by these historical factors. The producers in this industry were small-scale tenants, who, as a result of the restrictions of the land system and the action of merchant capital, no longer owned land. The early cotton industry expanded as sideline, handicraft-style commodity production whose purpose was to supplement the income of these tenants.

If we look at the question from a different angle, we can see that development in a new direction was blocked as long as the chief producers were such small-scale tenants, since they were bound by the fetters of the land system and the oppression of merchant capital. It is not only that such tenants were not an independent, self-managing class; even more than that was the fact that this new industry did not have the strength to create an independent, self-managing peasant class. For example, we do not find the manufacturing form of production in the early cotton industry. It was impossible even for a putting-out system to develop because the tenant producers could not free themselves from the restrictions of the land system. The putting-out system, which is a premodern form of capitalist control, is based on a certain relationship of trust between the merchant capitalist and the producers, and the producers gain some guarantee of profit returns. In the case of the early Chinese cotton industry, however, the merchant capitalists did not need to establish this relationship of trust. Merchant capital could control the producers at the beginning and end of the production process. Given the lack of stability in the living conditions of this non-independent producing class, merchant capital could take advantage of the gaps provided by the division of labor in the production process and expropriate the profits. This system was, of course, very profitable to the merchants. It would have been absurd for them to establish voluntarily a relationship of trust with the producers which would have required them to give income guarantees. These are the reasons why a putting-out system does not appear.

If what we have said so far is correct, then we can see that in its formation and structure the early cotton industry was a new rural industry that had developed within the supposedly stagnant Chinese society. It thus does not conform to the so-called Asian form, in which undifferentiated agriculture and industry are bound within a single community unit. It is, however, also a long way away from a "modern" form.

Thus in China rural industry existed as a special category.[161] In analyzing the early cotton industry we have seen it as a new industry developing in the most advanced economic region. It was different from both the older-style, complex form, which was based on the accumulation of miscellaneous goods, and from the imperial industries, in which production of luxury goods was carried out under government control. Unlike those forms it developed spontaneously and was directly related to the production of consumer goods for the masses. Our investigation has shown that the cotton industry was indissolubly linked to both the land system and the centralized, authoritarian power of the state. Even with the intervention of merchant capital, the basic characteristics of the cotton industry did not change, and the rural-industry sector continued to regulate the important urban handicraft sector.

In this type of rural industry and in the forms that are derived from it, it is difficult to develop the "sprouts" of modern forms. Moreover, when such industry was confronted by modern industrial capitalism it was unable to change itself. Even when faced with inevitable bankruptcy and defeat, it still had, initially at least, the capacity for resistance.[162] In the end it worked to block or postpone modernization and to leave China economically crippled.

Notes

[1] Nishijima Sadao, "Mindai ni okeru momen no fukyū," in Nishijima Sadao, *Chūgoku keizaishi kenkyū.*

[2] Katō Shigeru, *Shina keizaishi gaisetsu,* pp. 60–61.

[3] Nishijima, "Mindai ni okeru momen no fukyū."

[4] Ibid.

[5] This statement is attributed to the *WuXun zapei* [Miscellany from Wuzhou and Xunzhou], and is quoted in the section on cotton in the *Gujin tushu jicheng, juan* 303 of the botanical section, 1b–2a. It is not clear whether this book is still extant. According-ing to the 1663 *Songjiang fuzhi,* 50:11b: "All of the following books were written by Administration Commissioner Zhang Suowang: *Guitian lu, Bao chuang tang zaji, Wu Xun zapei, Yuegeng lu,* and the *Yue geng xulu.*" The same gazetteer tells us that Zhang had the style name of Shuqiao. Since he was a native of Shanghai, who passed the metropolitan examination in 1601, we can assume that this source, *Wu Xun za-pei,* was written during the Wanli era (1573–1615). In the 1504 edition of the *Shanghai zhi* we find a similar reference that says, "Cotton and patterned gauze clothe the whole nation." This statement predates that found in the *Wu Xun zapei.* See note 29 for a further discussion on patterned gauze. The reference to Shandong silk textiles can be found in the essay on geography, *Han shu,* p. 1660.

[6] 1534 *Nanji Zhi,* 16:4a.

[7] In the early Ming, Songjiang prefecture had only two subordinate counties, Hua-ting and Shanghai. By the late Ming, one additional county, Qingpu, had been added. (Qingpu was first established in 1542, abolished in 1543, and then reestablished in 1573). During the Qing it was further subdivided, adding on the following four coun-ties: Lou (established in 1656), Fengxian (established in 1725), Jinshan (established in 1725), and Nanhui (also established in 1725).

[8] See my essay "Chūgoku shoki mengyō shijō no kōsatsu."

[9] Fujita Toyohachi, "Sō-Gen jidai kaikō to shite no Kōshū," pp. 63–80. See the same author's *Tōzai kōshōshi no kenkyū.*

[10] *Dieshan ji,* 3:1a.

[11] *Gaiyu cong kao,* 30:28b.

[12] Other sources that make the same distinction include the *Chuogeng lu,* Chen Gao's *Tonghua shi,* and *Langya daizui bian.*

[13] Fujita, "Sō-Gen jidai kaikō to shite no Kōshū"; and F. Hirth and W.W.

Rockhill, *Chau Ju-kua*, p. 219.

[14] *Chuogeng lu*, 24:11a–b.

[15] *Wuxi ji*, 3:30b.

[16] According to Chu Hua's *Mumian pu*, written during the Qianlong period, the shrine was rebuilt and the Taoist nun Huang was later worshiped as the patron of weaving. She was referred to as Huang Niangniang. (This seems to be associated with the Niang-niang shrines whose patron spirit, referred to as Niang-niang, had as her chief function protection of sailors; she also interceded on behalf of women who wanted to bear children.—Trans.)

[17] The translation herè follows that of E-Tu Zen Sun and Shiou-chuan Sun, *T'ien kung K'ai-wu—Chinese Technology in the Seventeenth Century*, p. 63.

[18] The 1504 edition of the *Shanghai zhi*, 3:18a, lists cotton cloth and *fan* cloth as separate categories. The 1512 edition of the *Songjiang fuzhi* divides cotton cloth into two categories, *sansha* cloth and *fan* cloth. Since this gazetteer says that *fan* cloth was the type brought by the Taoist nun Huang, it would seem that *sansha* cloth was produced using traditional Chinese technology. The difference between the two categories seems to be based on differences in technology. This same Songjiang gazetteer suggests that there was exchange between the two different technologies.

[19] Gu Yanwu, *Rizhi lu*, 8:1a–4a.

[20] 1512 *Songjiang fuzhi*, 7:8a.

[21] 1631 *Songjiang fuzhi*, 10:29b.

[22] *Ming shi*, p. 1896.

[23] 1512 *Songjiang fuzhi*, 7:7b.

[24] 1631 *Songjiang fuzhi*, 10:31b–32a.

[25] Katō, *Shina keizaishi gaisetsu*, p. 150.

[26] Gu Yanwu's *Rizhi lu* (8:1a–4a) contains an essay on heavy tax rates in the Su-Song area which says, "Among the Wu people, only one in ten own land and nine out of ten tenant the fields of others. Their fields are quite small." This clearly shows the dominance of tenants in the agriculture of this region.

[27] With regard to the western regions, our source suggests that on arable land of 25 *mu*, the harvest would be 2.5 *shi* per *mu*, of which 1.7 *shi* would be paid in rent, leaving a return of 20 *shi*. However, since this was a region in which there had been great fragmentation of land, the actual area managed was probably quite a bit less than this, which raises doubts about the size of the returns. Further, I have questions about the actual differential between peasant budgets in the eastern and western regions of the prefecture.

[28] 1631 *Songjiang fuzhi*, 6:18a–b.

[29] In the Wanli edition of the *Da Ming huidian, juan* 24, there are figures for the summer and autumn tax assessments in South Zhili for 1502; *juan* 25 gives similar data for 1578. In each case there is a notation with regard to Songjiang prefecture of "floss silk and silk conversions." In the preface to the 1504 *Shanghai zhi* we find: "Songjiang prefecture alone has an annual land tax of 800,000 deliverable in the capital, of which more than 160,000 comes from Shanghai. The taxes are heavy because output was high and marine products are prominent. Its cotton and patterned gauze clothed the whole empire. It could be called a wealthy district." Both cotton and patterned gauze are cited as having national markets. This clearly suggests that sericulture and the silk industry were practiced in Songjiang. However, the 1631 edition of the *Songjiang fuzhi* (10:40b–41a) included a "Deposition on relapsed taxes" by Nan'an Eastern Seas Commander Zhang Gongbi which says, "Silk floss is not produced in Songjiang prefecture. However, in the past, Songjiang was administratively part of Xiuzhou, which is the present day Jiaxing prefecture. Therefore, it still has this silk-floss tax category." During the Song dynasty, Songjiang, which was then called Huating county, was administratively attached to Xiuzhou, a silk-producing region. The tax categories of that time had simply been maintained without change. This therefore does not mean that sericulture was practiced in Songjiang. The 1504 *Shanghai zhi* lists silk gauze in its native products section, a fact which might lead us to

think it was produced there. However, one of the special characteristics of such gazetteers is their practice of listing categories with no mention of volume; thus it is impossible to estimate volume. Therefore, we don't know whether this gauze is included in the statement "clothing the whole empire." Moreover, this same phrase is not really limited to Shanghai county, but refers to all of Songjiang prefecture. In the 1512 *Songjiang fuzhi* (5:18b) it says: "Large quantities of silk gauze are now produced in the prefectural city, particularly in the Eastern Gate area. In fineness of quality it is first in the empire. That produced in the Wu Gate area does not equal it. That which is forwarded to the court is broad and long and is called 'official silk gauze.' There is another kind that is very fine and light like crepe. It is called 'sealed window.' Both are produced by the Imperial Textile Works." While this shows that silk gauze was produced in Songjiang city, it was clearly not produced by ordinary weavers, but by the Imperial Textile Works as a luxury product. See Nakayama Hachirō, "Min dai no Shokusenkyoku." Thus this patterned gauze was produced in the cities and is in no way connected with rural, sideline handicraft industry.

30 1521 *Huating xianzhi*, 3:14b–15a.

31 Yuan edition of the *Jiahe zhi*, 6:3b. Jiahe was an early name for Jiaxing.

32 *Taizu shilu*, Hongwu 3 (1370), ninth month, *xinmao*, 56:1b–2a.

33 1588 *Shanghai xianzhi*, 1:14b.

34 1512 *Songjiang fuzhi*, 7:12a.

35 1631 *Songjiang fuzhi*, 10:41a.

36 1605 *Jiading xianzhi*, 5:7a–7b.

37 Nishijima, "Chūgoku shoki mengyō shijō no kōsatsu."

38 Feng Menglong, *Zhinang bu*, 4:6b. This is a copy of similar statements found in the classics.

39 1631 *Songjiang fuzhi*, 8:16a–17a.

40 1878 *Huating xianzhi*, 8:10a–b.

41 These tax-remitting households (*jiehu*) were also called "cloth-forwarding households" (*bujie*) and were part of the Songjiang prefecture service levy system. Several landholding households took on this responsibility in rotation. Of service levy duties this was the heaviest, and some families were forced into bankruptcy by it. This problem became the subject of a major controversy, and most of the arguments in that debate are included in the 1631 *Songjiang fuzhi*, 11:24a–b.

42 *Nongzheng quanshu jiaozhu*, vol. 2, p. 969.

43 1512 *Songjiang fuzhi*, 5:11b.

44 *Nongzheng quanshu jiaozhu*, vol. 2, p. 694.

45 The reference to Haishang here certainly is to Shanghai; the author Xu Guangqi, a Shanghai native, uses the phrase "Our Haishang." In the *Nongzheng quanshu jiaozhu* (pp. 964–65) we find the following: "The public, private, military colony, salt, and reclaimed lands of Haishang total 2,000,000 *mu*." The 1504 *Shanghai zhi* (3:2b) gives a figure for total land area in Shanghai county of about 2,000,000 *mu*. There seems to be no doubt that Haishang then is Shanghai.

46 1506 *Gusu zhi, juan* 10, section on waterways. "Lianqitang, also called Lianchuan, is a town in the neighboring county [Jiading]. It is 72 *li* from east to west." From this we know that Lianqitang was located in Jiading county.

47 Wu Weiye, *Meicun jiacang gao*, 10:15a.

48 J. Thorp, *Geography of the Soil of China*, 1936. Japanese translation by Itō Takakichi, *Shina dojō chirigaku*, 1941, p. 155, says, "One of the chief uses of the dry, alkaline soil of the eastern parts of Jiangsu province was cotton cultivation." Cotton was not necessarily incompatible with alkaline soil. The 1631 *Songjiang fuzhi*, 8:16a–17a, includes a proposal submitted by Governor Zhang Feng in 1511 which reports, "In the poorer fields near the sea, only cotton can be planted with a return of 50 to 60 *jin*."

49 1631 *Songjiang fuzhi*, 10:58a.

50 This pattern of using the profits from cotton to buy rice further increases in the Qing and led to debates over food policy. See the 1775 report, "A request to those

living near the sea to grow grain as well as cotton," by the governor-general of Li-angjiang (Zhejiang-Jiangsu) Gao Jin, included in the *Huangchao jingshi wenbian*, *juan* 37.
  [51] *Nongzheng quanshu jiaozhu*, vol. 2, p. 691-92.
  [52] In the section on raw cotton in the *Nongzheng quanshu jiaozhu*, vol. 2, p. 959-79 the words cotton field (*miantian*) occasionally appear. In the 1673 *Jiading xianzhi*, 14:9b we find the following: "Qi Rushan received his *jinshi* degree in 1559. In the year after he became an official, there was a great flood in the Jiangsu area. In the pe-riod between fall and winter, the rice price was not yet too high. He used 10,000 taeis of government funds to purchase 20,000 *shi* of rice from areas on the upper Yangzi, and this served to aid in emergencies. He then personally inspected the outlying areas and learned that the people planted cotton and rice. He ordered that taxes on rice paddies were to be paid in kind and on cotton fields to be converted and paid." Here we see the use of *daotian* for rice fields and *huatian* for cotton fields. In the "Cotton Poem" of Wu Meicun, there is a note to the original that reads, "All those who grow cotton call it *hua* and are distinguished from those who grow rice." Phrases like cot-ton field (*huatian*) and cotton rent (*huazu*) have become a part of the local dialect. In Luoyang, the people refer to peonies as *hua* (= flower; this is the same word that is used for cotton in the above); "they do not dare to disparage peonies, which are very valuable." As an aside, in the Guangdong area the phrase *huatian* refers to fields on which jasmine is planted (*Guangdong xinyu, juan* 72).
  [53] *Nongzheng quanshu jiaozhu*, vol. 2, pp. 964-65. *Guantian* refers to government land, *mintian* to private land, *juntuntian* to military colony land, and *zaohutian* to the fields of salt households in the coastal areas. According to the 1512 *Songjiang fuzhi*, 8:11a, these latter are different from the actual salt-producing households in the coast-al regions. While they are included in the salt-household registration, they do not produce salt but rather are primarily engaged in agriculture.
  [54] *Meicun jiacang gao*, 10:16a.
  [55] 1605 *Jiading xianzhi*, 7:1a.
  [56] Ibid.
  [57] *Nongzheng quanshu jiaozhu*, vol. 2, p. 961.
  [58] 1744 *Zhenyang xianzhi*, 1:13b.
  [59] *Nongzheng quanshu jiaozhu*, vol. 2, p. 965.
  [60] 1735 *Nanhui xianzhi*, 15:2a.
  [61] 1605 *Jiading xianzhi*, 19:44b-45a.
  [62] 1744 *Zhenyang xianzhi*, 1:14a.
  [63] Chu Hua, *Mumian pu*, 8b.
  [64] *Nongzheng quanshu jiaozhu*, vol. 2, p. 695.
  [65] 1673 *Jiading xianzhi*, 4:39a.
  [66] *Nongzheng quanshu jiaozhu*, vol. 2, p. 966. We should note that Xu Guangqi's section on fertilizer mentions bean cake together with the more traditional manure, ash, and creek mud. This is the first mention of the use of bean cake in the history of Chinese fertilizer. It is not clear whether this was being traded as a commercial ferti-lizer.
  [67] Mantetsu Chōsabu, ed., *Hoku Shina menka sōran*, pp. 213-76.
  [68] According to the 1744 *Zhenyang xianzhi*, 1:15a: "Cattail: The coastal areas in the eastern part of the county all cultivate it. It is called "cattail marshes." It is cut in the early fall and woven into bags which are used to wrap up cotton. Profits are higher than from rice. Reed: Woven into curtains which are used for drying cotton. They are also made into latticework used in the construction of earthen walls."
  [69] Chu Hua, *Mumian pu*, 15a.
  [70] Ye Mengzhu, *Yueshi bian*, 7:4b-5a.
  [71] [*Yuti*] *Mianhua tu*, eighth illustration.
  [72] 1631 *Songjiang fuzhi*, 8:20b.
  [73] *Nongzheng quanshu jiaozhu*, vol. 2, pp. 963-64.
  [74] The original is in Yuan Songzhou, *Zhongguo zuowu lun*, p. 232.

[75] 1663 *Songjiang fuzhi*, 4:9b.

[76] Nishijima, "Chūgoku shoki mengyō shijō no kōsatsu," pp. 873-903.

[77] 1631 *Songjiang fuzhi*, 10:29b.

[78] See the original note to Wu Meicun's "Cotton Poem" cited in note 52.

[79] Wang Zhen, *Nong shu*, section 19 of illustrations on agriculture implements, gives the following explanation of the *jiaoche* ginning machine: "In the past, a machine called the *nianzhou* was used, but now a gin called the *jiaoche* is used. It is much more convenient. Four pieces of wood form the frame, and at the top are two small uprights; it is about 5 *chi* high. A square board is placed at the top to stabliize the two uprights, with the axles passing through each upright. Cranks for turning the two rollers are placed at the ends of the axles. The end of the axles are blocked so that nothing can pass through. Two people turn the crank handles while a third feeds in the cotton. As the two rollers move, the branches and stems remain on the inside, while the cotton comes out on the other side. It is many times more efficient than the *nianzhou* style of gin." In this description, the gin requires the labor of three men. In the late Ming it was further improved, as we can see from the description in the *Nongzheng quanshu jiaozhu*, vol. 2., p. 977: "Using the *jiaoche* gin, one person can do the work of three. It is said that with the *jurong* style of gin, one person can do the work of four. With the Taicang-style gin, two can do the work of eight." The *jurong*-style gin referred to here is probably the same as the *ganche* referred to in *Tiangong kaiwu* (see pp. 60-61). As we can see from the illustration supplied there, one person using both hands and feet is able to do all the ginning work. The *yache*-style gin is described in the *Mumian pu* in the following way: "This machine is made of wood, with a triangular base. When one sits, the top will be level with the breast. Attached to the top are two uprights. A wooden roller is placed in the space between the two uprights. It is about 3 *cun* (inches) in diameter, and there is a handle on the left of the machine which is operated with the right hand. On the outside there is an iron roller, 0.5 inch in diameter. It is attached to a wheel on the right of the machine and is operated by the left foot. On the inside of the machine, there should always be wooden wedges to hold the frame firmly together leaving a foot or more of space in the center. The cotton is fed through the space between the two rollers, with both hands and feet operating the machine. The seeds fall out on the inside of the machine, and the seedless cotton comes out on the outside." This seems to be a slight improvement over the machine depicted in *Tiangong kaiwu*. It has a wheel to smooth the turning of the rollers. This seems to be the machine depicted in the [*Yuti*] *Mianhua tu*.

[80] 1735 *Nanhui xianzhi*, 15:2b.

[81] For illustrations, see Rudolf P. Hommel, *China At Work*, pp. 161-89.—Trans.

[82] *Nongzheng quanshu jiaozhu*, vol. 2, p. 971.

[83] Chu Hua, *Mumian pu*, 13a-b. This translation has been done in consultation with M.J. Hagerty's 1927 unpublished translation of the text, which is in the collection of the East Asian History of Science Library, Cambridge University.

[84] *Nongzheng quanshu jiaozhu*, vol. 2, p. 970.

[85] Chu Hua, *Mumian pu*, 13a-b.

[86] Ibid., 14b.

[87] The 1631 *Songjiang fuzhi*, 6:10b, includes the following discussion of changes in dyes in the late Ming: "Changes in dyes: at first the following reds were used: crimson, peach, refined silver-pink, and mauve red. Now we use clear pale pink, gold pink, lychee red, orange, and eastern red. In the past we had deep green, cedar green, and light green. Now we also have pale green, bright green, orchid green. In the past we used bamboo shoot green, peacock blue; now we have sky blue, jade green, moon green, and pale green. At first we used incense, tea brown, and soy brown; now we have ink black, rice color, hawk color, deep incense, and lotus tint. In the past we had ginger yellow; now we use canary yellow and pine flower yellow. In the past we used purple; now we also have grape blue."

[88] 1631 *Songjiang fuzhi*, 6:10b.

[89] 1512 *Songjiang fuzhi*, 5:17b-18b.

[90] 1663 *Songjiang fuzhi*, 4:13b.
[91] *Da Ming huidian*, 38:22b.
[92] *Xianzong shilu*, Chenghua 16 (1480), seventh month, *bingjia*, 205:4a–4b.
[93] *Shuyuan zaji*, 1:1b.
[94] 1663 *Songjiang fuzhi*, 53:5a.
[95] 1631 *Songjiang fuzhi*, 11:24a–39b.
[96] Ibid., 6:10b, 7:27a.
[97] 1512 *Songjiang fuzhi*, 5:17b.
[98] Ibid., 5:17b–18a.
[99] 1524 *Shanghai xianzhi*, 1:13a.
[100] 1512 *Songjiang fuzhi*, 5:18a.
[101] *Xiaozong shilu*, Hongzhi 5 (1492), fourth month, *wuwu*, 62:5a–b.
[102] See Xu Weinan, *Shanghai mianbu*.
[103] 1605 *Jiading xianzhi*, 6:27b.
[104] 1673 *Jiading xianzhi*, 1:6b.
[105] Chu Hua, *Mumian pu*, 14a.
[106] 1605 *Jiading xianzhi*, 6:27b.
[107] 1673 *Jiading xianzhi*, 1:7a.
[108] 1681 *Chongming xianzhi*, 6:7b.
[109] 1512 *Songjiang fuzhi*, 5:18a.
[110] 1631 *Songjiang fuzhi*, 6:10b.
[111] 1512 *Songjiang fuzhi*, 5:18b.
[112] 1681 *Chongming xianzhi*, 6:7b.
[113] 1512 *Songjiang fuzhi*, 5:18a.
[114] 1379 *Suzhou fuzhi*, 43:14b.
[115] 1506 *Gusu zhi*, 14:14b–15a.
[116] Chunyou (1241–52) edition of the *Yufeng zhi*, 3:61b.
[117] 1631 *Songjiang fuzhi*, 6:11a; 1524 *Shanghai xianzhi*, 1:13a.
[118] 1663 *Songjiang fuzhi*, 4:14a.
[119] 1576 *Kunshan xianzhi*, 2:23b; 1605 *Jiading xianzhi*, 6:37a.
[120] 1631 *Songjiang fuzhi*, 6:10b.
[121] 1673 *Jiading xianzhi*, 4:43b.
[122] 1631 *Songjiang fuzhi*, 11:34a–37b.
[123] 1793 *Nanhui xianzhi*, 15:44b.
[124] 1752 *Jianshan xianzhi*, 17:10b.
[125] Nishijima, "Chūgoku shoki mengyō shijō no kōsatsu."
[126] 1631 *Songjiang fuzhi*, 6:10b.
[127] 1744 *Zhenyang xianzhi*, 1:17a; 1605 *Jiading xianzhi*, 6:27b; 1631 *Songjiang fuzhi*, 6:10b; 1663 *Songjiang fuzhi*, 4:13b; 1752 *Jinshan xianzhi*, 17:10b.
[128] 1752 *Jinshan xianzhi*, 19:7a. (I have followed the translation in Mark Elvin, *Pattern of the Chinese Past*, p. 273.—Trans.)
[129] 1512 *Songjiang fuzhi*, 4:11a.
[130] This passage was frequently quoted in later gazetteers. For example, the 1521 *Huating xianzhi*, 3:9b–10a; 1588 *Shanghai xianzhi*, 1:12b; 1631 *Songjiang fuzhi*, 7:18a–b; and the 1878 *Huating xianzhi*, 23:4b.
[131] *Nongzheng quanshu jiaozhu*, vol. 2, p. 970.
[132] 1735 *Nanhui xianzhi*, 11:2a.
[133] 1517 *Jinshan weizhi*, 2:32b.
[134] 1624 *Haiyang xian tujing*, 4:12a.
[135] In a note in the copy of *Shangcheng yilan* that is in the collection of the Naikaku Bunko, in the section corresponding to the section cited from the *Shuilu lucheng* the boats are called cotton spinning boats. This seems to be an error, and probably the word "spinning" has been mistakenly written instead of "yarn." The full title of the *Shangcheng yilan* is *Xinke jingben huayi fengwu shangcheng yilan*. It is divided into two chapters and was edited by the vice magistrate of Xinyu county, Tao Chengqing. The date of the publication is unclear. However, according to the *Xinyu xianzhi*,

Tao Chengqing lived after the Longqing period (1567–72). This work therefore may be earlier than the *Shuilu lucheng*. In content it is almost identical to the latter. It would seem that both came from a common source that was then re-edited. In that process, cotton-yarn boats were incorrectly recorded as cotton-spinning boats. For more on these route books see Timothy Brook, "Guides for Vexed Travelers—Route Books in the Ming and Qing," *Ching-shih wen-ti*, 4:5(1981), pp.32–76.

[136] *Shuilu lucheng*, 7:17a. Small boats called cotton-yarn boats thus regularly went back and forth between Jiashan county and Songjiang prefecture. These boats would seem to be cargo boats whose main function was to transport cotton yarn. Their destination was the center of the textile industry, Songjiang prefectural city. Jiashan was located midway on the water route from Haiyan to Songjiang. The cotton-yarn boats which transported cotton yarn from Haiyan to Songjiang could thus conveniently be boarded at Jiashan by travelers going from Jiaxing county to Songjiang. The yarn referred to here seems to have been that part of the cotton yarn produced in Haiyan county which had not been consumed locally, and thus was transported to Songjiang as raw material for the weaving industry.

[137] 1512 *Songjiang fuzhi*, 4:11a.

[138] 1631 *Songjiang fuzhi*, 11:31a–b.

[139] 1735 *Nanhui xianzhi*, 15:15b.

[140] 1752 *Jinshan xianzhi*, 17:10b.

[141] *Yueshi bian*, 7:5a.

[142] According to the 1752 *Jinshan xianzhi*, 17:10b, the various kinds of coarse cloth described in the main text (small cloth, broad cloth, etc.) were produced by the people. It thus seems that although in the mid-Ming this area was only involved in spinning, it later also developed into a weaving area.

[143] 1793 *Nanhui xianzhi*, 15:38b–39a. (Most of the translation given here is taken from Elvin, *Pattern of the Chinese Past*, pp. 274–75. However, the sections in the middle of the poem were omitted in Elvin's translation.—Trans.)

[144] Nishijima, "Chūgoku shoki mengyō shijō no kōsatsu", pp.873–903.

[145] 1631 *Songjiang fuzhi*, 6:13a. (Elvin has translated this poem in *Pattern of the Chinese Past*, p. 274. He gives it a slightly different interpretation; this translation follows Nishijima's reading of the poem.—Trans.)

[146] *Da Ming lu*, vol. 2, p. 93.

[147] *Huangchao jingshi wenbian*, 28:12b.

[148] Xu Xianzhong, *Wuxing zhanggu ji*, 12:10a.

[149] *Yanshan wenji*, 81:5b–6a.

[150] *Lu Wending gong ji*, 5:25b, 27a.

[151] 1524 *Shanghai xianzhi*, 1:10b.

[152] Padre Alvaro Semedo's Chinese name was Lu Dezhao.

[153] P.A. Semedo, *The History of the Great and Renowned Monarchy of China*, p.14. This book was originally published in Madrid in 1624 and was then translated into many other languages including English, French, and Italian. There are many problems with the romanization of Chinese names. Shanghai comes out as "Xanhai" in the Madrid edition and as "Xanuchi" in the English and French editions and as "Xanuchie" in the Italian edition. These different forms all seem to be translator's errors. All of these errors seem to come from the Italian edition published in 1643. For a reference see H. Cordier, *Biblotheca Sinica*, vol. 1, no. 24. Since the later translations all seem to have been made from this 1643 version, they all have the same errors. However, since I have not seen the 1643 edition, I will not pursue this question any further.

[154] 1631 *Songjiang fuzhi*, 2:29a.

[155] Katō, *Shina keizaishi gaisetsu*, p. 86.

[156] 1631 *Songjiang fuzhi*, 11:31a–b.

[157] Ibid., 11:24a.

[158] Ibid., 11:24a–b.

[159] This interpretation may raise doubts about the use of "imperial manufacturing"

with reference to the court-supervised industries. In this case, it is also important to look not only at the surface form, but also at the structure of the industry including the nature of capital and labor.

[160] On markets, see my article "Chūgoku shoki mengyō shijō no kōsatsu." Although that article is incomplete, it does describe the conditions of a rural industry subordinate to merchant capital. With regard to the disruption of commercial activity as a result of military action and its impact on the weaving industry, see the report of Feng En in the 1631 *Songjiang fuzhi*, 49:42–43b. He reports that after pirate invasions, "trade and commerce ceased. The rural people stopped spinning and weaving." There were frequent pirate raids during the Jiajing period (1522–66), and the Zhexi area was one of the major areas affected. This external problem of lack of stability limited the method of payment used by wholesale merchants and was thus another factor which hindered the development of a putting-out system.

[161] On the historical role of rural industry in modern economic history, see Ōtsuka Hisao, *Kindai Ōshū keizaishi josetsu* and the same author's *Kindai shihonshugi no keifu*, reprinted as volumes 2 and 3 of *Ōtsuka Hisao chosakushū*. A comparison of the various types described by Ōtsuka Hisao with the rural industry of the early Chinese cotton industry clarifies the characteristics of the latter. It also suggests the prospects for this form in an industrial revolution.

[162] Early Anglo-Chinese trade did not follow the classic pattern of trade between advanced nations and colonial dependencies, in which the advanced country exports manufactured goods and imports raw materials. Rather, China was exporting large volumes of finished cotton textile goods and importing cotton as a raw material. This Chinese import of raw cotton continued for a long time. Chinese import of finished cotton textiles began to grow only in the 1830s. We should note that a significant portion of the import volume consisted of the semi-finished product, cotton yarn. On this point see Fujita Masanori, "Jūshichi-hachi seiki ni okeru Ei-Shi tsūshō kankei'; and Ubukata Naokichi, "Nankin momen kōbōshi." See also H.D. Fong, *Cotton Industry and Trade in China*, p. 39.

RURAL HANDICRAFT IN JIANGNAN IN THE SIXTEENTH AND SEVENTEENTH CENTURIES

TANAKA MASATOSHI

In his study of the Chinese cotton industry, Nishijima Sadao argued that the development of rural handicraft came in response to external pressures, particularly the state's increasing demand for taxes. Unable to meet those demands out of their agricultural income, peasants turned to handicraft production as a way both to meet their tax payments and to provide for their own subsistence needs.

In this article Tanaka Masatoshi takes issue with Nishijima's analysis, arguing that internal developments in the forces of production within the small peasant family farming unit were an important factor in the expansion of handicraft. Tanaka's argument focuses on the silk industry in the Jiangnan region, but the lines of the argument also apply to other rural handicraft industries. Although Tanaka disagrees with Nishijima's interpretation of the factors that played a leading role in the development of rural handicraft, both Tanaka and Nishijima agree in opposing the "sprouts of capitalism" thesis developed by Chinese scholars. Partisans of the "sprouts of capitalism" thesis believe that capitalist relations were already present in an embryonic form in the late Ming.

Tanaka's essay begins with a careful analysis of a hitherto unused late-Ming magistrate's report on rural raw silk production in the Jiangnan region. Tanaka draws very precise distinctions between the late-Ming rural handicraft industries and capitalist-style commodity production. He argues that "commodity exchange was slowly driving a wedge between agriculture and handicraft production," breaking the previous integration between the

This essay was originally published in *Wada hakushi koki kinen Tōyōshi ronshū* (Tokyo: Kodansha, 1961). This translation follows the revised version, "Jūroku-jūnana seiki no Kōnan ni okeru nōson shukōgyō"「十六・十七世紀の江南における農村手工業」, in *Chūgoku kindai keizaishi kenkyū josetsu* [中國近代經濟史研究序說] (Tokyo: Tokyo Daigaku Shuppankai, 1973), pp. 79–100. Translation by Linda Grove.

two pursuits within a single family unit. Capital shortage among
the direct producers led to a system in which small peasant producers would sell their unprocessed or semi-processed agricultural
raw materials and then repurchase raw materials for their own
handicraft production. Tanaka argues that this peasant involve-
ment in the market, which was leading to specialization and an increased division of labor, should not be regarded as embryonic
capitalism since the process did not allow for the capitalist-style
use of income for the expansion of production.

Tanaka's disagreement with Nishijima over the causal factors in
this process of development has important implications for the
interpretation of later historical developments. The Tanaka thesis,
which stresses the internal development of forces of production,
posits an increasingly tense relationship between peasants and
state authority, with the state attempting to expropriate all gains
made as a result of the development of productive forces. The
state's increasing demands were met by peasant resistance, sometimes in the form of armed struggle. The twentieth-century revolution is then seen as the culmination of this basic struggle. The
Nishijima thesis, which puts the basic stimulus to change outside
the production process, in the state, has much more difficulty explaining in a systematic way the origins of the revolution.

This essay represents a much condensed version of the author's
graduation thesis. In subsequent years he has had wide-ranging
research interests and published numerous essays on modern economic history, historiographical methodology, and popular rebellion. One of the most rigorous theorists among Japanese historians of China, he is currently working on a book-length study of
land relations in Ming-Qing China. Tanaka Masatoshi retired
from the University of Tokyo in 1983 and is now professor at
Shinshū University.

*   *   *

During the sixteenth and seventeenth centuries commodity production* by rural handicraft industries in Jiangnan had achieved a high
level of development. Regional specialization in certain commodities
which were exchanged throughout the country was quite advanced:
cotton textiles were produced in Songjiang and Suzhou prefectures,

Research for this article was conducted as part of a joint research project with
Saeki Yūichi, but the author alone is responsible for the argument and conclusions.
*Here and in the following discussion I am using commodity production in its
broad meaning; it does not refer to capitalist-style commodity production.

flax in Changzhou and Zhenjiang prefectures, silk textiles and raw silk in Huzhou and Jiaxing prefectures.[1]

Study of such rural handicrafts has been a major theme in postwar Japanese Sinology. This work has been stimulated by two major theoretical debates. The first was the postwar critique cf the earlier theory of the stagnation of Asian society.[2] The second was the concurrent debate in China over the genesis ("sprouts") of capitalism: handicraft was regarded as an important index for verifying the existence of the beginning of capitalist development.[3] This essay builds on all this earlier work but will make use of one historical source not adequately treated in the earlier debates.

The text

Jin Yipai, while he was magistrate of Chongde county, Jiaxing prefecture, from 1607 to 1609, made a penetrating study of local rural production of raw silk and silk textiles. Let us first look at his report:

> Jin Yipai reports: According to the 1251 gazetteer all available land in our area was solidly planted in mulberry. The rich, like ancient lords, had so much land that they did not even calculate it by *mu*. They fertilized their mulberry, and it grew thick and luxuriant. The poor, on the few feet of land around their dwellings, planted mulberry in every open space; there too it stretched up fresh and luxuriant. During the silkworm months, all households were engaged in its cultivation. They produced silk that was light and fine; the part of their output that was narrow in width was not directly turned over in taxes, but rather was taxed according to its price. At the peak of the season, resident merchants and large groups of traveling merchants gathered to trade in silk.

> [A wide variety of textiles were produced.] Coarse cocoons were used for making silk floss, and coarse yarn for pongee. Fabrics like figured silk, woolen cloth, cotton, brocade, and a thin silk called *sanfasha* were woven on handlooms. Hemp was planted in the spring and cut in the summer, while ramie crops were grown four times a year. Yellow grass (*huangcao*) was planted like rice in paddy fields. . . . Following local customs all the households spun and wove, and then sold any surplus beyond their own use. This system produced greater prosperity.

> From what I, as an official, have heard, the situation is now different. Present-day agriculture and sericulture are more developed

than in the past. Annual harvests reach as much as three *shi* per *mu*. [The peasants have their hands full gathering in all the worms;] they busily go "to lop the boughs far and high."⁴ For landowners 1000 *mu* is regarded as a large estate. Fields are being opened up. Silk is now of high enough quality to be part of the taxes offered to the throne. Weavers of pongee, both patterned and plain, figured silks, gauze, thin silk, and plain silk are particularly busy; everyday they are bent over their small looms. Silk traders flock to the area. Throughout the silk districts the looms and shuttles are always busy. But, even though they work this diligently, the peasants still cannot acquire enough to buy the necessities of life. Small peasants come out short at the year-end settling of accounts. The agricultural profits do not meet their needs, and in the final accounting the apparent wealth disappears. On the other hand, the merchants easily make profits.

What can be done about this situation? The problem lies in the fact that production is not able to keep up with demand. Even when we exclude the problems of natural disasters and excessively heavy taxes, and even if every year brought a good harvest, the most profitable crops produced here are silk and grain. Although silk is the more profitable of the two, it is a gamble for the poor to raise silkworms and produce cocoons. All the equipment for sericulture is borrowed from pawnshops. As the months go by, bitter work dims the eyes and turns the hair white; finally the silk is reeled just before the year is brought to a close. [At the end of the year,] public and private debts are settled at the silk market. The peasants' profits from the silk market all must come out of the purses of the merchants. After the big merchants and small merchants have grown fat on their profits, the little that is left is passed on to the peasants. The merchants have hundreds of ways of cheating: they use deceptive scales and debase good silver with unrefined tin. Before the payment of taxes to the officials, the pawnshops, whose expenses have been light but whose income has been great, confront the peasants: they squeeze out the last drop of blood, and the peasants are left, as before, with empty pockets. Moreover, the peasants have been following new, more extravagant customs, and it is impossible for a single family to remain frugal. When will they be able to put aside a little money? This is the result when production cannot meet demand.⁵

By the late Ming the Chongde peasants, despite advances in agriculture and sericulture and despite their diligent efforts to reclaim fields and produce textiles, were unable to supply even their own basic physical needs. Jin Yipai argues that the source of the problem was the fact that production could not meet peasants' demand. In the Jiangnan region, which was the major source of national funds, the peasants suffered from the burdens of tax and service levy exactions and from the difficulties in adjusting to the new exchange economy. As a result, they began to shift from rice production to the more profitable silk production. However, sericulture was impossible without equipment, and the required tools all had to be borrowed from usurers. This necessitated the bitter labor bemoaned by Jin. Only after the raw silk had been sold could public and private debts finally be settled. However, in selling the raw silk, the peasants were totally dependent on the merchants. These merchants used unfair scales and debased silver to enrich themselves, and in the end only a small proportion of the profits would reach the peasants' hands. In this fashion, even before the peasants had paid their taxes the usurers were squeezing out their life's blood, and the peasants remained as poor as they had been before. In addition, the standard of living rose steadily and customs became more extravagant. Thus it was even more difficult for a peasant family to be thrifty and much more impossible for them to set aside savings.

In interpreting this text, we should keep in mind two facts. First, most of the direct producers were tenants. The 1879 gazetteer for Shimen quotes the 1611 gazetteer for Chongde county as follows: "According to the Song gazetteer, much of the agricultural land in Chongde was not owned by the peasants themselves."[6] We should note that the 1611 gazetteer recognizes a similar situation in the late Ming. Second, the small peasants (xiaomin, xiangmin) mentioned in the above texts refer to those directly involved in production, i.e., the tenants. It is important to note that, contrary to the common assumption that the landowners were responsible for land tax and labor service levy, these tenants seem to be charged for the land tax and labor service levy.[7]

In this essay I will use Jin's report to explore the following issues: (1) the relationship between agriculture and domestic handicraft industry under the system of small peasant farming; (2) the relationship between the form of small peasant farming and the power of the authoritarian state; (3) the relationship between small peasant farming and usurious merchant capital; and (4) the historical development of small peasant farming in the late Ming.

Agriculture and domestic industry in small peasant farming

Jin states that at the end of the Southern Song, families sold their surplus textiles: they "sold any surplus beyond their own use." Thus, at that time commodity circulation (at least of textiles) meant simply the sale of surplus products. Furthermore, Jin indicates that within small peasant farming there was a close integration of agriculture (rice, hemp, ramie, "yellow grass" [flax?], and especially mulberry and silkworms) and domestic handicraft industry (spinning, weaving, cotton cloth, and particularly the production of silk thread and cloth). In this section I am interested in two problems: what form did this integration of agriculture and domestic industry take? And, through an examination of this relationship, can we determine whether commodity production existed?

Let us turn to the situation in the Southern Song. Even if we accept the evidence on weaving in the text above, we must determine whether the phrase "At the peak of the season, resident merchants and large groups of traveling merchants gather to trade in silk" refers to the commodity production of raw silk,[8] or simply to the sale and circulation of surplus raw silk. It is important to keep in mind that silk fabrics were not used by the peasants themselves but were regarded as surplus, over and above what was produced to pay taxes. So the question becomes: did rural commodity production of silk—that is, the production of silk for exchange purposes alone—exist at the end of the Southern Song?[9] Evidence from the Ming suggests that commodity production developed during that period only after the separation of agriculture and domestic industry. If commodity production did indeed exist in the Southern Song, what special factors enabled it to develop within a small peasant unit integrating agriculture and domestic industry?

Jin Yipai's report does suggest certain differences between the Song and Ming. His description of Song sericulture begins with the planting of mulberry "in every open space";[10] there is no mention of the purchase of raw materials. Therefore, there is no evidence for the theory that methods of commodity exchange were introduced into small peasant farming to supplement home-produced raw materials.[11] Secondly, it is clear that as a result of the development of productive forces in the late Southern Song (seen in our source in such phrases as "this system produced greater prosperity") merchants had begun to penetrate rural villages. Thus, although the development of commodity production in the late Song cannot be proven, the existence of commodity circulation is clearly evident in the fact that the direct producers or peasants sold their goods themselves. Within these limits, then, we can say at least that the development of the productive forces had broken down the original isolation of the rural community which had its origins in the integration of agriculture and domestic industry. This conclusion does not, however, solve the original problem: we still do not know how commodity production could have developed in the Song within a small peasant unit integrating agriculture and domestic industry; nor, indeed, do we know whether it developed at all. Unfortunately, there is no way to fully clarify the historical process that was in operation within late Southern Song small peasant farming. In leaving this question unanswered, it is important to recognize the problem this raises in judging the relative development of small peasant agriculture in the late Ming.

Although a similar integration of agriculture and domestic industry in small peasant farming could still be seen in the late Ming,[12] significant changes in the stage of development had occurred by this time, and those naturally affected the relationship between agriculture and domestic industry. In comparison with the Song, the forces of production in the late Ming were much more advanced: Jin explains, "Present-day agriculture and sericulture are more developed than in the past," and gives as examples the opening of fields and the high level of activity in silk weaving. It is clear that what is being described here is a peasant-managed handicraft-style production of raw silk for the market. Thus Jin's comment, "Public and private debts are settled at the silk market."[13]

A distinction must be made here between the beginnings of commodity production for the market and the earlier process in which surplus produce was simply made into a commodity. Of course, when simple commodity production involves merely the acquisition of cash for the purchase of daily necessities, it is still significant in its function as a base for the separation of agriculture and domestic industry. However we cannot identify this simple commodity production with the genesis of capitalism, since the process involved does not allow for capitalist-style use of the income to expand production. In looking at the beginnings of commodity production, I will ignore the question of the overall mode of production. And since we are looking at a gradually developing process, the intentions of the direct actors (i.e., the small peasants) will also be considered irrelevant. I am not suggesting that the peasants were consciously initiating commodity production. My major concern then is with the developing process itself and the results that we can observe from it.

The development of commodity production for the market followed roughly this pattern. First, the handicraft production of textiles was a process contained completely within the peasant farming unit—that is, peasants made textiles using agricultural raw materials which they had grown themselves. This system—the integration of agriculture and industry within one unit—existed, as we have seen, in the late Song. In the next stage of development, the market disrupted this integration: peasants sold their agricultural raw materials to merchants, who then sold them off to other textile-producing units. Finally a new, modified and somewhat unstable form of integration developed through the mediation of this kind of market exchange.[14] Here peasants would sell their agricultural raw materials to merchants, and then buy raw materials produced by other households, which they would turn into finished textiles, again to be sold through merchants. The whole production process came to be mediated by commodity exchange. At a glance it may appear that there was little division in the production process between agriculture and domestic industry within a single farming unit. But, in fact, commodity exchange was slowly driving a wedge between agriculture and handicraft production:[15] peasant producers no longer produced their own agricultural raw materials for use in their own handicraft industries. One of the results of this change was the decline of agriculture within small farming.[16] Furthermore, the dependence on preindustrial merchant capital and the need for rapid circulation of small amounts of peasant capital in order to meet obligations introduced increasing opportunities for exchange into the internal production process of agriculture and domestic industry. This process in turn encouraged the development of a division of labor.[17] We find, for example, that many small peasants were involved in a variety of exchange relations that might include selling raw silk for cash in the spring and then buying cotton or silk yarn in the fall to weave. The chief cause of this development cannot be found in external factors (i.e., market pressure or tax demands), but rather in the internal process of the work itself and in the development of the productive forces in which the separation of agriculture and domestic industry encouraged specialization, particularly handicraft specialization. We will return to this problem in the last section.

As sericulture developed, the profits that could be made from the sale of raw silk (a product of handicraft production) came to exceed those made from the sale of rice (a product of agriculture).[18] Jin explains, "Silk is the more profitable of the two." Now, taking into account the conditions of commodity production and circulation noted above, we can for the first time use prices to compare the relative economic advantages of the agricultural and industrial sectors within the small peasant management unit.[19] The 1611 Chongde county gazetteer provides evidence on the establishment of exchange prices for raw silk:

In Chongde city, paddy and dry fields are equal in area.[20] Harvest on paddy land is only sufficient to provide food for eight months of the year. For the remaining months, rice is obtained primarily through purchase. The meeting of both public and private obligations depends largely on the profits from silkworms. Therefore, sericulture is most important. Loan contracts are always drawn up with a repayment date at the end of the silkworm season. Therefore, at the time of the quota for the autumn tax assessment, many are unwilling to turn over their salable rice, thinking that perhaps as the days pass the price of rice will rise. Ordinarily rice is pawned at a pawnshop for silver; after the silkworms have matured, the profits are used to reclaim it. Therefore in paying taxes the people depend on the profit from silkworms; they do not depend on the profit from paddy fields.[21]

It is clear that, regardless of the mode of production, rice exchange had developed, and with it, price fluctuations. When we compare the exchange prices for agriculture and home industry, the higher profitability of silk handicraft production is overwhelming, and it is easy to see why people relied on silkworms to pay their taxes and their debts. Rice did, however, continue to play an important role in the circulation structure since, as noted above, it was pawned for silver.

From the evidence presented above, we can conclude that commodity production developed within peasant-managed handicraft industries during the Ming. This development was based to some extent on the breakdown of the previous integration of agricultural and industrial production within one peasant household. The capital shortage of small peasant farming units limited their ability to manage the total production and reproduction process, forcing them to depend on usurers' or merchants' capital. Since the latter carried on their activities outside the production process—at the market exchange level—their activities cannot be regarded as a stimulus to development: the activities of merchants can only be seen as a stimulus to the development of capitalism when they work within the production process itself—for example, within a true putting-out system.

Peasant farming and the power of the authoritarian state

In the late Southern Song period the authoritarian state, assuming the persistence of the integration of agriculture and domestic industry within the small peasant management unit, began to expand the objects of taxation, collecting a cash tax on silk fabrics of a certain quality. In accordance with traditional ideas three categories had been fixed as appropriate objects of taxation: land, labor (labor service levy), and handicraft goods (tribute). Thus state expropriation was not originally limited to the agricultural output of the peasant farm, but included also the products of domestic-enterprise processing of raw agricultural goods.[22] This expropriation did not stop at the collection of taxes *in kind*; assuming a market exchange value for cocoons and rough silk fiber as well as for high-quality raw silk (as our text notes, they "gather to trade in silk"), the government also collected a *cash* tax on sub-standard silk fabric.[23]

Following our earlier line of reasoning, the dominance of commodity production in the silk-yarn industry within the peasant economy proves that it was the most advantageous mode of production in the late Ming.[24] Two passages reveal that it also benefited the government system of expropriation through taxation: "public and private debts are settled at the silk market," and the peasants' "payment of taxes to the officials." Here I want to look at the specific historical conditions which allowed the development of such a system of expropriation.

The state—sometimes working directly, sometimes with the assistance of landlords—originally regarded the undifferentiated small peasant unit as the basic taxation unit. When taxation was limited to the collection of taxes in kind, agriculture and domestic industry were divided into different taxable spheres. The Ming tax system at first followed this pattern of expropriation.[25] As a result, first, domestic industry was not originally excluded as an object of expropriation, and second, the products of agriculture and those of domestic industry were not interchangeable as tax payments; each had to be paid under its own category.[26]

This situation began to change in the late Ming in conjunction with the development of commodity production. This development of rural handicraft production took place within the expropriation relationship itself rather than, as some scholars have tried to maintain, as a response to some form of external pressure such as increased taxation. This required a kind of change in the character of the basic taxation unit. Earlier handicraft production had been incorporated into a taxation system in which land and its related labor complement were the base of all state expropriation. Commodity production began to pull handicraft away from its former integrated relationship with agriculture and stimulated its development along independent lines. Since the state wished to control to the greatest extent possible the profits of the handicraft industry as it was assuming an increasingly important role in the small peasant economy, they increased their expropriation of the products not only of handicraft production but also of agriculture. The result at this stage was the conversion of tax payments to silver, a conversion that was based on an estimate of the taxes on agriculture and domestic industry combined. The establishment of a tax system based on silver conversion was possible because, by working through the exchange system, monetary equivalents for the taxes on the products of agriculture and domestic industry could be determined.[27] Naturally this kind of conversion to payment of taxes in silver was not simply the result of state initiative. It was only possible after the development of the productive forces as seen in the growth of commodity production and the expansion of commodity exchange.

Nishijima Sadao maintains that rural handicraft developed in part as a side industry, as a supplement to family income necessary to meet the heavy taxes imposed on the Jiangnan region from the late Southern Song on.[28] But this is to suggest that it was simply changes in the land tax system which caused the development of rural handicraft industry. Doubtless this factor did play a role in handicraft development, but it is essential to consider also the internal connections between the development of the forces of production and expropriation. As the above analysis of these connections suggests, there is no simple cause-and-effect relationship between the changes in the land system, the development of the forces of production, and changes in the method of expropriation. Even after the conversion to tax payment in silver, it was difficult to divest rural handicraft of its role as a means of supplementing the family budget. Certainly the development of commodity production no more "caused" the change in Ming taxation policy than the increase in taxation "necessitated" the development of domestic industry. The relationship is much more complex than either alternative suggests.

Peasant farming and usurious and commercial capital

Now it is possible to examine more closely an important new element in the development of commodity production in the Ming—the role of usurious capital in the whole production process. To return for a moment to our text, it seems possible to interpret the relevant section ("All the equipment for sericulture is borrowed from pawnshops") in two ways. If we follow the literal meaning of the phrase, we must assume that the tools themselves were borrowed. If, on the other hand, we assume that this is a symbolic expression, then the phrase would mean that the funds used to purchase the tools were borrowed.

The first case represents direct control over production by merchant or usurious capital. It resembles somewhat the classic putting-out system of domestic industry, in which the direct producers own the tools of production and borrow capital on account in the form of raw materials. When the finished product is collected the fee ("wage") received by the producer embodies the value of the unpaid surplus labor; thus, the direct producers have been turned into de facto wage laborers. In this case, however, the production tools are loaned to the direct producers by usurious capital. In this process, the price of the final product represents the labor of the direct producers plus the value of the borrowed tools. In this arrangement the direct producer himself controls the tools of production. Only through such a joint relationship between merchant and direct producer can the borrowed tools realize their utility. Just as the feudal landlord manipulated his land base to exert extra-economic pressure to expropriate land rent from his tenants, so too usurers used their ownership of the tools of production to expropriate the fruits of the peasants' usufruct. Since the profits associated with usurious capital do not equal those of the putting-out system of control, it must be regarded as a more primitive system. However, merchant-usurer capital, which originally simply extracted profit outside the actual production process, has here undergone certain changes. We cannot ignore these changes: they are intrinsically related to changes in the social structure and to the development of commodity production and are a direct reflection of the stage of development of the mode of production at that time.

According to the above interpretation, peasants borrowed the tools of production themselves from merchants or pawnshops. However, there is no evidence that such a putting-out system of production existed in the late Ming. It is not until the nineteenth century, when a more sophisticated distribution system had been created, that a real putting-out mode of production could develop. Thus, the second possible interpretation of the text—that peasants borrowed the funds for sericulture from usurious capital—is most likely.

Our text describes the practices of usurious capital as follows: "The pawnshops, whose expenses have been light but whose income has been great, confront the peasants: they squeeze out the last drop of blood, and the peasants are left, as before, with empty pockets." Pawnshop accumulation of high profits was in fact quite common at that time. Interest on loans according to one source was 100 cash per 1000 loaned (10 percent);[29] the 1892 gazetteer for Changxing county gives an interest rate of 200 cash on a 1000 cash loan (20 percent);[30] and the 1749 gazetteer for the same county gives an example of Huzhou prefecture rates in which there was a 1.5-percent monthly interest on loans above 10 taels, a 2-percent monthly rate for loans of one tael or more, and a 3-percent monthly interest on loans of less than one tael.[31] These rates, even when we compare them directly to the very different conditions of our own day, seem quite high. When we consider them in the light of the low level of productive forces of the day—and particularly when we consider that they were loans given under the conditions of uncertainty involved in the sericulture of that day[32]—then the interest rates in fact seem even more usurious.

Using the funds described above and passing the months in bitter work, the peasants finally completed the process of raising the silkworms and producing the raw silk. Then the finished product was transferred into the hands of merchant capital through sale at the silk market. This was clearly a buyer's market,[33] in which the "producers were not able to best their customers." Jin Yipai also described the methods of the merchants: they "have hundreds of ways of cheating . . . and debase good silver with unrefined tin." This was truly a preindustrial merchant stratum, in which one after another, "the big merchants and small merchants have grown fat on their profits"[34] by using all kinds of deceptive extra-economic methods, such as unfair scales.[35] However, no single individual merchant monopolized the outlet for peasant-produced commodities. Thus the merchant capital in both its local form and traveling form was completely outside the production process. It never took advantage of the opportunities offered by the new historical development in production to build a real capital-controlled industry but was content merely to extract and monopolize the transferred profits of one part of the exchange process. This is only possible in a closed socioeconomic system like that of rural China—a system characterized by the landlord-tenant relationship and a chronic insufficiency of funds resulting from the limited scope of the market. Moreover, merchant capital, in its use of extra-economic methods of expropriation, had simply adapted a preindustrial landlord style of expropriation. In such a preindustrial system, the landlord and merchant used similar methods. In the case of agriculture, the tenant-serf carried on semi-independent production with the landlord extracting the surplus (as rent) only after the completion of the production process. Handicraft followed a similar pattern, with the merchants extracting the surplus outside the production process; the role of the markets and prices in this extraction process merely represented a change in form, not a change in the system itself.

The following passage from the 1892 gazetteer for Changxing county gives a vivid summary of the tensions between the small peasants (direct producers) and merchant capital:

> In the raw silk market, those who are buying silk are referred to as "silk guests." Those who open wholesale stores and buy on behalf of others are called "silk masters" or "scalers." The "scalers" have sweet-talking mouths and greedy bellies; they practice countless deceptive methods. The honest countryfolk find that their heavy silk is weighed in as light, and what should bring a high price is reported as low. Those who start to leave their gates without selling are called back by the deceptive doubling of prices. Thus the "scalers" stop the countryfolk from going to other places to sell. Locally this is known as "beating the head when the customer enters the gate, building dikes when he leaves." The "beating" means that the merchant gives an impression of indifference when the customer enters; the "building dikes" means that he tries to pull back in those who are about to leave without selling their goods. For the poor men and women who have neglected sleep and missed meals in order to raise silkworms and produce raw silk, it is impossible to describe the bitterness of such treatment. A whole year's taxes, rent and debt repayment, food and clothing, and other daily necessities must all come out of their revenue from silk. Even when it is sold for a good price, they are still afraid that the income will not be sufficient. And the merchants will, in every possible way, bully them. This is truly intolerable. In Changxing the silk purchasers are commonly called "silk devils"; this is truly an apt description.[36]

Historical trends in late-Ming small peasant farming

Expanding forces of production in the late-Ming small-peasant farming form stimulated the development of commodity production. Although there was some development in the forces of production at the time, they were still at a sufficiently low level to allow preindustrial merchant capital to gain control of the circulation process and extract the major portion of the profit.[37] This extraction of profit took the form of extraction of interest by preindustrial merchant capital, in an amount equal to the value of surplus labor, which was itself the fruit of certain advances in the forces of production. This new system of expropriation was simply a variation on the landlord system of extraction. If we could stop time and take a cross section of the contemporary forces of production, what we would see would be not embryonic capitalism, but rather simple commodity production for the purpose of acquiring necessities. Jin's question—"When will they be able to put aside a little money?"—reveals that the peasants were concerned with their basic livelihood rather than with commercial profit. Here simple reproduction begins and ends with the acquisition of use value, and thus production produces no profits, as the foregoing Changxing gazetteer text suggests. The new advances in the forces of production and the accompanying increase in extractions indicate the intensification of the contradictions between the direct producers and the merchants.[38] Phrases like "silk devils" and "death shops"[39] express the bitterness of the relationship. Thus, the condition of peasant agriculture at the time, embedded as it was in this series of relationships, foreshadowed several major future developments.

There were two possible lines of development open. The first would lead to greater dependence on merchant capital; the second to a sharpening of the contradictions and peasant rebellion, with the potential to split the existing system. Let us turn to the first possibility, the growing dependence of the wholesale system on merchant capital. If we look at the actual situaton we can see that in the Jiangnan rural raw silk and weaving areas the most important role was played not by pongee wholesalers, but by raw silk wholesalers. In the early eighteenth century these raw silk wholesalers were distributing unsold raw silk to peasants and having them weave it in a kind of temporary putting-out system.[40] By the middle of the nineteenth century a permanent system of putting-out production in the process of silk twisting finally developed.[41] However, putting-out production was a system in which merchant capital which had originally been external to the production process came to extract its profits from within the production process itself. Production then became dependent on the total process of social reproduction. This process of social reproduction was still based on the feudal/small-peasant agricultural mode of production, and profit could only be produced within this outmoded production system. This fact is crucial, since it suggests that the possibilities for development in the nineteenth century were not, as has so often been maintained, limited to capitalist-style subordination to merchant capital. For example, there was nothing in this system that would make the continuation of the small-peasant farming mode impossible. It is also possible to see other paths of development: a class struggle growing out of the contradiction between putting-out style capital and the weavers, for example. At any rate, the important point is that there was nothing in the nature of the mode of production in nineteenth-century China which predetermined its development along a capitalist path.

The second possible line of development was an increase in anti-rent struggles directed against landlords—that is, peasant struggles against the controllers of the system. The 1879 gazetteer for Shimen county quotes the 1611 gazetteer for Chongde county as follows: "According to the local Song gazetteer, whenever there are times of drought or flood, inevitably the officials will be requested to reduce rent. . . . But now this is not automatically the case. According to a common saying, when there is flood or drought, neighbors watch each other before deciding on a rent-paying strategy. When there is a bad harvest, the cunning among the tenants do not always go to the officials and request a remission of rent; they simply reduce it themselves, and the landlord has to suffer the loss."[42]

According to the 1596 gazetteer for Xiushui county the tenants pawn their high-quality rice and pay rent with medium-quality or inferior rice, or they gather together in cliques and pledge not to pay their rent.[43] In the early nineteenth century we find similar evidence:

> More than half of the land cultivated by the peasants is rented. Rice is regarded as precious, and regular failures to pay rent are common. Even when some of it is paid, good rice is not used and empty husks are included. The landlord's wife and young are frightened by the slogans of the peasants, and for the landlords, rent collection becomes a perilous undertaking, and the possession of property a burden. Even in years when the crop is good, after all tax obligations have been paid there is almost nothing left. In years when there is some kind of natural disaster, then the fields are sold to meet the tax obligations. One cannot depend on landed property, and the decline in social morality is spreading.[44]

The rent-resistance struggles of what were called "stubborn" tenants mentioned here were not merely individual protests inspired by starvation conditions. Rather, they were rent protest struggles which naturally accompanied the new social climate created by the development of commodity production and circulation. Here, "stubborn" tenants have become a normal phenomenon. Although peasant struggles were increasing, the protests did not always end in victory for the peasants. As we can see from the 1596 gazetteer of Xiushui county it was often the landlords and the merchant and usurious moneylenders who ended up in control. Given the circumstances of the times, it was not easy for the peasants to defeat the system of landlord control. In spite of that, the peasants, strengthened by the development of commodity production, and frustrated by the tense economic relationships created by it, united in struggles against existing land relations. Their determination is clearly stated in the phrase "they joined together in cliques and pledged not to transfer rent payments to the rich." As a result of the developing process of such struggles, fixed property (in Chinese society this was land and was the most basic form of wealth and means of social control) for the first time became a burden rather than a reliable source of security.[45]

Ultimately this peasant unrest can be traced back to the economic disruption caused by internal developments within the mode of production throughout the sixteenth and seventeenth centuries. In the late Ming, the expansion of the forces of production and the resulting changes in the internal productive processes encouraged the development of commodity production within small peasant farming. Such farming had previously been organized on the basis of the integration of agriculture and home industry, but the development of commodity production and exchange, as explained above, disrupted this integration. Exploitation of the peasants both by usurious capital and by the state system of expropriation further undermined the system and exacerbated the contradictions between landlord and peasant, merchant and peasant, state and peasant. As these contradictions intensified in the course of the sixteenth and seventeenth centuries, the peasants were driven to attack at least one of these relationships (landlord-peasant) in an attempt to destroy the whole outmoded socioeconomic system.

Notes

[1] See Xu Guangqi, *Nongzheng quanshu jiaozhu*, pp. 959–90, on cotton; and Saeki Yūichi and Tanaka Masatoshi, "Jūroku-jūnana seiki no Chūgoku nōson seishi kinuori gyō."

[2] See Saeki Yūichi, "Nihon no Min-Shin jidai kenkyū ni okeru shōhin seisan hyōka o megutte." For further discussion of this methodological approach see my article "Ajia shakai teitairon hihan no hōhōronteki hansei," which is included in Tanaka Masatoshi, *Chūgoku kindai keizaishi kenkyū josetsu*, pp. 3–23.

[3] See my article "Chūgoku rekishi gakkai ni okeru 'shihonshugi no hōga' kenkyū."

[4] This phrase is a quotation from the *Shi jing* poem entitled "Seventh Month."

[5] The 1879 *Shimen xianzhi*, pp. 564–66. This is a revised edition of the 1683 *Shimen xianzhi*. The name of Chongde county was officially changed to Shimen in 1662. All further references to the Song gazetteer refer to the *Yuxi zhi* edited by the county magistrate Huang Yuanzhi in 1251. Yuxi was an early name for the Chongde area.

[6] 1879 *Shimen xianzhi*, p. 1849. According to the *Zhongguo difangzhi zonglu*, edited

by Zhu Shijia, manuscript copies of the 1611 edition of the *Chongde xianzhi*, edited by Jin Yipai, Li Taizhong, and Zhang Hongru, are in the collections of the Geography Institute of the Chinese Academy of Sciences, the Shanghai Library, and the Zhejiang Provincial Library.

[7] In dealing with the question of landlord and tenant tax responsibilities, one approach is to argue that while the landlord was nominally responsible, in fact the tenant was directly responsible for payment. At any rate, expressions of this kind are quite numerous in the sources of this period. See my article "Popular uprisings, rent resistance, and bondservant rebellions," which is included in this volume, and Tsurumi Naohiro, "Mindai no kireiko ni tsuite."

[8] As we see in the following discussion, the seasonal pattern in production and sales holds for raw silk, not silk cloth (see note 13). In cases where the market for raw silk was the urban silk-weaving industry in the Song, it was not unreasonable to limit rural commodity production to raw silk. This choice was a result of the lower technological level of silk weaving in rural domestic industries.

[9] In the 1863 edition of the *Nanxun zhenzhi* (Wucheng county, Huzhou prefecture), a stele inscription by Li Xinzhuang in the Baoguo Temple says, "Large crowds gather at Nanlin [old name for Nanxun]. Its wealth from agriculture and sericulture is superior to that of eastern Zhejiang. At this village where the traveling merchants and resident merchants gather, the officials do not investigate and collect taxes" (25:15b). According to an 1135 stele inscription from Shaoxing prefecture, there are examples of cash rents referred to as rent money and mulberry-leaf money (Sheng Xian, "Xuetian ji," in *Yuezhong jinshi ji*). See also Sutō Yoshiyuki, *Chūgoku tochi seidoshi kenkyū*, p. 134. From this we can see that mulberry leaves and raw silk were circulating as commodities, and that it is likely that commodity production had developed. Further, according to the 1683 *Shimen xianzhi* (2:15a), during the Song dynasty, silk and floss-silk taxes "were not paid in kind; rather, goods were exchanged for cash and then the taxes were paid." In spite of this account, we cannot consider cash payment of taxes in the Song period as the norm in that area. Rather, the section in our original source notes, "They produced silk that was light and fine; the part of their output that was narrow in width was not directly turned over in tax, but rather was taxed according to its price." This seems to be a more accurate description of the actual situation. Paying taxes in cash is simply a change in form, the regulation for payment in kind remaining unaltered.

[10] The separation of labor in raising silkworms (agriculture) and reeling silk (handicraft)—that is, the circulation of cocoons as a commodity—was limited by the fact that technology for killing chrysalises without damaging cocoons was not yet widespread. Such technology does not appear until the late Qing. See "Shuanglin ji zengzuan," which quotes Dong Xun, the Daoguang-era author of the *Nanxun zhigao*. Indications of the social division of labor in silkworm cultivation and silk-yarn production industries (for example, the circulation of mulberry seedlings, mulberry leaves, and silkworms as commodities, regardless of the mode of production involved, and the social division of labor for twisting in the process of silk-yarn production) demonstrate the introduction of commodity exchange within each internal process of agriculture and domestic industry. In silk weaving, raw silk is a commodity. See note 16 concerning this source.

[11] We should note that there are references to cotton weaving in late-Song Zhejiang but there is no record of any cultivation of cotton. This raises the question of commodity circulation of cotton; I note this question, but leave it for later research.

[12] Not only that, but we can see similar examples in the late Qing. See the "Mitchell Report," which is included in *British Parliamentary Papers*, China 33, pp. 663–71.

[13] According to the Wanli-era *Keyue zhi* by Wang Zhideng, "In Shimen the land planted in mulberry yields an abundant harvest. There are markets for raw silk, and large merchants from all directions gather. Every year they come in the fifth lunar month to buy raw silk and the gold is piled up like mountains" (1:2a-b).

[14] See notes 10, 15, 16, and 38.

[15] On the relationship between silk weaving or cotton weaving and silk reeling accompanied by silkworm raising, see the following note and Zhang Lixiang, *Bu nongshu*. On the special conditions leading to the integration or separation of the processes of silkworm raising and silk reeling, see notes 10 and 38. In the cotton industry, the degree of social specialization in cotton cultivation, ginning, spinning, and weaving varies with different management forms. See Nishijima Sadao, "The Formation of the Early Chinese Cotton Industry" in this volume. According to the 1879 *Shimen xianzhi* (p. 553): "The peasants in our area support themselves by spinning and weaving. Early in the morning they go to market, taking either cotton yarn or cotton cloth; after exchanging it for raw cotton, they return home and spin and weave. The next morning they again exchange their output. In addition to farming and silkworm raising, the peasants rely on this kind of work to provide for their food and clothing." Thus, in the late Qing agriculture and industry coexisted in a peasant-farming unit without a lineal relationship. That is, the individual peasant families did not usually produce the raw materials for handicraft and then process them themselves, but rather would sell some raw materials and then later might buy others for use in their own domestic industry. What we see here instead is the economic integration of silk cultivation, cotton spinning, and weaving under one management. According to the *Bu nongshu*, the fusing together of silkworm raising-silk reeling, cotton spinning, and weaving within the small peasant-farming unit had already made its appearance in this region by the early Qing. This same source also describes the spread of the production of cotton cloth and the prospects for a mass market for clothing material.

[16] According to "Shuanglin ji zengzuan," which refers to the town of Shuanglin in Guian county: "In several villages near this market town there are many who make their living from silk weaving. Some of the men work at silk twisting, and they must often go to the market to buy raw silk and sell silk fabric. As for farming, half of the fields are left to fallow, but still the peasants are able to wear fine clothes and eat fresh food. Many lounge about in teahouses and restaurants, getting drunk and raucous." The "Shuanglin ji zengzuan" is a late-Qing manuscript but is based on the late-Ming *Shuanglin zhi*, with some additions and corrections. This source describes conditions in the late Ming similar to those already mentioned in the text. (I have used an unpaginated, hand-copied edition of this work which is in the collection of the Seikadō library.)

[17] See the already cited works of Nishijima, Saeki, and Tanaka.

[18] In Jin's phrase, "the most profitable crops produced here are silk and grain." The word *di* is used for agricultural land in general and is not only being used to distinguish dry fields from paddy. "Grain" should be understood to mean rice, as this seems most suitable here. In the 1760 *Wuqing zhenzhi* we read the following: "In the past there was no gap between agriculture and mulberry cultivation. However, in western Zhejiang the profits from silkworm cultivation slightly exceed those from work in paddy agriculture, and work in paddy agriculture is thus considered backward." It should be noted that the text does not take up the question of silk weaving. The peasants were, of course, also diligently working at silk weaving, as we see in the *Zhenze xianzhi*, p. 946: "In the period before the Song and Yuan, work in the silk-damask industry was restricted to city people [in Suzhou]. During the Hongxi and Xuande eras [1425–35] of the Ming dynasty townsmen [living in the county seat of Wujiang] gradually began to make a living from silk and weaving. They were sometimes employed by the city people as weavers. From the Chenghua and Hongzhi eras [1465–1505] on, technically skilled country people also began to take up this work, and it gradually became quite common. With this the people of Zhenze market town and nearby villages also endeavored to gain the profits from silk damask." It is clear from this source that the development of rural silk-damask production is a special characteristic of the late Ming and early Qing. For small peasant farming, however, it was more profitable to stay out of the promising foreign-trade market and the urban, high-quality silk textile industry. Competition also came from the

cotton cloth industry with its expanding mass market. Instead, the peasants kept just enough raw silk for home use and sold the rest, using their time more profitably to weave cotton cloth for the mass market rather than coarse damask. In this same *Zhenze xianzhi* (p. 947) we find the following passage concerning the commercial possibilities of silk damask and raw silk which were the manufactures of different stages in the process: "According to historical records, the *Huangxizhi* [reports that] during the Jiajing era of the Ming dynasty [mid-sixteenth century], silk damask sold for 8 to 9 *fen* (silver) per *liang* of cloth, while raw silk sold for 2 *fen* per *liang*. In the middle of the Kangxi era [late seventeenth century], the price of damask was one *qian* of silver per *liang*, while raw silk sold for 3 to 4 *fen* per ounce. If we compare the present [1746] prices with those of the Kangxi era, the price of damask has only risen by one third, while the price of raw silk has doubled. The livelihood of damask weavers is becoming tighter every day."

[19] Of course within a given integrated relationship a distinction can be introduced as a result of the use of external symbols. In the 1748 *Haiyan xian xutujing*, II:7a, of the section on local customs we find: "If the silkworms do not mature, then the whole family cries. A peasant family relies completely on silk cocoons to provide the capital for agriculture. If the silkworms fail, then the fields will also be barren, and there will be no way to avoid the tragedy of borrowing money and selling children." This illustrates a kind of relationship in economic management between agriculture and domestic industry.

[20] In the 1624 *Haiyan xian tujing* (5:12a) it says: "Mulberry fields are numerous and as a result paddy land is gradually narrowing."

[21] 1879 *Shimen xianzhi*, pp. 1850–51.

[22] We can see this form of expropriation described in the Qing edition of the *Lixi zhengshun miaozhi*, which deals with conditions in Sanyuan market town (Sha county, Yanping prefecture, Fujian): "One wheat plot with the name of *hekangwei* pays an annual rent of four *zhang* of cloth." [One *zhang* is about 3.5 meters.] According to this source, the products of domestic industry (cloth) were being used for calculating rent assessment in a relationship that involved not state taxation but private obligations between landlord and tenant. This source is quoted in Fu Yiling, *Ming Qing nongcun shehui jingji*, p. 160, without giving editor or date of publication.

[23] See note 9.

[24] The 1684 edition of *Changzhou xianzhi*, volume 3, section on customs 1b, states, "In Wu county, mulberry is planted and silkworms are raised. Markets are held in the rural areas in the fourth and fifth lunar months. As a result it is easy to complete tax payments."

[25] During the Ming dynasty, handicraft products—divided into categories—were taxed in addition to wheat. The categories included raw silk, floss silk, silk fabrics, cotton yarn, and cotton cloth.

[26] With reference to cotton cloth in Songjiang prefecture, we know that following the regulation of Governor Zhou Chen with regard to premiums on tax commutation in 1433, collection of taxes in goods other than rice was officially authorized (see Nishijima on this point). The factors which would eventually form the base for reform were the development of rural domestic industry or handicraft within small peasant farming.

[27] In Zhejiang the Single Whip reform was implemented in 1565 by regional inspector Pang Shangpeng.

[28] Nishijima Sadao, "Jūroku-jūnana seiki o chūshin to suru Chūgoku nōson kōgyō no kōsatsu."

[29] According to "Shuanglin ji zengzuan," "Silk-cultivating peasants lacking capital borrow money from the rich households. When the cocoons are mature, they sell the raw silk to repay these loans. For every 1000 cash there is an interest of 100 cash; this is called adding one *qian*. Most loans come to term on the summer solstice. If the loan is not repaid on time, extra interest must be added. The rich

reap unfair gains, but the peasants who borrow funds in order to cultivate silkworms find it convenient."

30 1892 *Changxing xianzhi*, 8:13a.

31 1749 *Changxing xianzhi.*

32 *Shina sanshigyō taikan*, p.127. See also note 37.

33 In the late-Ming short story "Shi Runze Tanque yu you," which is included in *Xingshi hengyan*, ed. Feng Menglong, pp. 357–79, there is a description of such methods in a buyers' market.

34 According to "Shuanglin ji zengzuan" there are numerous specialists in the trade including the *chaozhuang* who acted as the representatives of the wholesalers, the *duozhuang* and peddlers who acted as middlemen between the producers and the wholesalers, the *chenghanchuan* who were their agents, and the *chaisizhuang* who sold small amounts of raw silk to weaving households. As the production process was divided into many parts because of the small scale of production, the commercial system also involved many small merchants with limited capital.

35 The 1879 edition of *Shimen xianzhi* (vol. 6, p. 185) quotes the 1611 edition of *Chongde xianzhi* as follows: "Among the masses, raising silkworms is like making pills of immortality. It requires the most exhausting labor, but success or failure is determined in an instant. The raw silk brokers hoodwink the countryfolk, constructing large scales with more than 20 *liang* in a *jin*. [The standard measure was 16 *liang* per *jin*—Tanaka] (In paying the peasants, the merchants) ought to use silver of 97.8 degree of fineness; however, they would mix in lower quality silver and claim it was of high quality. . . . Year after year the quality was lowered further. Time and again the officials issued prohibitions on these practices, but they could not bring them to a halt."

36 This source is from a later date (1892). Before the section that I have quoted there is a passage that reads, "The customs of the raw-silk market follow earlier practices."

37 The low level of development of the productive forces at that stage is revealed in the unstable nature of technology and its accompanying economically speculative character. A particularly severe example is the trade in mulberry leaves, the meeting point of mulberry cultivation, and silkworm raising. As a result of the unstable nature of sikworm-raising technology, it was difficult to decide whether to buy or sell silkworms, and so there was speculation (see the 1748 edition of *Haiyan xian xutujing*, section on *fengsu*, 7a–7b. The sale of almost mature worms is mentioned in *Shenshi nongshu* and in the 1808 edition of *Yuhang xianzhi*, 38:13a. The latter source also cites *Canshi tongji*, which mentions the same practice in the early Qing. This trade was stimulated or depressed depending on the quality and quantity of the silkworm and mulberry crops; the price of mulberry leaves varied accordingly. From the late Ming on, two types of mulberry-leaf markets developed: a futures market trade beginning in the winter, and a direct trade market during the silkworm cultivation season that same year. The price of mulberry leaves changed in proportion to the quality of the silkworms and the supply of leaves. This relationship is mentioned in the early seventeenth century in Zhu Guozhen, *Yongchuang xiaopin*, 2: 36a–36b: "The rise and fall of the price is quickly determined. There is a saying 'even the immortals find it difficult to guess correctly at the fluctuation of the price of leaves.' " Li Le's *Jianwen zaji*, 9:77b, describes the speculative nature of silkworm cultivation under these conditions in the following way: "The masses have wild hopes for great profits. Although they lack mulberry leaves of their own, they buy large numbers of small worms. They plan, if the price of leaves is low, to make a great profit. If the price is high, however, they quickly discard the worms in the rivers." In addition to the circulation of mulberry leaves, the roles of speculative leaf sales in overall silkworm cultivation and of the production relations and ground-rent relations associated with management of mulberry fields pose important questions which I plan to deal with in the future. See also Furushima Kazuo, "Minmatsu Chōkō deruta chitai ni okeru jinushi keiei."

[38] Lu Chongxing, who was the prefect of Jiaxing prefecture from 1675 to 1678, notes in his *Shouhe riji*, 6:35a–38a, that during that period more than 2000 weavers and small peddlers in Puyuan market town (Xiushui county), angered by merchants who "dominated the market and whose monopoly on profits had given rise to resentment," rose up shouting slogans, breaking into their shops, and burning them down. Puyuan was an important collection and distribution center for raw silk and a production center for Pu pongee. It was a regional marketing center that had grown up in the midst of silkworm rearing and raw-silk producing villages. In such rural towns there were also a number of professional weaving households. The class backgroud of these professional weaving households is a subject that still needs study. In this incident it is possible that those referred to as "weaving households" may be peasants. See also note 41.

[39] Silk wholesalers (*yahang*) are referred to as "silk devils," and cotton wholesalers (*buzhuang*) are called "death shops." See Nishijima Sadao's article also translated in this volume.

[40] The following poem by Shen Bocun, a 1733 scholar from Guian, is included in "Shuanglin ji zengzuan": "Merchants build up supplies of silk but do not weave it; they put it out to peasant households fixing the price in advance. As they work the shuttle, the dragon-and-phoenix pattern appears, twisting before the eyes. Working bitterly for nine days, they can weave only one bolt. Original commentary: When the wholesalers have extra silk, they put it out to weavers, gathering up silk cloth in exchange, and seeking great profit."

[41] In the 1844 *Zhenze zhenzhi* (2:10b–11a) we read: "There are some who both spin silk and weave brocade. Those who use their own raw silk spin it and sell it to the wholesale merchants (*yahang*). This is referred to as *xiangjing* (warping at home). Getting raw silk from the wholesaler, spinning it, and collecting payment is referred to as *liaojing* (warping for wages)."

[42] 1879 *Shimen xianzhi*, vol. 6, pp. 1849–50.

[43] According to the 1596 *Xiushui xianzhi*, vol. 1, p. 97, "Up to this time, the rich merchants have set up rice pawnshops. The tenants pawn their high-quality rice for silver and use middle- or inferior-quality rice to pay their rent. Even in years of a good harvest, they claim a poor harvest, and demand an extention of payment. Recently, cheating peasants along the shores of the Tiao creek joined together in cliques and pledged not to transfer rent to the rich. Although this particular situation has eased a little now, this kind of practice is gradually spreading. The officials and tax collectors are very busy and don't stop to ask whether one has 'reported' or not. ['Reported' refers to the notice from a landlord to the officials of a delay in rent payment—Tanaka] The peasants borrow from the pawnshop merchants to complete tax payment—with the losses taken up by the landlord. Small peasants who borrow silver from the pawnshop merchants spend it, and it is very difficult for them to complete tax payment. After this the profit goes to the pawnshop merchant. As time passes, more and more people flee their burdens, and this means of course that the number of people defaulting in rent payment are increasing." This passage gives a good description of the reorganization of the landlord system: the tenants' anti-rent struggles, the collapse of individual landlords, accumulation by usurious capital, and its direct efforts to control the tenants. In this case, we cannot ignore the role and structure of state power in extracting taxes from the people. See Fujii Hiroshi, "Shin' an shōnin no kenkyū."

[44] 1879 *Shimen xianzhi*, 11:4–b.

[45] It is not enough simply to prove the economic inevitability of the explosion of peasant struggles. It is very important—taking into account this inevitability—to make a concrete study of the practice and development of actual peasant struggles and the specific historical contexts in which they occur. See my essay on peasant rebellions also included in this volume.

LARGE LANDOWNERSHIP IN THE JIANGNAN DELTA REGION DURING THE LATE MING–EARLY QING PERIOD

OYAMA MASAAKI

Since the late 1950s the landholding system has been a major issue in Japanese studies of Ming-Qing history. The article translated here was one of the first articles to examine landownership through an analysis of the labor force as a basic unit of production and treating the land system in the context of rent resistance and water control.

Oyama's central argument is that the Ming dynasty was a slave society because until the late Ming-early Qing period production was based on slave labor; even tenants were bound to a landlord by patriarchal slave relations. This patriarchal system of control, however, began to break down as a result of the rise of rural hand-icraft production in the mid to late Ming, a trend which enabled slaves and tenants in the Jiangnan region to achieve independent reproduction. Once slaves and tenants could maintain themselves without assistance from landlords, old slave-owning landlords declined in number and feudalism appeared. Slaves turned into peasants (serfs) who were controlled by the state. With the Yong-zheng-period tax reform, which combined the poll tax with the land tax (*diding yin*), the base of state power shifted from the individual household to the village. This is the basis for Oyama's argument that the late Ming-early Qing period marks the begin-ning of the feudal era.

Though not acknowledged in the article, Oyama was strongly influenced by the innovative work of Araki Moriaki in explaining the formation of the *baku-han* system in Tokugawa Japan. Araki tried to identify and define the unit of production that was the basis for the power structure of the feudal *baku-han* state. He

This essay was originally published as "Minmatsu Shinsho no dai tochi shoyū: toku ni Kōnan deruta chitai o chūshin ni shite" [明末清初の大土地所有—とくに江南デルタ地帯を中心にして] in *Shigaku zasshi*, vol. 66 (1957), no. 12:1–30, vol. 67 (1958), no. 1:50–72. Translation by Christian Daniels.

was convinced that in village society before the Edo period the immediate producers were bound to large scale cultivators by patriarchal slave relations. Developing this premise, he argued that the *baku-han* system arose as a result of, and was therefore based on, an emerging class of small-scale peasant cultivators who had been emancipated from the patriarchal relationship. For an English summary of some of Araki's work, see Sumiya Mikio and Koji Taira, *An Outline of Japanese Economic History 1603–1940*, pp.26–28. In applying Araki's ideas to social and economic change in the late Ming-early Qing, Oyama did take into consideration the peculiarities of the Chinese situation. For example, in the Jiangnan region the old master-slave relationship turned into a landlord-tenant relationship, whereas in Japan the breakdown of the patriarchal slave system created a class of small cultivators.

The assertion that landlords used slave labor extensively in the Ming is perhaps the most controversial part of the article. Oyama assumes that all slaves appearing in the source materials are production slaves and fails to consider the possibility that they might have been domestic slaves. Oyama also neglects to define what he means by the term "slave". For example, he interprets the word *pu* to mean slave but provides no evidence for such an interpretation. The translation uses the term "bondservant" in rendering the words, *pu, nupu, nubi, tongpu, jiading*, etc., and reserves the term "slave" for *nuli*. This choice of words conforms to the standard English terminology; however, to Oyama all these bondservants are slaves. Oyama also regards tenants and their families as slaves. This is confusing because it is unclear whether he is treating slaves as a status group or a social class. The assertion that tenants were slaves is not accepted by many Japanese historians, who argue that, unlike slaves, tenants owned some of the means of production and to a certain extent were an independent economic unit. Although Oyama's interpretation of the material is controversial, this essay has been widely praised for its thoroughness in bringing together in one place a a voluminous collection of source materials on late Ming-early Qing land relations.

Oyama began his academic career with a graduation thesis on the cotton handicraft industry in nineteenth-century China. His aim was to extend Nishijima Sadao's work on the late Ming-early Qing cotton industry on into the late Qing. He soon discovered that the land system had to be explained before research on handicraft industries could proceed. This motivated him to undertake the study of landownership. In his subsequent publications on the tax and labor-service system in the Ming-Qing period, Oyama has endeavored to strengthen the basic themes he presented in the article translated here, albeit with minor modifications. Oyama Masaaki is professor at Chiba University.

*   *   *

During the late Ming-early Qing most of the cultivated land in the Jiangnan delta region was concentrated in the hands of a small number of large landowners who relied on tenants to till it. Gu Yanwu relates as much in his well-known diary, "Among the people of Wu, one in ten owns land, while nine out of ten work as tenants for the others."[1] Most of these large landowners were urban landlords, i.e., absentee landlords who resided in county capitals and market towns. The following two sources attest to this phenomenon. The 1765 gazetteer for the township of Puli in Wu county records:

> For over a hundred years of Qing rule great peace has prevailed and the population has been increasing daily. Local people settled in their occupation do not own a hundred *mu* of land, while all the rest is leased to tenants. Half of the first-class land belongs to wealthy households in the prefectural capital [i.e., Suzhou]. In Puli there are two or three wealthy families who are all diligent, frugal, and law abiding. Furthermore, they are poor and simple in their customs, unlike the wealthy households in the prefectural capital who live in luxury.[2]

Zhao Xixiao in his *Yaoyi yi* (A proposal for labor service) comments: "The people in Jiangnan have much landed property. Of these landowners, 40 or 50 percent reside in walled cities, 30 or 40 percent in market towns, while 10 or 20 percent are scattered in rural villages."[3] This article endeavors to examine in detail the conditions of such large-scale landownership. Let us begin by considering existing theories.

Matsumoto Yoshimi was the first person to offer an integrated theory on changes in the form of landownership from the Ming to the early Qing. He noted that the *lijia* service system, which was set up by the state in the early Ming to collect land tax and service-levy labor, consisted of graded household units (*hushu*). Furthermore, he observed that both "the division of the great estates," a result of peasant rebellions in the late Yuan, and the post-recovery policy of encouraging reclamation of wasteland had promoted small-scale landownership.

Matsumoto concluded that "the dominant form of landownership was small-scale private landownership with owner-cultivators (*jisakunō*) constituting the overwhelming majority." It was, then, this "small-scale private landownership" and the existence of these owner-cultivators which made possible the organization of the *lijia* system according to graded households. But, from the late Ming on, the expansion of the money economy based on the circulation of silver led to differentiation among the owner-cultivators who were the foundation of the *lijia* system. Matsumoto argued that this differentiation caused the gradual formation of large landownership, which in turn led to the collapse of the *lijia* system itself.[4] This outline of the changes in the land system has been adopted in postwar Ming historical research, especially in studies of the history of land-tax and labor-service-levy reform. As an alternative to Matsumoto's theory, Kitamura Hironao has attempted a more concrete and historical explanation of these changes.[5] Kitamura begins his analysis with the disappearance in the late Ming-early Qing of what he calls rural landlords (*kyōkyo jinushi*), the managerial land-lords living in villages who relied on bondservant labor. These rural landlords were gradually ruined by the development of the money economy, and their land was taken over by landlords living in cities. The new group, termed "urban landlords," used their resources as commercial usury capital. Kitamura first assumes the existence of an owner-cultivator stratum (*laonong*) in the early Ming, a group similar to Matsumoto's small-scale private landowners. He then compares the formation of rural and urban landlords in China with that of parasitic landlords in Edo Japan. Rural landlords used bondservant labor that derived from the differentiation of the owner-cultivator class. Urban landlords grew out of a further differentiation of these rural landlords. To Kitamura these urban landlords were "merchant landlords, who, living during the transition period from medieval feudal socioeconomic organization to modern capitalist socioeconomic organization, used capital to control land." Consequently, Kitamura regards the late Ming-early Qing as the period in which Chinese feudal society disintegrated.[6]

Both Matsumoto and Kitamura assume that owner-cultivators formed the base of the *lijia* system in the early Ming. They also agree that the breakdown of the *lijia* system followed the development of large land-ownership, which resulted from the differentiation of owner-cultivators. Nevertheless, Kitamura does not paint a monochrome picture of undifferentiated rural villages occupied only by owner-cultivators, but recognizes the existence of rural landlords even in the early Ming. He regards the owner-cultivator stratum as overwhelmingly important, in that the owner-cultivator stratum was in quantitative terms the foundation of the *lijia* system, and in that it was the differentiation of that stratum which caused the collapse of the *lijia* system. In this respect Kitamura and Matsumoto share a fundamentally similar view of the process of change.

Furushima Kazuo has published a trenchant criticism of these two accepted theories.[7] Furushima does not regard the development of large landownership from the differentiation of owner-cultivators in the early Ming as incompatible with the organization of the *lijia* system on the basis of graded household units. He points to a new force—the local power of the rural landlords as the cause of the breakdown of the *lijia* system. It should be noted that Kitamura identifies the owner-cultivators as the most important group in early-Ming rural society simply because of their overwhelming numbers. Furushima, in contrast analyzes the relations of dominance between the rural landlords and the owner-cultivators and concludes that the landlords had the greater authority despite their numerical inferiority. Furushima also asserted that the authority of rural landlords in their local areas was incorporated into the *lijia* system to guarantee the collection of land tax and labor service by the state. In doing so he avoids presenting rural society in the early Ming as a monotonous picture of an overwhelming number of owner-cultivators. Rather, he argues for another factor, the local power of rural landlords, as the cause of change in the system of landownership. Rural landlords controlled community regulations (*kyōdōtai kisei*) and the actual obligations arising from common land usufruct.* It was their local authority which constituted the base of the *lijia* system. Therefore, for Furushima the *lijia* system collapsed only as a result of changes in the local power structure. It was the local power of rural landlords that was the basis for the domination of society.

To determine what these changes were, Furushima compares rural managerial landlords in the first half of the Ming with those in the late Ming. During the earlier period, bondservants known as family servants (*jiaren, jiatong, jiading,* and *jianu*) comprised the main labor force of such landlords. In the late Ming this labor force was transformed into a hired labor force, although it was one still subject to patriarchal control. These hired laborers were bound by a mutual contractual relationship, but free from the status dependency which made unre-

---

*The term "actual obligations arising from common land usufruct" (*zaichi no gutaiteki na tochi yōeki*) means that all the people in the community shared the use of the natural resources there (water, forests, mountains) and were required to participate in group work. In practice it is equivalent to community relations (*kyō-dōtai kankei*). —Trans.

stricted expropriation possible. Such a change could not have occurred without some considerable shift in the local relations of dominance. Both this transformation in local authority and the development of "parasitic landlordism" are understood as indices of the breakdown of feudal society.

Our discussion of previous research allows us to draw the following conclusions: 1) Since both Kitamura and Furushima assume that the main labor force used by rural managerial landlords during the first half of the Ming dynasty were bondservants called "family servants" (*jiapu, jiading, jiatong*), such landlord operations should be defined as a slave management system (*doreisei keiei*).[8] 2) As long as community regulations were maintained by rural managerial landlords, such community regulations were bound to function as a means of upholding the management system based on servile labor. Subsequently, rural class differentiation of the peasantry subject to such community regulations only served to reproduce the various relations of servile labor. It did not give birth to new relations of production and could not be expected to bring about the *decisive* collapse of the *lijia* system. 3) Therefore the decisive breakdown of the *lijia* system had to be based upon the destruction of servile relationships. In that case, the urban landlord-tenant relationship, formed as a result of the destruction of servile relationships, appeared as a new social relationship in the late Ming-early Qing period. It logically fits in the category of feudal relations of production. The main aim of this paper is to demonstrate empirically the establishment of feudal relations of production during the late Ming-early Qing. This thesis contradicts the theory that Chinese feudal society was breaking down during this period and offers an alternative explanation.

In this paper, we will first investigate the management practices of Ming rural managerial landlords and then examine how these landlords changed during the late Ming-early Qing period. Our study of changes in landlord management will also clearly indicate the transformations in the form of landownership in the period under consideration.

Managerial landlord operations and bondservant labor

Most landlords in the first half of the Ming dynasty held managerial land cultivated by bondservants. This section will show how such land was cultivated. Let us begin with some examples from the delta region of Jiangsu province.

The *Baitian gengshe ji* (A record of the tillers' cottage at Baitian) by Gao Qi (1336–74), a poet and official from Changzhou county, records that a certain Ding Zhigong built living quarters at Baitian and assigned bondservants to cultivate the fields. The text reads: "Baitian is beside the Wusong River and thirty-odd *li* from the county seat. . . . Ding Zhigong lived east of the fields and had formerly built a house there; to the front it overlooked flat fields and to the rear it was lined with good trees. *Bondservants (tongnu) were assigned to work in the fields during the day*, and after finishing, rested in the dwelling. It was thus named the tillers' cottage at Baitian."[9]

In the collected works of Wang Ao (1450–1524) there is an epitaph of a Suzhou managerial landlord Chen Yu. Chen Yu reestablished the fortunes of his family, *"personally assigning bondservants (tongnu) to work at cultivation,"*[10] thereby greatly extending his land.

According to the collected works of Chen Huan, who lived at roughly the same time as Wang Ao, Zhu Li'an of Changshu was heirless after the age of 40 and took a daughter of Xie Qing, one of the Chiliad Commanders, as a concubine. After Zhu and his legitimate wife passed away the concubine "braved the cold, heat, dew and frost to *personally supervise the family servants (jiaren) working in the fields*, and prepared offerings to worship the ancestors in every season."[11] The family servants mentioned here are bondservants.[12] An engraved epitaph to Chen Mei of Changshu relates that "his father died early and was posthumously called Yingxuan. At the time Mr. Chen was only eight years old, and his mother, née Xu, twenty-eight. She went into seclusion, spinning and teaching him to study diligently. . . . In normal years he read widely the hundred philosophers and in books on medicine, divination, and arboriculture, and *had his family servants cultivate the few score mu beside the house to earn a meager livelihood*."[13] Chen Mei, as this passage indicates, also had family servants work several score *mu* beside his house.

The collected works of Wu Kuan (1436–1504), a competent poet and calligrapher, contain a biography of a certain Xu Nanxi which relates that Xu Nanxi's family had "for generations been natives of Changshu in Suzhou prefecture, . . . and lost their land and houses when rule was returned [to the Chinese] at the beginning of the Ming. Since Xu Nanxi was by nature sturdy and not content to be idle, he *led his bondservants (tongnu) in agricultural work* and was able to provide for his family needs again."[14] Here we have another example of a man providing for a family in distress by personally leading his bondservants in agricultural work.[15]

Gu Dingchen (1488?–1566?), in the epitaph he wrote for Wu Yu, related that Wu had "for generations lived in Jishan district in Kunshan county (in Jiangsu). . . . *Behind the house there were fields of several tens of mu which he had bondservants (nu) cultivate and harvest.*"[16] This is another example of the use of bondservant labor in agriculture. Another native of Kunshan county, Chai Qi (1465?–1566?) relates that after his youngest brother Dehong died, Dehong's wife, née Zhang, *"detailed the bondservants (tongnu) to work in the fields in order to provide for herself and her two children.* She personally led all the female bondservants *(bipu)* in weaving and spinning. Every evening they divided and needled the cocoons, never missing a day's work"[17]

Bai Yue (1488?–1566?) from Wujin county, in a letter to a friend, wrote that his family's fortune dehad clined since his father's generation and "although the family had not fallen into destitution, *they were unable to supply themselves with food for a whole year even with the male bondservants (dingnu) working in the fields.*"[18] It is clear that these male bondservants were set to work cultivating the land. A passage in Wu Kuan's collected works also relates that Wang Zongji from Wujiang county *"had bondservants (tongnu) cultivate"* his land for him.[19] This same source also records information about Li Duanqi from Changzhou county, who from an early age worked as a traveling merchant, journeying from Zhejiang and Fujian in the south to Beijing in the north. He bought land with his profits and *"directed bondservants (tongnu) in managing his work.* Inside he weighed goods and outside established fields. The family relied completely upon [these sources of income] and did not fall into destitution. People admired them greatly."[20] Li Duanqi also employed his bondservants in cultivation work The same source also notes that a certain Lu Zongbo owned a lot of paddy fields near Chen Lake in Songjiang prefecture. It relates: "When Zongbo was in his prime he was unceasingly diligent. Although he never personally cultivated the land for a living, he would certainly go over to see [the hired bondservants working his fields.] On windy days he walked in the wet mud, *enduring the same hardships as the hired bondservants (yongnu)."*[21] We can conclude that Lu used hired bondservants in his fields and supervised them closely.[22] Even Wu Kuan (from Changzhou prefecture) had a great number of bondservants: "My late mother, née Zhang, married my father when she was young. . . . She was a diligent wife and enlarged the property. Clothes and food were always given out equally to the many hired bondservants (*yongnu qianzhi*)."[23] As the citation shows, Wu employed a relatively large number of bondservants, many of whom were engaged in cultivation work, as "enlarging the property" indicates.

Zhao Kuan (1436?–87?) in his *Yuehu ji* (Record of moon lake) provides yet another example of landlord management:

> Moon Lake is 20 *li* southeast of the Wujiang county yamen and has several thousand *qing* [of arable land] surrounding it. . . . The estates of my friend Mr. Wang Sishan are located there. Around the lake there was much property that Wang's forefathers had established, but [by his father's time] it was almost completely run down. Sishan's venerable father, Leshan, not only restored the property to its original state but enlarged it greatly. He owns almost all of the excellent fields and rich soil there.[24]

In another essay Zhao Kuan provides further information on the undertakings of Wang Leshan.

> I knew him throughout his life. He was orphaned when only a few years old and his great family was forlorn. He inherited his ancestors' property, which comprised only several huts, a few *mu* of land, and some books. He was left alone and helpless. . . . He was particulatly gifted at making a living; he never missed an opportunity to work. By sowing with little grain and reaping great harvests, by feeding a large labor force with a meager amount of food *(liduo shigua)*, he gradually accumulated more profits. With land approaching several ten *qing* and many bondservants *(tongpu qianzhi)*, he was already wealthy.[25]

This passage makes it clear that Wang Leshan owned several thousand *mu* of land and about one hundred bondservants. Most of these bondservants were probably employed in cultivation.[26]

The 1766 Changzhou county gazetteer relates that a local man, Zhang Chang, who was engaged in agriculture, *"led his hired bondservants (yongbao) out to the fields to work before dawn,"* and that his family was flourishing.[27] The hired bondservants he used were also a type of servile labor. Xu Fang (1622–94), a native of Changzhou county, narrates a story about a certain Zhang Yingfu, who had been poor when young and had worked diligently with his wife at weaving. This man later made a tremendous profit by selling rice when rice prices rose during the transition from the Ming to the Qing. Xu Fang relates, "At that time his family was becoming increasingly prosperous and *he kept healthy men to cultivate one hundred mu."*[28] The healthy men mentioned here were also bondservants. Gu Qing (1460–1528) writes in an essay of 1489 that Xu Minwei, whose family owned several hundred *mu* of land on the banks of the Song River and had been engaged in agriculture there for generations, told him, "I work together with five or six bondservants (*jiatong*)."[29]

The title of a five-word ancient poem "Leading the bondservants out to the fields" (*Shuai tongpu chutian*)[30] by Lu Shen (1477–1544), a native of Shanghai, provides us with another example. Though this poem is in effect a description of a rural scene, the title shows that Lu Shen was probably using bondservant labor. Yet again we find similar evidence in Zhu Heling's (1606–83) autobiographical essay, *Jiangwan caoan ji* (A record of River Bay grass hut): "River Bay grass hut is a place where Zhuzi Changru [i.e., Zhu Heling] cultivates the land and reads. . . . *At times he comes back to supervise and manage the bondservants (geng-nu), assigning them cultivation work;* the irrigation ditches and foot-paths between the fields are covered with water, and the millet and grain are renewed. Though the income is not as much as that of a peasant cultivator (*laonong*), it is sufficient for the tastes of a farmer."[31] Zhu He-ling built a hut beside the Wusong river where he kept a lot of books and engaged in reading and writing. He also supervised and managed the bondservants at agricultural work.

Moving on to Zhejiang province we find that Qian Zhen, a native of Wucheng county who earned his metropolitan degree during the Jia-jing period (1522–66) and later became director of the ministry of war, *"personally led his bondservants in planting and sowing."*[32] Xu Yikui (1318–1400), in the preface to a poem extolling the chastity of a Ma-dame Pu, states:

Chaste Madame Pu was the wife of Pu Zonghui from Wuxiang in Chongde. . . . It was precisely a period of social disturbances, and wherever violent mobs went they would attack women without re-straint. . . . Fearing for her own personal safety she removed all her hairpins, jade earrings, and clothing apparel, [adopted] a disheveled hairstyle, made her face look ugly, and wore large clothes of ordinary cloth. *She supervised the bondservants (tongpu) in attending to culti-vation and the mulberry trees,* looking just like a peasant's wife. When-ever violent mobs passed their district they left without paying any attention to her.[33]

Here we see the wife of Pu Zonghui from Chongde disguising herself as a peasant woman, supervising bondservants, and engaging in cultivation during the upheaval at the end of the Yuan dynasty.

Tu Xun (1446–1516) in a seven-word ancient poem praised a certain Cao Shizhong, who would:

Accompany the children to
Hurriedly sow grain when it came to spring,
Shouldering his hoe and wearing a bamboo hat.
What a disgrace it is to me
If I do not cultivate and reap a harvest.[34]

The childern mentioned here constitute a servile labor force,[35] and Cao Shizhong used to work together with them in the fields. Zhou Shi (1522–66?) records that Xu Feng, a native of Renhe in Hangzhou prefecture, was: "sound in his administration of the fields, working at agriculture, plowing, and sowing. *In managing hired bondservants (yongpu) he would never work them too hard and from time to time would give them gifts of food.* Subsequently everybody gladly delighted in serving him. The remaining land was leased out to tenants who paid rent according to whether it was a good or bad harvest."[36] Xu Feng hired bondservants to work the land he managed himself and let tenants cultivate other spare land.

Another example, though not from the Yangzi delta region, is the account which Tao Yunyi (1522?–1615?) of Kuaiji presents of a relative, a certain Mr. Lou: "Mr. Lou established himself by passing the metropolitan examinations with excellent results. His grandfather had amassed a great fortune, and he handed it over to his brothers. He was not selfish about anything. *He assigned various bondservants (tong) to supervise agriculture and sericulture everyday.*[37]

Shang Lu (1414–69), a man from Chun'an in Zhejiang, "*made a living by personally leading the bondservants to* work in the fields."[38] The *Siyou zhai congshuo zhaichao* (Selections from the collected dissertations from the Siyou studio) by He Liangjun (1506–73) gives an account of Zhang Mao (1437–1522) of Jinhua, Zhejiang: "His household had 20 *mu* of land. The household had only ten members including male and female bondservants (*qinding*) and family servants (*jiaren*). Each person consumed 0.01 *shi* of rice per day, and 36 *shi* were needed every year. The harvests in Jinhua were poor, and the annual harvest was not sufficient for half of this amount."[39] Zhang Mao also cultivated his 20 *mu* of land in a managerial fashion, with bondservants and family servants.

From the enumeration of examples above we see that cultivation by bondservants was widely practiced in the Jiangnan delta region during the Ming. The 1521 county gazetteer for Huating sums up the situation by pointing out that even the literati directed the labor force on their land: "Peasants are most diligent. They are accustomed to taking [hard work] as the norm, and to toiling throughout the whole year without resting for even one morning. . . . *Metropolitan degree holders and literati who come from rural areas personally work in the fields.*"[40] As this passage indicates many landlords owned managerial land and personally operated it with a servile labor force of bondservants.[41]

Landlords and bondservants

In the previous section we have provided enough evidence to show that bondservant labor was used by managerial landlords during the Ming dynasty. In this section we will endeavor to go a step further and show how bondservants were bound to landlords and why they continued working on managerial land.

Once again we will start by considering the evidence available on these issues. The Suzhou author and art critic Du Mu (1459–1525) states that "*at present bondservants (nupu) all borrow their master's surname. It is the same even in literati households.*"[42] Dong Han, a native of Huating in Jiangsu who lived during the Qing, writes that "according to the customs in Jiangsu, east of the Yangzi, when the descendants of slave men and women *(nubi)* enter the prefectural or county school *they all adopt their masters' surnames.*"[43] The *Qingbai leichao* (Unofficial records of the Qing dynasty) clarifies the historical origins of this custom: "In antiquity the sons and daughters of criminals were implicated in the crime, taken in by officials and set to work as servants. They were known as bondservant men and women *(nubi)*. Later, people bought for a price who adopted their master's surname were also called bondservants *(nu)*."[44] These passages indicate that bondservants abandoned their own surnames for that of their masters.

In the early Qing, a man from Yangzhou, Shi Tianji, prohibited this practice within his own family: "Bondservants and family servants *(nupu, jiaren)* each have (their own) surnames. Despite differences between the eminent and the humble, each lineage has its main and branch families, and servants should never be permitted to adopt our surname; not only would it end their line of descendants, but it would also cause the false to be mixed with the true. Our lineage would be thrown into disorder as the years pass, and the children increase in number."[45] This prohibition against bondservants and family servants adopting their masters' surnames indicates that it was common for bondservants to take on their masters' surnames. Bondservants at that time were regarded as fictive members of the master's family, and once they had been made to adopt the master's surname, they were subordinate to his firm patriarchal control.

In some cases bondservants were known as adopted sons and adopted wives *(yinan yifu)*. During the Ming, a certain Xiao Yong noted, "The law does not allow commoners to keep bondservants *(nu)*. *Those that provide services are called adopted sons and adopted wives*. They are provided with food and clothing, and marriages are arranged for them at a suitable age."[46] Zhang Lixiang (1611–74), in one of his descriptions of slave management, recorded the following case of an affectionate landlord: "Chen Ganchu, personal name Que, wept very sorrowfully when a bondservant who cultivated his fields died. He would not eat luxurious food and shed tears when talking to people about him. . . . Previously he had clearly stated that the bondservant was his son. He said, *"Bondservants are called adopted sons,* and they should act according to the moral obligation between father and son. The master, in dealing with his bondservants, is bound by the moral obligation between elder and younger brother."[47]

Legal judgments also support this definition. In 1675 Lu Chongxing, prefect of Jiaxing prefecture, passed judgment on the case of a landlord Gong Mingyang, who had murdered his bondservant, Cao Wengui, and then seized his wife. He stated, "My examination shows that Gong Mingyang is a licentious rascal. *He bought Cao Wengui and his wife, née Hu, for a price, taking Cao on as an adopted son.* Originally they were to provide only labor for cultivation."[48] It is evident that the term "adopted son" refers to bondservants. Furthermore, Guan Zhidao (1536–1608), who investigated the state of master-servant relations, reports that

> upon examining the statutes and regulations we find that though there is a section on bondservants *(nubi)* meeting the head of the household, there is also a prohibition against bondservants committing crimes against the head of the household. But only dukes, marquises, and bureaucrats above the third grade are permitted to keep bondservants. People whose registration status has been suspended are granted as bondservants only to meritorious officials. They cannot be given to any other bureaucrats at all. *Scholar and commoner households merely call such people adopted sons, not bondservants.* Distinguished aristocrats can be masters of commoners, but commoners can never be masters of other commoners. Adopted sons are second best to one's own son, and they have never been prohibited from studying and serving as officials. Bondservants are subject to the same statutes as prostitutes, actors, underlings, and soldiers and

are not allowed to mix with the scholarly ranks. This distinction does
not clarify subtle [differences] in meaning between bondservants and
adopted sons to any great extent. Ministers and great officers are no
less important than meritorious officials, but if *they call their bondservants (jianpu) adopted sons,* the distinction between scholars and
commoners will not be preserved. How can the rich rascals in the villages presume to imitate the powerful people at court and *condemn
adopted sons to be slaves.* [If they call their adopted sons bondser-
vants], they will become proud and believe themselves equal to meritorious officials.[49]

It is evident that though commoners were prohibited from owning
bondservants, real bondservant ownership in the form of adoption
was widely practiced during the Ming. Bondservants employed on land
operated by managerial landlords abandoned their own surnames and
were made to take on those of their masters. Though as adopted sons
they were regarded as fictive family members, the master still wielded
the power of life and death over them. Zhang Lixiang relates: "From
what I have seen *masters do not treat bondservants (puli) in a benevolent
fashion.* When they are hungry, cold, tired, or in distress they do not
sympathize with them. The worst masters do not allow their bondservants to mourn for dead parents by wearing sackcloth and wailing.
They act as though it is all right to seduce their bondservants' wives and
daughters and take their property without asking them. *The very worst
ones secretly kill and cremate their bondservants and nobody dares to
take them to court.*"[50] To sum up, bondservants were classic patriarchal
slaves in that they were subject to firm patriarchal control. These
bondservants were either housed in the same building as the master
or in a nearby dwelling. They were provided for from the master's
household account.[51]

It is important to note the difference in the ways in which landlords
used bondservants and tenants. The difference is apparent in the description Zhang Lixiang offered He Shangyin in a letter about the management of land by a certain He Rushang in Haiyan county. Zhang advised landlords to build a house within a compound which "faced the
fields and gardens and had bamboo and other trees at the rear. *To the
north of the mulberry trees and pond you should set up a three-room barn as
a dwelling for the garden men.* [Build] a house to the east of the ditch."[52]
Zhang provided a sketch (see) leaving no doubt as to what he meant:
the part enclosed by the dotted line was surrounded by a wall, inside
which the landlord's residence and his managerial land (including mulberry tree land and a pond) was situated. Tenants cultivated the land

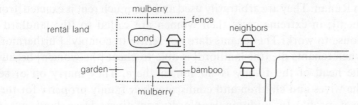

Enclose with bamboo fence on all four sides.
If there is not enough labor, the pond can be
used as the boundary on the southwest corner.
Later, a small wall can also be [constructed].

outside the wall. The garden men, the labor force employed in management, were housed in the barn on the north side of the pond. During the
early Qing, when this source was written, these garden men may have
been hired laborers, but during the Ming period bondservants were
probably assigned to live there and were fed and clothed by the master.
We can assume that Ming-dynasty managerial landlords lived in conditions much the same as those shown in this sketch.

Above we have seen how landlords managed their slave labor force
by a patriarchical system. We have also briefly touched upon the question of tenants. Tenants were given land to cultivate by the landlord and
were able to become independent from him to a certain extent. We will
investigate the relationship between landlords and tenants in the next
section.

Tenants: Labor on non-managerial land

Source materials on landlord-tenant relations are very scanty for the
Ming dynasty. This means that we have to infer these relations from
the evidence available for the late Ming-early Qing.

Let us begin with the areas surrounding the Yangzi delta region.
According to Jin Zhangzhen's *Qingyan zhupu* (Being strict with masters
and servants),[53] in 1658 bondservants in Guangshan, Shangcheng, Gushi,
and other counties in the southern part of Henan rebelled, demanding
liberation. This was one of the many bondservant rebellions that
occurred in the late Ming-early Qing. Jin Zhangzhen, who was responsible for the suppression of this uprising, divided the participants in
the rebellion into four groups:

One were the servants (*pu*) on tenant land. The tenant receives the
land and pays rent and is therefore different from a hired laborer
(*yonggong*). Colloquially they are often called tenant servants (*dianpu*)

in Runan. They are arbitrarily used and too much rent is exacted [from them]; in extreme cases their women are called to [the landlord's] house to work. The tenants dare not refuse to comply. Furthermore, when tenants die [the landlord] is able to cheat [the women] because the head of the family is no longer there. They marry off or sell the wives and children and confiscate their family property for their own profit. In addition, landlords sometimes lease land out to relatives. According to the various statutes and substatutes, when a tenant sees his landlord he should treat him with the propriety due from a young person to an elder, but if he is a relative then he is not bound by the rules of landlord-tenant relations. When landlord and tenant are relatives they have a relationship different from the regular landlord-tenant relationship. The difference between a relative and a tenant is clear, so how would it be proper for them to be kept as slaves (nuli).[54]

From this passage we can conclude that quite a large number of tenants were still kept as slaves in the southern part of Henan in the early Qing period. Further evidence is found in an article prohibiting the conversion of tenants into bondservants in the Li'an quanji (A collection of precedent cases, 1722), edited by Zhang Guangyue:

The Ministry of Revenue specially impeached powerful families who committed fraud, and submitted a report on their wicked habits in Wuyuan county and on various other affairs. The grand coordinator of Anhui, Xu Guoxiang, writes with reference to the former [memorial] that according to the 1660 item-by-item memorial by Jiangning Regional Inspector Wei Zhenyuan, a prohibition against treating tenants as bondservants (nu) was requested. The ministers requested that imperial orders be given to all grand coordinators and regional inspectors to strictly prohibit and reform [these bad habits]. These orders were implemented. At present gentry and grandee households cheat and oppress tenants and needy people into becoming bondservants. The viceroy and grand coordinator in each province should impeach them. This was approved by imperial order in the seventh lunar month of 1681.[55]

In 1681 the Ministry of Revenue prohibited the gentry and grandee households from turning tenants and needy people into slaves. This order was issued in response to a report by Anhui Grand Coordinator Xu Guoxiang.

Xu Guoxiang's memorial is included in a 1684 gazetteer for Jiangnan under the title *Tecan shihao lezha shu* (An exposition of the special impeachment of powerful families who committed fraud). It is an extremely interesting document, and we quote most of the text here, even though it is rather lengthy. After investigating a report from Wang Guotai, the surveillance commissioner in Anhui, which explained how Yu Kuang, an imperial student of Wuyuan county, was guilty of buying tenants and treating them as bondservants (*maidian zuopu*), Xu presented his findings. He wrote:

> Yu Kuang, the Wuyuan county elected assistant instructor, who was graciously ranked as an imperial student, [has acted in total disregard of others] and lacks self-respect. A nun, the daughter of Yu and therefore a member of the same lineage as Yu Kuang, drew up a contract which commended (*touxian*) three *li* of incense land from the Ruyi Temple, together with Yu Zi and the others who cultivated the land, to Yu Kuang. Yu Kuang subsequently forced Yu Zi and the others to become bondservants and provide labor services. Since Yu Zi refused to follow [these instructions], he was savagely beaten and compelled to buy back his freedom at a high price. First, he was made to write that he owed about 25 taels, but Yu Kuang and the others were not satisfied with just that. They sought a further 1.5 taels of silver and 4 taels of silver for a farm ox. Thereupon Yu Zi, in a fit of passion, pressed charges at the prefectural yamen. On the basis of the report from the prefecture, I approved an investigation by the surveillance commissioner.
>
> According to his report: "It is definitely true that Yu Kuang and the others drew up a false contract and compelled [Yu Zi and the others] to redeem themselves and sought to get silver for the ox from them. Furthermore, it is certain that they asked Hu Shangbin to write letters for them on many occasions. It is as if the powerful and mighty have [a right to] cheat the small peasants as they please. It is difficult for the law to be lenient and tolerant of this. Yet Yu Kuang is a recommended (*kaoshou*) assistant instructor, and a memorial should be submitted [demanding his] impeachment; an imperial decree should be requested to strip him of his position and title, and to have him investigated and punished according to the statutes."
>
> I have another request [to make to the throne]. Tenants are by nature poor people who till the land and pay rent. They are not the same as those who commend themselves [to large households in exchange for] undertaking labor service. If tenants have spare energy they should be allowed to open up more land in order to increase the amount of taxes to the state. If all the tenants who engage in

cultivation become bondservants of official families, then even the profits of the hard labor of small peasants will fall into the hands of wealthy households and will certainly create a waste of taxable land.

The item-by-item proposal report made to the Ministry by Wei Zhenyuan, the Jiangning regional inspector, in the first month of 1660 stated: "Large households in Fengyang and Yingzhou call their tenants manor serfs (*zhuangnu*) and do not allow them to go elsewhere. I request that this practice be strictly prohibited." The ministry answered that an investigation showed that these tenants were simply poor people, not bondservants. How can they be cheated, oppressed, and prevented from going elsewhere? I am afraid that it is not only Fengyang and Yingzhou that are like this. We must follow the proposal and ask for an imperial order instructing each grand coordinator and regional inspector to rigorously execute the prohibition and reform of this custom. If large gentry households cheat and oppress or forcibly seize tenants' wives and children, they should be called out, impeached, and punished. . . .

The law has been relaxed for a long time now, and the people are prone to be greedy. I suspect that the custom of ordering tenants to become bondservants is not only confined to the single county Wuyuan in Anhui. The Emperor's word should be sought to instruct that hereafter when landlords buy and sell land, the tenants should be allowed to do as they please, and that [landlords] are not permitted either to sell them together with the land or order them to undertake labor service. In this way the poor common people will be able to maintain a living and there will be no loss in taxes to the state.[56]

The first point to note here is that tenants were thought of as objects of sale. The commendation of the tenants Yu Zi and the others together with the land bespeaks the fact that these tenants were regarded as tenants accompanying the plot,[57] a term which appeared during the Song. This fact becomes even clearer from the account given in the latter part of the report. Furthermore, as the phrase "buying tenants and treating them as bondservants" indicates, some tenants in Wuyuan county were treated in the same fashion as bondservants in the early Qing.

The second point to be made is that large households in the Fengyang and Yingzhou region treated the tenants as manor serfs, not allowing them to move to other places. Also, since the report says that landlords "forcibly seized tenants' wives and children," we can assume that the spouses and children of tenants were either made to provide labor service or were sold, as was the case in the southern region of Henan. As a result Xu Guoxiang does not believe that the practice of treating tenants as serfs is confined merely to Wuyuan county. He suggests that in the future tenants should be allowed to choose whether they want to continue tilling land when it is bought or sold. He argues that the sale of tenants together with the land and compulsory labor service should be prohibited. Consequently, we can assume that tenants themselves were the object of trade. We can infer that tenants who were barred from moving to other places and sold together with the land existed on an extensive scale in Anhui province at that time.

Further evidence for this point is found in the Veritable records of the Yongzheng Emperor. An entry made during the fourth month of 1727 records the Yongzheng Emperor as saying:

Lately I have heard that there are servile tenants (*bandang*) in Huizhou prefecture, Jiangnan, and hereditary bondservants (*shipu*) in Ningguo prefecture. Locally they are called poor commoners, and they are almost the same as entertainer families and degenerate people (*duomin*). In even worse cases, in villages where the number of households is equally divided between two surnames, the members of one lineage become servile tenants and hereditary bondservants of the other. When there are marriages and funerals among families of the master surname, members of the families of the servile surname must go and provide labor service. If they are not prepared to do this, they are flogged. Upon inquiring when this bondservant labor service (*puyi*) began, I found that nobody had the vaguest idea and that there was no way of knowing. It is not that there is in reality discrimination between superiors and inferiors; it is merely that evil customs have been passed down from generation to generation. I have heard unconfirmed reports about this condition, and if they are really true, these people should be granted their freedom and treated as free men.[58]

This passage reveals the existence of subservient people who had been subordinate to their masters for generations and who were compelled to render them labor service. They were known as servile tenants in Huizhou prefecture, and hereditary bondservants in Ningguo prefecture, Anhui.

The fact that these people had been bondservants subservient to their masters for generations is clear from the following report in the *Yong-zheng zhupi yuzhi* (Imperial rescripts and edicts of the Yongzheng Emperor):

> Your servant, Liu Nan, the surveillance commissioner of Anqing prefecture in Jiangnan, respectfully memoralizes that . . . hereditary bondservants have been in existence for a long time in Huizhou and Ningguo. It is requested that they be set free. Your servant, the Anqing Grand Coordinator Wei Tingzhen, respectfully following the orders in the Imperial Rescript, has investigated the servile tenants in Huizhou and the hereditary bondservants in Ningguo prefecture. We have deliberated the matter of granting them their freedom and making them into respectable people and provide the following explanation by way of answer. In the second month of 1728 after due deliberation by the ministry, an imperial order was issued instructing us to abide by the results of the deliberations. Since receiving the order, the bondservants (*pu*) who have contracts themselves and the non-bondservants who live attached on leased land all abided by the instructions without any disobedience. But since many years have lapsed, some contracts have been lost and divisions have been created between those who have patrons and those who do not. This has been a constant source of disputes and of numerous accusations and lawsuits. I have investigated cases that report conflicts over hereditary bondservants and found that most of them originate from the Ming dynasty. These conflicts have persisted for one to two hundred years and over ten to twenty generations. Their male descendants have increased to tremendous proportions. It is only because one or two of [their ancestors] received the master's patronage or because they have been holding old, unstamped contracts for many years that the whole lineage, including their grandchildren, have not been able to leave their master. These people are really pitiable.[59]

According to this memorial there were hereditary bondservants in Huizhou and Ningguo who had been struggling with their masters for one to two hundred years. Whole lineages had been reduced to hereditary bondservant status because their ancestors had accepted the patronage of the master. Unfortunately, there is no record of the Imperial Rescript that was issued at that time, so it is difficult to completely understand the piece that reads "the bondservants (*pu*) who have contracts themselves and the non-bondservants who live attached on leased land all abided by the instructions without any disobedience." We can, however, infer that there were hereditary bondservants who cultivated the landlord's land while living in an independent house near the landlord's house. This point can be seen from the following passage in an imperial source providing information for the twelfth month of 1809:

> The Ministry of Rites has discussed and replied to Dong Jiaozeng's memorial, which requested that people who had been bondservants for many years be set free. What was decided has not yet been put into practice. The category of hereditary bondservants has been used in Huizhou, Ningguo, and Chizhou in Anhui province in the past. An investigation [showed that bondservants] generally claim that the contracts for the mortgage and sale of their person have been lost. . . . According to Dong Jiaozeng's previous memorial, the criterion for hereditary bondservants depends upon whether they provide labor service at present. If the master sets free those who are currently providing labor service, their grandchildren are only allowed to donate money and sit for the examinations three generations later. If they have stopped providing labor service and left the [master's] household over a hundred or a couple of hundred years ago, they are all to be released and regarded as free men even if their [ancestors] *had leased the landlord's land* and had been buried in his graveyards. This argument is most correct and reasonable. . . . We order that Dong Jiaozeng's memorial be followed. The status of hereditary bondservants is to be determined by whether labor service is rendered at present or not. If many years have lapsed and there are no reliable documents to go by, and if the people in question are not dependents who at present render [the master] labor service, we command that they all be released and made into free men, even though [their ancestors] may have leased the landlord's land and may have been buried in the landlord's graveyards.[60]

In the light of this decision, the report in the *Yongzheng zhupi yuzhi* quoted above probably signifies that those whose contracts were still in effect remained as bondservants subordinate to their masters, but that peasants who "live attached on leased land" (*fuju diantian*) were liberated from their bondservant status. The sources presented above show us that while hereditary bondservants were subordinate to a master for generations before the Qing dynasty, there were also tenants who tilled the master's land while living in a house independent from that of their master and maintaining a separate budget.[61]

Wang Si (1522?–1615?), a native of Xiuning county in Anhui province, in an essay about festivities given in honor of an ancestor, says:

"The grave of our tenth-generation ancestor Mr. Qi Wanfu is at Ling-nan in Xiuning county. Members of the Zhang family have continuously lived on the land beside the grave for almost three hundred years. During the Hongzhi period [1488–1505] some people encroached upon the land around the grave. Members of our lineage asked the officials for help [in protecting the grave] and the grave was left undamaged."[62] The Zhang family were probably both hereditary bondservants and tenants on the Wang family's land. Yu Zi, the tenant from Wuyuan county who was sold as a bondservant (see pp. 117–18) was most probably a bondservant on this type of land.

Fang Hongjing, a native of She county, records in his *Suyuan cungao* (Preserved drafts from the simple garden, 1611):

> The prefecture [i.e., Huizhou] has been stable for a long time. . . . How is it that not even several tens among the multitude can do as they please? Of course, it is sufficient for [the masters] to maintain [their rule] by using nine [relatively quiet people] to control one [rest-less person], just as a proper environment alone will correct evil. Large households use this technique to control their many bondser-vants and tenants (*pudian*). [These bondservants and tenants] are all used as freely as the hand moves the fingers. [This relationship] was not built up overnight. It is common practice for each [bondservant and tenant] to serve his master in times of trouble and for the master to feed them. Together they comprise an army of parents and chil-dren.[63]

The tenants here were clearly bondservants who had been given land by their masters.

Tenants were obviously subordinate to their master as bondservants (the so-called bondservants and tenants) and at least in the southern part of Henan and in Anhui province were themselves regarded as an object of sale. It is also evident that the sale of tenants with the land was still quite common during the early Qing. These tenants were given land by the master, lived in separate houses and ran an independent budget, even though they were regarded as bondservants. Accordingly, there is no essential difference between the historical characteristics of these tenants and those of bondservants who settled on land granted them by their masters. Both types should be included in the bondser-vant category.

All of these sources indicate that tenants and bondservants were trying to liberate themselves from their servile status. We can also infer that earlier in the Ming dynasty these bondservants were slaves under their master's firm control. Huang Xingzeng (1490–1540), the renown scholar and poet, in his piece on bondservant disobedience, relates, "It is a local custom in Huizhou for everybody to set young children to work. Only when they find a wife for them do they chase them out to live in a separate house. The masters provide them with the means to live separately and summon them only when they need them."[64] The master probably gave the bondservant family land to cultivate, calling them out to work his own fields when necessary. It is most likely that many of the hereditary bondservants in Huizhou who tilled the master's land while maintaining an independent house and budget established themselves in this way.This process is clearly seen in the following case from Fujian which was first cited by Tanaka Tadao.[65] Amano Motonosuke has skillfully summarized the details, so let me quote him:

> There are some rather old materials on serfs in the Xianlong village district of Longxi county. They were written by Huang Zhonggui, who traveled around this district in 1916 and published in the first issue of the journal *Minsu* (Folkways). At that time there were about three hundred-odd serfs. The ancestors of these serfs sold themselves during the Ming dynasty. The master provided them with servant girl spouses, annulled their old surnames, and made them take on his own surname.[66] Ordinarily, they till the land allotted to their ancestors by their master as well as engage in petty commerce. The men are required to carry sedan chairs for the master without receiving any compensation and provide all types of sundry services when there are marriages and funerals in the master's household. The women have to accompany the master's daughter to the bridegroom's house as maidservants when she marries; they are called felicitous girls [*xiniang*] or accompanying matrons [*song jiamu*]. They are permitted to marry only other serfs. When they meet members of the master's family, they can only speak to them standing up and are not allowed to sit down. When they have nothing to do they must squat beside the gate. Each of the master families with the four surnames Lin, Su, Liu, and Jiang reside in their own forts, which each has constructed. The serfs live in earthern towers outside the forts.[67]

In spite of being given land and attaining a certain degree of independence, these slave families still continued to be subject to the master's firm patriarchal domination (*kafuchōteki dorei shihai*). In effect, then, they were no different from the hereditary bondservants we saw in Huizhou above. The Kangxi county gazetteer for Macheng, Hubei, furnishes further evidence: "Few tenants till the land. *Grandee house-*

holds mostly use purchased bondservants to work at cultivation. If [these bondservants] have children and grandchildren, they are known as hereditary bondservants (shipu)."[68] Many of the grandee households in Macheng county evidently had bondservants farm for them. These bondservants were settled with their families on the land, and their descendants became hereditary bondservants, subservient to the master's family.[69] Why did landlords (bondservant masters) have bondservants settle on their own land as separate family units? A clear understanding of this point is most important when examining managerial landlords during the Ming.

First we had better note just what bondservant ownership meant to managerial landlords during the Ming. The historian and administrator Wang Huizu (1731–1807) expressed one opinion as follows: "Bondservants are mostly unintelligent and lazy. Unless the master supervises them properly, seldom will they be able to do their work."[70] Here, since bondservants were considered effective as a labor force only under the constant supervision of the master, it was both impossible and meaningless for the master to keep more bondservants than he could oversee as a labor force on his land. This condition, along with varying environmental factors, naturally limited the scope of landlord operations.[71] In cases where managerial landlords accumulated more land than they could handle, the spare land was put out to tenants. The bondservants whom the master had provided with families received a portion of this excess land.

Bondservant status includes several different degrees of subordination. Bondservants most subordinate to their masters were those reared in their master's household from a very young age. They were provided with wives chosen from the female bondservants, and their descendants retained their bondservant status within the master's household.[72] Consequently, managerial landlords who accumulated more land than they could administer had such subordinate bondservant families work their excess land for them. Bondservant ownership, therefore, provided managerial landlords with a service workforce for such activities. It also acted as a means of immediately replacing families settled on the landlord's land who were insubordinate. It was this threat of replacement that kept service families in their status as bondservants. Such conditions applied to hereditary bondservants in Hubei, Fujian, and the areas surrounding Huizhou, and to servile tenants in Anhui province and the southern part of Henan. They help to explain the entire structure of the Ming managerial system, in particular the relationship between landlord management and the use of excess land.

Zhang Lixiang, a managerial landlord from Tongxiang county, Zhejiang, who wrote extensively on Ming agriculture, drafted a plan for granting land to bondservants, or, as he called them, adopted men and women (*yinanfu*). His plan was as follows:

The amount of land granted: Adopted men and women. Recently I have noticed that bondservants (*puli*) are not well disposed to their masters. It has become so bad that it is harmful for masters to keep them, but the trend is such that they have to retain them. Therefore I propose to copy our predecessors' idea of public and private land [*gongsitian*, i.e., the well-field system]; we should consider making it the normal system and try to implement it with people who so desire.

A bondservant husband and wife should be presented with three *mu* of paddy and two *mu* of dry-field land as a means of living. The master is to take care of the labor service and the land tax for the bondservant husband and wife. The master should be careful not to interfere with the working labor of the bondservant family employed in cultivation.[73] Bondservant couples who receive a grant of wet and dry-field land have to cultivate two *mu* of paddy and one *mu* of dry-field land for their master without any remuneration —though those engaged in other labor services should be exempted from this kind of unpaid cultivation work. The bondservant managers (*jigang zhi pu*) who administer their master's land should be granted two or four times the amount of paddy and dry land given to ordinary bondservant couples, and they should not have to do any uncompensated cultivation work. When the people who have received grants of paddy and dry land reach 60 years of age, they should return the land they were granted[74] to their master, and the master will provide them with food and clothing. If they do not wish to return the land, they should be allowed to remain on it; they can stay on the paddy and dry-field land to provide for themselves. Also, if they want to leave the master, they should be allowed to do so. The children of bondservant couples have to engage in labor-service work for the master; one *mu* for children over five years, two *mu* for those over ten, three *mu* for those over fifteen (comprises two *mu* of paddy and one *mu* of dry field), and five *mu* for those over twenty years and those under twenty who are married (comprises three *mu* of paddy and two *mu* of dry land). However, children who do not want to engage in labor service for the master should not be forced to do so. In order to manage these lands two bondservants from the master's household should be allotted to every hundred *mu*,[75] and one bondservant manager (who receives a grant of land and is settled on the land) should be appointed if there are three hundred *mu* of land. Select bondservants who are especially respectful and honest to undertake this management and treat them with sincerity. Do not appoint cunning and indolent ones. (The above figures were arrived at by considering the actual situation on land in my own region, Tongxiang, in northern Zhejiang, and should not be used as a general example for other regions.)[76]

The measures that Zhang advocates indicate that the managerial system was no longer functioning efficiently by the late Ming.

Furushima Kazuo has said the following about the breakdown of this managerial system: "When the Ming managerial landlord operations that used bondservants broke down (in the late Ming-early Qing period), managerial landlords turned into a parasitic landlord group (*kiseiteki jinushisō*). It is certainly possible that [bondservants] also shifted to become tenants, forming the core of a different type of management."[77] Furushima interprets this breakdown in part as a result of "an idea of bondservant manumission." The following statement by Zhang Lixiang lends some support to this interpretation: "I will not buy men and women anymore and will allow those that have formerly served me to leave. When there is no other alternative, then I will feed and clothe one or two elders and children in the *li* to provide them with strength. They should be allowed to leave or stay. There should be no coercion."[78] Here Zhang is saying that he is prepared to release his bondservants (*pubi*).

It is certainly the case that the system of bondservant labor was breaking down in the late Ming. In cases when there is no other alternative, he advocates supporting a few elders or children, though he does not demand they be compelled to stay. That children of bondservant families are exempted from labor service and that bondservants over 60 are allowed to leave both indicate that landlord control over bondservant families had become fairly relaxed. But Furushima's description of this process of decay as bondservant manumission is not valid. Adopted men and women were not freed from their bondservant status when their master allotted them a portion of land, nor did they redeem themselves from servile status. "Recently I have noticed that bondservants (*puli*) are not well-disposed to their masters. It has become so bad that it is harmful for masters to keep them, but the trend is such that they have to retain them"; this passage indicates that bondservants still remained subordinate to their masters, even after they had received land allotments.

Further proof of this fact can be found in Zhang's reasons for advocating a return to the ancient well-field system. In the preamble to the section on adopted men and women, Zhang Lixiang writes, "The well-field system was abolished and the people were without land." In the passage on the amount of land granted he reports that they followed their predecessors' ideas of public and private land (i.e., the well-field system). Zhang's advocacy of the ancient well-field system was not an abstract plan based on nostalgia for an ancient ideal; it is evident from the amount of paddy and dry-field land granted that this was a proposal based on a realistic assessment of the situation. According to the passage quoted above, the total area of land to be cultivated by a bondservant and his wife was five *mu* of paddy and three *mu* of unirrigated land (including the land they were to cultivate for no compensation). If the amount of land that was granted to minors, who were not members of the labor force, is added, then it totals more than ten *mu* of paddy and unirrigated land. Zhang Lixiang, in his *Bu nongshu* (Supplemented treatise on agriculture) relates that "the most efficient peasants in my district are only able to cultivate ten *mu* of land."[79] In the same source he says, "One man can cultivate ten *mu* of land."[80] The largest area of land that a single most efficient peasant in Tongxiang could cultivate (in other words, a unit of the most productive labor force at that time) amounted to no more than ten *mu* of paddy and dry-field land. A grant of ten-odd *mu* of arable land was thus based on a realistic assessment of the amount of land tillable by a bondservant couple, already a backward labor force at that time. For this reason, Zhang Lixiang concluded the section by warning that these figures were arrived at through a consideration of the situation in his own region, and that this standard should not be used for other regions. The fact Zhang Lixiang proposed to grant land to bondservants shows that it was not bondservant manumission that was being demanded.[81]

Here I would like to briefly interrupt my argument to comment on the importance of the *Yangyuan xiansheng quanji* (The complete works of Master Yangyuan). It is an extremely useful source for studying agriculture in the late Ming-early Qing because of the concreteness of Zhang's observations. The author, Zhang Lixiang, consistently wrote from the standpoint of a managerial landlord. Furushima and Kitamura have demonstrated that the managerial system was an exceptionally stagnant type of operation: even though it had the potential to transform bondservant labor into hired labor, it was never able to develop into a more efficient system of management. We can conclude that the relations of production associated with the managerial system in the early part of the Ming persisted virtually unchanged through to the late Ming-early Qing. Therefore the section on the amount of land granted quoted above must be understood as a proposal reflecting the realities of land management in Tongxiang, where the managerial system had surpassed the limited scale of early Ming operations.

Next, let us turn to analyze the contents of Zhang's proposal. First, we should note that land was supplied in exchange for labor services provided to the landlord by the bondservant family. As a result the acquisitive relations between landlords and bondservants were founded on direct landlord domination of the labor force (the bondservant families), and on the levying of labor service upon the basis of this domination. Second, in return for receiving three *mu* of paddy land and two *mu* of dry field, a husband and wife had to cultivate, uncompensated, an extra two *mu* of paddy and one *mu* of dry field for their master; only if they engaged in other labor services were they exempted. This service can be categorized as uncompensated labor performed under the landlord's supervision on land directly managed by the landlord. However, since wet and dry land are particularly specified, it is also possible to consider it labor service performed without any remuneration on land other than the landlord's managerial land. Furthermore, we must assume that they paid rent on the three *mu* of paddy and two *mu* of dry land even though it is not clear from this passage whether rent was due or not. If they did not pay rent, a couple would only furnish rent for two *mu* of wet and one *mu* of dry land out of the total eight *mu* (five paddy, three dry field) they cultivated. This would be exceptionally light, compared with rents in other areas which generally amounted to half of the whole harvest. Furthermore, it is absurd to assume that bondservant managers, who were normally granted double or quadruple the amount of land issued to bondservant families, did not have any other responsibilities apart from overseeing, just because the text says "they do not have to cultivate for their master." We can infer that rent was due on wet and dry land that the landlord granted. Bondservant families were issued with land upon which rent was due and also had to work for nothing on the landlords' managerial land (or on land allocated outside of the managerial land). Judging from the general situation at that time, rent amounted to approximately half of the harvest. Third, rent would be due on eight *mu* of paddy and five *mu* of dry land in a bondservant family that was granted the largest amount of land possible (if calculated on the basis of a couple and two males, one over 20 and one over 15). If we take the highest yield to be 3 *shi* per *mu* for wet fields, then the total harvest would be 24 *shi* and the bondservant family would be left with 12 *shi* after deducting the rent. An adult consumes 0.015 *shi* per day which amounts to roughly 5.5 *shi* per annum.[82] This means that 20-odd *shi* are required for a family of four per annum. Even with what is left from their income from dry land, and the income from a second crop on paddy land, they could not possibly make up the disparity of approximately ten *shi* if minimum daily expenses and crop failure are taken into consideration. Therefore, bondservant families who received land grants were not able to maintain themselves independent of the landlord, and consequently could not avoid being subordinate to and dependent upon him.[83] In effect, these bondservants were slaves, and the landlords slave-owners. Fourth, leaving aside the question of whether the masters actually did demand that bondservants over 60 return their land, the very fact that they could reveals that the bondservant family did not have the cultivation rights to the land they were given. These four points indicate the realities of tenancy under managerial landlords during the Ming.

To sum up, managerial land operations were conducted by bondservants under a patriarchical system of control. Bondservants under such a system of control became fictive members of the master's family by taking on their master's surname. They were provided with a family and settled on spare land when the landlord had more than he could handle under the managerial system. Relations between the landlord and bondservant families who were settled on the extra land were based on the levying of labor service. The bondservant family undertook uncompensated cultivation on the landlord's managerial land (or land other than the managerial land) and on arable land that carried a rent equivalent to roughly half of the crop. Since it was impossible for bondservants to sustain independent reproduction with the amount left after they had paid rent, bondservants on this spare land remained in a continual state of subordination to the master. Moreover, it should be noted that these bondservant families did not have any cultivation rights to the land. This was the most rudimentary form of the managerial landlord system during the Ming dynasty, especially in the former half.[84] It was a slave system of management implemented under firm patriarchical regulations. The following entry in the *Taizu shilu* (Veritable records of Emperor Taizu (Hongwu)) in early 1387 confirms this conclusion: "The Provincial Administration Office of Zhejiang and the prefectures and counties of Zhili and Suzhou submitted the fish-scale maps and books. Thereupon the Emperor ordered the Ministry of Revenue to investigate the land in the empire. Wealthy people in Zhedong and Zhexi were avoiding labor service. They were always entrusting (*guituo*) their land to intimate neighboring field servants (*tianpu*). This is called iron-footed registration (*tiejiao guiji*)."[85] The field servant (tenant) mentioned here was a peasant, who, as we have shown above, was subordinate within the master's patriarchal slave system of control.

Rural class differentiation and land accumulation

Managerial landlord operations during the Ming, particularly the former half, were based on a slave system of management which was implemented under firm patriarchal regulations. In this context, rural class
differentiation taking place under existing community regulations
could only serve to perpetuate these servile relations. Such a situation
would persist as long as managerial landlords maintained their control
over community regulations. An entry for the second lunar month of
1479 in the *Huang Ming tiaofa shilei zuan* (Categorized sub-statutes and
regulations of the Ming dynasty) aptly describes how such landlords
benefited from their position in local society:

One: Honorary officials and those holding honorary titles should be
prohibited from breaking the law. Everywhere they ride on the best
horses, presenting grain to gain honorary posts and to glorify themselves with honorary titles. Most of them do not know the laws and
institutions. . . . The most scheming of them try to become tax
captains, riding on horses when going out and coming in, employing
poor people to carry four-man sedan chairs and wearing silver on
their belts at the waist. With copper gongs in front, under the cover
of open parasols they go down to the countryside to press for tax
payment, armed with forks, spears, and rattan cudgels *extorting private debts, taking away landed property and houses,* and raping the
women and girls. They monopolize petitions and there is nothing that
they do not do. . . .

Two: In order to lighten the troubles of the people, crimes by
powerful magnates (*haomin*) should be prohibited and their activities
reformed. Wu Gui, the provincial investigating official of Shouchang
county, Yanzhou prefecture, Zhejiang, reports: "I respectfully observe that people who contribute grain to the government in return
for a public post receive encouragement from the court. They are appointed as honorary officials and are exempted from miscellaneous
assignments (*zafan chaiyi*). They are honored for their whole lives.
. . . From early morning until late at night they stand in fear, respectfully keeping the law and regulations and protecting their family
background, yet they arbitrarily spoil and harm good people as they
please. When moving they ride in sedan chairs or on horses and take
along a group of three to five bondservant companions (*puban*) who
follow them on their rounds. *Relying upon their power and wealth they*

conspire to occupy the landed property of small peasants (xiaomin), forcefully drag away cows and horses and make the children of free people into bondservants (nu)."[86]

According to this report of 1479 by the Ministry of Rites, tax captains, because of their role as tax collectors, everywhere were obtaining land and houses from peasants in compensation for personal debts accrued. The magnates in Shouchang county, Zhejiang also, stole landed property and farm animals from small peasants and made their children into bondservants.

The following report for 1494, recorded in the same source, presents further evidence about the activities of the strong and powerful in local society:

> Rich and powerful families in the Jiangnan region either follow the custom of presenting grain to obtain honorary posts, or have retained the post of tax captain in their families for generations. They rely solely on their own wealth and do not follow the laws of the state. . . . [They] give shelter to people registered as soldiers, salt-makers, and craftsmen. Strong bandits and thieving robbers gather together the lazy good-for-nothings in the area. Gangs of actors and gamblers all escape to hide in this area because their ancestors committed crimes. *There are small peasants in the local area who commend (touxian) their children [to large households] in order to evade conscript service (chaiyi). Also, there are extremely poor households who are willing to give their boys and girls as payment for monetary debts.* The groups listed above are able to obtain shelter with the rich and powerful and then bully the weak on the strength of their connection with their patrons. . . . *Forcibly seizing small peasants' property, or cheating and raping the wives and women of poor people, they use their influence to oppress people in debt and to set up private jails. They falsely claim ownership of rented land and openly deceive and take [rent from the people].* They go beyond their social position and act improperly. There is nothing that they do not do.[87]

The powerful families which acted as the tax captains in the Jiangnan region took in unemployed people who had left rural villages, children commended by peasants who wanted to avoid conscript service, and boys and girls given in compensation for personal debts. With such groups of bondservants at their beck and call, powerful families often used violence in their efforts to accumulate land.[88]

What was the situation of peasant-tenants who cultivated land accumulated in this fashion? Qian Qi (1506?–21?) in his collected works describes the conditions in Xin'gan county in Linjiang prefecture, Jiangxi: "All matters, even the [requisition of] materials and labor services (*fuchai*), press upon [the peasants], so that they cannot stay there any longer, and they furtively move to other districts. They either become merchants in other provinces or *commend themselves to powerful people as family servants and servile tenants (dianpu)*."[89] On another occasion he says, "Grandee households in this area [Xin'gan county] *take in and raise unemployed people and fugitives and call them servile tenants (dianpu)*."[90] As these passages show, the land of peasants who were displaced because they could not bear the excess land and labor taxes became concentrated in the hands of grandee households. Dislocated peasants were taken in by powerful people and grandee households and ended up tilling their land as servile tenants.

Another report on the people in Xin'gan county, written in 1469 by the Ministry of Rites, says:

In this area, there are various local strongmen who set up landed estates and houses at 20-odd places. They still feel unsatisfied and begin scheming as soon as they see neighboring people who have good mountain gardens and flat land. They continually revise the conditions for long-standing debts and, against all previous regulations, charge interest. Reduced to the last extremity, poor people have no means of paying back the debt and have no alternative but to write out sale contracts for the garden, land, and houses mentioned above. [These strongmen] even receive [the property] without changing the name on the land register. Those who are unwilling to make out false documents flee from their homes in the middle of the night. Their property is then managed by the strongmen, and nobody dares argue with them. It is common practice for them to set up land and houses, invite fugitives, soldiers, and craftsmen from Ji'an prefecture and other areas and spread them out to live in each village. These village residents are no different from bondservants (*puli*). When the strongmen go out, they order them to carry their four-man sedan chairs and accompany their horses, with a large retinue in front and behind, like tigers and wolves. They search for expert teachers to practice martial arts. When they fight with people in the district, the masses of followers all hurriedly come, each carrying spears, knives, iron cudgels, bamboo poles, and other implements as soon as the strongman calls. They are like a big army going out to do battle.[91]

From the tactics of rural strongmen in Xin'gan county described above, we see that rural class differentiation in this region had had two effects. First, it encouraged the accumulation of land in the hands of strongmen. Second, it turned dislocated peasants into servile tenants (*dianpu*) who were in fact bondservants. These tenants were then put to work cultivating the land accumulated by the strongmen.

This mode of operation was not limited to Jiangxi province but was common also in Jiangnan. Zhou Chen (1381–1453), in a letter to the Ministry of Revenue, laments the difficulty of collecting land tax and labor service in Suzhou and Songjiang because the peasants, who could not bear the burdensome land and labor taxes, were running away. He drew up seven articles explaining where fugitive peasants went. In one of those articles he noted that they seek refuge under the patronage of grandee households. Zhou explains:

The so-called grandee privileged households (*dahu*) who provide the poor with protection are powerful and rich people who either take male labor power (*dingnan*) as payment on private debts or use their power to steal people's sons or hire whole families to work, giving them a house to live in. Some confer their own surname on these people and look upon them as adopted sons (*yinan*), while others change their names and order them to become bondservants (*puli*). All of these people have become subordinate to [strongmen] and never pay tax or provide labor service again. Every one of them is willing to depend upon [grandee households]. Because of this the number of subordinates held by magnate households increases while the number of peasants on the land decreases daily.[92]

Peasants, unable to maintain reproduction, were forced to give their families to grandee households, either as compensation for private debts, or as a result of a more direct form of violence. Sometimes entire households were hired by the powerful and rich. In other cases, landlords provided peasants with a dwelling and forced them into subordinate positions as adopted sons and bondservants. It was by such means that peasants were exempted from land and labor taxes. Those peasants who were given a place to live and made into adopted sons or bondservants probably engaged in cultivation as tenants. Qiu Jun (1420–95) clearly states that the land of the wealthy was being leased by slaves: "South of the Yangzi there are many people and a shortage of land. Residents [there] lease the land of rich households and become their slaves (*nuli*)."[93] The 1681 gazetteer for Chongming county also relates, "Tenants in the inland districts[94] are no different from bondservants."[95] The same source explains elsewhere: "Tenants are commonly called tenant bondservants (*dianpu*). It is the same in every juris-

diction in Jiangnan."[96] Consequently tenants in Jiangnan were known
as tenant bondservants and were in fact the same as bondservants.
Weng Shuyuan's (1633–1701) chronological biography records in 1663:
"My eldestbrother sold the 60 *mu* of land that he had bought from Mr.
Qu back to Qu again because he could not pay the land tax. A mes-
senger from the Qu family went to receive the land. . . . The land was
in Mr. Qu's district, and the tenants on it were all Qu's bondservants."[97]
The tenants on the land that Weng's eldest brother had purchased were
"all Qu's bondservants." In other words, they were all slaves owned
by Mr. Qu. Zhao Xixiao, in his proposal on labor service recorded in
the 1824 prefectural gazetteer for Suzhou, stated:

> The elders have informed us that prior to 1674, when imperial permis-
> sion for implementation of the equal field system was granted, con-
> scription and labor service were universally heavy. People in the
> district were always going bankrupt because of labor service. Small
> households attached themselves to grandee households, asking
> them to provide labor service on their behalf. *Grandee households*
> *employed them in labor service like slaves (nuli).* . . . *Small house-*
> *holds presented half of what they harvested in their fields to the grandee*
> *households.* Accordingly, many people deserted their property or ran
> away, and their land tax was in arrears.[98]

Before the equal field system was introduced in 1674, small households
had commended themselves to large households because they could not
bear the burden of excess conscription and labor service. In such arrangements half of their harvest was taken, and they were worked like
slaves. A more detailed example of such commendation is given by Gu
Gongxie, who relates:

> Even though the gentry of the former Ming had a reputation for
> uprightness, they often took possession of scenic spots and large
> tracts of land for their luxurious mansions, garden pavilions, well-
> positioned urban residential lots, and farms. [They were able to live
> this way] because they always had their students and former subordi-
> nates manage [their property] for them, and they never invested all
> of their own capital [in their land]. Brazen slaves and fierce bondser-
> vants relied upon the gentry's power to terrorize others. The common
> people in the district were not able to live in peace. Small peasants
> (*xiaomin*) in the towns *had no choice but to submit to such brazen slaves*
> *and bondservants* in order to live in cordial harmony with them.
> Moreover, since these bondservants were protected by the gentry

they could get away with doing evil. As a result, 20 to 30 percent of the people on the land in a county or district posted their names (*guaming*) as bondservants. It has been the same ever since the change of dynasties. [These brazen slaves and bondservants] *are extremely bossy and rebellious.* Watching the bondservant rebellion in Jintan county in 1662 I noticed that the gentry suffered the most terrible misfortune. As soon as something reaches its extremity, it reverses its course; the gentry got the punishment they deserved for evil done in the past.[99]

Peasants—tenants who were the cultivators of vast tracts of land which had been given to the gentry in the late Ming—were reduced to bondservant status when they commended themselves to the gentry. In some areas 20 or 30 percent of the people on the land were in bondservitude. The final section of this passage also indicates that these bondservants (i.e., tenants) were the chief participants in the bondservant rebellions which burst out all over China during the late Ming-early Qing period.[100]

From the evidence presented above, we can conclude that displaced peasants were gathered together by magnate households and treated as adopted sons (bondservants). Many of these tenants were also subordinated to a patriarchical system of control. Both these bondservants and tenants were reduced to a servile status and entered into fictive family relationships with their masters. The following incident recorded in the 1748 prefectural gazetteer for Suzhou indicates just how common the holding of bondservants was in the Jiangnan region. "After Liaoyang fell, the orders to recruit soldiers became even more urgent. There was a retired low-ranking official, Jia Xiang from Zhejiang, who, hoping to gain the favor of his superior officer and thus an appointment, said falsely that *there were several thousand family servants (jiading) living scattered over the rural community*, and that with effort he would be able to make them [into soldiers]."[101] After the Manchu army conquered Liaoyang, the Ming dynasty frequently recruited soldiers in Jiangnan. The several thousand family servants who, Jia Xiang claimed, could be used as soldiers were simply tenants controlled by fictive family relationships.[102]

To sum up, rural class differentiation progressed during the Ming through an expansion of the organizational principles of managerial landlord operations (i.e., the patriarchal slave system). But in the late Ming-early Qing period, this form of slave-system landownership was shaken at the roots.

Large landownership and the rent resistance movement

Tenant resistance took a new turn in the late Ming-early Qing period. Let us begin by providing an array of examples. A native of Jinkui county, Qin Huitian (1702–64), noted that the custom of resisting and defaulting in rent payment was common: "There are invariably two types of people working at agriculture: landlords and tenants. The landlord provides for the taxes and the tenant pays rent. Although their roles are different, their situation is the same; *at first we were troubled with intimidation by landlords, and now we are worried by tenant resistance and rent arrears.*"[103]

The 1814 gazetteer for Wuxi and Jinkui counties also relates that tenant resistance was detrimental to landlords: "The peasants work diligently and there is no barren land. As a result, land is several times more valuable than it was before. But tenants do not pay their rent and are always giving the landlords trouble."[104] The 1681 gazetteer for Wucheng county shows what consequences such rent resistance had for landlords: "At present poor scholars are rushing around trying to make a living. *The owners of land are constrained by their tenants.* They find it difficult to pay the land tax and do not provide congee."[105] Families owning land were pressed by tenants and were having trouble meeting their tax quotas. The 1673 gazetteer for Jiading county emphasizes the helpless position which landlords faced: "If tenant families are called [to cultivate land], they are obstinate and do not comply [with the landlord's wishes]. No matter whether the harvest is good or bad, they always default [in rent payments] and even if tenants are changed, it is still the same old thing over again."[106]

Here the author is lamenting the fact that tenants never pay the full amount of rent, irrespective of whether crops are successful or not, and that the situation does not improve even if landlords change their tenants. The 1879 gazetteer for Shimen county quotes the following passage from the Daoguang edition: "Most peasants cultivate the land as tenants. They regard rice as a treasure, and normally most of them are in arrears with the rent. When they do pay, it is never with good grain. In extreme cases the disabled and sick intimidate [the landlords]. The women and children yell and shout, and it is a fearful task for landlords to try and collect rent. Owning property is a troublesome affair."[107] As a result of such tactics landlords had a difficult job collecting rent and came to regard their land as a great burden.[108] Tenants organized themselves into groups to carry on resistance. Chen Hongmou

(1696–1771), who served as grand coordinator of Jiangsu during the Qianlong period, gives the following account of such tenant activities in a public notice he issued: "There are riffraff in each district who call themselves petition leaders (*chengtou*) and head pressers and advocate that tenants should not pay rent. Banding together cunning tenants they tell them that it is not necessary to turn over the rent. They control good tenants and do not allow them to fulfill rent obligations. Local officials should immediately arrest and interrogate such people."[109] As this passage shows, tenants resisted rent payment by organizing groups centered around people called petition leaders and head pressers.

Huang Zhongjian, a native of Wu county who lived during the early Qing, took special note of the way tenants tried to profit from natural disasters: "In times of very poor harvest there is no limit to the continual succession of cheating and hiding that occurs. Very bad people are unperturbed about defaulting in rent payments even in years of plenty. Recently, floods and droughts have occurred frequently in Wu and *tenants take blood oaths and form pacts to oppose the landlords*."[110] In this same source there is another passage which throws further light on tenant resistance: "At present all the poor people in the villages pool their money for play performances. They make pledges, take blood oaths, and form pacts to resist the landlords. Despite being warned many times by all the officials, they are fearless. Among them there are one or two good tenants who are willing to hand over rent, but if they do, the mob rises en masse to attack them. They even sink their boats, scatter their rice around, and destroy their houses. It is always like this."[111] From these two passages it is clear that neglect of rent payment was common, even when the harvest was good. Once there was a poor harvest, tenants pooled their money to show plays[112] and, cursing the landlords, organized pacts symbolized by having all the participants smear the blood of a slaughtered animal around their mouths. If any tenant behaved in a manner contrary to the agreement, he was punished. This served to strengthen group solidarity.

Zhang Lixiang in giving advice to a friend on how to handle tenants, wrote in a letter, "Since parting I have continually thought of your trouble in handling tenants. *The land is not infertile, but these people are obstinate* [and refuse to pay their rent].... *Even if you invite another tenant to cultivate, you will not necessarily* obtain a good one."[113] On a different occasion Zhang laments, "Of late few peasants are plain-minded. They manipulate their forces in order to impede us, and it is always difficult to make permanent plans."[114] As Chen Dashou, the Jiangsu grand coordinator, states in a 1745 memorial, "*Rent resistance by Suzhoua tenants has long been a fixed habit*."[115] It should be noted that

these passages are not referring to individual and specific cases of
"cunning and refractory tenants." Rather the evidence suggests the
formation of new objective material conditions which greatly strengthened the power of tenants to oppose landlords.

Next, let us take a closer look at the form of the anti-rent movement
by examining in some detail these new objective conditions.

We will begin with evidence from Xiushui county in Zhejiang province. The 1596 gazetteer for that county contains the following description of local tenant customs:

> In the tenth month grain and rice are ready for rent payment. Previ-
> ously, after the grain had already been harvested and the barley sown,
> rich peasants would submit the fixed tax to the officials and store
> a little away in the granary as reserve. Tenants paid rent to big
> households and kept what was left over for the spring planting. Every-
> one was pleased with this arrangement. Recently, wealthy merchants
> have instituted rice mortgaging (*midian*). Tenants pawn their best
> rice for silver, separately allotting lower- and middle-quality rice for
> the rent. Even in years of plenty they claim a bad harvest, pro-
> crastinating and neglecting rent payment. A little while ago crafty
> people assembled mobs every day on the banks of the Tiao River to
> swear mutual oaths not to pay rent to big households. Though it has
> eased off a bit lately, this practice is gradually coming to be regular
> custom. Officials press for the taxes with great urgency but take no
> notice of those who pay rent. Thereupon landlords have to borrow
> to meet their obligations to the officials and suffer as a result. Small
> peasants obtain silver from mortgaging merchants (*dianshang*) and
> squander it. Consequently, they find it difficult to fill their tax quota.
> Later the profit goes to the mortgaging merchants. Tenants are also
> ruined because debts are neglected and accumulate day after day.
> If both the landlord and tenant come to harm, how will the shortage
> in the granaries be filled, and how can the villages not be poor?[116]

By the late Ming rent resistance was gradually gathering strength in
Xiushui county. This also brought great changes with it. Previously,
when the new grain was harvested in the tenth lunar month, tenants
would pay their rent and keep the rest for planting in the spring of the
following year. Sometime in the late sixteenth century such practices
were interfered with by wealthy merchants who introduced rice mortgaging. Tenants would pawn their best rice for silver and use the middle
to bad rice for making rent payments. Moreover, since they were unwilling to pay rent, claiming a bad harvest even in years of plenty, land-

lords who were being pressed for tax had no alternative but to borrow money to pay the tax in full. The tenants, for their part, spent all the silver that they had obtained from mortgaging their rice and in the end were unable to pay the rent in full. As a result it was only the mortgaging merchants who profited from this practice. An account by Zhang Yanzhen (1662?–1722?) recorded in an 1863 source for the township Nanxun in Zhejiang relates a similar situation. It reads:

> In the tenth month grain and rice are ready for use. Previously, as soon as the grain was harvested wealthy peasants, after paying their taxes, would store the surplus in granaries, in preparation for bad harvests and famines. Tenants paid rent to the large households and saved a little to provide for the next spring's planting. Of late tenants are wicked and perverse. They pound and grind rice and grain before the normal harvest season, and either take advantage of the opportunity to sell it at a high price, or pawn it cheaply, fancying that they can engage in trade and expand their profits. In extreme cases, where tenants are discontent with their lot, they cunningly scheme to do evil. Also some tenants borrow from the wealthy households during the spring and summer and delay the rent rice for days and months, claiming crop failure and lean harvests. After winter has passed, they pay about half of the rent with broken husked rice. Officials press for the taxes with great urgency [and the landlords] demand their rent, but [the tenants] take no notice of them. Therefore, the landlord has to borrow to buy grain for the granary and suffers a loss as a result. Tenants borrow rice in a desperate effort to delay death for a while. They pawn and sell at high prices to do things which do not need to be done quickly. Later they suffer losses at trading and are forced to sell. The interest [on the mortgage] doubles. Thereafter the rent arrears increasingly accumulate and the tenant is also injured.[117]

The great similarities between these two accounts suggest that this passage was either based on the Xiushui account or that they were both compiled from a common source. In this latter case, tenants took advantage of the high price of new grain produced early to turn their grain into silver by selling or pawning it. Even if they borrowed rice from the landlord during the lean period between harvests, they would prolong rent payment, only handing over half of the rent due after winter, and paying it in rice damaged during the threshing. As a consequence landlords had to borrow money to pay taxes, and the interest on the tenant's mortgage acculumated, eventually rendering him incapable of paying rent.[118] The major reason given here for deficiency in rent payment is the fact that the tenant was changing his new grain into silver at the time when he should have been paying rent.

The following section from the Wanli edition of the Shimen county gazetteer provides more data on the process of pawning new grain:

> There are almost the same number of wet and dry fields in Chongde county.[119] Consequently, the harvest from wet fields is only sufficient to supply a peasant family with food for eight months. For the remaining months they buy rice to provide for themselves. They depend upon the profits from sericulture to pay taxes and for living expenses. As a result sericulture is most important. Loan contracts are always drawn up with a repayment date at the end of the silkworm season. *During the winter large amounts of official taxes are collected, [but the peasants] do not dare sell their rice to pay the taxes because they are afraid that rice prices will rise as time goes on. They usually pawn their rice in the pawnshops for silver and wait until sericultural operations are finished before redeeming it with interest.*[120]

Here peasants pawn their new grain for silver in order to pay taxes. Later they retrieve the rice they pawned with the income received from raw silk and use it for food. There is evidence that tenants as well as landed peasants engaged in such practices. For instance, take the following passage from a Yongzheng-period (1723–35) source:

> Every year when the new grain ripens in the counties belonging to Jiaxing and Huzhou prefectures, landed households, tenants, and small peasants (*xiaomin*) all pawn the rice they harvested, receiving silver to use for expenses according to the amount [of rice deposited]. It goes on for a while with a sense of urgency. The following year, after the sericultural work is finished and the barley is ripe, but before the new rice is harvested, they buy back [the rice in pawn] to relieve the food situation. People find it more convenient than selling on the spot, when the price of rice is uniformly cheap.[121]

Again it is evident that even tenants were pawning the new grain and redeeming it the following year with the income earned from silkworms and barley. The reclaimed rice then supplied their food in the period before the new grain was harvested, when the price of rice was at its highest. The practice of pawning new grain was, above all, designed to provide insurance against the high price of rice in the summer and autumn of the following year.

During the Ming the money economy gradually began to develop in response to an increase in the general forces of production and to the revival and growth of the rural economy after the disturbances at the end of the Yuan. The higher demand for money in turn stimulated the commercialization of rural handicraft industries from the fifteenth century on because it created an increase in the dynasty's demand for money. Based on the Songjiang cotton-weaving industry and the sericulture, silk-thread spinning, and silk-gauze-weaving industries in the region around the southern edge of Lake Tai, commodity production secured a firm position in the rural economy of the delta region during the sixteenth and seventeenth centuries.[122] Although it ultimately only served to perpetuate simple reproduction within existing management units, commodity production by the tenant stratum did bring about decisive changes in the tenant management of the reproduction process. A 1752 source for Wuxi and Jinkui counties describes the local situation as follows:

> Of the five counties in Changzhou prefecture, only ours do not grow cotton. Yet the profits from cotton cloth here are far greater than those of other counties. Local people only live off their land for the three winter months. After paying the rent they pound the husks off the rice that is left and deposit it in the granaries of the pawnshops, retrieving the clothes they had there in pawn. In the spring months they lock themselves in their houses to spin and weave, exchanging their cloth for rice to eat. There is no surplus grain in their households. In the fifth month, when the demands of field work become pressing, they once again retrieve the rice they pawned by returning their winter clothes. Colloquially this is known as "cultivating the fields for rice to eat." In autumn when the rains come, the sound of the loom is heard again in all the villages. They trade their cloth in order to have rice to eat. As a result, even when our counties meet with a bad year the local people are not greatly troubled as long as there is a crop of cotton elsewhere.[123]

The local people of Wuxi and Jinkui counties (here the author evidently is talking of tenants) imported cotton to spin and weave during the slack agricultural seasons. Clearly it was agricultural work which determined the distribution of the tenants' labor throughout the year. Therefore even with the expansion of commodity production, rural handicraft industry could not become independent of agriculture. It could only exist in a form subordinate to agriculture. In the cycle described above, the rural handicraft industry is part of the simple reproduction process of the tenants and serves to provide merely the minimum use value necessary for the purchase of rice. It is clear from the above passage that rice was pawned because there was no time for spinning and weaving during the fifth month, the busiest season of the farming year, and it was necessary to secure a supply of rice in preparation for rice price rises during lean periods. Subordinated to the autarkic management of the tenants, the rural handicraft industry could not become a true profit-making industry independent of agriculture. Rural handicraft industry at that time was entirely dependent upon external conditions. Commercial and usury capital intervened at each stage of production, from the purchase of raw materials to the sale of the finished product. Tenants, the main body of producers, had no say in determining whether reproduction was possible or not. It is impossible for a handicraft industry conducted on a tenant scale of management to disengage itself from agriculture. Tenants consequently had no alternative but to work to maintain their autarkic management as best they could. They gave first priority to agricultural work when apportioning their yearly labor. From the viewpoint of the social formation it should be noted that this type of tenant management does not indicate a commodity economy, but an autarkic economy.

Nevertheless, the commercialization of the handicraft industry under tenant management did play a positive role in a different sense. First, it was possible to obtain rice that was necessary for the maintenance of tenant households through this type of handicraft industry. Second, conditions that allowed the tenant to leave the landlord's care and enabled him to carry on independent reproduction were created. This fact is indicated in the statement "the local people are not greatly troubled as long as there is a good crop of cotton elsewhere."

Our next source, a Republican-period record for Jiangwan village in Binshan county, directly depicts the role rural handicraft industry played in the reproduction process. The demand for the type of cotton cloth produced in Jiangwan expanded during the Yongzheng period (1723–35), and, "for the most part, it was Cantonese merchants who competed to buy it. They strove for fine and delicate cloth, not worrying about its size. Though it only required a small amount of cotton to make the cloth, it fetched a high price. *In the surprise famine of the year Yinmao during the Qianlong period, it was precisely because the independent weavers relied on making fine cloth that they were spared the misery of weeping and wailing.*"[124] Tenants under the patriarchical slave-management system in the Ming had to depend on landlords to maintain reproduction. This was the fundamental condition which kept tenants in a servile state. However, once tenants acquired the objective conditions that enabled them to break away from the landlord and maintain independent reproduction, the patriarchical slave-management system of landlords lost its foundation and had to change.[125] All the materials quoted above describe the process in which tenants pawned their new grain for silver, rather than using it to pay their rents. This practice gave them two advantages: it ensured a food supply when costs were greatest, and enabled them to obtain funds to set themselves up when handicraft industries began each year. This practice indicates a decisive strengthening of the tenant's power to resist his landlord. Tenants' new-found ability to maintain independent reproduction was only achieved through the handicraft industry.

A 1760 source for Wuqing township provides evidence which illustrates the special characteristics of the rent-resistance movement at that time. The original reads:

Recently a crafty and cunning custom has appeared among the tenants. Even if their crop is fine, they try to keep rent payments as small as possible. Whenever there is a slight drought or flood, *they make tenant alliances by joining together all the tenants in the polders* (*lianyu jiejia*). They secretly discuss and decide the amount of rent they should pay, strengthen their solidarity by showing plays, and make contracts and pacts. If they discover anyone paying rent over and above the amount they have decided on among themselves, sly members of the group form a band to go to make a din at the offender's home, reproaching him for going against the group's wishes, and secretly bringing disaster upon him if he remains disobedient.[126]

The important point to note here is that the polder was the unit for tenant organization. We can conclude that the anti-rent movement developed on the basis of mutually integrated local ties between tenants. The 1642 gazetteer for Wu county provides more evidence of such tenant solidarity. It relates that late in 1638 some "cunning and wicked" people took advantage of a locust plague to band together. The people's organization is described in the following terms: "In 30-odd villages around Lake Tai the people slaughtered a beast and swore to the gods. [*Each*] *village elected a leader* to write down the people's names and make an agreement with the tenants that no one was to pay rent to the landlords. If the landlords pressed for rent, they would sink their boats and kill them."[127]

Tenants organized in much the same way as the villagers just described. Solidarity was based on groups of villages linked by special geographic ties. To examine the question of local ties a little more closely,

we should take a look at the situation of landowners and arable landholdings at that time. Let us begin with a report for Shanghai county
written in 1675: "Big gentry households own from several thousand to
several hundred *mu*. Holdings of middle and small households vary from
ten to a few *mu*. *How can this land all be in one place? Landholdings are
all comprised of small plots. In some cases one person owns land separated by several polders and the polders may be divisions apart.*"[128]
Zhao Xixiao also comments upon the subject: "Since boats can travel
everywhere in the watery land of Jiangnan, many people who live in
one ward (*tu*) also have land in another ward. Many people who live
in the cities or their suburbs also have land in each of the wards. *Even
if their property does not exceed several tens of mu it will still be scattered,
all over the countryside.*"[129] Landholdings were not made up of single
lots of land in an area, but rather of numerous small fragments of land
scattered over a number of villages or polders. A single landlord hardly
ever held a lot of land that included all the arable land in a village or
polder. It is evident that tenants who began the rent resistance movement and whose unity was founded on the village and the polders were
not subordinate to a single landlord. Rather, individual tenants were
subservient to different landlords. In such a context landlord-tenant
confrontation was not merely an antagonistic relationship between a
specific landlord and his tenant, but constituted a more general conflict
between the landlord and tenant classes. It should also be noted that
such antagonistic relations were only possible after the establishment of
strong local ties of solidarity among the tenants. As shown earlier,
in the Ming tenants were slaves, fictive family members who were subject to the direct and individual personal domination of the landlord.
It was impossible for tenants to build up a sense of local solidarity
among themselves under such conditions. Even if there was trouble
between a specific landlord and his tenant, it could never break out into
general conflict between the landlord and tenant classes. Therefore the
appearance of tenant solidarity and this type of antagonistic relationship indicates that landlord-tenant relations had reached a different
stage in development. Finally let us consider the conditions associated
with local tenant solidarity.

In the polder field regions of Jiangnan, where arable land was surrounded by creeks, water wheels known as square-pallet chain pumps
(*fanche* and *longguche*) were indispensable for wet-field rice cultivation.
Such pumps were required for irrigation work and for drainage in times
of flood. Xu Danfu described the operation of water wheels in an essay
contained in the 1863 gazetteer for Nanxun township. He writes, "The
biggest of the water wheels are driven by oxen walking around in a cir-

cle to rotate the axle, or by three or four people who stand [on the machine] and peddle to turn [the water wheel]. There are even some that are driven by wind sails. The small ones are operated by one person who sits turning it by hand. Actually we do not often see these in our district. The water wheels most appropriate to our district are ones operated by two seated people who peddle to turn the wheel."[130]

Although there were a wide variety of water wheels in use, this text indicates that the two-man, foot-driven machine was most commonly employed. The same text notes that "everybody attends to their own irrigation in years of drought."[131] Watering the fields was normally done by each family on an individual basis. It should, however, be noted that draining water from the fields was group work done by all the people in the polder. Xu Danfu explains this point in detail:

In rainy years when water submerges the fields, the entire polder comes out to work in what is known as collective pumping (*dapeng-che*). The number of water wheels depends upon the size of the polder. The person who provides the water wheel pays for the tax levied on the land upon which it stands and is known as the head of the water-wheel landing (*chebutou*). He divides the people according to their land and gathers them together.[132] Each time they begin work it is for a stretch of six days. When he summons them to come, those who are late for work are punished. In times of great urgency spun yarn is placed on top of the axle in order to record the number of revolutions and turns. The small axles of the wheels are connected with ropes in order to compare the speed of each treadler. If a person's yarn is frequently entwined and broken by another's, he should be punished. As punishment they have to provide everyone with wine.[133]

This source seems to indicate that the water wheels used for pumping were the private property of the head of the water wheel landing, but judging from the findings of Fei Xiaotong's field survey of Kaixiangong village on the southern banks of Lake Tai, that was not the case. This village was comprised of eleven polders. One of these polders, Xizhang polder, was further internally subdivided into four *qian*. In the northern subdivision (*qian* or *cien*) of this polder, Fei found:

The members of the *cien* are organized into fifteen teams corresponding to fifteen pumps. *Each year one of a group will be charged with contributing the pump and managing the team. This position is taken in turn by the members of the group. Among the fifteen groups, there*

is a chief manager. This position is also taken in turn. At the beginning
of the year, the chief manager calls the fourteen other managers to
a meeting. A feast is prepared as a formal inauguration. The chief
manager has authority to determine when the drainage should begin
and stop.

Whenever drainage is needed, the chief manager will give orders
to the managers. Early in the morning, these managers will inform
the workers on duty by beating a bronze brace. If anyone on duty
does not show himself at the pump half an hour after the signal, the
other two charged to work on the same pump will stop their work,
take the pivot of the pump to the nearest grocery, and bring back to
the spot 53 pounds of wine and some fruit and cakes, the cost of
which will be charged to the absentee as a fine.[134]

In this instance members of the polder subdivision (*qian*) took turns
in acting as managers of the drainage water wheels, so we may also
interpret the head of the water-wheel landing mentioned earlier as a
rotational position. Thus in the polder land region, drainage work,
which was an essential condition for each family's reproduction in
the polders, was conducted as the common responsibility of those who
cultivated land in the polders (mainly tenants in the late Ming-early
Qing) and who were subject to autonomous regulations. This shows
that community regulations which acted as a medium for reproduction
in peasant management had been disconnected from the control of
slave-owning managerial landlords and placed in the hands of an
alliance formed among tenants. In other words, it indicates the establishment of a community composed of tenants.[135] Tenant organizations which started rent resistance movements "forming alliances
by joining together all the tenants in the polders (*lianyu jiejia*)" were
founded upon this type of community. Such tenant organizations,
which had their origins in everyday participation in community
activities, served to decisively strengthen the tenant's power to oppose
landlords.[136]

We can draw the following conclusions from this analysis. First,
tenants were able to free themselves from their dependency upon landlords as a result of the commercialization of handicraft industries. With
this innovation simple reproduction independent of the landlord was
possible. Nevertheless, we must add that this sort of tenant management
was characteristic of an autarkic economy, not of a true commodity
economy. Therefore it did not significantly alter the mode of production.
Second, in response to this process of change in the method of reproduction, control over community regulations was transferred from

managerial landlords to the tenants who made up the community. Community ties also helped tenants carry on a form of management independent of landlords. In this context the independence of tenants from landlords took on new significance, as the following passage from the 1811 gazetteer for Taiping county demonstrates: "The rent on tenant land is collected once or twice a year, the custom varying according to the locality. In the north tenants cultivate people's fields according to the regulations governing the master-servant relationship (*zhupu mingfen*). In the south it is different, and the landlords are called the private heads of the field (*tiansitou*)."[137] It is clear that in the south tenants were liberated from bondservant status, and for the first time in Chinese history the landlord-tenant relationship was not legally defined as a master-servant relationship.[138] As a natural consequence Ming managerial landlords who had relied on the patriarchical slave system were forced to change their mode of operation. Since they had also lost control over the community regulations, the basis of the system of large landholdings, their property was gradually broken up into smaller lots. Such developments naturally caused changes in the nature of the tenants: they were transformed from operators of independent simple reproduction based on the labor force of the small nuclear family into feudal peasant proprietors or serfs. In order to maintain independent simple reproduction they established feudal communities (*hōkenteki kyōdōtai*).[139]

The landlord response

The late Ming-early Qing period then was a transition period in which tenants changed from slaves to serfs. How did the landlords respond to such a change? Before answering this question let us first summarize what we have learned so far. First, managerial landlord operations during the Ming dynasty, especially the first half, were carried on under a patriarchical slave system of management which used bond-servants as the main labor force. It is also noteworthy that bondservants were subordinated to the master in a fictive family relationship. Second, two other factors—landlord control of community regulations and rural class differentiation—resulted in a pattern of large landownership which served to perpetuate further the various relations of patriarchical slavery. Third, the commercialization of the rural handicraft industry, beginning in the mid-Ming, allowed tenants who were subject to patriarchical control to develop a form of management which made independent simple reproduction possible. The inevitable result was the breakdown of the Ming managerial-landlord system and the transfer of control over community regulations to the tenants. The community then became something that functioned on the basis of local ties among the tenants. The change in the nature of the community in turn caused the system of bondservant-owning large landownership to break down. Finally, the decay of this system resulted in a steady increase in the numbers of urban landlords in the delta region during the late Ming-early Qing. But how did these new urban landlords manage to collect rent from tenants in communities now unified against their landlords? Let us begin to answer this question by examining a report by Lu Chongxing, the magistrate of Jiaxing prefecture during the Kangxi period (1662–1722). Lu describes the methods used by landlords to deal with tenants tardy in paying their rent. He records the case of the tenant Bu Zhong, who cultivated 3.3 *mu* of Wu Mingyu's land and agreed to pay an annual rent of 4.95 *shi*. His report describes the crucial part of the incident as follows: "By the thirteenth day of the tenth month 1675 [Bu Zhong] had already paid 4.6 *shi* and the deficiency was a mere 0.35 of a *shi*. Wu Mingyu reported this to the county yamen and *received permission to send people from the tax office (liangya)*. Presuming upon the landlord's influence they schemed to frighten and cheat Bu Zhong."[140] The important point to note here is that rent arrears were handled by the tax office within the county yamen. Local county government was modeled on the central bureaucratic system and was divided into six departments: civil appointments revenue, rites, war, punishments, and works. The tax office in this passage probably refers to the revenue department (*hufang*), which administered tax collection. Accordingly, it is clear that the revenue department pressed tenants on behalf of landlords if there were deficiencies in rent payment.[141] This indicates the close relationship between the collection of rent, and the collection of taxes.

Next, let us look at the type of people who served in the revenue department. A useful source for this purpose is the *Zhang Hanru sugao* (Draft memorials of Zhang Hanru), which denounces, with plenty of concrete examples, the outrages and evil-doing in Changshu county, the native place of Qian Qianyi and Qu Shisi, the famous leaders of the Donglin faction during the late Ming.[142] The following episode on the evils of taxation is most revealing:

At present Qian Qianyi and Qu Shisi have appointed trusted bond-servants and managers in their service, such as Zou Risheng, An Rupan, Zhou Xianchang, Liu Shisheng, and Zhang Yongzuo as tax and granary clerks. [They control] the influx and outflow [of tax and grain], act aggressively, and do not obey orders. When they are sent out to collect taxes, under the name of official households they accumulate great quantities of grain. At one stroke all the tax grain in the granaries, which amounts to 400,000 *shi* for the entire county, is erased from the books. Also when the land tax is sent into the central government, tax clerk chiefs always covetous for more ask the county officials to release the tax money which should not be disbursed. As a result the deficits in the payment of top-grade silver and military provisions to the capital accumulate. From 1634 to 1636, several ten thousand taels of silver went unaccounted for. There is even a group of cunning clerks, a bunch of utter rogues, who buy up all the women, gamble day and night, counterfeit official stamps and documents. . . . Half of the silver in the treasury ends up in the pockets of clerks and the other half in the purses of officials.[143]

This case shows that Qian Qianyi and Qu Shisi, powerful gentry in Changshu, appointed many of their own bondservants to positions as yamen clerks, whose job it was to administer the collection of taxes. In such a capacity these yamen clerks continually misappropriated huge amounts of government money.

To make this point clearer let us examine yet another case in detail. We will take as an example a complaint leveled against the family of the early-Qing high official Xu Qianxue (1631-94), which was accused of many misdoings in its native area, Kunshan county. According to the complaint filed with the authorities, Xu Zhenfu, a nephew of the grand secretary Xu Yuanwen (1634-91) from Taicang, working in collaboration with Qian Laichen, a relative by marriage, was giving protection to many bondservants, unemployed people (*youmin*), and yamen clerks, stealing the people's land and misappropriating tax funds.[144] One of these bondservants, Chen Chaoma, was described as "*a bogus clerk in charge of dispatching court documents and a brazen bondservant of Qian Laichen. The officials use their authority and power to injure atrociously the myriad people.*"[145] Bondservants were evidently being appointed to positions as yamen clerks. There were many other cases of such people being nominated as yamen clerks with tax-collection responsibilities.[146] Finally, we will briefly examine how these yamen clerks could be connected with powerful people in local sociey. Once again let us refer to Lu Chongxing on this matter. Lu writes that in each county the watchmen of granaries, who were also in charge of the accounts, were under the control of powerful officials whom they addressed as "governing master" (*taozhu*). With the power of the governing masters behind them, these watchmen were able to engage in all types of illegal activities.[147]

In summing up this section it should be noted that powerful bureaucrats (i.e., the gentry who were also large landowners) during the late Ming-early Qing period put their bondservants and agents with whom they had close relations into the county yamen as clerks with tax collection responsibilities. Since the *lijia* system was in a state of disorder at that time, yamen clerks were collecting tax by proxy remittance.[148] As a consequence the real power over tax collection fell into the hands of the powerful bureaucrats who were the masters of bondservants.[149] The tax that these powerful officials paid to the state was in effect the rent collected from tenants on their own land. In other words, tax collection rights, the state's most fundamental form of manifesting its power, and the private right to collect rent came to mean one and the same thing to large landowners. Rent-in-arrears was regarded as evasion of tax payments due to the state. As a result, it was the revenue department administering tax collection that pressed for payment when there were defaults in rent payments. This indicates that the relationship between large landowners and tenants was one of direct political control and subordination.

The political control large landowners exercised over their tenants functioned as an extra-economic means of controlling the essentially economic production relationship between landlords and tenants; it guaranteed the collection of rent. These extra-economic impositions made it possible for landlords to accumulate large tracts of land.[150] The use of extra-economic force in rent collection was a measure taken by bureaucrats to counteract the changes in tenant conditions. By the late Ming-early Qing, tenants were no longer slaves dependent upon a master, but serfs capable of maintaining themselves independent of landlords; naturally this transformation forced landowners to develop new methods of controlling their tenants. The form of landownership that resulted from these changes was a type of feudal landownership peculiar to China.

Postscript

In this paper we have argued that the late Ming-early Qing period marked the beginning of feudal landownership in China. The urban landlords of the Jiangnan delta region were the feudal landowners, and their tenants, the direct producers, were the serfs. I am aware that at this stage my argument is largely speculative, and in the future I hope to build upon this preliminary study by considering the following two points. First, although there are numerous theories on feudal land-ownership, most of them have placed the origin of feudal landowner-ship in China in the late Tang-Song period when manors (*zhuangyuan*) were established as the dominant form of large landholding. This theory for the most part depends upon the empirical studies of Sutō Yoshiyuki. Given that the dominant form of management practiced by landlords in the Ming was a system of landownership based on bondservant labor, our next task is to reexamine the manors of the Song and to determine how the manorial system fits in with the bond-servant system of landownership. Second, in this paper I have dealt with only one aspect of Chinese feudal society, the transformation in the landlord management form. This form is only one of the several styles of production *(uklad)* within the dominant feudal mode of production and cannot be used alone to characterize the kind of feudal society peculiar to China. Certainly Chinese feudal society differed from its Japanese and European counterparts. In China, Asiatic despotism persisted through the establishment of feudal society, although the relative strength of this element varied, of course, from stage to stage. If we are to analyze the entire structure of Chinese feudal society, we must develop a theory which explains both the persistence of despotism and the relations within the various styles of production. Only after such an analytical framework has been developed can the production relations within the system of feudal landownership be understood.

Notes

[1] *Rizhi lu*, 10:15a.

[2] 1765 *Wujun Puli zhi*, 5:1b.

[3] This is the *Yaoyi yi* [A proposal on labor service] found in the 1824 *Suzhou fuzhi*, 10:23b–24a. Since there are omissions in the 1824 gazetteer, the missing characters have been supplied by referring to the *Yaoyi yi* in the 1933 *Wu xianzhi*, 49:11b. The same applies to all quotations from the *Yaoyi yi* below.

[4] See Wada Sei, ed., *Shina chihō jichi hattatsushi*, pp. 104–5.

[5] Kitamura Hironao, "Shindai no jidaiteki ichi," pp. 47–57; and Kitamura Hiro-nao, "Minmatsu Shinsho ni okeru jinushi ni tsuite," pp. 13–25.

[6] Kitamura has partially revised his former theory in "Chūgoku no jinushi to Nihon no jinushi," pp. 19–25, but his fundamental conceptions presented in this article have not altered.

[7] Furushima Kazuo, "Minmatsu Chōkō deruta ni okeru jinushi keiei," pp. 11–23.

[8] Furushima adds: "This bondservant (*jiapu*) type of existence was also possible under the large landlord strata and was not limited to small local managerial land-lords. Even if bondservants did not hold the rights of cultivation, they owned most

of the means of production themselves and their life was essentially much the same as that of a tenant." (See article cited in note 7, p. 14.) Therefore he does not see a substantial difference between tenants and those bondservants who had been granted land.

[9] *Gao Taishi fuzao ji*, 1:21a–b.

[10] 1536 *Zhenze Xiansheng ji*, 26:12a.

[11] *Jijiu qinxi Chen xiansheng ji*, 4:19b.

[12] The section on bondservants (*nupu*) in the *Rizhi lu*, 13:30a reads: "Zheng Kangcheng, in his commentary to the *Sili* section of the *Zhouli* [Rites of Zhou], states, "The male and female slaves (*nubi*) of the present day are the descendants of the criminals of ancient times."' According to the *Fengsu tong*, in the ancient system there were orginally no male and female slaves. Male and female slaves are all people who committed crimes. In Wu at present they are called family servants (*jiaren*) to avoid that appellation [i.e., *nubi*].

[13] Gu Yanwu, *Tinglin yuji* 19a.

[14] *Paoweng jiacang ji*, 58:14a.

[15] Furthermore, in Gong Liben's *Songchuang kuaibi*, p. 4a, Xu Nanxi (Xu Na) is mentioned: "Xu Na, personal name Minshu, was gentle, kind, and experienced. He personally assigned the slaves (*zanghuo*) to work in the fields."

[16] *Gu Wenkang gong wencao*, 6:8b, 12a.

[17] *Fu'an yigao*, 10:26a.

[18] *Bai Luoyuan yigao*, 8:32a–b.

[19] *Paoweng jiacang ji*, 65:9a.

[20] Ibid., 62:5a.

[21] Ibid., 36:9b.

[22] The term "hired bondservant" (*yongnu*) conveys a slightly different nuance from the word "bondservant" (*nupu*). Wang Ao's *Zhenze xiansheng ji*, 27:3b, provides us with the following evidence from an inscription on Lu Boliang's (d. 1492) grave: "The recluse was tolerant and generous. He managed his household very strictly. He is known to have said, 'Slaves (*zanghuo*) destroy people's households.' Subsequently, though the Lu family was wealthy, *he hired but not did keep bondservants* (*nu*) and did not allow even the smallest amount of untaxed salt into the household." From this epitaph it seems that there was an awareness of a difference between hired labor and bondservants even during the early Ming. However, Shi Tianji, who lived in Yangzhou during the early Qing, records in his *Chuanjia bao*, 2 *ji yiyan* under the *modangpu* entry (1834 Edition): "Family servants (*jiaren*) and bondservants (*nupu*) should only be hired by the year; the amount of their wages should be fixed each year and paid according to the season. If they are good then they can be employed for several years, if bad then their employment should be canceled. This is a system convenient for all." Thus the labor force hired on an annual basis was made up of family servants and bondservants. Also, the following passage from the *Qingbai leichao*, vol. 39, in the section on bondservants, p. 1, shows that in actual fact hired laborers were treated in the same way as male and female bondservants.

"In antiquity the sons and daughters of criminals were implicated in the crimes, taken in by officials and set to work as servants. They were known as bondservant men and women (*nubi*). Later, people who were bought for a price and who adopted their master's surname were also called bondservants (*nu*). '*Hired laborers*' *refer to those employed and receiving a remuneration, though they are generally regarded as bondservants* (*nu*)." An even more concrete example is the following section from the *Xing'an hulian*, 39:31a, 32a:

Chen Wenkui intentionally murdered his hired laborer (*gugong*) Zhang Xuecong. . . . The regulations state that cases where pawned family servants (*diandang jiaren*) and bonded personal servants (*lishen changsui*) (who have graciously been kept for over three years) kill or injure [their masters] should be dealt with according to the bondservant regulations. . . . During the first month of 1820

Chen Wenkui hired Zhang Xuecong as a hired laborer (*yonggong*). They agreed to make the contract valid for six years according to the regulations governing the master-servant relationship (*zhupu mingfen*). On the sixteenth day of the eleventh month, 1824, Chen Wenkui shouted at Zhang Xuecong and reviled him because he would not follow orders. Zhang Xuecong returned the abuse, and Chen Wenkui got angry and killed him. Over four years had passed since the contract was made, so Zhang was in effect the same as a pawned family servant who had been kindly kept for over three years. This was treated as a bondservant (*nubi*) case according to precedent.

Zhang Xuecong, though contracted as a hired laborer, was said to have the status of a servant vis-à-vis his master (*zhupu zhifen*). Since the murder occurred over four years after the time of contract, it was dealt with as a bondservant case according to precedent. This type of hired laborer was in fact treated as a bondservant. Hired laborers therefore can be regarded as bondservants who sold themselves for a certain period of time. An entry for 1587 in the *Shenzong shilu*, Wanli 15/10, p. 3585, reads:

> The left-capital censor, Wu Shilai, from the censorate reports that the criminal law is not clear and its clauses are incomplete. One clause states that commoner households are not allowed to keep bondservants (*nubi*). Only the households of meritorious officials are to be granted bondservants. Commoners must labor and toil themselves, so they are not permitted to keep (bondservants). *Criminals are all called hired laborers.* At first [the prohibiticn against keeping bondservants] did not apply to gentry households. There are many differences between hired laborers, some of them deliberately committed crimes [to gain this status]. . . . It was decided that: all people contracting for paid labor upon an annual basis in either official or commoner households are to be treated as hired laborers, while those receiving pay for small jobs only calculated in terms of days and months are still to be dealt with as commoners.

Despite the fact that a distinction between bondservants (*nubi*) and hired laborers (*gugongren*) had already been made in the *Minglu* [Ming statutes], during the late Ming it was clearly stated that long-term laborers were to be treated as hired laborers and short-term laborers as commoners. This indicates that hired labor was gradually establishing its position by this period as a labor force distinct from bondservants, as Kitamura and Furushima have already pointed out. There are many concrete examples of this in the *Xing'an huilan*. See also Niida Noboru, "Chūgoku no nōdo koyōjin no hōteki mibun no keisei to henshitsu—shuboku no bun ni tsuite." It also shows that commoner households, even though they were legally prohibited from owning bondservants before the late Ming, did in fact own bondservants who "were called hired laborers." Though they were labeled as hired labor, they were treated in the same fashion as bondservants (*nubi*). Zhou Chen, in a letter to the Ministry of Revenue included in the *Huang Ming wenheng*, 27:7a–b, relates the direction of rural class differentiation during the mid-Ming: "The so-called grandee privileged households (*dahu baoyin*) and the powerful and rich take male labor power (*dingnan*) as a discount on private debts, use their power to steal people's sons, hire whole families to work, or divide their households and have them live in. Some confer their own surname and look upon them as adopted sons (*yinan*). Others have them change their names and order them to become bondservants (*puli*)." "Hire whole families to work" shows that since the whole family was hired by one landlord, they were a servile labor force accommodated within the master's household. All these examples provide enough evidence to allow us to interpret hired bondservants (*yongnu*) as slave laborers [Note *yongnu* literally means hired slaves.—Trans.]

²³ *Yongnu qianzhi* (lit., "the thousand fingers of the hired bondservants") is a conventional expression. It indicates that Wu Kuan had a large number of bondservants, not necessarily exactly one hundred. *Paoweng jiacang ji*, 57: 13a.

[24] *Banjiang Zhao Xiansheng wenji*, 9:35b–36a.

[25] Ibid., 9:6a.

[26] Another example of a family keeping large numbers of bondservants is a certain Wang Yingxiang from Changzhou who also had many hired bondservants (*yongnu qianzhi*); cf. *Paoweng jiacang ji*, 74:18a.

[27] 1766 *Changzhou xianzhi*, 23:8a.

[28] *Juyi tang ji*, preface dated 1684, 12:19a.

[29] Gu Qing, *Dongjiang jiacang ji*, Jiajing era (1522–66); 4:13a.

[30] Lu Shen, *Yanshan wenji*, 1546: 4:7b.

[31] 1812 *Tongli zhi*, 23:20a–b.

[32] 1746 *Wucheng xianzhi*, 6:12b.

[33] 1678 *Tongxiang xianzhi*, 5:53a.

[34] *Tu Kangxi gong wenji*, 1:21a.

[35] We will explain later how adolescents raised as adopted sons (*yinan*) were made into a servile labor force.

[36] *Yulu xiansheng ji*, Ming dynasty, 11:6a–b.

[37] *Jingxin tang cao*, Ming dynasty, 11:16a.

[38] *Shang Wenyi gong ji*, 1603, 7:12a.

[39] *Jilu huibian*, 175:12b–13a.

[40] 1521 *Huating xianzhi*, 3:5a–b.

[41] The use of bondservants by managerial landlords during the Ming dynasty was not limited to the Yangzi delta region; it was widely practiced in other areas as well. With the materials at hand I can find examples from Taihe county in Jiangxi, Nanhai county in Guangdong, Nanyang prefecture in Henan, Xinjiang county in Shanxi, Laiyang county in Hunan, and the Hehou Wei in Shaanxi. If an extensive search was made for materials we could probably discover even more examples.

[42] *Tingyu jitan*, 10a.

[43] *Sangang shilue*, 3:7b.

[44] *Qingbai leichao*, vol. 39, section on bondservants, p. 1.

[45] *Chuanjia bao*, 2 *ji*, 1:7b–8a.

[46] *Chishan huiyue*, p. 14.

[47] *Yangyuan xiansheng quanji*, 32:10a–b, p. 564.

[48] *Shouhe riji*, 6:17a.

[49] *Congxian weisu yi*, 2:61a–b.

[50] *Yangyuan xiansheng quanji*, 19:35a–b, p. 379.

[51] Wu Kuan in the passage from the *Paoweng jiacang ji*, 57:13a quoted above; "My late mother, née Zhang, married my father when she was young. . . . She was a diligent wife and enlarged the property. Clothes and food were always given out equally to the many hired bondservants (*yongnu qianzhi*)."

[52] *Yangyuan xiansheng quanji*, 5:15a, p. 118.

[53] This source was introduced in Niida Noboru, "Chūgoku shakai no 'hōken' to fyūdarizumu," pp. 1–39.

[54] In Li Yu, (*Xinzeng*) *Zizhi xinshu quanji*, 1663, 31b–32a.

[55] 1737 *Li'an quanji*, 6:4b–5a.

[56] 1684 *Jiangnan tongzhi*, 65:43b–44a.

[57] Cf. Sutō Yoshiyuki, "Sōdai no denkosei—dorei kōsaku to no kanren ni tsuite," in Sutō, *Chūgoku tochi seidoshi kenkyū*, pp. 107–77.

[58] *Shizong Xianhuangdi shilu*, 5/4, p. 880

[59] *Yongzheng zhupi yuzhi*, vol. 3, p. 1823.

[60] *Renzong juihuangdi shilu*, I am grateful to Shigeta Atsushi for drawing my attention to this passage. 14/12, pp. 3288–89.

[61] There is a tendency to define servile tenants (*bandang*) and hereditary bondservants (*shipu*) in Huizhou, Ningguo, and Chizhou as lowly people and not as slaves. The following passage from the *Huangchao wenxian tongkao*, 19:6b, is the source material used to support this theory. The relevant passage reads: "There are servile tenants (*bandang*) in Huizhou prefecture and hereditary bondservants (*shipu*)

in Ningguo prefecture, Jiangnan. In the local area they are called poor commoners. They have the same occupational registration as entertainer families and degenerate people." The fact that their occupational registration is said to be the same as that of the entertainer households of Shanxi and the degenerate people in Shaoxing prefecture is firm evidence for this theory. Nevertheless, lowly people are defined as a special status group that was isolated from the whole of society because they engaged in a specific mean occupation; they would be neither subordinate to, nor in service to, a specific individual or family. It is difficult to call the servile tenants and hereditary bondservants mentioned above "mean people" because they were in fact subordinate to one specific master and only provided that one master with labor service. Moreover, since the liberation of servile tenants and hereditary bondservants meant freedom from the status of bondservancy to their masters, we can regard them as slaves subordinate to a specific family. For example, there is an 1825 case from Anhui of poor commoners beating a member of a grandee household to death. The essential point in deciding the severity of the crime was whether a legal master and servant relationship existed between the two parties. The relevant passage in this case reads:

> It should be requested that poor commoners (*ximin*) who in reality are clearly bound by master-servant status (*zhupu mingfen*) and those who have reliable documents to prove their personal mortgage and sale and who are continuing to provide the master with labor service and receive his patronage should be separately questioned and punished according to the regulations for bondservants if they commit a crime against the head of the family or his relatives. It should be requested that the lowly status of poor commoners be annulled if they are not bound by a manifest master-servant status, if they possess no documents for the sale of their person, and if they have neither constantly served the master nor received his patronage, even though they may have leased land from grandee households, lived in their houses, and had [their ancestors] buried in their graveyards. Crimes committed among them will be treated the same as those among commoners. (*Xing'an huilan*, 39:15b.

This source was first cited by Niida Noboru in "Chūgoku no nōdo koyōjin no hōteki mibun no keisei to henshitsu—shuboku no bun ni tsuite," p. 185, note 15, and p. 187, note 33.

[62] *Fangtang Wang xiansheng wenchi*, 1575, 7:1a.

[63] *Suyuan cungao*, 17:28a–b.

[64] *Wuyue shanren ji*, 4:7a.

[65] Tanaka Tadao, *Shina keizai no hōkai katei to hōhōron*, pp. 474–75.

[66] In the Xianlong district of Longxi county in Fujian, the slaves who had sold themselves during the Ming became fictive family members by taking on the master's surname. This provides a most interesting analogy with the bondservants in the Jiangnan delta region, whose case we have already discussed.

[67] Amano Motonosuke, *Shina nōgyō keizairon*, vol. 1, p. 369.

[68] The Kangxi edition of the *Macheng xianzhi*. This source is cited in Xu Daling, "Shiliu shiji shiqi shiji chuqi Zhongguo fengjian shehui neibu ziben zhuyi de mengya," p. 43; and in Han Dacheng, "Mingdai shangpin jingji de fazhan yu ziben zhuyi de mengya," p. 89.

[69] According to surveys conducted in the Republican period, it appears that similar conditions were still quite prevalent in the southwestern region of China during the first half of the twentieth century (cf. Amano Motonosuke, *Chūgoku nōgyō keizairon*, vol. 1, pp. 585–86).

[70] *Shuangjie tang yongxun*, 3:16a.

[71] The *Zhifu qishu*, anonymous, *5 zhong gu* records: "Since the basic criterion for moving one's abode is adequate food and since a precondition for an adequate food supply is agricultural activity, people live in a fixed place and have bondservants each attend to their tasks. *If there are ten people including master and bond-*

servants on the land, there must be [a harvest] of 60 shi. Therefore convenience of management depends upon the amount of land held; *if there are 100 mu of land, then have the bodnservants till 30 mu. The remaining land can be cultivated by tenants.*" Since the author is anonymous, we have no way of knowing when this book was written and what region he was from. The following passage from this same source (4b) does, however, provide a hint: "Apply 30 catties (*jin*) of mud from rivers and ponds, or sesame and bean cakes to each *mu*. Mix it with lime and dung, or with cotton-seed cakes and apply 200 catties to every *mu*." Since mud from rivers and ponds, sesame and bean cakes, and cotton-seed cakes were used as fertilizers, the book seems to be describing the Jiangnan region in the mid-Ming. Now returning to the main text, we find that if there are ten people, including the master and his slaves (four to five of the ten will probably be bondservants), they need land that yields a 60-*shi* harvest to maintain themselves. If they have a hundred *mu*, they can work 30 *mu* of it themselves and lease the remaining land out to tenants. Even though this was written with the Jiangnan region in mind, there was quite a range of local variation in the yield per *mu* in this same region. For instance, He Liangjun (1506–73) in his *Siyou-zhai congshuo,* 1579, reports that in the western district of Songjiang the highest yield was 3 *shi* and the average yield 2.5 *shi* while in the eastern district it was 1.5 *shi*. Local gazetteers also provide further examples of such differences. The 1539 *Changshu xianzhi,* 4: 13a (Zhongguo shixue congshu edition, p. 383), records that the most efficient peasants obtain 2 *shi*, the average peasants over one *shi* and the relatively inefficient peasants one *shi*, while the 1624 *Haiyanxian tujing,* 4:11b–12a, indicates that the most efficient peasants produce 2 to 5 *shi*. If we take about 2 *shi* per *mu* as an average yield, 30 *mu* of land will give roughly 60 *shi*. Since the *Zhifu qishu* stipulates that 30 *mu* out of 100 *mu* should be kept and the remaining land leased to tenants, we can conclude that 30 *mu* was the limit to the amount of land one master could manage. [The *Zhifu qishu* is in the collection of the Naikaku Bunko. The Naikaku Bunko catalogue lists the book under the name of Tao Zhugong, but he does not seem to be its author.—Trans.]

[72] The late Ming-early Qing saw the appearance of historical materials which attempted to redefine bondservant status. The following entry for 1588 in the *Shenzong shilu,* 16/1, p. 3655, clarified the position of bondservants (*nubi*) in official and commoner households. It reads: "People working under contract with a fixed term of employment are to be treated as hired laborers (*gugong*), while those employed for short periods with little pay are to be regarded as commoners (*fanren*). *Adopted sons (yinan) who have been bought, graciously kept for many years, and provided with a spouse are to be treated as family members (zisun).* Adopted sons who have only been kept for a short period and not provided with a wife are to be treated as hired laborers in commoner households and bondservants in gentry households." Since the penalty for crimes committed against the head of the household by children and grandchildren was most severe, adopted sons, in their position as fictive members of the family, were actually subject to a stronger slave-like subordination than other people. In an entry for 1727 in the *Shizong xianhuangdi shilu,* 5/4, p. 880, which earlier showed us the situation of hereditary bondservants and servile tenants in Ningguo and Huizhou, we find a memorial from Wei Tingzhen, the grand coordinator of Anqing which, says: "The categories of servile tenant and hereditary bondservant are still used in Huizhou, Ningguo, and various places in Jiangnan. I request that henceforth mortgaged and purchased bondservants and their descendants, owned by gentry families which possess reliable contracts and have not yet granted them freedom, must follow and obey their master. Even when they redeem their freedom, they themselves and the children and grandchildren who were born in the master's household are still bound by the legal status of master and servant. Those not born in the master's household should be set free according to the precedents for bannermen opening a household. It is strctily prohibited to ever call those who possess no contracts and have not been reared by the master for many generations hereditary bondservants."

An epigraphic inscription in the 1885 *Jiading xianzhi,* held by the Tōyō Bunko, 29:

28b relates: "In 1739 the county magistrate, Mu Wenhuan received instructions from the grand coordinator, Viceroy Yang, to set up a stone tablet within his jurisdiction. It said, "Prior to 1727, all of those who were either bought by contract or commended themselves (*toukao*), raised by their masters, and made to marry bondservant women who bore them sons were [regarded] as family servants (*jianu*). They were to provide labor services forever, and their marriages were all arranged by the master. If the deeds of sale are imperfect or have not been reported for registration, and when people who were not raised by their master [have contracts drawn up by] unreliable middlemen or have lost the original documents, the people should all be allowed to redeem their freedom, according to precedent. They should be prohibited from keeping their master's name, and they hsould not be made to work."

⁷³ The term "land tax and labor service" (*fuyi*) was normally used at that time to mean the land tax and labor services the state exacted from landowners. If it is taken in this sense, then we can understand this passage to mean that the master was responsible to the state for the land tax and labor service, and that the master was careful not to steal the farming time of slave families. The following passage in the *Bu nongshu* [Supplemented treatise on agriculture], however, offers the possibility of a different interpretation: "Formerly I read that Mencius said, 'The feudal princes have three treasures: land, people, and the affairs of government. Scholar and commoner households are also the same: household regulations are the affairs of government, land property the land, *and hired workers (gugong) and tenants the people* (50:19a).'" As Zhang Lixiang himself related, the master was considered a political ruler (feudal lord or the state) and bondservant families as the people. We can also interpret this idea to mean that the substance of the relations of acquisition between the two is equivalent to the relations between the feudal lords or the state and the people (i.e., the land and labor-service taxes). Whatever way it is taken, it does not contradict the explanation of this passage given later.

⁷⁴ The land in question here refers not to the paddy land alone but to all the paddy and unirrigated land they were granted.

⁷⁵ This line, which reads literally, "Two bondservants (*pu*) for every hundred *mu* of land" can also be taken to mean that in addition to what is mentioned in the text, two bondservants per hundred *mu* of land should be given to the master by the bondservant families cultivating that hundred *mu*. However, since the content of the passage from "Two bondservants (*pu*) for every hundred *mu* of land" to "do not appoint cunning and indolent ones" is coherently connected, the bondservants in the line "Two bondservants (*pu*) for every hundred *mu* of land" should be understood to mean bondservants allocated to manage land in the same way as the bondservant managers. Two bondservants from among those kept in the master's household were to be allotted a hundred *mu* to manage, and one bondservant manager was to be given land and to settle down to manage three hundred *mu*. Whichever way this is interpreted, it does not change the explanation of the contents given in my translation.

⁷⁶ *Yangyuan xiansheng quanji*, 19:26a–b.

⁷⁷ Furushima, "Minmatsu Chōkō deruta," pp. 14–15.

⁷⁸ *Yangyuan xiansheng quanji*, 19:26a.

⁷⁹ *Bu nongshu*, 50:18b.

⁸⁰ Ibid., 50:20a.

⁸¹ Considering that this region was a low-lying, damp creek zone, it may seem strange that there was a high proportion of dry-field land given out relative to wet field land. However, the following passage from the *Bu nongshu* clarifies this point: "There are an equal number of wet and dry fields in Tongxiang, where great profits are made from silkworm and mulberry. The counties of Jiashan, Pinghu, and Haiyan to the east and Guian and Wucheng to the west have many wet fields but few dry fields" (50:1a–b). In contradistinction to the surrounding districts, there were an equal number of wet and dry-fields in Tongxiang. This was the reason that a fairly high proportion of dry-field land was given out to bondservants.

158   OYAMA

⁸² Furushima, "Minmatsu Chōkō deruta," p. 17.
⁸³ As a result, bondservant families which received land in this way were compelled to borrow rice from their landlords every year. The author of the *Jiting waiji*, 1665, Chen Longzheng (1585–1645), a native of Jiashan county in the late Ming, relates that: "In normal years tenants borrow 0.2*s hi* of rice along with the land (*suitianmi*) at the interest rate of 20 percent [per annum] (4: 15a)." The term "rice along with land" refers to rice borrowed from the landlord.
⁸⁴ Many of these settled bondservant families were probably included among the large numbers in such expressions as "many bondservants" (*tongnu qianzhi*) and "many hired bondservants" (*yongnu qianzhi*).
⁸⁵ *Taizu shilu*, Hongwu 20/2, p.2726.
⁸⁶ *Huang Ming tiaofa shilei zuan*, vol. 1, p. 34, lower half page, to p. 35, upper half page.
⁸⁷ Ibid., vol. 1, p. 31, upper half page.
⁸⁸ If we compare what was said in the main text with the following passage from Ding Yuanjian's (1573–1620?) *Xishan riji*, we notice that large landholdings during the Ming, especially in Jiangnan, originated among members of the tax-captain stratum. The relevant passage from Ding's work reads: "Over half of the large gentry families in Wuxing began as tax captains. At present their children and grandchildren are extremely numerous. In our county (Wuxing), our family, the Zhu's, the Sun's, and the Li's, all began as tax captains." (*Shangjuan* section on daily assignments, p. 11b.)
⁸⁹ *Dongshe xiansheng jiacangji*, 14:5b–6a.
⁹⁰ Ibid., 14:8a.
⁹¹ *Huang Ming tiaofa shilei zuan*, vol. 1, p. 321, lower half page, to p. 322, upper half page.
⁹² *Huang Ming wenheng*, 27:7a–7b.
⁹³ *Huang Ming jingshi wenbian*, 72:10b–11a.
⁹⁴ At first Chongming county belonged to Suzhou prefecture, but it was put under the jurisdiction of Taicangzhou in 1497, when the latter was separated from Suzhou prefecture. Accordingly, what is meant by "inland districts" here is the region south of the Yangzi River.
⁹⁵ 1681 *Chongming xianzhi*, 4:11a.
⁹⁶ Ibid., 6:2b.
⁹⁷ *Weng Tie'an nianpu*, 11a–b.
⁹⁸ 1824 *Suzhou fuzhi*, 10:25a.
⁹⁹ *Xiaoxia xianji zhaichao*, 1785, vol. 16a–b.
¹⁰⁰ Cf. Niida Noboru, "Chūgoku shakai no 'hōken' to fyūdarizumu," pp. 107–8, The *Zhuo zhai shiyi* by Xiao Lianggan, a man who lived in the Wanli period (1573–1615), provides evidence that people who commended land during the Ming became bondservants of their landlord. The relevant passage reads: "At present, if the fertile land [of the empire] is not privately owned by Imperial concubines, it is used for the manors and houses of powerful people. Half of the hereditary property of the people, has been gradually encroached upon and annexed by these powerful people. . . . *They present the strong and powerful (shihao)* with land called either ownerless barren land or taxless official land, *express their faithfulness to them as bondservants (nu)*, and bring an insatiable acquisitiveness with them" (*Jingchuan congshu* edition, 7a–b).
¹⁰¹ 1748 *Suzhou fuzhi*, 78:35b.
¹⁰² During the upheavals of the late Ming tenants were often used by landlords as an armed force. Take for example the following case from the 1748 *Haiyan xian tujing* 6:2, 4b, describing the activities of a man called Sheng Dan, whose family had lived in the Xinfeng district of Jiaxing for generations: "During the late Ming when big groups of bandits were rampant everywhere [Sheng] Dan took the lead in organizing his brothers and clansmen in defense. When bandits came, he would direct the *tenant males (dianding)* and healthy boys in the fighting." Gu Gongxie, in his *Xiaoxia xianji zhaichao* (2:38a), relates the case of Lu Shiyao, who was "immensely wealthy.

He gathered together a mob of over a thousand who were all tenants. When the troops were defeated, he escaped with his life, shaved his head, and became a monk. It is not known where he died." There is yet another example, this time from the 1788 *Qingpu xianzhi*, 40:8b. This source tells of Shi Taocheng, who prided himself on clever planning. During the transition period from the Ming to the Qing, Shi Taocheng went and warned a marital relation of his, a certain Mr. Chen, that though he had made a fortune by charging compound interest, all the local people were very angry with him and were planning to take advantage of the disorder to pillage his house. Mr. Chen was greatly astonished and entrusted Shi with the task of getting him out of the fix. Shi devised a plan and he "gathered together every tenant, youth, and riffraff (*wulai*), took an oath before the gods with them, and, smearing their mouths with blood, went out to start a righteous uprising. Chen was elected as the covenant leader and agreed to comply with the agreement. Shi was appointed as a counselor, and affairs both large and small were all solved within the covenant." Tenants (*dianhu, dianding*) used by landlords as armed forces, as seen in the cases above, were all extremely subordinate to their landlord—indeed, they were probably slave-like.

103 *Huangchao jingshi wenbian*, 10:11b.

104 1814 *Wuxi Jinkui xianzhi*, 31:2b–3a.

105 1681 *Wucheng xianzhi*, 5:2b.

106 1673 *Jiading xianzhi*, 4:2a.

107 1879 *Shimen xianzhi*, 11:4a–b.

108 Here follows a list of specific examples. The 1744 *Zhenyang xianzhi*, 14:5a has: "There were great winds in the seventh month of 1631 which destroyed the grain and cotton. *Cunning tenants in the neighboring districts all plotted to evade paying rent. Acting in coordination with each other, they would set fire to landlord houses in the middle of the night.* They stopped these activities once winter was over."

The *Xijinzhi xiaolu*, 2:19b records: "In the summer of the sixth month of 1640, the local people were without food. They formed a group and plundered rice and barley from the wealthy households. It all began on the nineteenth day. *In every village it was the same, though they did not enter upon any agreement.* The county officials punished the disorderly people severely. Several score people were beaten to death, while a great many in every district were taken alive and either killed or burned to death."

The 1684 *Wujiang xianzhi*, 43:5a, also has a passage on the disturbances of the same year: "There was a drought and locust plague in 1640. The price of rice suddenly rose, and many wealthy people stopped selling grain. Disorderly people like the monk Zhu led over a hundred starving people to force the big households to sell their grain. If they did not comply, they smashed their houses. This was called beating for rice (*dami*), and *it was the same in every town and village.* Some used it as an excuse to get even with profiteers. The whole county was in disorder."

This incident was heavily colored with the elements common to smashings by poor people in Edo-period Japan. Now some more examples from the Qing dynasty. Dong Han, in a piece on the great famine in Songjiang prefecture from 1689 to 1693 in his *Sangang zhilue* (10:2b–3a), recounts that "a violent wind blew day and night without stopping from the twenty-seventh to the twenty-ninth of the seventh month. . . . Accordingly, the fields in the neighborhood were either completely ruined, half-destroyed or only yielded 0.1 or 0.2 *shi* per *mu*. *Crafty peasants used the bad harvest as an excuse not to pay even one grain of rice [as rent]. They even formed groups to resist and refuse [rent payment].* The officials did not prevent them from doing so, and there was nothing the landlords could do about it, except look at each other in dismay."

Qin Huitian (1702–64), in a memorial to the throne written in 1745 (*Huang Qing zouyi*, 41:14b–15a), reports that in Zhili province "people have been quarrelling in the yamen and pillaging the village markets because the local officials were a little tardy in distributing relief in the areas recently struck by disaster. . . . Ruffians in the villages, who have pet hates, band together and stop trade. They even fearlessly insult the senior officials. Ignorant officials at the subprefecture and county levels try every means to hide [their shortcomings] and are careful to smooth over [their faults] in fear of trouble occurring in their area or of their superiors becoming aware of the situation. *When they meet refractory tenants who resist rent payment, they should remember that the taxes come from paying rent and hurriedly press for and collect [unpaid rent]. But they vainly instruct the landlords to submit taxes, disregard the tenants' refusal to pay rent, and allow them to escape through cunning.*"

An entry for 1741 in the *Gaozong chunhuangdi shilu*, 6/9, p. 2248, has a memorial by the acting grand coordinator of Jiangsu, Chen Dashou, which reports a militia man (*tuanmin*) named Xu Yongxiang, who "gathered a mob and went to the county yamen carrying cotton tree branches that had been picked clean of cotton to argue and make an appeal. They used the reports of famine as a pretext for requesting the good fortune of a rent reduction." [Here rent refers to rent paid by tenants.]

Another entry from the same source for the twelfth month of 1776 has a memorial by Zhong Yin which says: "*Hu Tingsan, a tenant* in Yongjia county in Zhejiang, *gathered a mob to refuse rent payment.* The landlords had reported the matter to the officials, and the latter had ordered the prohibition of such behavior. The tenants did not comply, and the jail wardens who went to admonish them were beaten and detained" (p. 15,037).

Another passage for the same month of the same year continues: "Hu Tingsan and the others advocated rent reduction and were bold enough to rally together a mob of people, and to beat and detain the jail wardens. The circuit intendant led the soldiers to catch them, and when he went to arrest [Hu and the others, he found that Hu] was still relying on the power of the mob, which was rampaging around doing as it pleased. In the end they dared to take up cudgels and climb onto a bridge to resist. They were extremely unlawful (p. 15,041)."

The *Yongzheng zhupi yuzhi*, vol. 10, p. 6325, gives the following description of Chongming county, located at the mouth of the Yangzi River: "Chongming county is a solitary island off the coast. The customs of the people are fierce and hard. There is trouble at the slightest instigation. *The tenants in the villages become very tense when the landlords demand barley rent (maizu). They gather together, create turmoil, and force the closure of the market.*"

The 1741 memorial by Chen Dashou cited above also comments on the behavior of tenants in Chongming county. It reads: "*There are also cunning tenants in Chongming county.* They took advantage of the magistrate changing the place of the military examinations *to form a group and force the assistant county magistrate to agree to announce a rent reduction*" (*Gaozong chunhuangdi shilu*, 6/9, p. 2248).

An entry for 1741 in the *Gaozong chunhuangdi shilu*, 6/10, p. 2272, contains a memorial by Yang Zhaozeng, minister of the ministry of rites who was the acting viceroy of Liangjiang: "Chongming is an area struck by disaster. There are many local toughs *who gang together and incite mobs. They make disaster an excuse for not allowing [tenants] to pay rent.*"

The last example, once again from Chongming county, is taken from the entry for the eleventh month of 1758 in the *Gaozong chunhuangdi shilu*, 23/11, p. 8439. It is a report of a case about "*a cunning tenant, Yao Ba, and others in Chongming, Jiangsu, who resisted rent payment, burned and destroyed the landlords' thatched houses, and refused to participate in military service.*"

[109] *Peiyuan tang oucun gao* 45:26a–b.

[110] *Xu zhai ji*, 5:21b.

[111] Ibid., 4:21a–b.

[112] As the following passage from the 1760 *Wuqing zhenzhi*, 2: *Nongsang* 4a indicates, it was common practice for tenants to put on plays when they were resisting rent payment. "Recently a crafty and cunning custom has appeared among the tenants. . . . [They] solidify their mutual unity by showing plays." This practice is also mentioned in sources from the Taiping period, though in this case secret societies would band the peasants together while showing plays. For example, Mao Hongbin (1806–68), in his *Mao shangshu zougao* (10:7a–7b), reports that in 1863 there was talk that some rebels had infiltrated a temple in Yiyang county and were "*showing plays to*

band together a mob to plan to attack Yiyang [county city]." The rebels provided entertainments that would rouse the will to fight in tenants in order to strengthen their solidarity.
[113] *Yangyuan xiansheng quanji,* 8:18a.
[114] Ibid., 5:12a.
[115] *Gaozong chunhuangdi shilu,* 10/7, p. 3554.
[116] 1596 *Xiushui xianzhi,* 1:42a.
[117] 1868 *Nanxun zhenzhi,* 21:1a–b.
[118] A similar passage may be found in the 1760 *Wuqing zhenzhi,* 2: *Nongsang,* 2a–b.
[119] Chongde county was renamed Shimen county in 1662.
[120] Quoted in *Shimen xianzhi,* 11:5b–6a.
[121] *Yongzheng zhupi yuzhi,* vol. 7, p. 4399.
[122] For the cotton-weaving industry in Songjiang prefecture, refer to the following studies by Nishijima Sadao. "Shōkō-fu ni okeru mengyō keisei no katei ni tsuite"; "Shina shoki mengyō shijō no kōsatsu," later revised and included in Nishijima Sadao, *Chūgoku keizaishi kenkyū;* "Mindai ni okeru momen no fukyū ni tsuite," later revised and included in *Chūgoku keizaishi kenkyū:* "Shina shoki mengyō no seiritsu to sono kōzō," later revised and included in *Chūgoku keizaishi kenkyū;* "Jūroku-jūnana seiki o chūshin to suru Chūgoku nōson kōgyō no kōsatsu," later revised and included in *Chūgoku keizaishi kenkyū.* For sericulture, silk-thread spinning, and silk-gauze weaving in the region around the southern edge of Lake Tai refer to: Tanaka Masatoshi, Saeki Yūichi, "Kinuorimonogyō: sōsetsu, Chūgoku"; Tanaka Masatoshi, Saeki Yūichi, "Jūroku-jūnana seiki no Chūgoku nōson seishi kinuorigyō."
[123] *Xijinzhi xiaolu,* 1:6b–7a.
[124] 1924 *Jiangwan lizhi,* 4:1b.
[125] Furthermore, the foundation of the tenants' new forces of production in the face of the commercialization of this sort of rural handicraft industry formed the objective material conditions for the transformation and shitt in the content of landlord management. Managerial landlords whose operations were based upon the levying of labor services from tenants turned into urban landlords who collected feudal rent-in-kind. The transformation from "rural landlords" to "urban landlords" in the late Ming-early Qing, as described by Kitamura, took place in the context of such changes.
[126] 1760 *Wuqing zhenzhi,* 2: *Nongsang* 4a.
[127] 1642 *Wuxian zhi,* 11: 51a–b.
[128] *Songjun Louxian junyi yaolue* by Li Fuxing, p. 253b.
[129] 1824 *Suzhou fuzhi,* 10:21b–22a.
[130] 1863 *Nanxun zhenzhi,* 21:13a.
[131] Ibid., 21, 13b.
[132] The line in the text which reads, "He divides the people according to their land and gathers them together" is difficult to understand. Fei Xiaotong in his survey of Kaixiangong village on the southern banks of Lake Tai (Fei Hsiao-Tung, *Peasant Life in China, a Field Study in the Yangtze Valley,* p. 173) provides some relevant information. He writes that the labor for work on the drainage pumps is allocated in proportion to the amount of land cultivated by each household. In view of this information I interpret the line in question to be referring to the same practice Fei describes. Furthermore, it should be pointed out that Senba Yasuo and Shioya Yasuo, in their translation of Fei's book, entitled *Shina no nōmin seikatsu* (p. 207), rendered the English original "the size of his holding" as "in proportion to the size of the land owned," thus supporting this interpretation.
[133] 1868 *Nanxun zhenzhi,* 21:13b.
[134] Fei, *Peasant Life,* pp. 172–73. Senba and Shioya, *Shina no nōmin seikatsu,* pp. 208–9.
[135] In light of this evidence we must conclude that the animal-and-wind-driven large-scale square-pallet chain pumps mentioned earlier could not be maintained by poor tenants at that time. Such pumps were probably used by bondservant-holding managerial landlords. The following passage from the *Wong Zhen nong shu,* (19:12b)

records that such large-scale pumps were introduced during the Yuan period. It states: "The ox-powered square-pallet chain pump is nearly twice as effective as the one treadled by humans. It has been *newly constructed* together with the former water-driven square-pallet chain pump." From this piece it seems that the ox-driven square-pallet chain pump, which required nearly twice as much energy as the human-powered one, came to be used from the Yuan dynasty on, together with a similar pump that was powered by water. These big chain pumps and ones that required a comparatively large number of people to run them—from three to six people for one pump (e.g., 1521 *Huating xianzhi,* 3:6a–b)—went out of use, and the two-person pump was widely adopted toward the end of the Ming. The reason for this change was that whereas the former type of pump was suitable for use by managerial land-lords who had a lot of bondservants for a labor force, the latter type suited the scale of tenant operations—a small nuclear family based on the labor power of a husband-and-wife team. Such a changeover itself indicates that the control of the regulations for irrigation and drainage shifted from managerial landlords to tenants. Cf. Furu-shima Kazuo, "*Ho nōsho* no seiritsu to sono jiban," pp. 113–14.

[136] A source cited earlier stated that tenants who did not participate in anti-rent activities were punished. Such punishment was made possible only because tenant solidarity was founded on a community which was bound together through produc-tion.

[137] 1811 *Taiping xianzhi,* 18:43b. Fujii Hiroshi, who was the first to cite this source material, says that the north and south refer to areas within Taiping county and should not be interpreted as vaguely indicating north and central China on a broader scale (Fujii Hiroshi, "Mindai enjō no kenkyū," pp. 89–132, footnote 63). Nevertheless, in view of the fact that the legal status of master and servant disappeared after the late Ming, we regard this source as indicating the disappearance of such status.

[138] Cf. Niida, "Chūgoku no nōdo koyōjin no hōteki mibun no keisei to henshitsu—shuboku no bun ni tsuite."

[139] According to such a theory the fundamental reason for the transformation of Ming managerial landlord operations was the growth of tenants from slaves to serfs. Furushima would regard the shift from slaves, the managerial labor force, to hired laborers, as an index of the breakdown of local power, and as a phenomenon deriving from this basic process.

Studies of surface and subsoil rights in the Yangzi River delta and areas to the south have not made it fully explicit when surface rights were universally obtained by tenants, the direct producers. If we assume that this occurred during the late Ming-early Qing period, we would have to interpret the surface rights set up by tenants as the establishment of cultivation rights (feudal landholding rights).

[140] *Shouhe riji,* 4:35a.

[141] The landlords' use of official power in pressing for rent from tenants in default was already evident in the Song dynasty. In the Song it was simply a case of mobiliz-ing the police force; the assistant subprefect (*xianwei*) would lead archers to take tenants into custody. (See Sutō Yoshiyuki, *Chūgoku tochi seido shi kenkyū,* pp. 265–69.)

[142] For information on Qian Qianyi, refer to Wu Han, " 'Shehui xianda' Qian Mu-zhai," pp. 342–58.

[143] *Yuyang shuoyuan,* edited by Ding Zuyin; 1917 *Jiabian,* section on Zhang Hanru's draft memorials, 2a–b.

[144] *Wenxian congbian,* 4 *Ji* section on the suing of Xu Qianxue, 4b.

[145] Ibid.,7b.

[146] The same case also provides us with the specific names of other such yamen clerks. For example:

Wang Jubin is a *bogus clerk in the tax department.* He was appointed head of tax commutation for 1689 (ibid., 7b).

Yang Maofan is an inveterate offender. *He consecutively held the posts of head of tax transportation and tax commutation* and stealthily collected amounts of tax over and above the official level. The former provincial governor Hong Fang dismissed him. Now he has again been appointed as the head of tax commutation for 1690 and is also scheming for the post of head of tax transportation this year (ibid., 7b).

Yang Dianchen *is a bogus clerk in the tax department.* The previous provincial governor Hong Fang dismissed him, but now he has once again been secretly appointed in defiance of the regulations (ibid., 7b).

Chen Xiang is an inveterate offender who entered the yamen again in defiance of the regulations *and is at present acting as the head of post stations* (? *tiaozong*) (ibid., 7b).

Apart from such activities some of them had also become yamen officials in the departments of rites and civil appointment, as the two following cases from the same source show:

Wang Jude is a bogus official in the department of rites (ibid., 7b).
Zou Jinggong is a bogus official in the department of civil appointment (ibid., 7b).

[147] *Shouhe riji,* 3:10a–b.
[148] Hosoi Masaharu, "Shinsho no shori" *Shakai keizai shigaku,* 14:6, pp. 1–23.
[149] Powerful bureaucrats came to hold real power over tax collection in their home areas during the Jiajing period (1522–66). This occurred just at the time when it was becoming difficult to hide the fact that the *lijia* system was ruined. As evidence for the intrusion by powerful bureaucrats into local tax collection during the Jiajing period let us consider a memorial on tax arrears penned by Chen Ru: "The accumulated tax arrears in every province each year can be counted in the ten thousands. Among them there are some small peasants who fail to make payment. They pay their taxes to grandee households or others. Embezzlement and cheating are particularly terrible. . . . In the worst cases even, if the bureaucrat magnates and powerful families order their servants to collect tax in proxy (*lanna*), the officials do not dare to say anything against them (*Qinshan ji,* 1569, 3:17b)."
[150] Contemporaries pointed out that large landholdings were quite common in the Yangzi delta. For example, Zhang Juzheng, in his *Zhang Taiyue xiansheng wenji,* 1612 (26: 10a), says of the Jiangnan region: "Magnates hold 70,000 *qing* of land with a tax of 20,000." Chu Fangqing in his *Huangtian yi* (34:16b), described the situation in Yihuang county as follows: "During the late Ming there was a great amount of land annexation. Poor people could not own even an inch of land, while influential gentry families counted several tens of thousands of *mu* of adjoining land."

POPULAR UPRISINGS, RENT RESISTANCE, AND BONDSERVANT REBELLIONS IN THE LATE MING

TANAKA MASATOSHI

Tanaka Masatoshi, whose earliest work was on handicraft industries, began in the late 1950s to study various types of mass action, including peasant rebellions, urban uprisings, and bondservant revolts. He has published a number of articles and theoretical essays on the subject including a long masterful introduction to various forms of popular rebellion in the Ming which is translated here. Originally published in 1961, this essay has had a major impact on Japanese studies of peasant rebellions and is one of the starting points for most Japanese students of Chinese history. The essay was originally written for a survey of world history and, following the style of the series, included no notes. For this English translation, Professor Tanaka has provided a set of notes which should make the translation of greater use.

Tanaka's earlier research on and debate with Nishijima Sadao over factors leading to the development of vigorous rural handicraft activity in the late Ming had already begun to point in the direction of mass rebellions. In his earlier essay (in this volume), Tanaka had stressed the role of the developing forces of production which in creating the possibilities for the development of handicraft industry had set off a new round in the struggle for control of the surplus created. Tanaka views the relationships between the state and the peasants and between landlords and peasants as basically antagonistic. An examination of both of those relationships shows not only exploitation by the state and the landlord, but also a struggle against that exploitation by the masses. Such popular struggles have the potential to create new structures and relationships, altering the former situation.

In all of his studies of popular uprisings Tanaka tries to link

This essay was originally published as "Minpen, kōso, nuhen" [民変, 抗租, 奴変] in *Sekai no rekishi* [世界の歴史], vol. 11 (Tokyo: Chikuma shobō, 1961), pp. 41–80. Translation by Joseph McDermott.

a firm grasp of the economic and social base conditions to instances of political action. Drawing on a wide variety of both primary and secondary sources, Tanaka brings together data on a number of types of popular movements which are usually seen in isolation. While some of the rebellions he deals with have in recent years also been studied by Western scholars, the breadth of his vision and comprehensiveness of the coverage in a single survey cannot be matched anywhere else.

Tanaka was one of the leaders in the study of such popular movements and used a methodology shared by many others. This methodology, which stressed the links between economic conditions and political action, has been criticized by some younger scholars who feel that Tanaka's work puts too much stress on economic factors while neglecting the role of ideology, religion, and community. Tanaka's views on community may be summarized as follows. To Tanaka class conflict, which is the driving force of history, does not surface in pre-modern Asian societies in a simple fashion, but appears and functions through the medium of community. Formalistically it appears as if the peasantry built communities for themselves and that both landlords and peasants within the community rely upon each other to maintain their livelihood. In reality, however, landlords manipulate the idea of community to control the peasantry. Since landlords control the peasantry through community and use the idea of community to divert the attention of peasants away from class struggle, revolution in Asian societies has to destroy community as well as promote class struggle before it can succeed in abolishing the landlord system. Tanaka's critics, however, argue that community is more fundamental to the history of social structures than class conflict. They stress that community is often used as a means of constructing new alliances for revolution and that communities continue to exist after revolutions. Tanaka counters such criticism with the argument that landlords rule the peasantry through their control over peasant collective labor performed with land and water owned by landlords within the community. He also notes that though communities exist both before and after revolutions, new postrevolutionary communities are qualitatively different from prerevolutionary ones: that is to say, class struggle converts old communities into new ones with a completely different set of class relations.

Tanaka's career has combined research interests in both

economic and social history as a result of his belief that even though the system may reach a point where the old relations of production are in severe contradiction, it is only through class struggle that new relations of production can be created. Thus the study of economic history and problems in economic development led him to an interest in popular movements, and a sense of the dynamics of such popular movements fed back into and enriched his study of economic history. In the West, where these two fields of interest are too often isolated from each other, Tanaka's work may offer a more organic approach well worth consideration.

*　　　　*　　　　*

In the spring of 1644 the 277-year reign of the Ming dynasty came to a violent end. The next dynasty, the Qing, which was to be the last of imperial China, was established by Manchu conquerors. Despite the interpretation suggested by this sequence of events, the direct cause of the fall of the Ming was not the Manchu invasion, but the peasant insurrections which had arisen within China itself during the late sixteenth and early seventeenth centuries.

On 18th day, third lunar month, 1644, Beijing, the capital, had fallen to the peasant army led by Li Zicheng. This was well before the the Manchus were close to taking the city. The last Ming emperor, Yizong, saw to his sons' safe escape, beheaded his daughters and concubines, and hanged himself on Prospect Hill overlooking the Forbidden City. His final testament written on the lapel of his robe reveals his perception of the reasons for his failure: "His Imperial Majesty has reigned for 17 years and now the wicked rebels press on to his capital. His Imperial Majesty has striven to rule without thought of himself, but he has been lacking in virtue. In so doing he has earned the rebuke of Heaven. His ministers have all misled him. How can he face his ancestors in the afterlife? . . . Let the bandits then rend his body asunder. Only see that not even one of the common people suffer any harm." Resigning himself to his fate, the emperor expressed profound remorse at the failure of his rule. Yizong's reign came at the end of a despotic dynasty that had a bureaucracy more organized than any before it; although he personally believed he tried to rule virtuously, in the end, faced with popular rebellion and the desertion of his ministers, he was forced to realize that as emperor he was nothing more than a symbol of a harsh, autocratic despotism.

Where did the forces which destroyed this rule originate? How did they grow to such strength? Why, after destroying the autocratic rule of one dynasty, did they allow the perpetuation of despotism under the Manchu conquerors rule? Why were they unable to create a new form of government to replace the despotic institutions they attacked? The first step toward answering these questions lies in the investigation of the wide-scale social upheaval which characterized the late Ming and early Qing. In this essay I will discuss the most obvious expressions of this upheaval—the relationship between late-Ming popular urban uprisings, rent resistance struggles, and bondservant insurrections.

Popular uprisings: Hired silk workers' rebellion

Development of rural handicraft industry

The city of Suzhou was the site of several major urban uprisings in the seventeenth century, including the two that we will consider in some detail here, the rebellion of the hired silk workers, and the Kaidu (reading of the edict) rebellion. Located at an important transportation and trade crossroads, the city of Suzhou had been a leading urban center since the Southern Song dynasty (1127–1279). Although it had been partially destroyed in the rebellions of the late Yuan (1234–1367) and early Ming, by the middle of the fifteenth century it had recovered and was the central city in the lower Yangzi delta region, the most advanced area of the Chinese empire. Its key economic and cultural roles were recognized in the popular Chinese saying, "Above there is paradise, below there are Suzhou and Hangzhou." Suzhou, located at the center of a domestic and international network, reflected the splendor of Ming China. And yet a closer examination shows that the actual conditions in late-Ming Suzhou ill fit the popular description of the city as "prosperous and thriving."

Suzhou was famous throughout China as the center of the sericulture and silk-weaving industries. The development of those industries had brought great economic and social change to the greater Suzhou region. A 1746 gazetteer for Zhenze county(Suzhou prefecture) provides historical background for the development of the rural sericulture industry in Suzhou prefecture:

During the Song and Yuan dynasties work in the silk damask industry was restricted to weavers in Suzhou city. In the Hongxi and Xuande eras (1425–35) of the Ming dynasty the residents of

Wujiang county (Suzhou), for the first time began to weave silk, and men in Wujiang ran this industry by hiring weavers from the prefectural city of Suzhou. However, from the Chenghua and the Hongzhi eras (1465–1505), peasants outside the city wall of Wujiang mastered the skill of silk weaving. This then became the general practice, and peasants in the market town of Zhenze and its surrounding villages sought profit from weaving pongee and damask.[2]

It is clear that new central markets were growing up in the textile-producing areas to keep pace with the rapid development of commodity production in the sericulture industry.[3] These commercial developments, which were supported by the development of productive forces in rural Yangzi delta villages, were a response to the worsening crisis in the rural economy, to the heavy burden of land taxes and village labor services or tenancy fees.[4] For example, in the early Ming the village of Shengze had only 50 to 60 families, but during the Chenghua period (1465–87) merchants and other people came to reside there in ever increasing numbers. In 1561 it had become a market place for the floss silk and pongee industry, with several hundred families in residence. In the 1620s it contained over 1100 families, their pongee silk thread brokerage houses arranged in rows; and in the late seventeenth and early eighteenth centuries its population had surpassed 10,000 families. It could then be rightly called a first-rank market town in Wujiang county. At the time of the Ming-Qing transition it had become the focal point for the collection and distribution of pongee and damask produced throughout Wujiang. Swarms of wealthy merchants with vast sums of money gathered at this marketing center of Wujiang to buy the renowned Shengze damask.[5]

The market town of Zhenze, referred to earlier, had been a quiet hamlet of several tens of families in the mid-fourteenth century. By the latter half of the fifteenth century its residents had increased to three or four hundred families, then 1000 families in the mid-sixteenth century, and even more by the time Zhenze was made a county seat in 1726. In the latter half of the eighteenth century the population of the market town of Zhenze in Zhenze county reportedly numbered 2000 to 3000 families.[6] Such market towns had become new commercial and industrial cities as a result of the development of the sericulture industry in surrounding villages. This rural base enabled Suzhou to become a great center for the production and finishing of high-quality handicraft goods, as well as a commercial city within the market system of China and ultimately a symbol of the age.

From the seventeenth through the eighteenth century the satin and thin-silk-gauze industries in the weaving districts in the eastern part of Suzhou city employed many weavers. These men were hired on either a regular or temporary basis to weave satin and thin gauze or spin yarn. Regularly employed weavers received daily wages. The temporary weavers, however, were hired anew every morning by a contractor boss (*xingtou*, later known as *batou*) at a labor market. The labor market for satin weavers was located at Flower bridge, for gauze weavers at the Guanghua Temple bridge, and for yarn spinners at Lianxi ward.[7] At the start of the eighteenth century the calendering trade in the cotton cloth industry also had over 450 shops located outside Chang Gate in Suzhou city. Some 340 contractor bosses and, at the reasonable average of several ten a shop, 20,000-odd artisans were attached to just this sector of the cotton industry.[8]

As the economy developed the old order of Ming society underwent striking changes, a transformation clearly indicated in the signs of a political and social crisis in the late Ming. Enmeshed in the development of this commercial economy was an imperial court addicted by the late sixteenth century to a lifestyle of luxury. The three great military campaigns of the Wanli era (1573–1620), beginning with the rebellion by Bohai in Ningxia prefecture in Gansu province in 1592, the Japanese invasions of Korea under Hideyoshi between 1592 and 1598, and the rebellion by Yang Yinglong in Bozhou, Sichuan province, in 1597, brought on a greater economic crisis for already pressed finances of the dynasty. These military engagements ran up expenses of two million, seven million, and two to three million taels of silver, respectively.[9]

Then in 1597 three palace buildings—the Huangji, Zhongji, and Jianji Halls—were destroyed by fire. The government gathered building materials from places as far away as Sichuan, Guizhou, and the Huguang provinces, spending a grand sum of over 9,300,000 taels of silver. (As much as 9,000 taels was paid for a single tree.) The government wasted a hundred or thousand times more money than a private contractor would have, and yet the resulting buildings were less sturdy than private edifices.[10]

As the state's finances were increasingly depleted due to these expenses, some ministers took advantage of the crisis to suggest state profiteering: they forwarded to the Emperor proposals for the opening of mines and increases in the commercial taxes. In response to the development of a currency-based economy, the government began to stockpile silver in 1596. Furthermore, since the government sought to control the flow of commercial goods, imperial eunuchs were sent to every part of the empire in order to collect commercial taxes and levies on mine production.[11] These eunuchs treated tax stations already in existence as their personal property. They also set up tax stations at every point along the major highways and waterways. Attended by several tens or hundreds of domestic servants and riffraff they practiced extortion by every possible means, such as forcible seizure of property and false accusation. All of this was undertaken in the name of the Emperor.

The eunuchs' handling of the mines followed a similar pattern. In the mine exploration program which lasted from 1546 to 1577, the government spent over 30,000 taels of silver, but reportedly acquired no more than 28,000 taels of silver.[12] Much of the silver extracted from the mines opened during the Wanli era ended up lining the pockets of the eunuchs. Their extortions touched every market and natural resource and every person: "The mines they tapped were not necessarily only mountain mines, and the taxes they levied were not necessarily imposed only on commerce."[13] Such was the infamous "disaster of the mines and taxes" (*kuang shui zhi hai*).

Toward the end of the Ming the land taxes of the entire empire were increased in response to demands for the *liaoxiang* levies, that is, the military provisions needed to resist the Manchu onslaught on the Liaodong borders. The collection of further imposts, under names like "provisions for annihilation" (*chaoxiang*), "supply aid" (*zhuxiang*), and "training supplies" (*lianxiang*), followed one after another with intensified severity. An entire village in Dengzhou prefecture in Shandong province was reportedly abandoned. Children were hurled into ponds, and men hanged themselves on trees.[14] As I have explained more fully in another article, the basic cause of this social and economic disintegration was the increase in landlord, merchant, and state exploitation of the peasants, an increase made possible by the expansion of the forces of production in the sixteenth and seventeenth centuries. Ultimately the victims of this exploitation—the direct producers or peasants, who, ironically, were responsible for the expansion of production in the first place—rose in resistance against their oppressors.

Extortion by the eunuch Sun Long

The brutal government extortions, which had begun as an attempt to deal with the financial crisis brought on by the depletion of government funds, sharpened the already existing contradictions in late-Ming society. Fierce popular resistance shook the structure of Ming control and initiated a process that was ultimately to lead to its dissolution. The riot of the hired silk weavers in Suzhou in 1601 is an example of the convergence of these various forces.

The eunuch Sun Long was sent to the Hangzhou-Suzhou area as the grand supervisor of the Imperial Silkworks (*zhiranju*), with the concurrent posts of intendant of the Imperial Silkworks and tax office manager. His responsibilities entailed the collection of commercial taxes and the management of the government-operated weaving factories.[15]

In the fifth lunar month of 1601 Sun Long, under the pretext of inspecting tax evasion at the tax stations in the city of Suzhou, moved from Hangzhou to Suzhou with Huang Jianjie and other retainers in attendance. After Sun's arrival in Suzhou, Ding Yuanfu, a powerful member of the gentry (*xiangshen*) who was engaged in moneylending in the eastern part of the city, made presents of valuable goods and money to Sun to gain his favor. Ding also secretly gave sums of money to such riffraff as Tang Shen, Xu Cheng, and ten others in Suzhou, to bribe Huang Jianjie to give them appointments as tax collectors. They were all appointed as tax collectors and, by keeping watch on the major waterways and roadways, they openly plundered goods from passing merchants. Prices soared and trade came to a complete halt. Huang Jianjie tantalized Sun Long with additional projects for self-enrichment and plotted with him to levy a monthly tax of 0.3 tael of silver on each loom. Naturally, the people of Suzhou were disturbed. Rumors ran in all directions that new taxes would be imposed—for instance, 0.05 tael of silver on each bolt of satin and a 0.02 tael of silver on each bolt of thin silk gauze. The same rumor also held that it would be possible to sell woven satin and thin silk gauze only after they had received the official seal—upon payment of a tax fee—at the Taoist shrine of Xuanmiaoguan in Suzhou city. One after another, the weavers and the wholesalers halted work, and the hired laborers who worked for them lost their means of livelihood.[16]

The hired silkers uprising

In the midst of such events violent riots broke out in which the hired silk weavers of Suzhou played the principal role. On the third day of the sixth lunar month, Xu Yuan, Gu Yun, Qian Da, Lu Man, and more than two thousand hired silk weavers formed six divisions, each of which was headed by a man holding aloft a banana-leaf fan followed by hired workers wielding wooden staffs. They started their march from Feng gate in the silk-weaving quarter in the southeast section of the city. Upon arriving at Miedu bridge they first killed Huang Jianjie.

When Deng Yunxiao, who as the magistrate of Changzhou county was stationed inside the city, heard of this incident, he had Tang Shen and Xu Cheng thrown into jail. He made a public apology for the injustices of the tax collectors, but the anger of the crowd did not subside. For three days and nights their protests raged unabated.

On the seventh day of the sixth lunar month crowds of people besieged the homes of the ten other tax collectors. After drowning them in the river or exposing their corpses by the roadside, they destroyed the tax collectors' houses and furniture, sometimes even slaying their family members. Seeing that these forces would be hard to halt, Deng Yunxiao for the second time called Xu Cheng and Tang Shen for further punishment at the Taoist shrine of Xuanmiaoguan. The crowd immediately beat the two tax collectors to death and had their bodies sliced into pieces.[17] Knowing that the source of their problems lay with the eunuch Sun Long, the people then thronged to his office and demanded the abolition of the new taxes. Sun Long escaped only by leaping over a fence and scrambling to shelter in a private house. Having barely averted further trouble, he reportedly left for Hangzhou.

The next day the crowd set fire to the mansion of the gentry figure Ding Yuanfu. Later that same day the crowd was dispersed only after being pacified by the prefect of Suzhou, Zhu Xieyuan, and others.

At this point there unexpectedly came to the fore a certain Ge Cheng, a native of Kunshan county who had become a hired silk weaver. (Or, according to another reliable source, he and his elder brother had rushed from Kunshan to the city of Suzhou upon hearing of these events.)[18] When Ge Cheng learned that the official authorities were seeking to arrest the leaders in the incident, he raised aloft a banana-leaf fan, proceeded to the government offices, and turned himself in. He requested his own confinement, and the release of everyone else. He was then beaten and almost died from his wounds. The residents of Suzhou city were deeply moved by his sense of righteousness and, according to contemporary sources, called him "General Ge."[19]

These events were reported to the court in a memorial written by the censor-in-chief Cao Shipin, who expressed his profound sympathy for the hired workers:

These men did not carry even a single knife, nor did they plunder a single thing. When they set houses on fire, they forewarned the neighbors to prevent the spread of flames. They only beat to death those men who were the same as thieves, confiscating their wealth and doing no more than making them atone for their robbery. . . . Ge Cheng surrendered himself to the prefectural offices with the wish that he suffer the heavy punishment normally given for such behavior and that the government punish no one else. His indignation was not unwarranted. . . . These hired silk workers find themselves in a situation where they live by selling their labor. If they lose their jobs, they suddenly starve to death. From what I have recently seen, the weavers and dyers unemployed on account of the work stoppage by the weaving households and the dyers' shops respectively number several thousand each. All of these men are good people who make a living by their labor. But with one blow they have been driven to their graves. I personally have great pity for them.[20]

He then proceeded to propose that, since the tax increases these men objected to would bring in only 60,000 additional taels of silver, the government should abolish the tax immediately. Such action, he argued, would stabilize conditions in Suzhou, a valuable source of government finances. (Together with the three neighboring prefectures of Songjiang, Jiaxing, and Huzhou, Suzhou bore annual tax quotas of several million taels of silver.)

The power of the hired silk workers

Hired silk workers could not get a wage equivalent to the labor they expended. They were forced to accept a pre-modern form of labor control known as the overseer boss (*batou*) system. However, it was through this process of becoming "wage laborers" that they began to have a real impact on historical development. Their status, lowly as it was, gave them some degree of political sophistication: when they lost their jobs, they organized and attacked their exploiters in a highly disciplined way. Their protest was thus quite different in nature from that of an undirected mob. As wage laborers they had developed some conciousness of the root causes of their situation, and that understanding shaped the organization and leadership of their uprising. The incident itself may seem to have been nothing more than an accidental riot by hungry men against cruel tax-collecting officials, such as is likely to occur at the end of a dynasty when the government's control has weakened. But this incident had a greater social and historical significance.

The development of simple commodity production and market circulation had led, though slowly, to the widespread creation of a hired-labor work force which was gradually acquiring the characteristics of a free, wage-labor status. However, these hired laborers were restricted by the isolated and closed nature of the small-scale operations in which they were working, and by guildlike regulations involving vertical status distinctions. Some of them worked in units organized as patriarchical societies—all members were supposedly regarded as family members. But such a system in the end made it easier for the laborers to unite in resistance against their exploiters: a consciousness of mutual concern within the "family" units led to the establishment of horizontal linkages and greater worker solidarity. The riot that occurred in Suzhou was the product of all these changes. The well-disciplined organization, leadership, and clear goals which characterized their protest could not have occurred before the late Ming, nor in areas less advanced than Suzhou.

Hired silk workers and the weavers and merchants

What impact did this riot have on the society of that time? What sort of men sympathized with and supported the riot? Or, more broadly, what kind of cross-group solidarity was expressed in the riot?

First, was the relationship between these hired workers and the wholesale merchants and weavers hurt by the tax increase? Did the wholesale merchants and weavers support and join them in their fight? This relationship is mentioned only in the edict issued in response to the report of Cao Shipin.[21] Even there, however, we learn only that the weavers and silk workers in Suzhou had violated the law by murdering and destroying property. Some weavers, as small producers, may have spontaneously risen to participate in this anti-tax struggle. But, for the others the historical record is not very clear. The nature of class conflict between the hired laborers and the weavers, which was the fundamental relationship,* is also not clear. Nonetheless, it is important to recognize the historical significance of the emergence of the silk workers as the main element in this struggle at this time.

The fact that most immediate producers had to depend upon an individual and direct type of resistance, that class conflict between hired silk workers and weaver managers did not surface, and that hired silk workers made no criticism of imperial power all reveal the difficulties of overcoming a paternalistic and Asian-style autocracy.

Hired silk workers and the literati

There is evidence that some Suzhou literati actively supported the ac-

---

* The term "fundamental relationship" specifically refers to class relations and relations of production.—Trans.

tions of the hired laborers in this incident, or at least took advantage of it to criticize their fellow officials and gentry. As we have seen, some gentry members played quite an active role on the other side: the gentry figure Ding Yuanfu secretly manipulated Tang Shen, Xu Cheng, and the other riffraff in collaboration with a eunuch and his subordinates. Once the hired workers discovered the part Ding had played, they set his house on fire.

During these events another gentry member, an Imperial College student named Zhang Xianyi, drafted a document and led scholars and commoners in making sacrifices to Ge Cheng while he was still alive. He also sent letters to the local officials and Ding Yuanfu, demanding that they treat Ge Cheng generously.[22] When another literatus wrote a play, *Jiaoshan ji* (The banana-leaf fan record), which criticized Ding's role in the incident, Ding mistakenly thought that the play had been written by Zhang Xianyi and had a bandit kill Zhang. Then fearing that his crime would be discovered, he drowned the bandit in a river.[23]

Another Imperial College student, Qin Shuyang, wrote the *Shuiguan yao* (The song of the tax officials) and thereby aligned himself with the hired laborers:

A thousand men rouse themselves to action,
Ten thousand men watch them from both sides of the road.
Cut and sharpen your trees! Hold your poles up high!
Follow along with me,
And let us slay the tax officials![24]

Being spared the fate of execution Ge Cheng was released in 1613 at the request of the censor Fang Kezhuang after being imprisoned for over ten years. At that time everyone in Suzhou sang Ge's praises as a "righteous brave" and called him "Ge the Worthy." He was accorded the style name "Barely Alive" (*yusheng*) by Chen Jiru, a government student who lived in seclusion in his native Kunshan and who was extolled as a lofty scholar.[25]

The students sympathetic to the hired silk workers were almost invariably among the lower academic ranks—they were either students at the Imperial College or government students. There were clearly status and power distinctions within the broad group of official-degree holders. A man like Ding Yuanfu was called a gentryman (*xiangshen*) or a gentry official (*xianghuan*). Such people were either officials living in their native place on leave from a post elsewhere or officials who had withdrawn from their posts and returned home.[26] Those who had a degree but had not yet served in the bureaucracy were in a different category. This included imperial students, Imperial College students, government students, and especially the provincial-degree holders, who had not yet passed the palace or metropolitan examinations which were a prerequisite for entrance into an orthodox official career. Some literati without a metropolitan degree had in fact discarded any aspirations for an official career and lived in a town or the countryside.[27]

It is a mistake, however, to hierarchically divide the two groups of literati—that is, those who were on the official rolls and who had held official posts, and those who had never held official posts. Rather we should think of the two groups as standing side by side. One group, the gentry and gentry officials, regardless of their examination degree or official success, consisted of those who had dominant power in rural matters and who advised the local officials. The other group included urban recluses (*shiyin*) who were at best active champions of righteousness through criticisms of current situations and at worst, peevish critics considered "eccentric" by their fellow townsmen. They constituted a source of public opinion formed in seclusion in a town or village, and thus aloof from the pursuit of fame and profit.

Many wealthy and powerful households in the local areas were of the gentry strata (officials living in their home area), while most urban recluses were Imperial College students or government students. At that time, to take the palace examination the examinee needed at least six hundred taels of silver for essentials alone—expenses while staying in the capital, gifts to the examining officials, and tips to the officials in charge. Thus social differences derived in part from material resources: some students could simply not afford to try to become officials. There were also, among the urban literati, those who were not merely critics: discontented with their failure in official circles and angry at the conditions of landownership and rural control, they were ready to act. It was these literati who supported the wage laborers in their attack on the eunuchs and their gentry allies.

Hired silk workers and the peasants

What was the relationship between the peasants and the hired silk workers involved in this incident? In connection with this question it is noteworthy that Ge Cheng was a native of Kunshan county in Suzhou prefecture and a silk worker in the city of Suzhou who joined the people of Suzhou in the movement. Some time after his release from prison he himself declared, "I withdrew to farm in the countryside for several years."[28] It is probable that he had had previous farming experience, or that he had a home village to return to; perhaps his work in Suzhou was done to supplement farm work in the countryside.

None of these possibilities are at all surprising: it was quite common for peasants to migrate to the cities when they could not support themselves by farming. For example, in the early Qing some twenty thousand men had abandoned agriculture and left their native Jiangning prefecture (Jiangsu) and Taiping and Ningguo prefectures (Anhui) to work in the cotton-calendering trade on the outskirts of Suzhou.[29] Although these peasants had been separated from various relationships within their villages, they did not completely break their ties with their villages when they moved away.

In preindustrial China the distinction between town and village was not yet a sharp one. Since the city's structure was determined by relations in the villages, an indivisible unity can be said to have existed between town and village. Accordingly, it was difficult to establish a European-style city—that is, one which by its very atmosphere made men free. But it also meant that the fruits of a struggle by the peasants or the urban handicraft workers occasionally could be shared between the town and village. Although historical evidence of direct ties between the peasantry and the hired workers is lacking, it is still correct to treat holistically the two seemingly distinct phenomena—the urban struggles and the rent resistance of the tenants. Both these struggles are part of a single movement which naturally followed on from the development of commodity production in the sixteenth and seventeenth centuries.

Hired silk workers and the government authorities

What was the reaction of the bureaucrats and the government authorities to these riots? As our narrative of these events has indicated, the Suzhou officials, when confronted with the riots, showed some understanding and made some concessions. The same reaction was evident in the attitude of the central government. Upon receiving a report of the incident, the court issued the following imperial edict:

> The government ought to use the law to the maximum in investigating and punishing these rioters. However, being poor and empty-handed, the rioters had no weapons at all. They destroyed the homes of only those who had caused trouble, and they harmed no one without cause. After remonstration by Sun Long and the prefectural and county officials, they are to be released immediately. Their actions arose from public indignation and their feelings deserve our sympathy.

The ringleader Ge Cheng as well as Tang Shen and others who inflicted this misfortune are to suffer a harsh sentence. But all the rest
have been forced to commit this crime; they are to be pardoned and
spared investigation. We should aim for peace and stability at the
place where the riot occurred.[30]

What we see here is a stock practice of an authoritarian monarch. He
treats the leaders as harshly as possible, passing on them the sentence
of capital punishment by slicing. Meanwhile, he treats the ordinary participants leniently, assuming that they have been manipulated by their
leaders.

Probing further, we can discern in this edict a deeper meaning. First
the government tried to meet the financial crisis by intensifying its exploitation of the people. When this failed, that is, when the people resisted, it then cleverly made use of their indignation. Ignoring the deeper
causes of the resistance, it praised "public indignation" as a justifiable
outcry against the personal cruelty of a single official. It was able to
divert the people's attention away from the deep-seated contradictions,
and thus avoid dealing with the contradictions within its overall system of control.

This attitude cannot be treated simply as a retreat and concession
made by a self-indulgent and weak ruling power in general. Rather, we
see revealed here the true nature of the Asian form of despotism.
Wrapped in the trappings of ethical politics, this autocracy strove to
accomplish its goals by pretending to adopt the norms of the people
themselves. It then used these norms against people who endeavored to
rise against the patriarchal and communalistic formation of society. It
both praised the "righteous braves" and encouraged the expression of
"popular indignation"—exhortations and praise which in reality
amounted to nothing more than another variety of oppression.

This analysis reveals the tragic limitations of the attitude of Ge Cheng
and others toward the government, limitations which prevented them
from understanding the real nature of the despotic rule they struggled
against. When Ge Cheng was released, he lived of his own accord as a
tomb guardian at the graves of Yan Peiwei and four other men whose
lives were sacrificed in the Kaidu Incident (described below). Once he
wept over their deaths:

The life that remains for me is a gift from the Wanli emperor. Two-
thirds of all the tax officials murdered in Suzhou were certainly slain by
my hand alone. But the Wanli emperor stayed my death, and I could
leave prison after ten years. Later, I withdrew to farm in the coun-

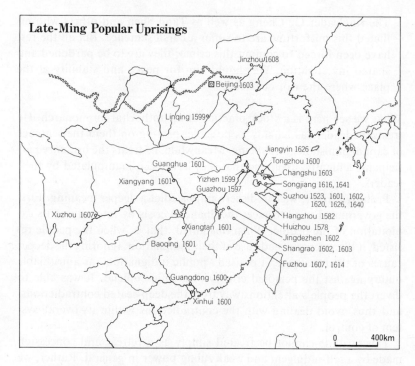

Late-Ming Popular Uprisings

Jinzhou 1608

Beijing 1603

Linqing 1599

Jiangyin 1626

Guanghua 1601   Tongzhou 1600
                             Changshu 1603
Xiangyang 1601   Yizhen 1599
                  Guazhou 1597   Songjiang 1616, 1641
                                  Suzhou 1523, 1601, 1602,
                                       1620, 1626, 1640
Xuzhou 1607
                                  Hangzhou 1582
                 Xiangtan 1601   Huizhou 1578
                                  Jingdezhen 1602
     Baoqing 1601   Shangrao 1602, 1603

        Guangdong 1600   Fuzhou 1607, 1614

           Xinhui 1600

                                          0   400km

tryside for several years, and 28 years after our disorders there occurred an incident in which five men, including Yan Peiwei, beat to death the guardsmen of the Imperial Secret Service. Before the Tianqi emperor Xizong knew of their plight, the officials imposed a sentence of capital punishment on these men at the eunuchs' request. It is for these five men that I weep. Not for myself.[31]

Ge Cheng shouldered full responsibility for the incident he was involved in, handing himself over to the authorities. After his sentence was commuted, he was respected as a living god. Believing that he was alive at the grace of the emperor himself, he thereafter identified his individual will with the wishes of the emperor. In short, he became a part of the very order he had previously attacked (i.e., the natural order).[32] Clearly Ge Cheng had a tendency to dramatize himself, but the very form his self-indulgence took reveals the power which the idea of the emperor and the state still exercised over the people.

In spite of these limitations, however, we should not underestimate the power of the masses, who were just beginning to attack the thick walls of the despotic structure. Popular uprisings did not stop with the hired silk weavers' riot in Suzhou. As can be seen from the map, from

1596 on, everywhere the eunuch Chen Feng was sent on assignments, struggles quickly erupted. Most of these struggles, which involved stoning, smashing, burning, and beating to death, were expressions of fierce resistance to the group of eunuch tax supervisors (*shuijian*) who collected taxes throughout the country. In 1599 transport workers in Linqing prefecture (Shandong) led a tax struggle. And in the Wuchang and Hanyang areas, officials were terrified by the possibility of a recurrence of popular uprisings like those of 1600. Such popular resistance was a product of the times corresponding in the economic sphere to the development of commodity production linked into a countrywide market.

One group of literati and officials, the Donglin (Eastern Forest) party, assisted this anti-tax struggle overtly and covertly by criticizing the cruel exploitation by the tax supervisors.[33] When officials of the Donglin party seized political power after the death of the Wanli emperor in 1620, the mines were closed, the new taxes voided, and the tax supervisor posts abolished.

The Kaidu revolt: Another popular uprising

The Donglin party and the eunuch faction

During the Ming dynasty bureaucratic factions were often formed by officials who shared a common birthplace. However, in the late Ming, when imperial rule was confronted with increasing social disorder, a different kind of group emerged among official ranks. These groups were based on common political stance and so transcended the locale-based nature of previous factional politics. Signs of this development first appeared when Zhang Juzheng gained power in the court. Opposition first surfaced during the 1586–1601 controversy over the successor of the Wanli emperor. Beginning in 1594 with the dismissal of Gu Xiancheng, the man who later founded the Donglin party, the dominant faction in the Grand Secretariat drove its opponents from office.

Gu Xiancheng was an official of exceptional learning and integrity. When he was relieved of his post, he returned to his native county of Wuxi in Jiangsu province, where he revived and lectured at the old Donglin Academy, which had been established some five hundred years earlier by the noted Confucian scholar Yang Shi. Gu and two other scholars, Zhao Nanxiang and Zou Yuanbiao, were known as the "Three Gentlemen," and together with their followers—including such famous figures as Gao Panlong, Yang Lian, Zuo Guangdou, Wei Dazhong, Yuan Huazhong, Miao Changqi, Zhou Zongjian, Huang Zunsu, and Zhou Qiyuan—they came to be known as members of the Donglin party.[34]

In contrast to this group, the men attached to the court, and criticized by the Donglin party, did not hold a uniform political viewpoint. In fact, the court group included three distinct factions—the Qi, the Chu, and the Yue—with officials joining and leaving for personal considerations. These court factions forged an alliance with the eunuchs and thus had some of the characteristics of a eunuch faction (*yandang*). The Palace and the government offices became the scene of a depressing political battle.

Some officials won over eunuchs in the Inner Palace with bribes, while the eunuchs extended their power in the bureaucracy by interfering in personnel administration. This union of officials and eunuchs was based on self-interest alone, and thus was in effect close to becoming a eunuch faction. Although groups similar to this faction had existed since the early days of the fifteenth century, it was not until the late Ming that one was able to extend its influence into official circles. Once the eunuch faction was established during the 1620s the illiterate eunuch Wei Zhongxian was able to carry out a campaign against his enemies, whom the eunuch faction and others often labeled as members of the Donglin party.

The Donglin party was not a unified political organization; indeed, it contained people from every social strata—not simply the gentry, but also soldiers, merchants, artisans, criminals, and a portion of the newly prominent commoners. Its central figures were deeply critical of the government, both while they were in and out of office. An examination of the characteristics of Donglin members reveals that they reflected many of the important social trends of the day.

First, many of these men had been born into landlord families with small- or medium-size landholdings. Their social and economic positions, however, had declined as taxation had increased and the social progress of the late Ming had undermined their control as landlords. Second, some members of the Donglin party began to realize that it was no longer possible for a family to rely on its past eminence as a literati family to overcome the present social crisis and thrive. More and more literati families were turning to trade to survive. Third, these men tried to maintain or change their social position by advocating, even if only passively, a policy designed to support the subjective development of small and medium peasants in the villages and the power of newly risen commoners in the towns.

After the death of the Wanli emperor in 1620, the Donglin party briefly held power, and then in 1624 Wei Zhongxian and his eunuch faction launched a counterattack. Having strengthened his position through his supervision of the Imperial Secret Service Office (*dongchang*; literally, "Eastern barracks"), Wei and his faction took successful advantage of Yang Lian's call for Wei's impeachment. Zhao Nanxing, Gao Panlong, Yang Lian, Zuo Guangdou, Ye Xianggao, Zhu Guozhen, and others were removed successively from office in 1624. At the end of the year Wang Wenyan was cast into prison for his criticism of the eunuchs' influence on the new Tianqi emperor.[35] Then in 1625 Yang Lian, Zuo Guangdou, Wei Dazhong, Yuan Huazhong, Zhou Chaorui, and Gu Dazhang were all charged with having taken bribes. Falsely found guilty, they were forced to undergo merciless questioning and were cruelly tortured to death.[36] Also in 1625 academies throughout the empire were destroyed, beginning, of course, with the Donglin Academy. In the twelfth lunar month the names of people suspected of membership in the Donglin party were posted on government placards everywhere in the empire.[37] The suppression of the Donglin party by Wei Zhongxian's faction had reached its peak.

Zhou Shunchang

It was in this context that the Kaidu incident took place. It occurred in 1626, right after the arrest of Zhou Shunchang, a Donglin party member. A native of Suzhou and a recipient of the metropolitan degree in 1613, Zhou Shunchang had first served as a judge (*tuiguan*) in Fuzhou prefecture (Fujian). In 1614, when small- and medium-sized merchants there protested against the extortions of the eunuch tax supervisor Gao Cai, Zhou had tried to protect them. Upon being appointed vice director of the Ministry of Civil Services Department of Civil Selections, Zhou proceeded to Beijing. However, because of his dissatisfaction with injustices within the department, he withdrew from this post and returned to Suzhou. He was so poor then that he had no more than several *mu* of land, and several small and shabby rooms. His wife, née Wu, had but one or two silver hairpins to her name, and they were almost always at the pawnshop. He focused his attention, however, on the problems of the common people. When taxes were collected after a flood or drought, he did not hesitate to petition the responsible officials. He associated with poor and simple scholars and did not begrudge assisting them. The people respected him as a man of virtue. In terms of the categories we suggested earlier, he can be described as an outspoken urban gentry recluse.

Several years passed, and the people placed their hopes on Zhou, a righteous gentry member of the Donglin party. During this time the eunuch supervisor of the textile workshop, Li Shi, had been harassing the silk weavers of Suzhou. In 1624 the prefect of Suzhou, Yang Jiang, reported Li's offenses to the emperor. Rather than punish Li, the court impeached Yang, and when the governor of the Nanjing-Suzhou area, Zhou Qiyuan, tried to shield Yang, he too was criticized in a memorial presented to the court by Li Shi. Making use of the ill feeling between Li Shi and Zhou Qiyuan, Wei Zhongxian, acting in the name of Li Shi, then reported to the emperor that Zhou Qiyuan had taken bribes of over one hundred thousand cash. In this denunciatory memorial, Wei also included the names of six opponents, all central figures of the Donglin party—Zhou Shunchang, Zhou Zongjian, Miao Changqi, Gao Panlong, Li Yingsheng, and Huang Zunsu. When the emperor in 1626 gave his approval to this memorial, later known as the fraudulent memorial (*wuzou*) of Li Shi, Zhang Yinglong, and others acting together with the guardsmen of the Imperial Secret Service immediately went south to Suzhou in the company of officials assigned to carry out the arrest of Zhou Shunchang.[38]

The Kaidu incident

Wherever the guardsmen, operating in the name of Wei Zhongxian, traveled, the local magistrate provided them with food and lodging. Lower-ranking officials were repeatedly whipped for even the slightest failure to meet the wishes of these emissaries. Even provincial governors were forced to defer to the guardsmen; and needless to say, commoners also regularly had to submit to their demands.

Before taking custody of any accused man from a local county office and despatching him to the capital, it was accepted practice to read aloud (*kaidu*) the imperial edicts to the accused and to the public. The guardsmen, after their arrival in Suzhou, pressed such exorbitant demands on the people that the ceremony for the public reading of the edict had to be postponed for three days. Zhou Shunchang's family had not a penny to its name, and his neighbors risked their fortunes to help him meet the guardsmen's demands. Poor literati went into debt, and even peddlers pawned their rags—everyone tried to help Zhou Shunchang by bribing the guardsmen.

At the same time thousands of people, both young and old, rushed to that section of the county office where Zhou was detained and awaiting the reading of the imperial edict that would seal his fate. The crowds

included many from impoverished villages in out-of-the-way places who
had rushed to Suzhou to catch a glimpse of Zhou. Cursuing Mao Yilu,
the provincial governor and a member of the eunuch faction, they
prayed for clemency. Students also joined the crowd, scurrying back and
forth in the mud, and the courtyard of the county offices was filled with
these people.

Once they knew that they could not resist the masses, the officials
moved Zhou from place to place four or five times a day. After each
move, the crowds immediately congregated at the new site. They entered
his room and bowed to him; those unable to enter bowed and called out
his name—they all acted as upset as if their parents had met with some
disaster. Hundreds and thousands of people were occupying the government offices and holding discussions about the case. It is reported that
a ghostly air hung over the city; during this time the gloom of a steady
drizzle assured that even the daytime was dark.

Finally it was decided that the public reading ceremony would be held
on the eighteenth day of the third lunar month. As soon as they heard
the news that Zhou was to be transferred to the guards compound (the
office of the surveillance commissioner in charge of the punishment),
the people gathered in huge crowds. While waiting for the gate of the
compound to open, they climbed atop the city wall nearby and stood in
thick ranks. They all burned incense in the rain, and smoke was so thick
that it seemed to conceal the sky. Shouts attesting to Zhou's innocence
echoed up and down the city walls and shook the heavens.

Such actions were part of a plan drawn up by students and other educated people to calm the crowd. "Because the hearts of the people are
flooded with anger," they reasoned, "we don't know what they might
do at the public reading. Therefore, let us act as their representatives
and make an appeal lest something regrettable happens to our community." Along with two or three elders, they went about pacifying the
crowd. They explained, "We will plan everything for Zhou and present
an appeal for his life to the provincial governor and the provincial
governor censor. So don't do anything violent." The people approved
this request; burning incense, they followed Zhou on foot as he was
taken from the Wu county office westward to the guards compound.

Previously, when the magistrate of Wu county, Chen Wenrui, had
come to his house to take him away, Zhou had declared, "It is a great
pity that I was removed from the rolls of the officials and so barred from
making an appeal in front of the emperor. If, as a criminal, I could
present a memorial to the emperor, I could teach the evil eunuch faction
of Wei Zhongxian a lesson—that it is impossible to kill all the loyal officials of the empire." But now, when he saw this unanticipated action

by the people, he turned to them with a request that they disperse, even though he was moved by "the friends' love for me."

When the gates of the compound opened, the crowds of commoners squeezed in along with some five hundred students in their official dress. Inside there was a raised platform with drawn curtains and insignia. Zhang Yinglong and others took seats on the platform with the guardsmen standing around them. Before the platform there was also a pair of shackles set up at the place where the accused would prostrate himself.

One of the students, Wen Zhenheng, came forward and made an appeal directly to Mao Yilu, "Today when the feelings of the people are as you see, why is it that you alone do not want to have your name treasured by posterity? Why can't you send a memorial to the emperor telling him the facts and asking him in his vast and magnificent mercy to leave the matter in the hands of the provincial governor?"

Other students bared their sleeves and responded aloud to what Wen had said, "Everyone knows the cause for this incident. That's why we have asked you to handle this matter." While the crowd watched, the students conducted the negotiations, urging the officials to present a memorial calling for an imperial pardon of the innocent Zhou. By then the provincial governor and the provincial governor censor were standing in the mud, their shoulders rubbing against each other. Since many people crowded into the compound, there was no empty space left.

Finally the students raised the examples of the eunuch Wang Jing and his ministerial underling Wang Chen. When they had encountered resistence from the students of Suzhou in 1482, Wang Chen was eventually sentenced to death. His head was sent to those Lower Yangzi delta prefectures which had suffered from his misrule. Mao Yilu, however, expressed his contempt for the strength of their argument and to the force of their numbers. Insisting that he could not alter an imperial edict, he refused to respond to the substance of their questions.

This unproductive repetition of questions and answers dragged on into the afternoon. The guardsmen grumbled to one another, "What have those students come to do? Why doesn't the provincial governor tie them up?" Finally, they grew so impatient that they hurled chains on the ground and shouted out, "Where is the criminal? The officials of the Secret Service Office would never allow you rats to poke your noses about!"

At this point Yan Peiwei and others came forth from the crowd and challenged them, "Does the order come from the Imperial Court or from the Secret Service Office?" The guardsmen angrily replied, "Cut out their tongues right now! Where else would the order come from if not from the Secret Service Office?"

Upon hearing this, the crowd said, "What we are talking about is the edict of the Son of Heaven. Such a place as the Secret Service Office has no right to arrest our Zhou Shunchang." They raised their fists and were about to attack. Then, in the words of a contemporary account, "the entire crowd grew angry and were like a mountain landslide or a wave surging forth. The crowd crawled up on the railings, broke the shields, and boldly attacked." The guardsmen all fled, covering their heads with their hands. Some climbed the rafters of the building, others hid in outhouses, and yet others, not knowing where to go, camouflaged their heads with leaves. When discovered, they would bow their foreheads to the ground and plead for their lives. Those who fled over the fence were met by people with whips. Finally, one of the guardsmen, Li Guozhu, was killed.

Thinking that the incident had ended in failure, the students all left the site. At dusk, however, additional guardsmen passed through the Xuguan Gate of Suzhou, on their way by boat to Hangzhou to arrest Huang Zunsu. They ordered the customs officials to get food and drink for them at extortionately cheap prices in the market. But the shop-keepers caught and beat these officials and climbed up on the city wall shouting in all directions, "Some more guardsmen have arrived!" Immediately, crowds of people gathered and sank the boats, forcing the guardsmen to swim to the west bank where peasants were waiting to chase them with hoes.

The atmosphere remained tense. The crowds still wished to halt the arrest of Zhou Shunchang. Rumors flew about wildly, and some of them were posted on roadside boards. The magistrate, after consulting Zhou Shunchang, daringly stated that he would not allow him to be transported to the capital until the edict had been read aloud publicly. One night, however, he sent Zhou off in secret, and it was only long afterward that the crowds learned of his departure.

Meanwhile, Mao Yilu sent a notice to the surrounding counties and prefectures demanding the arrest of the ringleaders in this incident, Yan Peiwei and twelve other men. They were subsequently arrested and put into prison simply on the basis of hearsay evidence. One source says, "In the most extreme cases, some men who had left the city before the incident and returned only after it was over were also arrested." A very detailed investigation report was conjured up, and people were arrested to fit the details.

Among the arrested victims were five commoners. The son of a very rich merchant, Yan Peiwei had not cared for trade and so had become a "chivalrous man." Although he had no personal acquaintance with Zhou Shunchang, he had spent four days rushing about collecting money to save him. Ma Jie was reputedly a "powerful man," and every morning during the incident he had cracked his wooden clappers to assemble people, burn incense, and organize a procession. Yang Nianru was a cloth merchant from Chang Gate, the cotton-cloth calendering quarters located outside the Suzhou city walls. He, like another arrested commoner, the wholesaler Shen Yang, had never met Zhou. Finally, there was Zhou Wenyuan, a palanquin bearer for the family of Zhou Shunchang.

These men had no regrets, since they were dying for Zhou Shunchang, and they were ashamed to make any plea in their own defense. They cursed Mao Yilu, saying, "You are the one who has trapped Zhou Shunchang and will have him put to death. Even if your official position is high, your standing as a man is low. We, however, will die for Zhou, and even if our status is that of commoners, out status as men will be great."

In the sixth lunar month of 1626 Zhou Shunchang died in a Beijing prison. A month later Yan and his four fellow commoners were beheaded, and their heads put on public display in the city of Suzhou.

When first informed of the incident, Wei Zhongxian was extremely frightened. He had a member of the eunuch faction request the construction of a temple in his honor even though he was still alive—a so-called Living Shrine (*shengci*) and similar shrines were built throughout the empire.[39] Then in 1627 the Emperor Xizong died, to be succeeded by Yizong. Later that year, in the eleventh lunar month Wei Zhongxian was executed. In Suzhou, Wu Mo, Wen Zhenmeng, Yao Ximeng, and some other literati bought back the five victims' heads in exchange for 50 taels and had graves made for them on the site of the destroyed Living Shrine of Wei Zhongxian. They named the place "The Graves of the Five."[40]

Here I would like to examine the character of the Kaidu Incident, an archetype of the many protests that occurred after the arrests of Yang Lian, Zuo Guangdou, Li Yingsheng, and Huang Zunsu. In particular, I hope to demonstrate the critical role of the masses in such incidents. Three phenomena reveal the importance of mass action in the Kaidu Incident. First, throughout the entire incident the masses and the literati had consciously arranged a place to discuss the issues. Their occupation of the yamen for several days is one example of this kind of organization. Second, the students conducted hours of negotiations in which they criticized Wei Zhongxian, tried to persuade the provincial governor to release Zhou Shunchang, and presented their requests.

These actions were possible because of mass support. Third, in some senses the five commoners were sacrificial victims, since the eunuch faction hesitated to take sanctions against the students directly involved in the affair. This intimidation of the eunuch faction, further indicated in the guardsmen's fear of "leaving the gates of the capital," was a response to the unified protest by the masses.

What role did the literati play, and with what sense of consciousness did they participate in the incident? With the elders acting as intermediaries, the students hoped to persuade the masses to carry out their protest in a moderate manner. At the same time, the presence of the crowd protected the students and allowed time for their attempts at persuasion. Consequently, when the masses turned their backs on such moderate tactics, the students interpreted it to mean that their efforts had failed, and they dispersed.

Next, let us discuss the reaction of Zhou Shunchang to the incident. When he saw the mass actions on his behalf, he expressed his surprise at this unexpected development. It was said that later he wondered why he was respected and loved by the people. Doesn't such a reaction suggest that his sympathy for the masses was not based on concrete, individual dealings with them but rather was a reflection of the more abstract concern of the rulers for the ruled? Furthermore, his sense of righteousness, as revealed in his own past administrative career, had led him to exercise his feelings for the masses simply as the objects of administration.

Thus there was still a significant gap in understanding and sympathy between the literati and the masses. Nevertheless even more significant than the gap between these two groups was the fact that they both acted together. And indeed, we must ask why the people were willing to risk their lives on behalf of Zhou Shunchang, a man they had never even met. What then was the source of the temporary unity between the two groups in this incident? It must lie in the particular historical circumstances of seventeenth-century China.

Urban residents' movement: The early stage

In recent years Chinese scholars have engaged in a debate on the origins or "sprouts" of capitalism in China.[41] In the course of this controversy scholars have quite frequently shown an inadequate structural understanding of the origins of capitalism and have thus been too easily distracted by a pursuit of phenomena falsely identified as signs of incipient capitalism. In spite of these problems, this Chinese research has made an important contribution: it has drawn attention to the economic nature of the origins of capitalism as well as elucidating the resistance movement and the formation of class consciousness among peasants and direct producers in cities, which arose from the economic development of the sixteenth and seventeenth centuries. Peasant class consciousness developed during the rural resistance movement, consciously initiated by the peasants to achieve certain goals. In the cities, popular uprisings, or, as Chinese scholars have named them, "early urban residents' movements," fulfilled much the same role.

The Chinese expression *shimin,* meaning urban residents, is found in documentary sources predating the late Ming. Today Chinese historians have defined this concept according to the class distinctions made by Engels in his *Peasant War in Germany.* Engels divided the early-sixteenth-century urban residents of Germany into three classes. First, there was the urban patriciate, which was able to practice monopoly and usurious capitalism because of its privileged, aristocratic-like position. The urban patricians taxed transport as they wished and publicly engaged in fiscal misappropriation. Opposing this patriciate were two other urban classes. One was the comparatively affluent middle stratum of urban residents, who were educated, had some wealth, and wished to oppose legally and moderately the way the urban patriciate used personal connections to attain their political goals. Also belonging to this burgher class were less affluent urbanites whose proportion in the overall urban population varied according to local conditions. The other urban class opposed to the patriciate was that of the commoners, formed from the multifarious strands of the handicraft workers, the day laborers, as well as the huge "lumpen proletariat" which appeared even in these early stages of urban development.

Chinese scholars have argued that in Ming China the first of these two anti-aristocratic classes consisted of a part of the merchant stratum as well as a part of the literati—as represented by the Donglin party. The popular disturbances can thus be thought of as urban riots undertaken by the second oppostion group, the commoners. Chinese scholars have thus viewed these two opposition groups as expressions of the new class relations resulting from the development of both commodity-production and market circulation during the late Ming-early Qing period.

We must, however, pay attention to two points directly related to Engels' analysis. First, class relations, and thus class conflict at this time, as already seen in our discussion of the socioeconomic background of members of the Donglin party, were many-sided and quite varied. Second, there were certain limits on the role the burgher opposition could play in the late Ming. Among the literati, we see a variety of reactions to Qing rule which were expressive of the complex historical trends at that time of great upheaval. It is often said that some of the lower Yangzi delta literati, such as Gu Yanwu, Wang Fuzhi, Lü Liuliang, and Huang Zongxi (the son of Huang Zunsu), belonged to the burgher opposition; as outsiders, they opposed the Qing dynasty's rule and founded a tradition which formed the "Statecraft School" of the late Ming. However, from the Donglin party there also came such lower Yangzi delta literati as Qian Qianyi who submitted to Qing rule and served that dynasty as an official.[42] Yet another pattern was evident in the actions of Shi Kefa. A member of the Donglin party, he sacrificed his life at Yangzhou on behalf of the Ming nationalist resistance to the southward march of Qing troops. The same man, however, had already acquired a reputation as an enthusiastic suppressor of peasant rebellions.[43]

In the late Ming the immediate producers, positioned at the bottom of the complex class structure, did unite with other classes in protest movements. We have seen such an alliance in the Kaidu Incident, in which a coalition of peasants and urban commoners greatly frightened the guardsmen, and also in the hired silk workers' disturbance in Suzhou. Likewise, in the summer of 1645, 172,000 people, including peasants, sacrificed their lives at Jiangyin county in Jiangsu after an 81-day struggle against the Manchus.[44] A further example comes from Jiading county, Jiangsu province, where militia were organized in every district and managed to wage a two-month resistance against the Qing.[45] But in these and other such actions the extent to which the peasantry and the handicraft workers were able to join together in an alliance played a decisive role in determining the conditions of armed struggle; when they were able to ally, it was possible, if only temporarily, to overcome the contradictions between the literati and the other classes, and they were able to join together in opposing Ming rule and the invading Manchu troops. The historical importance of these developments cannot be judged merely by the outcome of individual struggles. Rather, we must evaluate the historical significance and consequences of this entire series of struggles as one total process.

Rent resistance struggles and bondservant revolts

The popular uprisings of handicraft workers in the cities of the late Ming did not erupt accidentally. Rather, they were the inevitable results of the increase in the numbers of urban handicraft workers which accompanied the development of commodity production in many parts of China. The development of urban commerce and industry was linked to the development of commodity production in the villages, especially those in the lower Yangzi delta. Then the development of commodity-production in rural areas in turn intensified the social contradictions within the villages; and not surprisingly this tendency gave rise to peasant struggles, just as it had caused popular uprisings in the cities. These rural struggles were of two types—bondservant disturbances and rent resistance struggles. They are grouped together in this section because they often occurred together and were closely related to each other. I am particularly interested in the reasons for their frequent occurrence in the sixteenth and seventeenth centuries.

Bondservant uprisings

First, we must answer a few questions about the existence and conditions of bondservants (*nupu*)* during the period: What was their social position? Were they the basic direct producers in premodern Chinese society?

It is clear that bondservant status was a legal status during the late Ming and early Qing: signs of this fact are evident in every aspect of the society. In fact, the legal status of bondservant was abolished only at the close of the Qing, in 1909. Holders of this status were called by a variety of terms all meaning bondservant (*nubi, nupu, tongnu, tongpu*); in addition, they were given names which translate literally as family member (*jiaren*), family servant (*jianu, jiapu, jiatong*), adopted son (*yinan*), and adopted daughter (*yifu*). The names suggest that they were domestic bondservants who did not engage in productive labor. However, our major questions—Were bondservants the basic direct producers, and was China at that time a slave society?—have to be considered from a non-legal viewpoint; they must be treated in terms of the structure of production and *class* relations.

Men became bondservants through sale, gift, or commendation of themselves to their master's family under economic and social condi-

---

* The proper understanding and translation of this key term *nupu* is a matter of great controversy. After some deliberation I have agreed to the translation "bondservant" with the understanding that the servile groups here discussed as *nupu* can be considered as one kind of "slave," if one takes "slave" in a very broad sense as a dependent in servitude to another. I have refrained from using "slave" lest English readers think that Ming *nupu* were identical to the slaves of classical Greece and Rome, who were treated as objects and forbidden to marry and have families.

tions we shall discuss below. Others were driven by debt into bondservitude. As a rule, bondage was not restricted to just one generation; a bondservant held a hereditary status which essentially entailed master-servant relations. Yet many a bondservant took on the name of his master's family, and the nature of the bondservant's servitude and his relationship to his master and his family were shaped by his placement within a strong patriarchal system.

In agriculture, the basic occupation, tenant farming was widely practiced, particularly in southern and central China. In order to control their tenants and collect rent, some landowners used bondservants as their agents; they were called bondservant managers (*jigang zhi pu*). Bondservants were also used to farm land under direct managerial supervision of the owner. Bondservants were used in these ways most commonly in the houses of literati and in private family-run enterprises. Some officials retained over a thousand bondservants, sometimes having letters and official memorials written by, as contemporaries often called them, "brazen" servants (*haonu*).

As a group, however, these bondservants had two special features. First, some modern Japanese legal scholars have regarded the character of bondservants in China from early times as half-human and half-object. Because bondservants were given the right to have their own possessions and families, a great gap in wealth and economic position arose between the bondservants who owned nothing and could be used without restraint by their master and "brazen" servants, such as the bondservant managers, who were often able to acquire considerable wealth. In short, not all bondservants shared identical class interests.

Second, the increase in land tax, labor service, or tenancy fee exploitation, as well as the encroachment of merchant capital and usurious moneylenders on peasant production drove an ever greater number of small, independent farmers into debt and thus into debt bondage. Of course, not all debtors suffered permanent purchase or were forced into permanent debt enthrallment; nor were all debtors invariably transformed into bondservants. Rather, it can be assumed that there were many temporary debt bondservants with some autonomy who could redeem themselves through their work or, as had been agreed to in the original purchase, buy back their freedom.[46] Accordingly, those indentured servants who did not fall into the bondservant status seem despite their debt to have been no different in form from hired laborers who had, as it were, "given themselves over on loan."[47]

Bondservant uprisings: The role of tenants and hired laborers

In his *Rizhi lu* (Record of things learned daily) the noted scholar Gu Yanwu wrote, "In the Suzhou area bondservants are especially numerous, and their high-handed arrogance extremely cruel."[48] During the Ming-Qing transition years, especially in 1644 and 1645, and on into the early Qing such bondservants rebelled in the Suzhou counties of Jiading, Kunshan, Wusong, and Nanxiang. Bondservant uprisings erupted elsewhere in the lower Yangzi delta in Yixing county (Changzhou prefecture), Shanghai county (Songjiang prefecture), Chongde county (Jiaxing prefecture), Liyang and Jinling counties (Jiangning prefecture) and Taicangzhou. And north of the mouth of the Yangzi there were uprisings in Taizhou (Yangzhou prefecture). Similar insurrections occurred in Huizhou (Anhui), Guangzhou (Guangdong), and Quanzhou (Fujian), and in the three counties of Guangshan, Shangcheng, and Gushi in Runing prefecture (Henan).[49]

Among the incidents categorized as bondservant disturbances, two mutually distinct trends are evident. The first type of bondservant disturbance consists of cases in which several thousand bondservants in the employ of large and affluent clans, such as those of Qian Qianyi and Qu Shisi, relied on their master's power to back up their arrogant behavior toward the general populace. Or, it refers to incidents whereby such powerful brazen servants harmed their old master and commended themselves to a new master.[50] These cases reveal the power of bondservants who had economically transcended their bondservant status. Since their uprisings were not directly aimed at their liberation from bondservant status, these incidents must be clearly distinguished from the other type of bondservant uprising.

This second type occurred when bondservants rebelled in order to free themselves from their bondservant status and to destroy any proof that they had been sold into bondage. These incidents were the real bondservant rebellions, rebellions of class and status. They appear to have been concentrated in that period of anarchy brought on by the dynastic transition from Ming to Qing rule. An example of this second type of bondservant rebellion expressing the bondservants' motivation and growth as a class was the insurrection which erupted in Yi county, Huizhou, in 1645.[51]

A bondservant named Song Qi led several thousand fellow bondservants in Yi county in rebellion and built armed fortresses. This struggle then spread as far as Xiuning county in Huizhou. Over a hundred literati were killed, and almost all the households of great and middling wealth were attacked so that in the end almost no families dared to claim to be scholar-officials. At the start of the uprising Song Qi addressed his bondservant followers: "Ever since my grandfather became a bondservant, his descendants have been registered as bondservants, and we have been unable to cast ourselves free of these registers. Now we have a chance to do so, a chance given us by heaven. Our masters are all weak and cannot be expected to fight back."[52] He then announced his goal: "The emperor of the earlier dynasty has been replaced. Our masters also should become servants and serve us."[53] He demanded relations not of master to servant but of elder brother to younger brother for himself and his fellow bondservants. This incident expresses in archetypical fashion both the motivation of the second type of bondservant disturbance and the growth of bondservants as a class pursuing specific goals.

It is difficult to define the background or the motivations of the participants in the bondservant disturbances in simple terms. First, as a result of the considerable variation in types of bondservant status, there were some bondservant disturbances in which not all bondservants would join. The clearest example of such limited struggles is the first type of bondservant disturbance described above—the type generated by powerful and wealthy bondservants against their relatively weak masters. Second, the second type of "real" bondservant struggle was not necessarily generated by lower-status bondservants alone. Tenants and hired laborers, whose class interests, though not their legal status, were identical to those of the bondservants, often joined the bondservant disturbances.

In the agricultural as in the handicraft sector the use of hired labor had become quite common. Some hired laborers lent themselves out for labor, and as a result hired labor sometimes formally bore some features of indentured labor. However, labor was usually, even if only as a matter of form, sold on the labor market, and hired labor became a status with a greater degree of independence than that enjoyed by bondservants. With the emergence of such a hired-labor status, bondservants gradually gained a similar degree of independence. Through their struggles, they hoped eventually to change their legal status completely. However, it should be noted that these bondservant rebellions were inspired by the fundamental struggle of tenants against landlords, and as such the direct participation of relatively independent hired laborers and tenants in the bondservant disturbances merely serves to highlight this trend and does not indicate that the participation of tenants and independent hired laborers was essential for their success.

The 1658 bondservant uprising in Runing prefecture (Henan) provides an example both of tenant and hired-laborer participation in a bondservant disturbance and of the complex problem of motives that underlay many of these disturbances.[54] In Guangshan county a rumor spread that an imperial edict had been issued allowing for the manumission of bondservants. Assembling in crowds, the bondservants took up arms and pressed for the destruction of any evidence of their subjugation to their masters. The uprising then spread to Shangcheng and Gushi counties.

If we rely on the report of Jin Changzhen, the official who suppressed this rebellion, four types of motivation are evident among the participants in the uprising. First, there were those bondservants who had commended themselves out of self-interest and who were now trying to change masters. This motive is similar to ones most commonly expressed in the first type of bondservant disturbances, the opportunistic uprising of already powerful bondservants greedy for more wealth. Second, there were bondservants who had fallen involuntarily into the hands of local strongmen (*tuhao*) and who were now demanding their release: this motive is close to that of the second type of "real" bondservant disturbances and is an indication of the new power attained by bondservants. Third, there were hired laborers who upon the termination of their duties as indentured servants were sought by their masters as "renegade" bondservants; they rebelled rather than be forced to return to their masters. Fourth, there were tenants, who, though they had originally stood in a junior-senior relationship to their master, were now together with their families treated as bondservants; and so they too rebelled. Jin Changzhen is particularly sympathetic to these last two motives; he is quite critical of masters who treated their tenants or hired laborers as bondservants. At any rate, it is clear that the 1658 bondservant uprising arose from many different demands put forth by several different groups, including but also extending beyond the bondservants. The unity of all these forces at that time reveals the real power of the bondservants despite the limitations of their status as well as the determination of the tenants and hired laborers to gain the legal rights to which they were entitled.

Rebellion of 1645 (*Yiyou zhi luan*)

Bondservant uprisings often include such complex factors as class antagonism within the bondservant status, the integration of people from lower classes with small bondservants (*xiaonu*) through secret societies.

The 1645 rebellion is a case in point. In 1645 a bondservant Yu Boxiang in Taicang (southern Jiangsu) was the ringleader in plots against his rich and eminent master, the Wang family.[55] Believing that the change of dynasty meant that bondservants could expect to become free men (*liangren*), he called for them to recover any evidence of their sale into servitude. Thousands of bondservants responded to his cry, attacked their masters' houses, took whatever evidence they found of their bondage, set the houses on fire, and sometimes even tied up their masters. These bondservants were so consumed with bitterness over their past sufferings and by their desire for freedom that they did not allow personal compassion for the masters to stand in their way. They raised their hate-filled voices like tigers and wolves, and even forced the young maidservants working alongside their masters to join their ranks.

The rebellion spread from the town of Taicang to every market town and village in the area. Every day several thousand men engaged in murder, arson, and plunder. After several days, Yu Boxiang wanted to inscribe the accomplishments of the uprising on a stone tablet, so that the improvements in their status would be remembered by later generations. He appealed to the officials to establish a law restricting bondservant status to a single generation. However, Yu Boxiang was killed, and the rebellion merged with the uprising of the Black Dragon Association (*Wulonghui*), led by Gu Zhenqing, a bondservant of the Xu family, a local family with official status.[56] With a membership of several thousand, the Black Dragon Association was a society of bondservants and urban hired laborers who worked as vegetable sellers. During their uprising the lower-strata elements in the society seized the wealth of a certain Jin Mengtiao, a brazen bondservant of the same Xu family.

The secret society is often considered an antisocial and reactionary form of organization, but here the Black Dragon Association was the instrument of liberation for bondservants who otherwise could not have easily freed themselves from their status. Of course the role of secret societies is not always progressive, and the form of organization often functions in a reactionary way depending upon the historical circumstances. In a period when Chinese society was in the process of disintegration, with a greatly increased number of propertyless people there was always the potential for secret societies to play a vital role by organizing displaced people for the struggle against the old order.

The historical significance of the bondservant disturbances

The rich families learned a costly lesson from the violence of the bondservant disturbances, and they stopped using bondservants for a time. However, it is not enough to consider merely the short-term result of the rebellions. Rather, our evaluation of the historical significance of the bondservant disturbances must deal, once again, with the nature of the participants in these rebellions.

In the bondservant rebellions discussed above hereditary bondservants were the major participants, although several other social strata were also involved. These include the brazen servants, whose bondservant status was hereditary but who did not directly participate in what I have termed the real bondservant rebellions. Second were those tenants who, while holding the legal status of free men, had fallen into a bondservant-like relationship with their masters, each with its own special and individual conditions. Third were those hired laborers who likewise had a free legal status but actually suffered bondservant-like conditions. Fourth were the comparatively free tenants and hired laborers who were struggling to avoid payment of heavy rent and to raise their class position; even if they were not direct participants in these bondservant rebellions, they were on the outer perimeters. Fifth were the small peasants and handicraft workers driven by debt into temporary, non-hereditary servitude; they likewise were on the outer fringes of the rebellions.

In such a case as the 1645 rebellion, if the real bondservant uprisings are to be considered attempts by bondservants to abolish the legal existence of their status—not as blind outbreaks of violence or as efforts by individuals to liberate themselves from the bondservant status—then we can judge these uprisings to have been class struggles. Indeed, the presence of some comparatively free tenants and hired laborers and the example of temporary, changeable debt-bondage relations in the same age must have provided practical and attainable goals for those bondservants bound and fixed into permanent bondservant status. Such aspirations are evident, for example, in the demand for "order by seniority" among free men made by the bondservants in the 1645 rebellion in Yi county, Huizhou.

Unfortunately we lack the sources to show the concrete historical process of the tenants' and hired laborers' liberation from their servitude. However, we know that from the middle of the Ming on there had been two general changes in landlord-tenant relations. First, there were two types of absentee gentry; those that were officials, and those that made a living from high-interest loans and commerce. Second, there was a decline in landlord management of their own land—in other words, landlords switched from the use of bondservant labor to the use of hired labor in their farm management. Such a trend is perhaps evident in the decision by Zhang Lixiang, an archetype late-Ming and early-Qing managerial landlord, to free his bondservants and purchase no others. Confronted with the disappearance of obedient, "good" bondservants, he felt he had no alternative.[57]

If some bondservants in the late Ming and early Qing appear to have liberated themselves individually through disturbances, then why was the legal status of bondservant not entirely abolished? We must not explain this question away with the argument that bondservants were too weak to make their rebellions succeed. Rather, it is the structural character of Chinese society at that time, in which the status of bondservants could not be easily discarded, that must be examined.

The practice of commendation (*toukao*) helps us to understand some of the complexity of this issue. In his *Rizhi lu* Gu Yanwu wrote, "at present many literati in the lower Yangzi delta (Jiangnan) have the custom of keeping many bondservants. Once a literatus embarks on an official career, as many as a thousand men vie to assemble under his wing. This is called commendation."[58] Also, He Liangjun, a member of the rural gentry in neighboring Songjiang prefecture, wrote in 1569: "During the past forty or fifty years the taxes have increased daily, and the labor service duties have grown heavier by the day. The people cannot endure them, and they have all changed their occupations. Whereas formerly the rural gentry did not have so many bondservants, now ten times as many peasants as before leave agriculture to become bondservants to the gentry."[59]

Commendation was practiced to acquire wealth or avoid exploitation. For instance, Xu Yikui in his account "A silk worker answers" (*zhigongdui*) relates that a highly skilled silk worker who had been receiving twice the pay of other silk workers sought wealth by becoming a bondservant to a great official in the 1350s.[60] Other men commended themselves as bondservants to local gentry in order to escape exploitation by landlords and usurious moneylenders as well as the burdens of taxes and labor services.

If we add to such practices of commendation the fall of men into bondservant status due to debt, then we can see that there would be bondservants as long as the exploitative system of control by landlords and despotic government existed. The general liberation of the bondservants would be possible only with the overthrow of the system of which they were a natural by-product. Not surprisingly, contradictions arose among bondservants in their liberation struggles: sometimes the demands made during the struggles benefited only those brazen servants who were taking advantage of their masters' power; sometimes peasants could escape exploitation only by commending themselves to a master as a bondservant. As a result of this situation, the "real" struggle of bondservants for liberation could only succeed by collaborating with the rent resistance struggle of tenants who were striving in an uncompromising way to oppose those systematically controlling them—the landlord stratum (possibly, concurrently the bondservant masters), including the gentry, merchants and usurious moneylenders, and the despotic state which was linked to the landlord stratum.

Rent resistance struggles

From the latter half of the twelfth century tenants in the lower Yangzi delta had at various times opposed the payment of rent. Some tenants had even attacked and burned landlord residences and killed their occupants as part of their protests against rent payment. Other tenants had risked their lives fighting government troops dispatched in response to landlord appeals to pressure tenants who had fallen behind in their rent payments. From the mid-fifteenth century, and even more so in the late Ming and early Qing, such struggles occurred everywhere, but the greatest concentration of them was in the lower Yangzi delta.

Tenants, of course, have resisted paying rent for as long as landlords have been exploiting them. But from the mid-Ming on, rent resistance became much more frequent. The nature and quality of tenant resistance also changed. In order to define this change, we must look at the types of tenant demands, and their relationship with contemporary social changes, particularly that of the landlord-tenant relationship.

In discussing tenant resistance to landlords we must realize that "tenant" (*dianhu*) is a general term with meanings that vary over both time and place with everyday speech and historical documents. The Japanese term, *kosakunin*, commonly used to define "tenant," is inadequate as it merely refers to a managerial category which existed throughout Chinese history. The real conditions of a tenant are defined by his particular social relationships, relationships that varied widely from period to period. In the case of the tenants of the late Ming and early Qing, these social relationships were the relations of production and rent payment between tenant and landlords.

Antagonistic landlord-tenant relationships were expressed most plainly in the rent resistance struggles. Therefore, by examining the factors in the development of specific rent resistance struggles, we should be able to characterize the changes in the landlord-tenant relationship and in the meaning of tenant over time. The advantage of this method of using the rent resistance movement to define the term "tenant" is that it will reveal not only the nature of the tenant status in a particular period (here the late Ming and early Qing), but also the very way it developed. Let us keep in mind as we look at the concrete descriptions of rent resistance struggles below that these define both the actual situation of the tenant and the process by which the tenant reached that particular stage of development in history.

The rebellion of Deng Maoqi

In his miscellany *Nancun chuogenglu* (Writing and cultivating in Nancun), Tao Zongyi tells of a tenant who in the late Yuan tried to pawn the cultivation rights to a plot of land he had been renting.[61] A precondition of this practice, we can see, was a general recognition of a tenant's ownership of cultivation rights. But the earliest clear-cut example of tenants rising to oppose the payment of rent and to consciously assert a peasant-like claim to the land they cultivated occurred about a century later, in 1448 and 1449, when the rebellion of Deng Maoqi shook the province of Fujian.[62]

By that time the Ming dynasty had passed through its formative period and eunuchs had come to dominate court politics. Economically, an important trend was the increased use of silver. The circulation of silver which was later officially formalized with the adoption of the fiscal policy known as the Single Whip reform had only just begun to be used in the tax system with the establishment of the category of gold floral silver (*jinhuayin*). This early form of silver tax was instituted in response to the demands of military officials who wanted to be paid in silver rather than rice. Thus, although the Ming strove to suppress the circulation of silver through its emphasis on agriculture, the court and officials were caught up in the commodity economy and their need for silver by necessity led to the promotion of its usage. The silver deposits scattered throughout southern Zhejiang and northern Fujian were alternately opened and closed. Officials anxious to take advantage of this splendid opportunity to make a fortune paid bribes to eunuchs to get on-site assignments to the silver mines. There in office as silver mine operators and as tax collectors, they extorted silver from the mines, the miners, and the peasantry.

Some mine managers were dismissed as a result of these officials' monopolization of the mining enterprises, and they soon led their workers away to become "mine bandits" (*kuangzei*), roving about the mountains in search of mines to manage and work illegally for a profit. Poisonous mineral extracts seeped out of the officially run silver mines and destroyed the nearby fields. Men driven into vagrancy by such conditions and by officials' labor-service extortions joined up with the mine bandits. At first these groups conducted what were clearly simply bandit raids; but over time these raids developed, like the rebellion of the mine bandit Ye Zongliu, into struggles against the authorities.[63]

What then of the peasantry? Ever since the middle of the Tang dynasty an increasing number of migrants had moved from Zhejiang as well as from the North China plain to Fujian. By the end of the thirteenth century, Fujian was so fully developed that "its land was cramped and its population dense." Simple peasant commodity production had flourished there quite early; Fujian peasants specialized in such products as sugar cane, indigo, tea, lichees, paper, and hemp cloth. And as commerce also developed, peasants came to rely more and more on usurious loans to maintain their livelihood. This control by merchant and usurious capital was reflected also in landownership patterns. In the late Yuan fifty to sixty families owned 83 percent of the arable land in Chong'an county (Jianning prefecture), and they had others tenant it for them. The remaining 17 percent of the land was owned by some four hundred independent farmers.[64] A century later, in 1449, most of the farmland in Jianyang county of the same prefecture was reportedly owned by absentee landlords.[65] In addition to a high rent delivered personally to their landlord, the tenants were obliged to pay a supplementary rent, called the winter gift (*dongsheng*), in the form of firewood rice, chickens, or ducks.[66]

It is in the context of this potentially explosive economic situation that the exploitation of the silver mines and the miners became particularly dangerous for the security of the area. The central government should have carefully supervised the official managers of the silver mines and the officials who controlled the peasantry. Instead, it supported these officials and tried to repress the inevitable rebellions against their exploitation. As part of its policy toward the mine bandits the government had the peasants armed and organized into self-police groups through the comprehensive *jia* (*zongjia*) and small *jia* (*xiaojia*). To a certain degree it bestowed authority upon the heads of these units. Ironically, it was the establishment of this self-police system that stimulated the rebellion of 1645.

In the twenty-fourth ward (*du*) of Sha county in Yanping prefecture two of those appointed to the comprehensive *jia* were Deng Maoqi and his younger brother Deng Maoba. Using his position to present tenant demands, Deng Maoqi advocated the complete abolition of the tenants' traditional winter gift to the landlord. In 1447 he actually implemented this proposal and further demanded that the absentee landlords should come themselves to collect the rent due from the tenants. The landlords refused and attempted to have Deng Maoqi arrested. In the second lunar month of 1448 the tenants rose up to protect Deng, killing the magistrate and the chief of the county police. The tenants wasted much time in presenting their demands to the authorities, and by the seventh lunar month their protest had developed into a full-scale military conflict.

As might be expected of a centralized autocratic state, the Ming government dispatched its army to the rescue of the officials and the landlords. Prior to this, the peasantry, armed and organized under the comprehensive *jia* system, had crushed the government troops stationed in the area. They had taken over the two county seats of Sha and Youxi and pressed to the foot of the city walls of Yanping. One man then came forth from among the peasant army. Looking up at the city wall, he appealed to the officials within: "We are all good men, but we are pained and exhausted by the rich. Also, the officials of our county have shown no concern for us, and we have had no place to present our appeals. We were compelled to break the law by organizing our bands. Please intercede for us with the imperial court. If it shows generosity, we will immediately disband."[67] After some hesitation he later returned to make another appeal: "Our family wealth is depleted. Please give us three years of exemption from government labor services. For the sake of the country please let us live." It is significant that this request for a three-year exemption from labor services was put forth by tenants resisting their landlords. It would seem that these tenants were actually bearing the burden of the labor services and perhaps even of land taxes, in place of their landlords (although no contemporary source explicitly mentions either practice).

Upon receiving reports of these requests, the emperor accepted this appeal as an apology and decided to exempt the protesters from government service for three years and from payment of overdue taxes. But because of the stubborn attitude of the officials on the scene, the negotiations between the rebels and the government completely broke down in the tenth lunar month of the same year. Deng Maoqi, calling himself the "Evil eliminating king" (*chanping wang*), conferred military posts on his subordinates, strove to reorganize them under his leadership, and then fought. Wherever peasants were suffering similar conditions, they rose in rebellion. Their force totaled several hundred thousand, and the names of the leaders we know of today amount to thirty.

All of Fujian was turned into a battlefield for guerilla war. Tenant soldiers breached the walls of county seats with the aid of ladders attached to chariots.[68] Tenants also snatched the tax registers and the household registers of the county offices. The central government retaliated by dispatching more than 20,000 troops from the five armies, cannon troops from the miraculous garrison (*shenjiying*) in Beijing, and 27,000 grain-tax transport troops from Jiangxi and Zhejiang, in addition to a total of 6,000 other government troops from both Zhejiang and Jiangxi. Reportedly, only 20,000-odd troops remained in Nanjing.[69]

In the second lunar month of 1449 Deng Maoqi was killed in Yanping prefecture. However, his followers' resistance continued long enough to overlap with the Mongol capture of the Emperor Yingzong in the ninth lunar month, 1449, and so further disrupt Ming rule.

Deng Maoqi had underestimated the power of the centralized autocracy. He had not understood that the throne would back the the landlords and the local officials, and that his revolt against them would be considered an act of treason against the emperor. In fact, he had expected to receive the warm sympathy of the emperor himself. By repeatedly seeking government understanding he had given the central government time to come to the rescue of the local officials and landlords. Also, his actions were restricted by his narrow, fixed, peasant concern with the local area. Consequently, he did not seize control of the strategic nodes of transport and military movements. Lacking close ties with friendly powers, his army suffered everywhere from the self-defense resistance led by the landlords. The absentee landlords, composed of literati or powerful families were able to use their own funds to supply their armies. (They issued 1000 to 2000 *shi* of rice as supplies for the army.) They were able to recruit their armies from local militia and family servants to fight the peasant army. Attacked from all sides and shattered by the landlords' self-defense forces, the peasants had to contend with support for the landlords not simply from the government troops but also from the village elders in charge of government labor services (*lilaoren*) who also organized resistance to them. It was the treachery of a village elder in the peasant army that led to the defeat of Deng Maoqi's successor, his elder cousin Deng Bosun.[70]

Although the rebellion of Deng Maoqi had many limitations—that was of course unavoidable—it was nonetheless a part of the long struggle toward a new period in Chinese history. Deng's anti-rent peasant struggle was the first great rebellion in Chinese history genuinely led by the tenants themselves that approaches the concept of peasant war.*

* The term peasant war is used with Engels' *The Peasant War in Germany* in mind.—Trans.

Rent resistance struggles in the late Ming and early Qing

In the tenth month of 1638, Tang Zuogeng, Wang Si, Li Nanzhou, Cha Xian, and Han Foshou, under the pretext of having suffered damage from a locust attack, assembled a crowd of residents from some thirty villages around the shores of Lake Tai in Wu county, Suzhou. They killed a sacrificial beast, took an oath to a god, chose one leader for each village, and recorded the names of those present. They exchanged an agreement that they would not pay rent to their landlords and that if the landlords or some representatives came to collect rent, they would sink their boats and kill them. Subsequently, they took up arms, sounded the bells and great drums, burned the landlords' houses and confiscated their wealth.[71]

This incident is but one example of the numerous anti-rent struggles in Suzhou prefecture. From the sixteenth and seventeenth centuries onward such incidents were common in the provinces of Jiangsu, Zhejiang, Fujian, Huguang, and Henan. Finally, in the mid-eighteenth century it was said that "the refusal of Suzhou tenants to pay rent had become so endemic,"[72] that it reportedly made the landlords complain that "it is better to have good tenants than good land."[73]

In the great tide of late Ming-early Qing protests against the payment of rent one can discern some common features. Most notably, the tenants consciously made certain specific demands. The first of these demands, as seen in the rebellion of Deng Maoqi, was the abolition of supplementary rents and attendant labor services. Second, as seen in the rent resistance movement of the Grain Measure Society (*Doulaohui*) of Fujian,[74] they demanded that grain measures be corrected and made uniform; previously their size had varied considerably according to place, landlord, and tenant. Third, they sought a reduction in rent (normally half or more of the crop or its commuted form in a fixed amount). Fourth, they refused to pay rent. This resulted in the tendency to reject the landlord's ownership claims and the very existence of a landlord-tenant relationship. These protests differed from the temporary and unplanned rent resistance outbreaks of the Southern Song, since the late-Ming and early-Qing tenants organized their protests and systematically planned their demands. A protest against rent payment including these four demands could occur only after tenants had secured cultivation rights and acquired a high degree of independence.[75]

A second feature common to these rent resistance protests was the

manner in which the demands were made. They were made with
rational arguments, as when the peasant Huang Tong compared the
size of grain measures and presented his findings in the anti-rent
protest in Ninghua county in Fujian in 1646.[76] Furthermore, the tenants
submitted their demands not only to the landlords but also to the local
officials. Finally, these demands were the outgrowth of a pact already
made by the peasants themselves.

Third, we can notice a common method of struggle. As was evident
from the persistence of the Grain Measure Society, the tenants had
a permanent organization. This tenant organization, as we can see in
the example from Wu county (Suzhou prefecture), was based on the
village unit; tenant leagues were formed among different villages.
Landlord's estates were not geographically contiguous; they were so
scattered that often the tenants in a village had different landlords.
The organization of struggles based on the village unit or a league of
villages indicates the existence of territorial alliances which arose
among tenants with different masters. Alliances were often based on
irrigation labor and other activities in the village. Such ties indicate
that some class solidarity had developed among the tenants. These
ties were also the precondition for mutual cooperation among tenants
for the formation of such associations as the Grain Measure Society.
Of Wuqing market town, located on the border between Jiaxing and
Huzhou prefectures, in the mid-eighteenth century it was said:

Recently a cunning practice has gained currency among the tenants.
Even if their crop is fine, they try to keep the rent payment as small
as possible. Whenever there is even a slight drought or flood, they form
a union of polders and hamlets (lianyu jiejia) to resist rent payment.
They secretly discuss and decide the amount of rent they should
pay and solidify their mutual unity by showing plays and making
contracts and pacts. If they discover anyone paying rent over and
above the amount they have decided among themselves, sly members
of the group form a band to go to make a din at the offender's home,
reproaching him for going against the group's wishes and secretly
bringing disaster upon him if he remains disobedient.[77]

Such neighborhood communities (kyōdōtai), formed by tenants who
were becoming increasingly independent and united by the need to
engage in common work such as irrigation to maintain reproduction
on their own land, were behind the tenants' refusal to pay rent.

In response, the landlords colluded with the lowest-level officials
in order to strengthen their collective power.[78] In the late Ming and
early Qing, as the class opposition between the tenants and the land-

lords became sharper, alliances between local power-holders and the lowest level of the bureaucracy were forged. The two groups were part of a mutually dependent structure. This development meant that landlord control of the peasantry was based on the state's material support for the structure of reproduction in the village.

The historical significance of rent resistance struggles

In the late Ming and early Qing some tenants sold for personal profit grain that should have been used to pay rent. Others concealed their good rice and paid rent with poor rice, and yet others threatened the landlord with violence. We find in the sources such phrases as "stubborn tenants refuse to pay rent" and "the crafty tenants refuse to pay rent" (diaodian kangzu). During the late Ming and early Qing these peasants were not called "stubborn tenants," because of rent resistance struggles due to famine, natural disaster, or an individual landlord's extortion. Rather it was their daily stand against the landlords that won them such epithets as "stubborn," "bad," "deceitful," and "field overlords." This intensified opposition between tenants and landlords had grown out of broad social changes in the late Ming, in particular, the development of productive forces which had increased the surplus product of the tenants and so prompted even harsher exploitation by the landlords. By the seventeenth century rent resistance and other struggles against the landlords had become part of the daily life of many tenants.

As we have already seen, in the villages of central and southern China, particularly in the lower Yangzi delta, both domestic handicraft production and the planting of cash crops developed from the mid-Ming onward. The 1612 gazetteer for Quanzhou prefecture (Fujian) describes how the system of cash crops tended to encourage rent resistance: "The tenants in the morning go out to the fields to bring in the harvest, and in the evening they go off to the town to sell their crops to the merchants. The situation has reached the stage that tenants made pacts among themselves beforehand not to pay rent to their landlords [in order to maximize their profits from the market]."[79]

The 1879 Shimen county gazetteer explains the situation in Chongde county in Jiaxing prefecture in the late Ming:

Harvest on paddy fields is only sufficient to provide food for eight months of the year. For the remaining months, rice is obtained primarily through purchase. The meeting of both public and private obligations depends largely on the profits from silkworms. Therefore, sericulture is most important. Loan contracts are always drawn up with a repayment date at the end of the silkworm season. Therefore, at the time of the quota for the autumn tax assessment, many are unwilling to turn over their salable rice, thinking that perhaps as days pass the price of rice will rise. Ordinarily rice is pawned at a pawnshop for silver; after the silkworms have matured, the profits are used to reclaim it. Therefore in paying taxes the people depend on the profit from silkworms; they do not depend on the profit from paddy fields.[80]

Thus tenants acquired currency by selling their surplus products which had grown as the results of the development of productive forces or by speculating and investing part of their produce in the market. However, it was hard for them to save cash except to cover the family budget, since merchants exploited them when purchasing their products and their surplus produce went to pay back usurious loans. When confronted with early forms of merchant monopoly, where did landlords and tenants stand? An answer is found in the 1596 gazetteer for Xiushui county in Jiaxing prefecture, Zhejiang:

Previously when grain was already harvested and the barley sown rich peasants would submit the fixed tax to the officials and store a little away in the granary as reserve. Tenants paid rent to big households and kept what was left over for the spring planting [the following year]. Everyone was pleased with this arrangement. Recently, wealthy merchants have instituted rice mortgaging *(midian)*. Tenants pawn their best rice for silver, separately allotting lower- and middle-quality rice for rent. Even in years of plenty they claim a bad harvest, procrastinating and neglecting rent payments. A little while ago crafty people assembled mobs *(dang)* every day on the banks of the Tiao river to swear mutual oaths not to pay rent to the big households. Though it has eased off a bit lately, this practice is gradually coming to be regular custom. Officials press for the taxes with great urgency but take no notice of those who pay the rent. Thereupon landlords have to borrow to meet their obligations with the officials and are harmed as a result of it. Small peasants obtain silver from mortgaging merchants *(dianshang)* and squander it. Subsequently, they find it difficult to fill their tax quota. Later the profit goes to the mortgaging merchant. Tenants are also ruined because debts are neglected and accumulate day after day. If both the landlord and tenant come to harm, how will the shortage in the granaries be filled and how can the villages not be poor?[81]

In short, the tenants' surplus products are snatched away by merchant capital through exploitation when purchasing and through high interset loans, or by "landlordification" of the merchants.* Three conditions aggravated the contradictions between the exploiters consisting of landlords and merchants, and the immediate producers, the tenants: the growing power of tenants due to the rise in the forces of production, and the increasing exploitation of tenants both by merchants who purchased tenants' products at a low price and offered them usurious loans, and by landlords whose exploitation had also been able to increase as a result of the rise in the tenants' level of production. Under these circumstances it is not surprising that tenant rent resistance became more common.

From the mid-Ming onward the dual ownership system of land tenure (literally, "two masters on one field," *yitian liangzhu*) spread throughout the paddy-field areas of south and central China, such as Jiangsu, Zhejiang, Fujian, and Guangdong provinces.[82] This development occurred at the same time and in the same places as the rent resistance struggles. There was clearly an internal relationship between them, but it was more subtle and complex than a cause-effect relationship. Tenant's cultivation rights had matured into permanent tenancy rights, so his right to the land surface represented a definite material right. It was the acquisition of such a right which made the tenant such an important figure in the interconnected developments of the forces of production of commodity production and of the rent resistance movement. But this right to land surface was not necessarily preserved by the tenants as a fixed or constant right for the immediate producers themselves. Often it was sold and mortgaged after being used as collateral for usurious loans from merchants and usurious moneylenders. Just as certain merchants accumulated wealth through their ownership of rice pawnshops, so others made their fortunes through their acquisition of land surface rights. Merchants became landlords accepting the rents acquired from land surface rights as interest on loans.

However, we should not be sidetracked here by individual examples of how much merchants were able to appropriate surface rights and use them as a means of parasitic rent collection just at a time when tenants were beginning to use their surface rights, that is, cultivation rights gained through their own labor, as security to borrow money from merchants. Our subject here is not the development of usurious moneylenders into parasitic landlords but the conditions that made tenant rent resistance struggles inevitable. The cultivators, the tenants who labored

---

* "Landlordification of the merchants" means that merchants acquire land and manage it like a normal landlord. This does not preclude them from continuing to engage in normal commercial activities.—Trans.

under two layers of exploitation (by the old landlords holding subsoil rights and new parasitic landlords who in reality were moneylenders who obtained the surface rights as security on debts) were able to consolidate themselves because of the development in the tenants' forces of production. How were such tenants able to overcome the new contradictions? This is a vital question because the peasant struggle spawned by the contradiction between the development of the productive forces of tenants and increased exploitation on the part of landlords ultimately led to the dissolution of the system of landlord control, a system that included the dual ownership form of land tenure.

Directly before the Taiping Rebellion in the mid-nineteenth century, it was reported that landlords in Shimen county (Chongde county during the Ming) Zhejiang "viewed the collection of rent as dangerous,"[83] or that "one could not live off the income from landed property alone."[84] And in Quanzhou prefecture in Fujian, "it was difficult to eat off one's rents [alone]."[85] Thus the contradictions within the landlord-tenant relationship finally brought on the dissolution of this feudal relationship, a process fully evident in the concrete details of the rent resistance struggle from the mid-Ming through to the Qing.

Conclusion

It was against the background of these social changes in the late Ming that the rebellion of Li Zicheng took shape.[86] This fact is evident in the slow spread of the peasant rebellions throughout North China after 1628, and their eventual growth into Li Zicheng's rebellion. With an army composed of vagrant bandits from these earlier struggles, Li Zicheng's rebellion constituted not a short-lived uprising but a culmination of the upheavals of North China in the late Ming.

When Li's army entered Beijing in 1644, it could no longer be effective as a peasant army. Its conservative narrowness isolated it from the urban residents, and with its ranks divided, it was kept busy trying to maintain a new dynasty rather than dealing with the Manchu forces to the north. Eventually, Li's troops had to retreat from Beijing in the face of the superior military force of Wu Sangui and other members of the Chinese ruling elite. In order to preserve their position, these Chinese had submitted to the Manchu troops, formed an alliance with them, and turned their spears against their fellow countrymen.

The peasant army of Li Zicheng, however, did not engage in mere blind peasant riots. It had political principles, it was well disciplined, it believed in no superstitions, and it included Muslims and other minority groups. At the suggestion of Li Yan and Niu Jinxing, both holders of the provincial degree who had joined the peasant army, Li Zicheng's government at the end of 1640 chose policies aimed at stabilizing the people's lives: "It would not kill the common people, it would exempt them from taxes for three years, and it would distribute fields among them regardless of whether their status was noble or mean." Furthermore, it forbade its soldiers to hoard silver, to enter others' houses without reason, and made it a capital offense to rape women. Military discipline was strict. The army's slogan was "No Killing, No Greed, No Illicit Sex, No Plundering, Fair Transactions, and the Equalization of Wealth and Aid for the Poor." All of this shows that Li Zicheng's army was of a different character from those of earlier peasant movements.

Li Zicheng's army was eventually defeated; nor did other anti-rent movements and other forms of resistance to the Qing troops bring victory to the urban commoners and the peasantry. In light of the historical character of the earlier peasant rebellions we have discussed, it is quite possible that Li's rule too would have in the end become another traditional, despotic dynasty, had he proven able to conquer both the Manchu invaders and the native Chinese ruling elite represented by Wu Sangui and others. However, history never really repeats itself. Only if we ignore the historical context of the rebellions of Deng Maoqi and Li Zicheng can they and others like them be dismissed as completely insignificant failures. But when we consider their historical context and realize that the direct producers were the prime movers of these rebellions, it is clear that each rebellion signaled the emergence of important new forces and goals in its own time. These uprisings succeeded at least in undermining the power of the state and in shifting the locus of control in society. Through these changes they left a rich historical legacy to later generations.

Notes

1 Gu Yingtai, *Ming shi jishi benmo*, vol. 12, p. 87.
2 1746 *Zhenze xianzhi*, 25:15b.
3 Fu Yiling, "Ming-Qing shidai Jiangnan shizhen jingji de fenxi," *Lishi jiaoxue*, 1964:5, pp. 9–13.
4 See Tanaka Masatoshi, "Minmatsu Shinsho Kōnan nōson shukōgyō ni kansuru ichi kōsatsu," in the same author's *Chūgoku kindai keizaishi josetsu*, pp. 79–100. Translated in this volume.
5 1747 *Wujiang xianzhi*, 4:16a.
6 1746 *Zhenze xianzhi*, 1:2a, 4:1b.
7 1684 *Changzhou xianzhi*, 3: *fengsu*, 4b–5a.
8 It is interesting to note that in the calendering trade a kind of management

evolved in which the merchant capital of cotton wholesalers controlled and monopolized production. See Yokoyama Suguru, *Chūgoku kindaika no keizai kōzō*, pp. 63–143, and Terada Takanobu, *Sansei shōnin no kenkyū*, pp. 337–410.

[9] Mao Ruizheng, *Wanli san dazheng kao*.

[10] Xie Zhaozhe, *Wu zazu*, p. 454.

[11] Zhao Yi, *Nianer shi zhaji*, pp. 729–31. At that time the punishment of castration known as the Palace Punishment (*gongxing*), was inflicted only rarely. The palace eunuchs were selected from among those men who volunteered to be castrated. Competition for these posts was very intense. For instance, in 1621 over 20,000 self-castrated men applied for the 3,000 eunuch posts then available. The custom of having one's son hired as a eunuch had begun in general with the poor, for reasons which are self-evident. In the mid-fifteenth century the eunuch Wang Chen amassed some sixty treasure houses of gold and silver. In the early sixteenth century Liu Jin similarly accumulated 2,500,000 taels of gold and 50,000,000 taels of silver. Such fortunes were accumulated by eunuchs powerful enough in the court and elsewhere to receive gifts and bribes.

[12] *Shenzong shilu*, Wanli 24:7, p. 5594.

[13] *Mingchen zouyi*, p. 629.

[14] Wang Zaijin, *Sanchao Liaoshi shilu*, 3:4a.

[15] Factories for the Imperial Silkworks were set up in over twenty cities throughout the empire, including Beijing and Nanjing. Craftsmen in weaving-related jobs were officially registered as artisans, and through their obligatory labor services they produced high-quality silk goods used in the palace or for other government needs, such as official garments and rewards. As this work was done on the basis of a minute division of labor, the artisans' registers were divided up into as many as twenty different categories, including yarn spinners, dyers, and weavers. Although these categories do not necessarily reflect actual work assignments in private operated workshops we can suppose a certain amount of social division of labor as a precondition for such classifications. Since commodity production in the private sector developed from the mid-Ming on, the system of obligatory labor service in the Imperial Silkworks broke down due to resistance by the producers, who went into flight or otherwise evaded the service. By the mid-sixteenth century almost all the provincial Imperial Silkwork factories had been closed down, except for those in Suzhou, Hangzhou, and Nanjing. In order to meet the court and government demands for high-quality silk goods, the government bought most of its silk goods from independent weavers. (A private weaving industry had been developing in the weaving quarters of Jiangnan cities like Hangzhou, Nanjing, and Suzhou.) Furthermore, the eunuchs sent out by the court received private orders from the emperor which enabled them to extract goods beyond the set amount. Since these transactions were naturally handled at unjust prices, the system of buying up silk goods from independent weavers in fact amounted to expropriation.

[16] *Shenzong shilu*, Wanli 29:7, pp. 6741–43, 1748, *Suzhou fuzhi*, 78:34a–35a; Chen Jiru, "Wu Ge Jiangjun mubei," in *Jiangsu sheng Ming-Qing yilai beike ziliao xuanji*, ed. Jiangsu sheng bowuguan, pp. 415–17.

[17] 1642 *Wu xianzhi*, 11:39b–40b.

[18] 1748 *Suzhou fuzhi*, 78:34a.

[19] Ibid., 78:34b. There are other studies of the hired silk workers rebellion by Yokoyama Suguru, "Chūgoku ni okeru shōkōgyō rōdōsha no hatten to yakuwari: Minmatsu ni okeru Soshū o chūshin to shite"; and Mori Masao, "Jūnana seiki shotō no shokuyō no hen o meguru ni-san no shiryō ni tsuite."

[20] *Shenzong shilu*, Wanli 29:7, pp. 6742–43.

[21] Ibid.

[22] 1748 *Suzhou fuzhi*, 78:34b.

[23] Ibid.

[24] 1642 *Wu xianzhi*, 11:42a.

[25] 1748 *Suzhou fuzhi*, 78:34b.

[26] In this case, being a member of the rural gentry (*xiangshen*) made it easy to declare one's views to a local official.

[27] Miyazaki Ichisada, "Mindai So-Shō chihō no shidaifu to minshū," pp. 1–33.

[28] 1748 *Suzhou fuzhi*, 78:35a.

[29] Yokoyama, *Chūgoku kindaika no keizai kōzō*, pp. 63–143.

[30] *Shenzong shilu*, Wanli 29:7, p. 6743. It should be noted that the imperial edict assumed Sun Long was the remonstrator.

[31] 1748 *Suzhou fuzhi*, 78:35a.

[32] Quesnay, François, "Despotisme de la Chine."

[33] Liu Yan, "Mingmo chengshi jingji fazhan xia de chuqi shimin yundong."

[34] Ono Kazuko, "Tōrinha to sono seiji shisō."

[35] When Xizong, the Tianqi emperor, ascended the throne, a lady attendant named Li lived with him and tried to participate in court politics. Criticized by Zuo Guangdou, she was shifted to another palace.

[36] Jin Risheng, *Songtian lubi*, 21:11a–25a.

[37] *Xizong shilu*, Tianqi 5:12, p. 3131. Li Yan, *Donglin dang jikao*.

[38] The guardsmen were actually officials sent to carry out arrests.

[39] Zhao Yi, *Nianer shi zhaji*, pp. 744–46.

[40] This account of the Kaidu Incident is drawn from historical records written by actual participants in or eyewitnesses of the events, such as Zhang Shiwei, Wen Zhenheng, and Yao Simeng, friends of Zhou Shunchang. Although their records were all written separately, they do not contradict one another in their accounts of this incident. Also cf. Jin Risheng, *Songtian lubi*, 21:32b–33a, 22:1a–15a, 22:28a–30b; Wen Zhenmeng, *Wuren muji*, in *Jiangsu sheng Ming-Qing yilai beike xuanji*, pp. 411–14; Charles O. Hucker, "Su-chou and the Agents of Wei Chung-hsien, a translation of *K'ai-tu ch'uan-hsin*."

[41] Renmin daxue, *Zhongguo ziben zhuyi mengya wenti taolunji*; Nanjing daxue lishixi Zhongguo gudaishi jiaoyanjiushi, ed., *Zhongguo ziben zhuyi mengya wenti taolunji xubian*.

[42] Guoshi guan, comp; *Qingshi liezhuan*, 79:33b–35a.

[43] Wei Hongyun, *Shi Kefa*.

[44] Xie Chengren, *Yiliusiwu-nian Jiangyin renmin shoucheng de gushi*.

[45] Li Tianyou, *Mingmo Jiangyin Jiading renmin de kang Qing douzheng*.

[46] Kikuchi Hideo, "Tō-Sō jidai o chūshin to suru iwayuru 'koyō rōdō' ni kansuru sho kenkyū."

[47] "Hired labor" does not mean modern-style wage labor; it refers to the way in which indebted people indentured themselves to repay their debts. The said person would indenture himself for a set period of time during which the pawnshop or userer would put him to work, but the money he received to repay the debt was not merely for the labor power but for the leasing of the person himself.

[48] Gu Yanwu, *Rizhi lu*, 13:30a.

[49] Chen Shoushi, "Ming-Qing zhi ji shiliao: nubian"; Xie Guozhen, "Mingji nubian kao"; Nakayama Hachirō, "Banmin no nuka nuhen"; Jiang Ruizhen, "Ming-Qing zhi ji Wuzhong de nubian"; Wu Jingxian, "Ming-Qing zhi ji Huizhou nubian kao"; Fu Yiling, "Ming-Qing zhi ji de 'nubian' he diannong jiefang yundong," in the same author's *Ming-Qing nongcun shehui jingji*, pp. 68–153; Fu Yiling, "Mingji nubian shiliao shibu."

[50] Saeki Yūichi, "Minmatsu no To-shi no hen: iwayuru 'nuhen' no seikaku ni kanrenshite."

[51] 1871 *Yi xianzhi*, 15:13a–16b; 15:27b–29a; Wu Jingxian, "Ming-Qing zhi ji Huizhou nubian kao."

[52] 1871 *Yi xianzhi*, 15:14a.

[53] Jiang Tongwen, *Enyu shulue* [A brief account of benevolent preparation], quoted in Wu Jingxian, "Ming-Qing zhi ji Huizhou nubian kao."

[54] 1786 *Guangshan xianzhi*, 19:16a–18b.

[55] *Yantang jianwen zaji*, pp. 246–49.

⁵⁶ Ibid., p. 249; Mori Masao, "1645 nen Taisō-shū Sakeichin ni okeru uryūkai no hanran ni tsuite."

⁵⁷ Zhang Lixiang, *Yangyuan xiansheng quanji*, 19:25a–26a.

⁵⁸ Gu Yanwu, *Rizhi lu*, 13:29a.

⁵⁹ He Liangjun, *Siyouzhai congshuo*, 13:12a.

⁶⁰ Xu Yikui, *Shifeng gao*, 1:2a–b. Fujii Hiroshi, "Chūgoku ni okeru shin to kyū."

⁶¹ Tao Zongyi, *Nancun chuogenglu*, p. 162.

⁶² Xu Tiantai, "Mingdai Fujian Deng Maoqi zhi luan"; Miyazaki Ichisada, "Chūgoku kinsei no nōmin bōdō," later included in the same author's *Ajiashi kenkyū*; Tanaka Masatoshi, "Tachiagaru nōmintachi—Jūgo seiki ni okeru Chūgoku no nōmin hanran"; Saeki Yūichi and Tanaka Masatoshi, "Jūgo seiki ni okeru Fukken no nōmin hanran" (1); Tanaka Masatoshi, "Tō Moshichi no ran no shoden ni tsuite."

⁶³ Saeki Yūichi and Tanaka Masatoshi, "Jūgo seiki ni okeru Fukken no nōmin hanran."

⁶⁴ *Yuan shi*, p. 4373; Fu Yiling, "Ming-Qing shidai Fujian diannong fengchao kao," in the same author's *Ming-Qing nongcun shehui jingji*, p. 154.

⁶⁵ *Yingzong shilu*, Zhengtong 14:5, p. 3446.

⁶⁶ Fu Yiling, "Ming-Qing shidai Fujian diannong fengchao kao," p. 163.

⁶⁷ *Yingzong shilu*, Zhengtong 13:9, p. 3281.

⁶⁸ This type of battle cart is properly known as the Duke Lu Cart (*Lugong che*).

⁶⁹ *Yingzong shilu*, Zhengtong 13: 11, p. 3303.

⁷⁰ Ibid., Zhengtong 14:2, pp. 3363–64; ibid., Zhengtong 14:5, p. 3445.

⁷¹ 1642 *Wu xianzhi*, 11:51a–b.

⁷² *Gaozong chunhuangdi shilu*, Qianlong 10:7, p. 3554.

⁷³ Zhang Ying, *Hengchan suoyan*, in *Dusu tang wenji*, 3:9a. [For a complete English translation of this text see Hilary J. Beattie, *Land and Lineage: A study of T'ung-ch'eng county, Anhwei, in the Ming and Ch'ing dynasties*, pp. 140–51.—Trans.]

⁷⁴ Fu Yiling, "Ming-Qing shidai Fujian diannong fengchao kao," p. 174.

⁷⁵ See, for example, the account of a tenant in Tao Zongyi's *Nancun chuogenglu*, p. 162.

⁷⁶ Fu Yiling, "Ming-Qing shidai Fujian diannong fengchao kao," pp. 178–81; Mori Masao, "Jūnana seiki no Fukken Neika-ken ni okeru Kō Tsū no kōso hanran" (1)–(3).

⁷⁷ 1760 *Wuqing zhenzhi*, 2: *Nongsang*, 4a.

⁷⁸ Oyama Masaaki, "Minmatsu Shinsho no dai tochi shoyū" (2), pp. 67ff. Translated in this volume.

⁷⁹ 1612 *Quanzhou fuzhi*, 3:58a–b.

⁸⁰ 1879 *Shimen xianzhi*, 11:5b–6a.

⁸¹ 1596 *Xiushui xianzhi*, 1:42a.

⁸² The dual ownership system of land tenure refers to a custom common in south and central China from the late Ming onward, whereby former landownership was eroded by tenants and divided into ownership of the "field surface" (or soil) and ownership of the "field bones" (or subsoil); one field thus could be owned by two people. Since this system existed as a community custom, its existence and the maintenance depended on the power gained by the holders of the "field surface" within the landlord-tenant relationship.

⁸³ 1879 *Shimen xianzhi*, 11:4b.

⁸⁴ Ibid., 11:4b.

⁸⁵ 1763 *Quanzhou fuzhi*, 20:13b.

⁸⁶ Li Wenzhi, *Wan Ming minbian*; Beijing daxue wenke yanjiusuo, ed., *Mingmo nongmin qiyi shiliao*; Xie Guozhen, *Qingchu nongmin qiyi ziliao jilu*; Xie Guozhen, *Nan Ming shilüe*.

THE OTHER SIDE OF RENT AND TAX
RESISTANCE STRUGGLES: IDEOLOGY AND
THE ROAD TO REBELLION

KOBAYASHI KAZUMI

Although Japanese historians have long recognized the significance of rent and tax resistance struggles in the Ming-Qing period,
Kobayashi Kazumi was one of the first to examine the ideological
dimension of the struggles. This essay, published in 1973 in the
popular journal *Shisō*, created quite a stir in academic circles,
both because of Kobayashi's criticism of previous interpretations
of the rent and tax resistance movements and because of his application of contemporary political analysis to this historical issue.

Kobayashi criticizes previous scholarship on the rent and tax
resistance movements for its exclusive emphasis on the economic
causes—i.e., the role of the forces of production—in the development of the struggles. In his own analysis, Kobayashi certainly
does not neglect economic causes. Indeed, he begins with an explanation of how economic conditions shaped the aims and the
ideology of both the rent and tax resistance struggles. But he also
emphasizes the developing role of ideology in the formation of the
struggles. In contrast to earlier scholars, he sees the tax and rent
resistance struggles as two distinct movements divided by ideological differences which inhibited the potential for common action.
Finally, he recognizes the important transformative role of political and religious ideology in directing economic and social struggles toward revolution.

This essay is remarkable also for its application of certain
philosophical concepts, some developed by Kobayashi himself,
others drawn from the contemporary political situation of the
late 1960s. First, he uses the term "indirect producers" (*seikatsusha*) to denote members of the non-elite and non-landlord

This essay was originally published as "Kōso, kōryō tōsō no kanata—Kasō seikatsusha no omoi to seijiteki shūkyōteki jiritsu no michi" [抗租抗糧鬪爭の彼方—下
層生活者の想いと政治的宗教的自立の途] in *Shisō*, 2 (1973): 228-47. Translation by
Cynthia Brokaw and Timothy Brook.

classes who produce services rather than goods. The category includes doctors, martial arts masters, county runners, hired laborers, etc. Indirect producers are contrasted conceptually with direct producers (*seisansha*), primarily the peasants, whose attachment to the land made it difficult for them to create rebel organizations. Kobayashi is particularly interested in the process whereby direct producers are transformed into indirect producers, who are uniquely qualified by their more desperate socioeconomic circumstances to form rebel sects.

Second, Kobayashi has chosen to apply the dialectical mode of analysis popular during the Cultural Revolution to his study of rent and tax resistance movements. Thus his emphasis is largely on the tensions and contradictions that run through the movements—between the two types of struggles themselves, between the economic aims and religious ideologies of the struggles, between the leadership and the masses, and so forth. Kobayashi also employs certain philosophical concepts developed within Japan in the late 1960s as part of a neo-Hegelian attempt to transcend the limitations of the traditional Marxist concept of the state. He repeatedly speaks of the state or of an alternative anti-state world as a "vision of community" (*kyōdō gensōsei*) or a "fiction" (*kyokō*). These terms are derived from the theories of state and community developed by Takimura Ryūichi and Yoshimoto Takaaki. These two theoreticians emphasize the crucial role of ideology in actively creating and sustaining social formations. In a sense, their place in intellectual debate in Japan is analogous to that of Marcuse or Gramsci in the West. Takimura abandons the orthodox Marxist definition of the state as part of the social constituton that makes up the national community; rather, he conceives of it broadly as the national community itself.[1] For Yoshimoto, the state exists not as a community but as a secondary derivation or "vision" of community. Accordingly, the state functions in a conceptually different way from primary economic and social categories, playing an ideological rather than material role.[2] Yoshimoto defines "the vision of community" as "roughly signifying the entire conceptual world beyond the mental world of people as individuals and what is produced by individuals. In other words, it connotes those concepts related to the world of people not as individuals but as members of some community." This vision was first generated historically at the level of the family or clan, then at the level of the village, and finally at the level of the state.[3]

For Kobayashi the concept of a vision of community is applicable not only to the state but also to the alternative world created by the ideology of rebellion, a world in direct contrast to the legitimate state. As visions, both are structured out of what Kobayashi terms "fictions" or "deceptions." Politics and religion are two such fictions, contributing both to the vision projected by the legitimate state and to the vision of the alternative world offered by rebellion. Rebellion achieves a revolutionary character only when it challenges and negates the political fiction of the ruling state, thereby exposing its political reality and establishing the ideological conditions for taking over state power.

Kobayashi Kazumi is associate professor at Meijō University, Nagoya.

*   *   *

Identification of the problem

The discovery of rent and tax resistance struggles and the recognition of their historical significance has been one of the most valuable contributions made by Japanese scholars to the study of Chinese history. Thanks to the research of postwar historians, these struggles are now recognized as the major mass movements against the feudal system in pre-modern China. Rent resistance struggles may be defined simply as protests by tenants against the payment of rent to their landlords; tax resistance struggles as protests against state taxation of land ownership.

Up to the present [1973], Japanese historians have been guided in their research on these struggles by two related theories: the theory of historical stages of development and the theory of the forces of production. I do not want to suggest that these approaches are invalid; on the contrary, they are generally confirmed by the historical evidence, and they have produced important interpretive conclusions. For example, the idea that the landlord-tenant relationship was the major economic relationship in Chinese feudal society, the relationship which defined the very nature of that society, is a product of the theory of historical stages. Furthermore, this theory has helped historians demonstrate the inevitability of the socialist revolution in China—that is, to show that the Communist party program succeeded because it supported both the peasants' desire for land and their opposition to land taxes.

But when applied to rent and tax resistance struggles, the two theories have tended to limit our understanding: the struggles are perceived almost exclusively as expressions of economic interests. Their political and religious aspects and connections to political and religious rebel-lions are slighted. For example, the theory of the forces of produc-tion, developed during the debate over the sprouts of capitalism, has produced only the following rather crude picture of rent and tax re-sistance struggles: From the Song period forward the landlord-tenant system defined the basic economic structure of China. Political as well as economic power rested in the landlords' hands, since the state represented the class interests of the landlords. Rent resistance struggles were direct attacks on the economic system which supported the state, i.e., the landlord-tenant system. They became explicitly political only after uniting with tax resistance struggles.

The weakness of this argument lies in the assumption that there is an unmediated connection between economic and social struggles and religious struggles. It implies that political and religious struggles are merely intensifications of economic and social struggles. But political and religious rebellions are qualitatively different. They are spiritual transformations of economic and social struggles, transformations which purify everyday economic interests by subordinating them to a political fiction or religious vision. This ideological transformation also entails a change in the organization and material power of the struggles—indeed, the very nature of the struggles is changed. Only then can the rebels transcend their material existence, what Marx calls the "life of civil society," of "man in the proper sense, . . . in his sen-suous, individual, immediate existence."[4]

Now it is necessary to extend and refine our interpretation of rent and tax resistance struggles in view of their potential for development into political and religious struggles. What relationship did they bear to contemporary religious and political rebellions? What ideological elements were peculiar to both rent and tax resistance? At what stages, and under what conditions did economic struggles develop into politi-cal and religious struggles? What were the contradictions between these two types of struggles? How could they be resolved?

This dialectical approach to the issue grows out of a method of analy-sis developed in the late 1960s and early 1970s to resolve the contradic-tions raised during the Cultural Revolution in China and during the university struggles in the rest of the world. At that time the contradic-tions were between individual and party, family and political in-dependence, the forces of production and spiritual liberation, the idea of a political consensus and the reality of civil society, and nationalism and internationalism.

The dialectic at work in these contradictions will here be applied to the issue of rent and tax resistance. The central contradiction is between the aims of the rent and tax resistance struggles as economic and social struggles and those of political and religious struggles. For economic and social struggles, the urgent problem is capturing control of the state. But it is the basic nature of political and religious struggles to transcend such concerns with material and political power, with "natural necessity, need and private interest, and the preservation of property and the egoistic self."[5] Participants in political and religious struggles strive to attain spiritual liberation, to gain the status of "true men" (zhenren). But how can the aims of both of these struggles be advanced at the same time? Here lies the dilemma which has defeated mankind throughout history.

In this essay I will examine how the Chinese people dealt with this problem in the nineteenth and early twentieth centuries. I will concentrate on the two periods for which materials related to this issue are most numerous, the mid-nineteenth century, during the period of the Taiping Revolution and of several White Lotus uprisings, and the early twentieth century, around the time of the 1911 Revolution.

The ideology of rent resistance

Rent resistance struggles shared certain concrete but somewhat limited goals. Most attacked a variety of inequities: the collection of subsidiary rents, arbitrary rent increases, a lack of uniformity in measures used to calculate rent, the coercion of tenants to pay rent transport costs, brutal methods of collection, and the exaction of tenant security deposits. In addition, some struggles aimed at the reduction of rents to a 4:6 ratio (40 percent to the landlord, 60 percent to the tenant), the acquisition of surface or cultivation rights (tianmianquan; this right could be freely bought, sold, or transferred by the tenant), and the abolition of the field rotation system (yitian).[6] These are all precise and relatively narrow goals. There is no evidence that any rent resistance struggles grew out of a more comprehensive and more theoretical criticism of the whole landlord-tenant relationship as a deviation from an ideal social pattern. In this section I will examine the context of the rent resistance struggles, their ideology, and the limitations of that ideology.

First, let us consider what conditions the tenants labored under, and how these shaped their justification of rent resistance. From dire economic necessity, these men were completely absorbed in the daily routine of farming. They did not have the time for philosophical speculations about the social structure. Their attacks on the landlords grew out of their total dependence on the land for survival, out of a natural and overriding—albeit somewhat conservative—concern with material security. Under these harsh economic conditions, the acquisition of permanent tenancy and surface rights represented a significant improvement in economic status, so significant, indeed, that it was seen as the highest ambition for tenants. It is important not to slight the emotional elements of their struggles: they were moved not only by concern for their families, but also by personal bitterness over the years of exploitation by the landlords.

Understandable as this passion for permanent tenancy and surface rights may have been, however, it tended in the long run to hurt the tenants. These rights were limited and conservative, yet the tenants had invested so much labor and emotion in their acquisition that, after they had gained them, they tended to feel too easily satisfied and secure. They neglected possibilities of struggling for rights of even greater scope. Even worse, this feeling of security was completely illusory: tenants still faced a harsh and perilously insecure livelihood. Tao Xu, a scholar and local landlord living in the countryside of Yuanhe county, Suzhou prefecture, described in his *Zu he* the precarious existence of tenants in that area immediately after the Taiping Revolution:

When people acquire something, they want it for themselves alone, and they hate to share it with anyone else: this is a universal human feeling. [Now,] if we look at land [in this locality], the wealthy men [in the county seat] despise land, the surface and subsoil rights of which cannot be purchased separately, and refuse to buy it. They acquire only the subsoil rights and allow the tenants to keep the surface rights for themselves. . . . . The surface rights become the tenants' only material possession. Therefore, even if the landlords raise the rent, even if they raise the commutation rate for the rent, even if they force the tenants to pay rent when it falls due, even if they are brutally cruel to the tenants, the tenants cannot bear to give up their surface rights and move to another place. Their very livelihood and that of their descendants rely wholly on the possession of surface rights. In an extreme case, a landlord could seize his tenant's surface rights, extract the unpaid portion of the rent, and then, in the end, sell the rights to another man. At such a time, even though there would be nothing the tenant could do, the surface rights would be so precious to him that he could not leave the land.[7]

Thus the tenants' necessary attachment to permanent tenancy and surface rights, rather than ensuring greater freedom and prosperity, in fact could leave them even more vulnerable to landlord exploitation and control than they had been before.

During the Qing, many tenants gained surface rights throughout the lower Yangzi delta. Yet, under the conditions of heightened landlord oppression described above, the very poorest tenants were forced to give up agriculture for secondary or service occupations in order to survive: they became doctors, hired laborers, county runners, etc. It was at this stage, at the nadir of their economic decline, that they turned to the path of insurrection. To the end, however, they held to the logic of peasant cultivators, and their insurrection took the form of a counter-attack against the landlords. Ironically, they based this counterattack on the possession of those same surface rights which the landlords had previously used to intensify their exploitation of the tenants. Two con-temporary observers, writing in *Shen bao* in 1879, noticed the connection between the system of split property rights (*yitian liangzhu*; i.e., the creation of surface and subsoil rights which could be owned separately) and tenant uprisings: "The birth of the system of split property rights opened the floodgates of rent resistance."[8] "After the introduction of surface rights, all the land was seized by the tenants. . . . The landlords had to bear the loss."[9] Thus the desire for landownership was the real motive behind the tenants' rent resistance struggles.

The whole logic of these struggles was clearly based on a kind of quantitative thinking. It was not the nature or quality of the landlord-tenant relationship which was attacked; rather, it was the degree of exploitation which drove the tenants to resistance. A handbill from the 1846 rent resistance movement in Zhaowen county (Jiangsu) provides an example of this kind of reasoning:

The commutation rate for the rental of wheat fields has always been 2000 copper cash for each *shi* of wheat. How can they suddenly raise it to 2400 cash? The rent for cotton fields in autumn has always been 1000 cash for each *mu*. How can they now make it 1200 cash? If the rent is not paid on time, 30 cash is customarily added to each 1000 cash of overdue rent. How can they suddenly raise the penalty to 100 cash? When a landlord buys more land, he calls for us tenants and draws up contracts. They have always asked for 500 to 600 cash for each *mu*. It is our resolve to continue to work hard even if the rate is raised to 1000 cash per *mu*, but they say they will demand 2000 to 3000 cash for each *mu*. We are powerless—we can only weep as we pawn our clothing and borrow at high interest rates. Who could have foreseen the advent of such a frightful time?[10]

Here the peasants are not questioning the basic right of the landlords to extract rent. Even if the contract fees are raised to 1000 cash, they will continue to work hard on their land. It is their refusal to accept an even greater increase which is the cause of their resistance.

Because the landlords were able to use surface rights to exploit their tenants, a new kind of tenant resistance was necessary at this point. The kind of quantitative reasoning expressed above was no longer adequate. It was necessary for the peasants to change the ideological quality of their attack, to find a means of exposing and destroying the contradictions within their society. Furthermore, during the period analyzed here, the Qing state was in the process of disintegration, and that fact made it all the more important for an attack on the imperial system to be made from a sound ideological base. The necessary ideological leap would, of course, transform the organization and material power of the tenant movement also.

It may be objected here that some rent resistance struggles did achieve a revolutionary quality on their own. Admittedly, some became so violent that landlords were killed or wounded, officials attacked, and county offices and landlords' homes destroyed. But these struggles never really became more than economic and social struggles, since they never created a new political and religious ideology. Uprisings can be considered political or religious struggles only after they both develop an ideology in opposition to the state and its ideology, and unite with other sects to realize this ideology. When the people did in fact have the opportunity to make the transition to political and religious rebellion, they usually ended up either emulating the political fiction of the already-existing state, or acting according to a religious world view which they created in reaction against the state. Thus some rebel groups issued proclamations in the names of the descendants of the Han or Ming royal houses. Others developed a belief in the coming of the Maitreya Buddha, the King of Light (Ming wang), or Jehovah. Both the the White Lotus sect (Bailian jiao) and the God-worshipping Society (Bai Shangdihui), for example, awaited the coming of the Truly Mandated Son of Heaven (Zhenming tianzi).

However, before examining the development of rent resistance struggles in greater detail, I want to turn to tax resistance struggles, to analyze their ideology and their relationship to rent resistance struggles.

The ideology of tax resistance

In research to date, tax resistance struggles have been linked with rent resistance struggles as the major popular movements against the pre-modern Chinese state. These types of uprisings have been so closely associated that historians have referred to them together in the phrase "rent and tax resistance."

This linking of the two types of struggles has led historians to neglect the real differences between them. That these differences are decisive ones is suggested by the fact that the rent and tax resistance struggles never united in their attacks against the existing system.[11] These differences cannot be explained simply by economic geography, by such external differences as those between the advanced regions with a heavy concentration of tenants and the mountainous or backward regions with a greater practice of independent cultivation.[12] Rather, the critical difference lies between the aims of the two types of struggles. Rent resistance struggles arose from the tenants' absorption in their individual struggles for survival. In contrast, the tax resistance struggles, representing the class interests of the direct producers (independent and semi-independent peasants, and middle and small landlords who worked their own land), grew from an opposition to the real workings of the bureaucracy and the state. Rent resistance struggles were limited by the tenants' attachment to the land; tax resistance struggles by their acceptance of the validity of the existing political fiction.[13] They strove to purify this fiction—that is, to make the real operation of the state match its stated ideals. Thus they attacked the bureaucracy for not living up to its principles: the public sector (*gong*), instead of "aiding the people," acted in private interests (*si*); the bureaucracy, instead of safeguarding the laws, exacted unfair taxes from the people. By concentrating on the gap between reality and theory, the tax resistance struggles neglected the real point: it was the very idea of community in the dynastic system that was inadequate.

If we look at the statements of some tax resistance leaders and theoreticians, this basic flaw becomes very clear. In most cases these men were middle- or lower-level resident landlords, local figures of note, or village leaders.[14] Here, for example, is the speech of the military licentiate who led a tax resistance struggle in Tiantai county (Zhejiang) in 1874:

At first I joined the Nian bandits [Nian army]. . . . However, they did a great deal of harm to the people whenever they felt like it, so I captured some of them and turned them over to the government forces and devoted myself at that point to eradicating such bandits. I thought the officials would always adhere to the law and would reduce the taxes. But, contrary to my expectations, and despite the fact that the fighting had eased up, the officials, acting from selfishness, increased the taxes even more. How could the people bear this suffering? For this reason I set up the standard of "aiding the people." By uniting to take up this righteous banner, our goal is to save the people from the hardships they have suffered in the past.[15]

His anger is directed against the fact that public officials act for their private interest, that the officials whose duty it is to aid the people are in fact harming them. It is clear that he accepted the ideal of an autocratic dynasty; the problem for him was simply that the actual administrators did not live up to this ideal.

A similar attitude is expressed by a student who brought a suit against unfair tax collection in Jiashan county (Zhejiang). The examining official, Duan Guangqing, asked, "Why do you deny the responsibility of paying taxes?" The student replied, "The county officials are unjust in their tax assessments. Therefore I cannot pay the taxes. If such injustice is stopped, why should I oppose making my 'contribution to the empire'?"[16] This reference to "contributions to the empire" perfectly expresses the intellectual limitations of most leaders and ideologues of the tax resistance movement.

Furthermore, most tax resistance struggles specifically attacked administrative evils—that is, the arbitrary exactions of the county magistrate, the corruption of the clerks, and the inequity of the categorizations of classes made for the purpose of tax collection. For example, the 1852 tax resistance uprising in Yin county (Zhejiang), led by a National University student, Zhou Xiangqian, aimed at rectifying the unfairness of the tax assessment administered by the county magistrate. Sasaki Masaya evaluates the demands and attitudes of the local people and their leaders as follows: "The demands of the local people were the release of Zhou and five others from prison and the rectification of the unfairness of the tax assessment. By punishing the treasury and tax officials who had tried to enforce the taxes, they achieved fair taxes. They certainly did not deny their responsibility to pay taxes, and still less did they have any revolutionary aim."[17]

The central figures in tax resistance felt that "the harm done to the people in this way by the subordinates (clerks) of the unscrupulous magistrate was illegal. They expressed their indignation, in unity with the village people, but without any overall revolutionary plan."[18] In the end, they attacked the behavior of the clerks and evil officials as violations of the dynasty's absolute and supreme laws. Here there is no ideological disposition to deny the legal concept of absolutism or the legitimacy of the emperor. By protecting the existing concept of the state, tax resistance ideology fell into the trap of attributing all social and economic problems to the evils of policy or officials.

The relationship between rent and tax resistance

I have briefly outlined the ideologies and the ideological limitations of the two types of struggles under discussion, in an attempt to indicate the revolutionary potential of each. At this point it is instructive to compare the development of the struggles, to gain some idea of the degree to which they interacted with or reinforced each other.

Although the two types of struggles never united in their attacks against the existing system, there were certain logical relationships between them. We have seen that it was the tax resistance struggles that attacked the administration of state taxes, but the tenants involved in rent resistance were no less a part of this whole system of state taxation. It is through an examination of their participation in it that we can get some sense of the relationship between the two types of struggles and their relative revolutionary potential.

Taxes were considered contributions from the whole empire, but they were paid largely by landlords, who had a considerable stake in ensuring the stability of the state. During the period from the late-Ming Single Whip reform to the mid-Qing combination of the land and poll taxes, landowners became the real pillars of the state. They looked down on the propertyless tenants, who had no clear role in the Qing political system. By this time the definition of landlords and tenants together as "equally the [subjects and] children of the emperor" had completely lost its meaning.[19] They were in fact divided into two groups: politically powerful landlords and virtually powerless tenants. The state never acknowledged this reality but persisted in defining tenants and landlords as equals. As a result, the landlord-tenant relationship was never adequately defined in law. This anomaly left the tenants even more open to exploitation. Since the legal system did not protect them, they were completely dependent on the personality of their individual landlords.

However, one crucial fact has been omitted from this analysis. The tenants did ultimately, through their role as rent payers, have some power over the fiscal resources of the state. If tenants did not pay rent to their landlords, then the landlords could not pay taxes to the state. Thus the tenants as a group existed for the state only at the purely administrative level of tax collection. The following text of a song, written by Jin Luqing, the magistrate of Wujiang county (Jiangsu), in 1876, illustrates the connection quite clearly: "It is forbidden to default in the payment of rents. It is forbidden to default in the payment of rents. Everyone knows that the land tax comes out of rents. If the landlords do not collect the rents, then there will be a delay in the payment of taxes to the state supported by the landlords."[20] The following two passages from the *Shen bao* reinforce the point. "The land tax comes from the rents collected by the landlords; the rents are collected by the landlords from their tenants. Therefore, the landlords and tenants should be on cordial terms, and there must be no fighting between them."[21] "The land tax is part of the fiscal administration of the state. Truly the slightest default is not allowed. However, since the rents have not come in, even though the landlords exert all their efforts to collect them, the tax cannot be completely collected."[22] Thus, though lacking any effective legal status or political definition, the tenants could still pose a challenge to political power: if they did not pay their rent to the landlords, then the fiscal resources of the state, in the form of land taxes, could simply not be ensured. State power, by upholding the logic of taxation—"taxes are from rents, and rents are from tenants"—was in the end powerless against the tenants.

It is at this point, through the obvious relationship between rent and taxes, that tax and rent resistance struggles could have shared a certain common interest and could have usefully united against the landlords and the state. Why was this unity never achieved?

The major limitation lay with the logic of the tax resistance struggles. As long as their goal remained the harmonization of the theory of the imperial system and the acts of individual officials, they could never sympathize with or represent the economic concerns of the propertyless masses. Nor could they share the vision of absolute equity and absolute equality which arose among the propertyless masses and which became the basis for the Taiping, Maitreyan, or Datong visions of community. Both were impossible because the tax resistance struggles accepted as a premise the right of landownership—that is, the right of private landowners to exist within the feudal structure.

But it must be conceded that however severe the ideological limitations of the tax resistance struggles, they did help to undermine state power and the supports of the existing order. At least they were not a hindrance to rent resistance struggles: they gave these struggles some temporal margin and spatial latitude. But the ideology of tax resistance struggles was certainly not advanced enough to develop the political and religious world views necessary to the achievement of a real revolutionary advance. Indeed, the more tax resistance struggles developed, the more local power-holders—the upper levels of village society, the literati, and licentiates who still dreamed of official careers—

were absorbed into the movement. Because of this development, tax resistance struggles were in the end co-opted into the political system, to such an extent that they were almost destroyed by the tax-reduction policy of 1863. For this reason, the paths of rent and tax resistance split apart quite sharply.

Rent resistance struggles, in contrast, could not be absorbed into the false world of the existing political fiction, simply because they did not recognize any difference between the economic and political reality and the political image embodied in the emperor. The more the ideology of rent resistance struggles developed, the more firmly it opposed the concept of the imperial system and its principles. Thus participants in these struggles, in particular the propertyless tenants and vagrant peasants, turned more easily to political and religious rebellion. They were often forced into a life of vagrancy and were easily attracted to dreams of the worlds of Taiping or Maitreya, where they would be able to return to their homes, their parents, and the graves of their ancestors. Since they were not bound to follow the logic of the existing state system, they were drawn to a religious world view which attacked the fiction that the state was based on the common interests of all the people.

Of course, as we have seen in the section on the ideology of rent resistance, these struggles did suffer from certain limitations of their own. In the economically advanced region of the lower Yangzi delta, where tenancy was highest, even propertyless tenants were simply interested in obtaining permanent tenancy and surface rights. They first became involved in rent resistance struggles as *economic* struggles, and consequently it was difficult for them to cut their ties to the land and set off on the path of political or religious rebellion.

Despite all these limitations, some of the participants in both tax resistance and rent resistance struggles did in fact move on to political and religious rebellion. The great majority of the people who were the motive force in both struggles were from the lower strata of society, the poor independent, semi-independent, and tenant peasants. Though the leaders of tax resistance struggles may have been co-opted by the state, these lower-strata participants were left unsatisfied. Similarly, though certain tenants in rent resistance struggles may have been unable to transcend their personal economic concerns, others became aware of the dangers of such concerns and sought to move beyond them. It was these people who, drawing on some ideas of tax and rent resistance struggles, were able to make the necessary "ideological leap" into political and religious rebellion.

Political and religious rebellions

Under the revolutionary conditions of the Taiping and 1911 revolutions, peasants often went beyond the limits characteristic of rent and tax resistance struggles and rose to become true political and religious rebels. In certain cases, religious sects and political cliques—such as secret societies, the Taiping Heavenly Kingdom, and the White Lotus sect—brought world views, organization, and programs from the outside and led peasants who were resisting rent and tax. Only then could these peasants make the qualitative step toward a revolutionary movement.

The Taiping period furnishes numerous examples of this development. Once secret societies established the "Great State of Cheng" (Dachengguo) in Xunzhou prefecture (Guangxi), the perennial rent resistance struggles there in the counties of Hengchun and Guan achieved for the first time a revolutionary significance, as the following passage from a proclamation by one of the Dachengguo leaders suggests: "Land is the basis of agriculture, and all dry, slash-and-burn, and wet fields were opened by the peasants. Heaven is truly angry with the landlords for collecting rents generation after generation. Henceforth landlords are not permitted to collect rents as they did in the old system."[23] A second example is the "rent reduction and interest reduction" uprising in the Hunan subprefecture of Fengzhou and the Hubei counties of Songzi and Shimen. White Lotus sectarian Peng Zhengke of Songzi, boxing master Chen Zhengjie from western Fengzhou, and White Lotus organizer Deng Zhenglei united several thousand peasants under their leadership, and for the first time developed the struggle into a "revolutionary" uprising in sympathy with the Taiping Heavenly Kingdom.[24] The following conversation during the Taiping period between the Nanjing scholar Wang Shiduo and a peasant who participated in a rent resistance struggle provides a particularly revealing third example:

"Are the officials corrupt? Do they bend the laws?"
"I don't know."
"Why do you hate them?"
"Because they collect taxes."
"Do the Long Hairs [the Taiping armies] say that they will not collect taxes?"
"I would pay taxes to the Long Hairs, but I will no longer pay rent to the landlord."

"Doesn't your land belong to the landlord? Why will you not pay rent?"

"If I paid, I wouldn't have enough for myself."[25]

The straightforward and simple logic behind this peasant's refusal to pay rent is characteristic of a petty producer; yet it also confirms that, for the peasants, the Taiping Heavenly Kingdom had become a political state with enough power to challenge the legitimacy of the ruling Qing dynasty.

During the 1911 Revolution, there are similar instances of peasants who advanced from rent resistance to the advocacy of a peasant-style revolution that would give them ownership of the land they cultivated. The Society of the Thousand (Qianrenhui), formed by the tenants of Changshu, Wuxi, and Jiangyin counties (Jiangsu), proclaimed: "The emperor is now no more, so rent does not have to be handed over."[26] In the same vein, "the tenants of Shimen county demanded that, since taxes were rescinded in honor of the birth of the Republic, rents should also be rescinded, although in the end the collection of rents was carried out just as in any other year."[27] Similarly, in Tonglizhen in Wujiang county (Jiangsu), we read: "In recent times the tide of rent resistance everywhere has been strong. The tenants of 72 polders within the area of Tonglizhen have united in common agreement, refusing to pay rent to their landlords. At the same time they use violent means to wrest back the tenancy contracts from the landlords, saying, 'Since the government has now changed, this land no longer belongs to the landlords.' "[28]

Some tax resistance struggles also went beyond the limits of social and economic struggles and developed into rebellions that were political in their goal of taking state power. Although these struggles occurred under revolutionary conditions, they actually developed through the leadership of the White Lotus and other secret societies. Kojima Shinji cites as examples of such struggles the tax resistance uprising of 1842 in Chongyang county (Hubei) and the 1853 uprising in Qingpu county (Jiangsu), the latter merging with the Small Sword Society (Xiaodaohui) uprising in Shanghai.[29] Another example of the same development is the White Lotus uprising of the Five Great Banners, which later became the large-scale rebellion of Song Jingshi's Black Banner Army, one of the Five Great Banners. Beginning in 1860 as a tax resistance struggle in western Shandong, which arose in sympathy with the Taiping and Nian Army rebellions, the struggle developed into an attack on the county prison and then became a political rebellion in which the organization and world conception of White Lotus sectarians played a decisive role.[30] Without this organization, and without the martial training groups among the people, these tax

resistance struggles could not have developed into large-scale political
and religious rebellions.

As we have seen, struggles, such as rent and tax resistances struggles,
which were fundamentally economic in nature, had to wait for a revolutionary situation and the leadership of a religious sect or political faction before they could become political and religious rebellions that
challenged the legitimacy of the already constituted state. Local petty-
producer peasants, who were the main participants in rent and tax
resistance, approached this kind of rebellion only when they adopted a
sect's political or religious world view and accepted its leadership. Em-
boldened by the new visions conferred by this world view, they broke
their attachment to the small plots of land they cultivated or owned
and, as members of a fictitious higher political and religious community,
cast off the personal relationships that fettered them to family, clan,
and native place. That the small peasants, especially those in the Yangzi
river delta where narrowly economic struggles were endemic, were
willing to abandon their land and form a revolutionary group aiming
at state power indicates the depth of their desperation.

The world of religious and political rebels

The preceding discussion has suggested the decisive importance of the
role played by religious and political groups in facilitating rebellion.
The conditions under which these sects were formed is the subject of this
final section, in which I examine the rebellions of the White Lotus and
other heterodox sects during the first half of the nineteenth century.

Independent peasants, semi-independent peasants, and tenants were
the main participants in rent and tax resistance struggles, but on their own
they could not become rebels who possessed a vision of a higher community. They embraced all manner of economic livelihoods and social positions, and occasionally they joined together in common cause, yet their
world ended at the level of the particular village or county town where
they owned or rented land.[31] It is true that this local world of livelihood
and production was decisive in providing a starting point for the development of economic movements and social attitudes: had the peasants
been confined to a world of religious and political fictions abstracted
and cut off from the narrowly defined world of their own native place,
they would have had nothing to identify as a real object of resistance.
On the other hand, however, the tenants' thorough attachment to the
land they cultivated imposed limitations on rent resistance struggles.

As long as these struggles were successful in their limited aim of winning for the peasants possession of the land that provided them with the necessities of life, they were caught within almost the same limits as tax resistance struggles, which began from the premise that peasants naturally seek to keep the land that they own. Because of the success of these limited struggles in the most advanced regions of Chinese feudal society, the petty-producer peasants in these regions were in the end unable to move beyond the world of economic and social struggles to religious and political rebellion.

The central figures and charismatic leaders of religious and political rebellion, in contrast, were semi-proletarian intellectuals or impoverished semi-proletarian vagrants who had fled from their home villages. These were the people who stood at the extreme edge of power and caught a glimpse of its hidden workings: county runners, county school students, doctors working among the people, county clerks, Confucian licentiates, geomancers, martial arts masters, itinerant merchants, temporary hired laborers, fortunetellers, military deserters, and Hakka.[32] Some of them were drawn to the search for a new political authority because of the many setbacks that they had encountered after leaving their native places; others embraced a political vision because their social or occupational positions allowed them to see the degenerate reality of the ruling state. For such people, the world view of the White Lotus sect—"the native land of true emptiness, fatherless and lordless, and the unbegotten parents" (*zhenkong jiaxiang, wujun wufu, wusheng fumu*)—offered a spiritual redemption. They had no other course but to imagine themselves to be "true men" within a visionary heavenly community. Vagrants, outsiders, renegades from power, and higher-level intellectual lumpen, they first responded sympathetically to the world view of the White Lotus, and then went on to broaden that world view. Armed with this new religious and political vision, they harbored dreams of extending their ambitions and regenerating mankind.

These people inhabited a world very different from that of the peasants involved in local rent and tax resistance, for even the poorest tenant was tied to his land and even the propertyless cultivator clung to the plot he rented in order to go on living. The objective conditions that brought them to the leadership of religious and political rebellions were supplied by the great mass of desperate propertyless vagrants who were appearing in ever greater numbers from the late Qianlong era forward. Unlike the peasants in the economically advanced regions, the propertyless masses in less-developed regions had nothing that confined them to their native places. Forced into vagrancy, they drifted into the western provinces of Sichuan, Hubei, and Shaanxi, or else gathered in the border areas among the five central provinces of Hebei, Shandong, Henan, Anhui, and Jiangsu, or the southern border region in Yunnan and Guangxi.[33] These were the people who provided the core mass of religious and political rebellion in pursuit of a visionary paradise of absolute equity and absolute equality.

The Hakka, the name by which these migrants and outsiders were known, came into conflict with the long-established indigenous residents, as Suzuki Chūsei has observed: "Between the residents and the newly arrived there were unceasing problems over the question of taxation, which resulted in a large number of murders. . . . Those who entered from Huguang came into conflict with the indigenous residents of Sichuan and incurred a great deal of enmity. Among the drifters who came in from Hunan there were also criminals and tax evaders who frequently stirred up trouble in the new areas."[34] The indigenous residents perceived the immigrants to be their natural economic enemies, usurping their privately owned land, their cultivators, and other conditions necessary for production. The local people also accused the Hakka of laying waste to their native ancestral places, of being in effect enemies of traditional communal society. The personal discrimination which resulted was exacerbated by the immigrants' dialects, which identified them clearly as outsiders. To the end they remained blocked by the fundamental barrier created by the principle of the exclusive community and the rules that protected such closed villages.

The revolutionary border regions were the areas where these contradictions in personal and socioeconomic relations were most intense, and thus it followed that they were also the places where religious sects and political groups got underway. The drifters who organized such groups succeeded initially in going beyond the small universe of the closed village community and substituting for it an "independent" world by taking up such skills as medicine, geomancy, and martial arts. In time they came to those areas where autocratic exploitation had generated the greatest number of economic contradictions, but these are regions not easily delineated by simple economic geography.

Concrete examples of such people abound. Li Wencheng, one of the most important leaders of the Heavenly Principle (Tianli) sectarians' rebellion of 1813, made his livelihood as a hired construction laborer, though in fact he achieved prominence by practicing "computation and astrology."[35] Sun Dafeng of the One Stick of Incense (Yizhuxiang) sect in 1823 was respected by the people for "curing illness by giving incense."[36] Individuals such as these glimpsed worlds unknown to the common people and were the first to form religious sects and political factions that stood up to the political fiction of the Qing dynasty. Acting not out of private interest but out of a belief in their own absolute spiritual value, they practiced asceticism and believed themselves to be messiahs. A typical example is Liu Zhixie, one of the central White Lotus figures during the Jiaqing era.[37] A native of Taihe county in Anhui, he went to Gansu to revive the old teachings of Liu Song, who had been exiled there for the Murky Origin (Hunyuan) sect incident of 1775. Liu Zhixie returned home to lead his own rebellion, yet even in the midst of his struggles he managed to send 2000 taels in gold to his exiled teacher, which suggests his individual determination to maintain the bond with his master.[38] In a similar case, Liu Zhaokui went from Shandong to Xinjiang in 1791, traveling at great peril through Kucha, Aksu, Yarkand, and Kashgar until he reached the exiled Thunder Trigram (Zhengua) sect leader Wang Zitong, who had been made the slave of a Muslim. Liu received the secret transmission of the sect and the title "True Man of the Eastern Thunder Who Has Traveled the Hidden Road," though after returning home he was captured in the midst of rebel activity.[39] In yet another case, Zhang Xiaoyuan of Anhui "went at the command of his father Zhang Quan to Kashgar in central Asia in 1800 to deliver money to a fellow sectarian, Wang Fasheng;" he, however, deserted en route.[40] An earlier case is that of Xia Tianyou of Jiangyin county (Jiangsu), a believer of the Western Rice (Ximi) sect who in the early Qianlong era visited sect leader Zhang Baotai in Dali prefecture (Yunnan) and received scriptures from him.[41] In one final example, Zhang Wanxuan and Zhang Congzheng, the fathers of two White Lotus leaders of the Five Great Banners rebellion of 1861 in Shandong, were exiled in the Jiaqing era to Xinjiang for being White Lotus sectarians. They returned home in 1826, and at the time of the rebellion, Zhang Congzheng was still alive and, as an old White Lotus leader, had considerable influence on the rebels led by his son.[42]

Those suffering under the burdens of vagrancy and poverty looked for instruction and deliverance to such men: the powerful, the learned, and the ascetic seekers of truth. As vagrants, it was natural that they yearned for the actualization of a visionary community. This was especially true in north China, where poor peasants could support themselves only by traveling extensively and dealing in all manner of itinerant trading or, if they were women, by marrying into other families. The leaders to whom the masses of poor people turned sympathized with their aspirations and urged them on to a visionary utopia. They were "a stratum that stood outside or at the bottom of the already existing social hierarchy, so that in a sense they were standing at the Archimedean fulcrum in relation to the customs of their society. In other words, they had, to a certain degree, fallen out of their society's nominal order and customary attitudes. Because they were not fettered

Table 1. Rebellions during the Qing: Leaders and places of origin

Name	Uprising or sect	Date	Native place	Area of activity (including flight or exile)
Liu Zhaokui[1]	Eight Trigram sect (Bagua jiao)	1791	Weinan county, Shandong	Shandong→Central Asia→Shandong (this was his journey to see Wang Zitong; see p. 233)
Shen Xun[1]	The great rebellion of the White Lotus sect in the Jiaqing era	early Jiaqing (1796–1805)	Linxiang county, Hunan	Henan
Long Tongzhi[1]	"	"	Hengshan county, Hunan	Taiping county, Anhui
Tang Mingwan[1]	"	"	Hubei	Xixiang county, Shaanxi
Liu Song[1]	"	"	Luyi county, Henan	Longde county, Gansu (in exile)
Liu Zhixie[2]	"	"	Taihe county, Anhui	→Gansu→Sichuan, Shaanxi, Hubei
Chen Jinyu[2] Chen Guangyu[2]	"	"	Jianli county, Hubei	Tenants in Zhuqi county, Hubei → rebellion in Henan
Liu Qirong[2]	"	"	Taihe county, Anhui	Xiangyang→Gansu
Wang Mingzhao[3]	"	"	Xihua county, Henan	Luyi county, Henan→Xiangyang
Yang Mingyuan[4]	A heterodox sect	1823	Miyun county, Hebei	to An county, Shandong, then plotted rebellion in Wuqing county
Lian Fangcheng[4]	White Lotus sect	1822	Shan county, Shandong	Yucheng county, Henan
Lu Zhaochang[4]	White Lotus sect	1822	Shandong	Yucheng county, Henan
Zhu Mazi[5]	"	"	Xincai county, Henan	uprising in Xincai →Anhui

Continued on next page

Table 1—*Continued*

Name	Uprising or sect	Date	Native place	Area of activity (including flight or exile)
Ma Wan-liang (Jin-zhong)[6]	Heaven Trigram sect (Qiangua jiao)	1823	Linqing county, Shandong	Tianjin, Hebei
Zhou Tian-ming[7]	Mahayana sectarian bandits (Dacheng jiaofei)	"	Pingyuan county, Shandong	Linqing county, Shandong (his comrades were also in Lulong, Xian, and Qinghe counties)
Wang Er Dazui[8]	Four Palaces and Four Trigrams sect (Sigong sigua jiao)	"	Dongming prefecture, Henan	Lu Zongran of Juye county, Shandong, was his teacher
Li Shiming[9]	a sect member only, not a rebel	1826	Wucheng county, Shandong	Chengde prefecture, Hebei
Zhu Wen-xiang[10]	"	1827	Luyi county, Henan	Fuyang county, Anhui
Yuan Zhiqian[10]	Green Lotus sect (Qinglian jiao)	1828	Longli county, Guizhou	fled from Shaanxi, Sichuan to Hubei
Yang Shouyi[11]	"	"	Xindu county(?), Sichuan	according to orders to subordinates: one division of troops from Chengdu, Hubei, Henan→ Beijing; another from Jiading→ Yubiao→Beijing

[1]Suzuki, *Shinchō chūkishi kenkyū*, p. 134, n. 31.

[2]Yasuno, "Shindai no nōmin hanran," p. 213; Suzuki, *Shinchō chūkishi kenkyū*, pp. 97–104; and Sano, *Nōmin bōdō*, part 1, pp. 77–86, 92–100.

[3]Suzuki, *Shinchō chūkishi kenkyū*, pp. 98–101.

[4]*Xuanzong shilu*, Daoguang 3rd year (1823), 10th lunar month, 60:18a.

[5]Ibid., Daoguang 2nd year (1822), 12th lunar month, 46:28a; and Daoguang 3rd year (1823), 1st lunar month, 48:19b, and 2nd lunar month, 49:32b.

[6]Ibid., Daoguang 3rd year (1823), 12th lunar month, 63:23b; and Daoguang 4th year (1824), 1st lunar month, 64: 10b–11a.

[7]Ibid., Daoguang 3rd year (1823), 8th lunar month, 57:7a.

[8]Ibid., Daoguang 3rd year (1823), 8th lunar month, 57:18a.

[9]Ibid., Daoguang 6th year (1826), 4th lunar month, 97:12b.

[10]Ibid., Daoguang 7th year (1827), 5th lunar month, 117:31b.

[11]Ibid., Daoguang 8th year (1828), 7th lunar month, 139:13a–b.

by these customs, they were in a position to adopt a radically different idea of the meaning of the world and to promote a fervent moral and religious vision unobstructed by material concerns."[43] Accordingly, they frequently carried out their activities in areas far from their native places. This is demonstrated in Table 1, which outlines the places of origin and activity of religious rebels and heterodox sect leaders captured between 1791 and 1828.

The leaders and participants in religious rebellions lost their homelands and were forced by poverty to abandon their parents. An impression of the mental world inhabited by such people may be derived from the case of the sectarian leader Lian Fangcheng, who as a boy was obliged to leave his native place with his mother after his father had been exiled during a suppression of the White Lotus sect.[44] A memorial submitted in early 1823 reported that Lian Fangcheng and another White Lotus sectarian, Lu Zhaochang, had been discovered in Yucheng county (Henan) preparing banners and weapons and calling together sectarians from Henan and Hubei for an uprising scheduled for the twenty-third of the previous month. Officials crushed them with government troops, and it was reported that Lian and Lu resisted and died in battle. Many members of the Lian clan took part in the planning of this uprising, among them Lian's paternal cousin, his uncle, and his uncle's three brothers-in-law. His father, Lian Zaiyou, was no longer living at the time of the rebellion. He had been exiled in the Qianlong era, first to Guangdong and then to Heilongjiang, for practicing a "heterodox religion," probably White Lotus, but had later returned home under pardon. While his father had been in exile, Lian Fangcheng and his mother had left their home in Shan county (Shandong) and gone to Yucheng county in the neighboring province of Henan, probably because his mother was unable to make a living in Shan. Lian Fangcheng's plans for rebellion betray traces of his father's will.

We may surmise that Lian Fangcheng held the core world view of the White Lotus from a remark in a memorial by Yan Jian, the governor-general of Zhili province: "Recently in Henan and Shandong, a series of heterodox sectarian bandits have been captured. They believe in the teaching of 'the native land of true emptiness and the unbegotten parents.' " If we interpret the meaning of this doctrine within the context of Lian's life, his father exiled and his family driven from home, we could identify "the native land of true emptiness" as his old home in Shan county, a home that he wished to recover in a spiritually higher world. This White Lotus formula cannot be restricted simply to this literal interpretation, however, since Lian also used it to attract his entire clan, which was still living in their native village in Shandong. In a

similar vein, the idea of "the unbegotten parents" was for Lian a puri-
fied, universalized expression of his father's anger and his mother's
loneliness. Lian Fangcheng brought to this world view a dimension
of personal enmity, a fact which indicates that "the native land of true
emptiness and the unbegotten parents" provided the people with an
important spiritual opportunity to break through to a universal religious and political realm and construct a world that embodied a vision
of higher community. The expression "fatherless and lordless" was also
sometimes included in this formula, bringing into the core White Lotus
world view the concept of resistance to authority.[45]

Religious and political uprisings, besides having a comprehensive
world view, must also come to terms with the problem of militarization.
Obliged to create armed groups, they turned to the tradition of martial
training among the people.

Plentiful evidence concerning the link between martial training and
rebellion may be found in the Veritable Records of the Daoguang era.
In 1821 in Zhongmou county (Henan), "the criminal civilian Liu
Shunyi taught combat skills, . . . concocted rumors, and fomented
rebellion" among the many companions he gathered around him.[46]
In 1824 there was a group in Xiayi county, also in Henan, whose anti-
Qing character was expressed in the title "Great King of the Restored
Ming" given to its central figure, a county runner named Zhu Xiaohe.
This was a group that trained itself: "They drank together in a Taoist
temple, gathering at night and dispersing at dawn. Every morning at
the first light of dawn they faced north and kowtowed to Zhu Xiaomeng (Zhu Xiaohe's elder brother). They practiced with swords,
rifles, and fowling pieces, and their arsenal included several hundred
items."[47] In an incident of 1827, a devotional group with no plans for
rebellion was judged to be a heterodox sect: when it was found that
Zhu Wenxiang "taught combat skills" at the home of sect leader Wang
Huilong, the group was suppressed.[48] As the result of another incident
in 1827, "Na Wu, Quan Ge, Wang Qi, Wang Ba, Yan Da, Lai Si, and
many other unidentified people who practiced combat skills and gathered together to rebel" were pursued for arrest.[49] In an earlier anti-Qing
uprising in 1765 in Jingmen subprefecture (Hubei), Sun Dayou, one of
its leaders, wandered about as a monk, practicing combat skills and
proclaiming that "he had learned martial arts from an extraordinary
person who had also given him heavenly writings (holy scripture) and
a spirit whip (a ritual implement)." Sun also claimed that he was a
descendant of the Ming royal house and gathered a group of companions
to whom he taught combat skills.[50] Wang Lun, who led the Shandong
rebellion of 1774, "was a native of Shouzhang county in Shandong but

lived in neighboring Yanggu county, where he 'cured illness by the circulation of psycho-physical energy (*qi*)' and taught combat and the art of refining one's energy so as to be able to go without food for half a month without dying."[51] The widespread practice of martial training is further attested in Suzuki Chūsei's studies of secret society rebels known as *guofei* and of the Jiaqing-era White Lotus rebellion.[52]

The martial arts tradition was prominent in north China, but it was to be found in central and south China as well, and thus should be understood as a nationwide phenomenon. A few examples from the abundant historical material on the tradition of martial training in the south are offered here. Liu Que, who led an uprising in Taiwan in 1702, "worked as a tax agent but was highly skilled in boxing: his martial ability made him the outstanding man in his district."[53] In Gan Feng-chi's anti-Qing uprising of 1792 in Jiangsu and Zhejiang, the martial arts practitioners Zhang Yunru, Gan Fengchi, Zhou Kunlai, Yu Lian, and Fan Longyou were all famous as "intrepid knights-errant."[54] Finally, in the Iron Ruler Society (Tiechihui) in Shaowu county (Fujian) in 1753, "the criminal civilian Du Qi excelled in the art of boxing."[55]

The state feared that the tradition of martial training among the people could become a vehicle for rebellion and prohibited it in an imperial edict of 1727: "The governors-general and governors of all provinces are to order local officials to vigorously prohibit combat practice. Should anyone continue to offer or receive instruction in combat skills, he is to be investigated and arrested."[56] In the northern Jiangsu region of Xuzhou, Huaian, and Haizhou, "wearing dangerous weapons on one's person" was said to be common in 1826. The authorities regarded this as a dangerous practice and formulated a prohibition and issued strict regulations against it.[57]

The tradition of martial arts training, however, was not necessarily tied to revolutionary activity or popularly based armed uprisings. In some cases, martial skills were readily used to vandalize the people, as in the following examples. In Fuyang county (Anhui) in the early nineteenth century, it is recorded that "most of the younger men in the county practice combat skills, and they lead the lives of scoundrels. They are usually intimate with the county runners [scoundrels themselves for the most part] who are constantly inviting them to drink and sleep in prostitutes' houses, where they plot intrigues. They even set up their own private offices in these places and lock up many people there. Their depredations are daily getting worse."[58] It also often happened that many martial heroes among the people were absorbed into the landlords' counterrevolutionary armed gangs.[59] Both possibilities show how combat practices could be turned against the people.

The question here is not whether the greater number of martial arts practitioners joined the rebels' camp or went over to the side of counterrevolution. What is important is the ideological significance of martial training. Those with martial skills who personally experienced the difficulties of either the petty producers or the indirect producers did not just develop military prowess but adopted a new world view as well. Only then could they succeed in going beyond the village, the limited small universe of the producers, and set out on the long task to become the political and religious true man. Through their selfless absorption into martial training, they experienced a great spiritual liberation as they sought both to actualize a shared vision of community and to assault the status quo with an enthusiasm so exalted that it induced the reckless belief that swords and guns could not harm them. Obtaining military power inspired a feeling of liberation for the masses.

The martial arts tradition served as the concrete foundation for the qualitative transformation of religious groups into armed factions. The religious and political leaders and charismatic figures, who identified themselves as the "Truly Mandated Son of Heaven" or the "King of Light" or as a descendent of the Ming royal house, united with martial organizations. The White Lotus sect, for example, made a revolutionary advance in group militarization by having both civil (religious) and military (martial) sections under its leadership. This is illustrated in the case of Wang Lun, the leader of the Shandong rebellion of 1774 (mentioned above), who followed the Qingzhou branch of the White Lotus, known as the Pure Water sect (Qingshui jiao). "Those he trained in the circulation and refinement of psycho-physical energy he called his civil disciples, and those he trained in combat he called his military disciples. His followers gradually increased to the point that he harbored the desire to rebel."[60] The same combination of civil and military sections can be found in other cases. Among the groups that drifted into a later Shandong uprising, the Five Great Banners uprising of 1861, there were both armed groups drawn into White Lotus sectarian activities and martial heroes who, like the Black Banner leader Song Jingshi, were not sectarians. In 1952, a peasant who had voluntarily become a White Lotus member, Li Taiping, related his own experiences to a team of historians investigating the Black Banner rebellion: "The White Lotus was divided into a civil section and a military section, the civil leading the military. The civil section had 'Disciples within the Gate,' and the military section had 'Disciples outside the Gate.' In the civil section, one teacher was allowed to take only one disciple," whereas military teachers could take an unrestricted number of disciples.[61]

Without this organized unity between the civil and the military, the Black Banner rebellion would probably have been impossible. This conjunction between the religious world view of the sectarians and the martial tradition among the people enabled the rebel leaders to envision the ideal of the living "true man" and then to go on to construct an actual, practical program for attaining that vision.

Concluding thoughts

None of the uprisings initiated by religious societies described above succeeded in attaining their goals. What were the reasons for these persistent failures? The major problem seems to have been the power structure of the sects themselves, and the rift this structure created between the sect leaders and the mass of followers.

The sect leaders can generally be characterized as highly mobile, ambitious, and semi-proletarian in outlook. These qualities separated them at the very beginning from the mass of direct and indirect producers who were their followers. In addition, the charismatic nature of sect leadership and the internal power structure of the sects deepened the gulf between leaders and followers. Increasingly the leaders became enmeshed in their own ideological fictions, and as a result, they gradually lost touch with the demands of the direct and indirect producers, who were concerned largely with the basic struggle for livelihood. Although some sect leaders succeeded in forging armies with a strong unity of purpose, in the end their organizational skill served only to distance the struggles from the lives of the producers and from the "reality of civil society." Using these armies as a base, the sect leaders formed political cliques not all that different from traditional power cliques. As they themselves became more deeply enmeshed in the world of religious illusions, they set themselves up as "mini-emperors," in imitation of imperial absolutism.

Thus on the eve of the Taiping Revolution the masses were confronted with a choice: should they follow such leaders once again on their path to traditional-style absolutism, or wait for a new type of leader? The people needed leaders with a strong ethical and religious vision and a coherent world view that could reconcile and unite the multiplicity of values and vague religious teachings of the sects linked to the White Lotus. More importantly, they needed leaders who could meet the revolutionary demands of the propertyless poor and the lower-strata peasant producers in the lower Yangzi delta.

The Taiping Revolution did not succeed in becoming a mass movement. From the research of Kojima Shinji, we know that it was ultimately defeated by exactly the kinds of contradictions between the leadership and the masses that plagued all other religious sect uprisings. Nonetheless, if we study closely the development of the Taiping Heavenly Kingdom, and the process by which peasant political power was established through it, we can discern that this problem was recognized and that some tentative efforts were made to solve it. Only after we have acknowledged these efforts can we fully understand the real dramatic tensions of the "failed" Taiping Revolution.

Notes

[1]Takimura Ryūichi, *Marukusushugi kokkaron*, pp. 15–18.

[2]Yoshimoto Takaaki, "Kotai, kazoku, kyōdōsei to shite no ningen," vol. 14, pp. 229–31.

[3]Yoshimoto Takaaki, *Kyōdō gensō ron*, pp. 7, 231.

[4]Karl Marx, "On the Jewish Question," in *The Collected Works of Karl Marx and Frederick Engels*, vol. 3, p. 167. The complete passage is: "Man as a member of civil society is held to be man *in the proper sense*, homme as distinct from the citoyen, because he is man in his sensuous, individual, immediate existence, whereas *political* man is only abstract, artificial man, man as an allegorical, juridical person."

[5]Marx, "On the Jewish Question," p. 164. Marx is discussing the relationship between the individual and civil society: "None of the so-called rights of man, therefore, go beyond egoistic man, beyond man as a member of civil society, that is, an individual withdrawn into himself, into the confines of his private interests and private caprice, and separated from the community. In the rights of man, he is far from being conceived as a species-being; on the contrary, species-life itself, society, appears as a framework external to the individuals, as a restriction of their original independence. The sole bond holding them together is natural necessity, need and private interest, the preservation of their property and their egoistic selves."

[6]Tanaka Masatoshi, "Tachiagaru nōmintachi," pp. 194–96, 211, 214–20; and, by the same author, "Popular Uprisings, Rent Resistance, and Bondservant Rebellions in the Late Ming," translated in this volume. See also Mori Masao, "Min-Shin jidai no tochi seido," pp. 236, 260–64.

[7]Tao Xu, *Zu he*, 11b.

[8]"Tianzhu kulei" [The burdens of the landlords], *Shen bao*, Guangxu 5th year (1879), 12th lunar month, 22nd day, reprint, vol. 29, p. 18672.

[9]"Changguan pianjian" [The prejudice of the underlings in the salt office], *Shen bao*, Guangxu 5th year (1879), 11th lunar month, 27th day, in reprint, vol. 28, p. 184723. The materials in footnotes 8 and 9 were pointed out to me by Kojima Yoshio.

[10]Zheng Guangzu, "Xiangmin bufa" [The illegal acts of local people], *Yiban lu*, zashu 7:43b–44a.

[11]In the *Daqing lichao shilu* [Veritable records of the Qing dynasty], a struggle with the slogan "rent and tax resistance" is mentioned in only one place, so we cannot really confirm the existence of struggles fought in resistance to both rents and taxes. See *Xianfeng shilu*, Xianfeng 1st year (1851), 1st lunar month, 25:17a–18b.

[12]Kojima Shinji, "Taihei Tengoku to nōmin."

[13]Yokoyama Suguru, "Jūkyū seiki chūyō no kōryō fūchō," pp. 227–28. He writes:

"In their basic nature the tax resistance struggles were economic struggles whose purpose was the defense of peasant livelihood. They did not consciously make political demands against the Qing or against feudalism."

[14]Yokoyama, "Jūkyū seiki chūyō no kōryō fūchō," pp. 239–42; Kojima Shinji, "Taihei Tengoku to nōmin," part 1, pp. 48, 55–57, 70–75; part 2, section 2, p. 86; Sasaki Masaya, "Kanpō ni-nen Gin-ken no kōryō bōdō," pp. 189–92, 199; Fujioka Jirō, "1853-nen 'Katei nōmin kigi' to sono rekishiteki haikei," pp. 164–68; and Banno Ryōkichi, "Shanhai Shōtōkai no hanran," pp. 4–5, 7, 10.

[15]Shen bao, Tongzhi 13th year (1874), 11th lunar month, 20th day, in reprint, vol. 11, p. 6642.

[16]Duan Guangqing, Jinghu zizhuan nianpu, p. 153.

[17]Sasaki, "Kanpō ni-nen Gin-ken no kōryō bōdō," p. 192.

[18]Ibid., pp. 192–93.

[19]This phrase appears in an announcement of the governor of Jiangsu province dated Tongzhi 7th year (1868), 12th lunar month. The whole passage reads: "The prefectural and county officials are the parents of the people. Landlords and tenants are equally the children of the emperor." Jiangsu shengli, 3:35a.

[20]Jin Luqing, "Quanmin huanzu ge" [A song urging the people to pay their rent], Shen bao, Guangxu 2nd year (1876), 1st lunar month, 28th day, in reprint, vol. 15, p. 9254.

[21]An announcement of the Xinyang county (Jiangsu) magistrate Shen, dated Daoguang 14th year (1834), 8th lunar month, in Baxi zhi, zaji p. 9.

[22]"Qianliang chijin" [Tax default grievances], Shen bao, Guangxu 5th year (1879), 7th lunar month, 9th day, in reprint, vol. 27, p. 17392.

[23]Kojima Shinji, "Taihei Tengoku to nōmin," part 1, p. 66.

[24]Ibid., part 2, section 2, pp. 86–88.

[25]Wang Shiduo, Yibing riji (1856–57 diary), quoted in Kojima Shinji, "Taihei tengoku," pp. 147–48.

[26]Qi Longwei, "Qianren hui qiyi diaochaji," p. 201.

[27]Kojima Yoshio, "Shinmatsu Minkoku-shoki Kōnan no nōmin undō," p. 121.

[28]Ibid., pp. 120–21, quoting from local records of Tonglizhen.

[29]Kojima Shinji, "Taihei tengoku kakumei," p. 289.

[30]Chen Baichen, Song Jingshi lishi diaochaji, pp. 46–58.

[31]Yokoyama Suguru evaluates rent resistance struggles as economic struggles. He writes: "In order to develop an economic struggle into a political one, or a struggle against one official to a fight against the Qing, a separate, regimented force must appear to overcome the principle of the village community." Yokoyama, "Jūkyū seiki chūyō no kōryō fūchō," p. 231.

[32]I wish to extend my thanks to Sōda Hiroshi, from whose study of White Lotus uprisings in the Ming I have benefited greatly. (This was published subsequent to the present essay as "Byakuren-kyō no seiritsu to sono tenkai." —Trans.) It seems that the leaders of religious uprisings in both the Ming and the Qing came from almost the same stratum. Kojima Shinji deals with the Hakka, who suffered social and personal discrimination, addressing in particular the question of how their association with the visionary community of the Taiping Heavenly Kingdom took them beyond the world of the local residents. He makes an important point when he writes: "Besides intense poverty, it was the discriminated status and situation of the Hakka peasants that was above all the condition that induced them to join the God-worshipping Society, the intention of which was the total negation of the presently existing order." Kojima, "Taihei Tengoku," pp. 323–24.

[33]Suzuki Chūsei, Shinchō chūkishi kenkyū, p. 29; Yasuno Shōzō, "Shindai no nōmin hanran," p. 203.

[34]Suzuki, Shinchō chūkishi kenkyū, pp. 68–69.

[35]Sano Manabu," Nōmin bōdō" [Peasant uprisings], in Shinchō shakaishi, vol. 3, part 2, p. 17.

[36] *Xuanzong shilu,* Daoguang 3rd year (1823), 10th lunar month and 12th lunar month, 60:3b, 63:11b.

[37] Sano, *"Nōmin bōdō,"* part 2, p. 22; Suzuki, *Shinchō chūkishi kenkyū,* p. 98; Yasuno, "Shindai no nōmin hanran," p. 213.

[38] Suzuki, *Shinchō chūkishi kenkyū,* p. 115.

[39] Sano, *"Nōmin bōdō,"* part 1, pp. 44–45.

[40] Suzuki, *Shinchō chūkishi kenkyū,* p. 134, n. 31.

[41] Ibid., p. 134, n. 31.

[42] Chen, *Song Jingshi lishi diaochaji,* p. 52.

[43] Orihara Hiroshi, *Kiki ni okeru ningen to gakumon,* p. 192.

[44] Ibid., Daoguang 2nd year (1822), 12th lunar month, 3rd year (1823), 1st and 2nd lunar months, 46:27b–49:32b.

[45] Yasuno Shōzō comments on this White Lotus idea: "As is generally known, the White Lotus took as its mantra the eight-character phrase 'the native land of true emptiness and the unbegotten parents.' . . . The idea of 'the unbegotten parents' must have been established to negate the traditional arbitrary family order in which ranking is by age and the head of the family wields ultimate power. When this is combined with 'the native land of true emptiness, fatherless and lordless,' it becomes sufficiently serious to confront directly the politically centralized state as well as its supplementary elements, the communal earthbound society and the autocratic monarchy supported by Confucian morality." Yasuno, "Shindai no nōmin hanran," p. 200.

[46] *Xuanzong shilu,* Daoguang 1st year (1821), 2nd lunar month, 13:25a.

[47] Ibid., Daoguang 4th year (1824), 2nd lunar month, 65:25a.

[48] Ibid., Daoguang 7th year (1827), 5th lunar month, 117:31a.

[49] Ibid., Daoguang 7th year (1827), 3rd lunar month, 115:19b.

[50] Sasaki Masaya, *Shinmatsu no himitsu kessha,* vol. 1, p. 190, quoting a memorial of Qianlong 33rd year (1768), 4th lunar month, 9th day.

[51] Sano, *"Nōmin bōdō,"* part 1, p. 50.

[52] Suzuki, *Shinchō chūkishi kenkyū,* pp. 83–85. Did the skill of going without food perhaps evolve as a necessity of economic life in this particular region of Shandong?

[53] Sasaki, *Shinmatsu no himitsu kessha,* p. 217, quoting the Kangxi gazetteer of Zhuluo county, *juan* 12.

[54] Ibid., p. 81, quoting a memorial of Yongzheng 7th year (1729), 12th lunar month, 4th day.

[55] Ibid., p. 184, quoting a memorial of Qianlong 18th year (1753), 10th lunar month, 6th day.

[56] Suzuki, *Shinchō chūkishi kenkyū,* p. 65, n. 75.

[57] *Xuanzong shilu,* Daoguang 6th year (1826), 3rd lunar month, 96:22b.

[58] Ibid., Daoguang 8th year (1828), 12th lunar month, 148:28a.

[59] Chen, *Song Jingshi lishi diaochaji,* p. 138.

[60] Sano, *"Nōmin bōdō,"* part 1, p. 50.

[61] Chen, *Song Jingshi lishi diaochaji,* p. 46.

RURAL CONTROL IN THE MING DYNASTY

TSURUMI NAOHIRO

Tsurumi Naohiro, professor of Chinese history at Yokohama National University, wrote this essay on the *lijia* and local control for the authoritative Iwanami lectures on world history series (*Iwanami kōza sekai rekishi*), which was published in 1971. The essay was quickly recognized as a classic description of the origins, operation, and decline of the *lijia* system during the Ming dynasty, with emphasis on its function within rural society. Tsurumi's wide-ranging study of the *lijia* focuses on an organization which has often been studied merely as a tax-collection unit, discussing the changing class relations within rural Ming society from the beginning of the dynasty to its decline, and the impact of those changes on the *lijia* system.

Tsurumi Naohiro began his research in Chinese history with a graduation thesis on the Ming mining industry. His interest in mining had been sparked by the debates over handicraft industry in the Ming and Qing. Following completion of that thesis, he began to turn in other directions, believing that a study of handicraft industry had to be linked to a deeper understanding of the dominant agricultural sector and related land and class relations. He focused on the *lijia* system as both an administrative unit and as a system of local control, seeing it as a good way to understand the workings of rural society. He has published a number of essays on various aspects of the Ming *lijia* and its broader social functions.

Tsurumi argues that the *lijia* was at the center of Ming administrative attempts to control rural society and that it played a vital role in the rural reproduction process. The concept of rural reproduction, which is crucial to Tsurumi's understanding of the *lijia* system, is a category in Marxist historiography which is now commonly used by most Japanese historians. "Reproduction" is used to

This essay was originally published as "Mindai ni okeru kyōson shihai" [明代に
おける郷村支配] in *Iwanami kōza sekai rekishi* [岩波講座世界歴史], vol. 12 (Tokyo: Iwanami shoten, 1971), pp. 57–92. Translation by Timothy Brook and James Cole.

denote both the production process itself and the resources necessary to enable producers to maintain and reproduce themselves in the short term as well as command sufficient resources to sustain subsequent production cycles. When used with reference to peasants, it means that the peasant family has had sufficient return from their productive efforts to supply food and other necessities to family members (including the conditions necessary for the propagation of children which constitutes the reproduction of the work force), and to put away sufficient seed, fertilizer, etc., to sustain the next year's planting. In this essay, Tsurumi argues that the Ming state established the *lijia* and attempted to regulate land relationships in such a way as to insure a stable base that allowed for peasant reproduction.

In addition to supervising tax collection, the *lijia* organization also played a role in the supervision of certain crucial community functions. The concept of community (*kyōdōtai*, taken from the German *gemeinde*) has been used in many ways by various Japanese authors, and at least a sketchy understanding of its meaning is crucial to understanding Tsurumi's analysis. Arguments about community assume that there were certain basic social organizations in all premodern societies which so organized social production as to insure the survival of the members of the group; without such communal functions, survival was certainly less secure, if not impossible. In the European case, such communal functions included the use of common lands held by the village community. In the case of China, such communal functions are less easy to isolate. Japanese scholars have focused their attention on agreements related to water control and to shared arrangements for labor exchange. In this article, Tsurumi argues that the *lijia* has an important supervisory role in such communal functions and thus plays a major role in assuring communitywide reproduction.

Tsurumi's solid knowledge of the sources of Ming history and clarity in argument make this essay an excellent introduction to the study of Ming rural society.

*   *   *

The basis of village organization in the Ming dynasty was the *lijia* system.[1] This system did not serve simply as an organization for collecting taxes or ensuring mutual security, as has often been maintained; rather, it must be seen as an integrated structure of social control by the state, of which taxation was but one component. The *lijia* was not merely a tax-collection system that ignored existing class relations, but was instead a system of control that was based upon those relations and could be implemented only when the state exercised control over them. Accordingly, the *lijia* system was designed to support the local reproduction process crucial for the security of the community and to play a role in the community functions geared to that reproduction. The significance of the *lijia* system of control lies in its relationship to the total social structure.

From this understanding we shall proceed to the following issues. First, which peasant strata constituted the core of society, and how could that core be used as the basis for the *lijia* system? This question will be examined in the context of the aims and implementation of early Ming agrarian policy. Second, we shall examine the establishment of the *lijia* structure of control, its relationship to the previous dynasty's rural systems, and the nature of community functions in the rural reproduction process. The important question here is the relationship between the hierarchy within the *lijia* and the multiple class relations in the villages. Third, we shall address the systemic contradictions and class conflicts within the *lijia* system.

However, due to the limitations of sources, as well as the persistence of certain unresolved issues, our conclusions must remain incomplete. Among the issues for further research are the actual nature of the landlord stratum's control over the community order and the role of such internal factors as class and subject in the dissolution of the *lijia* system. In this article we shall not deal with the *lijia's* relationship to the village covenant and *baojia* systems, which were local organizations of importance from the mid-Ming forward,[2] since I do not view the *lijia* system as a village organization for mutual security and self-defense.

Peasant policy under the founding Ming emperor

Early–Ming agrarian policy: Fostering owner-cultivators[3]

The momentum of peasant rebellion at the end of the Yuan dynasty put a former peasant named Zhu Yuanzhang on the throne as the founder of a new autocratic dynasty. Ever conscious of his peasant origins, Zhu remarked, "Having risen from the peasantry, we know full well the hardship of tilling the soil."[4] In the course of laying the social and economic foundations of the new Ming dynasty, Taizu, as Zhu was known by his posthumous title, keenly felt the need to give land to the peasants, reduce the burden of their taxes, return to agricultural production the land laid waste in the turmoil of rebellion, and stabilize the social order so as to win the support of the peasantry.

Zhu Yuanzhang's agrarian policies emerged clearly as soon as he had established a territorial base. In 1356, after breaking with the rebel leader Guo Tianxu, Zhu crossed the Yangzi River and captured Jiqing (present-day Nanjing), the Yuan headquarters in the Jiangnan region. Once he had established his base there, Zhu turned to the administration of Jiangnan. He established the Bureau of Civilian Cultivation (*Yingtian si*) that same year, setting in order the water-control and irrigation facilities that were of special importance in Jiangnan. Thereafter, he encouraged local officials throughout the region, promoted large-scale water-control projects, and worked for the restoration and expansion of the forces of agricultural production. In 1368, as part of his effort to encourage land reclamation, Zhu conferred ownership on those in each locality who brought untilled land under cultivation, regardless of prior claims of ownership. He also granted a three-year tax exemption on such reclaimed land and even devised tax exemptions and reductions in areas where new land was not being opened. Zhu strove for good order among the peasantry by resettling the large numbers of landless peasants in Jiangnan, Shanxi, and Guangdong beginning in 1370; in addition, he invited displaced peasants to return to their fallow fields and cultivate them. He also moved rich Jiangnan households into north China and regions north of the Yangzi River where the problem of war-devastated land was most severe. As a result of such policies, the cultivated land reported to the central government doubled between 1368 and 1381: out of a total of 3,667,000 *qing* reported in 1381, 1,800,000 *qing* was reclaimed land. The land reclamation policy was continued, and by 1391 the total amount of cultivated land had increased to 3,874,746 *qing*.[5] Even though this figure is colored by the deception and embellishment that often characterizes the official statistics of autocratic regimes, we can derive a fairly accurate sense of the vast amount of land newly cultivated or brought back into production during the first 20 years of the dynasty.

This widely enforced early-Ming policy of resettlement and reclamantion needs to be examined more closely.[6] In the fifth lunar month of 1370, it is recorded that the Bureau of Agriculture (*Sinong si*) was established and a policy of "enumerating the population and allotting land accordingly" was adopted for land in the central north China plain which had lain fallow since the fighting in the late Yuan.[7] An edict promulgated in the fifth month of 1372 states that "in cases where the present adult male labor of displaced peasants who return to cultivate their land is low in proportion to the amount of land originally held, ownership shall not be recognized to its previous extent. Conversely, additional land may be granted for cultivation in cases where the amount of adult male labor has increased beyond its previous figure and the area of land has become disproportionately small following an official investigation of the amount of adult male labor available."[8] According to this edict, households that tried to own a disproportionately large amount of land by reason of previous extensive holdings were to be punished in accordance with the *Statutes*. Thus, the policy of resettlement and reclamation promulgated in the early Ming was known variously as "enumerating family size and allotting land accordingly," "enumerating population and allotting land accordingly," and "inspecting the amount of adult male labor and allotting land accordingly." Landholdings that were proportionate to adult male labor were granted legitimacy, but those that exceeded it were not.

What exactly was this category of "adult male labor"? The following evidence suggests that "adult male labor" was not meant to include slaves or tenants. The ownership of slaves was forbidden by imperial edict: "Those who have been forced into vagrancy by the fighting and become the slaves of others are to be sent home immediately."[9] "Commoners harboring slaves shall receive one hundred strokes."[10] Moreover it was forbidden to accumulate land and then turn it over to tenants to cultivate: "Greedy rascals who occupy much land, make it their own property, and have poor peasants cultivate it for them are to be punished."[11] Slaves and tenants therefore were legally outside the category of "adult male labor," which included only owner-cultivators capable of performing labor service. In other words, "adult male labor" refers to the labor power in small-landowning families composed of blood relatives.

Allotting land according to family size was part of the policy of fostering owner-cultivators; it was, however, not tied to a standard determining how much land ought to be allotted. For example, in Suzhou prefecture, where the forces of production were most highly developed, Prefect Song Xin in the Hongwu era allotted 16 *mu* per unit of adult male labor in Taicang subprefecture.[12] This would appear to be the minimal amount necessary to sustain the reproduction of one Jiangnan owner-cultivator at that time. On the other hand, each household in Jinan prefecture in north China was allotted only 17 *mu*,[13] a figure which seems inadequate given the contemporary level of the forces of production in north China. Nevertheless, since "those with extra adult male labor are not restricted by acreage," a household was not necessarily restricted to this average allotment of 17 *mu*. Examples of military colony land attest to grants of land ranging from 20 to 100 *mu*.[14] The early-Ming practice of allotting land by quota was quite different from the equal field system of earlier times, which in brief stipulated a uniform quota of allotted land for the entire country. The early-Ming policy of allotting land according to family size did not have the revolutionary significance that a wholesale, nationwide enactment might have had. Rather, by supplementing inadequate holdings, this allotment was a policy adapted to existing realities, and as such it was carried out in piecemeal fashion and varied according to regional discrepancies in productivity and land-labor ratios.

This peasant policy also included provisions stipulating the cultivation of mulberry, hemp, and cotton. An edict of 1365 required that peasants owning from five to ten *mu* of land devote half a *mu* to such crops, and that those who had over ten *mu* allocate one *mu*.[15] Through this requirement the state sought to foster self-sufficient owner-cultivators. It reveals at the same time the general trend for the state to deal with peasant enterprise as a combination of agriculture and household industry. Products of household industry, such as raw-silk thread, raw-silk fabric, and cloth woven from vegetable fibers, were as much the object of exactions as were agricultural products.[16]

The aim of the early-Ming policy of resettlement and reclamation was therefore conceived as one that could create an economy based on the small landowner and on the labor of the blood-related family. It was designed to foster the self-sufficient peasant who combined agriculture with household industry and who could provide for the fiscal needs of the state. In this way the state sought to establish the economic base necessary for dynastic control.

Contradictions in early–Ming agrarian policy

What measures were taken in agrarian policy, especially in relation to landownership, to create the conditions whereby the economic base of the new dynasty would be translated into a social reality capable of supporting the dynasty?

As we have seen, Taizu's policy of land allotment was intended primarily to limit landholdings to a size suitable for owner cultivation and also to reduce the amount of uncultivated land. To this end he sought to preserve those conditions of production that were suitable to the labor of owner-cultivators. His bans on tenancy and slavery indicate his dislike of land annexation, as well as his further goal of

abolishing landownership by landlords. The emperor was both aware
of and opposed to landlord ownership and sought instead to make
owner-cultivators the social base of the dynasty. But did reality conform
to the emperor's wishes? Let us consider first the tenants, who, along
with slaves, were officially prohibited.

In early-Ming regulations on equalized labor levy (*jungongfu*),
a local labor service system centered on Jiangnan, it is written that
"tenants may be used for labor service when the amount of adult male
labor is disproportionately low in respect to the amount of land held."[17]
According to the equalized labor service system, one man was to be
provided for public works projects from every hundred *mu* of land.
Landlords who had large amounts of land in proportion to their adult
male labor were allowed to assign their tenants to fulfill the labor
service requirement. As Mori Masao has pointed out, "the relationship
that existed between landlords and tenants was much more than a
simple contractual relationship between renter and rentee: it was a
personal status relationship mediated on a daily basis by community
regulations."[18] The promulgation of such a regulation in the early
Ming indicates that state power acknowledged and utilized the de
facto existence of the relationship of class between landlords and
tenants. The labor service system reflected the various actual relations
between the two. In an edict concerning the rural banquet cermony,
the purpose of which was moral instruction and the stabilization of
the rural order, it is specified that "seating should be arranged such
that the eldest occupy the superior positions. When tenants and their
landlords encounter each other, their respective ages are irrelevant:
the decorum should be that of youths attending their elders."[19] Although
the banquet was supposed to observe an order based on age superiority,
this edict required that elder tenants defer to younger landlords. The
state extended official recognition to the actual relationship between
tenant and landlord within village society, for it sought to use this
relationship to ensure rural social order.

The Ming was also unsuccessful in curtailing slavery. Prohibitions
and manumission orders were promulgated in the early Ming, as we
have noted, and others followed.[20] The fact that such bans were repeated
suggests that slaves continued to exist in spite of them. Slave owners
manipulated loopholes in the law, either by disguising their slaves
under other categories such as bondservants, or by giving them their
owners' surnames.[21]

In conclusion, the dynasty established "adult male labor" as the
standard unit of labor and, in spite of its own express wishes to the contrary, allowed tenants and slaves to be included within that category.

In the Ming, tenants had noticeably greater social importance than slaves. Since the dynasty could not avoid mobilizing them in the labor service system, their de facto existence was openly acknowledged in the workings of the tax system, even though official state policy prohibited the practice of tenancy.

Early–Ming policy toward landlords

Early-Ming policy conceived of the category of owner-cultivator as contrasting to the relationship of landlord and tenant. In fact, however, this category was premised on the full development of the landlord-tenant relationship. The government's policy toward landlords must be viewed in the context of the political aim of fostering owner-cultivators in the early Ming.

Taizu adopted severe policies toward landlords. In the case of landlords possessing special status privileges, he wanted to overthrow them because of their association with the old system of Mongolian control and their power as an exploitive force in competition with the new dynasty. As for the landlords without status privileges, he sought to restrain their power as an exploitive force parasitic on the society newly under Ming control. The Ming state took a harsh stance against Jiangnan landlords in general, confiscating their land on the most trivial of pretexts, implicating them in the frequent political scandals, forcing them to resettle outside the region, and saddling them with gargantuan levies to build the capital city. Because Jiangnan was a key economic area for the Ming, the new Ming state thoroughly extirpated from its villages all vestiges of the power exercised by the Mongols or by its former rival, Zhang Shicheng. Once landlord exploitation had been brought under control, the material (fiscal) foundation of the Ming's power was assured. However, the attack on the landlords was limited to the expropriation of individuals and to the formulation of restrictions on them as a group. A revolution in the system of landownership by landlords was not attempted. Dependent on landlordism, and himself the largest landlord of all by virtue of his policy of state land, Taizu established himself as the absolute ruler of a landlord-based society. Landlordism was the cornerstone of his fiscal foundation.[22]

After his initial victory built on the strength of peasant rebellion, Zhu Yuanzhang began to shift his base of support from the village poor to the village leadership. He originally rose to power through the support of the lowest peasant strata, and poor peasants and tenants appeared within the leadership of his peasant army. Yet from the time of his attack on Jiqing in 1356, Zhu Yuanzhang began to foster a new set of contacts with the indigenous village leaders, known as "elders."[23] The nature of his peasant army gradually changed as he gained support from the elders and Confucian literati, and his regime gradually adopted landlord traits. In his frequent audiences with elders, Taizu reassured them, sought their advice on matters of policy, entrusted commoners and children to their guidance and exhortations, and had them supervise water-control and irrigation projects and the mass mobilization involved.[24] All this demonstrates that, despite the disorder at the end of the Yuan, the elders managed to hold onto their social position as local leaders, and that the state had learned it not only could not reject the landlord class but needed it to gain control at the local level of each and every peasant. When selecting officials in 1376 before the civil service examination system was fully restored, the Ming state publicly resorted to a policy of appointing wealthy people. The officials who were later selected through the examination system virtually all came from landlord backgrounds. By virtue of the special privileges that these officials received, such as exemption from labor service, they formed the social base of the dynasty's structure of power. Similarly, the officers and elders at the heart of the *lijia* system and the state's structure of local control were selected from among the landlords. The state made use of their already existing relations of local control to achieve its domination of the rural areas and, by making these people responsible for tax collection, sought to secure its fiscal well-being.

The characterization of the Ming dynasty as a landlord regime becomes clearer as we consider state land. These state-owned holdings, especially prevalent in Jiangnan, served as a basic fiscal source for the state. Under this system, the state was a landlord, and the directly producing peasants on this land were "state tenants." The state looked to this arrangement as a way of maintaining for itself the rights of both rent and tax collection. The Yuan dynasty had set up the same system of state land when it had taken over from the Song, but when the Ming set up its official land, it did so on an even larger scale. This system embodied the legal recognition of landlord-style exploitation. Within this context, the relations of production between landlords and tenants, which had underpinned Jiangnan landholding since the Song and Yuan periods, were firmly established and won wide social acceptance. State land had the reputation of bearing a heavy rent, even though its rent was in fact lighter than for regular, non-official land. This suggests that the direct producers paying the heavy rent were not paying directly to the state but to a stratum of landlords that had inserted itself between the state and the direct producers. Thus, the landlords were the ones who first rented state land, and under them stood the stratum of rent-paying peasants known as "cultivators" (*zhonghu*).[25]

As we have seen, although Taizu's policies were designed to foster and protect owner-cultivators,[26] they did not in fact represent the interests of the poor peasants. Taizu intended to rely on exactions from owner-cultivators as the major contribution to the dynasty's fiscal base, but he had to rely on the power of the landlords in order to carry out his program. By supporting the local structure of reproduction that was based on already existing landlord-tenant relations, the Ming state ended up incorporating the landlord class into its ruling system and making it the social and economic foundation for a unified structure of control.

The owner-cultivators protected by the state's policies in actual fact spanned a variety of small-landlord strata, from landlords harboring non-kin labor to the smallest landowners relying exclusively on family labor.[27] Although the state did not publicly approve of this situation, it accepted the fact that it depended on the social relations in which these people were involved. The state relied on an institutional abstraction that was capable of adapting to this ambiguous situation by organizing the people on the basis of existing landlord-tenant relations. This system of rural control was the *lijia*.

The *lijia* system: Its establishment and structure

The establishment of the *lijia* system

Previous scholars have assumed that the *lijia* system of rural control began in 1381,[28] but recent research has shown that the *lijia* in some form was already in operation by the late Yuan or the very early Ming.[29] In this section we shall examine the earliest forms of the *lijia* system and consider their relationship with the *lijia* after 1381.

Two systems of rural organization were practiced during the Yuan, the township-ward (*dubao*) system and the community (*she*) system. In the Jiangnan township-ward system, rural areas were divided into districts (*xiang*) and townships (*du*). Each district had a supervisor (*lizheng*), and each township had several headmen (*zhushou*). The size of one's landholdings determined eligibility to serve as a supervisor or headman. In Huzhou prefecture landlords owning at least one hundred *mu* of land were eligible to serve as supervisors. Their duties involved tax collection, census-taking, and the maintenance of public order, and in this last duty they were assisted by the headmen. The community system began first in north China and only later spread to Jiangnan. Under this system, 50 families formed one community (*she*) led by a captain (*shezhang*) whose duties included the encouragement of agriculture, moral instruction, and the supervision of mutual aid. In actual practice the two systems mixed, such that captains, supervisors, and headmen were often considered the same post.[30]

Continuities with the township-ward system of the Yuan can be detected in early-Ming village organization. For example, in Jinhua prefecture in Zhejiang, we find that in 1371 one tax captain (*liangzhang*) was appointed per township (*du*) and one captain (*lizhang*) per ward (*bao*) in Jinhua county.[31] In 1368 in the same prefecture, duty appointments in Yiwu county were decided on the basis of the township-ward system, with each township having a township captain and each ward having a ward captain.[32] We know that this prefecture in the late Yuan had one chief and one assistant captain per township,[33] from which we may conclude that the Yuan system of organizing rural control by means of captaincies continued uninterrupted in this prefecture into the early Ming. Similar cases may be found in Huzhou prefecture and the subprefecture of Chuzhou, both in South Zhili.[34]

A new organization of rural control, contrasting with the Yuan township-ward system, emerged in Huzhou prefecture and was known as the *lijia* system. There in 1370 "small yellow registers" were compiled to serve as the basis for organizing the *lijia*.[35] This system worked according to the number of households, with one hundred households forming one ward (*tu*). Those households having the most adult male labor and paying the most land tax served as captains and were responsible for collecting taxes and supplying military provisions. This system had much in common with the *lijia* system that went into effect in 1381, though it also differed in several respects. There was, for instance, no attempt to distinguish between marginal landowners who were too poor to meet the service levy and those for whom sickness or age made any kind of labor service impossible. At the same time that the small yellow registers were being compiled in Huzhou, units of village organization know as *li* and *jia* were in use in Wujiang county in neighboring Suzhou prefecture. These units, which appeared in Wujiang at least as early as 1369, became the standard divisions for the nationwide *lijia* system enacted in 1381.[36]

Thus, beginning around 1369 or 1370, the new *lijia* system was taking shape in Jiangnan. Intimately connected with this development was the compilation of Yellow Registers.[37] In 1370, prior to the introduction of the Yellow Registers, a nationwide system of household registration was already in operation. The household register recorded a household's address, the number of adult males, and its members' names and ages. Since property was also recorded, this register was no mere population census, for it could also serve as a vehicle for levying taxes.[38] Probably on the basis of these early household registers, Yellow Registers were compiled in Huzhou prefecture in 1370 and in Jiaxing and Huizhou prefectures in 1371.[39] Since the compilation of the Yellow Registers was the essential prerequisite for the widespread implementation of the *lijia* system, it is clear that the emergence of the two systems was closely linked.[40]

The various types of *lijia* organizations at the end of the Yuan and the beginning of the Ming served as the means by which the peasants were ruled. Because many of these local units were originally part of the Yuan dynasty's system of peasant control, the Ming had to create a new structure of its own in order to effectively supersede Yuan control. The *lijia* system as it was implemented in Jiangnan in 1369–71 was based on new principles that differed from those underlying Yuan village organization. At that point the *lijia* system was not yet institutionalized, so its implementation took many forms. Increasing uniformity developed as the dynasty secured its power, and full uniformity was achieved in 1381.

The new *lijia* organization was conceived as institutionally distinct from the pre-existing villages. The fundamental principle on which it was based was household enumeration. However, as we can see in Table 1, the *lijia* units that were actually formed took their divisions and boundaries from the dimensions of the villages that had existed ever since the Song. Even when *lijia* units were reorganized, one unit was rarely divided among several other units. Instead it was usually amalgamated in its entirety into another *li*. In those cases in Jiangnan where *lijia* boundaries were altered, they were altered within the township— the next higher administrative unit dating from the Southern Song—and did not cross over into other townships. Jiangnan was densely populated and had many polders requiring special water-control and irrigation works. Because of this, the unit of reproduction within a locality was not necessarily the small area constituted by a unit in the *lijia* system but could embrace several *lijia* units or even an entire township.[41] Since township boundaries were never crossed when *lijia* units were organized in Jiangnan, as Table 1 illustrates, we can see that the object of *lijia* organization was not to keep to an artificial number of households but to maintain the local process of reproduction.

Table 1. The Amalgamation and dispersal of wards in Luoyuan county, Fujian, from the Song to the Ming dynasty.

Name of district (xiang)	Name of township (yu, li)	Song or Yuan	1381–91	1403	1412–52	1462	1472–1542
Chongde	Dongyu	x	x	*x*	x	x	x
	Beiyu	x	x				
	Xiyu	x	x	*x*	x	x	x
	Nanyu	x	x				
	Xinshun	x	x	x			
	Meixi	x	x				
		x	x → *x*		*x*	x	x
	Anjin li	x	x				
		x	*x* → *x*		*		
	Baijing li	x					
		x → *x*	x	x → *x*	x	x	
		x → *x*	x	x			
	Shanhua li	x	x				
		x	x → *x*	x	x	x	
		x	x → *x*	x	x	x	
Changshu	Zhaoxian li	x					
		x → *x*	x				
		x	x	x → *x*	x	x	
		x	x	x			
		x → *x*	x → *x*	x	x		
	Linji li	x	x				
		x	x				
		x	x	*x*	x	x	x
		x	x				
	Xinfeng li	x	x				
		x	x → *x*	x	x	x	
		x	x → *x*	x		x	
	Xugong li	x	x				
		x	x → *x*	x	*x*	x	
		x	x				
	Luoping li	x	x				
		x	x → *x*	x	§	x	
Tongle	Huangchong li	x	x	x	x	x	x
		x	x	*x*	x	x	x
	Huokou li	x	x				
		x	x				
	Linyang li	x	x				
		x	x → *x*	x	x	x	
	Total number of wards:	38	36	21	16	14	16

Source: *Luochuan zhi* (Luochuan gazetteer, 1545), 2:38b–41b.

Notes: * Anjin li was dispersed among Dongyu, Xiyu, Linji li, Baijing li, and Xugong li. §Luoping li was temporarily dispersed among Dongyu, Xiyu, Xinfeng li, and Shanhua li.

The existence of wards is indicated by an x. Amalgamated wards are indicated by *x*. Here the terms *tu* (ward) and *li* are interchangeable.

Lijia organization

The *lijia* system of the Ming was implemented throughout the entire country in the first month of 1381. In that year the first Yellow Registers were compiled using *li* and *jia* as census units. The earlier household registers had distinguished individual households according to the four occupational categories of military, civilian, artisan, and saltern. These categories were meant to be hereditary. The Yellow Registers, however, registered all households uniformly into *li* and *jia* regardless of occupation.[42] When the second compilation took place in 1391, more detailed regulations were drawn up to rectify previous omissions. According to these new regulations, one *li* (known in the cities as *fang* and in the suburbs as *xiang*) was composed of 110 households of spatially contiguous landowners, regardless of their occupational registration. Within the *li*, the households were divided into either three or nine grades on the basis of their adult male labor and their landholdings. The ten households that were graded most highly were designated as *li* captains (*lizhang*, or alternatively *fangzhang* or *xiangzhang*). The remaining 100 households, designated as *jia* heads (*jiashou*), were divided into ten *jia*. Each *jia*, therefore, had ten *jia*-head households, and for every *jia* there was one *li*-captain household. During any one year, one of the ten captain households had to serve as that year's *li* captain, and one of the ten head households in each *jia* had to serve as *jia* head. This service was rotated among the registered households, the cycle of responsibility being completed every ten years.

   This *lijia*'s ideal was to construct artificial villages by organizing households into units of 110, but the system could not ignore the natural villages that already existed. It was, of course, impossible to organize exactly 110 households into every *li*, and there were often many households existing outside the regular *lijia* membership. These were known as "attached households."[43] Exempt from regular *lijia* responsibilities, they were attached to particular *jia* and assigned various miscellaneous labor duties. In addition there was the category of "supernumerary households," those who were exempted from labor service because they were living alone and lacked sufficient means of support. This category included elderly persons over 60 years of age, the chronically ill, children under the age of ten, widows, and transients. Although in principle exempt from labor service, these supernumerary households were often not strictly distinguished from the attached households. It was a common practice that, when the regular members of a *li* were selected from the higher-grade households, the excluded lower-grade households were lumped together as supernumerary households.[44] In such an instance, the attached households owning small amounts of land were classed together with those that qualified as supernumerary households in the strict sense of the term. This unavoidable discrepancy between *lijia* theory and practice was due to the theory's strictly observed distinction between those who bore *lijia* responsibilities (the regular members) and those who did not. The minimal landownership qualification in Jiangnan for regular membership was 10 *mu*,[45] presumably the level at which the lowest stratum of regular households could independently sustain their own reproduction. Distinctions below this level became blurred: since neither those who owned less than 10 *mu* nor those who were entirely landless could sustain their own reproduction, both petty landowners and tenants came to be included in the category of supernumerary households.

The labor service of *li* captain and *jia* head was distributed over a ten-year period on the basis of the decennial compilation of the Yellow Registers.[46] When a household previously ranked as a *li*-captain household lost its qualifications due to a decrease in its membership or wealth, or when a household died out, it was replaced by a new *li*-captain household selected from among the *jia*-head households that were closest to it in terms of size and wealth. If the number of *jia*-head households was insufficient, attached or supernumerary households were reclassified as regular-member households in order to fill the gap. In the case of *li* that had no attached or supernumerary households, they were permitted to bring some in from a neighboring *lijia* unit. However, since *lijia* units were organized within townships, which in Jiangnan was the next administrative unit above the *li*, households could be transferred between individual *li* within the same township but not across township boundaries.

Households that cultivated state land, as we have noted, were formally tenants but actually landlords; accordingly, they were deemed regular-member households and had to form *lijia* units also. Finally, *lijia* regulations strictly forbade households from splitting into subhouseholds, dividing fiscal responsibility among several *lijia* units, or arbitrarily changing grade within the *lijia* hierarchy. Nonetheless, many households engaged in such practices in order to evade regular and miscellaneous labor-service responsibilities within the *lijia*.[47]

Regular *lijia* posts[48]

Li **Captains and** *Jia* **Heads.** *Li* captain and *jia* head were the most common and also the most fundamental regular posts in the *lijia* system.

As a rule all regular-member households had to serve in these posts once every ten years, and service could not be avoided even by the families of government officials. In each *li*, one *li* captain and ten *jia* heads took up their posts every year according to a regular succession. The *li* captains supervised the *jia* heads and were in charge of regular *jia* duties. The *li* captain serving in a given year was called the current-year captain, and the other nine were known as successive-year captains.[49]

The responsibilities of the *li* captain and *jia* heads were fourfold.[50] First, they had to collect and ship the tax for the *li*, which in the Ming was set according to a prescribed quota. Since these officers were made directly responsible for seeing that taxes were paid in full, tax collection entailed the further responsibility of ensuring that there would be no deficit. This could include investigating land and population to forestall fraudulent tax declarations, inspecting land and filing reports for areas suffering from natural disaster, routinely supervising water-control projects, and encouraging agricultural production among the people. Many of these duties overlapped those of the tax captain, to be discussed below, and where both systems were in effect, the two captains carried them out jointly.[51] The second responsibility of *li* captains and *jia* heads was to maintain good order within their *li* and take care of such matters of public business as apportioning the tax levy among the *lijia* members and adjudicating minor disputes. Together with the elders, they were responsible for moral instruction, through which intra-*li* organization could be strengthened. The third responsibility was to furnish specified tribute items to the central government and supply various necessities required by the local county office. They were also responsible for the transport system within the *li*. Furthermore, the *jia* heads were required to perform miscellaneous services at the county office, and as these duties multiplied, problems arose over how they should be delegated. The fourth responsibility was the compilation of the Yellow Registers.[52] The so-called major compilation (*dazao*) took place once every ten years, and the *li* captains and *jia* heads for that particular year were in charge of the job and had to bear the costs involved. The compilation procedure began when local officials distributed empty registers and tax registration receipts (*hutie*) to the *li* captains and *jia* heads. Local officials had every household within their jurisdiction register the names of their members, their total number of adult males, and their property. Changes over the preceding ten years were noted by checking this information with the last Yellow Register and then the new data was used as a base for determining the taxation grades for the next ten years. Once registers for each *jia* and *li* were compiled, maps of the *li* were appended to the front of the *li* register. The completed registers were then forwarded to the county office. In Jiangnan, registers were also compiled at the next higher administrative level, the township.

In principle, the term of service for *lijia* posts was only one year in ten. As the burden on the current-year captains increased, a portion of their regular duties gradually devolved upon the other successive-year captains. These reassigned duties included taking care of the registration of military and artisan households, investigating lawsuits, apprehending escaped prisoners, and managing water-control projects at the polder level.

Lijia **Elders.** Although the system of appointing *lijia* elders was implemented nationwide and constituted a main component of the *lijia* system, there exist very few sources explaining its origins, organization, and function. The year when it was established is in dispute. Obata Tatsuo said 1389, Matsumoto Yoshimi gave 1394, and recently Hosono Kōji claimed 1398.[53] Even the number of elders per *li* is in question. Formerly it was assumed that there was only one, but Hosono believes that in the early Ming there were three or ten per *li*, plus other elders who assisted them.

What we know of the responsibilities of the elders is summarized in the 1398 "Proclamation on Instructing the People."[54] The proclamation stipulates such functions as minor adjudication, moral instruction, encouragement of agriculture, water-control management, and mutual aid within the *li*. Along with the *li* captain, the elders played their part in maintaining the *lijia*'s system of control by keeping good order within the *li* and intervening in the *lijia* members' process of reproduction. Those who became elders had to be men of good reputation and intelligence who were known among the people for their honesty. In times of rent resistance and peasant rebellion, the *lijia* elders repeatedly sided with the government in suppressing the peasants. By organizing self-defense corps within the villages, they were able to resist rebel forces.[55] Thus we many hypothesize that the *lijia* elders were powerful local landlords who supported the local authorities and enjoyed the backing of state power.

Tax Captains. Tax captaincies were first established along the middle and lower reaches of the Yangzi River, an area of key economic importance for the state's fiscal administration.[56] They were initiated in 1371, at which time each tax captain was responsible for collecting 10,000 *shi* of grain on the average. The post was temporarily abolished in 1382 but was revived in 1385. Although subject to various changes from the Jiajing era forward, the post of tax captain survived into the early Qing. As of 1385, the tax captain's basic unit was the *qu* (division), which was formed by combining several *li* that were not necessarily within the same township. In 1397 a total of one tax captain and two assistant tax captains were set up in each division, and powerful landlords were appointed to the posts. The position of tax captain was originally an annually rotated post, but as of the Xuande era in the first half of the fifteenth century it became a lifetime appointment. From the Zhengde era in the early sixteenth century, one tax captain's duties were shared simultaneously by several persons under an arrangement known as the associate-appointment (*pengchong*) system.

The main responsibilities of the tax captain were collecting tax grain from every *li* within his division and forwarding it to the designated granary. In addition, he drew up and implemented the division's labor service assignment roster and also participated with *li* captains and elders in legal adjudication. As the officer supervising the *li* captains and polder captains, he also devoted himself to maintaining the peasants' reproductive capacity, directing his attention primarily to water control and irrigation. The tax captain's motive for encouraging agriculture in this way was to ensure that the district could meet its tax quota. When natural disaster struck, it was the tax captain's job to investigate and report the extent of the damaged fields and to apply for appropriate tax relief for the stricken areas. These tax captains were probably selected from among the most powerful *li*-captain households in a district. Since their duties extended to every aspect of village control, households appointed to the tax captain's position were said to be on a par with real officials, so great was their power as the ruling stratum in the village.

In addition to the posts that have been discussed, there were occasionally other local labor-service posts within the *lijia* system, such as embankment captain (*tangzhang*), *jia* overseer (*zongjia*), and *jia* warden (*xiaojia*).[57] Although these were considered regular posts, they were minor and are omitted from the present discussion.

The *lijia* system as a structure of control

The number of small landowners temporarily increased in the early Ming as a result of Taizu's policy of resettlement and land reclamation in the wake of late-Yuan peasant rebellion. This did not, however, lead to a transformation of landlord-style landownership. Accordingly, the same multilayered relations among the various strata of local landlords, owner-cultivators, tenants, and slaves continued in the villages through the transition from the Yuan to the Ming. Reproduction was maintained on the basis of the rights of use specified within the community constituted by these various relations. The Ming dynasty was able to use the *lijia* system to impose its mechanism of control on these multiple relations among the village strata. Village landownership and power remained in the hands of the landlords because of the support extended to them by the *lijia* system of community control.

The fact that the *lijia* system relied on a fixed quota of 110 households should not be allowed to obscure the fact that, in many cases, *li* and township boundaries often conformed to the contours of villages that had existed from the Song and Yuan. Passages in the "Proclamation on Instructing the People" make it clear that the organization of the *li* and *jia* units was often done with full attention to existing spatial relationships:

To be an elder in the *lijia*, one must live among the people of the ward or *li*, have land that borders theirs, and know the day-to-day good and bad of the locale. . . .

In each ward or *li*, a large wooden clapper is to be set up. . . .

If the villagers' houses are scattered and far from each other, each *jia* should also set up a wooden clapper to facilitate communication.[58]

The formula of 110 households per *li* was not strictly adhered to in practice. The *lijia* used individual households as the building blocks in its structure of control, but its actual organization was not the neat sum of 110 parts. Since the social substance of a *li* was constituted not by the number of households but by the relations among the village strata, the system saw fit to maintain 110 or more households as a structured clique within village society.

All of the regular *lijia* members were assessed for labor service as captains and heads and, as well as serving in these regularly rotated posts once every ten years, were also responsible for filling such posts as tax captain or embankment captain. Since the *lijia* system operated as a mechanism both for tax collection and for ensuring the maintenance of conditions necessary for tax collection, the captains and heads were concerned with maintaining the stability of reproduction within their units of jurisdiction, the essential precondition for the performance of their duties. Consequently, those assigned to labor service were not merely tax collectors. Indeed, it was a matter of course that they should concern themselves with and take charge of virtually every aspect of the peasants' process of reproduction. From this perspective, one can say that the *lijia* system was not simply a village tax-collection organization. It was at the same time deeply involved in community functions designed to support the process of local reproduction on which such tax collection depended.

What were the village community functions embraced by the *lijia* system? The crucially important natural factor for agricultural production, apart from land, was water. This was true for both northern Chinese dryland agriculture as well as the paddy fields of central and south China. The clearest example is the low, damp region of Jiangnan where polder fields constituted a major base of rice production. The constant repair of polder banks, creek-dredging, and irrigation by treadmills, work that had to be repeated every year on schedule, were essential to reproduction in this region. These operations were without exception carried out by collective labor, and the assignment of the necessary labor was done through the *lijia* system by the designated *lijia* officers.[59] For example, in fifteenth-century Suzhou and Songjiang prefectures, peasants pooled their treadmills to pump water out of paddy fields when they were inundated by rain. Able-bodied men and women were compelled to sign up for community labor in which, supervised by the tax captain and the *li* captains, they turned the treadmills to the sound of drums and wooden clappers.[60] Undoubtedly, this borrowed use of labor was closely related to the existence of customary community activities based on the *lijia* units. In the busy season, the cooperative pooling of labor among the small peasants also took place: this was called "exchange of labor" and was similar to the "customary collective activities" in Japan.

Previous research has already pointed out that water-control organizations outside Jiangnan were formed on the basis of the Yuan community (*she*) system which incorporated intact village organizations for mutual collective aid.[61] It has also testified to the existence of a range of customary collective activities in north China.[62] This leads us to conclude that during the Ming, even in areas outside Jiangnan, customary collective activities not only survived but were linked in some way with the *lijia* system of control, although concrete evidence of this is not yet available. Nonetheless, we can read in the "Proclamation on Instructing the People" a list of activities concerning the encouragement of agriculture with which *lijia* elders would be involved when handling litigation, such as "agricultural land," "unauthorized consumption of garden and orchard produce," "domestic animals trampling and eating of rice plants," "equal water rights," etc.[63] We must surmise that, in order to make these community regulations effective, they had to fall within the jurisdiction of the *lijia* system. North China, even into the twentieth century, also had village structures for watching crops,[64] and they functioned within the same terms as the articles for litigation mentioned in the "Proclamation on Instructing the People."

Although collective labor and customary community activities in relation to water control sustained the reproduction of the peasants, the unit of peasant reproduction, at least in Jiangnan's polder region, was basically that of the individual petty peasant carrying on production on a very small scale. The means and objects of production, including not only cultivated land but also water and non-agricultural land where wild herbs could be gathered, were probably utilized on an individual basis. However, this individual utilization could not possibly have been totally divorced from the various actual regulations governing water use within the community. Consequently, the labor services for maintaining reproduction, primarily labor for water control, were carried out on the basis of *lijia* or tax division units, which in turn were based on the various relationships within the community.

The *lijia* organizations were within the power of the landlords who as *lijia* officers could control community regulations. These landlord households also were the principle owners or suppliers of the tools essential for irrigation, such as treadmills and water sweeps,[65] which meant that these tools served as the material foundation for the concrete exercise of control over the petty peasants within the *lijia* system.

Dominating the structure of the various class relationships within the community were the landlord strata whose households served as tax and *li* captains. They likewise dominated the social and status hierarchies. Within this group were the tax captains, who, "both in their social status and in their daily style of life comprised a social stratum that had much in common with officialdom. They held a clearcut status that put them on a par with the officials vis-à-vis the *li*-captain households and the common peasants. The tax captains together with the government officials constituted a single ruling status. . . . Moreover, there also existed a gap between the *li*-captain households and the common peasants, between whom was observed the distinction between 'honored' and 'base,' such that the peasants dared not rank themselves with the captain households."[66] Up to the present no historical materials have been discovered showing that a relative status ranking also existed between the regular, *jia*-head households and the attached and supernumerary households. However, since the regular members controlled the operation of the *lijia* system, we may assume that a differential status ranking developed between them and the households classed outside the service hierarchy.

Thus, the *lijia* system organized its units by establishing a level-differentiated hierarchy of households in which every household had its place, be it as a *li*-captain, *jia*-head, attached, or supernumerary household. In doing so, the *lijia* system recognized a variety of de facto class and status relations in the villages. From the state's viewpoint, incorporating these various social relations into the *lijia* order made these relations even stronger; and by placing the landlord strata, the local powerholders, at the core of the *lijia* system's embodiment of autocratic power, these households became the medium by which an autocratic, unified structure of control, culminating in the emperor, could be erected.[67]

The breakdown of the *lijia* system

The *lijia* in the context of tax reform[68]

In the early Ming, taxes and labor services were apportioned among the households in the *lijia* and levied according to the units of *li* and *jia*. Among the regular-member households, labor service was equally distributed on a ten-year cycle. Despite the intent to equalize fiscal burdens both among and within each *li* and *jia*, discrepancies immediately developed among the abilities of each *li*, *jia*, and household to meet its burdens. These discrepancies resulted because households were not ranked according to a uniform, nationwide criterion but were subject to variations relative to regional differences. Tax collection inequalities were further aggravated by the use of decennial quotas, for the taxes recorded in the Yellow Registers were in principle not to be changed despite changes in actual conditions during the ten years between compilations.[69] The system nevertheless implied that all *li* and *jia* were equally able to bear their fiscal burdens. By adhering to this principle and collecting taxes at uniform rates, however, real inequalities among *li*, *jia*, and households intensified over time. This systemic contradiction existed within the *lijia* from the very first.

As one might expect, the *lijia* system was plagued right from the beginning by a succession of schemes to avoid taxes: commending the ownership of one's land to a powerful person (*touxian*), transferring the registration of one's land to another person (*guiji*), making a false declaration (*yingshe*), and shifting land registration to another place (*nayi*). Rich households colluded with the clerks who compiled the Yellow Registers, concealing the sizes of their families and tampering with their household's status and ranking. As a result, taxation was thrown into confusion.[70] Levies were comparatively light in the early Ming, but as they were increased by new exactions over time, disparities among the *lijia* members increased. Thus, from the mid-Ming on, systemic contradictions intensified. Attempts were made accordingly to reform the *lijia* system. For instance in areas where there was a conspicuously small number of regular-member households, *li* were combined or reorganized. Also, as of the Jingtai era (1450–56), the government conditionally approved the previously interdicted practice of splitting up households so that *lijia* units could maintain an adequate number of member households.[71]

Changes in the assessment of taxes also occurred. Under a system known as equalized labor service (*junyao*), initiated in Jiangxi in 1443 and implemented nationwide in 1488, miscellaneous labor services were levied at fixed instead of irregular intervals as they had been in the past. Also, the severity of the levy was made to depend more on the amount of the taxpayer's landholdings.[72] Similarly, from the second half of the fifteenth century, it became common to convert part of the regular *lijia* service to a payment in silver, known as "*lijia* silver." This testifies to a change in tax-levy principles from a variable levy per household based on that household's ranking to a uniform levy on adult male labor and land.[73] This trend culminated in the first half of the sixteenth century in the "ten-sections system."[74]

These tax reforms occurred against a background of increasingly serious tax fraud through land commendation, transferred registration, and subdivision of registration. At the same time, greater limitations were being imposed on the special tax exemptions accorded to government officials and gentry.[75] As the basis for taxation shifted to land, the ordinary landlords who bore most of the labor-service burden within the *lijia* commended their land or conferred its registration to the officials and gentry. From the mid-Ming on, the gentry was emerging as a distinct social stratum, and their large-scale landholding intensified the systemic contradictions within the *lijia* system.

The Single Whip reform, the single most important tax reform in the Ming, developed in central and south China on the basis of the ten-sections system. The Single Whip was applied initially in the first half of the sixteenth century to taxes, equalizing them on the basis of adult male labor and land. Then it was applied in the second half of the sixteenth century to labor services as well. The effect of the Single Whip system was to convert into a single payment in silver such regular *lijia* labor services as furnishing tribute (*shanggong*), meeting county expenses (*gongfei*), and providing county services (*gongshi*). The same was done for miscellaneous labor services. In this way it abandoned the early-Ming principle of assessing taxes on the basis of household rank within *lijia* units and shifted the unit of tax assessment from the *li* to the county. Among the new methods of tax payment that were also introduced under this system was the practice of making each taxpayer responsible for delivering his tax payment in person to the county treasury.

Despite this reform, some of the regular labor services at the local level were still handled by the *li* and *jia* units.[76] The *li* captain continued to compile the Yellow Registers, supervise tax collection, maintain law and order, and manage water-control facilities. The tax captain similarly continued to supervise water control and forward tax payments. But in time these various duties were gradually divided up and performed separately as specialized categories of labor service. Later, when the land-based service levy equalization (*juntian junyi*) system was implemented, these categories were abolished. In this manner the Single Whip destroyed the substance of the *lijia* system, and the equalization system eradicated all lingering vestiges of it.

The collapse of the *lijia* system

The *lijia* system dissolved because of formal contradictions external to the system itself. However, this analysis does not sufficiently explain the role of the relations of production and the class composition of the peasants, which were the internal factors by which the *lijia* system was maintained. What then was the real cause of the system's collapse?

Furushima Kazuo has postulated the following conjuncture as the major factor in the collapse of the *lijia* system: "The basic problem lay in the collapse of the local power relations of the smaller landlords, the households in the first two ranks of the system who were most liable for the fiscal burden of serving as *li* captains, tax captains, or tax-remitting households (*jiehu*), the key posts within the *lijia* system."[77] These local landlords, lacking connections with the tax-exempt world of officialdom, were forced to bear not only the burden of their own taxes but also the burden of the taxes which officials and gentry could avoid, thereby becoming the state's major taxpayers. Furushima also points out that the local landlords were the ones responsible for maintaining the conditions necessary for peasant reproduction, on which the parasitic large landowners, who were well connected with officialdom, relied to collect rents from their tenants. According to Furushima, this double social burden borne by the local landlords resulted in a weakening of control over the tenants, such that the tenants' surplus labor could not be completely exploited by the landlords. On land that was managed directly by landlords, there is no sign that tenant labor was used; rather, the primary source of labor was bondservants (*jiapu*). In order to counter the weight of the political exploitation exerted by the *lijia* system, these local landlord operations required an intensification of agricultural technology. Since the low productivity of enslaved labor was not equal to the task, this system of landlord-managed bondservant labor collapsed. From the mid-Ming on, hired labor became the primary form of labor power, from which followed a deterioration of the power of the local landlords.

This argument by Furushima was an attempt to counter earlier explanations by Matsumoto Yoshimi and Kitamura Hironao of the transformation of landholding based on external conditions.[78] They argued that the *lijia* system's collapse was due to the decline of the owner-cultivator and rural landlord. That decline was caused by the growth of absentee urban landlords, a phenomenon predicated on the development of a monetarized economy. Furushima in contrast probed the internal links holding the *lijia* together by focusing on the structure of local power and control. However, Furushima's explanation becomes problematic when he refers to the development of an intensive system of agricultural technology that necessitated a transformation in the form of labor in local landlord enterprise. As Saeki Yūichi has already noted, "This merely points out the general development of technology, which has been conceptualized in complete separation from the various conditions necessary for the development of the forces of production by the directly producing peasants in whose hands this agricultural technology lay."[79] Thus Furushima's argument amounts in fact to a one-dimensional argument based on managerial systems external to the relations of production. If such an intensification of the technological system of Ming agriculture took place, what must be asked is, what brought about this kind of development in the technological system? Such a development would have been possible only through the production and labor of the peasants working on a small scale, for it was they who utilized that society's forces of production.

To understand the role of the peasants, it is essential to examine the nature of the parasitic large landowners at the local level in the early Ming who were being promoted to official posts and appointed to the labor-service posts of captain and elder, and who from the late Yuan on were expanding with state backing their already large landholdings. As Tanaka Masatoshi has argued, the management of these large holdings was basically being done on a tenancy basis. While some plots were cultivated by the landlords themselves, these were relatively tiny plots, such as vegetable gardens from which the landlords supplied only their own families. It was the large landholdings that dominated the actual

pattern of local land use.[80] These parasitic large landowners are the
social stratum that Furushima pointed out as comprising the core of
the *lijia* system.

On the other side of the production relationship were the tenants in
whose hands rested the forces of production. Niida Noboru has stated
that from the Ming forward the legal system no longer categorized landlords and tenants as "masters" and "servants" respectively.[81] We also
know that the tenant's right to cultivate the land on which he was situated was already established in the late Yuan, as shown in cases of
Jiangnan tenants pawning the land they rented.[82] In other areas of production, we know that a social division of labor had occurred in the
Jiangnan cotton industry, as well as in the silk-thread and silk-weaving
industries. In the opening years of the Ming in Songjiang prefecture,
cotton cloth was being widely sold in the streets, produced by small-
scale peasants in order to pay their land tax.[83] Thus we see that simple
commodity production had already developed in the villages of four-
teenth-century Jiangnan. This production conferred considerable
autonomy on small-scale peasants, including tenants; although subject to control by community regulations which were the tools of the
parasitic large landowners, they could sustain their reproduction autonomously. On the basis of such self-managing peasants, the various
forces of production developed further, but the taxes and rents extracted
from them also got progressively more severe. In this dual context of
rural economic crisis and growing commodity production, the tenants
struggled against the exactions of the landlords. This struggle contributed to the further development of the forces of production and also
enhanced their own autonomy. For example, Deng Maoqi's 1448 rebellion in Fujian enumerated clear, peasant-style demands, and the
tenants who rose up in revolt succeeded in abolishing the practice of
paying a "winter gift" (*dongsheng*) to the landlords in addition to the
regular rent.[84] Such an accomplishment was possible only in the context
of an increase in the tenants' autonomy as self-managing peasants.
Bianmin tuzuan (Illustrated guide for the people), published in 1502,
reflects this relationship between landlord and tenant in its depiction of
"the joys of the farmer." As described by Amano Motonosuke: "It
portrays a thank-you drinking banquet in full swing, to which the
landlord has invited to his house his tenants and hired laborers (?), . . .
testimony to the rise in the social status of the Ming peasantry."[85]

It has already been noted that the peasantry in the early Ming existed
in a variety of social strata. In conjunction with the unprecedented development in the forces of production from the mid-Ming on, these various strata were moving toward and cohering in the most important

relation of production of that society, that between landlord and tenant. However, just as this happened, their coherence began to disintegrate. Accompanying this disintegration was the continuous reproduction and cyclical reappearance of a clearly defined stratum alienated from the means of production, namely, a stratum of slavelike bondservants. Bondservants became the inevitable concomitant to the dissolution of independent management among the peasants. These bondservants cannot be defined simply as slaves, for the definition of their character must be made in relation to the development of the structural relationships constituting the contemporary social totality.

How then should we assess landlord management of cultivation? What must be borne in mind here is the fact of unprecedented expansion in commodity production for the market, bolstered by the growth in the forces of production from the early Ming. For directly producing, self-managing peasants, the road to rich-peasant status was blocked off for the time being by the state's and the landlords' increasing exactions. It was the landlords who controlled the local community regulations and usually as well the commercial capital that was the key to the circulation of commodities. Nevertheless, the peasants struggled against state and landlord exactions and in the process of production and labor advanced the forces of production during the Ming. This advance was simultaneously manifested in the intensification of class contradictions between landlord and tenant. On their side, the landlords in sixteenth- and seventeenth-century Jiangnan complained that "recently simple-hearted peasants have become more scarce," and that "with the petty obstinacy that reigns these days, one cannot be sure of finding two or three good men out of ten."[86] As Oyama Masaaki has pointed out, these complaints do not typify just a few idiosyncratic relationships between recalcitrant tenants and their landlords; on the contrary, such remarks reveal a class opposition.[87] Through their collective labor day after day in irrigation work and agricultural production at the village or intervillage level, the tenants gradually achieved organizational strength in their struggle against the landlords. As well, unity within particular localities was forged.[88] It was against such a background that the rent-resistance movement in the sixteenth and seventeenth centuries gained momentum throughout central and south China, with Jiangnan its center. By the mid-eighteenth century, rent resistance in the Suzhou region had become chronic, and contemporary landlords lamented: "Good land is less valuable than good tenants."[89]

Faced with this intensification of class contradictions with their tenants, brought on by the growth in agrarian commodity production, the local landlords found it increasingly difficult to expropriate from the self-managing tenants the fruits of the development of the forces of agricultural production. At this point, the local landlords came up with a new response: exploitation under the direct management of the landlord himself.[90] The landlords tried an intensive style of agriculture, overseeing the cultivation of their land by bondservants or hired laborers rather than renting it out to tenants who managed production themselves. From the late Ming into the early Qing, there was much debate on the subject of landlord management. However, the class confrontation between landlords and tenants was also driving a wedge between landlords and bondservants. Whereas bondservants had previously been subordinated to their masters through fictive kinship ties, now they were altering that relationship. As one landlord remarked, "Nowadays bondservants who are obedient and respectful are scarcer than they used to be"; and again, "Recent customs are such that there are no good bondservants anymore."[91] As a result, even when managerial landlords used bondservant labor in their personally supervised enterprises, they could not get away with maintaining servile relationships with their bondservants because of what was happening in the relations between landlords and tenants. In the midst of that intensifying confrontation, dependence either on bondservants or on nominally free, hired laborers was a novel but at best temporary response.

As these class confrontations between tenants and managerial landlords increased, the local landlord stratum's position of local control was growing shakier. As Furushima has pointed out, these were the households forced to bear the brunt of the tax burden that was not being shared by the parasitic large landowners who had good connections with official circles. As gentry landownership grew, so did the tax burden.[92] Thus the local landlords were beset by intensified class confrontation with their tenants as well as by increased exactions on the part of the state and the official and gentry landlords. At the same time, their relations with other strata were also deteriorating. At this point, their authority crumbled, thereby depriving the *lijia* system of its foundation. The system then collapsed. Looking at this process leading to the collapse of the *lijia* system from the perspective of landownership, we can see it as one segment in the further expansion and development of landlord-tenant relations.

The state and the landlords both recognized that a decline in community functions at the local level due to the dissolution of various social relationships would have made their exactions impossible to realize. Therefore, maintaining and securing these community functions continued to be an essential prerequisite for state and landlord rule. Even after many of the labor-service duties within the *lijia* had been canceled by the Single Whip system, those pertaining to water control and irrigation, which were indispensible to local reproduction, became distinct and independent posts. The survival of this supervision of community functions meant that landlord control could continue. In the Wanli era, there are many examples of gentry who participated in water-control activities, although they had the privilege of refusing.[93]

The trend from the Kangxi era forward was for greater state intervention in the process of local reproduction. Backed by landlord control in the sense already described, "a reorganization of community relations through the intervention of state power"[94] was carried out. Water-control practices were gradually reestablished on the unit of the polder.[95] No longer was water control governed by the local unity of the tenants; instead, it was essentially a vehicle for the landlord's control of community functions.[96] In the polders of Huzhou prefecture in the first half of the eighteenth century, "such things as the custody of the sluices and the management of irrigation machinery (?) were by customary arrangement the province of the landowners. The responsibility is rotated annually among the landowners, with costs apportioned according to the amount of acreage owned. The repair of polder walls and irrigation ditches is carried out in the same way."[97] Whatever concerned water control, a necessary prerequisite for the peasants' reproduction, had to be handled according to "customary arrangement." In other words, the local landlord strata were still in control of this, just as they had always been.

What we speak of as gentry landownership was a necessary phase in the development of the relations of production between landlords and tenants. As such, it could not have been established either directly or through the agency of the state's labor service system, were it not for its close link with the local community's structure of reproduction. This view forward into the subsequent developments in landlord-tenant relations in the Qing allows us to recognize more clearly the character of the *lijia* system in the Ming as a form of local organization whose rise and decline were irreversibly tied to that society's class relations and its structure of local control.

Notes

  [1] "Village" refers throughout this article not to the so-called administrative village but rather to the real, historical, social village. This historically formed unit is often called the natural village, but this nomenclature is not entirely appropriate.

[2] For studies of the village covenant (*xiangyue*) and *baojia* systems, see Matsumoto Yoshimi, "Mindai," pp. 120–26; Shimizu Morimitsu, *Chūgoku kyōson shakairon*, pp. 340–88; Obata Tatsuo, "Mindai kyōson no kyōka to saiban"; Sakai Tadao, "Mindai zenchūki no hokōsei ni tsuite"; and Saeki Tomi, "Shindai no kyōyaku chiho ni tsuite."

[3] In speaking of "owner-cultivators" (*jisakunō*), I follow the convention in East Asian historical scholarship. It should be noted, however, that although these owner-cultivators managed their enterprises independently, they worked under a system of landownership which was subject to an autocratic regime placing certain historical constraints on their "private ownership" of land. The reader is referred to "Nihon ni okeru Chūgoku kenkyū no kadai," p. 56.

[4] *Taizu shilu*, Hongwu 4th year (1371), 5th month, *yihai*, p. 1232.

[5] Fujii Hiroshi, "Mindai no dendo tōkei ni kansuru ichi kōsatsu," pp. 101–2.

[6] This section is based on my oral presentation at the Ōtsuka Historical Association convention in 1960, abstracted as "Shoki Min-ōchō no nōmin shihai." Those views have since been revised on the basis of a critique made on that occasion by Tanaka Masatoshi and also on the basis of his oral presentation at the Conference on Oriental History at the University of Tokyo in July, 1963, entitled "Minsho tochi mondai no ichi kōsatsu."

[7] *Taizu shilu*, Hongwu 3rd year (1370), 5th month, *jiawu*, p. 1012.

[8] Ibid., Hongwu 5th year (1372), 5th month, p. 1352.

[9] Ibid.

[10] *Da Ming lü*, vol. 2, p. 72.

[11] *Taizu shilu*, Hongwu 4th year (1371), 3rd month, *renyin*, p. 1198.

[12] Mori Masao, "Minsho Kōnan no kanden ni tsuite," part 2, p. 437. A biography of Song Xin is included in *juan* 22 of the 1512 prefectural gazetteer of Songjiang. There it states that men aged 15 or older were each allotted 60 *mu* of land. I reject this statement on the grounds that one person could not cultivate that much land under conditions prevailing at that time. Instead I follow Zhou Chen's testimony that they were allotted 16 *mu* each: see Zhou Chen, "Yu xingzai hubu zhugong shu" (Letter to the officials in the Ministry of Revenue at the emperor's temporary residence), in *Huang Ming wenheng*.

[13] *Taizu shilu*, Hongwu 3rd year (1370), 6th month, *dingchou*, p. 1049; cited in Kataoka Shibako, "Kahoku no tochi shoyū to ichijō benpō," p. 140. A different interpretation of this source, with which I disagree, may be found in Shimizu Taiji, "Min no Taiso no sengo tochi keiei," p. 79.

[14] Shimizu Taiji, "Minsho ni okeru gunton no hatten to sono soshiki," p. 34.

[15] *Taizu shilu, yisi* (1365), 6th month, *yimao*, p. 231.

[16] Tanaka Masatoshi, "Rural Handicraft in Jiangnan in the Sixteenth and Seventeenth Centuries," translated in this volume.

[17] *Taizu shilu*, Hongwu 3rd year (1370), 7th month, *xinmao*, p. 1060.

[18] Mori Masao, "Jūyon seiki kōhan Sekisai chihō no jinushisei ni kansuru oboegaki," pp. 71–73.

[19] Niida Noboru, *Chūgoku hōseishi kenkyū: dorei nōdo hō, kazoku sonraku hō*, p. 175.

[20] *Taizong shilu*, Hongwu 35th year (1402), 7th month, *renwu*, p. 146. The relevant passage is quoted in Niida, *Chūgoku hōseishi kenkyū*, p. 183, n. 4.

[21] Oyama Masaaki, "Large Landownership in the Jiangnan Delta Region During the Late Ming-Early Qing Period," translated in this volume.

[22] Saeki Yūichi and Tanaka Masatoshi, "Jūgo seiki ni okeru Fukken no nōmin hanran," p. 1.

[23] "Elders" (*fulao*) appear in late-Yuan and early-Ming documents under a plethora of names: *gulao, qiru, rushi, fuxiong*, etc. This seems to indicate that the elders' composition was broad and their nature complex, cautioning against generalizations based on the few sources at hand. See Moriya Mitsuo, "Furō."

[24] For references to elders in the Veritable Records, see *Taizu shilu, wuxu* (1358),

12th month, *gengchen*, p. 71; *bingwu* (1366), 4th month, *wuchen*, p. 283; 11th month), *yimao*, p. 305; Hongwu 1st year (1368), 6th month, *wuchen*, p. 569.

[25] Tanaka Masatoshi, "Chūsei Chūgoku ni okeru kokka kenryoku to tochi shoyū kankei"; Fujii Hiroshi, "Min: shakai, keizai," p. 419.

[26] Tanaka, "Minsho tochi mondai."

[27] Fujii Hiroshi, "Ichijō benpō no ichi sokumen," p. 573; Kataoka Shibako, "Kahoku no tochi shoyū," pp. 144–45; Oyama Masaaki, "Mindai Kahoku fueki seido kaikakushi kenkyū no ichi kentō," p. 110.

[28] Matsumoto, "Mindai," p. 94.

[29] Fujii Hiroshi, "Minsho ni okeru kinkōfu to zeiryō to no kankei," p. 24; Oyama Masaaki, "Rikōsei setchi no nendai ni tsuite"; Tsurumi Naohiro, "Mindai no kireiko ni tsuite," p. 38; Yamane Yukio, *Mindai yōeki seido no tenkai*, pp. 14–15.

[30] Umehara Kaoru, "Gendai saekihō shōron."

[31] *Su Pingzhong wenji*, 6: 23, cited in Shimizu Taiji, "Mindai hanseki no kenkyū," p. 42.

[32] Oyama, "Rikōsei setchi."

[33] Ibid.

[34] Tsurumi, "Mindai no kireiko," p. 38; 1614 *Chuyang zhi*, 3:3b–5b.

[35] Tsurumi, "Mindai no kireiko," p. 38; Yamane, *Mindai yōeki seido*, pp. 16–18.

[36] Tsurumi, "Mindai no kireiko," p. 37.

[37] Concerning Yellow Registers, see Wei Qingyuan, *Mingdai huangce zhidu*; Yamane, *Mindai yōeki seido*, pp. 16–36.

[38] Yamane, *Mindai yōeki seido*, p. 36.

[39] For Huzhou, see Tsurumi, "Mindai no kireiko," p. 38. For Haiyan county in Jiaxing, see Oyama Masaaki, "Mindai no jūdanhō ni tsuite," part 2, p. 38, n. 17. For Huizhou, see "Wushi fenshandian jingli zongbu," p. 2.

[40] Wei, *Mingdai huangce zhidu*, pp. 46–53; Yamane, *Mindai yōeki seido*, p. 36.

[41] This point has been inferred from the fact that there was one tax captain in each district. Furthermore, according to the 1488 *Wujiang zhi*, 3: 22b, there were 530 rural supervisors in Wujiang county during the Yuan in addition to 9 urban ward supervisors (*fangzheng*). In 1369 Wujiang county had 530 *li*. We cannot immediately conclude from this that the locations and boundaries of the Ming *li* were carried over intact from the Yuan, but there is little doubt that the Ming *lijia* system in Jiangnan was founded on an intimate connection with the Yuan ward system.

[42] There are many studies that explain how the *lijia* functioned as an institution. The following are among the best: Matsumoto, "Mindai," pp. 95–119; Obata Tatsuo, "Minsho no chihō seido to rikōsei"; Yamane Yukio, "Jūroku seiki Chūgoku ni okeru aru kokō tōkei ni tsuite—Fukken Keianken no baai," pp. 161–65.

[43] "Attached household" is a translation of *daiguanhu* in the narrow sense of the term: households whose landholdings made them potentially eligible for *lijia* membership. *Daiguanhu* is also used in a broad sense to mean those who are not regular-member households, and as such includes the "supernumerary" households (*jilinghu*) discussed below.

[44] Tsurumi, "Mindai no kireiko," pp. 43–44.

[45] Ibid., p. 49.

[46] Matsumoto, "Mindai," p. 99.

[47] Yamane, *Mindai yōeki seido*, p. 85.

[48] *Lijia zhengyi* (regular *lijia* labor-service posts) can be interpreted in broad and narrow senses. Here I interpret it broadly to denote those labor-service posts that were essential to the maintenance of the *lijia* system. See Yamane, *Mindai yōeki seido*, pp. 37–39.

[49] Current-year captains were known alternatively as *xiannian*, *jiannian*, or *gainian* captains. Successive-year captains were called *painian* captains: for the meaning of *painian*, see Okazaki Hiroshi, "Mindai ni okeru jinushi no shisō no ichi kōsatsu," p. 58.

[50] On the duties of the *lijia* officers, see Matsumoto, "Mindai," pp. 99–101;

Yamane Yukio, "Mindai richō no shokuseki ni kansuru ichi kōsatsu," pp. 79–87; Iwami Hiroshi, "Mindai chihō zaisei no ichi kōsatsu: Kanton no kinpeigin ni tsuite," pp. 77–80; Yamane, *Mindai yōeki seido*, pp. 40–52.

[51] Oyama Masaaki, "Mindai no ryōchō ni tsuite," p. 46.

[52] Wei, *Mingdai huangce zhidu*, p. 50. The compilation of the Yellow Registers was supposed to take place once every ten years. The third compilation should therefore have been carried out in 1401, but it was deferred till the following year due to the succession crisis. This apparently is the reason that later compilations all took place one year behind schedule (see Matsumoto, "Mindai," p. 98). However, Wei points out that the third compilation actually took place in 1403, twelve years after the second compilation, and that the fourth was conducted nine years later in 1412. Thereafter, compilations were made at ten-year intervals until 1642.

[53] Obata Tatsuo, "Mindai kyokusho no rōjinsei," p. 65; Matsumoto, "Mindai," p. 112; Hosono Kōji, "Rirōjin to shūrōjin," p. 66.

[54] Concerning *lijia* elders, see Matsumoto, "Mindai," pp. 84–127; Obata, "Rōjinsei," pp. 61–70; Hosono, "Rirōjin," pp. 51–68; Kuribayashi Norio, "Mindai rōjin kō." ["Jiaomin bangwen" (Proclamation on instructing the people) constitutes the ninth *juan* of *Huang Ming zhishu*, vol. 1, pp. 467–76.—Trans.]

[55] Tanaka, "Tachiagaru nōmintachi: Jūgo seiki ni okeru Chūgoku no nōmin hanran," pp. 225–26; Sakai, "Mindai zenchūki no hokōsei," p. 598.

[56] Concerning tax captains, see Liang Fangzhong, *Mingdai liangzhang zhidu*; Oyama, "Mindai no ryōchō," pp. 24–68.

[57] Concerning embankment captains, see Hoshi Ayao and Funabashi Sadao, "Mindai no tōchō ni tsuite"; Morita Akira, "Minmatsu ni okeru tōchōsei no henshitsu ni tsuite"; idem, "Shindai no tōchōsei ni tsuite." Concerning *baojia* overseers and wardens, see Yamane, *Mindai yōeki seido*, pp. 63–64.

[58] "Jiaomin bangwen," pp. 467, 470.

[59] Hamashima Atsutoshi, "Mindai Kōnan no suiri no ichi kōsatsu," pp. 7–17; Oyama, "Mindai no ryōchō," p. 43.

[60] Oyama, "Mindai no ryōchō," p. 45.

[61] Among the many studies on this subject, see for example Toyoshima Shizuhide, "Chūgoku saihokubu ni okeru suiri kyōdōtai ni tsuite." An appendix to Song Lian, *Song xueshi quanji*, 33:66b, itemizes 20 *mu* of ceremonial land (*jichan*) attached to a sixteenth-century shrine to Song Lian in Pujiang county, Zhejiang. An irrigation pond was designated to supply water to irrigate 5 *mu* of this land, and it is recorded that this water was "not allowed to be used to irrigate other land," which amounts to a prohibition on the recirculation of water. This appears to have been a common practice at this time.

[62] Sōda Hiroshi, "Genmatsu no hanran to sono haikei," p. 15.

[63] "Jiaomin bangwen," p. 468.

[64] These crop-watching societies were called *kanqing hui* or *kanmiao hui*. They are discussed in Fukutake Tadashi, *Chūgoku nōson shakai no kōzō*, pp. 440–47.

[65] Oyama, "Mindai no ryōchō," p. 46.

[66] Ibid., pp. 52–53. The first study to note this point was Yasuno Shōzō, "Minmatsu Shinsho Yōsukō chūryūiki no dai tochi shoyū ni kansuru ichi kōsatsu" p. 76.

[67] Tsurumi, "Mindai no kireiko," p. 58.

[68] Ming tax reform is treated in Oyama Masaaki, "Fueki seido no henkaku."

[69] Matsumoto, "Mindai," p. 97.

[70] Shimizu Taiji, "Mindai no zeieki to kiki"; Yamane, *Mindai yōeki seido*, p. 85.

[71] Gao Jie, *Houhu zhi*, 4:5b–6b.

[72] Yamane, *Mindai yōeki seido*, p. 108.

[73] Iwami, "Mindai chihō zaisei," pp. 80–81; Kuribayashi Norio, "Rikōgin ni kansuru kōsatsu," pp. 344–45; Yamane Yukio, "Teiryō to kōgin"; idem, *Mindai yōeki seido*, p. 130; Kuribayashi Norio, "Sekkō no teiden ni tsuite."

[74] The "ten-sections system" (*shiduan fa*) redistributed the silver-commuted service levy on all households within a county rather than a single *lijia* unit. Oyama

Masaaki discusses it in a two-part article entitled "Mindai no jūdanpō ni tsuite."—
Trans.

[75] Hamashima Atsutoshi, "Minmatsu Sekkō no KaKo ryōfu in okeru kinden kin' eki hō," p. 164.

[76] Kuribayashi Norio, "Mindai kōki no nōson to rikōsei," p. 386; Yamane, *Mindai yōeki seido*, p. 147.

[77] Furushima Kazuo, "Minmatsu Chōkō deruta ni okeru jinushi keiei," p. 13.

[78] Matsumoto, "Mindai," pp. 104–8; Kitamura Hironao, "Minmatsu Shinsho ni okeru jinushi ni tsuite," pp. 13–15.

[79] Saeki Yūichi, "Nihon no Min-Shin jidai kenkyū ni okeru shōhin seisan hyōka o megutte," p. 285.

[80] Tanaka Masatoshi, "Minmatsu Shinsho no dai tochi shoyū ni tsuite—gakuse-tsushiteki tenbō."

[81] Niida Noboru, "Chūgoku shakai no hōken to fyūdarizumu," pp. 104–5.

[82] Tanaka Masatoshi, "Ichiden-ryōshu-sei to ganden kōsō"; idem, "Popular Uprisings, Rent Resistance, and Bondservant Rebellions in the Late Ming," translated in this volume; Sōda, "Genmatsu no hanran," p. 7.

[83] Nishijima, "The Formation of the Early Chinese Cotton Industry," translated in this volume.

[84] Miyazaki Ichisada, "Chūgoku kinsei no nōmin bōdō," p. 6; Tanaka, "Tachi-agaru nōmintachi," p. 235.

[85] Amano Motonosuke, "Chin Fu no *Nōsho* to suitōsaku gijitsu no tenkai," p. 40.

[86] Zhang Lixiang, *Yangyuan xiansheng quanji*, 5:12a, 7:18b.

[87] Oyama, "Large Landownership in the Jiangnan Delta Region During the Late Ming-Early Qing," translated in this volume.

[88] Furushima Kazuo, "*Ho nōsho* no seiritsu to sono jiban," p. 111.

[89] Tanaka, "Popular Uprisings, Rent Resistance, and Bondservant Rebellions in the Late Ming," translated in this volume.

[90] Comment by Tanaka Masatoshi in "Chūgoku no kindaika," (China's moderni-zation), in *Sekai no rekishi* (World history; Tokyo: Chikuma Shobō, 1961), vol. 11, p. 307.

[91] Zhang Lixiang, *Yangyuan xiansheng quanji*, 48:136, 19:25a.

[92] Hamashima, "Minmatsu Sekkō no KaKo ryōfu," p. 185.

[93] Hamashima, "Mindai Kōnan no suiri," pp. 54–56.

[94] Ibid., p. 57.

[95] Ibid., p. 52.

[96] Ibid., p. 57.

[97] Yao Tianpu, *Huangzheng jiyao*, 8:26b–27a.

REFORMS IN THE SERVICE LEVY SYSTEM IN THE FIFTEENTH AND SIXTEENTH CENTURIES

YAMANE YUKIO

This essay, by Yamane Yukio, professor of Chinese history at Tokyo Women's Christian University and leader of the Ming history research group at the Tōyō Bunko, provides a clear and authoritative description of the development of the Ming tax system by one of Japan's leading experts in the field.

In taking up the study of the Ming tax system, Yamane follows a long line of Japanese scholars who have examined the details of Chinese institutional arrangements. Such studies began in the early twentieth century as the Japanese government searched for administrative policies to deal with the recently acquired colony of Taiwan. Assuming that it was necessary to know something about Chinese administrative tradition before formulating colonial policies, scholars were mobilized to collect and analyze data on Qing administrative and legal practices. Researchers attached to the project collected large numbers of documents, including legal contracts and other records. The study and analysis of such new materials stimulated a lively academic interest in analyzing Chinese administrative and legal history. Studies were begun on Chinese administration, going back in the past to the days of the legendary well-field system, and continuing through the Ming and Qing.

Interest in administrative history led to a project developed at Tokyo University under the leadership of Katō Shigeru, pioneer in Chinese social and economic history, and his colleagues Wada Sei and Shimizu Taiji, to study and translate the fiscal treatises from the standard dynastic histories. As the research project progressed, their interest expanded from simple study and translation of the treatises to investigation of their accuracy; this in-

This essay was originally published as "Jūgo-Jūroku seiki Chūgoku ni okeru fueki rōdōsei no kaikaku: Kin'yōhō o chūshin to shite" [十五・六世紀中国における賦役労働制の改革―均徭法を中心として] in *Shigaku zasshi*, vol. 60 (1951), no. 11:43–68. Translation by Helen Dunstan.

volved the comparison of data given in the dynastic histories with other sources, particularly with the data that could be found in local gazetteers.

After World War II, Japanese historians quickly realized that land tax and the labor service system were important factors linking the state and peasantry. Many studies of the Ming tax system were made, though there is a conspicuous paucity of work on land tax. Nevertheless, convinced that tax was an important way of explaining the changes in state-peasantry relationships, Japanese historians have produced a new subfield of tax history.

Yamane Yukio, a student of Wada Sei, has continued the study of Chinese administration, particularly the study of the Ming tax system. Though he has shown little interest in engaging in theoretical debates, he has worked untiringly at producing empirical studies. His published work includes a wide variety of essays on local marketing and local elite studies. He is the editor of a number of very useful bibliographies, editor of the journal *Minshi kenkyū* [Historical studies of the Ming], and leader of the Ming research group at the Tōyō Bunko.

*   *   *

For dynasty after dynasty the *fuyi* taxes and the state monopolies were the chief sources of revenue. *Fuyi* represented the land taxes (*fu*) assessed on agricultural land, plus the services (*yi*) assessed principally on the individual adult male.[1] In Chinese taxation history, the service levy system was just as important as the land tax. The Chinese service levy system differed from European and Japanese corvée practices which involved agricultural production on the manorial demesnes of feudal lords. In the Chinese case, the labor service system served the various manpower needs of the state apparatus at its lowest reaches. The service system was implemented through the coercive powers of the centralized bureaucratic state.

The system, which originated in pre-Qin times, continued to exist down to the Qing dynasty. The distinctive character of the Chinese service levy system is related to the fact that in Chinese fiscal history there was no separation between central and local finance. All aspects of collection and disbursement of the revenues operated through the unitary labyrinthine system of the central state. Thus standing behind the system was the great power of the premodern, centralized, and bureaucratic Chinese state.

This distinctive Chinese labor service system underwent major reforms during the Ming dynasty, particularly from the middle of the fifteenth century to the sixteenth. This was one element in the larger fiscal reform in which changes in the service levy system played a central role. For this reason, I hope in the present article to trace these changes and to investigate the transformations in the social and economic structure underlying them.

The pre-Ming service levy system

Before embarking on a discussion of the Ming system, I wish to give a simple sketch of earlier arrangements. The service levy system of antiquity involved taking up arms in defense of the state or participating in construction projects, but it appears that the period of service did not exceed three days. During the Han, the burden of the service levy gradually became more severe, but at the same time it was possible to buy release from actual service through a monetary payment. During the period of the Northern and Southern dynasties, the service levy by and large seems to have occupied some twenty days a year. Then with the adoption of the celebrated equal fields system (*juntian fa*) the *zu-yong-diao* (land, service levy, cloth) taxation system was established, and the service levy became a uniform and standard institution. It should not, however, be forgotten that besides the *yong* therewere some other, miscellaneous service duties under this system. When the equal fields system collapsed in mid-Tang times, change was inevitable for the *zu-yong-diao* system as well, and it was replaced by the dual tax system. As a result, the *yong* was absorbed within the dual tax, and it appears that subsequently the old form of service levy disappeared. But what was the so-called service levy (*yi*) of the Song dynasty and after? According to Sogabe Shizuo: "In China, from the time of the Zhou dynasty, the compulsory services demanded of the population were of two kinds: the service levy and official service duty (*zhiyi*). The former meant performing manual labor for the state for a fixed period; the latter, carrying out administrative tasks within the governmental apparatus, chiefly at the local level—in other words, serving as honorary functionary. This second form . . . was found in Song times also and was indeed the institution designated by the word *yi* during that period."[2]

This is the theory not of Sogabe alone, but also of Ma Duanlin, compiler of the *Wenxian tongkao*.[3] But was the service levy of the Song dynasty exclusively a matter of the community self-governmental *zhiyi*? Of course, the *li* captains (*lizhang*), household captains (*huzhang*), elders

(*qizhang*), bowmen (*gongshou*), stalwart men (*zhuangding*), etc., corresponded to the *sanlao, tingzhang, sefu, youjiao*, etc., of the Han, but
can such errand-runners and miscellaneous yamen menials as the
chengfu, renli, shouli, sancong, yuhou, and *zazhi* really be deemed to have
been honorary functionaries? My inclination is rather to believe that
distinct from the community self-governmental service duty, the Song
service levy system also embraced the running of errands and performance of miscellaneous tasks within the governmental offices. We find
the following passage about the Song service levy system in the *fuyi*
section of the treatise on population of the *Min shu*, a gazetteer on
Fujian compiled by He Qiaoyuan in 1630:

> There was a division into district labor service (*xiangyi*) and bureau-
> cratic labor service (*liyi*), and there were five gradations. In the dis-
> trict labor service system, the *li* captain supervised taxation payments,
> the household captain took responsibility for tax returns, and the
> elder investigated [crimes of] robbery. . . . In the bureaucratic labor
> service system, at first the Supply Master had charge of official prop-
> erty;[4] the *renli tiesi*, and *shushou* processed the documents; and
> the *shouli* and the *sancongguan* were there for running errands. As for
> the *zazhi, yuhou*, and the like, these were all drafted equitably from
> the tax-paying households.[5]

Thus in fact the labor service system of the Song had two divisions, district labor service and bureaucratic labor service. The former was the
"official service duty" of which Sogabe speaks; the latter was the
duty of performing errands and other miscellaneous tasks within the
governmental offices, and it would seem that one ought to distinguish
between it and the district labor service. At the present time, however,
I am unable to speak with any confidence on the relationship between
this "bureaucratic labor service" and the service arrangements of earlier periods.[6]

The service levy system of the early Ming

Next I should like to give a summary of the service levy system of the
early Ming. In the fiscal treatise of the *Ming shi* the first entry on this subject concerns the equalized labor levy (*jungongfu*) fixed in 1368. This was
a matter of levying the labor necessary for the construction works at
the new dynastic capital [Nanjing] from the population of the surrounding area; it was assessed on landowners, and the rate was one able-

bodied adult male for each *qing* [100 *mu*] of land. The area affected was
the fourteen prefectures and four subprefectures of the Metropolitan
Jurisdiction plus a part of Jiangxi;[7] and since moreover those who were
subject to this levy were exempted from the land tax, it must be admitted
that the equalized labor levy, being assessed over a specially designated
region in the place of land tax, was a little different from what normally is understood by the service levy system.

It was in fact with the compilation of the Yellow Registers (*fuyi
huangce*)[8] in 1381 that the early-Ming service levy system was established. The Yellow Registers combined the functions of the household
register and the taxation ledger, and the territorial units known as *li*
were established for the purpose of their compilation. A *li* was composed of 110 households: the richest 10 were chosen to be *li*-captain
households, leaving the remaining hundred to be *jia*-head households.
A *jia* was constituted for every ten households. Thus in effect a *li* was
made up of ten *li*-captain households plus ten *jia* households. This was
the so-called *lijia* system of the Ming, and throughout the whole of the
dynasty it performed the lowest-level functions in the tax-collection
mechanism. From the beginning, the *lijia* also had some local self-
government functions, but it was the tax-collection functions that were
paramount. The one *li* captain (*lizhang*) and the ten *jia* heads (*jiashou*),
serving their turns in a decennial rotation, were responsible for these
functions. Serving as *li* or *jia* head was known as the regular *lijia* service
(*lijia zhengyi*), or more simply as the regular service levy (*zhengyi*),[9] *li*
service (*liyi*), or household service (*huyi*); and it corresponded to the
"district labor service" (*xiangyi*), that is to say the service duty of the
Song dynasty. There were cases in which further offices—those of elder
(*laoren*), tax captain (*liangzhang*), and embankment captain (*tangzhang*)
—were also included in the regular service levy.

All other forms of service were by contrast known as miscellaneous
services. They corresponded to the bureaucratic labor service of the
Song. In the Song, the district labor service and the bureaucratic labor
service differed only in the kind of work that they involved: there
was no real differentiation in the method of assessment. That is to say,
district labor service was levied principally on the upper-grade households, bureaucratic labor service on the middle-grade ones. In the Ming,
however, the relationship between regular and miscellaneous was different. The regular labor service came around uniformly and inevitably
once a decade to each and every household, with the sole exception of
the supernumerary households (*jilinghu*).[10] The miscellaneous service,
on the other hand, was allocated among households on the basis of "the
number of their adult male members (*ding*) and the land taxes due

(*liang*),[11] and the extent of their property": a household was allotted light or heavy service duties in accordance with its rating. This was done by means of the household grades of the ninefold classification system. The classification of households into nine grades was already carried out in Tang times and seems to have prevailed in early Song times also. The establishment of household classification in the Ming took place in 1385. In the Veritable Records for the first lunar month of that year we read: "The officials of all the prefectures, subprefectures, and counties in the Empire were commanded to rank the households in their jurisdictions into three grades, upper, middle, and lower; and (so) to prepare service levy system registers (*fuyi ce*). These were to be kept in the official compound. Whenever there arose some service task, the registers should be brought out, and the service assessed according to the degree of its onerousness."[12] It is not clear from this entry whether or not the three grades were each subdivided into three, but the nine-fold classification was certainly an institution of rather ancient standing. From the time of the second compilation of the Yellow Registers, the classification data were appended to these documents and formed the basis for the service levy allocation.[13]

The objects of this miscellaneous service allocation process were only the civilian households (*minhu*), that is to say, the rural landholders (landlords, independent farmers, and part tenants). The Ming population was divided into four main registration categories[14]—military, civilian, artisan, and saltern—and each category was liable for different forms of service. Those subject to miscellaneous service were the land-holding civilian households only.

But how was service allocation actually carried out in early Ming times? Although it is somewhat late evidence, we may cite the following from the Veritable Records for the eighth lunar month 1466: "In former times before the equalization of the labor service system (*junyao*) was adopted, [the authorities] simply made their allocations by assessment of the households at their disposal in accordance with [the dictates of] the times. In a given year it might suffice to use no more than three or four households, and then the others could remain at ease pending a subsequent assignment."[15] And from the 1519 edition of the Chaoyi county (Xi'an prefecture, Shaanxi province) gazetteer: "Before the Hongzhi period [1488–1505], once the adult male (*ding*) impost and labor service draft had yielded adequate resources to meet the year's requirements, [the authorities] left off assessing them. It was therefore possible, with 36 *li* (all within Chaoyi county), to alternate service and rest among them."[16]

Thus the miscellaneous service duties were allotted on an *ad hoc*

basis, according to the needs of the time; compared with the regular
lijia service levy, which came round regularly once every ten years, it
was entirely irregular.[17] It is probable that in this early period when
governmental institutions were still relatively simple, the needs for
labor-power requisitioned from the population were not so very great,
and so arrangements such as those described above were altogether adequate.

As for the functions covered by the miscellaneous service levy, I think
they may be grouped as follows: 1) the performance of miscellaneous
duties at central and local governmental offices; 2) participation in official transport and communications work; 3) maintenance of local law
and order; 4) collection and transport of taxes.

The first of these involved quite a variety of types of service, and the
numbers of individuals required were also rather large. The assignments
were sometimes classified, according to the place of service, as capital
duty, prefecture duty, and county duty. Lictors, runners, door-keepers,
jailers, college instructors' cooks, college servitors, storehouse keepers
and grain measurers come under this head. As examples of servicemen
involved in transport and communications functions, one may cite the
hostel porters, grooms, boat hands, postmasters, dispatch bearers, and
guardsmen. Under law and order come the bowmen of the local police
stations, and the militiamen set up on the occasion of the Tumu incident
of 1449. Under tax collection and delivery come tax captains,[18] delivery
agents, business-tax collectors, and so forth.

Equalized labor service

As we have seen, the service levy system of the early Ming was very
simple. Not yet definitively institutionalized, it amounted to no more
than an irregular and variable burden. As time passed governmental
institutions grew more complex; and as it grew in size, the government
came gradually to lay heavier demands for service on the population.
Although the household grades of the old ninefold classification system
could serve as the basis for the allocation of these now excessive burdens, in practice allocation was left entirely to the arbitrary judgments
of local officials. Among the excerpts from the Yongkang county (Jinhua
prefecture, Zhejiang province) gazetteer included in the *Tianxia junguo
libing shu* (The strengths and weaknesses of the various regions of the
empire) we find the following: "The authorities are able to administer
[the allocation of miscellaneous service] according to their own will

and pleasure: it is not like *lijia* [allocation] where there is a predetermined sequence. For this reason they commit malpractices of shifting and switching, letting off the rich, and burdening the poor."[19] Thus the official personnel, taking advantage of the imperfections of the system, colluded with the rich and powerful, or other ill-intentioned persons, to commit injustices when allocating service. As the number of abuses grew, the desirability of a thorough overhaul of the whole system came to be keenly appreciated.

In early Ming times, landholding had been comparatively equalized, particularly in north China. However, by the Xuande and Zhengtong eras (1426–49) landownership was beginning to concentrate and the gap between rich and poor was gradually becoming an issue for public debate. As we have seen, the elements which determined household grade —the basis of service allocation—were the number of adult male members in a given household, its land taxes due, and the extent of its property. It was, however, the size of the landholding that received the greatest emphasis. Landlords and influential persons who were rich in land ought naturally to have borne the heaviest service burdens; but it was also natural that they should have conspired to the detriment of justice with official personnel in order to evade the heavy service duties. It was thus in the Jiangnan region, where concentration of landownership was most advanced, that such abuses first became an issue. The reform of the service levy system therefore began in Jiangnan.

During the Xuande era (1426–35), the Jiangnan grand coordinator Zhou Chen proposed the following measures for Suzhou and Songjiang in order to remedy the overcomplication of the services and the unfairness of their allocation:

The assignments are to rotate year by year among the ten *li* captains[20] of each ward (*tu*) in every township (*du*),[21] excluding the current year *li* captain (*xianyi*)[22] and the *li* captain with responsibility for land tax dunning (*cuiliang lizheng*), in accordance with the sequence appointed. . . . Following former practice, the *li* captains are to take responsibility for the filling of such posts as that of yamen runner, while the *jia* heads make supporting contributions on an equal basis. Many hands make light work: the people will feel no hardship. As for such burdensome assignments as those of serving as boat hand, groom, or relay-station hand, persons of substantial means shall undertake them.[23]

Thus a system was established whereby the off-duty captains were allotted miscellaneous service duties corresponding to their means, and served in rotation following a predetermined schedule and supported by the *jia* heads. This was an attempt at overhaul of the service levy allocation system, and it resulted in a lessening of the hardships suffered by the population. It is not clear how thoroughly Zhou Chen's reform was implemented.[24]

The next development was the so-called equalized labor service system put into successful operation in Jiangxi by the assistant surveillance commissioner Xia Shi. The fiscal treatise of the *Ming shi* says no more than this about the equalized labor service system: "Early in the Zhengtong era (1436–49) the assistant surveillance commissioner Xia Shi initiated it in Jiangxi, and the other provinces adopted it in imitation. The service levy was thereby made somewhat more equitable."[25]

Further information comes from the *Ming shilu* (Veritable records of the Ming) for the eighth lunar month of 1444, where we find the following (passage A) from a memorial by Jie Ji, the administration commissioner of Guangxi: "Of late, in accordance with the proposals of the Jiangxi assistant surveillance commissioner Xia Shi, [the authorities] have been compiling Equitable Service Levy Tables. However, the territory of Guangxi is near the frontier; people are few and duties numerous, and it is difficult to adhere to a fixed pattern. We ask leave to go back to the old system and make assignments through assessing [the requirements of] the time."[26]

This was granted. Similarly, in the Veritable Records for the twelfth lunar month of 1445 we find the following account (passage B) of the abolition of the equalized labor service registers in Jiangxi and elsewhere:

Now (Xia) Shi had been made assistant administration commissioner and in his tour within the province he had reached Linjiang prefecture. He was assigning the tax-paying households (? *lianghu*) of this prefecture for service as attendants at the provincial administration office and the provincial surveillance office. The Jiangxi administration vice commissioner of the right in (temporary) charge of Linjiang prefecture, Zhu De, submitted a memorial to the effect that Shi was tending to use the top-grade tax-paying households for the attendants, his intention being to call them up year after year. This could not but be harmful to the people. He [Zhu] begged that the equalized labor service registers be abolished.

The matter was referred to the court ministers. They gave as their opinion that, whereas the basic purpose of the equalized labor service registers was to oblige the people, Shi's proposals had not been in force three years, yet he himself had been the first to violate them. It was truly not an idea that would stand the test of time. [The registers] should be abolished as De had proposed. This was accepted.[27]

Then we have the following (passage C) from a memorial by Jin Da, a supervising secretary in the Office of Scrutiny for Rites (Veritable Records 1450, 11th month):

I take the liberty of observing: the assistant surveillance commissioner of the Jiangxi Provincial Surveillance Office Xia Shi asked leave in a memorial to carry out the equalized labor service system [under which] the regular service levy was imposed after five years, and the miscellaneous service levy after another five years. This system was quite excellent, yet one fine day the administration vice commissioner Zhu De resentfully trumped up some allegations and submitted a memorial to get it stopped. I beg that the operation of the equalized labor service system be resumed.[28]

Assent to this was granted. Finally (passage D), in the Veritable Records for the eighth lunar month of 1457, we find:

Earlier, in the service levy (allocations), the captains had tended to release the rich for a consideration, and to assign the duties to the poor. During the Zhengtong period, the Jiangxi assistant administration commissioner Xia Shi[29] initiated the idea of making registers which classified (the households) on the basis of their land-tax liabilities. The authorities then fixed the labor service allocations (in accordance with this), and the registers were called the equalized labor service registers. At first the people found it helpful.[30]

Passages A, B, C, and D comprise the sum total of the material concerning Xia Shi's equalized labor service system to be found in the Veritable Records for the whole of Yingzong's reign (1436–64). They would seem to lead to the following conclusions:1) In the first lunar month, 1446 court ministers note that Xia's proposals had not yet been in operation for three years (B), therefore the date of the inauguration of the equalized labor service system would seem to have been 1443.[31] It is also possible that Xia's original memorial was submitted in 1442. 2) The equalized labor service took the *jia* as the unit of service rotation; five years after a given household had performed the regular service levy, it became due for miscellaneous service (C). The miscellaneous service, which had previously been allocated on an irregular basis, now became a regular decennial obligation. 3) In addition to the Yellow Registers, equalized labor service registers were compiled (A, B, C) to serve as the documentary basis for the equalized labor service allocation. The extent of the individual household's land-tax liability was the principal determinant of its classification in the registers (D).

It is thus clear that the outstanding feature of Xia Shi's equalized labor service system was the shifting of irregularly levied miscellaneous service so that it was allocated on a regular basis like the regular service levy and came around once a decade.

The equalized labor service system inaugurated in Jiangxi by Xia Shi around 1443 was temporarily abandoned in 1446 (B), revived in 1450 (C), and subsequently adopted over many regions of the empire. During the Jingtai period (1450–56) it was introduced in Guangdong by the assistant administration commissioner Zhu Ying, in Shanxi by the administration vice commissioner Yang Xuan, and again in Jiangxi by the administration commissioner Cui Gong;[32] by the beginning of the Tianshun period (1457–64) it was known in Sichuan;[33] and subsequently it was introduced in Jiangnan by Cui Gong when he was regional governor there,[34] and in Fujian and Shaanxi by Zhu Ying, who served as administration commissioner successively in each of these two provinces.[35] From a remark in a memorial submitted by the supervising secretary Qiu Hong during the Chenghua period (1465–87)—"Now that the equalized labor service system is in operation, each decade's worth of service assignments is settled on the assumption of (the full) ten *jia* worth of households"[36]—we may sense the extent to which the equalized labor service system had spread. By the first year of the Hongzhi period (1488) it was employed throughout the empire.[37]

The chief characteristic of the equalized labor service was that the miscellaneous service duties came to be fixed on a decennial basis. For explanation in more concrete terms, we turn again to the excerpts from the Yongkang county gazetteer included in the *Tianxia junguo libing shu*: "The system is that . . . every year one *jia* is responsible for service. The obligation alternates on a quinquennial basis with that of regular service levy."[38]

Speaking in terms of a single *li*, when at the beginning of the cycle *jia* one was due for regular *lijia* service, *jia* six would be responsible for the equalized labor services. Five years later, *jia* one would be liable for the equalized labor services, and *jia* six for the regular *lijia* service. The grouping due for equalized labor service in a given year was normally referred to as the current year equalized labor service household, a term corresponding to the current year *li* household of the regular *lijia* service rota. As for the equalized labor service registers which served as the basis for assessment, in every county-level juris-diction these set out the households of the equalized labor service system in order of their household grade, noting beneath each house-hold's name the service which should be allotted to it. The lighter duties would be performed unassisted, but for the more taxing ones a group of households might be set to share the load.[39] Where a middle-grade household would receive one assignment, an upper-middle one would be given several, while the very top households might each have several tens to perform. Among the low-grade households several individuals might share one assignment.[40] The basis of the ranking of the households in the equalized labor service registers ought naturally to have been the Yellow Registers, but in many cases these were disre-garded,[41] and sole emphasis was put upon the size of the landholding (or of the land-tax payment due). That this is so is clearly shown in the following passage from a memorial by one Deng Qi of Yongchuan county (Chongqing prefecture) written in 1457, when the equalized labor service system was introduced in Sichuan: "If, as now, the service assignments are fixed solely on the basis of the land tax [payments], then labor service obligations will not touch rich merchants and big traders. Meanwhile the farming people enjoy not a single day of respite from their toil all year long. I fear that in a few years' time the people will all have fled the basic occupation for the parasitic sectors (i.e., commerce, etc.)."[42]

The same situation is revealed in a letter by Wang Ao (1450–1524) discussing the land taxes of the Suzhou region: "The equalized labor service system, generally speaking, is fixed on the basis of landholding. Those who have much land are designated upper households, and they are heavily assessed. Those who have but little land are assessed lightly, and those with none more lightly still. No account is taken of other resources."[43]

In this section we have concentrated on the establishment of the equalized labor service system. In summary, it may be said that it began in Jiangxi around 1443, and that by 1488—about half a century later—it was in operation on an empirewide basis.

The commutation of the equalized labor service

From 1436, commutation of the land tax was put into practice over quite a wide area. This was the so-called gold floral silver (*jinhua yin*). Besides representing a slackening of the Ming government's control over the circulation of silver—hitherto kept under severe restraint—this development may also be seen as a manifestation of the strong governmental craving for silver receipts. However, in no sense was any such provision part of the equalized labor service reform brought in seven years after this institutionalization of land-tax commutation.

In the past the equalized labor service has been automatically glossed as the system of silver assignments (*yinchai*) and labor assignments (*lichai*). It has been assumed that this differentiation existed from the adoption of the equalized labor service system.[44] From what we have said so far, it ought to be clear that this was certainly not so. Of course, in special cases, commutation of service assignments occurred at an early time. For instance, in the 1510 edition of the *Da Ming Huidian* (Collected statutes of the Ming dynasty) we find: "During the Xuande period, those who did not wish to serve as lictors-in-attendance were directed to pay one tael of firewood silver for each month."[45]

And in a memorial by Zhu De, Jiangxi administration vice commissioner in temporary charge of Linjiang prefecture, included in the Veritable Records for the seventh month of 1438: "At the present time, the surveillance vice commissioner Yin Tang has repeatedly instructed this prefecture to draft attendants, 55 in all. [Only] a minority [actually] serve: the majority send in a payment."[46]

The payment here was probably in silver. Further examples of the commutation of labor services into silver payments are to be found from 1466, 1468, 1471, and 1473.[47] However, these are almost all exceptional cases and amount to no more than commutation with regard to certain special forms of service. It is not until a little later that instances of commutation emerge upon a broad and general scale. Nonetheless, it would seem that from the beginning there existed within the labor service system certain factors making commutation possible.

In the first place, from early times there were provisions for service by proxy. Under the *jungongfu* system it was recognized that "those who have much land but few adult males (*ding*) use tenants to stand in as servicemen"; and in Qiu Hong's memorial of 1466 cited above we find the following: "In former times before the *junyao* (system) was adopted [the authorities] simply made their allocations by assessment of the households at their disposal in accordance with [the dictates of] the times.... The poor supplied labor, the rich funds, each being allowed to suit his own convenience in accordance with what he possessed."[48]

Qiu Jun, in his discussion of the equalized labor levy, writes, "The poor employ their strength; the rich draw on their wealth."⁴⁹ It would thus seem that, whereas the poor gave direct labor service, the rich were able to hire others to stand in for them, although there may also have been cases of the latter making direct payments to the authorities and thereby gaining exemption from the labor service. Once service by proxy had been recognized, it was only a logical step for the rich to pay the authorities, who then hired servicemen rather than finding and paying replacements themselves.

Second, with the equalization of labor services—though not with every other type of labor service—there was a distinction between chief households (*touhu* or *zhenghu*) and auxiliary households (*tiehu*). In the *Min shu* we find: "In the past, when labor services were being allocated, X would be a *touhu*, and Y a *tiehu*."⁵⁰

And in a sixteenth-century edition of the Wujiang county gazetteer: "In accordance with the Yellow Registers, once these had been finalized, and in an annual rotation, the households designated upper and middle on the basis of the number of their adult male members and the amount of taxes due were assigned to labor service, while the lower households were assigned auxiliary roles. It was called the equalized labor service system."⁵¹

Thus chief households and auxiliary households collaborated on a given service assignment. The former actually performed the service, while the latter rendered assistance. The form of this assistance is made clear by a passage in the 1642 edition of the Yuanshi county (North Zhili, Zhending prefecture) gazetteer: "For every assignment . . . one head is appointed who when his year comes around reports to the authorities and performs the service. The remaining households assist variously in silver or with labor."⁵²

There thus existed both the payment of silver to help with the serviceman's expenses, and the furnishing of labor to assist him with his task. It was, however, the former which was the more important mode; and this practice of silver contribution by the auxiliary households seems to have been another factor spurring on the commutation of the labor services.

Third, as Qiu Jun pointed out,⁵³ when the services of two or three households of the equalized labor service *lijia* sufficed for the fulfillment of the task allotted, the remaining, surplus households might be required to make substitution payments. In the taxation section of the 1519 edition of Chaoyi county gazetteer, we find:

Before the Hongzhi period, once the adult male labor impost and labor service draft had yielded adequate resources to meet the year's requirements [the authorities] left off assessing them. It was therefore possible, with 36 *li*, to alternate service and rest among them. Subsequently, all became subject to requisition. The reason for this was that the allowed assignment (*tingchai*) system was adopted. The meaning of *tingchai* is that once the requirement is fulfilled and there is nothing more to do, assignments are "allowed." That is to say, the authorities collect silver all round and deposit it within their treasury.[54]

In the days before the equalized labor service system had been introduced, labor services were allotted according to the requirements of the time; when these were met, assessment stopped. However, after the adoption of the equalized labor service system when there were no labor services to be allotted—that is to say, when there were surplus households within the equalized labor service *lijia*—the surplus households were required to pay silver, which was stored in the local treasury against future expenditure. This was the arrangement termed "allowed assignment," and the fact that it and similar arrangements were rather widely practiced also no doubt contributed to the commutation of the services themselves.[55]

While the above seem to have been factors in the progress toward commutation, there were also promptings from the side of social policy. For the small peasants who could not afford to hire substitutes, service in person meant complete desertion of their agricultural activities. On top of this, travel to the place of service might take several days and mean heavy expenditure, and on arrival the draftee might be subjected to all sorts of squeeze and extortion by the clerks. Thus for the ordinary people commutation was preferable to service in person. That this was so may be readily imagined from the following found in the 1612 edition of the Yongfu county (Fuzhou prefecture, Fujian) gazetteer: "With silver assignment (*yinchai*) . . . there is a set payment, and where more is exacted it does not exceed 10 to 20 percent. With service performed by the taxpayer in person (*lichai*) . . . the excess over the [proper] quota is several-fold."[56]

Thus at the beginning commutation was adopted with the small peasants in mind. The "Examination of the equitable assignments" included in the 1606 edition of the Shangyu county (Shaoxing prefecture, Zhejiang province) gazetteer includes the observation: "The original intention of the system was that the silver assignment was for the poor people, the service performed by the taxpayer in person, for the rich houses."[57] A memorial submitted by the Nanjing minister of personnel Ni Yue in 1499, and another by the northern metropolitan area regional governor Liu Yingchen of 1506, both testify to the same effect.[58] The fact is that from the point of view of the overburdened peasants, the commutation of the labor services represented an alleviation. This also suggests the existence of factors making for the change. Nor is it difficult to imagine that the empire-wide extension of the commutation of the land tax that took place during the Hongzhi and Zhengde periods (1488–1521) should have exercised a powerful influence.

But when was it that commutation within the equalized labor service system became general? The answer to that is, at the time when the differentiation between silver assignment and service performed by the taxpayer in person in the equalized labor service system emerged. But when did this differentiation crystallize? In the 1564 edition of the Huizhou gazetteer we find the statement "from the former edition of the gazetteer [it would appear that] by 1501 the equalized labor service system was not yet divided between silver assessment and service performed by the taxpayer in person. In the edition of the gazetteer of Xinghua prefecture (Fujian) compiled in 1503 distinction is made among the labor services, between "assignments met with silver" and "assignments met with manpower" (yongyin fuyi and yongli fuyi.[59] And yet no such distinction may be found in the labor service sections of two Yangzi delta region gazetteers compiled in the Zhengde period, the Gusu (Suzhou) gazetteer of 1506 and the 1512 gazetteer of Songjiang prefecture. But then in the Guangdong provincial section of the Tianxia junguo libing shu under Leizhou prefecture we find, "From the time of the Zhengde period the system of silver assessment and service performed by the taxpayer in person was instituted for the first time . . . .," and under Zhaoqing prefecture, "In 1520 the Censor Cheng Chang memorialized and had the yinchai/lichai system instituted. . . ."[60]

We may thus perhaps conclude that in most places it was probably in late Hongzhi or during Zhengde (the beginning of the sixteenth century) that the yinchai/lichai system was established. However, the distinction was not absolute. In a paragraph headed "Examination of the origin of lichai, yinchai, and tingchai" excerpted from the Songjiang prefectural gazetteer in the Tianxia junguo libing shu we find: "As for the service performed by the taxpayer in person . . . still later silver was levied and servicemen hired (so that) the lichai turned into silver assessment."[61] And in the 1618 edition of the gazetteer of Jianchang prefecture (Jiangxi province): "During the Zhengde and Jiajing periods, silver and manpower [assignments] were sometimes swapped around."[62]

Thus there was constant interchange between the two. Since from the

Table 1. Silver and manpower assignments in eight districts of southeastern China

Name of administrative unit	Date	No. of silver assignments	No. of manpower assignments	Source
Jianning prefecture (Fujian)	1541	884	2,147	1541 *Jianning fuzhi*
Longyan county (Fujian)	1557	63	276	1557 *Longyan xianzhi*
Haining county (Zhejiang)	1557	664	483.5	1557 *Haining xianzhi*
Youxi county (Fujian)	"of old"	120	303	1636 *Youxi xianzhi*
Leizhou prefecture (Guangdong)	"	107	84	*Tianxia junguo libing shu*
Haikang county (Guangdong)	"	66.5	239	" " " "
Suixi county (Guangdong)	"	63	283	" " " "
Qiongzhou prefecture (Guangdong)	"	942	1,645	1617 *Qiongzhou fuzhi*

point of view of the small peasants the manpower assignments represented the heavier burden, they were one by one transformed into silver
assignments.[63] Thus, as can be seen from Table 1,[64] at first the manpower
assignments by far outnumbered the silver assignments; subsequently
silver assignments gradually grew in number. In the labor service sections of many local gazetteers of Jiajing date, a silver quota figure appears for each item of the manpower assignments, and the overall total
quota for the manpower assignments is in turn expressed in terms of silver. This does not necessarily imply, however, that all of the manpower
assignments were actually commuted. Again in the Guangdong section
of the *Tianxia junguo libing shu* we find: "For manpower assignments
. . . again (an amount of) silver is calculated equivalent to the (cost of)
wages . . ."; and under Yongkang county (Jinhua prefecture, Zhejiang): "With labor performed by the taxpayer in person an equivalence
is merely set in terms of silver so as to fix the assignments: silver is not
(actually) levied. Individuals may either serve in person or hire substitutes."[65]

Thus it was precisely the standard for manpower assignment fulfill-
ments that was being indicated by means of the silver figures. A similar
phenomenon is to be observed in European history also.[66]

As to the question of how the division of assignments between silver
and manpower was determined, we may quote the following excerpts
from the gazetteer of Daming prefecture (North Zhili) included in the
Tianxia junguo libing shu: "Distances, however, vary. Thus reporting for
duty in person is called *lichai*; the services that are required within the
boundaries of the given prefecture, subprefecture, or county take this

Table 2. Manpower and commuted assignments in ten southeastern districts (M = manpower assignment, S = silver assignment)

Type of service	Fujian						Zhejiang	Southern Metropolitan area		
	Longyan	Jianning	Datian	Fuqing	Yongfu	Sha	Yongjia	Wujiang	Ningguo	Chunyang
Delivery agent (*jiehu*)	M				S	M	M	S	M	M
Archer (*gongbing*)	M					M		M	M	M
Attendant (*libing*)	M		M	M		M				
Door-keeper (*menzi*)	M		M	M		M		M	M	M
Grain measurer (*douji*)	M			M	M	M	M	M	M	M
Storehouse keeper (*kuzi*)	M		M	M		M		M	M	
Hostel porter (*guanfu*)	M			M	M		M	M		S
Dispatch bearer (*pubing*)	M			M	M	M		M	M	M
Runner (*zhihou*)	S		S	S	S	S			S	
Lictor (*zaoli*)	S					S		SM	SM	SM
Groom (*mafu*)	S	S	S	S	S	S		S	S	S
College servitor (*zhaifu*)	S	S	S	S	S	S		S	S	S
Instructors' cook (*shanfu*)	S	S	S	S	S	S		S	S	S
Business-tax collector (*xunlan*)		S		M		S		M		M
Jailer (*jinzi*)				M		M		M	M	M

form. Tendering the value of one's turn of duty and letting the authorities do the engaging is called *yinchai*; the services that are required at the yamen of the capital or in the relay stations of other county-level jurisdictions, and so on, are of this form."[67]

And from the 1624 edition of the Haiyan county (Jiaxing prefecture, Zhejiang) gazetteer: "With the equalized labor services required at the different yamen, those that involve some distance are levied as silver assignments, and there is still some limit to the wage expenses. As for the local ones, these are raised as manpower assignments and the embarrassment to individuals and their families is infinite."[68]

It seems indeed to stand to reason that commutation would begin with the distant assignments. As for the local services, it began with the slighter ones. Thus in Table 2 almost all the straightforward menial miscellaneous services—duty as lictor, groom, or college servitor or cook, for instance—appear as silver assignments. Manpower assignment was retained in the case of the more important tasks—that is to say, those in which the burden was heavy—for which it was difficult to find suitable recruits. Examples are the posts of storehouse keepers and grain measurers, the caretakers of the official stores and granaries; of archers and jailers, involved in maintenance of law and order; and of dispatch bearers, who played a vital part in the official communication system. However, these remnant manpower assignment services also were destined to an eventual transformation into silver assignment.

We have shown above that commutation in the equalized labor service system took place some half a century or more after the land-tax commutation, and was an early-sixteenth-century development. Whereas the land-tax commutation was imposed as a matter of fiscal policy arising from the government's demand for silver, the labor service system held within itself the seeds of commutation, and this commutation was adopted with a view to lessening the burden of the services. Naturally, empire-wide the process took place in ways adapted to the particular conditions obtaining in the different localities.

Emergence of the ten-section method

In his *Daxue yanyi bu*, Qiu Jun wrote as follows: "The equalized labor service system is suitable for use south of the Yangzi River, but not north of the river. It is suitable for use in large counties, but not in small ones. It is suitable for use on the great households, but not on the poor commoners."[69] The reason given for this is that where, as in small counties and north of the Yangzi River, the population is small but the demands for service numerous; it is difficult to adhere to the principle of "one turn of service in a decade," and there arise situations in which it is necessary to make people serve twice or three times in the decade. Besides this, there was the consideration that small peasants with inadequate resources found even one turn of a heavy service duty more than they could bear. In actual fact, in jurisdictions where the "once-a-decade" principle could no longer be maintained, the rule became once in every five years, once in every three years, every other year, or even annually. As a result the burden on the population grew in inverse proportion as the time between the turns of service shortened. Thus people began to consider the expedient of transferring the labor service burden onto landed property, thereby preserving the decennial principle and avoiding an increase in trouble to the people.

From the beginning of the dynasty, land had held an important place as part of the basis for the allocation of the labor services, and this tendency had become particularly marked in the context of the equalized labor service system. It had, however, been a mere matter of emphasis on landholding as basis for assessment; now a certain proportion of the labor service burden was being levied directly on the land. The earliest example of this occurred in Jiangnan under the governorship of Zhou Chen, when on the basis of the "scheme for encouraging lending" the shortfall in the services requirement was made up from the land taxes. The proportion was, however, no more than 20 to 30 percent of the whole.[70] Subsequently, the proportion of the service burden transferred onto landholdings gradually rose until, as represented in the formula *ding* 4 *liang* 6/*ding* 3 *liang* 7, 60 to 70 percent of the requirement had gone onto the land (or land tax). There were two methods of doing this. One was to assess the service requirement directly onto land or land tax. Thus in the 1577 edition of the gazetteer of Ningguo prefecture we find: "At first the equalized labor service levy was assessed decennially. Before the Hongzhi period, 0.02 tael odd was assessed on every *mu* of land. This was subsequently increased to 0.05 tael."[71]

Thus a labor service silver charge was raised from every *mu* land. Naturally, where the land tax was the basis of assessment, the charge was levied in respect of every *shi* payable. The second method was to convert the landholding or land tax payable to adult male equivalents (or vice versa), and then to charge so much per adult male equivalent (or *mu* or *shi*). For example, one frequently encounters instances of five to ten *mu* of land or one *shi* of land-tax liability being deemed equivalent to one adult male.

Behind these developments lay not only the variety of geographical conditions in the different jurisdictions, but also the surfacing of contradictions in the equalized labor service allocation system, based as it was upon the *lijia* structure. Whereas in early Ming times landholding within the agricultural communities was relatively evenly distributed, with the passage of time landownership became progressively more concentrated, while the number of small peasants falling into ruin mounted. Thus in *li* A landholdings might be concentrated, while in *li* B impoverished small peasants would predominate; alternatively, within the same *li*, there might be a great imbalance between *jia* X and *jia* Y. There was also the problem that the quota of services for annual apportionment was more or less fixed. In the gazetteer of Jiangxi province (1597 edition), we read: "Under the equalized labor service system, the annual labor service silver quotas applicable throughout each county, once fixed, cannot be reduced. The different *jia*, meanwhile, vary in their strengths in adult males and taxes due. If a *jia* is well off with regard to adult males and taxes due, its annual silver allocation will be (felt as) light; if the adult males and taxes due are few, the allocation will be (felt as) heavy. There is already inequality, and the service assessment only adds to it."[72]

It was a natural development, in these circumstances, that people should attempt to flee from heavy-burdened *jia* into lightly burdened ones. This process is also described in the same source; "The evil-doing people, fleeing the onerous and making for the easeful, often enter into registration in a *jia* where the adult males and taxes due are numerous, with the result that overburdened [communities] become still further overburdened, lightly burdened ones still further privileged. Besides, the assignments filled are ever multiplying."[73] In other words, it was a vicious circle.

In addition to this trick of moving *jia* so as to reduce one's service burden, sundry other artifices were employed by those intending to evade their service liabilities. In essence, these were deceptions over land-holdings—trying to hide the land which had become the principal object of service assessment, or passing it off as someone else's. There were in fact two main forms of trickery employed. One was to escape duty by putting one's own land under someone else's name, and this was called commendation (*guiji*).[74] We find an account of it in the 1579 edition of the gazetteer of Hangzhou prefecture:

In the first section[75] of the regulations exemption privileges are given, but plain commoners share none of them. When commoners with large amounts of land are scheming to obtain exemption, they variously ask the local dignitaries—the degree holders—the clerks, the statute saltworkers, and paupers[76] to represent themselves as householder [in respect of a specific parcel of land]. When one person's land is parceled among several households, what cannot be exhaustively protected by a lofty dignitary or great functionary will still all be exempted. This is called *guiji*.[77]

This passage makes it clear that the prime objects of commendation solicitation were such holders of exemption privileges as the families of

Table 3.   Exemption entitlement*

	Shi of land tax assessment	Acreage exempt (in mu**)	No. of adult males exempt
Grade 1	30	1,000	30
Grade 2	24	800	24
Grade 3	20	670	20
Grade 4	16	535	16
Grade 5	14	470	14
Grade 6	12	400	12
Grade 7	10	335	10
Grade 8	8	270	8
Grade 9	6	200	6

* I.e., the amount of land/no. of adult males not taken into account for purposes of labor service liability assessment for capital officials of each of the nine grades.
** 30 shi of land tax assessment are converted to 1,000 mu of land. Thus in cases where the labor service liability was assessed directly on the land, up to one thousand mu might be exempted. The same conversion ratio is used throughout.

mandarins and saltern households. For the former, there was at first nothing more laid down than that they should be exempted from the miscellaneous labor services; but as the services began to be assessed on land, official families began to use their privileges to aid and abet would-be evaders by accepting the entrustment of their land. Finally, in 1545, in response to the increasing popularity of commendation, limits were set on the exemption entitlements of officials.[78] For capital officials (officials serving in the central govenment departments), these were as shown in Table 3. They were the same for palace officials, but reduced by 50 percent for officials serving in the provinces. For educational officials, students of the Imperial Academy, juren, and shengyuan, the entitlement was two shi of land-tax assessment (or forty mu of land) and two adult males. Retired officials were entitled to a 70 percent exemption rate. However, even though such limitations might be set, it is

Table 4. Equalized labor service exemptions in late-sixteenth-century Shanghai

	Adult males	Land (in qing*)
A) Overall county quota	70,623	14,806
B) Exemptions:		
a) accounted for by households of officials	705	252
b) accounted for by saltern households	12,084	2,453
Total Exemptions	12,789	2,705
B total as percentage of A	18.11%	18.27%

*1 qing = 100 mu

not difficult to imagine how very problematical was their observance. Thus, although it may not have been the exemption privileges of officials only that were involved, in Suzhou by the time of compilation of the 1642 Wu county gazetteer, things had reached the following pass: "For the annual assessment of the three-grade labor service levy, there are over forty thousand *mu* available. Landowners with labor service exemption occupy 70 percent."[79] There may of course be a certain element of exaggeration here, and it is perhaps something of an extreme example.

According to the 1588 edition of the Shanghai county gazetteer, the scale of exemptions from the equalized labor service allocation was as shown in Table 4. Here, for both adult males and land, the exemptions occupied something approaching 20 percent of the overall quota, and the exemptions claimed by officials occupied no more than one-tenth of all exemptions. For the most part, these belonged to saltern households. Not that anything can be inferred about the total picture from the single case of Shanghai county; but in any case, we may assume that other individuals attempted to evade their service liability by sheltering their own land under the exemption privileges of mandarins and salt-boilers. Naturally, some nominal fee must have been paid the latter in return for their cooperation. Indeed, it may be suspected that the practice of commendation was one contributory factor in the growing concentration of landownership. Besides this, since pauper households enjoyed immunity from labor service liability, there were also cases of landowners partitioning their holdings among a number of such households.[80] Such abuses known as *nayi* (shifting registration to another place), *huafen* (subdividing household property), and *feixi* (removing property from tax registers) were basically similar in nature.

A different evasion technique was for the rich and influential to hold land outside the jurisdiction of their registration. In the 1548 edition of the county gazetteer of Xiangshan (Guangzhou prefecture) we read: "Rich and influential households purchase landed property in other counties, setting them up as outside land interest (*jizhuang*). They sit and enjoy the revenues from rent and do not pay the land tax. When it comes around to levying labor service, they again rely upon their separation to refuse submission to the draft. . . . The land taxes of Xiangshan amount to no more than 20,000, but outside land interests account already for 8,000."[81]

Taking advantage of the distance of their outside landholdings, such people openly contrived evasion of their obligations. There was a tendency everywhere for outside land interests to grow in size and number. In Shangyuan county, South Zhili, for instance, the number of households with outside land interests gradually grew from a mere 10 percent at the beginning of the dynasty.[82] The phenomenon was particularly marked in Jiangnan. It goes without saying that as households with outside land interests were all rich and influential people, they would undoubtedly have had to bear a heavy service burden if the place of their registration had been identical with the location of their landholdings. And so in order to prevent this form of cheating, there emerged talk of levying labor service on the land instead of on the adult males in cases where the land was located outside the family's place of registration. Thus Yao Ruxun could write as follows concerning this problem: "Nowadays, those who take part in discussions tend to show a wish to suppress outside land interests on the pretext of compassion for the poor. At each re-registration, the land located outside the family's place of registration is reported in terms of adult males."[83]

Yao puts forward the following criticism of this assessment method that converted acreage to fiscal individuals. Labor service is something assessed on adult males: if landholdings are converted into adult males, one individual will be faced with two assignments, which is irrational. Essentially, Yao seems in this opinion to be representing the position of households with outside land interests. It was inevitable that a measure of the kind outlined above should be proposed in order to put a stop to labor service evasion through extrajurisdictional landholding. The ten-section method (*shiduan fa*) was devised in order to assess labor service with the maximum degree of rationality and fairness, maintaining the principle of decennial equalized labor service and correcting the misdeeds of influential landowners.[84] The first application of this system—though without the name ten-section method being used—seems to have been during the Tianshun period when the regional inspector Sheng Yong introduced it in Fujian. We read as follows in his biography in the *Min shu*: "Previously, the labor services within the prefecture had tended to be levied by the *li* clerks. . . . Yong took the acreage and adult male figures for each entire county, established ten divisions *(jia)*, and had each year's services met from the adult male levies and taxes due pertaining to that year."[85]

Next came a scheme inaugurated during the Zhengde period (1506–21) in Changzhou prefecture (South Zhili). The excerpts from the Wujin county gazetteer included in the *Tianxia junguo libing shu* contain the following: "During the Zhengde period, Vice Prefect Ma proposed that the land of the entire county should be divided equally into ten sections, and that a separate ten-section register (*shiduan wence*) should be compiled. One section would be assessed each year. At first this was found highly convenient."[86]

Table 5. Ten-section method conversion in Wujin in 1535

	Actual amount (in *mu*)	Conversion ratio	Amount after conversion (in *mu*)
Private land	1,295,881.4	—	1,295,881.4
State land	139,662.7	1:5	27,932.5*
Hillside and marsh land	75,478	1:10	7,547.8
Adult males	124,398	1:1	124,398
Total			1,455,759.7

* The figure actually given in the text is 25,933.5, but this is evidently erroneous.

From this passage one would understand that the ten-section method meant dividing only the acreage of the given county-level jurisdiction into ten equal parts and levying the labor services upon one part each year. This in fact was definitely not the case. It was the total of the acreage and the adult male numbers that was so divided. In the *Min shu* we read: "With the ten-section method, one takes the adult males and taxes due of the whole county that are actually subject to assessment and divides them into ten sections, establishing the sequence on the basis of the *jia*. Each year one section is assessed for labor service in rotation."[87]

Thus it was both adult males and taxes due (or acreage) that were divided into ten. So far, however, we have little idea of how the method actually worked. Fortunately, there is a very detailed record of the system put into operation in Wujin in 1535 by the magistrate Ma Ruzhang.[88]

In this case, the method chosen was to convert adult males and land of every category into acreage of arable in private ownership. Thus as shown in Table 5, every five *mu* of state-owned land, every ten *mu* of hillside and marsh land, and every individual adult male was each converted to one *mu* of privately owned arable. The total thus obtained was then divided into ten, and each year's labor service assessment was levied on one of the sections.[89] (While this conversion system took the *mu* for its unit, there could also have been cases where the adult male was made the unit.) It seems, however, that this ten-section method of Ma Ruzhang's did not remain in operation long in Wujin county. In a proposal for reform of the abuses in the equalized labor service levy written in 1542, the magistrate Xu Liangfu advocated the *revival* of Ma's system:

It is not as satisfactory as the ten-section registers of earlier years, in which the adult males and acreage of the entire county were divided into ten sections, the distribution being even, more or less. Each year one section was assessed, and everything was plain and unequivocal. [This system] was able to put down the *nayi* malpractices of the old days, and would spare [the population] the chill winds of recent years. Both the authorities and the population would find it convenient. It is something that will stand the test of time and ought to be adopted.[90]

It appears that the system so carefully devised by Ma was dropped almost as soon as he left office.

But it was not only in the Jiangnan region that the ten-section method was carried out. For instance, in a memorial excerpted in the Veritable Records for the intercalary seventh moon of 1539, the regional inspector of Fujian Li Yuanyang writes: "The *junyao* is apportioned in ten sections so as to shut out deceit and trickery." Since the term "ten-section register" occurs in the land-tax and labor service section of the Sha county (Yanping prefecture, Fujian) gazetteer of 1545, we may say—setting apart Sheng Yong's initiative of almost a century earlier—that during the second and third decades of the Jiajing period the ten-section method was known in Fujian also. It appears that by the end of the Jiajing period the method was in operation throughout the whole of Quanzhou prefecture (Fujian). In the 1612 edition of the gazetteer of Quanzhou prefecture we read, "During the closing years of the Jiajing period . . . each county was instructed to divide the adult males and rice actually subject to the service levy into ten sections and so make the assessment."[91]

Although we cannot be sure about the date, the ten-section method was applied in Yunnan also. In the provincial gazetteer printed in 1576 we read, "The adult males and acreage of each county-level jurisdiction, irrespective of their quantity, were in every case divided into the sections, and one section was assessed each year."[92] And since there is an explanation of the ten-section method in the *Jiangxi sheng dazhi* of 1597, it may have been adopted in Jiangxi as well.

The most celebrated ten-section system was that put into practice in Jiangnan by Wen Ruzhang in 1565 under the name of ten-sectioned brocade register method. The entries in the Veritable Records and the 1587 *Da Ming Huidian*[93] being extremely vague, the distinctive features of the ten-section method do not emerge with any clarity. What is clear is that Wen advocated the adoption of this method actuated by his understanding of the need to check the abuse of exemption privileges by ranking officials and the use of the technique of setting up land outside the household's place of registration. There were also cases where the ten-section method was adopted at the time of the assessment of the *lijia* silver.[94] After the introduction of the Single Whip reform it was sometimes used in the assessment of the labor service dues associated with the land tax.[95]

Two final quotations. In the Yongjia county section of the fiscal treatise of the 1605 gazetteer of Wenzhou prefecture (Zhejiang province), we read: "In 1572, in response to a directive, the magistrate Wu Shiwang proposed that all receivables due under the *junping yin*, etc., should be (divided) equally to form a ten-sectioned Single Whip and allotted to the *li* and *jia* to pay year by year. Warrants would be issued to be proof for the decade."[96]

And, also from Wenzhou prefecture, in the 1572 edition of the Leqing county gazetteer, in the labor service section: "The Regional Inspector Xie (Tingjie) further established the ten-sectioned Single Whip method."[97] Although the details are unclear, it appears that a system seemingly compounded from the ten-section method and Single Whip reform was put into practice in Wenzhou.

In the section now to be concluded, we have noted the intensification of the transfer of the labor service burden onto landholdings, a measure directed against the defects of the equalized labor service levy and conforming with the social and economic conditions of the early sixteenth century; we have further discussed the consequent emergence of the ten-section method. Although it goes without saying that the ten-section method itself was not put into practice everywhere throughout the empire, the direction taken indicated the way forward for the reform of the labor service system generally. Not all the problems of the labor service system were resolved by the adoption of the ten-section method, however, and it was necessary to wait for the establishment of the Single Whip reform.[98]

Conclusion

In the present essay, I have examined the reforms that took place in the labor service system of the Ming, focusing upon the equalized labor service levy inaugurated in Jiangxi in the mid-fifteenth century. Behind the reforms there lay great changes in the structure of Chinese agricultural society, particularly the concentration of landownership wrought by the rich and influential. In the face of such a situation, in order to secure the income represented by the labor services, the authorities were forced to shift the burden from the shoulders of the ruined small peasants to the holdings of the rich and influential. And thus the impetus for the transfer of the labor service obligations onto land. At the same time, the authorities contrived some lightening of the burden on the small peasants by promoting commutation of the labor services. Since, however, the expedient of shifting service obligations onto land provoked all kinds of unfair practices on the part of the rich and influential landowners desirous of evasion, the authorities devised the ten-section method as a countermeasure, and sought means of rationalizing the equalized labor service system. Then in the middle of the sixteenth century, the problem of reform of the taxation system moved beyond the single focus of the equalized labor service levy, as an overall reform embracing land tax and such other forms of service imposition as *lijia*, postal relay system, and militia emerged as a necessity. The Single Whip reform then appeared on the scene.

Notes

[1] In the case of China, *fuyi* does indeed mean *fu* and *yi*, but there also came to be occasions on which the expression was used to refer to the second element, the labor service only. It is also used to indicate the corvée of Japan and Europe. In the title of the present article, *fuyi* naturally means the *yi* alone, but in the text I have as far as possible employed a less ambiguous term in order to avoid confusion.

[2] Sogabe Shizuo, *Sōdai zaiseishi*, p. 91.

[3] In compiling the *Wenxian tongkao*, Ma Duanlin inserted an "Examination of the official service duty system" (*zhiyi kao*) as a distinct entry, and all subsequent political encyclopedias followed suit. As to the meaning of the term "*zhiyi*," if we look at the memorial of the Palace Censor Lu Chong included in the *Xu Zizhi tongjian changbian*, *juan* 12 under the year 971 (1st month), and the commentary on *xingshi hu* in the *fuyi* section of the *Qingyuan tiaofa shilei*, it becomes clear that it covered petty functionaries, clerks, *li* captains, elders. household chiefs, etc. However, the entry in the *Lishu zhinan* reading, "when an officer is called *zhiyi*, it means that he has administrative duties," gives us cause to think that in the Yuan, *zhiyi* did not necessarily still bear its original significance. In Ming times, moreover, *zhiyi* normally refers to official functionaries, *shengyuan*, and the like.

[4] In a memorial dated 1068 included in the labor service section of the fiscal treatise of the *Song shi* (177: p. 4299), the Administrator of the Bureau of Policy Criticism Wu Chong writes: "Among the *xiangyi* (offices) of the present day, that of *yaqian* is the most burdensome." *Yaqian* is here regarded as a district labor (*xiangyi*) service. The details of the classification given in the *Min shu* are perhaps not necessarily definitive.

[5] *Min shu*, 39:4b–5a.

[6] Cf. Nie Chongqi, "Song yifa shu."

[7] The area of Jiangxi from which equalized labor levy (*jungongfu*) was drafted initially comprised the three prefectures of Raozhou, Jiujiang, and Nankang; but from an entry in the *Ming shilu* for 1375 (*Taizu shilu*, p. 1671) it seems that eventually it came to be applied in all the 13 prefectures of Jiangxi.

[8] See Shimizu Taiji, "Mindai no kokōsatsu (kōsatsu) no kenkyū."

[9] The regular *lijia* service levy was essentially a matter of serving as *li* or *jia* headman, but the duties of these offices did not stop at tax collection and the compilation of the Yellow Registers. What with defraying various expenses incurred at the local yamen, entertaining visiting officials, and so on, regular *lijia* service involved the expenditure of considerable sums of money. As the payments increased in complex-

ity, they came to be replaced by a lump sum silver payment called the *lijia* silver (*lijia yin*) or, in certain regions, amalgamated payment (*gangyin*) or equitable silver levy (*junping yin*). In company with the equalized labor service levy, postal-relay (*yizhuan*), and militia (*minzhuang*) levies, this was one of the "four duties" (*sichai*). I plan to examine the early history of *lijia* silver in a subsequent article.

¹⁰ At the time of the creation of the *lijia* "supportless and solitary persons unfit for labor service" were excluded from the 110 households and termed supernumerary households (*jilinghu*).

¹¹ The *ding* were the adult male members of each household, as entered in the household registers: the term does not include the labor power of slaves or servants. The *liang* were the land-tax payments due, and they were a reflection of the size of the landholding.

¹² *Taizu shilu*, 170:3a (facs. repr. p. 2585).

¹³ See Matsumoto Yoshimi, "Mindai," p. 101.

¹⁴ Although generally speaking the Ming population was divided between these four categories, there were some other, special kinds of registration such as that of scholar household (*ruhu*), geomancer household (*yinyanghu*), medical household (*yihu*), guardsman household (*lishihu* and *xiaoweihu*), dispatch bearer household (*pubinghu*), archer household (*gongshouhu*), kitchen household (*chuhu*), musician household (*yuehu*), *sangha* household (*senghu*), and Taoist household (*daohu*). Each of these was treated in a special way for labor service purposes.

¹⁵ *Xianzong shilu*, 33:2b (facs. repr. p. 650); and *Xiaokan ji*, p. 131.

¹⁶ 1519 *Chaoyi zhi*, 1:7a.

¹⁷ We may also give the following as an example of a particular labor service allocation method in use before the adoption of the equalized labor service levy. In a letter included in his collected works, *Wang Wenke gong ji*, Wang Ao (1450–1524) writes as follows of the practice in Changzhou and Wu counties (Suzhou, modern Jiangsu), *juan* 36: "The old method [i.e., that used prior to the adoption of the equalized labor service] was to count the *li* but not the households. If for the moment we confine ourselves to Changzhou and Wu, these two counties put together had in total 1,252 *li*, and their joint annual quota came to altogether 1,155 assignments (*yi*). The number of *li* and the number of assignments roughly matched. . . . If every *li* collectively took on one assignment, although the expenses would be heavy, they were not crippling when shared among ten households. As the *li* headman knew each household's resources and could make slight adjustments, people could bear it."

¹⁸ Whether service as tax captain is to be counted as part of the miscellaneous labor service is somewhat problematical. I am inclined to think that it should be regarded as corresponding to the regular labor service.

¹⁹ *Tianxia junguo libing shu*, 22:127a.

²⁰ The term used here, *lizheng*, is synonymous with *lizhang*.

²¹ The *du*, township, was a territorial division higher than the *li*; it had existed since the Southern Song. *Tu* was synoymous with *li*, and often used in place of it in Jiangnan.

²² The *xianyi* is the *lizhang* in service at the given time. The terms *xiannian*, *zhinian*, *gainian*, etc., were also used.

²³ 1503 *Changshu xianzhi*, 3:104b–105a.

²⁴ In gazetteers compiled at later periods, such as the *Jiangnan tongzhi* [Jiangnan comprehensive gazetteer] of 1736 or the 1881 edition of *Jiading xianzhi* [Jiading county gazetteer], we find such entries as the following about Zhou Chen's reform: "Labor service was levied triennially from each household and commuted, so that each individual was made to pay one tael." It is, however,questionable whether this is accurate. It would seem more probable that such an idea arose from misquotation of the entries in the labor service section of the 1539 edition of the Changshu county gazetteer, etc. To equate Zhou Chen's reform with the adoption of the equalized labor service levy, as does Bekkuya Hideo, "Kinsei Chūgoku ni okeru fueki kaikaku," p. 52, must therefore seem a little hasty.

[25] *Ming shi, juan* 78: (1905).

[26] *Yingzong shilu*, 120:5a (facs. repr. p. 2425).

[27] Ibid., 136:2a–b (facs. repr. pp. 2697–8); and *Xiaokan ji*.

[28] Ibid., 198:3b (facs. repr. p. 4202).

[29] There is a reference to "the Jiangxi assistant administration commissioner of the left, Xia Shi," in the Veritable Records for the eleventh month of 1442 (*Yingzong shilu*, 98:7b; facs. repr. p. 1974), which means that Xia's promotion to the post of assistant administration commissioner must have taken place before that date. This in turn would mean that it was not the assistant surveillance, but, as in source D, the assistant administration commissioner Xia Shi who carried out the equalized labor service levy. It may, however, be unreasonable to make up our minds about the date of Xia's promotion on the basis of this single source alone.

[30] *Yingzong shilu*, 281:3b (facs. repr. p. 6032).

[31] If we accept 1443 as the date of the adoption of the equalized labor service system, the expression "early in the Zhengtong period" found in the *Ming shi* (see above) would seem to stand in need of correction.

[32] See *Ming shi*, 178: (4740) (Biography of Zhu Ying and Biography of Cui Gong); 1682 *Shanxi tongzhi*, 18:42b.

[33] *Yingzong shilu*, 281:3a–b (reprint, pp. 6031–6032).

[34] 1736 *Jiangnan tongzhi*, 76:5a–b.

[35] *Ming shi*, 178: (4741) (Biography of Zhu Ying); and Xu Wei, *Xu Wenchang quanji, juan* 25, memorial inscription for Pang Shangpeng.

[36] *Xianzong shilu*, 33:2b (facs. repr. p. 650; date 8th month of 1466).

[37] 1510 *Da Ming huidian*.

[38] *Tianxia junguo libing shu*, 22:127a.

[39] Qiu Jun, *Daxue yanyi bu*, 31:13b–14b.

[40] 1590 *Yixing xianzhi*, 4:23a.

[41] Shi Jian, *Xicun ji*, 5:14b–15a (letter to the provincial governor).

[42] *Yingzong shilu*, 281:3a (reprint, p. 6031).

[43] *Wang Wenke gong ji*, 36:10b.

[44] The fiscal treatise of the *Ming shi* is of this view, and the compiler of the *Qinding Xu Wenxian tongkao* (16:27b) in turn writes as follows: "When we examine the system of *yinchai* and *lichai*, there is a lack of clarity . . . as to its origin. According to the fiscal treatise (of the *Ming shi*), the equalized labor service method was proposed at the beginning of the Zhengtong period. [Under this reform, it says] the original silver and manpower requirement figures were to be matched to the adult male and land-tax figures. . . . The *yinchai/lichai* system must [therefore] have been (already) in existence before Yingzong's reign." He thus suspects that the *yinchai/lichai* duality antedates equalized labor service. Matsumoto Yoshimi tends to see the establishment of the equalized labor service method and the appearance of silver assignment as contemporaneous developments (*Shina chihō jichi hattatsu shi*, p. 102). The same point of view is represented in Bekkuya Hideo's article cited in note 24 above, and in Iwami Hiroshi's "Min no Kasei zengo ni okeru fueki kaikaku ni tsuite."

[45] 1510 *Da Ming huidian*, 125:5a (Ministry of War).

[46] *Yingzong shilu*, 44:3a–b (reprint, pp. 853–54).

[47] *Xianzong shilu*, 33:2b (reprint, p. 1466); 95:7a (1471: the gate-duty receivers, *jianchao fuyi*); and 121:5a–b (1473: the Yizhou charcoal-burners, *chaifu*). 1510 *Da Ming huidian*, 163 (Ministry of Works) (1468: wood-cutters, *kanzhaifu*).

[48] *Xianzong shilu*, 33:2b. Matsumoto, "Mindai" (p. 105) regards this as an early example of the *yinchai*, but, as is indeed clear from the text itself, it is the situation before the adoption of equalized labor service that is described. Service by proxy is probably what is indicated.

[49] *Daxue yanyi bu*, 31:14b.

[50] *Min shu*, 39:12b.

[51] 1561 *Wujiang xianzhi*, 10:11a.

⁵² 1642 *Yuanshi xianzhi.*
⁵³ *Daxue yanyi bu*, 31:16b.
⁵⁴ 1519 *Chaoyi zhi*, 1:7a.
⁵⁵ Cf. Wang Ao, *Wang Wenke gong ji*, 36 (letter discussing equalized labor service): "When assignments are few and people many (the silver equivalents) are stored to meet public expenditures. This is called *yusheng junyao* (surplus *junyao*)."
⁵⁶ 1612 *Yongfu xianzhi*, 2:21a–b.
⁵⁷ 1606 *Shangyu xianzhi*, 8:37b.
⁵⁸ *Xiaozong shilu*, 147:3a (p. 2579); *Wuzong shilu*, 19:2a–b (pp. 561–62).
⁵⁹ 1564 *Huizhou fuzhi*, 8:27a; 1503 *Xinghua fuzhi*, *juan* 12 (the labor service section). It is, however, worthy of attention that the terms *yinchai* and *lichai* are not yet in evidence.
⁶⁰ *Tianxia junguo libing shu*, 28:47a and 27:53a. See also 1548 *Xiangshan xianzhi*: "It (the *yinchai/lichai* system) was first established as an institution at the time when Cheng Chang was regional inspector."
⁶¹ *Tianxia junguo libing shu*, 6:63b–64a.
⁶² 1618 *Jianchang fuzhi*, 3:11b.
⁶³ 1617 *Qiongzhou fuzhi*, *juan* 5 (the *junyao* section of the treatise on taxation).
⁶⁴ In fact, according to Table 1, in the cases of Haining county (Zhejiang province) and Leizhou prefecture (Guangdong province) the *yinchai* predominate; but overall it seems correct to say that the *lichai* formed the majority.
⁶⁵ *Tianxia junguo libing shu*, 22:127b.
⁶⁶ In many English thirteenth-century land registers there are entered sums of money corresponding to the corvée services. Such monetary valuation appears in French sources also, but according to Henri See, commutation payment occurred rather infrequently. In England, similarly, the records do not necessarily imply actual commutation, but only that there was the choice between service in person and commutation payment. See Suzuki Shigetaka, *Hōken shakai no kenkyū.*
⁶⁷ *Tianxia junguo libing shu*, 2:28b.
⁶⁸ 1624 *Haiyan xian tujing*, 5:48a.
⁶⁹ *Daxue yanyi bu*, 31:13a.
⁷⁰ See 1593 *Shangyuan xianzhi*, *juan* 2 (land tax) and *juan* 12 (literary anthology): Yao Ruxun's Discourse on "*ding*" and "*liang*."
⁷¹ 1577 *Ningguo fuzhi*, 8:8b–9a.
⁷² 1597 *Jiangxi sheng dazhi*, 2:72a–b.
⁷³ Ibid., 2:1a–b.
⁷⁴ For a detailed examination of this practice, see Shimizu Taiji, "Mindai no zeieki to kiki."
⁷⁵ The expression used is *lingjia*, which means the first section in a regulation.
⁷⁶ The expression used is *pinjia*, which seems to mean a household headed by a woman, or one whose members were infirm and elderly, and so on. Such a household was exempt from labor services. There is, however, some uncertainty here.
⁷⁷ 1579 *Hangzhou fuzhi*, 31:8b.
⁷⁸ See 1587 *Da Ming huidian*, 20:19a–20, under 1545; and 1603 *Yuyao xianzhi*, 10.
⁷⁹ 1642 *Wuxian zhi*, 9:29a.
⁸⁰ Cf. Shi Jian, *Xicun ji*, 5, for use of the term *daiguan* in such a context. Such pauper households with immunity from labor service liability were often called *daiguanhu* households.
⁸¹ 1548 *Xiangshan xianzhi*, 2:6a–b.
⁸² See 1593 *Shangyuan xianzhi*, 2. Although Shangyuan is a special case, it still seems representative of a general tendency.
⁸³ Ibid., 22.
⁸⁴ There also existed such other terms as *shiduan jince fa* (ten-sectioned brocade register system). In his article "Mindai ni okeru ekihō no hensen," Shimizu Taiji treats them as differentiable, but in my view it is more accurate to identify them with the *shiduan fa.*

[85] *Min shu*, 45:27b.

[86] *Tianxia junguo libing shu*, 7:9b.

[87] *Min shu*, 39:12a.

[88] What follows is based again on *Tianxia junguo libing shu*, 7:9b–10a. Iwami Hiroshi touches on the *shiduan fa* in his "Min no Kasei zengo ni okeru fueki kaikaku ni tsuite."

[89] In fact, however, since the first and second *jia* had already served their turns, the remaining 1,164,607.7–odd *mu* (145,575.97 × 8) was divided into 8, and every year the *junyao* assessment was made on 133,075.9 *mu*. Exact division by eight would, of course, have meant 145,575.97 *mu* per section.

[90] *Tianxia junguo libing shu*, 7:11a.

[91] 1612 *Quanzhou fuzhi*, 6:13b.

[92] 1576 *Yunnan tongzhi*, 6:4b. [Without the context, it is impossible to know whether to use the past or present tense in the translation. I have opted for the former. —Trans.]

[93] *Shizong xianhuangdi shilu*, 543:3b–4a (pp. 8774–75; 2nd month 1565); 1587 *Da Ming huidian*, 20:14b.

[94] 1576 *Yunnan tongzhi*, 6.

[95] According to the 1622 gazetteer of Quzhou prefecture (Zhejiang) and the 1631 Kaihua county gazetteer (Quzhou prefecture), Yi Fangzhi (in office 1589) put the *shiduan fa* in operation so as to assess the *dahu* (great households).

[96] 1605 *Wenzhou fuzhi*, 5:12b.

[97] 1572 *Leqing xianzhi*, 3:19b.

[98] On the Single Whip reform, the following may be consulted. Shimizu Taiji, "Ichijō benpō"; and *Chūgoku kinsei shakai keizaishi*; Numata Tomoo, "Ichijō benpō josetsu"; Matsumoto Yoshimi, "Mindai"; Liang Fangzhong, "Yitiao bianfa;" Bekkuya Hideo, "Kinsei Chūgoku ni okeru fueki kaikaku"; and Iwami Hiroshi, "Min no Kasei zengo ni okeru fueki kaikaku ni tsuite."

AN INTRODUCTION TO THE
SHANDONG JINGHUI LU

IWAMI HIROSHI

Textual criticism, a longstanding academic tradition in both China and Japan, has provided many of the essential methodological tools used in the modern historical study of China. Textual criticism, which was developed to a very high level in China in the early Qing by such famous scholars as Gu Yanwu, was adopted by Japanese scholars during the Edo period. Using a wide variety of linguistic and semantic approaches, textual critics intensively studied classical texts to determine their authenticity, dating, and authorship.

In the twentieth century, Japanese students of Chinese history are still trained in the techniques of textual criticism which are assumed to be an essential adjunct to the other skills of a competent historian. Texts are rigorously examined, and disputes over interpretation are buttressed with comparative data on the use and meanings of words and terms from a wide variety of texts.

In this essay Iwami Hiroshi shows the rich rewards that can be reaped through the application of this method. Iwami's essay takes as its subject a rare book that was once in the library of the famous Kyoto University scholar Naitō Konan. Since no other copies of the book are known, Professor Iwami begins with an examination of the text to determine its date and authorship, and provides a general description of its content. Comparing the book with a number of other better-known Ming fiscal texts, he offers convincing hypotheses on its compilation and use. With the basic data established, he then uses the text to explore larger questions related to Ming taxation and the history of the Single Whip reform in the late Ming.

The essay is of interest both for its excellent demonstration of the

This essay was originally published as "*Santō keikai roku* ni tsuite" [山東經會錄につ
いて] in *Shimizu hakushi tsuitō kinen Mindaishi ronsō* [清水博士追悼記念明代史論
叢] (Tokyo: Daian, 1962), pp. 197–220. Translation by Helen Dunstan.

311

uses of the textual criticism method and for the new light it sheds on the important Ming tax reform. The text itself comes from Shandong province in North China and is of special interest for the detailed picture it gives of the reform in an area previously little studied. Iwami suggests that earlier assumptions that the implementation of the Single Whip came considerably later in the north than in the south need to be reconsidered.

Iwami Hiroshi is a professor at Kobe University and at present is serving as Dean of the Faculty of Letters.

*   *   *

The work which I would like to introduce in the following pages belongs to the collection of the late Naitō Konan. In the summer of 1958 and again in the spring of the following year, I was able, through the generosity of Professors Naitō Kenkichi and Naitō Boshin, to borrow it and make a photographic copy. This book is rich in source material for the study of the Ming taxation system. Not only does it shed new light on a variety of topics when set beside the other literature; there also seems to be a considerable amount of new information. Furthermore, I have never read elsewhere of its existence; neither have I been able to discover mention of it in any of the catalogues I have examined. Both because of its content and rarity, the *Shandong jinghui lu* is an extremely valuable source. Although I used an extremely limited portion of it in an article published last year,[1] the full-scale exploitation of the work remains a task for the future.

The text: An explanation

The *Shandong jinghui lu* is printed in 12 Chinese chapters (*juan*) and 14 separate volumes, each measuring just over 24 centimeters by just over 17. Neither the printing nor the paper are of good quality, and there are even places which are barely decipherable. There is a difference in the number of folios per volume, ranging from 45 to 105; the average would be a little over 68. The ccart on the following page is an outline of the volumes and their contents.

Unfortunately, part of the preface which would normally explain the background of the compilation and publication of this work is missing. The first folio of the preface has been lost, and the lower half of the second folio has been torn away. Consequently, the text begins from the

Vol. no.	*Juan* no.	Contents	No. of folios
1	—	Preface	5
	—	Table of Contents	1
	1	Table of the land taxes of Jinan, Yanzhou and Dongchang prefectures	48
2	1 cont'd	The same continued	67
3	2	Table of the land taxes of Qingzhou, Laizhou and Dengzhou prefectures	50
4	2 cont'd	Aggregated quotas for the land tax	49
5	3	Retrospect on the land tax	69
6	4	Appendix to the land-tax section	45
7	5	Table of the equalized labor service allocations	105
8	6	Aggregated quotas for the equalized labor service	54
9	7	Retrospect on equalized labor service I	84
10	8	Retrospect on equalized labor service II	94
11	9	Appendix to the equalized labor-service section	82
12	10	Tables, aggregated quotas, retrospect and appendix for the *lijia* service system	55
13	11	Tables, aggregated quotas, retrospect and appendix for the postal-relay service system	91
14	12	Tables, aggregated quotas, retrospect and appendix for the horsebreeding service system	49
		Tables, aggregated quotas, retrospect and appendix for the salt-distribution system	16

third folio. Since the fifth folio ends at the fourth line, the preface is only 44 lines long. Neither the date nor the author's name has been appended to the preface; on the inner side of the fifth folio, however, we find the record "Printed on the (blank) day of the tenth lunar month of the fifth year of the Longqing period [1571]." Thus although the preface is undated, the printing date is clear.

Incomplete as the preface is, it is evident that it differs considerably in tenor from prefaces to more ordinary types of work. It is a kind of official document, and relates the background to the publication largely in terms of exchanges between the provincial governor and the provincial administration office, and between the regional inspector and the same agency. Though the extant preface does not indicate the date and author of this work, judging from the text itself it seems practically

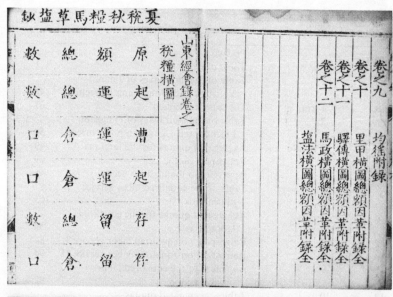

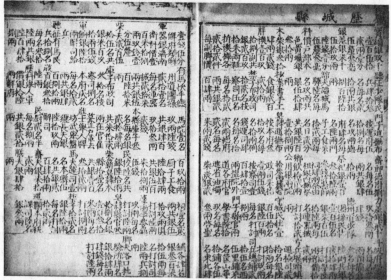

Tables from the *Shandong jinghui lu*, 1571. (Top, left): First page of *juan* 1 with the heading summer and autumn taxes, fodder levy, and salt-ration tax entered at the top. The six sections ruled horizontally across read: aggregated original quotas; aggregated figures for outside deliveries; grain-tribute destinations; outside deliveries destinations; aggregated figures for retained revenue; and retained revenue destinations. (Top, right): Last page of the contents page, listing chapters 9 through 12 of the *Shandong jinghui lu*. (Bottom): Double-page spread itemizing taxes for Licheng county, Jinan prefecture, showing the commutation of various labor services.

certain that the author was the provincial administration commissioner.

As we can see from the preface, a bureau was established for the compilation of this work. The chief directors of the project were three prefectural judges named Zhou Yude, Qian Pu, and Jing Song. The printing costs were met out of the revenue from incense fees stored in the administration office treasury, and Niu Ruoyu, vice-prefect of Jinan, was put in charge of management. A rescript transcribed at the end ordered the printing of the work, its distribution throughout the jurisdiction, and its eternal observation. It would seem reasonable to suppose that the missing opening explained who devised the compilation and for what reasons.

The preface also describes the work's layout and principal divisions. A presentation of this discussion should serve to explain the organization of the entire text. The principal divisions were: 1) land tax and fodder levy, 2) equalized labor service, 3) the *lijia* service system, 4) the postal-relay service system, 5) the horsebreeding service system, and 6) the salt-distribution system. This is exactly as shown in the outline above, except that the "fodder levy" of item 1 is omitted there.

The outline shows that each of these major sections consists of four parts: a table, aggregated quotas, a retrospect, and an appendix. This format is explained as follows in the preface.

The Tables. These set out the quotas assigned each county-level jurisdiction. The rows of figures are arranged on squared paper, making it easy to follow.

If we test this explanation against the land-tax tables, we find that each double page is ruled horizontally into six sections, devoted respectively to: 1) the aggregated original quotas; 2) the aggregated figures for outside deliveries; 3) the grain-tribute destinations; 4) the outside deliveries destinations; 5) the aggregated figures for retained revenue; and 6) the retained revenue destinations. The name of the given county-level jurisdiction is entered in the margin at the top, as are the three subheadings: summer and autumn taxes, fodder levy, and salt-ration tax. In the lower frames we find itemized the details subsumed within the major aggregates (see illustrations).

Although each section is referred to as a table, the division of the page varies in both form and logic from one section to another. Thus, for instance, in the equalized labor-service (*junyao*) section, the top four frames are allocated to silver assignments (*yinchai*), while the remaining two are used for manpower assignments (*lichai*). It would have been adequate in this case to simply divide the table into two frames; it was doubtless for the sake of visual effect that the six-frame division was

maintained. In the *lijia* service system section all six frames are allocated differentially: 1) blue-and-white-liveried attendants, 2) torchbearers, 3) dispatch bearers, 4) jailers, 5) horses, mules, and donkeys
and 6) bedding and entertainment funds. The *lijia*-service table is
basically complete with this six-fold division, though the land-tax table
is further subdivided. The only subdivisions in the *lijia* table are the
separate listings of blue-liveried attendants and white-liveried attendants in the first frame, horses and mules in the fifth (despite the
fact that the heading is "horses, mules, and donkeys," donkeys in fact
do not appear), and bedding and entertainment funds in the sixth.
We may remark in passing that the six headings given here relate to
the "service-men and horses" aspect of the *lijia* system, and in that
respect highlight the character of *lijia* as an auxiliary institution for the
postal-relay service system. In addition, we note that burdens frequently
apportioned to the *lijia* in the southern regions do not appear at all here.
The fact is that the many impositions corresponding to the *lijia* silver
levy (*lijia yin*) or equitable silver levy (*junping yin*), etc., of the South[2]
were for the most part to be found within the commuted services division of the equalized labor service in the case of Shandong province.

In the postal-relay service system table, the six frames are allotted to
1) the land for stations originally established, 2) numbers of horses, 3)
numbers of donkeys, 4) boat hands and cart hands, 5) supplementary
provisions and horse-replacement funds, and 6) extra stations. The six-
frame format has been maintained up to this point, but in the succeeding
horsebreeding service system section only four frames are used. The
division is between stud horses, occupying the top two frames, and
horses for use, taking up the bottom two. A two-frame division would
have been sufficient, but a greater number of frames are used simply
to convey the impression of a tabular presentation. The final table is
on the salt distribution system. The part of it concerned with the production yards is divided into two frames, license salt in kind and silver
commutation payments. Here it should be noted that the production
yards entered in the upper frame are entirely distinct from those entered
in the lower, and barring considerations of consistency of format there
is no reason for the juxtaposition. In the one remaining item, the levy
on civilian and saltern land, the county names and silver-payment
quotas are also arranged in two frames, the division of which is equally
pointless.

The Aggregated Quotas. Whereas the figures in the tables are those
for individual county-level jurisdictions, the aggregated quotas sections
are explained as "setting down the aggregated figures for the province

as a whole for ease of reference." When we check this against the text, we find the provincial totals arranged item by item and broken down into prefectural subtotals.

The Retrospect Sections. These present changes over succeeding years; that is to say, the increases, decreases, and shifts in different items and the particulars of proposals advanced by various administrative agencies. As the preface remarks, "these sections are the fullest and most detailed," and from a scholarly point of view they contain a great quantity of interesting material.

The Appendix Sections. These include items for which there was no room in the respective retrospect, and proposals recommended for adoption at a future date. For historians the appendix sections seem of equal or greater value than the retrospects. The retrospect and appendix sections cover material beginning from the 1540s and give special attention to the 1560s. There are occasional rare references to such early reigns as Chenghua (1465–87) but such references are not consecutive and only appear as citations of past practice included as support for present argument.

New materials on the Single Whip reform

In this section a few entries relating to the Single Whip reform (*yitiaobian fa*)[3] will be used to illustrate the kind of interesting materials in the retrospect and appendix sections. Let us begin by examining the origins of the Single Whip reform in Shandong.

In the Land-Tax Retrospect (*juan* 3) we find the following:
The magistrate of Feicheng county, Wan Pengcheng, and some other county magistrates submit:
In the summer tax for 1563 the four categories of the farmland silk impost amount in all to 25,148.60781 taels. Each year they have all been assessed separately, outside the Single Whip. If now we were to amalgamate them with the other taxes into a [revised] Single Whip so that the commuted value of each *shi* was not increased by more than a small fraction of a tael, not only would the people benefit, but abuses would also end. Besides, last year the prefectures made all-in-one assessments. This year we ought to integrate [these imposts] with the Single Whip for their assessment.

From this we may infer that by 1563 a mode of tax collection called the Single Whip was already in operation, and that it seems to have amalgamated and commuted quite a proportion of the many categories of taxation.[4] There is no more on this in the retrospect, but in the appendix to the land-tax section (*juan* 4) there are a large number of entries relating to the Single Whip reform. Although it is rather lengthy, let us begin by presenting the first of these documents in which the provincial governor censor-in-chief Liu, upon examination, issued in 1555 the document "Investigation of means of correcting longstanding abuses in land-tax assessment so as to relieve the people's hardships." It reads:

I hereby instruct the [provincial administration] office, in conjunction with the provincial surveillance office, the taxation and the general surveillance circuits, to deliberate the proper measures to be taken with regard to tax assessment in the long term. If in the subordinate territories of a given prefecture there are no great disparities in landholding and taxation or great distance between rich and poor, then the Single Whip reform should be adopted; if on the other hand the territories of a prefecture show marked differences in the fertility and state of cultivation of the land, and in the wealth and stability of the population, it will be necessary to use the ninefold classification (*sandeng jiuze*) system. . . .

I have subsequently noted a representation from Jinan prefecture. The prefect Xiang Shouli reports: "Among the territories subordinate to this prefecture, Licheng and Changqing counties have both over successive years been using the Single Whip in making allocations. Zhangqiu and a further 25 county-level jurisdictions have been using a threefold classification; Xintai and Laiwu counties have used a fourfold one. Although there are dissimilarities in the systems, all are alike in being riddled with abuses. The ordinary people suffer, and it behooves us to decide on steps. There would be no better time for the [provincial administration] office to implement the Single Whip system than the present, when they are settling the tax allocations. A comprehensive survey is to be made for each county of: the number of *shi* earmarked for each of the granaries in the capital and the northern frontier; the quantity of silver to which this is to be commuted; the number of *shi* of retained revenue earmarked for each granary; and how much wheat or rice is to be gathered in each case. [It should determine] how much silver altogether is due each granary, and how much [grain] in kind. It should take the county's standing tax quota and prepare an overall and even allocation. It should state the commutation rate, noting what fraction of a tael and how much rice and wheat in kind is to be taken in respect of every *shi* [of original assessment]. This should be clearly set out in a document to be issued to the prefecture for transmission to the county. One *shi* may be multiplied to make ten or a hundred; one *shi* may be divided to make a tenth, a hundredth, or a thousandth. The people will all naturally be able to make the calculation on this principle. The prefecture should also ascertain the quantity of silver and of uncommuted grain receivable in lieu of every *shi* in each county and not permit the great households to take the slightest fraction more than the amount due. A notice should be printed and distributed throughout each jurisdiction for display, so that the people all know clearly that there is a set valuation for each *shi* of assessment for the current year. Each should take his individual standing tax assessment, check it against the notice, and simply make the payment to the great household at his own convenience. He need not be told which granary his tax is for; nor should the *li* clerks be ordered to parcel out the allocations. As the taxpayers will have their settled figures, the collectors naturally will not dare to cheat.

The senior official of the given county should further be instructed to have registers prepared for every *li*. The *li* should be grouped together in an equitable manner, so that a large county is divided into eight divisions (*qu*), and a small one into four or six. Each division should have one chest, and four great households per division ought to be appointed: two to collect the uncommuted revenue, and two the silver payments. Each should be issued with a tax-chest warrant and required to gather what is due. Again, it is not necessary to specify the granary of destination. The great households should make the *li* captain responsible for prompt deliveries, the *li* captains the *jia* captains (*shipai*), and the *jia* captains the tax-paying households. As there will be a settled system for collection, the deliveries outside the county must also be made on time. . . .

One might perhaps have Yanzhou and Dongchang proceed according to the Jinan method, while the ninefold classification system might still be applied in places in Qingzhou, Dengzhou, etc.

It is evident from the opening of this document that by 1555 the Single Whip reform was in operation with regard to land-tax payments in at least some of the county-level jurisdictions. In addition it is notable that both the provincial governor and the prefect of Jinan distinguish between the Single Whip and the ninefold classification system. The threefold and fourfold classification systems referred to in the preamble by the prefect of Jinan may doubtless be regarded as variants or terminological abbreviations of the full ninefold classification form. I am not aware of any previous citation in the literature of a case in which the ninefold-household ranking system enters the picture in this way in connection with land-tax assessment. The precise nature of the ninefold classification system will be dealt with later.

Since the Single Whip system is mentioned antithetically to the ninefold classification system, it would naturally seem to follow that the Jinan method of the closing sentence of our long quotation must refer to the Single Whip. The Jinan method is the tax-collection system explained in detail in the quoted passage. It certainly seems to fit the category of the Single Whip system. All the same, the scheme's proposer, Xiang Shouli, does not himself employ the term Single Whip or, for that matter, any other. It is not clear whether, although the system was in substance Single Whip, there would have been some inexpediency in calling it explicitly by that name; or whether the name was simply understood. However, further on in the land-tax appendix chapter we find a passage telling how this same provincial governor Liu Cai,[5] adopting Xiang Shouli's proposals, restored the Single Whip method in 1555, so it seems that the system outlined by Xiang was indeed the Single Whip system. This means that the piece quoted above represents a detailed exposition of the Single Whip system as it was practiced in Shandong at that time.

The expression "Single Whip reform" is generally believed to designate the fusion of a miscellany of items into a streamlined payment mechanism, either right across the land-tax and service-levy system or in one or the other segment of it.[6] As far as Shandong is concerned, there has been nothing to compel a change in our interpretation in the material adduced so far. There does, however, appear in the land-tax appendix section of the *Shandong jinghui lu* a usage of the term "Single Whip" which seems a little different. The passage in question reads as follows:

In Licheng county, the basic wheat quota is 13,673.2138 *shi*. Out of this amount, 9,800 *shi* are for outside delivery, and for these 0.43 tael of silver have been charged in lieu of every *shi*. This makes 4,214 taels altogether. The difference, 3,873.2138 *shi*, is retained revenue and is (receivable) in kind. A Single Whip is to be applied comprehensively to the entire county, without distinction between outside landed interests (*jizhuang*), upper households, middle households, and lower households. That part of every *shi* of wheat quota which is in fact to be collected in silver for outside delivery comes to 0.71673 *shi*. If every *dou* is charged for at the original rate of 0.043 tael, the (new) silver charge (on every *shi* of assessment) will be 0.308194 tael. That part of the *shi* which is receivable in kind for retained revenue comes to 0.28327 *shi*. For each *dou*, 0.008 *shi* wastage shall be added; thus with the wastage [the uncommuted element charged on each *shi* of assessment] will be 0.3059316 *shi* plus 0.00435 tael matting levy. There is no need to designate the granary of destination; it is only necessary to charge the individual households to make payments of silver and wheat according to the figures entered on the warrants (*youtie*).

The remaining county-level jurisdictions shall all make their assessments on this model. Places such as Yizhou, Tengxian, Jiaozhou, and Juzhou, where inspection has shown there to be land that has gone out of cultivation, shall also order the households actually farming land to make up the payments through a Single Whip. On the one hand, the prefectures involved shall be instructed to direct the county-level senior officials to strictly ascertain the quantities of wheat and silver due from the land gone out of cultivation; on the other hand the peasant households still in operaton shall be made to share [this burden] equitably among themselves and pay it with their own assessments in a Single Whip.

From the wording of the lines of the first paragraph, it appears that here the term "Single Whip" denotes "without distinction of household grade." This resembles the antithetical use of the terms "Single Whip system" and "ninefold classification" in the piece we cited earlier. If the former term was used in opposition to the latter, it is natural to imagine that there was some point of contact between household rank and Single Whip as well. This point of contact appears in the instruction "ignore the distinctions between the household grades and apply a Single Whip." From this it would seem that in Shandong the meaning of the Single Whip reform was slightly different from previous interpretations. It implies the equalization of households for assessment purposes.

Yet there is no impediment to applying the traditional interpretation of the Shandong Single Whip system to the tax collection methods described in either of the two passages quoted above. Such a prescription as "there is no need to designate the granary of destination; it is only necessary to charge the individual households to make payments of silver and wheat according to the figures entered on the warrants" is precisely the Single Whip method as previously understood. This means that there are two interpretations for the same tax-collection system. The new interpretation appears to differ from the old, but is really only another aspect of the same system: the two are not mutually exclusive.

It is a well-known fact that although the simple term "land tax" (*shui-liang*) is used, it covers a complex variety of constituent elements. First there is the distinction between items receivable in kind and those commuted, and that between items for outside delivery and those to be retained within the locality. These two latter categories were further subdivided according to the precise location of each payment's final destination. There were also varying wastage rates attached to the different items, and sometimes surcharges were added. There were also variations in the commutation rates for the commuted items. Thus a single *shi* of assessment would in reality not necessarily entail the same degree of burden for each taxpayer. On the contrary, there would be quite a disparity. In order to distribute the burden fairly and remove the disparity the circumstances of the individual taxpayers would naturally have to be taken into account. It is in precisely this connection that the ninefold classification system enters the Shandong land-tax scene. Its significance stands out still more plainly where, a little further on in this same section, we find the statement: "[the purpose of the] ninefold classification system is to allocate the onerous tax payments to the upper households, the medium tax payments to the middle households, and the light tax payments to the lower households."

It seems that although the expression "ninefold classification" was employed, the actual division was, as the case of Jinan suggests, into three or at the most four grades. The collected works of Ge Shouli (1505–78) provide some explicit information on the matching of the burden to the household grade. They contain a letter, "Yu Jiang Mengquan zhong-cheng lun tianpu" (Discussion of the land tax with Provincial Governor Jiang Mengquan),[7] which partially reads, "I have heard that these days when the Provincial Administraton Office allots taxes, it distinguishes three grades. Those in the top grade pay 0.9 tael per *shi*, those in the middle 0.8, and those in the bottom grade 0.6." The recipient of this letter was the vice censor-in-chief of the right Jiang Tingyi who was provincial governor of Shandong from 1567 until 1570.[8]

Thus consideration of the household grade in connection with land-tax assessment took place in response to the existence of the multiplicity of different items into which the land-tax burden was divided. It follows that when these subdivisions were eliminated and the undifferentiated total allocated in an even fashion, the necessity to take account of household grade would also disappear. Conversely, if it were proposed to find a method that dispensed with the necessity for household grading where such a correlation was already in existence, there would be no option but to take the sum of all the subdivisions as the aggregated total and reallocate it evenly. In the past the Single Whip reform has only been understood to mean this consolidation of the different items. It is now clear, however, that in Shandong it occasionally referred to the equalization of the households for assessment purposes. We do not know whether the demand for such equalization emerged first and sparked off the Single Whip reform in Shandong or not. I guess that since—as can be seen in the case of the "gate silver" assessment— there was strong consciousness of household grading in Shandong, the Single Whip reform also placed special emphasis on rendering this system obsolete. This gave rise to understanding the term as referring to the removal of household gradings.

A variety of other developments connected with the Single Whip reform and dating roughly from the 1560s are set out in detail in the land-tax appendix section. Although they are in large part presented as the opinion of the provincial governor, there are nonetheless proposals for the promotion of the Single Whip reform, proposals against it, the various grounds advanced for such proposals, and in between some concrete information on the workings of the tax-collection system at the time. In summary, this appendix is composed mainly of entries focusing upon the Single Whip reform.

There is also material on the Single Whip land-tax reform in the equitable service levy appendix chapter, *juan* 9. This is of interest because it indicates an upper limit for the date of the adoption of the Single Whip reform, and the absorption of a portion of the service levy into the land tax. It appears in a document by Censor-in-Chief Liang,[9] provincial governor in 1570. The Single Whip reform is discussed under an item headed "Yiding qu min zhi zhi" (Deliberation of the means of taking from the people) in a memorial by a certain Guang, supervising secretary of the left in the Office of Scrutiny for Personnel. This was included in a Ministry of Revenue memorandum dated the thirteenth day of the fourth month, 1570, which Liang quotes. An extract follows:

For some unknown reason, after 1551, without receiving clear authorization [those who had direction of local affairs] all of a sudden changed over to the Single Whip scheme. There were no longer precise statements of amounts and destinations, and each year differed from the one before. Even the authorities could not work out the details; how were the ordinary people to know what was going on? Not only this, but according to the old regulations the beeswax, firewood, charcoal, and paint levies, etc., were all charged through the equalized labor service, and those engaged in trade and commerce also had their share to pay. Now that these levies are absorbed within the land tax, rich merchants and large-scale traders get off scot-free. The hardships of the peasant families are redoubled.

For the ministry's opinion on this, we cite their concluding comments:

> It behooves us to make an explicit supplication, and then to await respectfully the [Imperial] decree [commanding us to] issue instructions to the provincial governors of Shandong and elsewhere, and a memorandum to the censorate for transmission to the regional inspectors. [The purport of these documents will be that the recipients should] strictly instruct the senior officials of the [provincial administration and surveillance] offices, prefectures, subprefectures, and counties to make a most particular investigation. If the Single Whip method of the recent past is truly void of advantage for the common people, they are with unbiased minds and at their earliest convenience to consider how to put an end to it without submitting to constraint of usage. As for the beeswax, paint, firewood, and charcoal levies, and the like, since according to the old regulations both *ding* and landholdings were levied on an equitable basis, the present practice of assessing them within the land tax is to be put right at once. Henceforward the prefectural, subprefectural, and county officials subordinate to the two metropolitan jurisdictions and the 13 provincial administration offices are not to take it upon themselves to change established laws. . . .

And so instructions passed from the Ministry of Revenue to the provincial authorities. Liang Menglong, taking his stand upon the views of the central government, issues directions concerning the 1571 and 1572 assessments to be carried out in 1570. The lines relevant to the Single Whip reform in this decree are: "As for such items as the beeswax, firewood, charcoal, sacrificial animals, fruit, and materials-purchase levies, in keeping with established law they are once more to be assessed within the equalized labor-service levy." The fact that these levies were originally equalized labor service ones implies that they were imposed as a form of service levy (*yi*). Since these levies had been incorporated into the land tax and the land tax was collected by the Single Whip method, it would seem that here the Single Whip united land tax and a portion of the service levy.[10]

At this point I should like to add a word about the upper limit for the date of adoption of the Single Whip reform in Shandong. In his study on the subject, Professor Shimizu Taiji cited a passage in the collected works of Ge Shouli indicating that in Shandong the reform had been in operation since 1541.[11] In my earlier studies of this reform, I deliberately ignored this piece of evidence for two reasons: First, I found it difficult to understand the Ge Shouli text because of a lack of further records on the Single Whip reform in Shandong during the Jiajing period (1522–66). Second, I was preoccuppied by the idea that a reform adopted as part of the commutation movement at the end of Jiajing in central China could not have possibly been in operation 20 years before in economically less-advanced Shandong.[12] However, the *Shandong jinghui lu* states that the reform began after 1551. Such evidence forces us to revise the view that the reform began in North China during the Wanli period (1573–1619) and go back to Professor Shimizu's material. It goes without saying that we are here concerned only with the name Single Whip: we do not claim that the Jiajing system was the same in substance as the later one. The details of the difference must await investigation at a future date, but it is naturally anticipated that in the post-Wanli system the integration of the various taxation categories had become more advanced.

It should be noted that the Single Whip reform appearing in the *Shandong jinghui lu* is not simply the land-tax Single Whip reform. The following entry concerning equitable (*junyao*) Single Whip reform also comes from *juan* 9:

As for the Single Whip assessment method, in 1568 the deputies Vice Prefect Yi Zheng and others made the following report upon the allocation for equalized labor service: We submit that within the equalized labor service whereas the services performed in person (*lichai*), incurring as they do additional expenditure, are all assessed upon the wealthy households for performance, commuted services (*yinchai*), in which collection stops at the set quotas, pass through the procedure of allocation by the responsible official: for the revenues the sequence is determined by the statements of requirements issued by the provincial administration office, while for the objects of taxation it follows the disposition of the *li* in the given county. The requisitions are assessed in order, item by item, and the system does not lack in equity. However, there are differences in the urgency of services and in the wealth of the *li*. When an urgent and essential service comes around to a poor and wretched *li*, dunning will not yield results; when something less pressing falls to the turn of a prosperous *li*, they will follow their old custom and default. Thus is the collection stymied. Speaking from the point of view of fairness, there are still the former disadvantages. There is also the selection of rich commoners to fulfill the firewood, groom, and other duties, for the sole furtherance of their own selfish purposes; it is just as His Governorship fears. What with the bribery performed by evil-doing magnates and the shifting around [of burdens] perpetrated by clerks, it would be hard to list the malpractices exhaustively. In essence, all derive from the establishment of differentiated impost items. As a plan for the present situation, it would be well, in accordance with the Single Whip scheme originally put in operation by the governorship, to make an overall computation for each county-level jurisdiction [first] of the commuted service silver due for every item, and [second] of the [amounts receivable in respect of the] gate and *ding* (*mending*) charge. Apart from the requirement on the upper households to make up the services performed in person, the remaining sum of silver plus the amounts due from the lower households would be consolidated with any necessary adjustment to ensure that it agreed exactly with the commuted service quota. The item headings would be eliminated. A single warrant would be issued every household in every *li* stating only the amount of silver due: it would not specify an item. Four prosperous great households would be appointed to keep the books and jointly oversee collection. As for [the disbursement of] the silver taken, an examination would be made of the original requirements. If a certain item was an urgent one, it would be paid first in full. An item whose delivery was a less pressing matter would wait its turn. Items such as [commuted] turns of service at the capital, firewood, and materials purchase which must be dispatched to the capital would be handed over for delivery with the land tax. As for such items as padded jackets which have to be made, the great households should be instructed to disburse the sums appointed, have them made, and send them. In this way, it may be hoped that commuted service will become equitable, and will not be increased; shifting of burdens and other malpractices in registration and computation may be avoided also. The above is submitted to Provincial Governor Censor-in-Chief Jiang for his approval.

The Single Whip reform discussed here concerns only the commuted service element of the equalized labor service system. It is a question of amalgamating the different items of the commuted service element and carrying out an allocation and collection procedure that involves specifying nothing more than the amount of silver due. That is to say, it involves the consolidation of the subcategories of one portion of the service levy. The date of the adoption of this kind of Single Whip reform is problematical. When did "the Single Whip scheme originally put in operation by the governorship" begin? If it was not instituted in 1568, we have no way of knowing when it was adopted. Nevertheless, it is evident from our document that even if the Single Whip scheme had been applied earlier, it was not the norm in 1568. Or was it being adopted for the first time in 1568 never having been put in practice previously? Finally, previously it has been vaguely assumed that when the Single Whip was adopted, the services performed in person and the commuted service elements of the equalized labor service merged. It should be noted, however, that the appearance of a Single Whip reform of the above description precludes such a simple understanding of the problem. In other words, it is for the time being necessary to separate commuted service, services performed in person and the all-out commutation of the service levy conceptually from the Single Whip reform. Alternatively, if we prefer to link them up, we must divide the reform into several stages according to its import and consider at what stage the services performed in person disappeared. The *Shandong jinghui lu* shows that in Shandong, even with the Single Whip reform in operation, services performed in person remained as before, unfused.[13]

The *Shandong jinghui lu* and local taxation registers

As mentioned at the outset, I have not been able to locate the *Shandong jinghui lu* in any of the Chinese and Japanese catalogues available. I suspect that the book was never entered in a catalogue at all, at any rate before the end of the Qing dynasty. As this suspicion is derived from consideration of the book's character, I should like to conclude with some consideration of the nature of this work.

It stands to reason that in a country such as China where bureaucratic government had existed from early times, a wide variety of registers would have been created to meet the needs of administration. Recent research upon Han documents on wooden strips has clearly demonstrated that a minute form of organization had already emerged by the Han dynasty. The various discoveries made in the Dunhuang documents relating chiefly to the Tang period are also common knowledge. Nor should it now be necessary to explain the status of the Yellow Registers and Fish-scale Registers as representative basic documentary materials for administration in Ming times. These latter two did more than provide data: they were actually used as ledgers at the time of the assessment of the land tax and the service levy. We also know of other Ming registers of this kind, diagrammatic records of the equalized labor service levy, and equalized labor service.[14] Both appear to have been service-levy imposition ledgers designed to meet specific purposes.

However, changes appeared in every aspect of the taxation system, and the reforming late years of the Ming saw the creation of registers presenting the standard figures for fiscal administration in certain jurisdictions. There, registers differed somewhat in character from those just mentioned. They may have been similar to the statistical ledgers in that they were registers designed for overall control of actual fiscal administration; but it would appear that they came to take on a new, and more important, kind of significance. By "standard," we do not mean only that they were basic documentary materials; they also came to be invested with strong normative significance. To be sure, each individual figure was based on the actual situation at a certain time; nonetheless, overall the figures were abstractions from the specific circumstances of succeeding years deemed proper for adoption as the standard for the future. A major distinctive feature of these works is that they were printed. In many cases, registers of this sort were compiled on the occasion of the adoption of some reform; there were also instances of the contents being confined to one single sector.

To take an example, the *Guangdong yongping lu* (The Guangdong everlasting equity book), produced in 1559 on the occasion of the regional inspector Pan Jixun's readjustment of the *lijia* service burdens, was evidently printed with the intention that it should present norms to be followed in the future. It concerned itself exclusively with the equitable silver levy, and one would imagine that it consisted of detailed entries relating to the entire area within the jurisdiction of the Guangdong provincial administration office. Unfortunately, the original is not extant but the Jiajing period edition of the Guangdong provincial gazetteer appears to include a portion, or perhaps an epitome, of it.[15] Another extant work, similar in content, is the *Qinyi Liangzhe junping lu* (The imperially approved Zhejiang book of equitable dispensation). This was prepared chiefly under the auspices of Pang Shangpeng, the Zhejiang regional inspector in 1566, and a copy is held by the Sonkeikaku Bunko in Tokyo. Judging from the resemblance in title and content, and from the fact that, being a native of Guangdong, Pang would doubtless have had an opportunity to examine Pan's compilation, we may perhaps assume that the *Qinyi Liangzhe junping lu* was modeled on the *Guangdong yongping lu*. Moreover, the history of the work's printing is recorded in its preamble in the form of a document appearing in the name of the Zhejiang provincial administration office, and headed "Wei jie rongfei ding fashou yi su *lijia* shi" (Cutting back superfluous expenditures and establishing firm guidelines in order to relieve the *lijia*). This resembles the preface to the *Shandong jinghui lu* in format, and the similarity emerges once again in the stated purpose of the printing; the work was to be distributed, and its prescriptions followed evermore.

There are earlier examples of normative printed registers, and ones that cover the whole range of land taxes and service imposts. We know, for instance, from references in the sources, of the *fuyi ce* (land-tax and labor-service registers) of the Jiangnan region, although it is not clear whether any originals survive. The compilation of these registers was associated with the tax reform that took place in that area around 1537, and as the region fell within a so-called metropolitan area, individual prefectures were taken as units. Whether such registers were actually compiled throughout Jiangnan is unclear; at least they‸seem to have been made by Yingtian, Suzhou, Songjiang, Changzhou, and Zhenjiang prefectures.[16] Since the originals are not accessible, it is not possible to give a detailed account of their contents. However, some of the late-Ming local gazetteers include records which give us a general outline, and there are even some that appear to provide partial transcriptions. The *Shihuo zhi* (Fiscal treatise) section of the 1561 Wujiang county gazetteer, for instance, makes extensive use of something which it calls "the register approved and printed by the prefect Wang Yi in 1538";[17] in particular, it transcribes the detailed breakdown of the figures in the land-tax and labor-service sections, thereby transmitting some idea of the original. There can be no doubt but that this "register approved and printed by Wang Yi" is the same thing as the Suzhou land-tax and labor-service registers. Furthermore, the preamble to the land-tax section of the 1593 Shangyuan county gazetteer explains its aim of arranging the material on the principle of the register compiled by the regional governor Ouyang Duo in the following words:

When in olden times Ouyang Duo from Jiangxi was governor in the Southern Capital, Nanjing, he had the local chief officials wrack their brains about the hardships suffered by the populace and exhaust their ingenuity in considering the state's finances. He made two registers, one extracting the main points for the general information of the people, and one specifying the particulars for official reference. In plan, the work had four divisions: eight heads for settling the land tax; twelve heads for settling the *lijia* [impositions]; two heads for examining the equalized labor-service levy; and six heads for examining the postal-relay service [imposts]. These were handed down as established norms and left no room for evildoing. The people benefitted for some length of time. As the generations receded and men passed away, the threads that bound the volumes broke, and only handwritten copies have been transmitted by the elders. Although some alterations have by now been made in the subcategories, taken as a whole they do not vitiate the general plan. Thus our basic format for compiling the *Tianfu zhi* (Treatise on land tax) retains the old, while our subcategories are adjusted to accord with present circumstances.[18]

And in the text itself the four subtitles "Eight heads for settling the land tax," etc., are employed without change of wording. There are several other references to the land-tax and labor-service registers and their arrangement besides these.[19]

To the best of my knowledge, the land-tax and labor-service registers discussed here are the earliest example of this genre of printed registers. I believe that subsequently registers of the same kind came to be printed everywhere. Still within the Jiangnan region, there were the *Jingfu ce* (Registers for regulating the land tax) compiled in 1588.[20] The recent Catalogue of Rare Books held by the National Library of Beijing lists a *Henan fuyi zongkuai wence* (Statistical register of the land tax and service-levy imposts of Henan) printed in the Jiajing period in two volumes, and a *Sichuan chongkan fuyi shuce* (Reprinted register of land tax and service-levy imposts for Sichuan) printed in the Wanli period in four volumes.[21] It is a matter of common knowledge that *Fuyi quanshu* (Complete books of land taxes and service levies) were compiled everywhere during and after the Wanli period. My own view is that the registers produced under a variety of titles from Jiajing times onward came to be standardized under the title *Fuyi quanshu* during the later decades of the Ming dynasty, and it was not until early Qing times that a coordinated *Fuyi quanshu* covering the whole empire was printed. The *Shandong jinghui lu* is surely one of the products of this trend. Since it is a comparatively early example, it is particularly valuable.

As we have already noted, these registers were published with a normative intention, but since their distribution was restricted to the ordinary local yamen of the given jurisdiction, the number of copies printed must have been extremely small. Similarly, the works were never more than documentary materials for the local administrative officers, and so despite the fact that they were bound and printed, they were probably never regarded as books. They thus presumably failed to attract the interest of collectors. On one hand the chances of their surviving through the care of private individuals were exceptionally slight; while on the other, as the years passed and their records came to differ markedly from contemporary reality and the official point of view, they lost both their usefulness as reference works and their normative significance. Thus they were often discarded. The truth of this comes over in the passage we have quoted, which tells how by the time of the compilation of the Shangyuan county gazetteer, some fifty years later, only handwritten copies remained of the Yingtian registers prepared in 1537 or 1538. The absence of the *Shandong jinghui lu* from Ming and Qing catalogues would seem to derive precisely from such circumstances. The catalogues recorded "books," and the likes of the *Shangdong jinghui lu* did not qualify for recognition. It was not until more recent times, when concepts had changed and the scope of catalogues is broader, that such works could find a place upon their pages.

It is hoped that this essay, though brief and sketchy, is sufficient to demonstrate the value of the *Shandong jinghui lu* as a source. The evidence contained in this source shows beyond doubt that we need to revise the standard theories about the origin and contents of the Single Whip reform.[22]

Notes

[1] Iwami Hiroshi, "Mindai no minsō to hokuhen bōei." [Leif Littrup has noted that the *Shandong jinghui lu* is mentioned in Liang Fangzhong, "Mingdai yitiao bianfa nianbiao." It would seem that Liang saw the *Shandong jinghui lu* in the 1930s. Readers may also be interested in Leif Littrup, *Subbureaucratic Government in China in Ming Times: A Study of Shandong Province in the Sixteenth Century.* This work makes extensive use of the *Shandong jinghui lu,* a copy of which Dr. Littrup obtained from Professor Iwami.—Trans.]

[2] For concrete detail on these institutions, the reader is referred to Yamane Yukio, "Mindai richō no shokuseki ni kansuru ichi kōsatsu"; my own "Mindai chihō zaisei no ichi kōsatsu: Kanton no kinpeigin ni tsuite"; and Kuribayashi Norio, "Rikōgin ni kansuru kōsatsu."

[3] Such variant forms as *yitiaobian* and *yitiaobian paifa* are also found within the text, but I have chosen to use the standard form, *yitiao bianfa,* throughout.

[4] Cf. note 54 of my article "Min no Kasei zengo ni okeru fueki kaikaku ni tsuite."

[5] It appears from *juan* 4 of the *Ming du fu nianbiao* that the 1555 Shandong Provincial Governor Liu was Liu Cai, who had taken up office the previous year.

[6] See Iwami, "Min no Kasei zengo ni okeru fueki kaikaku ni tsuite," p. 17.

[7] *Ge Duansu gong wenji,* 15:17b–18b.

[8] *Ming dufu nianbiao,* 4. The "these days" of the letter must naturally refer to the period in which Jiang Tingyi was provincial governor of Shandong.

[9] Ibid. This must have been Liang Menglong

[10] The beeswax, firewood and charcoal, etc., levies would appear, after commutation, to have become the imposts known as *liaoyin* ("materials silver"), or other such blanket terms. If this is so, then instances of their being incorporated into the land tax are not necessarily unusual. The case of 1529 Guangdong is one such. On this point the reader is referred to Yamazaki Takeji, "Ichijō benpō no sōkō ni tsuite." It seems, however, that in the case of Shandong the incorporation of the *liaoyin* with the land tax served neither as the cue for the establishment of the Single Whip reform, nor as the inspiration for the name. When considering the introduction and diffusion

of the Single Whip, therefore, it would seem appropriate to relegate the question of *liaoyin* to mere associated status.

[11] Shimizu Taiji, "Ichijō benpō."

[12] See my article "Min no Kasei zengo ni okeru fueki kaikaku ni tsuite." Nor was I alone: in the postwar period Professor Shimizu's discovery has passed almost out of mind, and the majority of scholars appear to believe that the adoption of the Single Whip reform in North China dates from the Wanli period (1573–1619).

[13] Though this text provides much information on the land-tax Single Whip reform, it does not tell us a great deal about the service-levy Single Whip. The term "Single Whip reform" (*yitiaobian* and *yitiao bianfa*) do not appear at all in *juan* 7 and 8, or the equitable service levy retrospect. Even in *juan* 9 there are no further entries on it worthy of remark. As a result this discussion has unavoidably had to focus itself on the land tax aspect of the reform.

[14] See Yamane Yukio's article translated in this volume; and idem, "Minsho no kinkōfu ni tsuite."

[15] See my article, "Mindai chihō zaisei no ichi kōsatsu."

[16] On the tax reform that gave rise to the compilation of these registers, see my article referred to in note 4. Now the *Ming shi* uses the term *jingfu ce* (Registers for regulating the land tax) in its fiscal treatise (*Ming shi*, 78 [1900]), but as we shall go on to show, insofar as local gazetteers are to be taken as a guide, *fuyi ce* would seem to be correct. Where this latter name does not appear, such vague expressions as "the 1537 register," "Wang Yi's register," or "Ying Xia's register" are used. The *Ming shi* seems to have confused the *fuyi ce* with the *jingfu ce*, which were of similar content prepared in more or less the same area in c. 1588–89 (1537 was the 16th year of the Jiajing period, and 1588 the 16th of Wanli). On the *jingfu ce* the introductory section of the 1605 *Jiading xianzhi* has the entry: "In 1588 Military Censor Li Lai published the *jingfu ce*, and for the first time clarity was brought to bear upon the land tax." More detailed information is to be found in *juan* 5, the land-tax section, of the same work. Something referred to as "Provincial Governor Mr. Li's *jingfu ce* of 1589" or "the 1589 *Jingfu ce*" is quoted repeatedly in the taxation and labor service section of the 1597 *Zhenjiang fuzhi*.

[17] 1561 *Wujiang xianzhi*, 9:6a. This is in the collection of the Tōyō Bunko.

[18] 1593 *Shangyuan xianzhi*, 2:4b.

[19] In the case of Yingtian prefecture, the above-quoted *Shangyuan xianzhi* is the most detailed source, but the prefectural gazetteer (Wanli edition) also quotes from what it calls "the 1537 register." As for Suzhou prefecture, apart from the Wujiang gazetteer already cited in our text, the 1539 *Changshu xianzhi*, 2:51a, records "Responding to censorial direction, Wang initiated the *fuyi ce* and promulgated it within the jurisdictions subordinate (to Suzhou prefecture)." The Wang referred to here is Prefect Wang Yi, and the censor, Regional Governor Ouyang Duo. The land-tax section of the 1605 *Jiading xianzhi* has the record, "Originally Wang Yi took the annual land-tax requirements issued by the Ministry of Revenue and compiled them into a book, which he called the *Fuyi ce*. Thus in the future would there be something to consult." The name *fuyi ce* appears also in the service-levy section of this work. At the end of his "Min no Seisō-chō ni okeru Soshū chihō no jōryō," Professor Shimizu cites from the 1642 *Wu xianzhi* the expressions "the *Jingfu ce* approved and printed in 1538," and "the *Yaoli ce* ('*junyao*' and '*lijia*' register?) approved and printed in 1538." As has been explained in note 16, however, the first of the two names appears to be an error caused by confusion with a Wanli period compilation.

As for Changzhou prefecture, the tax-collection section of the 1618 prefectural gazetteer quotes from "the 1538 register," and it would seem that the "prefect Ying Jia's old regulations on tax collection" appended to this chapter is probably also an excerpt from the same work. In Ying Jia's biography in this gazetteer there is mention of his having made a *Yumin zhouzhi ce* [Register for the general information of the people]. This doubtless corresponds to the first of the two registers mentioned in the passage from the *Shangyuan xianzhi* presented in our text, and if this is so another register, that is to say the *fuyi ce*, must presumably have been compiled at the same time. Still within Changzhou prefecture, the tax-collection section of the Wujin county gazetteer (transcribed in *Tianxia junguo libing shu*, 7:21a–39b) quotes from "the prefect Ying Jia's register."

Moving to Zhenjiang, the 1597 *Zhenjiang fuzhi* has a treatise on land tax and labor service that extends from *juan* 5 to *juan* 10; the postal-relay-service section appears to consist entirely of transcription from the work. For Songjiang no clear evidence has come to light, but the land-tax section and the labor-service section of the 1588 *Shanghai xianzhi*, recording reform carried out by the prefect Huang Run in 1537, mention that he "examined [*sic*] the land tax through eight heads" and "examined the *lijia* [impositions] through nine [*sic*] heads." Since the name *fuyi ce* appears elsewhere in the gazetteer, the position would seem to have been as in the other prefectures that have been mentioned.

[20] See Yamane Yukio's article translated in this volume; and idem, "Minshō no kinkōfu ni tsuite."

[21] *Beijing tushuguan shanben shumu* (Beijing: 1959).

[22] After I had already sent the draft of this article to press, I received from Professor Fujii Hiroshi a copy of his article, "Sōkōki no ichijō benpō—Fu Kanshin no jōgen o meguru sho mondai." The fifth section of this article, entitled "The Single Whip reform chez Ge Shouli," discusses how in Shandong, as Ge Shouli relates, the Single Whip reform had been in operation, partial at least, since c. 1541, and how it started on the land-tax front. On the question of the proper evaluation of Ge Shouli's remarks, and consequently of the reality of the adoption of the Single Whip reform in Shandong, Professor Fujii corrects the error of the received view in no small way. It seems to me that the publication of Professor Fujii's article renders certain points made in this paper superfluous. However, since the basic purpose of the present paper is to introduce a source, I have made no revision at the proofreading stage. I ask for Professor Fujii's and the reader's understanding on this point.

THE ORIGINS AND STRUCTURE
OF GENTRY RULE

SHIGETA ATSUSHI

In his short lifetime Shigeta Atsushi produced a series of studies on state power which dealt with taxation, merchants, landlords, and the gentry during the Qing dynasty. Shigeta's work is pervaded by an underlying preoccupation with the issue of the autocratic state first raised by Nishijima Sadao, one of his teachers. While Nishijima was seeking to understand the origins and development of the despotic state in ancient China, Shigeta was concerned with the question of when the ancient state ended. Like Matsumoto Yoshimi, Shigeta emphasized the immense strength of state power and its decisive position in Chinese history.

Shigeta argues that the ancient and traditional elements embodied in the Chinese state continued to exist until quite late. The fact that the poll tax was not finally abolished until the early eighteenth century, when it was incorporated into the combined land and poll tax (*diding yin*), is evidence of this continuity. The abolition of the poll tax indicated that the ancient and traditional elements had been removed from state power. The new tax system also implied changes in the nature of state power. Feudalistic landownership had existed prior to the early eighteenth century, but the introduction of the combined land and poll tax meant that now the Qing state was dependent on feudal landlords for the collection of the land tax. In this sense, after the early eighteenth century the Qing dynasty, according to Shigeta, became a feudal state that was based on landlord landownership. In such a feudal state despotic emperors were unable to ignore landlords.

Synthesizing the findings of research done on the landholding

This essay was originally published as two separate articles in *Jimbun kenkyū*, 22:4 (1971), and *Iwanami kōza sekai rekishi*, vol. 12 (1971). This translation follows "Kyōshin shihai no seiritsu to kōzō" [郷紳支配の成立と構造] in *Shindai shakai keizaishi kenkyū* (Tokyo: Iwanami Shoten, 1975), pp. 155–206. Translation by Christian Daniels.

system and on landlords and peasant struggles during the 1950s and 1960s, Shigeta presented his theory of gentry rule in 1971 and reinterpreted Qing society using the gentry as an analytical tool. He traced the rise of the gentry from the mid-Ming showing how antagonism within the landlord-tenant relationship forced the gentry to join hands with the state. Since Shigeta emphasized the importance of state power, it was only natural that he should see the state as fostering gentry rule through tax exemption and other privileges; however, he did not insist on defining them rigidly according to that system. Rather his approach was to take a much broader theoretical stance that encompassed the entire society.

To Shigeta the gentry are basically landlords, though the opposite is not true; all landlords cannot be called gentry. After the early eighteenth century, when the combined land and poll tax was instituted and the Qing dynasty became a feudal state based on landlord landownership, it was mainly landlords who had the means to take the examinations and gain admittance to the gentry. The gentry, at the apex of society but below the state, used state power to dominate the whole of non-bureaucratic society, which included landlords, tenants, and owner-cultivators.

A major defect in Shigeta's work is that he tends to deal only with the question of state power, neglecting the economic base of society. He does not attempt to relate his research on state power and arguments for a feudal state to the question of whether the peasants were slaves or serfs as Oyama does. In many cases Shigeta relies on the work of Oyama Masaaki for his ideas on the peasantry. In this respect the work of Shigeta and Oyama are to a certain extent complementary.

Most regrettably Shigeta's untimely death in 1973, when he was associate professor at Osaka City University, deprived him of the chance to explicate his ideas further. A common criticism leveled against Shigeta is that his theory, which posits gentry domination of the entire non-bureaucratic society, is still merely a "hypothesis yet to be proven" by a full scale empirical study (e.g., Yamane Yukio, "Trends in Postwar Japanese Studies in Ming History," p. 121). It is only fair to note, however, that Shigeta did provide source materials to support his theory of gentry rule as well as leaving a theoretical framework with which to undertake further studies on the subject.

*　　　　　*　　　　　*

The role of the gentry in Chinese society has been a controversial subject among historians. Theories range from a positive appraisal of the gentry as powerholders and leaders in rural society to an outright condemnation of the gentry as "local bullies and evil gentry" who were the chief targets of the anti-feudal struggle. Some of these evaluations coincide with the well-known thesis that there was one ruling class in China made up of bureaucrats, landlords, and merchant usurers, with little real difference between the three component groups. In spite of the differences in interpretation, there is common agreement that the gentry played a major role in the changes that swept over China in the post-Opium War period. Moreover, although in an earlier period the activities of the gentry were often hidden from view, in the late Qing as the dynasty faced crisis after crisis, the activities of the gentry were increasingly exposed to view.

These changes began with the Opium War. The gentry provided leadership in the anti-British struggles, taking on a role that in an earlier day would have fallen to the central government.[1] During the Taiping rebellion, which followed the Opium War, however, the gentry stood in opposition to peasant forces. Their private militia, the village braves (*xiangyong*), played an important role independent of the regular Qing army. Many scholars have seen these developments as the emergence of Han Chinese power in late-Qing political history. While this is one noteworthy aspect, it is important to note that the gentry were concurrently establishing their own position in the overall political process.[2]

The term *xiangshen* (gentry) first came into common usage during the mid-Ming.[3] This does not necessarily mean that the gentry, as a group, first appeared at this time; some scholars place the formation of the gentry much earlier, others put it considerably later. This article aims to trace the historical origins and development of the gentry during the Ming-Qing period. Emphasis is placed on achieving a comprehensive understanding of the gentry through a concept that I have developed, the dominance of society by the gentry. An examination of some of the scholarly interpretations put forward about the gentry will serve as an introduction to my own analysis.

Japanese interpretations of the gentry

Let us begin by looking at Negishi Tadashi's still influential characterization of the gentry. The distinctive feature of Negishi's conception was the notion that the gentry were a "strata that guided and led the masses," existing "in spite of some differences, at certain times and in certain geographic regions, regardless of time or place."[4] According to this view the rulers, knights, and monks in European feudal society can be compared to the "industrialists and the salaried people who are subordinate to them" in modern capitalist society. Negishi is in effect arguing that the gentry were members of the ruling class. However, Negishi regards the gentry as representatives of civilian autonomous organizations and sharply distinguishes them from the official rulers, the state and its bureaucrats. In their *actual* relations, however, he calls them the leadership strata. As influential people in local society, gentry were close to the people; this closeness allowed the gentry to function as intermediaries between the populace and the bureaucracy. The gentry were the leaders, representatives of clans, guilds, and groups which traditionally practiced a self-governing way of life. They acted as spokesmen who conveyed the wishes of the lower to the higher, and also as agents of the bureaucracy. They passed on orders from above to those below, and cooperated in their execution. They were appointed to posts for "maintaining order and securing food for the populace, mediated in disputes (justice, mediation, settling disputes), acted as liaison between the people and the officials, carried out benevolent action, exhorted work, and improved public morals."

Negishi's theory is based upon Wang Huizu's (1731–1807) view of the gentry, which Negishi quotes as an apt explanation of civil administration during the Qing period:

An official [the district magistrate] is far from the people, but the scholar [the gentry] is close to them. The people trust scholars more than they trust officials. The laws and regulations of the court cannot be completely understood by the people, but can be easily explained by the scholar. By first informing the scholar, and having him explain them to the people, it is easily made clear and moral education is easy to implement. If there are good scholars within an official's jurisdiction, they will assist him in spreading moral values. Each district is different in its suitability for crops, susceptibility to flood and drought, and in its good and bad customs. The words of yamen clerks cannot be believed, only the opinions of scholars can be trusted.[5]

"Liaison between the people and the officials" which Negishi treats as a function of the gentry should not be simply lined up along with the others, since that function is fundamental to his understanding of the position of the gentry. Various other aspects of local rule, which by right were the responsibility of the state, were set up as responsibilities of the gentry's liaison work. The gentry were socially active in a supplementary capacity to the bureaucratic system.

Many scholars have been attracted by Negishi's characterization of the features of Chinese society. He argued that apart from tax collection and the maintenance of social order, the state was not greatly concerned with the livelihood of the people; such tasks were left to the resources of various intermediary, civilian, self-governing organizations. The gentry maintained their position in society by acting as an intermediary group, connecting the people and the officials.

Such a theory is transhistorical. In arguing that the gentry functioned as "intermediaries between the people and officials," it makes the gentry inseparable from the Chinese bureaucratic system and suggests that they were as old as the history of the bureaucratic system itself. Though the term *xiangshen* first came into popular use during the Ming-Qing period, the gentry as a group existed much earlier. Negishi's theory traces the origins of the gentry to the Han dynasty. He does make some distinctions between periods, but such distinctions are not drawn from his definition of the gentry itself. Neither is his definition consistent.

An assumption that the characteristic feature of Chinese despotic rule and bureaucracy was its separation from society (i.e., from the masses) underlies this theory of the gentry. Although such assertions are rare today, historians in the past commonly argued for the "separation of state and society" in Chinese history.[6] For analytical purposes they divided China into two spheres: the state, the sphere in which state power prevailed, and society, the sphere to which it did not extend. Both spheres developed in their own individual way without any close connection. This dualism fits well with the common image of the dynastic cycle. This dichotomy allows for many variations on the theme: a state with a history and a society without a history (a stagnant one); a dynamic and a static world; a world of the literati and the illiterate; Confucian and Taoist worlds; a world of exploiters and the exploited; etc. These dichotomies shaped the ways people thought about China; they were the master keys that were to open the doors to understanding Chinese society.

Soon after World War II Matsumoto Yoshimi joined others in criticizing this "theory of the special characteristics of society in prerevolutionary China."[7] Matsumoto's analysis began with a criticism of Sano Manabu's *Shinchō shakaishi*. Sano manifested a strong mechanistic inclination in his interest in finding laws for the operation of society. For example, "the separation of state and society" became the "law governing the separation of state and society." Sano's first law was "the law of the predomination of intermediary social groups"— this was precisely Negishi's main assumption with regard to the gentry. The two Sano laws noted here were contradictory. No matter which law is taken as fundamental, it can always be interpreted in the opposite way, because the laws were mutually binding. On the one hand, since the state was only concerned with tax collection and maintaining social order, and the masses only expected the state to attend to such matters, the people were normally forced to entrust their livelihood to the intermediary social strata (lineage, family, village, guild, etc.) as a means of ensuring safety. On the other hand, it is also possible to argue that state power could not reach down to the level of the masses because of the strength of autonomy at the intermediary group level. The latter argument is the more appropriate of the two.

Nevertheless, Sano differed from Negishi in that he did not see the gentry as the leaders of intermediary groups. In his third law, "the law regarding the mutual alienation of classes" which substantiated the first two, he included the gentry within the ruling class. The two great classes, the bureaucrats, who monopolized the organs of state, and the semi-slave-like peasants, who did not participate in government, originated in the late Warring States period and were the model for class relations thereafter. Change over time separated the former into bureaucrats, aristocrats, landlords, and magnate gentry (*haoshen*), while the latter became peasants, house slaves, unfree handicrafters, and the urban poor. The means of living and thought of both of these classes differed, and there was no interchange between them. The bureaucrats made the state their own property, while the peasants remained indifferent to the fate of the state.

This conception had its precedents in the analysis of Tachibana Shiraki: "While China's bureaucrats constitute a division within the entire society of the nation or state, at the same time they also comprise a social class and, by virtue of being the ruling class, occupy the highest position in the state or nation. . . . The bureaucratic class at the top of society vertically confronted the masses which included peasants, artisans, and merchants."[8] Civil and military officials or people who fit those requirements are categorized as bureaucrats. Subsequently, the gentry were equated with bureaucrats and put into the ruling class. Sano also held that "bureaucrats in old China were the masters of the state, and not mere organs of it. In that capacity they comprised a social class, not a simple social stratum."[9] Furthermore, he regarded bureaucrats and the gentry as one and the same thing. For example: "The state in pre-revolutionary China was the exclusive possession of the landlord class in its broadest sense, that is, as the ruling class. *This class included bureaucrats in office, magnate gentry (haoshen) out of office, and large landlords.* When bureaucrats retired from office and went home they became magnate gentry, and magnate gentry became bureaucrats once they took up office" [my italics].[10] Here, Sano's chief concern is with the real nature of the ruling class in the dynastic system and not with an intermediate group. In other words, he has abstracted the difference between bureaucrats in power and the gentry out of office. In his theory, the fundamental social relation was that between bureaucrats (landlords and gentry) and the masses, rather than the relationship between the emperor and the people or the bureaucracy and the people.[11] Therefore the origins of the gentry obviously date back much earlier than the Ming-Qing period.

From this it is evident that there is quite a disparity between Negishi's view of Chinese society and that of Tachibana and Sano. To put it simply, both theories agree in making a division between state and society, but one includes the gentry in the state as rulers, while the other places them in society as leaders of intermediary groups out of office. Sano, instead of seeing these intermediary social groups functioning as autonomous organizations, as his law of the predomination of intermediary social groups suggests, claims that as a class they were alienated from the masses. Without provision for class alienation these intermediary groups would be unreal, nothing more than leaderless small-scale peasant groups (no gentry, no landlords). In short, Sano's third law, the law of class alienation, is inconsistent with the first two laws described here, at least with the law of the predomination of intermediary social groups.

Post-war Japanese theories: Matsumoto and Niida

Matsumoto Yoshimi criticized the theory of the separation of state and society, which was the common premise of Negishi, Sano, and Tachibana. He developed a more flexible approach designed to understand Chinese society in the context of the relations between the political process and the social and economic structure by emphasizing the penetration of state power into society. Matsumoto criticized Sano's idea that "the state did not have any political ambitions to interfere with the autonomy of villages as long as the peasants paid their taxes." He argued that it was primarily because of tax collection that the state intervened in the villages and official rule reorganized the so-called autonomous villages. He held that it was principally the establishment of an organized system of controlling the peasants that made it possible for the state to recede into a position in which it appeared separate from society. This emphasis on state power naturally saw the landlord class as little different from poor peasants who were subservient to the state. At the same time, they enlisted the aid of the state in expropriating the peasantry. Matsumoto's theory stresses an organic understanding of state and society, the supremacy of state power, and its relative independence from class relations. The end result is that he has to argue for the concept of despotism.

Matsumoto's theory raises questions about state power that are still at issue today. The general meeting of the influential Rekishigaku kenkyūkai (Historical Science Society of Japan) took this issue as the center of its debate in 1950.[12] As part of that debate Nishijima Sadao directed attention to the question of the origins of despotism in China. He has consistently pursued this problem through an analysis of the formation of the Qin and Han empires, attempting to deal with the question of society—in this case community (kyōdōtai)—in the context of the formation of power in the ancient state. In contrast, Masubuchi Tatsuo (and Taniguchi Michio, who developed Masubuchi's theory in an original—in some ways too original—way) criticized Nishijima,[13] but even when they stress the significance of community, their own conception of community is pervaded by the influence of the "theory of the separation of state and society." These contrasting views also served to influence the debate as to whether the equal field system (juntian) was actually implemented.

What was Matsumoto's conception of the gentry?[14] He presents the gentry in the following context: "Natural villages that were still isolated and secluded comprised the local foundation which bolstered the absolute state in the Qin and Han periods. But since the local magnates (haozu) either turned the autonomous organization of the villages into instruments for their own despotic rule, or split them asunder, during the Sui and Tang periods the state was forced to act more positively to maintain these villages."[15] "State power clearly penetrated into the internal organization of the villages through the Sui and Tang reforms, and these administrative villages created by political power from outside"[16] were fragile. Signs of the disintegration of village solidarity showed as soon as cracks appeared in the various institutions connected with the equal field system. It was the expansion of the manor as a new form of social integration—to dislocated peasants from equal field land this meant life in a world outside areas which the state designated as their homes—and the development of associational cohesive relations (sheyi or yi) which grew up among the masses that destroyed the equal field system. While both the manor and the *sheyi* or *yi* were developing in the direction of medieval villages, their transition in this direction was incomplete, and according to Matsumoto "the fact that the gentry, *the illegitimate offspring of bureaucratism*, tyrannized the autonomous organization of the village eventually became apparent in the next period."[17] Here Matsumoto quite deliberately describes the gentry as appearing on the historical stage as "the illegitimate offspring of bureaucratism." He has them unexpectedly come down from above in a form that blocked the development of the social and economic structure. In his own words, "whenever new cohesive relations constantly arising from below became powerful, they were quickly absorbed into organizations created from above,"[18] or "they were turned into organs backing up such organizations."[19] This certainly agrees with the fact that the examination system, which began in the Sui and Tang, absorbed groups rising from below into the bureaucratic stratum and in the process obstructed new class organization.

Matsumoto's fundamental stance thus tries to subsume the social and economic structure within the concept of the predominance of state power. Even so, representatives of the village later lost their position as powerholders within the village: to be specific, with the shift from the prefectural militia system (*fubing*) to the hired militia system (*mubing*), the position of the village representative became a burden, not a privilege, and for that very reason a rotational system was devised. Since Matsumoto says that the gentry as powerholders in the village turned into robots of the state and were "quasi-officials that should be called gentry," it is clear that to him they were not formed by local historical changes.

In reality, there are two sides to the historical characterization of the gentry given by Matsumoto. On the one hand, he is plainly aware of a transformation of the village elders into the gentry; this is one of the phenomena that indicates what he calls "the inclination toward feudalism." On the other hand, they are not seen as representatives of the village (nor as manor owners), but rather as the illegitimate outcome of the bureaucratic system, quasi-officials originating from the bureaucracy. It should be noted that Matsumoto also holds that magnates and gentry (*haoshen*) were the social group which linked the officials and the people together. Although Matsumoto criticized the Tachibana/Sano line of analysis, his view is actually closer to theirs than it is to Negishi's.

Niida Noboru shared at least some of Matsumoto's assumptions, arguing that the gentry were "the illegitimate offspring of bureaucratism."[20] Niida's theory of the gentry, and the understanding of Chinese social

structure that lies behind it, has nuances different from Matsumoto's.
For example, in examining the connection between penal authority
and social structure, Niida first follows Matsumoto by acknowledging
the need to overthrow "the dogma" of "the separation of state and
society," and understands state power's penetration of society as
"the human application of the state's law designed to directly apply
to each individual person. The household registration system of ancient
China is a good example of a measure aimed at achieving individual
personal subjection (*kobetsuteki jinshin shihai*). . . . regarding the
power of punishment . . . (especially in ancient times), it was the intention of the state to diffuse its rule to the bottom of society with the
aim of achieving a state monopoly over the power of punishment."[21]
Nevertheless, he does qualify these statements saying:

> [in contrast to the modern state] state power was probably only
> able to first fully extend penal authority to the people using the
> community within society as a medium. . . . The state probably even
> entrusted a part of its penal power to the family and village com-
> munities. Ruling power within the community—for example, that
> of landlords—was also connected with state power, and there were
> probably common points between these two powers. Nevertheless,
> power within the community was removed from the penal authority
> of the state, so powerholders inside the community were probably
> able to wield their own independent power of punishment.[22]

Here Niida has reiterated the significance of the so-called intermediary
social group which both constrained and supplemented absolutism.
This was a natural consequence of Niida's research since studies of
guilds and family-villages based on field surveys were one of his central achievements.

Finally, in order to adjust these two processes of constraint and
complement, Niida adds the following qualifier. After repeating the
earlier criticism "can villagers controlled by *powerholders within a
village*—such as the *gentry*—be treated as separate from state power
as some people assert?" he goes on to argue that

> these various medieval-like groups were not separate from state
> power; state power had probably penetrated the groups—the people
> inside the groups submitted to dual control . . . group rule and state
> rule. Moreover, state power was in a noncommittal relationship
> with the leaders in the groups. When their interests were opposed to
> those of state power, the leaders in the village were even bold enough

to join the common villagers, including tenants, in resisting. Never-theless, there were also simultaneously areas in which their interests coincided with those of state power. *Gentry-landlords also belonged to the side of ruling power*; for the state to effectively enforce its own rule, it was necessary to *drag the gentry-landlords onto their side.*[23]

It is clear that Niida's conception of the gentry shared some common base with Negishi's. At the same time, in Niida's scheme of things, the gentry were the rulers. In this sense, his analysis shares similarities with those of Tachibana, Sano, and Matsumoto. As a result the magnetic placement of "state power" overlapped conceptually making the gentry "ambiguous"; they fit into both society and state. In the final analysis Niida settled for a conclusion that argued that while state power "called 'Asiatic' or 'Eastern' . . . was notorious for its immense strength in pre-revolutionary China, there was a limit to the extent to which that power could penetrate and the state was connected with various groups in a complicated fashion."[24]

Subsequent theories: Yasuno, Tanaka, and Oyama

In contrast to the series of theories about the gentry presented above, recent theories argue that gentry power should be understood as a stage in the development of large landholding or landlord systems. Moves in this direction were already apparent in Saeki Yūichi's expression "of-ficial-gentry landownership (*kanshinteki tochi shoyū*),"[25] but the first scholar to consciously work out the concept was Yasuno Shōzō.[26] Ya-suno defined the commonly accepted idea of the development of large-scale landownership in the late Ming as "the general formation of land-holdings *by the gentry strata.*" He clearly recognized the gentry as the prime movers in land accumulation. Regrettably, Yasuno's definition merely reworded the details of previous insights. He contrasted "the gentry-landlord strata" with the resident landlord stratum. which Furu-shima Kazuo had asserted held up the structure of the *lijia* system in the early Ming, and maintained that the gentry and landlords arose in place of resident landlords after the collapse of the latter as a social group. Since these gentry and landlords were also termed "gentry within city walls," the schema of "from resident landlords to gentry landlords" was nothing more than a rewording of Kitamura Hironao's formula "from resident landlords to absentee landlords." However, there are still subtle differences in these theories. Yasuno's conclusion gives the impression not of analyzing these differences, but rather of welding them together.

He furnishes us with the concept of the gentry and the substance of land-lordism as given premises, but fails to ask whether the two concepts must necessarily be linked. He does not pose the questions of whether land-lordism could validly be termed "gentry-like" or whether "gentry-land-lords" incorporated their social relations as landlords into a higher di-mension. Similarly Yasuno's logic, which holds that the destruction of the resident landlord system gave rise to the gentry, regards this change as occurring in inverse proportion; the gentry continually gained power as resident landlords declined. Such changes were due to the different posi-tions the resident landlords and gentry held in the structure of state exaction which was based upon the *lijia* system. The precedent for this is in Furushima's work. However, since it is founded on the assumption that the landlord-tenant system was the fundamental class relationship from the early Ming onward, class differentiation of the peasantry should naturally be elucidated in the context of the development of that funda-mental contradiction. The concept of the state and peasantry cannot be invoked without reference to an intermediary landlord class.

At roughly the same time, Tanaka Masatoshi presented a new method of studying the gentry designed to examine all aspects of the rise of the gentry within the context of the disintegration of the *lijia* system.[27] He approached the gentry structurally, correlating their appearance with the development of the forces of production and the spread of the cir-culation of commodities, focusing "not on interpreting them simply as direct resident rulers, but on asking how the gentry differed from former local landlord rulers."[28] On the one hand, that meant "it was possible to interpret the gentry strata in the local context as the concrete amalga-mation of merchant capital, landlords, and bureaucrats."[29] On the other hand, "at a time when the *lijia* system was disintegrating and the role of the gentry was being questioned, many warnings were issued instructing the gentry not to encroach upon and destroy agricultural production in the villages."[30] The inference is that the former *li* captains (*lizhanghu*) of the early Ming had maintained their position in rural society through their control of various positions in the wider village community. In other words, the gentry had changed: "not participating in production (parasitic), they practiced non-economic expropriation based upon nominal owership, and were no longer indispensible to the process of reproduction."[31]

This observation, which agrees with previous interpretations of the origin of merchant landlords (equivalent to urban landlords) and absen-tee landlords, is used here with reference to gentry-like landlords. Tanaka says that the common strata of literati and gentry should not be the cen-tral concern for analysis; rather, attention should be given to the problem

of stratification leading to the formation of a stratum that was critical
of the regime and that can be distinguished from a strongman type of
gentry. He probably had in mind the stratum that joined the masses in
popular rebellions. Such a viewpoint, however, is inconsistent with the
transformation of landlords described above. Since Tanaka does not dif-
ferentiate between the gentry and landlords, he seeks to find stratification
in other aspects of the gentry. Tanaka divides them into favored gentry
and "urban recluses" [*shiyin*] who were critical of society, and by doing
so improves upon the simple distinction between gentry and students.
In this sense, Tanaka's image of the gentry is fluid, though it is evident
that he is not trying to frame a precise definition of landlords. These
points together with Tanaka's periodization which puts the appearance
of the gentry "in the period when feudal society was at its zenith" sharply differ from Oyama Masaaki's theory, which we will discuss next.

At the symposium mentioned above, Oyama argued that the concept
of the gentry was still ahistorical. He later presented a brief outline of
the gentry as a historical category.[32] He made a new study of the existing
form of landownership after the late Ming-early Qing, which he posited
as the origin of feudal landownership in China.[33] His theory began with
the premise that the gentry were a new ruling stratum that arose in place
of the rich local families (*xingshi hu*) of the Song and the tax captains of
the Ming. Oyama sees both of them as historically homogenous entities.

Oyama saw two forces at work in the formation of the gentry. The
first force is related to his view of the breakdown of the Ming landholding system, which he describes as follows:

The *lijia* system could not be maintained. The older form of landownership practiced by wealthy local families and tax captains lost
its existential base. It was inevitably dismantled and transformed because the later Ming period saw the growth of independence in small-
scale agriculture due to the development of commodity production
and a money economy, the establishment of local community-like
integration within the village, and the organization of anti-rent movements as a united effort by whole villages.[34]

He sees "the gradual formation of large-scale landholdings by the gentry" filling the vacuum left by the downfall of former landowners. The
gentry are depicted as clearly setting themselves up as the mainstay of a
new form of landownership through this process. On the other hand,
Oyama also looks at the gentry as "the social status of the rulers who
appeared in place of the former rich local families and tax captains, . . . the main significance of their formation being the transfor-

mation of the social function of the examination system as a means of official appointment."[35]

The second force at work was the connection the gentry had with the examination system.During the Song the provincial graduate was qualified to sit for higher examinations only once, but in the Ming the holders of the lowest degree and provincial graduates were allowed to hold their ranks for life. Oyama further explains that the lowest degree holders and provincial graduates (quasi-bureaucrats) together with bureaucrats comprised a social stratum that enjoyed certain privileges and, in contrast to other commoners, came to have a great deal of influence in local politics. Changes in the social function of the examination system, and not the examination system in general, are seen as stimuli for the formation of gentry status.

What is the connection between this process and the two factors noted above which he regards as producing the gentry? We may conjecture whether the second factor described above was the premise for the development of the first or, vice versa, whether the first induced changes in the second. Whatever the sequence, this two-pronged theory lacks definite internal links, and in the end fails to create a vivid picture because it presents a double image of the gentry. This compels us to recognize the fact that the category of gentry neither uniformly defines a form of landownership, nor can it be defined succinctly by a form of landownership. Doubtlessly, the main significance of the gentry category to Oyama was its role in changing landlordism. There are, however, inherent inconsistencies between the two premises of his theory.

The historical nature of the gentry

Oyama's complex two-pronged theory, which is similar to Tanaka's conceptionalization, was connected with the antagonism between the form and content of the gentry. Judging from the arguments presented, the two aspects of Oyama's theory can be reworded to correspond to the concepts of state and society.[36] That is to say, the forces of change in both state and society determined the historical existence of the gentry. Even though recent theories of the gentry have tended to regard the the mode of landownership as the substance of society, they cannot avoid the issue of form endowed by the political structure. Generally speaking, in current attempts to achieve a coordinated analysis of state and society there seems to be a contrast in methodology, with each field trying to subsume the state within its own system of logic. The predominance of state power is stressed in ancient history, while real relations in society—for example, landlord and tenant relations—are emphasized in research after the Song. This is not merely a discrepancy in approach that has grown up from a difference in research fields, but in fact is assumed to reflect the historical development of Chinese society. It supposedly indicates that a change in fundamental class relations occurred during the Song period. Prior to the Song the fundamental class relationship was between state and society, while after the Song it turned into a landlord-tenant relationship.* Nevertheless, the gentry problem arises precisely at a point where such changes cannot be accurately ascertained. The assertion that the gentry are "the illegitimate offspring of bureaucratism" directly reflects this indeterminateness.[37]

The gentry and their rule appear to be a Chinese manifestation of that universal tendency for power to be turned into the semi-independent private property of certain specially privileged strata which grew up under the umbrella of a centralized system. It was a process of decentralization that ordinarily occurred in ancient centralized states. If we call this trend feudalization from above—strictly speaking, it is feudalization in the sense that it indicated decentralization, and accordingly is not complete as a historical category—we have to acknowledge that a move similar to the one that encouraged the formation of the so-called aristocratic officials was at work behind the formation of gentry rule. This type of methodology which is typically found in studies on Byzantine feudalism cannot simply be used to explain the formation of gentry rule.[38]

Needless to say, the core of the gentry comprised a reserve of potential officeholders, officials on leave and retired bureaucrats. The formation of the gentry followed a fundamentally different course of development from that which promoted decentralization and the dissociation of power. Nor did it correspond to the process whereby bureaucrats in office appropriated the powers of authority, and turned regional power into their own private property and secured immunity from taxation.

This is closely connected with the fact that the Chinese bureaucratic system did not allow the inheritance of official status. For this reason, special privileges obtained through the bureaucratic system were continually distributed among different families and were not held permanently by a specific family line. Apart from the period in the late Tang, when provincial military governors and provincial commanders were rampant, this phenomenon did not occur in China. Moreover, since bureaucrats were continually recruited from the people through the examina-

* Despite these changes in class relationship, however, Shigeta still argues that the gentry were created by state action and not because of the development of landlordism. —Trans.

tion system, the formation of the gentry first presupposed the existence of a social stratum that had adjusted itself to the examination system. We can probably safely identify this stratum as the landlord stratum of society.[39] It is possible to regard the contact the landlord stratum had with the bureaucratic organization as a means of bolstering their control over society and not as the origin of their rule.

If we understand landlord-tenant relations as an expression of the feudal relations of production, then gentry rule is nothing more than the integration of the energy of feudalization from below in the social and economic structure with the tendency to feudalization from above. This arose because the gentry were able to openly combine their special privileges with personal rule only when they acted in their non-office-holding, unofficial capacities. Looked at in this way the gentry cannot possibly be used as a category designating the specific, existential form of landlords per se. Even though there was a specific type of gentry-landlord that was spawned at a specific historical stage, to be a member of the gentry meant more than being a mere landlord.

Essentially the gentry were landlords who dominated owner-cultivators and organized other landlords by virtue of their position in society. The privileged position which made the gentry what they were was after all guaranteed by and within the framework of centralized dynastic rule. Landlordism was not established according to the principles of feudal rule in the strict sense. Gentry rule was in effect the domination of feudal rulers unable to become feudal lords, and it developed to the utmost under the protection of centralized power. Under such conditions the principle of state rule, which determined gentry status (i.e., their special privileges), and the reality of the gentry's social position, though always close to each other, could never be completely united until the mantle of dynastic rule was finally thrown off.

The origins and structure of gentry rule

The late Ming-early Qing is without question one of the periods of great change in Chinese history, but what exactly was that change? This period has been approached in many ways, including study of the sprouts of capitalism, the reorganization of the feudal system, the failure of modern thought, the early townsmen movement, the first stage of serf manumission, and the establishment of feudal landownership. This part of the paper will probe the historical significance of the Ming-Qing transition on the basis of these approaches. The task is to try to examine the transition through the framework of gentry rule, focusing on questions related to the social form of economic organization created by the dynastic change, and what type of structure and contradictions that social form of organization embodied.

As already noted above, the word *xiangshen* only came into common use after the mid-Ming, though it can be found as early as the Song.[40] The term "gentry" generally referred to officials from the same locale irrespective of whether they were retired, on leave, or in office, as is related in the 1694 *Fuyi quanshu*: "Among the local gentry some are appointed to places outside the capital, some are home on leave, and others are living leisurely at home with nothing to do."[41]

Bureaucrats were the agents of centralized imperial rule. A characteristic feature of the Chinese bureaucratic system was the policy of not posting officials to their native places. This policy recognized the fact that local society was the place where gentry rule flourished. Some contemporary sources show that it was local officials either home on leave or retired that formed the main body of the gentry in local society.[42] The government refused to send officials to their native areas precisely because they feared that retired officials or bureaucrats home on furlough would exert undue influence on them. However, it was not until the late Ming that the privileged status group known as the gentry formed. They comprised a reserve team of potential office-holders, mainly provincial graduates and lower-degree holders who had obtained their qualifications through the examination process as well as regular bureaucrats and degree holders with bureaucratic experience.[43] From the late Ming the gentry began to strengthen their de facto rule within the centralized power system, monopolizing the various functions of culture, economics, and politics in local society. As respected people (*wang*) in the villages, the gentry were expected to be paragons for the villagers.[44]

In recent years there has been heated debate about the nature of the gentry. In this part of the paper I want to build on the positive significance of this theorizing by treating the question of the gentry as a question of gentry rule; I will attempt to use the gentry category as a systematic concept related to the entire structure of Chinese society, and at the same time amplify it by elaborating its historical and developmental characteristics. Ultimately this is part of the task of liberating premodern Chinese history from its image as a continual repetition of the same pattern of development, and replacing it with a more dynamic view that stresses the irreversible development of social organization.

We know of several groups of powerful people who acted as an intermediary ruling stratum within the absolute state from the Qin-Han period onward. These groups stood between the emperor, who monopolized the right to rule, and the people, who, in theory, were all ruled alike by him. The magnates (*haozu*) of the Han dynasty, the aristocrats of the Six Dynasties, Sui, and Tang, the rich local families of the Song, and the gentry of Ming and Qing periods can all be cited as examples. Their peculiar historical and developmental nature will not emerge as long as we define them simply with reference to absolute rule. We have to avoid defining them as existing autonomously within absolute rule, as de facto rulers, or as intermediaries between officials and the people (i.e., the leadership strata). Studies up to the present have tended to proceed in this fashion, suffering from two basic faults.

First, the structure of dynastic rule itself is generally thought to have remained much the same from the Qin-Han period to the Qing, although it has been pointed out that there was a strengthening of the autocratic system after the Song. Second, the dialectical relationship with the social and economic structure has not been elucidated. As long as such intermediary groups are only seen within the framework of imperial rule, they will appear to be traditional and inflexible in nature. That in turn makes it difficult to identify the historical character of imperial rule, since change is obscured.[45] If, however, we make the intermediary ruling class (particularly the Ming-Qing gentry) the object of our study, we can identify a clearer historical image even within our common set of ideas. By deliberately searching for changes in the relationship between the gentry, dynastic control, and the peasants who comprise the social base, it is also probably possible to treat the development of the entire intermediary group as a successive, developmental process. Subsequently, the first aim here is to understand the gentry and their rule from the late Ming on as a mark of the historicity of their stage of development, and further to distinguish those aspects that differ both from the former intermediate strata and from the formal organs of bureaucratic rule in general. The purpose is to use these differences to refine the concept of gentry rule as a historical category. Our inquiry will try to investigate the whole range of political, social, and economic relationships embodied within the gentry, and not simply the gentry themselves as a social stratum. This is the reason that this paper is not merely concerned with the gentry, but with gentry rule.

If the ultimate purpose is to try to trace the successive development of the social structure through the emergence of the gentry, then the concept of gentry rule must be a special structural category that embodies the pattern of social organization at that particular stage. In reality the gentry were for the most part landlords. The term "gentry landownership" merely focuses on this aspect. But, fundamentally the term "gentry" is a socio-political category, and limiting it to the dimension of landownership is not the way to make full use of it as an analytical tool. The land-lord-tenant system, which has been posited as the relations of production (i.e., class relations) that formed the basis of Chinese feudal society, was almost completely developed by the mid-Ming. Nevertheless, it was not the universal foundation of feudal social organization, even though in the Jiangnan delta region it was said that 10 percent of the people were landowners while 90 percent were tenants. Small peasant proprietors, the so-called owner-cultivators who were not directly subordinate to landlords, were continually differentiated and reproduced. Therefore we cannot deduce the entire social structure from an analysis of the landlord-tenant relationship.

At the opposite end of the social spectrum to the owner-cultivator was the dynastic system of absolute rule which resisted the decentrali-zation of power to the last. The fact that this type of class structure cannot be uniformly reduced to a landlord-tenant relationship, but ap-pears compounded with the relations of dominance of the absolute state is taken as a characteristic feature of feudal social organization.[46] Gentry rule, therefore, is a category that indicates far more than mere rule by landlords. Gentry rule was the basic unit of control in Chinese society. It was not founded on landownership, but maintained by the gentry domination of other social strata, mainly owner-cultivators as well as tenants, through the medium of a neutral relationship with state power and by economic and non-economic relations. Gentry rule is essentially a category that connotes landlord-owner-cultivator relations, even though its axis is the landlord-tenant relationship.[47] As such this category unites the relations of dominance of the absolute state with landlord-tenant relations producing a systematic concept capable of ex-plaining organically the whole structure of Chinese society. It is for this reason that the issue of the gentry should be treated as a question of gentry rule, something of far greater dimensions than landownership.

The framework of gentry rule with landlord-tenant relations as its axis should offer a new way of interpreting the whole of Ming-Qing so-ciety, and at the same time provide a logical basis for understanding modern Chinese history by positing the fundamental contradictions in that framework. Here in the limited space left in this paper we will only attempt a preliminary study that will try to raise questions rather than present final and conclusive empirical proof.

The origins of gentry rule

The categories of gentry landownership and gentry landlords were part

of a larger analysis of structural changes in the landlord system during
the late Ming-early Qing. These concepts presented an integrated image
of privileged and absentee landlords, the so-called urban landlords.[48]
However, a search of source materials quickly reveals numerous examples of gentry that do not fit these categories. It is my contention that the
core of the gentry was actually made up of rural-dwelling gentry who
still held to many of the older managerial and paternalistic patterns.
The remainder of this section will offer a number of actual examples of
such gentry.

First let us look at the case of Pu Shanlin, who appears in the literary
collection of Lin Xiyuan (1480–1560), a representative member of the
gentry in Fujian during the mid-sixteenth century. Pu was "industrious
and frugal as of old, despite serving as an official for a long time," and
retiring from office he "had bondservants cultivate several *mu* of land
outside the city wall; leaving at dawn and returning at dusk he was an
unusual old country gentleman."[49] Until his father's generation Lin Xiyuan's own family had rejected Confucianism and engaged in agriculture. His father "calculating the number of mouths and surveying the
land by himself had bondservants till it for him, leading them personally."[50] The Lin family's attitude to life was industrious and frugal to the
extent that to them "even the grass and the trees were all created by heaven
and earth; one peck of grain and one coin of cash are invariably produced
only when three factors—the weather, productivity of the soil, and human endeavor—are provided for. They also cautioned against waste-
fulness. The unknowing all thought them parsimonious. It was a life in
which they were content with plainness in clothes and sleeping quarters.
They never rode in horse carriages, and would even walk several hundred *li* if there were no boats available."[51]

This type of lifestyle forms a striking contrast to the more conventional descriptions of gentry life. It should be compared to the thought
and lifestyle of local landlords.[52] Though Lin and his family personally
engaged in cultivation, they also possessed some attributes of the landlord as the following statement shows: "If the tenant does not pay the
full amount of his rent, he should be treated leniently."[53] Lin Xiyuan,
who inherited this mode of thought distinctly displays this paternalistic
aspect of gentry life, despite the fact that he was the founder of the maritime smuggling trade.[54] In his family precepts Lin exhorted, "tenants
till the fields and entrust their lives to us, and we depend on them for our
livelihood. They should be treated with benevolence," and warned his
descendants against "treating tenants too unkindly."[55] The actual situation of landlord-tenant relations which made this way of thought possible was far removed from the image of the so-called urban, or absentee,

landlords. In this case the predominance of landlords and the directness of their patronage is striking.

At this stage direct management by landlords was still possible and was in fact quite common. There are many examples of successful secular gentlemen (*chushi*), who shunned official life. The collected works of Lin Xiyuan mention a man named Huang, "a most prosperous secular gentleman," whose family had for generations relied solely on the productivity of the soil to become one of the "great families of Changxing." He "supervised the bondservants at plowing, sowing, planting fruit trees and vegetables, working day and night . . . ordinarily living among and working together with bamboo-hatted old men," though he did not register his name for land tax and labor service. He lived a natural life, eating when hungry, drinking when thirsty, sleeping when tired, and arising upon waking.[56] Pu Xian, who is mentioned in a 1752 supplement to the Wuxi and Jinkui county gazetteers, "made his wealth by working hard at agriculture."[57] Another man, Xue Dan, "accumulated the wealth of a thousand households by engaging in the fundamental occupation, agriculture." In this way it was possible to attain greatness and maintain direct landlord management without being connected with the bureaucratic system. Such direct management and control of tenants was symbolized by personally working together with the peasants, and we assume such control was administered through direct human relations. The same source also relates an anecdote about Lu Mou who though inheriting vast wealth, did not want his son Yunlong (county prefect of Yihuang in 1615) to take up office when he passed the provincial examinations. The father calmly admonished his son, saying, "You should know satisfaction. The road to office is very thorny. It is best to be content with working on the land to spread virtue for the ancestors."[58] Furthermore, the fact that his son eventually became a county magistrate shows that the core of the gentry lay precisely in this social stratum.

Local strongmen present a very different image. For example: "Strongmen devour the land in their area, and the official administration is unable to stop them."[59] "There is a county strongman called Liao who tyrannizes the villages and wields power in the prefecture and counties."[60] "In Xinghua and Quanzhou prefectures there are many magnates (*haoyou*) and powerful families which are known as hard to control."[61] Categorically speaking, these strongmen are little more than conspicuous members of the gentry as described above. Since they were able to maintain a type of personal rule which stood in clear opposition to state power, the state considered them "hard to control." This type of landlord also formed part of the nucleus of the gentry.

This is plainly shown in the case of Lu Shusheng, a famous member of the gentry from Songjiang prefecture who lived during the Jiajing-Wanli periods (1522–1619). Lu had been one of the "four great surnames in Wu since the Three Kingdoms period," and the Lu family had resided in Songjiang from Shusheng's great-grandfather's generation. His father, who was the youngest child of his grandfather, only received 10 percent of the family property when it was divided. They fell into such straitened circumstances that his mother had to return to her parents' home and his father wove to help his stepmother. The eldest brother supported the whole family by farming, while Lu Shusheng studied for the examinations. Later he "abandoned Confucianism for agricultural work, following his elder brother in carrying farm tools." Three years later, when Lu Shusheng was 20, his father took pity on him and in the end allowed him to resume studying.[62] This serves to show that the frugality and industriousness of Lin Xiyuan were not simply due to the peculiarity of a backward region, but were characteristic features of the gentry.[63]

None of these cases hint at traits associated with urban or absentee landlords. This further suggests that dividing the gentry into so-called rural and urban landlords is of questionable use. A static analysis of landlords clearly indicates the existence of both types, but when we look at these two landlord groups dynamically, we discover that both followed similar paths and were subject to the same forces of uncertainty. Lu Shusheng's family is a good example. His grandfather had been minister of the Board of Rites, and in the family precepts he delivers the following admonition: "Remember rise and decline are unfixed. People who lose their property today are either the people who formerly built up the property or their descendants."[64] Lu was not optimistic about the stability of his family's social position as gentry.

Zhang Shiyi is another example. The Zhang family registered at Huating in Songjiang prefecture (Jiangsu) after the southern migration in the Song and for generations had cultivated the land and studied, but from the time of Shiyi's father they moved into the county city, and in due course when the family was in financial difficulties, Shiyi asked: "Why do we have to restrict ourselves to abide by the chapters and sentences of the Classics? . . . [He] abandoned Confucianism and became a merchant. With Confucian intentions and accumulated reason he disdained fine detail and selected people to take care of calculating revenue and expenditure."[65] Eventually his estate doubled and he was able to see his elder brother successfully through the *jinshi* degree. In addition to the usual activities of rural and city landlords, commercial activity was also incorporated as a complementary measure to maintain and vitalize a family trying to become official gentry.[66]

Although these groups are usually referred to as gentry landlords and their mode of operation as gentry landownership, these terms lack historical specificity. In looking for a link between a form of landownership and the existence of a specific ruling class, it is important to remember that gentry privileges were obtained through contact with the bureaucratic system. To put it in another way, the gentry for the most part were essentially landlords who constituted a special status group on the basis of status privileges conferred from outside. Status privilege could only be held for one generation. These privileges were nonhereditary, and could not be held in the family forever; they had to be maintained by continual effort. (Just how difficult this was can be seen from the way Lu Shusheng and most of the gentry families recorded by Ye Mengzhu were described as having "gradually declined.")[67] Even so, as long as the privileges and status of the gentry were allocated by the state, we cannot deny that "feudalism from above" was an essential factor in the formation of gentry rule. Ideally speaking, in a centralized dynastic form of social organization heredity made aristocrats of bureaucrats who should by right have served regal authority, and excess power allowed regional officials to enfeoff themselves. *These regional officials divided state landowning rights and civil rights* taking possession of the land and the people. The classic case of such decentralization of power is Byzantine feudalism.[68] But fluidity based upon the openness of the examination system and the special characteristics of Chinese bureaucratic organization did not in the end allow the formation of a bureaucratic aristocracy, and for that reason there was no alienation of state power.[69] Momentum from above functioned as a brake, confining feudalization from below within the landlord strata (i.e., the social stratum most adapted to the examination system). The upshot—roughly speaking—is to assume that this force from above created a special Chinese phenomenon, gentry rule.[70]

The formation of gentry rule

What position did the core of the gentry occupy in the early-Ming system of rule which was founded on the *lijia* system? First, let us look at what Lu Shusheng's father said on his deathbed, "My old friend alternatively served on the court in the *li*. You should take good note of this, remembering his poverty and trouble."[71] We can infer from this that even the distinguished Lu family could not hold a privileged position in the *lijia* system at first (though in the early Ming they were exempted from labor). They had probably formerly been assigned as a *li* captain (*lizhanghu*).[72] The common interpretation since Furushima Kazuo's study has been that the organizational principle of the *lijia* system was not inconsistent with the development of landlordism. There is agreement that the *lijia* system was based on the power and control which local landlords had established in the villages.[73] According to this line of thought, these landlords were the foundation of the *lijia* system. They were a declining stratum which found it difficult to resist the changes taking place in society. Besides becoming the main group paying dynastic land tax and meeting service-levy exactions, the burden of maintaining conditions which ensured the reproduction of ground rent on estate land, donated land (*citian*), and other land held by privileged (absentee) landowners was shifted to these local landlords.

In the past I have argued that the *lijia* system was set up according to the principles of traditional dynastic rule using the power relations of local landlords as a lever to institute the system.[74] The argument that the *lijia* system formed in response to certain developments in the landlord system has difficulty in explaining why local landlords were ruined by dynastic exactions. It is illogical to assume that the political power of landlords unavoidably ruined the landlord strata, even if the existence of privileged large-scale landownership is admitted. Rather, the *lijia* system should be seen as the adoption by the state of an organizational system based on the traditional standard of small-scale peasants which was unrelated to the decline of a particular landlord stratum.[75] The conception of magnates as "hard to control" is also based on the idea that landlords were at the opposite pole to dynastic rule. At this stage the antagonism of state versus the peasantry, that is, a lord versus the people, still existed as the fundamental contradiction determining class relations. Such political and economic relations broadly determined trends in the various social strata and even embodied the main turning point in the progressive differentiation of the peasantry. The fundamental form of progressive differentiation of the peasantry was the contemporaneously all-too-common pattern of peasants ruined by burdensome service levy, evading such service by entrusting their lives to the wealthy and becoming their tenants, or of the poor being sold into debt slavery. It is precisely because gentry landownership also presupposes this type of contradiction between the state and the peasantry that the special privileges held by the gentry, such as exemption from the service levy, are meaningful.[76] These privileges were used to shelter peasants. On the one hand, the state used its control of small-scale peasants as a lever to ruin the local landlord stratum, while on the other hand, state action inevitably created a new landlord stratum. Quite understandably this sort of bipolar arrangement of power spurred local landlords on toward gentry status. Furthermore, given that the development of large-scale landownership from the mid-Ming on was interpreted as a crisis demanding a fundamental transformation of the dynasty's traditional way of controlling the peasantry, dynastic rule was doubtlessly trying to produce a different system. There is no question that such large-scale landownership represents a major change in the Ming-Qing transition. The situation is described in the well-known testimony of Gu Yanwu (1613–82) on the Jiangnan delta region: "Among the people of Wu, one in ten owns land, while nine out of ten work as tenants for others."[77] Lin Xiyuan also generalized about the growth of large-scale landownership all over China: "At present 50 or 60 percent of the land in the empire is in the hands of the rich houses, and almost none of the people cultivate private land."[78]

The process of land accumulation was accompanied by the advance of the gentry, an example of which can be found in He Liangjun's statement about Songjiang, in his *Siyouzhai congshuo* (Collected dissertations from Siyou studio, 1579): "At present [the number of] resident officials in Huating is already ten times greater than before."[79] Other sources directly point to the gentry as the prime force behind land concentration. Chu Fangqing in his *Huangtian yi* (Proposal on deserted land) evaluates their role as follows: "During the late Ming there was a great amount of [land] annexation. Poor people could not own even an inch of land, while influential gentry families counted several tens of thousands of [*mu*] of adjoining land."[80]

The formation of large-scale landownership was not solely due to the work of the state. Just as Lin Xiyuan stresses the role of "rich people," we cannot dismiss the part played by "moral leaders" or "secular gentlemen." They had not completely disappeared with the rise of the *lijia* system. We should evaluate the role of land accumulation which drove history on to a new stage of development by seeing the formation of large-scale landownership as the moving force in a feudalistic differentiation (i.e., as a constant feudalization occurring at the base of society), which arose in opposition to despotism. Gentry used their special privileges to develop a relationship with rich people (i.e., moral leaders) that helped the rich avoid state control by commendation. For example, Zhang Lixiang comments that: "In Jiangnan it is the custom for most of the *rich people* to evade labor service by putting their land under the name of *official households* (i.e., *guiji*). If gentry lack their own land they can bribe officials and have other people's land exempted from service levy."[81] Pang Shangpeng reports that "recently big powerful wealthy families (*fuhao dahu*) wishing to avoid burdensome [tax payments] take the easy way out by practicing fraudulent trusteeship (*guiji*) by setting up small lots of untaxable size under false names or by allocating their land to a multiple number of poor households who are exempted from tax (*huafen*), and dishonesty prevails."[82]

As these examples show, it was the wealthy strata that mainly practiced fraudulent trusteeship and not small-scale peasants. Obviously the gentry were in a special position, different from that of ordinary landlords in their association with the wealthy.[83] Wealthy people nestled under the wings of the gentry to protect and maintain their own personal relations of dominance. This created a sort of multilayered landowning relationship.

A fundamental point about the gentry was that they were basically large landowners who subsumed other landlords both by means of special privileges from above and also on the basis of the power they derived from large-scale landownership. As a result the gentry went beyond ordinary landlords; they became more important. This was one of the characteristic features of the formation of gentry rule. More importantly, by looking at the gentry in the context of feudalization from below we can also see that the gentry utilized state power to establish their own domination. On the one hand, this created the upper-class rule of the gentry, while on the other hand, the gentry absorbed the power of small and medium landlords in the villages who were in danger of ruin in the *lijia* system. In the process the gentry protected the landownership of close relations and relatives and brought order to other landlordistic forms of landownership. Though this provided some individual relief, as a whole it served to consolidate the system of landlord rule.[84]

Despite the fact that gentry rule was established using privileges conferred by the state, it was not simply born as "the illegitimate offspring of bureaucratic control." Gentry rule ran counter to state aims, and, therefore, the gentry were regarded as devils.[85] A 1752 source for Wuxi and Jinkui counties sums up the situation: "During the former Ming dynasty, gentry households were exempted from labor service, and much of the land owned by the wealthy was fraudulently entrusted (*guiji*) to these gentry. Therefore the poor people had to work in place of grandee households (*dahu*), and it was a period of much misgovernment."[86] Lu Zhenfei in his record of the Fushe movement reports that "the gentry in Jiangnan are numerous, and there is much exemption from labor service (*youmian*). Only 50 or 60 percent of the land provides labor service. . . . Influential grandee households are also connected with official slaves with whom they practice fraudulent trusteeship (*guiji*). Only 30 or 40 percent of them provide service-levy labor, and they are all bankrupt from overburdensome labor service."[87] This process was accompanied by a series of illegal actions which are interpreted as "the tyranny of the gentry." Gentry rule was, in reality, created through such malpractices.

The gentry wielded more control over local society than the landlords, and their domination ran counter to the aims of state rule *at that time*. This was the prototype of gentry rule. Yet, the specially privileged position that provided the gentry with opportunities for the accumulation of large tracts of land also presented them with the means to legalize their domination over the peasantry as a whole through the legitimacy afforded by the state; the state in turn was willing to recognize gentry rule because of the peculiar role the gentry played in its network of power. This was another way in which the gentry superseded the ordinary landlord.

The formation of gentry rule should not be taken as a temporary spout of "tyranny"; rather it developed over time within the existing social form of organization. In summary, the two premises necessary for setting up a new symbiotic relationship between the state and the gentry were state recognition of landlordism and the need for the landlords on their part to be associated with centralized bureaucratic power.

Gentry rule within the social formation

Certain structural changes also made a new cohesion between gentry and state inevitable, and at the same time indicated the maturity of the landlord-tenant system. Kitamura Hironao first suggested this interpretation, noting the stratification that the development of a money economy had brought about in the landlord strata and the changes in their life style. The changes included the removal of the upper landlord stratum to the cities (i.e., absenteeism), a phenomenon that coincided with the control of land by merchant capital, which in turn counterbalanced the release of land by landlords and small-scale peasant farmers. Furushima Kazuo later reconsidered the problem from the viewpoint of class struggle. His study concentrated on an evaluation of the rent-resistance movement, and Niida Noboru's research showed a rise in the legal position of tenants. Oyama Masaaki also reinterpreted this structural change in an original way. Oyama treated it as the formation of feudalistic landownership which was based on the independence of the tenant as a feudalistic small-scale peasant farmer.[88] All of these the-

ories dealt with the loss of the local character of landlords, the subsequent human and spatial alienation of landlord-tenant relations, and
the role that the development of commodity production and a money
economy played in these changes.[89]

Landlords were isolated from agricultural management. Lin Xiyuan,
who provided evidence of direct landlord management, reported, "In
my *li*, the wealthy people mostly live in idleness, seldom working at
agriculture and sericulture."[90] In fact, praise lauded on landlords engaging in direct management was designed to warn against such alienation from production, but by Zhang Lixiang's time alienation was
already a fact of life: "Recently, I notice that landowners in wealthy
families and large houses always remain inside, never going out. They
do not go out into the fields, and they do not know their tenants' faces;
everything is entrusted to bondservant managers (*jigang zhi pu*)."[91]
"Gentry families leisurely spend their time inside their houses, never
coming out all year. The people who cultivate their fields are never able
to see their faces."[92] "The master has no ties of friendship to his tenant;
he is indifferent to and unconcerned about him, not paying his respects
at times of sickness and death, and not caring about intimidation and
lawsuits. The masters sit and enjoy their revenue even more than the
emperors of old."[93] These changes also coincided with the following
evaluations of tenants: "Of late few peasants are plain minded."[94]
"Bondservants at present are crafty and wicked, and not even 20 or 30
percent of them are good."[95]

Zhang attributed this to "the lord and tenant not practicing mutual
kindness,"[96] and looked in vain to a revival of direct human relations
for a solution to the problem. Zhang's hopes were frustrated, as the
landlord-tenant relationship continued to deteriorate. The idea of
"mutual aid and mutual fostering" (*xiangzi xiangyang*), which had regulated the relationship between landlords and tenants, changed to one
of "mutual suspicion and mutual grudges,"[97] and rent resistance was
pervasive, increasingly becoming a general practice among tenants. A
representative source indicating such change is the 1760 Wuqing town
gazetteer, which records:

> Recently a crafty and cunning custom has appeared among the
> tenants. Even if their crop is fine, they try to keep rent payments as
> small as possible. Whenever there is a slight drought or flood, they
> make tenant alliances by joining together all the tenants in the
> polders (*lianyu jiejia*). They secretly discuss and decide the amount
> of rent they should pay, and solidify their mutual unity by showing

plays and making contracts and pacts. If they discover anyone paying
rent over and above the amount they have decided among themselves,
sly members of the group form bands to go to make a din at the
offender's home, reproaching him for going against the group's
wishes and surreptitiously bringing disaster upon him if he remains
disobedient.[98]

Oyama's theory, which argues for the independence of tenant management and the formation of a new class solidarity based on community
(*kyōdōtai*), deserves attention. This tenant struggle for greater economic
independence reached a climax during the late Qing, as illustrated in the
Jiangsu Shanyang shouzu quanan (Complete documents concerning
rent collection in Shanyang county, Jiangsu [1827]).[99] The Shanyang
gentry, who except for one provincial graduate were all lower degree
holders, published a detailed account relating how their inability to
deal with tenant rent resistance had led them to ask local officials to
issue a proclamation prohibiting such behavior. Their action was a
direct product of the class struggle; a struggle that involved not merely
the landlord-tenant relation, but a more general gentry-tenant relationship. In this struggle, the position of tenants had strengthened as seen
in the fact that the tenant was allowed to keep his second crop of barley.
Such changes occurred at a time when rent resistance was the order of
the day; tenants patronized and sent "customary gifts" (*xianggui*) of
firewood, rice, and barley to the constables, officials in the villages
who were supposed to act in gentry interests. They even went so far
as to win over rent-collectors with bribes.[100] In the intense conflict
between landlords and tenants, the landlords needed more effective
political backing if they were to continue to dominate their tenants
(i.e., collect feudal rent). It was this new antagonistic relationship which
forced the gentry, who had originally stood in opposition to the
dynasty, to move over and support dynastic power. This changed relationship between the gentry and the dynasty first appeared in the most
advanced regions, the areas which played a determining political role.

Another factor which encouraged gentry absenteeism was merchant
capital. Merchant capital is an indispensible attribute of the gentry
concept, and it played an important role in determining the structural
characteristics of gentry rule. Huang Xingzeng (1490–1540) in his *Wufeng lu* (Record of the customs of Suzhou) says the following about
gentry profit: "These days many of the gentry are busy increasing their
wealth."[101] He Liangjun remarks: "Prior to the reigns of Xianzong and
Xiaozong [latter half of the fifteenth century] scholar-officials still

did not amass wealth. . . . The property of high-standing families was only of medium size. . . . By the Zhengde period [early sixteenth century], they all competed in running businesses to seek profit."[102]

He also cynically continues on to say that once scholar-officials in Songjiang become metropolitan graduates (*jinshi*), they weary of associating with their former fellow students and other "scholars who talk of literature and discuss morals." He stresses that they only delight in receiving "profit-speaking fellows" who talk about: "How much profit can be made every year from certain manor land. How much interest someone gets every year by lending several hundred taels of silver. When somebody seeks a favor for doing something, how much silver can be received without moving from one's seat."[103]

The main aim of the gentry in seeking profit, as can be seen in the above quotations, was to accumulate land, lend money, and use their social position to extract mediatory and advisory fees. Speculative buying and selling of rice was a fundamental attribute of Chinese landlords in general who as a rule collected their rent in kind.[104] When considered in the light of the unprecedented development of commodity production that enveloped direct producers in this period, it was more than anything else the enlargement of the function of merchant capital through which these aims were attained—frequently expressed as "monopolizing the market"—that constituted the special characteristic of gentry profit.

The development of this type of commercial profiteering coincided with the isolation of landlords from direct management in agriculture. This in turn was coupled with peasant resistance and the desire of the gentry themselves for a luxurious lifestyle. In the long run commercial profiteering encouraged landlords to reside in the cities. The so-called urban landlords are significant as a historical category not simply because they were absentee landlords, but also because of their attributes as specific merchant landlords. These changes, combined with the intensification of rent resistance, demanded the creation of a new force to guarantee domination over the peasantry and ensure the expropriation of feudal rent. Commerce and money-lending thereby became nothing more than a means of ruling the peasantry.[105] Later we will explain the main significance of the innumerable bondservants (*tongpu*), who appear in historical sources as living in perfect harmony with the gentry in this period, and how they were related to gentry profit. Here suffice it to say that these structural changes within landlordism—changes which drove landlords into the gentry camp—were also connected with another premise upon which gentry rule as a category was based, the combined land and poll tax (*diding yin*). The institution of this tax reform in effect recognized landlordism as the social form of economic organization.

As mentioned above the functioning of the *lijia* system presupposed that landlordism had developed to a certain extent, despite the fact that landlordism was not the social form of economic organization. Once the *lijia* began to break down, landlordism proceeded to develop further, finally emerging as a most important social category. A series of land tax and labor service (*fuyi*) reforms were introduced to rectify the situation.[106] The combined land and poll tax, which appeared as the final solution to the problem, in the end accepted landlordism as the social form of organization through which the state was to maintain its control over the peasantry.[107] To sum up what I have said about this point elsewhere,[108] by abolishing the poll tax (*yi*), one of the two pillars of the ancient Chinese taxation system, this reform finally did away with the principle of a lord ruling over all the people. The incorporation of the poll tax into a one-system land tax put landless tenants beyond the reach of direct state control and meant that landlords were openly entrusted with the task of ruling them. Furthermore, as the idea "rent comes out of the tax" indicates, land tax fundamentally depended on the landlord rent, thus broadening the character of landlord rent as a part of feudal rent. Therefore the state backed up the collection of rent in order to secure its tax, and the conflict between the state and landlords over tenants was dissolved since their interests were *basically* the same. This made the Qing dynasty one of the most stable landlord regimes in the history of the Chinese centralized state.

Gentry rule, strictly speaking, was a form of landlord rule that appeared following changes of a class nature. It arose because of a principal transformation in the domination of the people by the state which categorically incorporated particularistic gentry rule. Landlordism at any rate acquired official sanction and support because it was subsumed into state rule via the gentry. Landlord domination did not completely abandon the traditional system of centralized rule—the main factor that restricted the development of landlord domination per se was the growth of tenants as a class. In order to counteract tenant rent resistance, landlords had to operate within the framework of gentry rule. This meant that landlord domination was incorporated into the social formation as a special type of gentry rule, though landlordism itself was not regulated by the centralized state.

In other words, the landlord style of production preserved (did not negate) the centralized state which traditionally monopolized the right to rule; landlords acting under the umbrella of the state exercised their authority by making themselves a part of the state. For this reason not all landlords were able to become rulers; only landlords of gentry status, who were connected with the bureaucratic system, could obtain a good deal of authority, and at the same time control other landlords. Furthermore, this system subsumed owner-cultivators and other strata of society under the guise of the traditional authority of centralized rule. As a result a broad rule based on landownership, as well as a particularistic and personal domination also founded on landownership, was created with official protection. It was "gentry rule" based on this type of domination that brought feudal rule in China to fruition.

Gentry rule and other social strata

The institution of the combined land and poll tax marked the beginning of the real recognition of gentry rule within the entire social formation. It was clearly de facto rule, so it often appears in the sources as gentry oppression and as something the central government should keep in check. In that sense its essential qualities were plainly visible in the formative period before the introduction of the combined tax system.

First let us look at the darker side of the gentry. Lü Kun (1536–1618) in his work on government, first published in 1593, presents a general description of gentry rule in the following passage:

> Rural dwellers [refers to the gentry in contrast to office-holding bureaucrats] are guilty of many crimes: using force to buy land and houses, extorting interest on debts, requesting the yamen to do things for them, controlling the market, letting their children and bond-servants (*puli*) loose to tyrannize the neighborhood, taking revenge upon their enemies with the help of old friends in the yamen, resisting and obstructing the payment of land tax, arbitrarily trying to get exemption from labor service (*youmian*), frequently using [public] labor, and demanding to have everything done at their convenience. The district magistrate is afraid of their local power (*pingshe*), and nobody dares to do anything [to stop them].[109]

Zhu Wan's (1494–1550) impeachment of the activities of Lin Xiyuan, who is regarded as a typical member of the gentry in the late Ming, reveals another aspect of the gentry. Zhu charged that Lin Xiyuan was guilty of:

> Hanging up the two characters for "Lin prefecture" to bolster the prestige of his family, opening private courts at will, extorting confessions

by torture, issuing unauthorized proclamations, and infringing on the rights of officials. Specially building large ships of the prohibited type under the name of ferryboats and solely using them for carrying stolen goods and prohibited cargo. . . . These resident officials are a kind of misappropriating worm. . . . They lead a retired life with no regard for the laws and institutions. Inviting deserters and gathering rebels, they dispatch their lackeys to arbitrarily determine [the law] in remote rural areas and control the affairs of government.[110]

Lin's greatest offense was constructing large boats that were unlawful and engaging in smuggling, though it should be noted that he acted like an independent monarch. For the most part he maintained complete control: posing as an official, exercising jurisdiction (i.e., wielding penal authority), and issuing proclamations. He had armed power to back up his authority; he took in refugee rebels and organized them as his private militia. This militia kept order in remote rural areas. Needless to say, the Lin family was not the only family engaging in such activities.

Of course, there was also a positive side to gentry rule; it was not all negative. A good example is the case of what the administration commissioner of Yunnan, Chen Jingting, did after retiring: "Simple by nature he lived plainly without ever being lavish. He did not begrudge spending several hundred in gold in building the Guanyin dykes, where seven floodgates were constructed over several hundred *li*, and in administering the various mountain roads in Ciyun."[111] As seen in this example, the gentry ideally should support the facilities necessary for peasant reproduction and also provide their services in the fields of mediation, relief, and charity. These actions, rather than being good deeds intentionally performed by gentry of superior character, were designed to maintain the conditions necessary for domination; such deeds served to supplement gentry rule as a whole.

A complete examination of the various aspects to gentry rule as listed above goes beyond the original aim of this paper. Here we will limit ourselves to trying to discover the logic underlying gentry rule by concentrating on its power structure.

We have already stated that the gentry were landlords who were more important than ordinary landlords. Idiomatically speaking, they constituted a group of privileged landlords who perfected landlordism as a social form of organization by maintaining patronage relationships with ordinary landlords. Another characteristic feature of gentry rule was their peculiar privileged position. This position was the lever that allowed gentry landlords to extend their control beyond those

peasants they directly supervised through the landlord-tenant relationship to include small peasant proprietors in general. This is also evident
from the examples above, which nearly all illustrate this point. Nevertheless, class relations which formed the nucleus of gentry rule were
concluded with tenants, and it was precisely the new strained relations
between landlord and tenant, especially symbolized by the pervasive
spread of rent resistance on the part of refractory tenants, that was a
basic factor in forcing the landlord camp to participate in gentry rule.
This shows the historical nature of gentry rule.

Special studies of this problem have been made elsewhere,[112] so
here for convenience of presentation we will endeavor to examine the
relationship between gentry rule and other social strata by focusing on
the issue of bondservants (i.e., slaves). However, by "bondservants"
(*jiapu*) we do not mean the bondservants that Kitamura and Furushima
regarded as the labor force used by landlords in direct management,
nor what Oyama saw as the base of patriarchical slave management
(*kafuchōteki doreisei keiei*) during the former half of the Ming.[113] Here
we understand bondservants as flocking to the gentry, a phenomenon
that paralleled the development of gentry rule as Gu Yanwu indicates:
"Many of the literati (*shidafu*) in Jiangnan today practice this custom
[of keeping bondservants]. As soon as they pass the examinations,
these people compete to be admitted to their families, large followings
numbering a thousand people. This is called submitting oneself to
another (*toukao*)."[114] Bondservants often appear in the historical
sources, as they do in the quotation above, as a concrete aspect of the
social problems surrounding the gentry. The following passage from the
1752 supplement to the Wuxi and Jinkui county gazetteers highlights
this point:

> During the Jiajing period [1522–56] the tyranny of bondservants from
> the two families Wang and Yu was terrible. Wang had 500 bond-
> servants, while Yu had over 100. They liked elegant clothes and fresh
> food and maltreated the people in neighboring villages, always seizing
> market goods. At that time it was rumored that "Yu divided evenly
> and Wang stole in broad daylight." In those days 70 to 80 percent of
> the gentry had their reputation ruined because of [the actions of]
> retainers, and 50 to 60 percent because [of the behavior] of brazen
> bondservants (*haonu*).[115]

He Liangjun explains the cause of these social problems in the following
fashion:

Prior to the Zhengde period [1506–21] one in every ten commoners was an official, and nine out of ten were working on the land. . . . During the last 40 to 50 years the land tax has been increasing daily and service labor getting heavier. The people cannot bear it, and they, all change their occupations. In former days resident officials (*xiangguan*) did not have too many family servants (*jiaren*). At present the number of people that give up agriculture to become family servants of resident officials is already ten times what it was previously.[116]

Bondservants therefore were the end result of rural class differentiation based on exactions by the state. This differentiation arose for various reasons, due to debt, to parents selling children, etc., and the fact that the profit motive was at work in cases of commendation (*toushen* or *toukao*) exhibits a complexity which makes it difficult to define consistently the bondservants of this period.[117]

Needless to say, some of them did constitute a labor force that engaged in agricultural production. There are many more examples of this than we have presented here. Since large landholdings by the gentry were not operated on an extensive farming basis, even in cases like that of "King Zou Donghu [name of a gentry man], who had 3000-odd *mu* of land and 3000 bondservants,"[118] we can only conclude that production slaves were of little importance. Bondservant labor did not constitute the basis of the system of social production.

If that is the case, then what role did they play? Previously, it has been pointed out that they were responsible for management, appearing in the sources as bondservant managers (*jigang zhi pu*).[119] Doubtlessly, their main function was to manage tenants; in the materials presented above they appear in place of the gentry when the latter were alienated from land management. An episode from the *Yanzhou shiliao* relates this in an intriguing way. One day a handsome young man came to a gentry man, Wei Zhong, who had retired from office after serving as an official in Henan, and begged him to take him on as a slave. He was an expert horseman and archer and good at calligraphy and arithmetic. The text continues:

Zhong favored him greatly. After staying for two months, he was entrusted with more important tasks than anybody else; he was trusted with all the receipts and expenditures of money and grain. One day they went out to the estate together collecting interest and pressing for the land tax from followers and tenants. Upon returning in the evening [family members?] found Zhong lying dead on the ground, decapitated, and the youth and the fine horse in the stable gone.[120]

This handsome bondservant was actually an assassin sent by someone who held a grudge against Wei Zhong as a result of his conduct while in office. Apart from being an interesting episode, this passage shows that bondservants functioned in a managerial capacity above the tenants on large estates while simultaneously inferring that their relations with their masters were extremely intimate. It was probably this intimacy that closed the alienation gap between landlords and tenants.

Lu Shusheng in his family precepts has a section on the selection of bondservants which reads: "The best bondservants are those that are honest and sincere without any ideas of cheating in their minds. Next come those that are adept at managing affairs. Others that only engage in clever, meaningless, idle talk are mediocre."[121] Here, too, we have the same situation. Attention is directed to the honesty of bondservants as well as their managerial skills. Furthermore, it is most interesting that Lu is so concerned about bondservants that he fails to mention anything about tenants, despite having written a section on the purchase of land. This stands in contrast to the way Zhang Lixiang gave serious consideration to the selection of tenants in landlord management. Separation from direct management was probably an axiomatic assumption in the case of Lu Shusheng. For Lu the crucial point in land management had shifted from picking tenants to the selection of bondservants who controlled direct management.

The new significance of bondservants corresponded to the diversification of gentry management. In the case of Lin Xiyuan, besides working the smuggling trade in which "panther and tiger-like brazen bondservants (haonu) sailed large ships with several masts to communicate with barbarian countries," bondservants, together with retainers, were also responsible for generating gentry profit. Saeki Yūichi analyzed the work done by managerial bondservants in a study of the brazen bondservants of the Dong family during the late Ming. He showed that brazen bondservants used other bondservants to collect rent and were responsible for revenue and expenditure in pawnshops owned by their master and investments in other stores, speculative selling of accumulated stores of rice, beans, and other agricultural produce, and the buying and selling of land and houses.[122] The significance of bondservants at this stage is that they were a management staff responsible for operating all the household affairs of the diversified gentry. They even intruded into the domain of the gentry, writing memorials and letters for them. These managerial bondservant staffs were subject to a patriarchical system of control.

Nevertheless, the most outstanding feature of bondservants was the way they were used to control remote rural areas. We cannot, however, claim that from a few hundred to a thousand-odd bondservants were all on the gentry's management staff. Here follow examples showing that bondservants were a direct violent force openly used in implementing gentry rule. First, a passage from the supplement to the Wuxi and Jin-kui county gazetteers: "Many bondservants of official households in the county tyrannize the market at will using force. Many of the people fear force and dare not say anything, and accordingly their masters are condemned."[123]

Ye Mengzhu also relates: "Recently there are a great many gentry and high officials in Songjiang. Their children and bondservants use force to tyrannize, subordinating small peasants and squeezing commoners. The property of middle ranking people bears the brunt of their outrages and is all ruined."[124] Here attention should be drawn to the fact that small peasants, commoners, and particularly middle-ranking people were the victims of such violence. This indicates that gentry rule had extended to owner-cultivators. It is in this sense that the stock phrase "the gentry use force" appears. It is generally assumed that the tyranny of bondservants was a reflection of the influence and power of the gentry; at the same time, however, the gentry were equally dependent on their bondservants, and despite criticism and resulting damaged reputations, they could not get rid of them. Together with bondservant managers, this type of private militia gave new meaning to bondservants in this period.

Bondservants were the direct advance guard for the general domination of the peasantry which had surpassed the earlier level of ordinary landlord control. They were the practical administrators who enforced the gentry's domination over tenants and used physical violence to back-up their non-economic compulsion. Accordingly, in slave revolts they opposed rebels who had the same slave status as themselves. As mentioned above, the new absentee relationship that grew up between landlords and tenants, and the subsequent alienation of landlords from the reproduction process caused the breakdown of the real base of landlord control over the peasants, which had been founded upon a direct personal relationship. Bondservants were the strength for the mechanism that was required by the gentry rule which arose out of this breakdown of former landlord-tenant relations.

The feudal essence of gentry rule is evident in the attempt to maintain direct and private control. A clear outline of this can be seen in Lin Xiyuan's creation of Lin prefecture, where he opened courts, imposed punishments, and issued proclamations. Lin was thus able to effect a subrogation of the authority of the local prefectural officials seizing "control" of their prerogatives.[125] The general possession of de facto tax-collecting powers, proxy remittance, and tax resistance in addition are noticeable. There are also many other cases of people being "styled a prefecture."[126]

We should, however, not lose sight of the fact that in the final analysis gentry rule did not become a part of the social formation as the end result of the extension of personal gentry rule. Rather, gentry rule was accepted within the social formation because it abandoned personal rule. Even though the acceptance of the gentry by the state was basically necessitated by the class growth of tenants, the changeover was facilitated by the fact that impersonal elements were inherent as a fundamental attribute of gentry rule.

Gentry rule and state power

The main factor in gentry rule which restrained the development of the personal landlord element and hastened its union with centralized bureaucratic power was the privileges that the gentry were granted. These privileges were an official mantle which colored the landlord reality of the gentry. Personal elements and privileges did not normally stand in such a relationship; personal landlord elements were the historical content of gentry rule, while privileges only acted as a lever to maintain it. This in reality was the dominant pattern in the formative period of gentry rule. "Controlling official [authority]" and "conspiring with officials" are direct expressions of this phenomenon. In this part of the paper we will approach the question of the power structure of gentry rule by centering upon the gentry's relationship with local officials.

We should note that the gentry were, as a matter of principle, supposed to be paragons for the people. He Liangjun states this explicitly: "When the prefectures and counties have good government and a complete set of prohibitions and regulations, the literati should all lead the way in observing them, thereby being models for the people."[127] In this case, the gentry should not exercise their own rule. Here the gentry were expected to assist in realizing the monistic rule of the emperor. To that extent the gentry should have been nothing more than helpers or representatives for officials. The *Xiangshen yue* (Gentry oath) by Shi Chengjin, who lived in the early Qing period, rationalized the role of the gentry in the following fashion:

There is only one senior official at the prefecture, subprefecture, and county level, respectively, but several tens of gentry. Senior officials are responsible for half of the proper guidance of the people, and the gentry should be entrusted with the other half. The gentry's good deeds are equivalent to a million deeds by ordinary people. Senior officials are not clear on the situation in the areas to which they are appointed, but the gentry are thoroughly familiar with it, and, unlike the ignorant peasants and commoners, they are able to report to the officials. Accordingly, the responsibility for voicing the interests of the people lies with the gentry.[128]

The agent of the officials was at the same time a representative for the people, and the gentry were regarded as the medium for these two roles. In this view, the gentry neither merely enjoyed various privileges on an individual basis, nor did they implement their rule separately through blood relationships. From the outset the gentry were treated as essential participants in local politics, and to that end a certain amount of de facto authority was assigned to them. Gentry rule was nothing more than a realization of such functions. Intercourse between the gentry and local officials was founded upon this logic, and from an early stage we can discern a certain intimacy between these two groups. For example, the gentry as a matter of formality would jointly implore a local official to stay when he was transferred to a new post.[129]

However, if we were to limit our explanation to this aspect of gentry rule, the gentry would merely become subcontractors for dynastic rule. This was not the case at all. The essence of gentry rule lies in its having an independent foundation and possessing historical and social characteristics which forced a certain amount of change in dynastic social organization. The fact that the gentry virtually controlled local politics can be seen in the way local officials consulted about local affairs with powerful gentrymen, like Lu Shusheng, who had held posts as high-ranking officials. On such occasions the gentry frequently differed from the official norm and expressed their own class logic.

The great influence the gentry had on local officials is evident in the problems concerning large landownership. For example, in his report to the surveillance commissioner concerning the limited amount of taxable land, Lu Shusheng said:

It is easy to accumulate land in Wu, but hard to keep it. It is a simple
matter to amass [large tracts of land] when the price is low, but difficult to hold on to if taxes are heavy. During years of bad harvest no
[tax] exemption is granted and the taxes have to be paid. Heavy un-
reduced taxes are collected on damaged fields that do not yield produce. Small peasants work until they are calloused, and grandee households are burdened by having to pay compensation. Accordingly,
the burden is always heavy if much land is held, but this does not necessarily limit [landholdings].[130]

Here Lu stresses the unprofitability and pains associated with large-
scale landownership. He later defends the special privileges of exemption from labor service and commendation (guiji), opposing the reform
designed to assign labor services according to the amount of land held
(zhaotian paiyi) on the grounds that it would infringe upon these privileges: "If labor silver (yaoyin) is arranged according to land, and permanent exemption (limian) is not permitted when calculating labor
service, both those who receive land in trust (ji) and those who give it
in trust will be unhappy."[131] This passage is plainly pleading the case
for large gentry landowners.

Lu, while supporting gentry landownership, did not display equal
sympathy with the peasantry. It is evident that he feared the peasants:
"What we should worry about at present is not solely the straitened
circumstances of the people, but how the people's minds are set on disorder and how they are easy to stir and hard to settle." Lu's fear of peasant rebellion betrays the fact that he was not representing the interests
of the people and was primarily concerned about the damage any disturbance would cause to his person and property.

One of the greatest defenders of landlordism in this period who wrote
for the gentry cause was Yao Ruxun. In his Jizhuang yi (A proposal on
landowning outside of the place of registration) he comments: "All
households that own land outside their place of registration are wealthy
ones, and the poor people depend upon them and cannot do without
them."[132] This reflects the standpoint of imperial administrators. The
Shizheng lu (Notes on effective administration) says that it is the administrator's duty to exalt diligent peasants and punish lazy ones. In that
context it is clearly diametrically opposed to the following statement
from the same work: "Landlords should not be permitted to use hired
tenants as a temporary expedient."[133]

Similarly, there was naturally a difference in the standpoints that were
revealed in the praise and criticism surrounding Hai Rui (1513–87), who
appeared as most loyal to the ruling principles of the despotic state by

"crushing the magnates" and was renown for his integrity and incorruptibility. The following criticism was leveled against Hai Rui: "This custom has arisen, and literati households are unwilling to buy land and put out capital, while the good people sit waiting for death. They cherish these people, yet in reality they force death upon them."[134] Yet at the same time Hai Rui was credited for "not having the style of a literatus."[135]

A reflection of this type of gentry standpoint can also be seen in the case of Lin Xiyuan. In the proposals contained in a memorial he presented to the throne, he suggested that it would be best for all concerned, officials, the people, and merchants alike to promote peasant relief on a commercial basis, and he advocated price restraint. Such ideas came about because of gentry activity in commerce and are strikingly different from the traditional concept of physiocratic methods.

The gentry were plainly able to accommodate their own private interests by utilizing their contacts with officials. These contacts were founded on the principle that the position of the gentry and officials differed. The gentry, however, forced their viewpoint upon the government by "falsifying the public good" (*jiagong*). This is neatly summarized in the idiomatic expression "rely on officials to occupy property and forcefully seize [land], to cheat, to hide grain, and to swindle people of their wealth."[136] The following passage from the source quoted earlier on Wuxi and Jinkui counties shows that gentry in fact could control the appointment and dismissal of county magistrates:

After 1603 the county gentry lectured at the Donglin academy and spoke straightforwardly on the interests of the county. Much profit was gained by one or two mean men. Only one in ten falsified the public good to serve their own selfish ends. But the issue of transferring magistrates was interfered with to a great extent. If a newly arrived magistrate showed the least sign of not complying [with the gentry's wishes], he was transferred before long, and someone they liked was selected and recommended for office. The county people spent over a thousand *jin* at the coming and going of magistrates.[137]

Here follow some illustrations of how the gentry got what they wanted from the local yamen. He Liangjun records that recently the gentry had been asking the prefecture and county for coolies, whose use was normally extremely limited even for bureaucrats holding office. They continually asked despite constant prohibitions, and when the prefectual and county authorities did not comply with their requests, the gentry slandered and created rtouble for them.[138] As this trend developed further, it made the lower gentry yamen toughs parasitic on the bureaucracy. The same source on Wuxi and Jinkui counties also furnishes us with a vivid description of the function, action, and influence of yamen toughs:

> Lower degree holders have access to the yamen and control the officials. During the Shunzhi and early Kangxi reign periods [mid-seventeenth century] oppressors of the local people were called the 13 bullies (*shisan taibao*). . . . These yamen toughs were backed by unworthy county gentry and had local ruffians from every district as their lackeys. When there were lawsuits between local people, the local ruffians dragged [one party] in and ordered them to treat the yamen toughs as their patrons. At first they consoled them with sweet words while secretly gauging the wealth of their household. No settlement could be reached until the toughs had used almost all of their property. If they were prosperous and afraid of creating a scene, toughs used that as a pretext for intimidation and did not stop until they had what they wanted. There is probably no easier way of picking out a person for beguiling than to raise the issue of their tax evasion. . . . Furthermore, some surreptitiously lined their own pockets by profiting from the proxy remittance of tax grain, and colloquially they were known as granary rats. This custom only ceased after the Yongzheng period [1723–35].[139]

In this instance the yamen toughs were evidently encroaching upon the domain of bureaucratic authority. Particularly noteworthy is the fact that their domination clearly extended to local residents (*xiangguan*), a group which mainly included wealthy people. This domination was achieved by intervening in judiciary procedures, or by clinging to the tax-collecting organization—practicing extortion of the wealthy by taking advantage of their weak position concerning tax evasion, and pocketing the balance left after contracting grain tax.[140] In the above citation there was a conspiracy with the lower gentry whose leading strata were *shengyuan* and *jiansheng*. As the "Lin prefecture" example shows, this type of threatened violence was a not uncommon constituent part of gentry rule. Gentry rule meant much more than working through the medium of the bureaucracy. There was a personal side to it. Yet, it was also achieved by "falsifying the public good" while leaching onto officialdom and devouring their authority.[141]

The introduction of the combined land and poll tax macroscopically extended the gentry's connection with state power. It restricted the personal elements, the tendency toward decentralization embodied within gentry rule, and incorporated them within the social formation. The conflict between the gentry and the state which accompanied large-scale landownership should fundamentally have been resolved if the landlordization of central bureaucratic power is taken as a measure of change. Also, state power absorbed and executed by proxy the apparatus of extraeconomic impositions (including physical violence by bondservants) which individual gentry had previously enforced themselves. The article inserted into the *Qing lu* (Qing code) in 1725 which specified penal regulations in imperial law for tenants refusing to pay rent carried double implications. While it indicated that state power served landlord interests, on the reverse side of the coin punishment of tenants by the gentry was prohibited.[142] The 1725 *Da Qing lü jijie fuli* (The annotated Qing code with substatutes appended) explicitly states: "Lawless gentry who set up instruments of torture and arbitrarily punish tenants should, if they are gentry (*xiangshen*), be punished according to the statutes for disobedience (*weizhi lü*), and if they are scholars, lower degree holders, and yamen clerks, be stripped of their robes, caps, and official titles."[143]

Our source for Wuxi and Jinkui counties also verifies that the gentry's relationship with the law had changed between the late Ming period and the mid-eighteenth century: "Now, we rarely hear of the extravagance and selfishness of the gentry, nor of arbitrary oppression by their bondservants [that prevailed in the Ming dynasty]. After the Kangxi period there were occasionally one or two such gentry. Recently they have become more courteous, careful, and afraid of the law."[144] "[Now], there is none of what people called equally dividing [things] stolen in broad daylight (*pingfen baiduo*), and nobody keeps lots of brazen bondservants (*haopu*) anymore."[145] The reduction in the number of bondservants kept by the gentry referred to here should not be simply explained as a change in gentry customs, but can be understood as the elevation and absorption of the gentry into the structure of state rule. Even the activities of the yamen toughs, which "only ceased after the Yongzheng period," suggest the epochal nature of this change in the gentry's relations with dynastic power.[146]

For the traditional dynastic state, this process was one form of overcoming the crisis. This inevitably led to two changes: one, the relinquishment of direct control over the landless tenant stratum, and two, a transformation in the significance of land tax which came to depend on landlord rent. These changes transformed the despotic character of dynastic rule. They absorbed the energy of gentry rule that was founded upon the base of an unmistakable feudalization from below. As a result the state and the gentry formed a new symbiotic relationship. Dynastic rule subsequently strengthened its position as a special framework for dominance and as a power-exercising organ. It also refined its methods of coercion and violence. In fact, the whole Manchu race was organized according to military principles into an eight-banner system.

The use of coercion is also substantiated by facts that suggest a decline in the function of agricultural promotion which had been an important state function and a mark of legitimacy since ancient times.[147] In times past the state demonstrated its important role in maintaining conditions necessary for reproduction and thus reinforced its character and authority as a community (kyōdōtai). Naturally, this shift must mean that the job of promoting agriculture had passed over to the real local rulers, the landlord-gentry stratum. As we saw in the case of Chen Jingting, such a changeover was definitely taking place.[148]

Nevertheless, it is important to bear in mind that at this stage of historical development landlords were fundamentally separated from agricultural work. Furthermore, it was not just individual landlords, but the whole of the gentry that was becoming alienated from the process of production. In connection with this point, Hamashima Atsutoshi stresses that irrigation communities (suiri kyōdōtai) which the gentry could not control were reorganized by the state.[149] Certainly, the promotion of agriculture by state administration never disappeared, even during the Qing, but it should be noted that there were no special officials appointed for that purpose.[150] The fact that state promotion of agriculture continued during the Qing should be interpreted as an indication of the extent to which the state had absorbed and started to execute by proxy tasks for which landlords were originally responsible, This, however, did not merely constitute a restoration of the traditional function of the state.[151]

The incorporation of gentry rule into the state explains why the dynastic authority of the Qing, which in substance was a mechanism for rule by the landlord class, appeared to be an unchanging replication of traditional dynastic practice. The Yueshi bian records the fact that 2,171 gentrymen (xiangshen) and 11,346 shengyuan were demoted for defaults in tax payments during the Kangxi reign period.[152] Such severity would seem to exclude the theory of a simple landlord regime. Nevertheless, after passing through such trials and tribulations gentry rule strengthened its multilayered regional domination as the indisputable internal support of Qing dynastic authority and at the same time provided the substructure. Because of this, the veneer of dynastic rule faded in the late Qing. As it disappeared, gentry rule revealed itself in naked form as the substantive relationship in society. The Shanyang county magistrate Zhu Xiang, in his preface to the *Jiangsu Shanyang shouzu quanan* dated sixth lunar month, 1827, notes:

Literati (*shidafu*) with real estate are not able to till in spring and harvest in autumn. This is the reason they lease their land to peasants in the county, having them cultivate it for them, collecting rent every year to pay the taxes and provide for their livelihood. Landless peasants, if they are capable, can obtain a living by working industriously all year. Literati by calculating the number of *mu* and collecting rent do not let their land go to waste. The intention is laudable and the method excellent.[153]

The author of this preface clearly supports landlordism. Judging from the fact that all authors who penned prefaces, apart from one prefectural magistrate, defended the landlord side, we must conclude that the substance of the landlord regime had certainly permeated social thought.[154]

Conclusion

This article has endeavored to throw new light on the nature of state power in the Ming-Qing period through an examination of the gentry. The gentry are seen as a social group one cut above ordinary landlords who maintained a special relationship with the state through the examination system. The gentry originated in the mid-Ming and gradually gained political power with the rise of landlordism. Antagonism within the landlord-tenant relationship, which surfaced in the form of rent resistance by tenants, drove the gentry over to the side of the state. The gentry soon found that they held the same interests as the state. The marriage between the gentry and the state was finally consummated with the introduction of the combined land and poll tax. This state-gentry alliance was an open recognition of the fact that the Qing state had come to represent landlordism.

What I am suggesting is that the concept of gentry rule allows us to understand Ming-Qing society in a uniquely organic fashion. My analysis puts forward the idea of a society dominated by the gentry. The Qing dynasty, operating through the landlords, was a society in which the gentry were at the apex below the bureaucracy. This put the gentry in a position to dominate landlords, tenants, and owner-cultivators. This theory, therefore, expresses something far more comprehensive

than mere landlord control of tenants. It posits gentry domination
of the whole of nonbureaucratic society.

Notes

¹ Suzuki Chūsei, "Shinmatsu jōgai undō no kigen."

² Ichiko Chūzō, "Kyōshin to Shingai kakumei" is a work that emphasizes the specifically modern turnover of the gentry and regards them as the actual leaders of the
1911 revolution. (Hereafter the term "political process" (*seiji katei*) is used to collectively indicate the state and the superstructure.—Trans.)

³ Sakai Tadao, *Chūgoku zensho no kenkyū*.

⁴ Negishi Tadashi, *Chūgoku shakai ni okeru shidōsō—kirō shinshi no kenkyū*.

⁵ This is a free translation of Wang Huizu's *Xuezhi yishuo*, 1:13b–14a.

⁶ Recently Nomura Kōichi has given new meaning to this viewpoint in "Kindai
kokkakan e no chōsen."

⁷ Matsumoto Yoshimi, "Kyū Chūgoku shakai no tokushitsuron e no hansei."

⁸ Tachibana Shiraki, *Shina shakai kenkyū*, pp. 430, 443.

⁹ Sano Manabu, *Shinchō shakaishi*, Part 2, I, p. 47.

¹⁰ Ibid.

¹¹ This idea is still prevalent at present. Cf. Ishida Yoneko, "Daikanryō to kyōshin."

¹² Rekishigaku kenkyūkai, ed., *Kokka kenryoku no shodankai*.

¹³ For details on this point cf. Shigeta Atsushi, "Chūgoku hōkensei kenkyū to
hōhō—rikuchō hōkenseiron no ichi kentō."

¹⁴ Matsumoto Yoshimi presents his view of the gentry in Wada Sei, ed., *Shina
chihō jichi hattatsushi*.

¹⁵ Mainichi Shimbunsha tosho henshūbu, ed., *Sekai no rekishi*, 3, p. 146.

¹⁶ Ibid., p. 146.

¹⁷ Ibid., p. 149.

¹⁸ Ibid.

¹⁹ Ibid.

²⁰ Niida Noboru, *Chūgoku hōseishi kenkyū: keihō*, p. 23. Katayama Seijirō also
holds similar views on the gentry. In "Mindai kaijō mitsubōeki to enkai chihō kyōshinsō" he states, "the gentry strata, which was spawned by the bureaucratic system
from the Song onwards and which acted as an unofficial leading force, structurally
ought to be regarded as belonging to the same social strata as bureaucrats in office"
(p. 23).

²¹ Niida Noboru, *Chūgoku hōseishi kenkyū: keihō*, pp. 5–6.

²² Ibid., p. 6.

²³ Ibid., pp. 26–27.

²⁴ Ibid., pp. 27–28.

²⁵ Saeki Yūichi, "Minmatsu no Tō-shi no hen: iwayuru 'nuhen' no seikaku ni
kanreshite."

²⁶ Yasuno Shōzō, "Minmatsu Shinsho Yōsukō chūryūiki no dai tochi shoyū ni
kansuru ichi kōsatsu."

²⁷ Tanaka Masatoshi, "Minpen, kōso, nuhen," which is included in this volume,
and his comments at the symposium entitled "Chūgoku no kindaika" [China's
modernization], appended to *Sekai no rekishi*, vol. 11.

²⁸ "Chūgoku no kindaika," p. 306.

²⁹ Ibid.

³⁰ Ibid.

³¹ Ibid.

³² Oyama Masaaki, "Chūgoku shakai no hen'yō to sono tenkai."

³³ Cf. Oyama Masaaki, "Minmatsu Shinsho no dai tochi shoyū" [translated in this volume].
³⁴ Oyama Masaaki, "Chūgoku shakai no hen'yō to sono tenkai," p. 53.
³⁵ Ibid., pp. 50–51.
³⁶ Of course, this is unrelated to the theory which holds that state and society are separate from each other.
³⁷ As noted earlier, this concept was first presented by Matsumoto Yoshimi.
³⁸ Cf. Watanabe Kin'ichi, "Bizantsu teikoku ni okeru hōkensei no mondai"; and Yoneda Haruyasu, "Bizantsu hōkensei kenkyū no dōkō."
³⁹ There is a common view that the gentry were scholar officials. This is connected with a major debate about the definition of the character of the gentry, and we will not deal with this problem in the limited space available in this paper, since it differs in methodological dimension.
⁴⁰ Fujii Hiroshi, "Kyōshin"; Sakai Tadao, *Chūgoku zensho*. Also note that there are various types of gentry such as retired gentry (*jinshen*), bureaucrats, resident local officials (*xiangguan*), local gentry (*yishen*).
⁴¹ 4: 9a, Kyūko Shoin reprint, 1973, p. 55.
⁴² For example, in Wang Shizhen's *Yanzhou shiliao*, *juan* 35 in the section entitled *jinshen canhuo*, pp. 346–76, all the accounts begin from officials being retired or on leave with such statements as "[he] returned [to office] as a prefect," or "[he] returned [to office] as a censor."
⁴³ But it is said that the gentry and these scholars (*shiren*) were distinguished from each other too (Sakai, *Chūgoku zensho*). Tanaka Masatoshi, as mentioned, above has suggested that the differentiation of a strata critical to the dynasty (for the most part identified as *shengyuan*) within the gentry should be distinguished (see "Minpen, kōso, nuhen," pp. 305–7.
⁴⁴ In the context of the ideas presented in this paragraph, the concept of the "gentry" first appeared as a group known as "gentry landlords" (*kyōshin jinushi*). Cf. Yasuno Shōzō, "Minmatsu Shinsho Yosukō."
⁴⁵ See Shigeta Atsushi, "Hōkensei no shiten to Min-Shin shakai."
⁴⁶ Nishijima Sadao, *Chūgoku keizaishi kenkyū*, p. 907.
⁴⁷ For the same kind of analytical orientation in studies of Song history refer to Tokyo kyōiku daigaku Chūgoku shakai keizaishi kenkyūkai, "Chūgokushi no sekai haaku wa dō susunda ka (2)—chūsei kenkyū no kadai."
⁴⁸ Kitamura Hironao, "Minmatsu Shinsho ni okeru jinushi ni tsuite."
⁴⁹ *Lin Ciyai xiansheng wenji*, 14:31a.
⁵⁰ Ibid., 14:33a.
⁵¹ Ibid., 14:33a–b.
⁵² Kitamura, "Minmatsu Shinsho."
⁵³ *Lin Ciyai xiansheng wenji*, 14: 33b.
⁵⁴ Katayama Seijirō, "Mindai kaijō."
⁵⁵ *Lin Ciyai xiansheng wenji*, 12:18b.
⁵⁶ Ibid., 13:21ab.
⁵⁷ *Xijinzhi xiaolu*, 7:27a.
⁵⁸ For Xue Dan see ibid., 7:28a, and for the Lu Mou episode, ibid., 7:27b.
⁵⁹ *Lin Ciyai xiansheng wenji*, 10:43b.
⁶⁰ Ibid., 14:3a.
⁶¹ *Lu Wending gongji*, 4:6b.
⁶² Ibid., 23:3b.
⁶³ Sakai has already pointed out (Sakai, *Chūgoku zensho*, pp. 207–8) that several of the materials Oyama Masaaki presented to posit the management of managerial landlords by family servants in the early Ming (Oyama Masaaki, "Minmatsu Shinsho no dai tochi shoyū") can be understood as directly indicating the situation of the gentry.
⁶⁴ *Lu Wending gong ji*, 23:15a.
⁶⁵ Ibid., 7:41a–b.

⁶⁶ This point was mentioned in my study of Huizhou merchants during the Qing dynasty, and it was a general characteristic not confined to the Huizhou merchants. Cf. Shigeta Atsushi, "Shindai Kishū shōnin no ichimen."

⁶⁷ *Yueshi bian*, 5:1a–10b. Also the *Xijinzhi xiaolu*, 4:11a, relates that "During the Yongzheng era all the old established families in the county were ruined, and many of their children turned to engaging in agriculture and trade, not having the means to study."

⁶⁸ Cf. Watanabe, "Bizantsu teikoku"; and Yoneda, "Bizantsu hōkensei."

⁶⁹ Therefore it is something of a simplification to define Chinese feudalism as bureaucratic feudalism.

⁷⁰ By contrast it should be kept in mind that Matsumoto Yoshimi in Mainichi Shimbunsha tosho henshūbu, ed., *Sekai no rekishi*, 3, p. 127, and Niida Noboru (*Chūgoku hōseishi*, p. 23) both regarded the gentry as "the illegitimate offspring of bureaucratism (bureaucratic rule)."

⁷¹ *Lu Wending gongji*, 8: 27b.

⁷² Yuan Liaofan, who played a big role in popular religion and the diffusion of the so-called didactic books from the late Ming, was also one type of gentry and his family had been *li* captains (*lizhang hu*) in the early Ming. Okazaki Hiroshi, "Mindai ni okeru jinushi no shisō no ichi kōsatsu." [Okuzaki has recently made a full-scale study of Yuan Liaofan. Cf. Okuzaki Hiroshi, *Chūgoku kyōshin jinushi no kenkyū.*—Trans.]

⁷³ Furushima Kazuo, "Minmatsu Chōkō deruta ni okeru jinushi keiei."

⁷⁴ Shigeta Atsushi, "Shinchō nōmin shihai no rekishiteki tokushitsu."

⁷⁵ For the relationship between the *lijia* system, state power and the landlord system see Tsurumi Naohiro, "Mindai ni okeru kyōson shihai" [translated in this volume].

⁷⁶ For the regulations concerning exemption and the exact amount granted see, Sakai Tadao, *Chūgoku zensho*, pp. 199–207, and Yamane Yukio, *Mindai yōeki seido no tenkai*, p. 121.

⁷⁷ *Rizhi lu*, 10:15b.

⁷⁸ *Lin Ciyai xiansheng wenji*, 2:8a.

⁷⁹ *Siyouzhai congshuo*, 34:11a.

⁸⁰ Chu Fangqing, "Huangtian yi" [Proposal on deserted land], in *Huangchao jingshi wenbian*, 34: 16b.

⁸¹ Zhang Lixiang, *Yang Yuan xiansheng quanji*, 32:7a, p. 563.

⁸² Pang Shangpeng, *Baike ting zhaigao*, 1:62a.

⁸³ In the first half of the Ming rich people commended their land (*guiji*) to dukes and marquises, meritorious ministers and powerful people (*shiyao*), but after the mid-Ming the gentry assumed the role of accepting land in commendation (*guiji*). (Sakai, *Chūgoku zensho*).

⁸⁴ This naturally means that subordinate relations grew up between the gentry and ordinary landlords, and that these relations embodied secondary contradictions.

⁸⁵ Katayama Seijirō, "*Mindai kaijō.*"

⁸⁶ *Xijinzhi xiaolu*, 1:11b.

⁸⁷ *Fushe jilue*, 2:9b.

⁸⁸ Kitamura Hironao, "Minmatsu Shinsho ni okeru jinushi"; Furushima Kazuo, "Minmatsu Chōkō deruta"; Oyama Masaaki, "Minmatsu Shinsho no dai tochi shoyū."

⁸⁹ The anti-rent activities of tenants are interpreted together with these changes, though a different significance is attached to them.

⁹⁰ *Lin Ciyai xiansheng wenji*, 14:33a.

⁹¹ *Yang Yuan xiansheng quanji*, 50: 19b (p. 899).

⁹² *Lin Ciyai xiansheng wenji*, 8: 19b–20a (p. 176).

⁹³ Ibid., 32:25a (p. 572).

⁹⁴ Ibid., 5:12a (p. 116).

⁹⁵ Ibid., 8:18b (p. 175).

[96] Ibid., 8:19b (p. 176).
[97] Such changes in landlord-tenant relations are noted by Xu Jie in his *Shijingtang ji*, 22:22a.
[98] 1760 *Wuqing zhenzhi*, 2, *Nongsang*, 4a.
[99] Held by the Niida Bunko in the library of the Tōyō Bunka Kenkyūjo.
[100] See Imahori Seiji, "Shindai no kōso ni tsuite"; and Mori Masao, "Min-Shin jidai no tochi seido."
[101] *Wufeng lu*, 5a.
[102] *Siyouzhai congshuo*, 34:4ab.
[103] *Wufeng lu*, 34:5a–b.
[104] See Shigeta Atsushi, "Shinsho ni okeru Konan kome shijō no ichi kōsatsu." Furthermore, in the *Xijinzhi xiaolu*, 10:27b–28a, there is an episode about gentry who were rebuked by the district magistrate for praying for rain not to fall during a drought when rice prices were high. The masses subsequently pillaged rice from several of their granaries with the approval of the enraged magistrate.
[105] Rent bursaries (*zuzhan*) were organizations run by specific gentry who received commissions from other landlords collectively to collect taxes and feudal rent, and control tenants for them, as well as doing the same on their own land. Muramatsu Yūji has unearthed many documents concerning such bursaries in Jiangnan during the late Qing. These bursaries were a social institution that grew up in response to this type of demand (Muramatsu Yūji, *Kindai Kōnan no sosan*).
[106] Oyama Masaaki, "Fueki seido no henkaku."
[107] Though there were precedents for the combined land and poll tax in the Ming, it was not instituted until the Yongzheng reign period in the early eighteenth century. See Hamashima Atsutoshi, "Minmatsu Sekkō no KaKo ryōfu ni okeru kinden kin'eki hō."
[108] Shigeta Atsushi, "Shinchō nōmin shihai no rekishiteki tokushitsu."
[109] *Shizheng lu*, 1:15a–b.
[110] *Piyu zaji*, 2:19b–20b.
[111] *Lu Wending gongji*, 6:37a.
[112] Cf. Mori Masao, "Min-Shin jidai no tochi seido."
[113] Kitamura Hironao, "Minmatsu Shinsho ni okeru jinushi ni tsuite"; Furushima Kazuo, "Minmatsu Chōkō deruta"; and Oyama Masaaki, "Minmatsu Shinsho no dai tochi shoyū."
[114] *Rizhi lu*, 13:29a.
[115] *Xijinzhi xiaolu*, 10:2a.
[116] *Siyouzhai congshuo*, 13:11b–12a.
[117] Cf. Tanaka Masatoshi, "Minpen, kōso, nuhen."
[118] *Xijinzhi xiaolu*, 10:10a.
[119] Refer to quote from *Yang Yuan xiansheng quanji* in note 91. Saeki Yūichi, "Minmatsu no Tō-shi."
[120] *Yanzhou shiliao*, 35:36a–b.
[121] *Lu Wending gongji*, 23:13a–b.
[122] Saeki, "Minmatsu no Tō-shi."
[123] *Xijinzhi xiaolu*, 6:28a–b.
[124] *Yueshi bian*, 4:7a.
[125] Though Chinese state power is generally reputed for its strength, there were limits to the extent to which it exercised its power. In reality it invested various groups with autonomous powers of penal authority and allowed them to open their own courts. See Niida Noboru, "Chūgoku kyūshakai no kōzō to keibatsuken." But this should be distinguished from the authority which supplemented dynastic power.
[126] Katayama Seijirō, "Mindai kaijō."
[127] *Siyouzhai congshuo*, 16:16b.
[128] A summary of the original which is quoted in the *Deyi lu*, 15:2:1a–b. The passage from Wang Huizu's *Xuezhi yishuo*, 1: 13b–14a, translated at the beginning of this article presents a similar view of the gentry from the standpoint of a local official.

[129] *Xijinzhi xiaolu*, 4:11a–b.
[130] *Lu Wending gongji*, 13:45b.
[131] Ibid., 13:45b–46a.
[132] Quoted in *Tianxia junguo libing shu*, 8:58a. Yao Ruxun explained the reason for this in the following fashion: "Before the Single Whip reform was implemented there were problems surrounding labor service (*lichai*). Labor services were always destroying people's households, and people all regarded landowning as a great burden. As a consequence, wealthy households were unwilling to buy land, and the abandonment of land ensued. The people deserted, taxes were in arrears, and there was much corruption at the county level. . . . Once the Single Whip system was instituted and profits began to be made from land cultivation, wealthy households in the cities started to buy land, and poor families in the villages were not willing to give up their land easily. The fact that there is no abandoned land, no deserting people, and no defaulting in tax payments is all due to wealthy households buying land. . . .

"Often poor people neither have oxen power, dung, or grass to cultivate their fields, nor do they possess the ability to dredge their ponds deeply or the capability of building solid dykes and levees. When they are struck by flood or drought, [there is nothing they can do], only leave it up to heaven. Now, wealthy households strive to prepare [for such disasters] beforehand. Therefore as long as there are no big droughts or floods, everyone can obtain a [sufficient harvest]. Needless to say, wealthy households are not able to cultivate themselves, and land cultivation has to be undertaken together with poor people. Even though poor people discard their property, in reality their interests are in common with those of the wealthy. . . . Poor people only have to provide the labor for cultivation, and they can easily enjoy the fruits of their efforts. This is the reason why I say all households that own land outside their place of registration are wealthy ones and the poor depend upon them and cannot do without them." (Quoted in *Tianxia junguo libing shu* 8:58a–b.)
[133] *Shizheng lu*, 2:6b. The following passage from the 1673 *Xiaogan xianzhi*, 5:3a (held by the Naikaku Bunko), indicates that even at the beginning of the Qing dynasty it was normal to regard self-cultivation as the norm and the use of bondservants and hired labor as extravagant: "There are landed peasants and landless peasants. Landless peasants do not all engage in agriculture themselves. Current customs are gradually becoming wasteful; normally they feel it beneath them to cultivate themselves, so they either assign bondservants to work or hire labor."
[134] *Siyouzhai congshuo*, 13:7b.
[135] Ibid., 13:7a.
[136] These were selected from a list provided in (*Santai*) *Wanyong zhengzong*, 8:5a, lower half of page. This list is also quoted in Sakai, *Chūgoku zensho*, p. 121.
[137] *Xijinzhi xiaolu*, 9:23b.
[138] *Siyouzhai congshuo*, 35:1b.
[139] *Xijinzhi xiaolu*, 1:13b–14a.
[140] Proxy remittance (*baolan*) become especially marked as the tax-collecting function of the *lijia* system deteriorated and repeatedly presented problems, even during the Qing dynasty. Proxy remittance is generally regarded as the concrete form of gentry domination over independent petty peasant proprietors. Muramatsu Yūji, however, regards this tax-collection commission agency work as an important item in the management of bursaries by influential gentry (*Kindai Kōnan no sosan*, pp. 681–747). According to Muramatsu, proxy remittance can also be understood as a means for the gentry to rank landlords.
[141] Lin Xiyuan evaluates the common gentry in the following fashion without touching upon his own conduct at all: "Scholars in this degenerate age have lost all sense of morality. They certainly have their own way; in their local areas they plunder villages, and when in office they devour living people. They are most aggressive and violent, relying upon their fame and force which ranges from being intimate with those inside and out [of government] to controlling followers in the villages. Even when their title and position is gone, they still use force to mix

with officials and practice aggression and violence as before" (*Lin Ciyai xiansheng wenji*, 10: 47b–48a).

[142] Cf. Shigeta Atsushi, "Shinchō nōmin shihai no rekishiteki tokushitsu," p. 113.

[143] *Da Qing lü jijie fuli*, 20:18b.

[144] *Xijinzhi xiaolu*, 10:9b.

[145] Ibid., 1:15a.

[146] The prohibition against government students and elders participating in petitions and litigation could be cited as a more concrete reason for the decline in yamen toughs.

[147] The agricultural administrators (*zhinongguan*) at the subprefecture and county level, who were set up by Ming Taizu and had a history that went back to the great agricultural administrator (*dasinong*) of the Han dynasty, were abolished during the Jiajing period (1522–66) on the grounds that they were "superfluous staff," and the Department for the Promotion of Agriculture (*quannongting*) was turned into the Silk Manufacturing Agency (*zhizaoguan*) (*Yehuo bian*, 12:20a–21a; *Siyouzhai congshuo*, 14:12b).

[148] The *Jizhuang yi*, quoted in note 136, stresses the fact that landlords provided the conditions necessary for reproduction as a factor supporting the legitimacy of their existence. Also, in the *Hunan shengli cheng'an*, which attaches relative importance to the state's function of promoting agriculture and provides many examples of dyke building and opening up of fields for cultivation by gentry and landlords, a local official comments that in his home area, Jiangnan, it is conducted without "supervision and pressure from local officials" (*gonglu*, 2:4a–5b). The *Da Qinglüli anyu*, 81:103b, records: "Rivers, streams, marshes, and ditches were originally the common irrigational property of the people. However, *powerful households are coercive and evil; they forcibly build ditches and dykes claiming the waterways as their own property*, or choose to build ponds on public official lands, etc." This indicates that such a process of obtaining the conditions necessary for production was inseparable from peasant rule.

[149] Hamashima Atsutoshi, "Mindai Kōnan no suiri no ichi kōsatsu."

[150] Rinji Taiwan kyūkan chōsakai, ed., *Shinkoku gyōseihō*, vol. 2, p. 280.

[151] The argument Mori Masao presents in his article "Jūroku-jūhachi seiki ni okeru kōsei to jinushi denko kankei" seems to be founded upon the key point that there was a change from the "argument for landlords to provide relief to tenants," which advocates that landlords should provide tenants with relief upon an individual basis, to making the state responsible for such relief. He observed in the concluding section that the Qing state, unlike the Ming, abandoned direct intervention in landlord-tenant relations and firmly guaranteed the landlord's right to collect rent. He further pointed out that the state tried to provide relief for tenants "in place of landlords." I understand Mori to mean that the role of relief work, which should have guaranteed reproduction for the tenant stratum (the direct producers), reverted once again to the state, which was a landlord regime, after the function of agricultural promotion changed in the Qing.

[152] *Yueshi bian*, 6:2b–3a.

[153] *Jiangsu Shanyang shouzu quanan*, Preface, 10a–b.

[154] Accordingly, this indicates that the bureaucratic standpoint and the class interests of gentry (landlords) were in agreement.

FOREIGN TRADE FINANCE IN CHINA, 1810-50

HAMASHITA TAKESHI

The youngest of all the authors translated in this volume, Hamashita Takeshi has been instrumental in opening a new field of inquiry in modern Chinese historical research in Japan, the relationship between world capitalism and China. Wide reading of works on economic history and theory has forced him to come to grips with China's external relations in the broader context of a Europe–America–Asia trade relationship which was developing within the world market created by capitalism. His work stresses the role of the Asia-wide economy within the world market and attempts to understand China's external relations within that Asian economic framework.

In the article translated here, Hamashita shows how the sale of English manufactures in China between 1820 and 1850 created a new trade structure based upon British industrial capital. British merchants in China found that the only way to dispose of surplus cotton goods was to barter them for Chinese produce. This soon gave rise to a barter trade in which tea was exchanged for cotton goods and silk for opium. The special feature of this barter trade was that it was accompanied by both credit sale and speculation, two features not usually associated with simple barter. Barter trade had two effects. First, it expanded the market for British industry in China. Second, it paved the way for the advance of British capital into China, giving foreign banks an opportunity to establish themselves there to provide both Chinese and foreign merchants with funds for the barter trade. Hamashita concludes that these two effects indicate: one, that the Chinese market had been incorporated into a new triangular structure of trade between England, America, and China, pivoted upon the British

This essay was originally published as "Kindai Chūgoku ni okeru bōeki kin'yū no ichi kōsatsu—jūkyū seiki zenpan no ginka tōki to gaikoku bōeki kōzō no henka" [近代中國における貿易金融の一考察——一九世紀前半の銀價騰貴と外國貿易構造の變化] in *Tōyō gakuhō*, 57: 3/4 (1976), pp. 116–77. Translation by Takechi Manabu.

cotton industry; and two, that the Chinese financial market had
been drawn into an international financial system centered on the
London financial market and united with the triangular trade.
One characteristic feature of Hamashita's work is his insistence
on the importance of understanding the position of Asia within
the structure of world capitalism. This is all the more significant
because of the tendency in the reappraisals of imperialism beginning with S. B. Saul, J. Gallagher, R. Robinson, and E. C. M.
Platt, and also evident in Japan in Mōri Kenzō's book, *Jiyū bōeki
teikoku shugi* [The imperialism of free trade] (1978) to treat Asia
in a negative way. Hamashita is very critical of such negative descriptions of Asia. In this respect his commitment to explaining the
role Asia and China played in the development of world capitalism represents an attempt to fill in the lacunae of previous research.

Most of Hamashita's subsequent work has been on foreign banks
in nineteenth-century China. His choice of finance as a subject
of inquiry was by no means accidental. His graduation thesis was
on the establishment of a Shanghai cotton spinning mill, but he
soon gave up the study of the cotton industry because he saw the
conceptual limitations of trying to explain the whole economic
structure through a single commodity or a single element of capital. He chose finance because he regards it and not modern
industry as a key to understanding the economic development of
both modern Asia and modern China. In finance he sees a method
of discovering the historical principles of economic development
in nineteenth- and early-twentieth-century China. This methodology is in effect a critique of previous research on modern
Chinese economic history which has primarily been concerned
with industrialization. Hamashita hopes to use finance to develop
a new conceptual picture of modern Chinese economic history.
His interests, however, are not merely limited to China's external
relations. He also plans to study Chinese financial and trading
institutions, such as native banks, guilds, and the Chinese inland
market. His primary concern will be to show how external economic factors interacted with internal Chinese economic institutions, and how such contact influenced the development of world
capitalism.

Hamashita Takeshi is now associate professor at the Institute
of Oriental Culture at University of Tokyo

*   *   *

Silver was China's chief means of settling accounts in both the domestic economy and foreign trade from the late 1830s to the First World War.[1] Since there were no institutional controls over the exchange rate of silver until the monetary reform of 1935, the price of circulated silver coin or bullion was determined, in principle, by the value of its components. As a result, the Chinese monetary market was directly influenced by fluctuations in the price of silver on the world market. Thus when the capitalist countries—which were themselves supported by the circulation of silver in the international market—set out to "open" and control the Chinese market, the status of Chinese silver was a chief factor making it both easy and strategically important for them to advance into the areas of money and banking.

With this data as introduction, let us turn to the pattern of influx and outflow of silver up to the end of the nineteenth century; for analytical purposes, we can divide this time span into four periods:[2]

1) From the end of the sixteenth century until the 1830s: during this long period silver flowed into China, first from Spain and Portugal, and then predominantly from Holland and Britain. This silver inflow was in exchange for silk and tea.

2) 1830s and 1840s: the direction was reversed during these two decades and silver flowed out of China and other parts of Asia. This change was brought on partly by the increase in industrial exports from Britain to India after the British East India Company lost its monopoly of Britain's India trade, and partly by a much larger volume of Indian opium making its way into China.

3) 1850s and 1860s: around 1850, silver began to pour into China again, and until the end of the 1860s, the Western powers kept up a steady, all-out advance into China's monetary market. It was during this period that foreign banks, chiefly British, laid the foundation for later activities in China.

4) From the early 1870s until the end of the nineteenth century: as more European economies adopted the gold standard, the influx of silver into Asia increased, stimulating the powers to compete for monetary control in the region.[3]

Although silver was its chief currency, China had to acquire the metal from outside; this fact had serious repercussions during the second period, when large quantities of silver left China. During the 1830s and 1840s, a shortage of the metal as a means of settling accounts caused the value of silver to rise in China's external trade. Internally, the value of the qian (cash coin) was forced down while the value of silver, which was growing increasingly scarce as a medium of exchange, rose rapidly. The Qing government did not exert direct control over the circulation

of silver, though it collected taxes and conducted financial affairs mainly in silver. The inherent contradiction in this system surfaced during
those two decades and was further exacerbated by the debasement of
standard cash (*zhiqian*) and by a sharp increase in privately minted
coins which lowered the value of cash coin.[4]

The high price of silver from the 1830s to the end of the 1840s was
closely related to China's foreign trade. The focus of this discussion is
the relationship between external trade and silver, particularly during
the late 1840s. An examination of those years clearly shows that the flow
of silver out of China was not just a consequence of structural change
in China's foreign trade at that time. Equally important was the role it
played in paving the way for new and portentous developments in the
activities of the Western powers in China, particularly in trade finance
and banking. This new type of activity shaped the manner in which
foreign powers advanced into—and gained increasing influence over—
China's economy and the directions of subsequent changes in China's
domestic monetary market.

Rising silver prices and silver outflow

During the first half of the nineteenth century, the Chinese debated
the cause of the sharp rise in the value of silver and the outflow of the
metal. Opinion was divided roughly between two positions. One side
held that cash payments in silver for opium had caused a large drain
of silver from China leading to a shortage, with the result that silver
rose sharply in value. The other side argued that when low-quality
foreign silver coins were exchanged for the high-quality Chinese *sycee*
(minted in the shape of a horse's hoof and 94–98 percent pure), the
principle of currency value by weight was ignored, and the foreign coins
were valued over parity with the *sycee*. Thus, speculation drew large
volumes of *sycee* out of China which gave rise to a shortage, pushing up
the price of silver in China.

Let us first examine the former opinion. In the fourth intercalary
lunar month 1838, Huang Juezi, director of the court of state, wrote:

In recent years the value of silver has been steadily rising. One tael
of silver is now worth more than 1,600 standard cash. The silver is
not used within the country but flows overseas. When opium started
coming into China, the Jiaqing Emperor (r. 1796–1820) clearly saw
how harmful the drug was. He urgently warned against its use and

issued prohibition laws. At that time, however, no government official had any idea of how much harm the drug would actually cause. If they had foreseen its devastating effect earlier, they would certainly have imposed severe laws and punishments and would have checked the coming disaster. As a rule, all foreign ships arriving at Canton were required to provide a foreign merchant's written guarantee that they carried no opium. Only then were they allowed to enter port. However, disregarding this regulation, they continued to bring opium into China. Between 1823 and 1831, a total of seventeen million taels of silver left China annually; from 1831 to 1834 twenty-odd million taels flowed out each year, and from 1834 to the present, the amount of silver going abroad has increased so much that China sometimes loses thirty million taels in one year. Besides Canton, tens of millions of taels have also been taken out of China from ports in Fujian, Jiangsu, Zhejiang, Shandong, and from Tianjin.[5]

Huang thus took the position that the silver shortage and the high price of silver were brought about by the transfer of large amounts of silver to foreign traders for opium imports, such opium trade continuing despite efforts by the Qing dynasty to ban and control it. He seemed to assume that the amounts paid out for opium were equivalent to the volume of silver being taken out of China. If we calculate figures taken from Chinese sources, presented in Table 1, the total amount of silver which left China from the 1820s to the 1840s would be about 480 million taels. It seems that Huang and others were too ready to assume that the outflow of silver could be calculated in direct relation to opium imports. Consequently their figures are ten times those given by Indian sources (see Table 3). According to another contemporary source, the amount of silver circulating in China during the Daoguang era (1821–50) was approximately 360 million taels[6] or $500 million. If we compare this with the figure given by Huang and others, 130 percent of the silver in circulation was taken out of China! Even in the mid-Xianfeng era (1851–61), when silver was flowing back into China, the amount of silver circulated annually was 1,200 million taels,[7] or about $1,670 million. What Huang Juezi overlooked was how far the outflow of silver was balanced by silver coming in from exports of tea and raw silk. In other words, we must consider the special character of China's overall trade structure, not simply the influx and outflow of silver used for the settlement of transactions, which are only a product of the trade structure.[8]

The relationship between Chinese trade and specie as a means of settling accounts appears in the rough trade estimates published in an

Table 1. Silver drain from China, 1823–51 (Estimates by Taiping Shanren)

Year	Volume of outflow	Documented by	Source
1823	Several million taels	Huang Juezi	a) *Xianping shuwu chuji nianji, juan 3* b) *Chouban yiwu shimo: Daoguang chao* Note: Estimates given by Huang Juezi below are from one of the two sources, a) or b).
1824–28	17–18 million taels	Huang Juezi	
1829	17–18 million taels Several million taels	Huang Juezi Zhang Yuan	*Donghua lu*
1830	17–18 million taels	Huang Juezi	
1831	20-odd million taels	Huang Juezi	
1832	20-odd million taels Several million taels	Huang Juezi Sun Lanzhi	*Lin Wenzhong gong zhengshu*
1833	20-odd million taels	Huang Juezi	
1834	20-odd million taels 20-odd million taels	Huang Juezi Liang Tingnan	*Yi fen jiwen*
1835	20-odd million taels	Huang Juezi	
1836	20-odd million taels 20-odd million taels Over million taels	Huang Juezi Yuan Yulin Xu Naizhi	*Chouban yiwu shimo* *Chouban yiwu shimo*
1837	30 million taels from Canton; at least 10 million taels each from Fujian, Zhejiang and Jiangsu; and 20 million taels from Tianjin 22 million yuan exported to England; 9.6 million yuan to America	Zhu Zenglie Wei Yuan	*Huangchao xu wenxian tongkao* *Haiguo tuzhi*
1838	30 million taels from Canton; a total of several tens of million taels from Fujian, Zhejiang, Shandong and Tianjin	Huang Juezi	
1841	40–50 million taels	Bao Shichen	*Qimin sishu*

Continued on next page

Table 1—*Continued*

Year	Volume of outflow	Documented by	Source
1846	Approx. ten million	Xu Mei	*Chaobi tonglun*
1851	Approx. ten million	Feng Guifen	*Xianzhi fang gao*

Source: Taiping Shanren, "Daoguang chao yinhuang wenti," p. 64.

1847 report written by Sir Rutherford Alcock, the British consul in Shanghai. In the report he stated: "The bulk of Chinese trade, so far as it affects the adjustment of foreign accounts, has been correctly described to consist in transactions with England, British India, and the United States. But the result is very different as regards each of these countries, and the inference to be drawn from this difference is important."[9] Table 2 shows China's balance of trade as estimated by Alcock. He subtracted the favorable margin of China's trade with the United States and Britain from the unfavorable margin in its trade with India, which left China a $10-million (7.2 million taels or £2.4 million) deficit. Alcock concluded that the excess of imports over exports was equiva-

Table 2. China's balance of trade in 1847 (Alcock's estimates) (dollars)

England, with her Exports to China	10,000,000
and her Imports thence of	20,000,000
Leaves a balance of trade in favour of the Chinese of	10,000,000
The United States in like manner exports into China	3,000,000
And imports thence to the amount of	9,000,000
Leaving a balance in favour of China of	6,000,000
British India exports into China in Opium	23,000,000
In Raw Cotton	5,000,000
	28,000,000
And imports from China raw Silk and other products	2,000,000
Leaving a balance of trade against China upon the Indian trade of no less a sum than	26,000,000
Which the balance in its favour from England of	10,000,000
And from United States only partially covering	6,000,000
	16,000,000
Leaving a final annual balance of trade against China of to be paid in specie.	10,000,000

Source: BPP., *Returns of the Trade of the Various Ports of China, for the Years 1847 and 1848*, pp. 72–73.

lent to the amount of silver taken out of China.[10] According to the Alcock report, Chinese commercial transactions were settled as a rule among two or more nations, and it was an ultimate consequence of the multilateral pattern of settlement that so much silver made its way from China to India at that time. The silver that left China was not, therefore, all paid out in exchange for opium. The amount of outgoing silver represented the final margin of deficit in China's overall trade, in which silver both entered and left China in separate transactions with two or more nations. But, according to an 1845 report on the Canton trade, instead of the *sycee*, which had long been China's medium of payment to India, the chopped dollar circulating in the Canton market came into use because *sycee* now carried a premium of 7–9 percent.[11] Table 3 shows the movement of various forms of silver between India and China. Looking at the amount of silver taken out of China, we see first that it showed a sudden, rapid rise in 1833 and 1834 when the East India Company's monopoly on the China trade ended. The outflow reached a peak in 1838 and 1839. After the outbreak of the Opium War, it began rising again, to reach another peak in 1844 and 1845. The bulk of silver remitted to India from China was in *sycee*, but the proportion of dollar coins gradually increased also. The rise in the outflow of *sycee* after the Opium War ended was a result of the designation of *sycee* as the medium for reparation payments.[12]

According to Alcock's calculations, China's excess of imports over exports in 1847 came to about 2.4 million pounds. However, the British consul at Canton estimated the amount of silver transported to India that year at 2 million pounds.[13] Moreover, according to F.W. Prideaux, who worked for a British trading firm, China's silver payments had been increasing over the previous two years because of reparations from the Opium War,[14] and so presumably the 2 million pounds noted by the consul in Canton included reparations. Thus we must account for the gap that emerges between the amount of silver that actually left China, and the value of the import surplus in China's trade. Two factors must be considered in seeking an answer. One is an inflow of silver into China in the form of bullion, which the United States used in trade settlements with China and which helped keep the net volume of outgoing silver low. The other was that, if we go by the testimony of Samuel Gregson, vice-chairman of the East India and China Association of England and entrepreneur in tea and other commodities from China, most remittances from China to India were conducted in drafts.[15]

The former can be disregarded because, as Table 4 shows, the amount of silver going from the United States into China was low; in 1847 it came to only 33,000 dollars (8,250 pounds[16]), far from adequate to compensate for the gap. Payments in drafts, therefore, emerge as a key point in examining the issue of trade with China. Before going into that, however, let us review the second opinion mentioned earlier, the argument that speculation caused the rise in the price of silver.

Speculation could occur in various ways. For example, *sycee* was estimated by a mint in Calcutta to be 15 percent more valuable in content than the foreign-made silver coin of the same weight, but its circulating value in Canton in 1815 was only 7 percent higher than the foreign coins. This led private trading merchants to focus on the *sycee* as a profitable medium of remittance to India.[17] Or, again, when the value of silver in Canton began to decline as the supply increased during the Opium War, a huge amount of *sycee*, to be exact, six million dollars worth, was sent from Canton to England on the account of the British government.[18] One more example: the British Bell & Company purchased, outside of China, Carlos dollars priced on parity with several other silver coins of the same purity and sold them in Canton at a premium of 14 to 15 percent. The same company also bought Mexican and South American dollars in Canton at a reduction of 6 to 7 percent, and the subsequent transactions reaped them as much as 20 percent profit from speculation on silver.[19]

However, silver shortage as the result of speculation tended to be eased by subsequent developments. When many merchants sought *sycee* at the same time, the premium on silver was high enough to make it unprofitable to ship it out of China. When silver was in short supply and became expensive in Canton, Shanghai silver flowed in.[20] Furthermore, when the premium on *sycee* grew too high, it became a common practice in Canton to melt down dollar coins and remint the silver into *sycee*.[21] It is therefore incorrect to assert that speculation caused a one-way outflow of silver from China. Incidentally, the question of silver speculation per se must be examined in light of fluctuations in the market price of silver because the metal figured so prominently in trade settlements. Without going into that question here, let me simply stress that silver shortages caused by speculation had a tendency to level off. Let us go on to the question of remittance in drafts.

Drafts in multilateral trade settlements

Remittance by draft was a means of settlement that required no actual transfer of silver. Sir John Bowring, who in 1849 was appointed British consul at Canton and superintendent of trade in China, offers some

Table 3. India's import and export of gold and silver vis-à-vis China (unit: 1,000 rupees or taels)

Year	A Import Bengal Gold (rupee)	Silver (rupee) sycee, bar silver	dollar coin	rupee coin	total	Bengal Total (rupee)	Madras Total (rupee)	Bombay Total (rupee)	Total of import (rupee)	Total of import (tael) 1 rupee = 0.326 taels	B Export Total of export (rupee)	B Export (tael)	C Excess of import over export (A–B) (tael)
1832–33	56	2,213	91	0	2,304	2,360	6	3,538	5,904	1,925	34	11	1,914
1833–34	67	3,836	100	7	3,943	4,010	–	9,078	13,088	4,267	47	15	4,252
1834–35	280	2,899	330	0	3,229	3,509	7	8,559	12,076	3,937	12	4	3,933
1835–36	17	3,208	210	79	3,497	3,514	21	9,567	13,103	4,272	46	15	4,257
1836–37	9	2,141	181	0	2,322	2,331	–	10,074	12,406	4,044	58	19	4,025
1837–38	93	2,411	2,994	9	5,414	5,507	4	11,850	17,361	5,660			5,660
1838–39	36	3,543	4,120	51	7,714	7,750	–	13,622	21,372	6,967	54	18	6,949
1839–40	8	403	1,718	2	2,123	2,131	0.3	2,845	4,975	1,622	1,140	372	1,250
1840–41	21	1,695	2,157	6	3,858	3,879	4	5,373	9,256	3,017	124	40	2,977
1841–42	71	10,078	1,476	83	11,637	11,708	–	5,672	17,380	5,666	2,005	654	5,012
1842–43	18	3,770	2,091	654	6,515	6,533	6	15,105	21,644	7,056	1	0.3	7,056
1843–44	137	7,568	2,092	879	10,539	10,676	201	28,623	39,501	12,877	1,022	333	12,544
1844–45							18	17,504	27,364	8,921	1,013	330	8,591
1845–46													(6,000)

Year	Total of import gold (tael)	Total of import silver (tael)	Export gold (tael)	Export silver (tael)	Excess (tael)
1846–47	1,308	4,350	–	–	5,708
1847–48	1,548	1,560	–	96	3,012
1848–49	2,802	6,522	–	–	9,324
1849–50	1,902	5,076	–	180	6,798
1850–51	2,085	3,450	–	3	5,532

1851–52	2,079	4,824	–	9	6,894
1852–53	1,704	5,586	30	63	7,197
1853–54	774	1,182	6	1,005	945

Sources: 1) A: BPP., *East India and China*, A Return "of the Value of Bullion Imported into each of the Indian Presidencies from China, in the Year 1830 to 1845, respectively, distinguishing, if practicable, the Value in Spanish Dollars from other Bullion" 1846.

BPP., *Returns of the Trade*, 1846, Canton, p. 36

BPP., *Report from the Select Committee*, 1847, p. 353.

2) B: BPP., *East India and China*, A Return "of the Value of Bullion Exported from the Indian Presidencies to China, in the Years 1830 to 1845, respectively."

BPP., *Report from the Select Committee*, 1847, p. 353.

3) Figures from 1847 onward are from Thomas Tooke, *A History of Prices, and of the State of the Circulation during the Nine Years 1848–56*, vol. VI, appendix XXIII, table M.

Notes: The figure in parentheses is an approximate figure.

Calculated on the basis of one rupee against 0.326 taels and one pound against 3 taels.

During the Opium War, 6 million dollars (4.32 million taels) were sent to England (BPP., *Select Committee Report*, 1847, p. 341).

interesting information on the currency and exchange of China at that time. He cites the observations of an "experienced and intelligent" banker regarding the effects of the 1849 discovery of California gold and the subsequent rise in the Chinese import of California gold on the bullion market in Canton and on the exchange rates in the world market. The banker was quoted by Bowring as saying:

The large balance [of trade] that is annually paid by England and America to China, is made to liquidate a great portion of the balance due by China to India, inasmuch as the most profitable modes for laying down funds in China for payment of the balance due by the first-named countries are:—

1st, The negotiation of bills of exchange on London, which are bought up for remittance to India.

2nd, The purchase of drafts from the East India Company in London, drawn upon the Bengal or Bombay Presidency, which are easily negotiated in China.

3rd, The remittance of money from England to India for the purchase of opium to be sold in China.

The rates of exchange at which the bills forming the first and second modes are obtainable in China, being generally more favourable than those afforded by remittances of bullion or specie to India, the bullion or specie received in exchange for opium is of course generally invested by the holders in such bills; and thus it is only to the extent of the general balance of the whole foreign trade that gold and silver are exported by China.[22]

The banker thus certified that bullion sent to India was destined only to settle the balance of total foreign trade, and that silver obtained from opium sales was reinvested in China for profit. "It has been seen," the banker concluded, "that nearly the whole foreign trade is settled through Great Britain; that India remains the creditor of China for a large amount; that gold or silver, to the extent of this creditor's claim must be exported; and gold or silver is of course preferred according to the respective prices of the day. It is evident that this export must be either to India or to some country whose debt can be transferred to India; and it is equally evident that Great Britain is the only other country with which China has commercial relations, whose debt can be so transferred."[23]

Those statements verify the assertion that China's trade was not always settled through silver (or gold) alone. Silver obtained from sale of Indian opium in China was invested in drafts, which were used as a means of remittance. At the same time, inherent in the problems of trade settlements was the question of investing in such a way as to preserve and reproduce trade activities. Drafts not only expanded the means of remittance but also functioned as an investment medium and thus could affect the entire trade. They were remitted through the agency of the East India Company between India and Britain and were supported by the entire international financial network centered on the money market in London.

This multilateral system of trade settlements in the exchange market in Canton was described as follows:

The principal places on which bills are negotiated in Canton, are London, Calcutta, and Bombay. The transactions with Manila, Singapore, Batavia, Sydney, &C., are so trifling, that it can hardly be said there is any course of exchange with these places. Neither is there any course of exchange with the continent of Europe or with the United States of America, although the exports to both these parts of the world are sufficiently large to lead one to presume the existence of a direct exchange.

The exports to Europe are settled by bills on London; and the rate of exchange for the few Government and private bills on continental towns that come into the market is fixed by an equation of the estimated rate in London, on those towns on the arrival of the bills there, with the rate on London ruling in Canton at date of negotiation.

The exports to America are settled by imports of American manufactures, and by bills on London drawn under credits from houses of high standing, who receive cover for such drafts from America, either by remittance of American bills on London, or by consignments of American produce.

In calculating exchanges, China receives the variable price; so many pence per dollar, or so many ruppees per hundred dollars.

Large transactions in bills drawn upon Canton are only to be found in Calcutta and Bombay, drawn against opium and cotton.[24]

This is a good description of the linkage among bilateral trade relations between England and the United States, the United States and China, China and India, India and England, and England and China, with the money market of London as the pivot in the whole network. No two countries had a complete and separate relation with London. U.S.–Chinese trade settlements were transferred into U.S.–British trade settlements—American merchants exported agricultural products (cotton and grains) to Britain in payment for the tea and other commodities that the United States imported from China—which provided a realistic basis for the United States to settle trade with China by remitting bills instead of specie.

It was in the latter half of the 1820s that American traders began to rely in principle on drafts drawn on the money market of London to settle transactions with China. Though its financial power had been waning since the beginning of the nineteenth century, the East India Company still monopolized Asian trade. These circumstances created a hospitable framework for a rise in the volume of opium brought into China by private traders. The demand for bills as a means of payment rose, and bills on London issued from the United States became more common. This means of remittance was used not only by American traders to settle transactions with China, but also by English traders in China.[25] U.S.–Chinese transactions settled in such a manner were facilitated by the decline of the East India Company in India. While the company had monopolized Patna opium, Malwa opium was handled by private merchants who gained sufficient leverage that the East India Company lost control of the economic cycle structured around a monopolistic supply of opium. Wider use of drafts drawn in America on London was encouraged further by the "boom" in American cotton exports to Britain in the 1830s.[26] Thus, in the 1830s, American ships bound for China used drafts on London, chiefly on Baring & Co., to settle more than half the goods they handled, including English manufactures.[27]

In reaction to the enormous sums that were represented in credit extended to Americans, in 1836 the Bank of England refused to accept drafts from America. In 1837, there was a financial panic, which hit hardest in Manchester's cotton industry and the London money market,[28] and the Chinese trade was suspended because of the Opium War. These events worked to sever credit relations between China and other countries, and the export of opium to China stopped from 1838 to 1842. As a result, trade between the United States and China plummeted.[29] Trade relations between the United States and China picked up again in 1845, after the five ports of Canton, Xiamen (Amoy), Fuzhou, Ningbo, and Shanghai were opened to foreign trade in accordance with the Treaty of Nanjing, as described in the following statement:

> They [the Americans] imported goods to a much larger amount than in the year preceding [1844]; and even had recourse to purchases of manufactures in the British markets, in preference to availing themselves of credits on London, in part payment of the teas exported

to the United States. Their shipping in the China waters was more numerous than in 1844, and had a fair share in the carriage of goods coastwise. They sent out their own vessels to Calcutta and Bombay for the opium they required in the China trade. They succeeded in getting the management of great part of the [European] continental business into their hands, which, independently of pecuniary abvantages, offers the facility of employing their own drafts on London, to some extent, in remittances for consignments received, in lieu of appearing with their bills in the market, which occasionally, and particularly at so critical a juncture as the present, is attended with some inconvenience.[30]

Here we see stated the fact that America brought British manufactures into China for the purchase of tea, and testimony that the United States, functioning as an exporting country by trading in tea on the European continent, made settlements with China through the money market of London, even when its drafts were not purchased in Chinese markets. American trade activities thus widened and were backed up by expanded, more flexible means of settlement. But the importation by America of English manufactures into China was not to be steadily profitable, as was evident in the Canton market in 1849:

As many drafts on American account being offered in October, the rate of exchange was 4s. 3d. [to the dollar] for that month; and the number of drawers increasing as the shipments to America gained more importance during the last two months of the year, the rate of exchange told proportionately against the drawer, and ultimately reached 4s. 6d. at the close of the year.

This rate is exclusively attributable to the great number of American drawers, who were obliged to procure funds for the payment of their rather considerable shipments of teas to America during this season. During the preceding season they imported a considerable quantity of British goods, employing them as the medium of placing their funds here; but as the prices of goods and yarns in the manufacturing districts of England advanced rapidly during the last six months of the year 1849, they were prevented from repeating the operation, and had recourse to their usual mode of procuring funds by drawing on England under credits granted them by English banking houses.[31]

Since importing British manufactures into China could no longer be a very profitable means of trade settlement, Americans began to use drafts in conjunction with cotton sales to Britain, a very "circuitous method" in the eyes of British traders.[32] This use of American drafts which produced new relationships in the wake of the Opium War developed as more British merchants who dominated the China trade, purchased drafts drawn by Americans. British industrial capitalists, working through the money market of London, concluded partial settlements on American cotton by purchasing drafts Americans had drawn to import Chinese tea. That was the origin of the trilateral trade relationship among Britain, the United States, and China.[33]

British traders at that time obtained the funds to purchase American drafts through opium sales, chiefly in Canton. T.A. Gibb of the Gibb, Livingstone Company, a British trading firm in China, described how British traders passed their surplus funds, including the proceeds of opium sales, to American merchants in order to buy American drafts on Baring & Co. and others.[34] They used the American drafts both as a means of remitting the proceeds of opium sales to Britain and as a medium for investment. The "triangular trade" among England, India, and China was connected, through opium, to the trilateral trade relationship among the United States, England, and China. These multilateral relationships were buttressed by the international finance and credit network whose center was the money market of London. For this reason the "Old China Hands," the long-term private British merchants, continued to coexist with the industrial capitalists in the home country.

The historical process which led to the use of American drafts was based on the formation of a commodity distribution system centered around the British cotton industry, in which America supplied the raw materials and Asia imported the products. Both were incorporated into a "linkage structure" revolving around the money market of London. This was the way in which international financial capitalists, who were influenced by the movements of the London money market, created conditions conducive to their advance into Asian markets, regardless of who was directly responsible for the financing of the China trade.

British trading firms in China controlled most of the financing of the China trade through their entrepreneurial activities there. More importantly, the international financial network was organized around London's money market, which was supported by the British cotton industry. On the one hand, British companies in China were compelled to accommodate themselves to the international financial network, and on the other, the organization of this network made it possible for British financial capitalists to advance into China. From here it takes little imagination to predict two later developments—the establishment of hegemony over the Chinese money market by world financial capitalists led by the British and the appearance of their banking houses in China, both of which did in fact occur from the 1860s on. American drafts were not only a convenient tool in trade; their growing use also had a decisive effect on the financial structure of the China trade and on the Chinese money market.

It might be instructive here to discuss briefly the role played by American China trade in determining the use of American drafts. The hallmark of the American China trade were the swift, sleek clippers that plied the seas with large shipments of cargo. The earliest clipper ship was the *Rainbow* (450 tons) built in New York in 1845. It shortened the length of the voyage across the Pacific from 175 to 80 days. The period between the early 1840s and early 1860s is called the "clipper age" in marine transport history, for clippers carried a great deal of the world's tea and opium during this period.[35] Tables 4 and 5 show some characteristics of American trade with China in those days. First of all, America carried a large unfavorable balance in the trade, but this was probably offset to some extent by silver with the rest covered by drafts.

Table 4. America's trade with China (unit: 1,000 dollars)

Year	Export Domestic goods	Export Foreign goods	Export Total	Import	Silver, silver coins Export	Silver, silver coins Import	Balance against the U.S.
1842			1,444	4,935			3,491
1843			2,419	4,386			1,967
1844			1,757	4,931			3,174
1845	2,079	197	2,276	7,286	159	27	4,878
1846	1,178	154	1,332	6,594	113		5,149
1847	1,709	124	1,833	5,583	33		3,717
1848	2,064	126	2,190	8,083	72		5,821
1849	1,461	122	1,583	5,514	10		3,921
1850	1,486	119	1,605	6,593	25		4,963
1851	2,156	329	2,485	7,065	147		4,433
1852	2,480	183	2,663	10,594	20		7,911
1853	3,213	524	3,737	10,574	489		6,348
1854	1,294	104	1,398	10,506	156	108	9,060
1855	1,533	186	1,719	11,049	675		8,655
1856	2,048	510	2,558	10,454	634	1	7,263

Source: BPP., *Select Committee Report*, 1847, p. 356. The U.S. Bureau of Statistics (Treasury Department), *Commerce of Asia and Oceania*, 1898. Re-cited from Qing Ruji, *Meiguo qin Hua shi*, vol. 1, pp. 93–94.

Table 5. Tonnage of foreign trading vessels entering
Canton (unit: 1,000 tons)

Year	England	America	Other	Total
1844	111	23	7	142
1845	86	39	12	137
1846	93	30	8	131
1847	89	28	9	126
1848	72	31	7	110
1849	93	37	12	142
1850	75	41	18	134
1851	104	49	24	177
1852	124	60	26	210
1853	85	48	27	160
1854	69	46	40	155
1855	71	65	44	180

Source: BPP., *Report by Mr. Parkes, British Consul at Canton, on the Trade of that Port during the year 1856*, p. 30.

The difference between America and Britain in total tonnage of ships entering Canton was small when we consider the much larger volume of transactions carried out by England (see Tables 9 and 10 for figures on the volume of trade between England and China). American trading activities, including shipping, in fact had become an important part of China's total foreign trade.[36] Clippers had indeed outpaced all contemporary ships, giving Americans a definite advantage. The active American China trade was given yet another boost by preferential tariffs established by the American government. These tariffs allowed American traders to buy Chinese teas at higher prices than English merchants, giving them a strong competitive leverage in the tea trade.[37] By bringing in raw cotton and yarns from home, America was able, also, to edge in on the India-China trade.[38] A protective foreign trade policy and high domestic agricultural and industrial production placed the United States in a position to change the structure of the entire China trade. And that position grew increasingly strong as American trading companies fought to gain an advantage in transactions with China by becoming agents for and joint-investors with Chinese merchants.[39]

These are some of the factors which make it clear that the silver shortages and subsequent high price of silver in China around the time of the Opium War were not only a problem of the volume of silver outflow over the years. Rather, the historical significance of the status of silver at that time lies in its relation to two new and influential developments: 1) a new structure of trade settlements had emerged in which actual outflow of silver represented only a residual margin in the total outflow-inflow balance; and 2) the use of drafts as a means of remittance incorporated the Chinese market into the London-centered world money market. Correlating these two factors, we must then ask what was the relationship between bullion (silver and gold) and drafts. The following passage dealing with the fluctuations in the gold prices in Canton in 1849 is enlightening on this point.

The price of gold in Canton is therefore determined:—lst. By the relative value of silver in Canton. 2nd. By the price of gold and silver in India and Great Britain. 3rd. By the course of exchange between China and India. 4th. By the course of exchange between China and London, and simultaneously between India and London. The price of gold, and these various causes of change have a necessary tendency towards mutual adjustment, and fluctuations in the price of gold rarely exceed those in the exchanges. They are also nearly simultaneous. It seldom happens that there is much difference between the estimated outturn of bullion and the course of exchange on India direct, and the export [of gold] therefore goes on gradually throughout the year, being greatest when bills are scarce and dear, and least when bills are plentiful and cheap. The export [of gold] in ordinary years is almost wholly to India; but when, from any cause, the rate of exchange between India and London falls to such an extent that China bills on London can be sold in India at a price that, whilst it gives a better return than bullion from Canton to India, permits of the bills being purchased in Canton at a lower rate than the bullion par between Canton and London, then the bullion is exported to London instead of to India; and bills of exchange drawn upon London in Canton against such bullion, and sold there for remittance to India, are so many deeds of tranfer, by which the claim of China on London is transferred to India in liquidation of the claims of India on China.[40]

This passage indicates that a final settlement was made between China and India, but payments did not always flow from China to India. Decisions on where they were sent and the means of remittance depended on the quoted bullion rate and the exchange rate in India, London, and Canton. If the rate of exchange in Canton was higher than the quoted bullion rate in that city, China sent bullion to India. If Canton drafts on London were cheaper than the bullion quotation, and if the exchange rate and quoted bullion rate in India were unfavorable, then China remitted bullion to London to pay its debts to India, and against such bullion bills of exchange were drawn upon London in Canton. In this way, the choice between bullion (specie) or draft as a means of remittance was decided according to fluctuations in their rates. The rates did not fluctuate independently on the basis of respective absolute volumes of circulation; rather, they influenced each other.

In the latter half of the 1840s, several new phenomena began to affect relations between bullion and draft. Tables 6 and 7 show fluctuations in draft and silver rates in Canton and fluctuations in draft rates in Shanghai. Extrapolating from the tables, the characteristics and causes of exchange rate fluctuations in Canton (and Shanghai) can be summarized in the following four points:

1) The drafts on London payable six months after sight were expensive between late December and March, declined between April and June, remained at a low level between July and September, and then rose again between October and December. Thus the fluctuations in the draft rate had a seasonal annual cycle which was divided into four

Table 6. Exchange rate and silver quotation in Canton

Year	Month	Six-month sight bill on London (per dollar)	Bill on Calcutta (per 100 Spanish dollars)	Sycee (premium)
1845	1– 3	4s. 4 d.–4s. 6 d.	223–226 rupees (Yearly average: 224 1/2 rupees)	3–5%
	4– 6	4s. 3 d.–4s. 4 d.		
	7– 9	4s. 2 d.–4s. 3 d.		5–6%
	10–12	4s. 4 1/2d.–4s. 5 1/2d.		
1846	1– 3	4s. 5 1/2d.–4s. 6 d.	212–218 rupees (Yearly average: 217 rupees)	7–9%
	4– 6	4s. 3 d.–4s. 3 1/2d.		
	7– 9	4s. 4 d.		
	10–12	4s. 4 d.–4s. 5 d.		
1847	1– 3	4s. 5 d.–4s. 5 1/2d.	212–217 rupees (Yearly average: 214 1/2 rupees)	8–10%
	4– 6	4s. 4 d.–4s. 4 1/2d.		
	7– 9	4s. 4 1/2d.–4s. 5 d.		
	10–12	4s. 4 d.–4s. 5 d.		
1848	1– 3	4s. 5 d.–4s. 6 d.	cheaper than the previous year	9–10%
	4– 6	4s. –4s. 0 1/4d.		
	7– 9	3s. 11 1/2d.–4s. 2 d.		
	10–12	4s. –4s. 2 1/2d.		7–8%
1849	1– 3	4s. 2 d.	212–216 rupees	7–8 1/2%
	4– 6	4s. –4s. 1 d.		
	7– 9	4s. 2 d.		8 1/2–9 1/2%
	10–12	4s. 3 d.–4s. 6 d.	219–225 rupees	4 1/2–8 1/2%

Source: BPP., *Returns of the Trade of the various Ports of China, 1846; 1847; 1848; 1849; 1850,* Canton.

Table 7. Exchange rate in Shanghai (Annual average per dollar)

1843–44	4s. 0d.	1849	4s. 6d.	1854	6s. 3d.
1845	4s. 0d.	1850	5s. 0d.	1855	6s. 5d.
1846	4s. 2d.	1851	5s. 0d.	1856	7s. 0d.
1847	4s. 2d.	1852	5s. 0d.		
1848	4s. 4d.	1853	6s. 6d.		

Source: BPP., *Report by Mr. Robertson, Her Majesty's Consul at Shanghai on the Trade of that Port during the year 1856*, p. 46.

periods of almost equal length. This cycle corresponded to the fluctuation in the demand for bills, which was influenced by tea shipments.

2) The yearly average rate of exchange had an upward tendency until 1847. (In Shanghai it was more conspicuous until the mid-1850s.)

3) The market price of the *sycee* was gradually given higher premium, mirroring the silver shortages. The drastic decline of the premium in late 1849 was caused by the inflow of Shanghai silver.[41]

4) Particularly important was the decline in the exchange rate in 1848 and its rise in late 1849. In the former case, the 1847 financial panic in England brought to the fore the negative effects of excessive trade in China which had been continuing for several years. The tea trade conducted on Chinese accounts tended to raise the exchange rate,[42] but the trade volume of tea and cotton products dropped when the economic crisis hit England. This caused a decline in the exchange rate in 1848. The rise in late 1849 was stimulated by a large volume of drafts offered by American merchants to export tea to the United States.[43]

The first two points make it clear that fluctuations in the rate of exchange and in bullion (silver) were affected by the status of trade at the time. They were not, however, merely a reflection of rise and fall in the volume of trade; the second two points demonstrate that silver shortage and excessive trade also caused fluctuations in the rate of exchange and the rate of bullion. Here a basic change emerges in the relationship between bullion and drafts. Turning first to the silver shortage, three factors were largely responsible for siphoning off much of China's silver. They were: the sharp increase in opium imports in the latter half of the 1830s; large transfers of silver from China to England and India during the Opium War; and the silver outflow to India in payment of reparations after the war (see Table 3). Abundant before the outbreak of the Opium War, there developed a shortage of silver even in Shanghai from 1845 on.[44] The decline in the net volume of silver was accelerated by a growing demand from foreign traders who, wanted more *sycee* to pay customs duties, as the volume of the products they brought into

China increased.[45] The shortage and rising price of silver affected remittances in the China trade. Alexander Matheson stated: "When silver is at a high price, as it is just now, it remains in China, and the opium merchants purchase bills on India and on England, which are remitted to India in return for opium; they give a better exchange than silver would give."[46] After a long tradition of settling accounts in silver, China was now faced with a virtually unrelieved deficit caused by increased opium imports and dwindling supplies of silver to pay for it. Perhaps it was inevitable that, as Matheson pointed out, even in the opium trade drafts eventually replaced silver. This was the case in spite of the fact that it was difficult to purchase tea by draft.

Oversupplies of goods also brought about a shift in the means of settlement to a system much like barter trade. The silver shortage and changes in the international trade structure were important factors in this shift, which means that the new "barter" form of settlement is crucial in analyzing the character and working of the Chinese trade market in the latter half of the 1840s.

We can identify a historical progression from settlement by silver cash to draft. That progression is a straightforward reflection of the incorporation of China into the world financial network. But when a form of barter trade or barter settlement emerged in the latter half of the 1840s, was this not historically retrogressive? Contemporary industrial capitalists in England and English merchants in China described the Chinese trade as barter. Generally, "barter trade" means a mutual exchange of goods taking place at a pre-money economy stage—a primitive form of exchange as economists see it. But the "barter" in the China trade of the latter 1840s seems to have been somewhat different. If trade settlement meant settling the total debt incurred between the two parties, then, irrespective of whether this ultimate balance is settled by draft or any other means, that portion of trade conducted before either side incurs a debt can be regarded as barter. In the case of China, exchanges of goods were settled by drafts. It would seem inconceivable, therefore, that the "barter trade" referred to in descriptions of the latter-nineteenth-century China trade meant barter pure and simple. There were probably some elements of primitive barter in the exchange of goods, but in an international economic system where the draft was an established means of settlement, this so-called barter must have had its own special features. Why did such a unique pattern of barter emerge in the China trade? An analysis of this question will yield a clear picture of the structure and features of the China trade at that time. The new structure evolving in the China trade drew the attention of the British

Parliament, to which English businessmen operating in China were summoned to testify. Their testimony sheds some light on this topic.

Changing trade structure and the emergence of "barter"

In March 1847 a Select Committee on Commercial Relations with China was established within the British Parliament. The committee met 16 times between March and July. Among its 15 or 16 members were people active in the commercial, financial, diplomatic, and other areas of Anglo-Chinese relations, people who joined the committee chiefly to represent the interests of their own spheres. One was James Matheson, a founder of Jardine, Matheson & Co., a firm heavily engaged in both the India and China trade. Another was Francis Baring, a powerful figure in London's financial world whose firm, Baring & Co., controlled an international network that reached as far as the United States and Asia. Sir George Staunton (the younger), another committee member, had been sent to China by the British government before the outbreak of the Opium War to try and smooth out British commercial and diplomatic relations with China.[47]

After hearing the testimony of witnesses, the Select Committee on Commercial Relations with China presented the following summary of the China trade:

> We find that on a great proportion of the trade for the same years [1845–46], the loss, taken both ways, i.e. that on the Manufactures sent out and on the Tea brought home in payment, may be fairly stated at from 35 to 40 per cent.; so great indeed that some manufacturers have abandoned the trade altogether, and that much of the Tea lately sent home has been sent on Chinese account, the English merchant declining to run the risk of the venture.

> We find that the difficulties of the trade do not arise from any want of demand in China for articles of British manufacture, or from the increasing competition of other nations. There is no evidence that foreign competition is to be seriously apprehended in the articles of general demand. The sole difficulty is in providing a return.[48]

In its summary of British trade with China between 1843 and 1847, the committee raised the question of acceptable returns for British exports to China, something other than unprofitable teas. This issue came up precisely because the China trade, which in extreme instances involved shipping tea to England on Chinese account, was conducted in the manner of "barter." Let us listen to the words of some contemporary industrial capitalists who, as witnesses, told the Select Committee about the way "barter" was conducted between England and China.

William Nicol, chairman of the East India and China Association of Liverpool, an organization which functioned to protect the interests of the British cotton industry in Asian trade, testified as follows:

(Section) 337.[49] . . . A dispute arose between [merchants and] a manufacturer who had sent out goods to China entrusted to a house in Liverpool connected with China, who got the returns chiefly in tea. The trade, as has been generally the case, was a very losing one to them. A dispute arose, which was referred to arbitration. I was arbitrator along with two other merchants, and I had occasion to go very minutely into the matter, in order to see the bearing of the different points. I have got the results here in a small compass. The first transaction was in 10 bales of twist and 20 bales of shirting, which with the charges upon them amounted to £886 19s. 8d.; that was the invoice cost. The manufacturer fixed his own price, but we had occasion to see that the invoice price had been tested, because an advance was made upon the goods.

338. Mr. Moffatt.] To what extent?—To the extent of two thirds.

339. Chairman. (Viscount Sandon)] It was a fair invoice?—It was a fair invoice. The sale of those goods in China produced, valuing the dollar at 4s. 4d., converting it into English money, £717 4s. 9d.; so that there was a loss, taking the sale in China, if they converted it into English money, of £170. If the return had been made in bills, I think a further abatement must have been made of something like 12 to 15 per cent., the difference between bills and tea being about that. They had authority from those parties to invest the product in the best manner they could. They found it impossible at Shanghai to procure dollars, and therefore invested the returns wholly in tea. The tea when sold in England produced £470 15s. 4d., leaving a loss upon the consignment to China, and the returns of tea, to the amount of £416. 4s. 4d. Now this is the exact transaction, which we found, on investigating both the quality of the tea and the invoice of the goods sent out, and all the circumstances connected with it, to be, although a serious loss,[50] not unusual.

340. Mr. Beckett.] What was the date?—The date of the invoice was the 5th of November 1844. The date of the sale of the goods was

1845, in China.[51] The teas were purchased the same month; the teas were returned to Liverpool.

345. Dr. Bowring.] Was this a case of out-and-out barter, or a case in which goods had been sold for money, and the money employed in the purchase of tea?—This was a case of out-and-out barter, and so close was the purchase connected with the sale, that the teas were bought, I believe, to be paid for with the goods.

349. Then there was no question of money between them?—I presume that a sum must have been named, but it was as a goods' payment.

350. How would the transaction be carried on?—A value would be fixed for the teas.

351. Mr. Brown.] Is it not done in this way, that so many taels are fixed as the price of the British goods, and then you agree to take the tea at so many taels in exchange?—Yes; as explained to us, the quantity of teas, far exceeding these, had been purchased by the house at Shanghai, agreeing to pay for them not in cash but in goods, without stating the particular price, that being left to be discussed afterwards.

353. Dr. Bowring.] You do not imagine that a bill of exchange could have been obtained for that value?—No; a bill of exchange could not have been got, except at an exceedingly high rate, unless, as shown in the next transaction, the bill of exchange was their own bill of exchange.[52]

Christopher Rawson, a Liverpool merchant, submitted to the committee the details of trade transactions as shown in Table 8. The balance shows two important facts. First, an overwhelming proportion of the remittance to Britain of the proceeds from the sale of cotton products was made in tea; only 2 percent was made in draft. Second, while the loss from cotton goods themselves was small,[53] the loss on the tea—which was obtained through barter in exchange for cotton products—was huge. The latter loss totaled about 20 percent of the proceeds from the cotton.

These are verbatim reports on the process of barter in the China trade, made from the point of view of people closely related to the British cotton industry. Since that industry was trying to expand exports of cotton products to China, the testimony was framed within the concern for transactions of cotton products alone. The witnesses' statements corroborate the following three facts: 1) barter did occur between cotton products and tea; 2) in long-term British-Chinese trade relationships—which included a contract stipulating that excessive pur-

Table 8. Sale and returns from the ship *Flora* (and one part from *Sarah Louisa*) at Shanghai

					£.	s.	d.
Sales							
Oct. 1844	61 cases white shirtings	3,042 pieces					
	123 bales grey shirtings	6,500 pieces					
		9,542 pieces		sold at $26,311.32			
					£.	s.	d.
	Exchanged in Shanghai, Nov. 1845				5,920	–	6
	Cost price				5,938	10	6
	Loss on sales				18	10	–
Returns							
			£.	s.	d.		
Bill	$ 619.64		139	8	5		
Tea	25,691.58 (produced Oct. 1846)		4,539	19	–		
	$26,311.22 (= £5,920 0s. 6d.) (A)		4,679	7	5	(B)	
	Loss on returns (A) − (B) £1,240 13s. 1d.						
	Cost price				5,938	10	6
	Total loss on sales and returns				1,259	3	1
					4,679	7	5
Percentage	Loss on sales	9/32%					
	Loss on returns	20 13/16%					
	Total loss on sales and returns	21 3/16%					

Source: BPP., *Report from the Select Committee on Comercial Relations with China*, 1847, p. 151.
Notes: All charges, including insurance and interest at the rate of 5% p.a. included.
(A) = barter price; (B) = resale price at home market
The exchange rate in all cases was 4s. 6d. to the dollar.

chase of tea in an individual barter transaction would be paid for in British goods—the Chinese tea and British products were exchanged in lots that were of almost equal value in China, but when the tea was sold in Britain, the proceeds netted nowhere near enough to cover total expenditures for production and sale of cotton goods, thus bringing a loss to the cotton cloth manufacturers; and 3) because of the very high exchange rate, the use of drafts as a means of remittance was very limited.

W. Ewart, a woolen manufacturer in Stroud, stated that remittance in U.S. dollars was profitable for British manufacturers, but according to him, that applied only to the year 1844.[54] In reaction to losses suffered in barter, British manufacturers and exporters asked their agents in China to make the remittance not in goods but in any drafts that could be obtained.[55] However, partly because the rate of exchange was extremely high and partly because the premium demanded to obtain drafts ate further into the total, their losses rose higher.[56] We have seen that the growing American demand for drafts had pushed the rate of exchange up steadily, and that limited the means of remittance increasingly to kind. That being the case, the testimony by William Nicol and Christoper Rawson seems to lead to an inevitable conclusion: if one regarded barter as an established form of Chinese trade and took into account the fact—proven by figures—that cotton product sales brought small losses or even profit, while tea sales brought huge losses, one would very likely try to strengthen the English market for tea (the market was for some time saturated from over-purchasing) in order to increase cotton sales in China. One would, therefore, demand that the tax on tea be reduced in Britain.[57] That was exactly what British industrial capitalists did to expand the Chinese market for British cotton products.[58]

Testimony nowhere relates why and how barter started in the China trade, nor is it clear whether barter was confined only to trade in British cotton goods, or whether it was used generally in transactions in the Chinese treaty ports at the time. The testimony does not tell us much about the peculiarities of the China trade or the position of British cotton goods in it. As a practical matter, a predictable loss from the sale of tea obtained by barter should have been calculated beforehand and accounted for in the sale price of cotton products. But the two English witnesses only talked about final losses in net income and made no reference to the interim procedures that led to such poor results. So, let us now look at the statements of British merchants in China, who were concerned about individual transactions in the China trade.

Alexander Matheson had pursued and built up the opium trade along the coast of China for 21 years, from 1826. He testified:

> 4526. Mr. Spooner] Did our merchants get any of it [*sycee* silver] in return for their goods?—Very little for manufactures. We have sent [*sycee* and other] silver to England as a remittance at times when we could not get bills at a better [lower] rate than 4s. 3d. the dollar.
>
> 4527. Then silver did, in point of fact, make the payment for the goods, because you drew against that silver to pay for the goods?— It might have been so, but in the case I refer to, it was not so; we sent home silver on account of people at Bombay as returns for opium, and they drew from Bombay upon England [as returns for English products].
>
> 4528. The Committee have had a great deal of evidence as to the great difficulty in the China trade of getting returns for British manufactures sent out; can you account for that difficulty of getting returns during the time when you say that the Sycee silver was so plenti-

ful in China?—At that time silver might have been bought for dollars, and sent home if the merchants chose; I am not aware that any was sent.

4529. Can you account for it, why such a transaction did not take place?—In this way, that nearly all the goods sent out from England were bartered for produce, for tea chiefly. There was such a quantity of goods sent forward to China, that the Chinese would not give money for them so long as they could get them in exchange for their tea, which they could supply in any quantity.

4530. By the evidence before the Committee, it has appeared that the profit upon the goods exported from this country to China was completely swallowed up by the loss occasioned by the importation of tea; can you explain why, when there was an article like Sycee silver that could come here at a profit, the merchants took tea that came here at a loss?—For several years past the agents in China have been expecting a reduction in the duty on tea; a great deal of tea has been sent home, speculating on the prospect of a reduction of duty, which probably would not have been sent otherwise.[59]

4546. Mr. Moffatt.] Is it your impression that the British trade in opium has caused a general extension of our trade with China?— I am convinced of it. When the trade in British manufactures commenced upon the east coast [of China] they could only be sold in very small quantities. Unless the vessels sent with the piece goods had contained opium, it is impossible that they could have paid their expenses.

4547. So that the opium was the precursor of the general trade which now exists?—Yes; unless the opium trade existed we should not have anything like the trade in piece goods which we have now. The trade would not bear the expense of carrying it on.[60]

After the opening of the five treaty ports, Alfred Wilkinson of Bell & Company, manager of the firm's agency in Canton from 1835 on, visited all the ports except Ningbo. He testified:

1305. Mr. J.A. Smith.] If the demand for tea here [England] was larger, you do not think that it would increase the sale of cotton goods?—I do not think that the sale of the one article should influence much the purchase of the other.

1306. Not when it is a case of barter?—I do not understand the barter trade as many gentlemen with whom I have conversed on China affairs appear to do.[61]

1307. Chairman.] Will you explain how you understand the barter?

—The barter that has been in China lately has been from over-sup-
plies of certain kinds of goods [cotton products]. It is of very little
use one merchant attempting to sell such goods for cash, except at
a very disproportionate price, when his neighbour will consent to
take merchandize.

1308. Dr. Bowring.] Would not increased facilities either here or
there tend to the extension of the demand?—Yes, it would certainly.
The greater the value of produce you can take from the Chinese, the
greater inducement for them to take goods from you in return,
provided these be suitable for their wants. But I do not see how you
can put one particular article against another; for instance, cotton
manufactures [not opium] against tea.[62]

For Matheson and Wilkinson, both of whom lived in China and had
vested trade interests there, the chief articles of trade were tea and
opium; cotton goods later imported into China were an "intruder."
They noted that oversupplies of cotton goods caused merchants to
barter them off. Their views on the place of British cotton goods in the
entire framework of China's foreign trade and on the cause of barter
are quite different from the testimony of Nicol and Rawson, who represented the cotton industry. Although both the English merchants
in China and the industrial capitalists in England described the trade
process as "barter," their views about the content and cause of the
barter were different, reflecting their different interests. Matheson and
Wilkinson's choice of cotton goods alone as their target was certainly
one-sided, without conceding the general tendency to oversupply (in
their own opium trade as well) after the five treaty ports were opened.
However, the fact that they talked about excessive trade (which
in itself means excessive supply) and concentrated their criticism on
cotton goods implies that "excessive trade" did not mean simply an increase in the number of trade items or a rise of the volume of trade;
it also meant a structural or qualitative change in the China trade that
would affect the interests of British merchants in China.

From the increase in the number of trade items, we can see that the
relationship between cotton goods and English merchants in China
was remarkably similar to the old relations between English woolens
and the East India Company. Both cottons and woolens were profitless
goods, and they penetrated the Chinese market only by dumping.
(How this was received within the Chinese market shall be discussed
later.) When woolens were made available as British trade items, the
government forced the East India Company to export them to China.
Cotton goods, however, had structural support in both production and

finance in their advance into China. An international system of trade
settlement supported by the British cotton industry had already been
established with the money market of London at the center, and China
was incorporated into that system. For that reason, cotton goods were
by definition export goods—for China or anywhere —regardless of the
the interests of individual merchants. The real cause of excessive trade
lay within the British cotton industry and the system of financing that
supported the production of cotton goods. Let us examine how the
structure of the China trade was affected by that system.

W. Brown, who was one of the members of the Select Committee
and familiar with trade affairs in Liverpool, testified on those engaged
in the China trade after the opening of the five treaty ports:

4730. Mr. Harcourt.] Is there not this difference, that the American
shipments are chiefly conducted by merchants, whereas here
[England] they are conducted by the manufacturers themselves?—I
think they are partly conducted by the manufacturers in the United
States, but to a more limited extent.[63]

This affirms the active participation of British industrial capitalists
in trade activities in China. On the other hand, G.T. Braine of Dent
& Co., Jardine, Matheson & Co.'s chief rival, stated: "A great
number of new houses have come out since the alteration of the
[trade] system in China [i.e., the opening of the five treaty ports],
and the business of the large houses has not increased in proportion to
the increase of the trade, owing to the large number of competitors who
have taken a portion of the business."[64] Here we have contemporary
evidence that new companies were reaching into the Chinese market
to become competitors with the large established houses.

Using these statements, we can make a broad summary of trade activities in China after the treaty ports were opened. England's industrial
capitalists provided funds for trade activities. Using these borrowed
funds, the private traders acted as agents for the industrialists and received commissions on sales. This enabled many British merchants who
did not have capital to enter the China trade and gradually to compete
with the large houses established decades before. Moreover, as already
noted above, American merchants were responsible for the export of
some English manufactures to China on their own account, another factor which encouraged trade expansion. All these activities were at work
to bring about the excessive trade Matheson referred to, and that is what
caused a major change in trade relations and generated the formation
of a new trade structure with English industrial capital as the axis.

Thus the circumstances that dictated the operation of the Chinese market changed to create a new structure of trade and production whose influence extended worldwide, with the British cotton industry as the center. The barter trade emerged as the result of a combination of two factors—a shortage caused by an unrelenting outflow of silver as the chief means of trade settlements and lack of other means of settlement because of trade expansion.

The excessive trade, which gave rise to barter, did not refer to the activities of trading merchants; it was "excessive" in terms of the volume absorbed by the Chinese market.[65] Rutherford Alcock, then English consul at Shanghai, bemoaned the inability to sell English cottons in China with dispatch. He cites the following reason: "It can scarcely be a matter of surprise that the opium trade under these circumstances should thrive and increase from year to year, while imports of British manufactures, nominally free, but de facto prohibited all access to the interior, seek in vain a profitable market in the most limited quantities."[66] On the other hand, the import volume of cotton cloth into Shanghai continued to rise, and in 1847 as many as 700,000 to 800,000 bolts of shirting were stockpiled in the Shanghai market.[67] Such oversupply led to barter trade, but how was it conducted in the treaty ports? Let us analyze the concrete operation of barter.

When did "barter" begin? After Shanghai was opened to foreign trade, payment for English manufactures there was made in silver until around 1843 and 1845,[68] and in kind thereafter.[69] In 1847, English goods were handled only by the silk and tea merchants,[70] and their volume was determined by the volume of teas purchased by the traders.[71] In his trade report in 1847, Alcock reported: "The trade here [Shanghai] has now become almost exclusively a barter trade, so far as our imports into China can be pushed into the market, opium and cotton goods being exchanged for silk and tea, the surplus opium alone therefore being paid for in silver by the Chinese consumer. The opium, and silk, and the tea, and piece goods are chiefly exchanged against each other respectively, although not to the exclusion of the long cloths for the silk, or the tea for the opium."[72]

We see here that in 1847 opium and cotton goods were bartered for teas and silk. Opium and silk had long been bought with silver but in 1845 silk became an item of barter,[73] and opium, the last to become an item of barter, began to be exchanged with silk in 1846,[74] because silk could be sold at higher prices than tea in England.[75] This shift to a barter trade in Shanghai was caused by trade expansion which occurred as Shanghai began to replace Canton as China's central mercantile port. Tables 9 and 10 show the movements of trade in Shanghai

Table 9. Valuation of the British trade at the port of Shanghai, from 1843 and 1844 to 1850 (unit: 1,000 dollars)

Imports

Description of goods	1843–44	1845	1846	1847	1848	1849	1850
Manufacture of cotton	1,671	4,255	3,080	3,311	1,836	3,052	2,618
" " wool	557	804	623	782	327	809	501
Sugar	2			43	170	82	147
Miscellaneous	292	136	186	176	200	470	643
Total dollars	2,522	5,195	3,889	4,312	2,533	4,413	3,909

Exports

Tea	322	2,221	2,027	1,834	1,654	2,019	2,427
Silk	2,003	3,806	4,430	4,819	3,331	4,417	5,520
Miscellaneous	35	19	35	73	96	78	65
Total dollars	2,360	6,046	6,492	6,726	5,081	6,514	8,021

Source: BPP., *Report by Mr. Robertson, Her Majesty's Consul at Shanghai on the Trade of that Port during the Year 1856*, p. 46.

Table 10. British import and export trade at the port of Canton from 1844 to 1850 (unit: 1,000 dollars)

Imports

Description of goods	1844	1845	1846	1847	1848	1849	1850
Cotton Manufactures	4,727	2,764	2,755	2,501	1,213	1,476	1,617
Woolen Manufactures	2,899	1,875	1,387	1,627	1,867	768	993
Metals	223	88	62	40	48	138	232
Miscellaneous, raw and manufactured	58	48	39	30	20	34	29
Raw cotton	6,816	4,728	4,925	4,686	2,792	4,770	3,432
Other Indian and Straits produce	783	1,213	830	741	595	717	594
Total dollars	15,506	10,716	9,998	9,625	6,535	7,903	6,897

Exports

	1844	1845	1846	1847	1848	1849	1850
Tea	13,433	15,826	11,113	11,848	7,382	9,336	7,673
Silk raw	2,172	2,425	1,344	1,808	444	860	1,010
Silk manufactured	401	522	426	386	167	415	486
Sundries	1,919	1,961	2,496	1,680	660	875	750
Total dollars	17,925	27,734	15,379	15,722	8,653	11,486	9,919

Source: BPP., *Report by Mr. Parkes, British Consul at Canton on the Trade of that Port during the Year 1856*, p. 30.

and Canton after the opening of treaty ports. In Shanghai trade was increasing in contrast to a downward trend in Canton. Except for silk, the net volume of trade in Shanghai was still small, but we have written records which indicate that domestic tea and silk were being brought to Shanghai[76] and that 20 to 50 percent of the foreign goods imported into Canton were transshipped to Shanghai.[77] Clearly China's central trading port was in the process of shifting from Canton to Shanghai.

The shift occurred only because Western traders saw in Shanghai the most strategic entry way to the huge potential markets in the interior in North China and along the Yangzi River. Long confined to restricted coastal trade, foreign merchants saw Shanghai as a base for inland expansion, although they were wary of a possible increase in the tax on the shipment of goods up the Yangzi.[78] Furthermore, they hoped that Shanghai would replace Canton, the center of the old triangular India–China–England trade, and become the center for the new trade between China and England, Europe, and the United States. Reports show that English merchants selected Shanghai or Canton as the destination for their goods after estimating the relative profitability of each market. It sometimes happened that goods first sent to Shanghai were transshipped to Canton if the market conditions there were better.[79]

When Shanghai became China's main international port, it did not become simply another Canton. That distinction was clearly evident in a bankruptcy case involving the Esang Company run by a Cantonese by the name of Allum, or Alum; the bankruptcy was apparently caused by a decline in tea export and a reduction of the tea price in Shanghai between 1846 and 1848. When Shanghai was opened to foreign trade, Allum tried to set up a Canton-style business: he borrowed $8,000 from foreign merchants and started a warehousing and agency business for Chinese merchants and foreign traders. In 1845 he was said to have a hand in two-thirds of all the dealings in Shanghai. In 1846 he disappeared, leaving behind a debt of 900,000 taels following a monumental failure from cornering.[80] The event galvanized Shanghai's commercial community, leading to debate over the question of how to launch and carry on direct dealings between Chinese merchants and foreign traders. One solution was barter trade. T.A. Gibb of Gibb, Livingstone Company, who had been trading in China for ten-odd years, first in Canton and then in Shanghai, testified before the Select Committee.

563. Will you explain distinctly the process in carrying out the barter trade?—Supposing I have 1,000 pieces of shirtings, of Manchester cottons; I exhibit my musters to various parties; none of them will make me a cash offer for them, or a credit of so much. They say, "I will pay you for these goods in Congou teas, at the market price of tea," if they have no teas on the spot to show me. But credit is so shaken in Canton since the dissolution of the Co-Hong, that there

are but few men that we can trust, and therefore we seldom deliver our goods till we get our teas.

572. How do you make an estimate as to what you sell your shirtings at, if you merely are to have so much tea, according to the prices in the market, that market being very doubtful?—We settle the price of the shirtings, but not of the tea.

573. Do you mention a money price for the shirtings?—It is a barter price. I should sell the shirtings for three dollars, and it is understood to be paid for in tea at the market price, within two months.[81]

Gibb noted that credit was so unstable that cottons and teas were exchanged simultaneously; that in settling a barter price, the price of cottons was determined by the English merchant and that of teas by the Chinese merchant, and the latter price was decided on the basis of market price; and that cash price and barter price were taken together in deciding a transaction.[82] The first two points lead one to ask: 1) how was commercial credit secured? and 2) on what basis was a barter price for cottons calculated? Bearing in mind the conditions imposed by the silver shortage and silver demand, let us examine these questions.

If we start with the question of how the price of cottons was determined in barter, we note that while Gibb stated that the tea price was settled on the basis of market price, he only stated that the price of cottons was settled by English merchants. He did not specify on what basis. Was the price of cottons determined arbitrarily by the English merchant? Did the conditions on the side of the buyer not affect the determination of price? Table 11 shows the movements in the price of grey shirtings in Shanghai. In the table a downward trend in the price is very clear. In addition, as a result of the 1847 financial crisis, cotton prices dropped further, although this is not evident in the table. If we keep these price movements in mind and recall the sales slump in the Chinese market, we can conclude that formally the price of cotton in barter trade was declared by the seller, but in actuality the price did not show an increase; efforts by buyer to reduce the price were at work in the determination of the price by the seller. If the seller (foreign merchants) did not actually determine the price, then why did he declare it? It is likely that a price adjustment function inherent in the barter trade made it practical for the seller to set up a price in this case. Barter was carried out as an immediate solution to the problem of, first, preventing a one-sided decline in the market price of English cotton goods which did not sell well and, second, creating an effective balance between the price decline and sales of dumped goods. To see this mechanism more clearly, let us take a look at the process of settling the price of the teas

Table 11. Price fluctuations of grey shirting in Shanghai

Date of shipment	Manchester, price of one piece shirt- ing, 72 reed		Date of sale	Prices realized, per piece	Turned into sterling at exchange 4s. 6d. per dollar		Net remittance, including all charges in England, as well as duty and charges in China	
1844	s.	d.	1844	$	s.	d.	s.	d.
January	9	9	June	3.75	16	10 1/2	14	3
April	11	–	September	3.50	15	9	13	2 1/4
July	10	6	December	3.50	15	9	13	2 1/4
			1845					
October	10	–	March	3.50	15	9	13	2 1/4
1845			1845					
January	10	3	June	3.40	15	3 1/2	12	9 1/4
April	10	4 1/2	September	3.15	14	2	11	8 1/2
July	10	6	December	3.20	14	4 3/4	11	11 1/4
			1846					
October	10	3	March	3.20	14	4 3/4	11	11 1/4
1846			1846					
January	9	9	June	3.00	13	6	11	1
April	9	6	September	2.95	13	3 1/4	10	9 3/4
July	9	3	December	2.95	13	3 1/4	10	9 3/4
October	—							

Source: BPP., *Select Committee Report*, 1847, p. 148.
Note: The duty in China is 14 cents per piece, or at 4s. 6d. = 7 1/2 d. per piece.

which were bartered against cottons.

The price of teas in England declined as imports rose, as is shown in Table 12. In China, however, the market price of tea showed a rapid rise, reflecting the growing demand for teas. The higher demand was brought about by the addition of new factors into the opium-tea trade, including increased volume of teas bought by American traders and in- creased exports of teas to be bartered against cotton cloth.[83] This was symptomatic of an imbalance in supply and demand, in which teas did not sell in England unless they were priced low but were nevertheless a target of speculation.[84] In barter, if the price of tea rose, it pushed up the price of the cotton barter goods. Furthermore, a sharp rise in tea price in China had little to do with tea consumption in England. So in order to prevent the price of cotton goods from falling further and to promote higher sales, the tea price had to be boosted, which made speculation in tea necessary.

Barter was an indispensable method for determining the price of cotton and as such was a vitally important form of trade to the English

Table 12. Fluctuation of congou tea price

Year	Quantity of tea imported (unit: 1,000 lb.)	Sold or retained for consumption (unit: 1,000 lb.)	Revenue received (unit: 1,000 lb.)	Average price per pound
1838	40,414	32,352	3,362	1s. 1d. to 2s. 4d.
1839	38,158	35,127	3,659	2s. 3d. to 3s.
1840	28,022	32,253	3,473	2s. 2d. to 2s. 8d.
1841	30,788	36,676	3,974	1s. 9d. to 2s. 3d.
1842	40,742	37,356	4,089	1s. 1d. to 2s. 3d.
1843	46,613	40,293	4,408	11d. to 2s.
1844	53,147	41,368	4,524	10d. to 2s. 4d.
1845	51,057	44,193	4,833	8 1/2d. to 2s. 2d.
1846	56,503	47,534	5,199	8 1/2d. to 2s. 1d.

Source: BPP., *Select Committee Report*, 1847, p. 503.

industrialists and the industry as a whole.[85] Barter was passive, conditioned by trade surplus (excessive trade) and shortage of silver as a means of settlement. These conditions were deliberately created by the English industrialists in their attempt to widen their market in China. Barter thus has a function in expanding the market for the English industrial capitalists, and at the same time it offered the English traders in China the opportunity to increase their sales. In that connection, Alfred Wilkinson of Bell & Company testified about credit in barter:

1325. Mr. Matheson.] . . . You take goods because you cannot get money?—We cannot get money. We do not like to run the risk of the failure of the buyer.

1326. Mr. Spooner.] You said before that barter was occasioned by oversupply; will you explain how you reconcile that with the last answer which you have given?—The oversupply of some goods causes us to sell to people who are less trustworthy of credit, but with whom we are willing to transact business in barter for produce.[86]

In this case, then, barter was employed partly to secure Chinese buyers who would join in transactions if payment was conducted in goods, and partly to make it possible to sell to untrustworthy buyers.

Here the advantage of barter was that it functioned as a form, albeit a primitive one, of commercial credit, as a mechanism for assuring trading partners and avoiding risks. Even Wilkinson, who like other traders was critical of the "invasion" of cotton goods, attests to the practicality of the system.[87]

So far we have examined the outlines of the barter trade in the Chinese treaty ports in the latter half of the 1840s. Although the constants at that time—excessive trade and silver shortage—were in themselves passive, they became integral conditions necessary for the expansion of the English cotton industry into the Chinese market, insofar as the industry itself gave to barter the active function of price adjustment.

As a result, to carry on through barter they had to supply funds to the traders, especially in China, to cover the overhead of cotton cloth export on the one hand, and to cover the costs of tea transport, on the other.[88]

The English banks took on the job of supplying funds. The first foreign bank in China was the Oriental Banking Corporation, which opened a branch in Canton in 1845 and another in Shanghai in 1848. The English consul at Canton, Francis MacGregor, sent home a message in 1847 that reveals something of this bank's activities vis-à-vis Chinese merchants. "The system now followed by the Chinese of shipping teas largely on their own account seems to have a tendency also to maintain a higher rate of exchange on England, since an advance made here [Canton] on such shipments is generally, if not always, paid for in cash, to raise which bills are drawn against the produce [teas]. Towards carrying out this system the Oriental Bank now established here has afforded great facilities."[89]

Both this report and the Select Committee's summary report cited earlier indicate that bartered Chinese teas were exported on the account of Chinese merchants between 1845 and 1847. While foreign banks lent funds to Chinese merchants for the export of tea, they also purchased highly priced drafts at the same time. Thus they ran a lucrative business. With regard to the operation of the Oriental Bank, R. Alcock reported in 1848 that "the specie imported [to Shanghai] has been chiefly for the Oriental Bank which has an agent at Shanghai, and the [financing] facilities that establishment has afforded have been to the extent of 180,000 to 200,000 dollars [annually]; whether such facilities have really proved advantageous to the interests of the port, as they may be assumed to have a tendency to promote trading upon credit, may perhaps admit of some question."[90] Here we see evidence that in the late 1840s specie was used, although the function of the bank was not necessarily utilized fully.

An examination of the activities of the foreign banks in relation to barter trade confirms the historical significance of barter: barter opened the way for the advance of British capital into China. Foreign banks were able to import from their home countries the silver which was running short—and was, therefore, in great demand—in China, and could lend the silver to Chinese merchants to facilitate barter trade. Of course, the same banks also lent Chinese trade funds to English merchants who did not have capital.[91]

Thus, the barter trade and the expansion of financial capital were closely connected, an apparently paradoxical phenomenon in the trade market that was actually promoted by the reactivation of barter. In this manner, barter at that time in China performed the financial function of cultivating the market in the China trade. Thus it had a very special place in the history of the establishment and growth of foreign banks in China.

Epilogue

Barter as a means of trade settlement, arose in response to a surplus of goods and a shortage of silver. These were the two main factors that influenced the way the treaty ports operated after the Opium War. Barter chiefly involved the exchange of English cotton goods and Chinese teas. However, it was not merely an exchange of goods. For barter evolved both out of the process of incorporating the Chinese market into a new triangular structure of trade among England, America, and China—with the English cotton industry as the axis—and out of the process by which the financial market of China was brought into the international financial system centered on London and united with the triangular trade. Thus the barter emerging in those particular circumstances was utilized for and geared toward expanding England's cotton industry. It was facilitated by two tendencies: the oversupply of cotton goods and speculation in Chinese tea. Consequently both English traders and Chinese merchants began to demand operating funds, which were indispensable even in barter trade for both importing and exporting goods. Hence, foreign banks took on the role of satisfying that demand by bringing British capital into China.

Although China's foreign trade was for a time conducted in the form of barter, the inland market operated on the basis of a money economy, largely in silver and copper. In 1849 Alcock made the following report concerning trade dealings in Shanghai and China's inland market:

The tea-merchants bring teas to Shanghae, and sell them for silver, or barter them for long cloths.

These long cloths they either sell to Soochow brokers at Shanghae,[92] or entrust the [native] bankers of Shanghae with their sale. The bankers pay them advances on the cloths (sometimes as much as 80 per cent.) in promissory notes of say twenty days' sight, on which they charge interest of 1 1/2 per mensem. They then send the cloths to Soochow, sell them there, and then account with the tea merchants, whether for profit or loss, the latter paying all expenses. The bankers are generally able to complete the transaction within the twenty days; but as their paper is good, the tea merchants find no difficulty in cashing it at once at a slight discount. The tea merchants sometimes take their cloths themselves to Soochow, but the more usual way is to sell them here [Shanghai] to Soochow brokers. The tea merchants either take back silver, or buy promissory notes from Hang-chow merchants.[93]

Alcock thus confirms that the advance of foreign cotton cloth into China's inland market was made through the medium of native Chinese bankers.

In the 1850s the Chinese bankers of Shanghai performed an important trade financing function, as we can see in the following report published in the *North-China Herald*:

The other [native] Banks have each a capital ranging from 5,000 to 10,000 Tls., and consist of two classes, one confining its operations to advance to dealers in manufactured goods, Straits produce, &C., the other advancing to the Opium brokers. The business of these Banks is to make advances to men of known respectability, in notes payable in 10 or 20 days, for the purchase of goods or opium, the borrower engaging to repay the amount in time to meet the orders when due. This gives time for opium, &C., to be sent to Soochow and realized, before the broker has to find the money, and foreigners knowing that the Banks have a capital to fall back upon, take these notes as payment for what they sell.[94]

The above shows that as the activities of native Chinese banks (*qianzhuang*) mushroomed, foreign merchants began to use them for their inland trade in China.

With a silver shortage and high silver price, foreign capitalists not only lent out funds to foreign traders but also began to prepare to lend funds to local merchants in order to procure local products. Such trade was essential to smooth the sale of their industrial products.

In the 1850s, bent on cultivating the markets of the interior, industrial and financial capitalists from Western countries began themselves to carry out the financial and credit functions utilizing the networks local Chinese bankers had set up in the Chinese inland market. In the latter half of the 1850s, the Shanghai market experienced the worst financial overheat since the five treaty ports were opened.[95]

Notes

[1]With regard to monetary standards, there are basically three different theories about the currency system of modern China: 1) that standard coin in a broad sense did not exist—the true coin in China was copper. See Edward Kann, *The Currencies of China*, 2nd ed., p. 1; 2) that the silver standard (*Silberwährung*) was maintained. See Bao-Seing Liao, *Die Bedeutung des Silberproblems für die Entwicklung der chinesischen Währungsverhältnisse*, pp. 6–7 (Japanese translation by Katsuya Arito, *Shina heisei no seikakuteki kenkyū*, pp. 13–14); and 3) that in structure, the modern Chinese currency system was bimetallic, based on silver and copper simultaneously. But since the value of silver was 100 times higher than that of copper cash of the same weight, and since each had its own sphere of circulation, the simultaneous use in China of the two metals did not constitute bimetallism as used in other modern currency systems. See Ye Shichang, *Yapian zhanzheng qianhou wo guo de huobi xueshuo*, pp. 5–7. One must not, however, treat the subject of a monetary standard merely as a matter of domestic administrative concern. International monetary circulation, credit, market relations, and other factors all have some bearing on its structure and operation. In the case of modern China, the monetary system cannot be analyzed without careful reference to the network of international financial relationships in which China's—and Asia's—currency system was formed, developing within a silver circulation sphere which itself was conditioned by the international gold standard system centered on London.

As Ye Shichang noted in (3), China had a dual, sometimes mutually contradictory, circulation system in which a currency measured by value (copper coin), and a currency measured by weight (silver) were used concurrently. Also, the inflow and outflow of silver, because it was so heavily influenced by international movements, were hard to control. Thus the modern Chinese monetary standard cannot be described on the basis of only one, silver or coin. That is why silver was described as modern China's "chief means of settling accounts," and not as the *sole* monetary standard.

[2]A "period of influx" or "outflow" as used here should not be taken to imply a one-way stream; it simply indicates whether the balance of China's incoming and outgoing silver was positive or negative during that period; this issue will be discussed later.

[3]The four-period division was made on the basis of the following sources: H. B. Morse, *Chronicles of the East India Company Trading to China, 1635–1834*; Edward Kann, *The Currencies of China*; Otake Fumio, "Min-Shin jidai ni okeru gaikoku gin no ryūnyū"; Momose Hiromu, "Shindai ni okeru Supein doru no ryūtsū"; Tan Bi'an, "Zhongguo jindai huobi de biandong"; and Wei Jianyou, *Zhongguo jindai huobi shi*.

[4]Besides the shortage of silver caused by the outflow, there were other reasons for the steep rise in the silver price: a growing demand for expensive currency stimulated hoarding, a de facto increase in taxes (resulting from higher conversion rates), and rigging of the silver quotation by local Chinese bankers. The decline in the value of *qian* (cash coin), on the other hand, was caused by deterioration in the quality of

newly minted *zhiqian* (standard cash), a rising volume of privately minted coins, and overissue of *qianpiao* (government notes and native banks' privately issued notes in *qian* denominations). The upswing in silver and downswing in cash coin together had a strong influence on society, though the impact and ramifications varied among the different strata. (Yang Duanliu, ed., *Qingdai huobi jinrong shigao*; Peng Zeyi, "Yapian zhanhou shinian jian yingui qianjian bodong xia de Zhongguo jingji yu jieji guanxi."

[5]Huang Juezi, "Yan sai louzhi yi bei guoben shu," in *Chouban yiwu shimo, Daoguang chao*, 2: 4a–5b.

[6]Calculated on a $1.00 = 0.72 tael basis according to 1) R. Montgomery Martin, *China, Political, Commercial and Social; in an Official Report to Her Majesty's Government*; and 2) E. H. Pritchard, "The Crucial Years of Early Anglo-Chinese Relations, 1750–1800," p. 103.

[7]British Parliamentary Papers (hereafter referred to as BPP.), *Extracts from a Despatch from the Governor of Hong Kong*, dated 4th September 1855, which was forwarded to the Treasury from the Colonial Office, in a letter dated 1st March 1856. All the BPPs to be introduced hereafter are contained in vols. 6, 38, 39, and 40 of Irish University Press Area Studies Series, *British Parliamentary Papers*, China, 42 vols., 1971–72. Calculated on a £1 = 3 tael basis in accordance with H. B. Morse, *The International Relations of the Chinese Empire, the Period of Conflict 1834–60*, p. xxxix.

[8]The idea of a "balance of trade" was not totally lacking. For example, concerning the trade situation in 1837, Wei Yuan reported: "The volume of goods the foreign countries export to China annually is valued at only 20,148,000 *yuan* of silver. The annual total of imports from China comes to 35,093,000 *yuan*. Thus China's foreign trade has a favorable balance of 14,945,000 *yuan* every year on a barter basis. If it were not for the "poison" of opium, silver would not leave China but would pour in instead. Chinese silver would grow cheaper daily and the profit would be incalculable." (*Haiguo tuzhi*, 2:21b.)

The volume of silver outflow officially reported to the emperor was often exaggerated, probably in an attempt to achieve the purpose of the report. Some reports to the emperor, however, presented statistics similar to those given by foreign countries, and they stated their sources of information. Among them was one presented to the Daoguang Emperor on the first day of the sixth month, 1829, by Li Hongbin, governor-general of Liangguang, who said, "We also surveyed the trade books of Chinese merchants trading with Western firms (thirteen of them in Canton authorized by the Qing government)." (Gugong bowuyuan, *Qingdai waijiao shiliao*, Daoguangchao 3, 3:11a.)

The figures shown in Table 1 are not accurate; some were obtained by equating the value of opium imports with the volume of silver leaving China. I listed these incorrect figures for the sole purpose of bringing out the problems that would arise if the figures presented by Chinese bureaucrats were regarded as correct. This chart clearly shows where their approach fails.

[9]BPP., *Returns of the Trade of the Various Ports of China, for the Years 1847 and 1848*, presented to the House of Commons by Command of Her Majesty, August 1849, No. 5, Mr. Bonham to Viscount Palmerston—(Received June 21) Inclosure 5, *Report on the Present State and Prospects of British Trade, in Reference More Especially to the Imports of Opium and Export of Specie*, p. 72.

[10]Ibid., p. 73.

[11]BPP., *Returns of the Trade of the Various Ports of China for the Year 1846*, p. 42, Canton. (Hereafter place name or year, listed after the page number, will indicate the port or the year concerned on that page.)

[12]BPP., *Report from the Select Committee on Commercial Relations with China; Together with the Minutes of Evidence, Appendix, and Index*, ordered by the House of Commons to be printed, 12 July, 1847 (hereafter simply referred to as *Select*

Committee Report, 1847), p. 46. Testified by T. A. Gibb.
[13]BPP., *Returns of the Trade of the Various Ports of China for the Year 1846*, p. 36, Canton.
[14]BPP., *Select Committee Report*, 1847, pp. 354, 363.
[15]Ibid., p. 25.
[16]In accordance with Pritchard, "Crucial Years," calculation was made on the basis of £1 = $4.
[17]M. Greenberg, *British Trade and the Opening of China, 1800-42*, pp. 159-60.
[18]BPP., *Select Committee Report*, 1847, p. 340.
[19]Ibid., p. 107. Chinese sources also note silver speculation by foreign merchants, as, for example, in the following:

The reason why there is an outflow of *sycee* silver is that Cantonese like foreign currency and have a proclivity for using it that is gradually spreading to Jiangsu and Zhejiang. Thus the foreign merchants secretly use *sycee* to purchase foreign currency, and then they engage in commerce with tea merchants from Jiangsu and Zhejiang. That activity is pushing up the value of foreign currency. (Guizhou District Inspector Huang Zhongmu's report of 1822/2/12, is included in *Qingdai waijiao shiliao*, Daoguangchao 1, 14a.)
On the pretext of selling goods, foreign ships loaded with foreign currency come to the ports of the several provinces to purchase *sycee*. In the interior, silver currency is dwindling in volume and foreign currency is growing more abundant each day. In recent years, as a result of this situation the value of silver has been rising daily. Opium, also, is much in demand in the interior, and the number of smokers is increasing day by day. (An Imperial rescript sent to Li Hongbin, the governor-general of Liangguang dated 1829/12/11, included in *Qingdai waijiao shiliao*, Daoguangchao 3, 21b.)

[20]Greenberg, *British Trade*, p. 160. BPP., *Returns of the Trade of the Various Ports of China, for the Year 1849*, p. 9, Canton. BPP., *Select Committee Report*, 1847, p. 341
[21]In 1832 the Indian minting bureau estimated that one pound of *sycee* contained 12 grains of gold while the same weight in Spanish dollar had less than 4 grains of gold. Based on that estimate, J. H. Palmer of Palmer & Co., an English trading house in India, testified at a special committee meeting held in the House of Commons in 1832 on the question of the East India Company that Chinese *sycee* silver could not possibly be reminted from Spanish dollars. (K. N. Chaudhuri, ed., *The Economic Development of India under the East India Company, 1814-58, A Selection of Contemporary Writers*, pp. 191-93). From this it can be assumed that foreign silver coins were reminted only during the period in which China's silver shortage continued.
[22]BPP., *Returns of the Trade of the Various Ports of China, for the Year 1849*, p. 9. Canton.
[23]Ibid., p. 10.
[24]Ibid., p. 12.
[25]Most of the bill purchases in Canton were conducted by an English trading firm, Jardine, Matheson & Co. (In 1832, the company transacted three-fourths of all purchases of bills.) Since it was much more profitable to send bills as remittance to England, Bombay merchants brought huge quantities of Malwa opium into Canton every year to obtain such bills. (Greenberg, *British Trade*, pp. 162-65.) For further discussion on this question, see Motoyama Yoshihiko, "Igirisu shihonshugi no sekaika to Ajia—ahen o meguru Higashi Indo Gaisha to Kanton shōsha no kakuchiku."
[26]On China's trade structure until the Opium War, see Tanaka Masatoshi, "Chūgoku shakai no kaitai to ahen sensō."
[27]W. T. C. King, *History of the London Discount Market*, p. 96; Greenberg, *British Trade*, p. 162; L. H. Jenks, *The Migration of British Capital to 1875*, p. 360.

[28]Hamada Yoshimichi, "Sangyō shihon dankai ni okeru Amerika no gaikoku bōeki."

[29]Jenks, *Migration of British Capital*, p. 360.

[30]BPP., *Returns of the Trade of the Various Ports of China, down to the latest period*, presented to the House of Commons, in pursuance of their order of January 22, 1847, p. 51, Canton.

[31]BPP., *Returns of the Trade of the Various Ports of China, for the year 1849*, p. 9, Canton.

[32]BPP., *Select Committee Report*, 1847, p. 356.

[33]America's unfavorable balance in Chinese trade and American cotton exports to England after the five ports were opened are shown in Appendix 1. The table shows that America's unfavorable balance in trade with China accounts for only 3 to 7 percent of its cotton export to England. However, the fact that this small amount could be easily covered in cotton exports by the huge favorable balance gave an enormous potential for expanding the means of settling accounts in the China trade, albeit subject to trends in the English cotton industry.

[34]BPP., *Select Committee Report*, 1847, p. 63.

[35]Toyohara Jirō, *Amerika shōhin ryūtsū shiron*, pp. 214–19.

[36]Appendix 2 shows the content of America's China trade in 1846, and the many regions it covered.

[37]William Nicol, chairman of the East India and China Association of Liverpool, stated that the difference in purchase price was 20 percent at the highest. (BPP., *Select Committee Report*, 1847, p. 49.)

[38]Ibid., p. 296. Testimony of Robert M. Martin, who was sent by the British government to China as a financier.

[39]Ibid., p. 357. Testimony of W. Brown from Liverpool, who was familiar with the tea trade with China.

[40]BPP., *Returns of the Trade of the Various Ports of China, for the Year 1849*, p. 11, Canton.

[41]Ibid., p. 9, Canton.

[42]BPP., *Returns of the Trade of the Various Ports of China, for the Year 1846*, p. 42, Canton.

[43]This, and the information in note 41 also, was noted by Sir John Bowring, British consul at Canton.

[44]During the Opium War as much as six million dollars in *sycee* left Canton for England (see note 19). At that time Jardine, Matheson & Co. alone transferred nearly one million dollars in *sycee* (BPP., Select Committee Report, 1847, p. 341.)

The abundance of silver was pointed out by A. Matheson (ibid., p. 207), and the reduced volume of silver in Shanghai after the Opium War was attested to by G. Balfour, first British consul at Shanghai (ibid., p. 363).

[45]Ibid., p. 208. Testimony of A. Matheson.

[46]Ibid., p. 340.

[47]Ibid., p. ii.

[48]Ibid., p. iii.

[49]Each set of questions and answers produced when witnesses were summoned before the Select Committee was given a number. *The Select Committee Report* has numbers up to 4911.

[50]The loss comes to a high 53 percent of the total production and sales expenses of cotton cloth. Expenses were £886 19s. 8d., but the net income from the teas was only £416 4s. 4d. The balance was £470 15s. 4d.

[51]In this case it took eight months to sell the English goods in Shanghai after they left England. Appendix 3 shows the time needed ranged from six to fourteen months. Clippers of the 1860s could sail between London and Shanghai in 100 to 115 days (B. Lubbock, *The China Clippers*, App. f), and so it probably took four to

five months for English goods to reach China in the late 1840s. That means that goods were stocked in Shanghai for many days before they were sold. See Table 11.
[52]BPP., *Select Committee Report*, 1847, pp. 46–48.
[53]As Appendix 3 shows, some profit was gained when cotton goods were bartered, while losses were sustained in cash transactions.
[54]BPP., *Select Committee Report*, 1847, p. 300.
[55]Ibid., p. 235. Attested by J. Garnett, from the cotton spinning and weaving industry.
[56]Ibid., p. 48. Attested by W. Nicol.
[57]Ibid., p. 55. Attested by W. Buchanan, an employee in an English trading house, who was involved in the company's export trade to Singapore and sending of remittances to China.
According to T. Bazley (president of the Chamber of Commerce in Manchester), Manchester employed a measure to facilitate tea consumption. Bazley stated that he and many others shared the benefits of a tea-related bonding system, under which importers did not have to immediately pay taxes when they brought in tea. They could transport the tea elsewhere or they could store it in a bonded warehouse until a good "deal" came their way. Only then were they required to pay the tax and carry out the necessary import procedures (ibid., pp. 78–79).
The Select Committee also received a request, from the first British consul at Shanghai, Captain G. Balfour, that the tea taxes be reduced (ibid., pp. 371–72).
[58]Some also stressed the necessity for reducing opium exports in order to expand cotton goods export. Two examples are W. Norton, who was engaged in the export of English industrial goods (ibid., pp. 45–46), and R. M. Martin (ibid., pp. 291–92).
[59]According to W. Norton, if the tea tax were reduced from the present 2s. 1/4d. per pound of tea to 1s., the total expense could be cut down by 33 1/3 percent (ibid., p. 444, Appendix, No. 2).
[60]Ibid., pp. 341–42.
[61]On this point, see A. Wilkinson's statement on the functions of barter within the Chinese treaty ports. See also note 87.
[62]Ibid., p. 105.
[63]Ibid., p. 358.
[64]Ibid.
[65]In the 1850s there were several foreign (English) reports which analyzed distribution, market, and agricultural production in inland China. These reports include the "Mitchell Report," and J. A. T. Meadows' report on Ningbo. The original Mitchell report and an analysis of it are included in Tanaka Masatoshi, "Seiō shihonshugi to kyū Chūgoku shakai no kaitai—Mitcheru hōkokusho o megutte." The Meadows report is introduced in Sasaki Masaya, "Kanpō ni-nen Gin-ken no kōryō bōdō."
[66]BPP., *Returns of the Trade of the Various Ports of China, for the Year 1849*, p. 50, Shanghai.
[67]BPP., *Select Committee Report*, 1847, p. 64. If we assume on the basis of Table 11 that the price of one piece of shirting was three dollars, then 2.1 million to 2.4 million dollars worth of shirtings were stockpiled in Shanghai. This accounts for 23 to 27 percent of the total import of cotton goods between 1843 and 1846.
[68]BPP., *Select Committee Report*, 1847, p. 65. Testimony by T. A. Gibb of Gibb, Livingstone Company.
[69]Ibid., p. 364. Testimony by G. Balfour.
[70]Ibid., pp. 370–71. Testimony by G. Balfour.
[71]Ibid., p. 123. Testimony by J. W. Robberds, an English merchant who exported camlets to China.
[72]BPP., *Returns of the Trade of the Various Ports of China, for the Years 1847 and 1848*, p. 74, Shanghai.
[73]BPP., *Select Committee Report*, 1847, p. 42. Testimony by W. Norton and T. A. Gibb (ibid., p. 64).

[74]Ibid., p. 56. Testimony by W. Buchanan.

[75]Ibid., p. 91. Testimony by C. Turner.

Barter was practiced at the other treaty ports besides Shanghai (except for Amoy). At Ningbo, goods for barter came in from Shanghai via Suzhou (BPP., *Returns of the Trade of the Various Ports of China down to the Latest Period*, pp. 45–46, 1846, Ningbo). At Fuzhou Chinese tea merchants received foreign goods in exchange for the teas sought by foreign merchants. This barter was very profitable for both parties (ibid., p. 9, Foo-chow-foo). At Canton, the barter price of Chinese produce was high (BPP., *Returns of the Trade of the Various Ports of China, for the Years 1847 and 1848*, p. 63, Shanghai).

[77]*North-China Herald*, July 3, 1852.

[78]Ibid.

[79]BPP., *Select Committee Report*, 1847, p. 335. Testimony by G. Balfour.

[80]*North-China Herald*, December 7, 1850. G. Lanning and S. Couling, *The History of Shanghai*, pp. 404–405. As of 1883, Allum was a comprador at Fuzhou for the Jardine, Matheson & Co. See Yen-P'ing Hao, *The Comprador in Nineteenth Century China: Bridge between East and West*, p. 232.

[81]BPP., *Select Committee Report*, 1847, p. 62.

[82]There was a 6 to 25 percent difference between the two, according to C. Turner, vice-chairman of the East India and Chinese Association of Liverpool (ibid., p. 90).

[83]In his reports for January and October 1846, R. Thom, British consul at Ningbo, stated that a large number of foreign merchants vied with each other in purchasing teas, and speculated in teas (BPP., *Returns of the Trade of the Various Ports of China, down to the Latest Period*, 1846, pp. 49, 104, Ningbo). See Appendix 4 for price fluctuations of raw silk in Canton.

[84]It might be useful to compare tea speculation by Chinese merchants in the early 1880s (and its collapse) with the tea speculation during the "barter" period. Speculation in the 1880s is discussed in Hamashita Takeshi, "Jūkyū seiki kōhan Chūgoku ni okeru gaikoku ginkō no kin'yū shijō shihai no rekishiteki tokushitsu—Shanhai ni okeru kin'yū kyōkō to no kanren ni oite."

[85]Two conditions gave rise to Chinese barter: in England, there was a demand for tea and a need to sell cotton goods; in China, tea was the only major export.

[86]BPP., *Select Committee Report*, 1847, p. 106.

[87]Simple barter is usually carried out in the absence of credit and it leaves little room for speculation. Nevertheless, the barter trade in China in the 1840s was accompanied by both credit sale and speculation.

[88]This has been referred to above.

[89]BPP., *Returns of the Trade of the Various Ports of China, for the Years 1847 and 1848*, pp. 45–46, Shanghai. This amount of 180,000 to 200,000 dollars accounts for only 9.8 to 10.7 percent of the tea export at Shanghai in 1847 (which amounted to 1,834,000 dollars), but 100 to 110 percent of the cost for the transport of the tea (about thirty dollars per ton, totaling 180,000 dollars; ibid., p. 45).

[91]In 1852, Rathbone Bros. & Co., Liverpool, received a report from its branch office in Shanghai stating that "it [the Oriental Bank] could not advance dollars unless it could sell its own bills on England or on India. On other occasions, however, it proved quite helpful" (Sheila Marriner, *Rathbones of Liverpool*, 1845–73, p. 200).

[92]A memorial presented on February 27, 1855, to the Xianfeng Emperor by Lü Quansun, the grand coordinator of Fujian, states that Suzhou was both a distributing center in China's inland market and a financial base of inland trade. The memorial reads in part: "Merchants gather at Jiangsu and Zhejiang. There all the goods from Fujian and Guangdong are sold. The market price of the *sycee* and foreign currency is decided in such way that Fujian and Guangdong follow Jiangsu's and Zhejiang's exchange houses, Zhejiang follows Jiangsu, Jiangsu follows the exchange houses in Nanhao Street in Suzhou. Thus the sharp rise and fall in the

value of the sycee and foreign currency is decided simply by the whims of the exchange houses" (*Zhongguo jindai huobi shi ziliao*, vol. I-1, pp. 192–93).

[93]BPP., *Returns of the Trade of the Various Ports of China, for the Years 1847 and 1848*, pp. 73–74, Shanghai.

[94]*North-China Herald*, June 12, 1858.

[95]For a study of this topic, see Hamashita Takeshi, "Shihonshugi—shokuminchi taisei no keisei to Ajia."

Appendix 1. U.S. trade with England and China (unit: $1 million)

Year	U.S. Deficit in China Trade (A)	U.S. Cotton Export to England (B)	A/B × 100 = (%)
1842	3.5	64	5.5
1843	2.0	61	3.3
1844	3.2	78	4.1
1845	4.9	73	6.7
1846	5.1	73	7.0
1847	3.7	105	3.5
1848	5.8	89	5.9
1849	3.9	97	4.0
1850	5.0	101	5.0

Source: Materials used for Table 4, and Stuart Bruchey, *Cotton and the Growth of the American Economy: 1790–1860, Sources and Readings*, pp. 16–17, 22.

Appendix 2. U.S. shipping activities in Chinese trade in 1846 (unit: 1,000 Spanish dollars)

(Imports) Major articles*	Source of imports	Estimated value
Manufactures of wool	Liverpool, Boston, New York	5
Manufactures cotton	Liverpool, Boston, New York	801
Betel nuts	Singapore and Batavia	76
Cotton	New York, Calcutta, Bombay, Rio	113
Ginseng	New York, Boston, Manila	313
Rattans	Singapore, Batavia	54
Rice and paddy	Lombock, Singapore, Manila	54
Skins and furs	New York	27
Treasure		426
Total value of imports		2,034

(Exports) Major articles	Destination of exports	Estimated value
Cassia lignea	New York, Boston	75
Silk, raw	Mazatlan (Mexico), New York, Boston	58
Sugar, raw	Valparaiso (Chile), Callao (Peru), Sandwich Islands	26
Tea	New York, Boston, Valparaiso	4,756
Silk thread and riband; silk piece goods	New York, Boston, Rio Mazatlan, Valparaiso, Callao	946
Total value of exports		6,207

Source: BPP., *Returns of the Trade at Canton and Hong Kong, 1847*, pp. 2–3.
* These import articles include cross trade items (for example, the "ginseng" that American ships transported included the ginseng produced in America, Korea, and Japan. Cf. E. Watson, *The Principle Articles of Chinese Commerce*, 2nd ed.

Appendix 3. Profit and loss in sale of English cotton goods

Date of shipment	Name of ship	Number of pieces, & c.	Invoice amount, including charges in England £ s. d.	Date of sale	Net proceeds (in dollars)	Exchange (per dollar) s. d.	Total in pounds £ s. d.
1844 April	Eleanor Russell	43 bales	1,279 19 5	Dec. 1844	6,238.36	4 5	1,377 12 8
							23 10 2
June	Charlotte	1,300 pieces	667 19 –	March 1845	3,595.35	4 3	1,401 2 10
						4 3 1/2	771 3 7
July	Charles Jones	800 "	462 2 –	Sept. "	2,157.94	4 4	467 11 1
31 October	Monarch	60 "	133 9 9	"	670.44	– –	145 5 3
1845 31 October	New Margaret	1,500 "	807 3 10	July 1846	2,813.32	– –	*609 11 –
1846 2 January	Monarch	2,000 "	1,173 12 –	"	4,345.0	– –	*941 8 4

Source: BPP., *Select Committee Report*, 1847, p. 149.
* Loss resulted from cash sales at Shanghai.

Appendix 4. Price changes of taysaam and tsatlee silk

Date		Taysaam (per picul)	Tsatlee (per picul)
1842	Mar. 8	450–500 dollars	500–520 dollars
	Dec. 6	365	465–75
1843	Feb. 21		470–80
	Nov. 24		525
1844	Feb. 23		500–520
	Nov. 29	510–550	
1845	Feb. 28		460–70
	Nov. 29	360	490–525
1846	Feb.–Mar.	no quotations	
	Nov. 28	260–300	300–410

Source: BPP., *Select Committee Report*, 1847, p. 33. Original source is *Canton Register*.

Reign periods of the Ming and Qing periods

Ming

Hongwu	1368–1398
Jianwen	1399–1402
Yongle	1403–1424
Hongxi	1425
Xuande	1426–1435
Zhengtong	1436–1449
Jingtai	1450–1456
Tianshun	1457–1464
Chenghua	1465–1487
Hongzhi	1488–1505
Zhengde	1506–1521
Jiajing	1522–1566
Longqing	1567–1572
Wanli	1573–1619
Taichang	1620
Tianqi	1621–1627
Chongzhen	1628–1644

Qing

Shunzhi	1644–1661
Kangxi	1662–1722
Yongzheng	1723–1735
Qianlong	1736–1795
Jiaqing	1796–1820
Daoguang	1821–1850
Xianfeng	1851–1861
Tongzhi	1862–1874
Guangxu	1875–1908
Xuantong	1909–1911

Measure equivalents

The equivalents given here are standard approximations; during the Ming and Qing periods, each marketing area had its own standard measures and thus there were local deviations from these approximations.

Chinese measure			Approximate metric equivalent
cun	寸	(inch)	3.2 centimeters
chi	尺	(foot/10 inches)	0.32 meter
zhang	丈	(10 feet)	3.2 meters
li	里	(150 zhang)	0.5 kilometer
liang	兩	(ounce/tael)	37.30 grams
jin	斤	(catty/16 liang)	596.8 grams
sheng	升	(volume measure for grain)	1.0355 liters
dou	斗	(10 sheng)	10.355 liters
shi	石	(10 dou)	103.55 liters
mu	畝	(land area measure)	6.144 ares
qing	頃	(100 mu)	614.4 ares

GLOSSARY

The definitions of the terms in the glossary are based on their use in the essays in this volume only. No attempt has been made to provide a complete listing of all the possible uses of the various terms. For references to specific essays, check the terms in the index.

Chinese

bandang 伴儅 servile tenants
bao 保 ward, 100-household unit in the *baojia* system
baojia 保甲 system of mutual responsibility
baolan 包攬 proxy remittance, engrossment
batou 把頭 overseer boss (system), which controlled hiring and labor of silkworkers
bipu 婢僕 female bondservants
boche 撥車 machine used to turn cotton yarn into finished warps
bujie 布解 cloth-forwarding households; under the Songjiang prefecture labor system, those households responsible for collecting the commuted taxes from peasants, purchasing cotton cloth with these silver payments, and turning the cloth over to the government (also called tax-paying households, **jiehu**)
buzhuang 布莊 cotton wholesalers

chaisizhuang 拆絲莊 those who sell small amounts of silk to weaving households
chaiyi 差役 conscript service
Chanping wang 剗平王 "Evil-eliminating king" (Deng Maoqi)
chaoxiang 勦餉 "provisions for annihilation," impost levied to provide military supplies for defense against the Manchus in the late Ming
chaozhuang 抄莊 representatives of silk wholesalers
chebutou 車埠頭 head of the waterwheel landing
chengfu 承符 errand runners and yamen menials
chenghan chuan 撐旱船 agents of silk wholesalers
chengtou 呈頭 petition leaders
chuhu 厨戶 kitchen household, a category of Ming population registration used in part to determine labor services
chushi 處士 secular gentlmen
cien 阡 a subdivision of a polder; also called **qian**
citian 賜田 donated land

439

cubu 粗布 a collective term for coarse cloth

cuiliang lizheng 催糧里正 *li* captain with responsibility for land-tax dunning

dabu 大布 a kind of coarse cloth called standard or large cloth; it includes **pingxiao** and **taoduan**

dahu baoyin 大戶苞蔭 grandee privileged households

daiguanhu 帶管戶 "attached households," households whose landholdings made them eligible for *lijia* membership; also refers to non-regular-member households, including the "extra households" (**jilinghu**)

dami 打米 "beating for rice," smashing the houses of the large households to force them to sell rice during famines

danchuan 單穿 a name for wide cotton cloth (**xibu**), also called **shuangkou**

dankou 單扣 a kind of thin cloth (**xibu**)

daohu 道戶 Taoist households, a category of Ming population registration used in part to determine labor services

daotian 稻田 fields used to grow rice

dapengche 大棚車 collective pumping

dasinong 大司農 great agricultural administrator (Han dynasty)

dazao 大造 major compilation (of the Yellow Registers, **fuyi huangce**, done once every ten years)

dengfu 燈夫 torchbearers, a category of the **lijia** service system

di 地 agricultural land in general; may also be used to distinguish dry from paddy land

diandang jiaren 典當家人 pawned family servants

dianding 佃丁 male tenants

dianpu 佃僕 servile tenants

dianshang 典商 mortgaging merchants

diaodian kangzu 刁佃抗租 lit., the crafty tenants refuse to pay rent, rent resistance by "cunning tenants"

diding yin 地丁銀 combined land and poll tax

ding 丁 adult male, fiscal individual

dingnan 丁男 male labor power

dingnu 丁奴 male bondservants

dongchang 東廠 Eastern Barracks, the imperial secret service office

Donglin dang 東林黨 Donglin (Eastern Forest) party

dongsheng 冬牲 "winter gift," one of a tenant's payment obligations to his landlord

Doulaohui 斗栳會 Grain Measure Society

du 都 rural township, parish, ward

dubao 都保 township-ward (system)

duomin 惰民 degenerate people

duozhuang 掇莊 middlemen between the producers and wholesalers in the silk trade

fan, fanbu 番,番布 a general name for a variety of cotton cloth (usually colored, patterned weaves)

fanche 翻車 a square-pallet chain pump, a kind of waterwheel; also called a **longguche**

fang 坊 a **li** (100-household unit) in the cities

fangkuobu 放濶布 a wide cotton cloth

fangsha 紡紗 spinning (in the Suzhou and Songjiang areas)

fangxian 紡綫 spinning (in the north)

fangzhang 坊長 a **fang** captain

feihua, feihuabu 飛花, 飛花布 "flying flower" cotton cloth

feixi 飛灑 an abuse in land registration whereby landowners would partition their holdings among a number of pauper households, and thereby gain exemption from labor services; see also **huafen, nayi, touxian, yingshe**

fen 分 a measure of silver

fenqing shengbu 粉青生布 a type of dyed cotton cloth

fu 賦 land taxes

fubing 府兵 prefectural militia system

fuchai 夫差 labor services

fuhao dahu 富豪大戶 large, powerful and wealthy households

fuju diantian 附居佃田 peasants who lived attached on leased land

fulao 父老 elders (late Yuan, early Ming)

fuxiong 父兄 elders (late Yuan, early Ming)

fuyi 賦役 land taxes assessed on agricultural land, plus labor services assessed principally on the individual adult male

fuyi ce 賦役冊 land tax and labor service registers; labor service registers (also **fuyi huangce**)

fuyi huangce 賦役黃冊 Yellow Registers, registers combining the functions of household registers and taxation ledgers, used to assess labor service

gainian 該年 current-year **li** captains (see also **jiannian, xiannian**)

ganche 赶車 a type of cotton gin (see also **jurong**)

gangyin 綱銀 amalgamated silver payment, a lump-sum silver payment covering a variety of **lijia** service expenditures (see also **junping yin, lijia yin**)

gengnu 耕奴 bondservants

gongfei 公費 meeting county expenses (a **lijia** service)

gongshi 公事 providing county services (a **lijia** service)

gongshou 弓手 bowmen (Song dynasty)

gongshouhu 弓手戶 archer household, a category of Ming population registration used in part to determine labor services

gongsitian 公私田 public and private land (i.e., the well-field system)

gongxing 宮刑 the Palace punishment (castration)

guaming 挂名 to post one's own name, to register

guanbu 官布 "official cloth," "cloth collected as taxes

guiji 詭寄 commendation, the practice whereby landowners registered their land as belonging to another household or several other households, in order to evade labor services

guituo 詭託 to entrust one's land to others, in order to avoid labor services

gulao 故老 elders (late Yuan, early Ming)

haonu 豪奴 "brazen" servants

haopu 豪僕 "brazen" bondservants

haoshen 豪神 gentry magnates, magnates and gentry

haoyou 豪右 magnates

haozu 豪族 local magnates

hongfang 紅坊 red workshops (for dyeing cotton)

hongsha guanbu 紅紗官布 red-yarn official cloth, cloth paid as taxes, with red borders woven into the ends to prevent people from shortening the bolts

huafen 花分 a method of tax or labor service evasion, whereby wealthy landowners would allocate their land to a number of poor households exempt from taxation and labor service; see also **feixi, guiji, nayi, touxian, yingshe**

huangcao 黃草 a yellow grass used to make cloth; a kind of cloth

huayi 花衣 ginned cotton

huazu 花租 "cotton rent," payment of rent in cotton

hufang 戶房 revenue department (of the county yamen), in charge of tax collection

hushu 戶數 graded household units in the Ming **lijia** service system, used to determine the land tax and labor services

hutie 戶帖 tax registration receipts (used in the compilation of the Yellow Registers)

huyi 戶役 household service, service as a *li* or *jia* head in the **lijia** system; also called **lijia zhengyi** or **zhengyi** regular (**lijia**) service levy, and **liyi, li** service

huzhang 戶長 household captains (in the labor service system of the Song dynasty)

ji 寄 land in trust

jia 甲 ten-household unit, in the *lijia* and *baojia* systems

jiading 家丁 "family servants," bondservants

jiagong 假公 "falsifying the public good," a technique practiced by the gentry to force their interests on the government

jianbu 間布 checkered cloth of blue or purple and white thread

jiang 匠 artisan, one of the four main Ming population registration categories; each category was liable for different forms of labor service (see **jun, minhu**)

jianghua 淨花 a superior quality ginned cotton

jiangsha 漿紗 low-quality cotton cloth

jiannian 見年 name for a current-year *li* captain (see **gainian, xiannian**)

jianpu 賤僕 bondservants

jiansi, jiansibu 兼絲, 兼絲布 a collective name for blended fabrics which used silk thread for the warp and cotton thread for the weft

jianu 家奴 "family servants," bondservants

jiaoche 攪車 a cotton gin

jiaohuabu 澆花布 a blue and white dyed fabric (see **yaobanbu**)

Jiaomin bangwen 敎民榜文 Proclamation on Instructing the People

jiaoqihuang 矯萁黃 a kind of cotton

jiapu 家僕 "family servants, "bondservants

jiaren 家人 "family servants," bondservants

jiashou 甲首 heads of **jia** (ten-unit households in the **lijia** and **baojia** systems)

jiatong 家僮 "family servants," bondservants

jibei 吉貝 "lucky cowry," a name for a kind of cotton cloth

jichan 祭產 ceremonial land

jiehu 解戶 a tax-remitting household or tax delivery agent, a post in the **lijia** system

jigang zhi pu 紀綱之僕 bondservant managers, in charge of administering their masters' lands

jilinghu 畸零戶 extra households, a **lijia** category of individuals exempt from labor service because they lived alone or lacked sufficient means of support

jingbu 經布 a blended fabric using ramie as the warp and cotton as the weft

jingbu 荆布 cloth used in making garments worn by commoners

jingche 經車 a warp wheel

Jingfu ce 經賦册 registers for regulating the land tax

jinhuayin 金花銀 gold floral silver, commutation of the land tax into silver payments

jinshen 縉紳 retired gentry, gentry

jizhuang 寄莊 outside landed interests, land held in a jurisdiction other than that of the owner's registration; "harboring estates," land purchased by wealthy households in other counties to avoid the land tax and labor services

jun 軍 military, one of the four main Ming population registration categories; each category was liable for different labor services (see **jiang, minhu**)

jungongfu 均工夫 equalized labor levy

junping yin 均平銀 equitable silver levy (in the labor service system)

juntian, juntian fa 均田, 均田法 equal field system

juntian junyi 均田均役 land-based service levy equalization system

juntuntian 軍屯田 military colony land

junyao, junyao fa 均徭, 均徭法 equalized labor service, whereby the irregularly levied miscellane-ous service levy was allocated on a regular basis

jurong 句容 a kind of cotton gin, like the **ganche**, with which one person can do all the ginning work

juxiang 居鄉 rural dwellers

Kaidu 開讀 "Reading of the edict" (uprising)

kanjian fu 看監夫 jailers (in the **lijia** service system)

kanmiao hui 看苗會 crop-watching societies; also **kanqing hui**

kanqing hui 看青會 crop-watching societies; also **kanmiao hui**

kaoshou 考授 recommended for an office, as "recommended assistant instructor"

kongyinji 空引機 a kind of draw-loom

koubu 扣布 sheeting, a kind of coarse cotton cloth (**cubu**), also called small cloth (**xiaobu**) and middle loom

kuandayi 寬大衣 a kind of cotton, with a white stalk and a high fiber content

Kuangshui zhi hai 礦稅之害 "disaster of the mines and taxes," widespread extortion practiced by the eunuchs in charge of the government mine exploration program (1547–57)

kuangzei 礦賊 mine bandits; unemployed mine managers who led bands of mine workers in search of mines to work for their own profit

lanna 攬納 to collect taxes by proxy, a term used of cases when bureaucratic magnates ordered their servants to collect taxes for them

laonong 老農 owner-cultivators,

private landowners (early Ming)

li 里 a 110-household unit in the **lijia** system

liang 糧 land taxes

lianghu 糧戶 taxpaying households

liangren 良人 free men

liangya 糧衙 tax office of a county yamen

liangzhang 糧長 a tax captain

lianxiang 練餉 "training supplies," an impost levied in the late Ming to provide military supplies for defense against the Manchus (see also **chaoxiang** and **zhuxiang**)

lianyu jiejia 連圩結甲 tenant alliances formed by all the tenants in a polder

liaojing 料經 warping for wages, the process whereby a peasant would get raw silk from a wholesaler, spin it, and collect payment on it (in contrast to **xiangjing**, warping at home)

liaoyin 料銀 "materials silver," a term for the commuted beeswax, firewood and charcoal, etc., levies, incorporated into land-tax payments under the Single Whip reform

lichai 力差 services performed in person, a division of the equitable labor service system (see **yinchai** commuted services)

liduo shigua 力多食寡 feeding a large labor force with a meager amount of food

lijia 里甲 population service system, system of population division whereby groups of ten households were responsible for sharing out taxes and labor services equitably among their members

lijia yin 里甲銀 **lijia** silver levy; see also **junping yin,** equitable silver levy

lijia zhengyi 里甲正役 regular **lijia** service, service as a **li** or **jia** head in the **lijia** system; also called **huyi,** household service, **liyi, li** service, and **zhengyi,** regular labor service.

lilaoren 里老人 village elder in charge of government labor services

limian 例免 permanent exemption from labor service

lingjia 令甲 first section in a regulation

lishen changsui 隸身長隨 bonded personal servants

lishihu 力士戶 guardsmen household, category of Ming population registration used in part to determine labor services

lizhang 里長 a **li** captain

lizhanghu 里長戶 **li** captain households

lizheng 里正 district supervisor or headman (in the **lijia** system)

liyi 里役 **li** service, service as a **li** or **jia** head in the **lijia** system; also called **huyi,** household service, **lijia zhengyi** or **zhengyi,** regular (**lijia**) service levy

liyi 吏役 bureaucratic labor service, a division of the Song labor service system; see also **xiangyi**

longguche 龍骨車 a square-pallet chain pump, a kind of waterwheel; also called a **fanche**

maidian zuopu 買佃作僕 buying tenants and treating them as bondservants

maizu 麥租 barley rent

mazheng 馬政 horse-breeding service system

meizhibu 眉織布 "eyebrow weave" cloth, a high-quality cotton cloth

miansha 棉紗 finished cotton yarn

miansui 綿縗 finished cotton yarn

miantian 棉田 fields planted in cotton

midian 米典 rice mortgaging, a system instituted by merchants whereby peasants could pawn their rice for silver

minhu 民戶 civilian households, rural landholders subject to the miscellaneous labor service allocation

mobu 捺布 cotton fabric, similar to Suzhou rubbed brocade

morongbu 抹絨布 a blended fabric, a "cloud" cloth using silk yarn blended with cotton as the weft

mubing 募兵 hired militia system

nayi 那移 shifting land registration to another place, an abuse within the **lijia** system, practiced to avoid taxes (see also **guiji, huafen, touxian, yingshe**)

nianzhou 輾軸 a kind of cotton gin

nongshu 農書 agricultural manuals

nu 奴 bondservants; slaves

nubi 奴婢 slaves, children of criminals, who in ancient times were taken over by the bureaucracy and set to work as servants; bondservants

nuli 奴隸 slaves, bondservants

nupu 奴僕 bondservants; slaves

paijiang 拍漿 a kind of small cloth (**xiaobu**), called "beat starch"

painian 排年 successive-year **li** captains

pengchong 朋充 associate-appointment system, under which a tax captain's (**liangzhang**) duties were shared by several people

piaofang 漂坊 bleaching workshops

pingmi 平米 leveling grain assessment, used to pay the expenses of the tax grain transport

pingxiao 平稍 a kind of cloth 16 *chi* long

pinjia 貧甲 household headed by a woman, or one whose members are infirm and elderly (meaning uncertain)

pu 僕 servants, bondservants

puban 僕伴 bondservant companions

pubi 僕婢 bondservants

pubinghu 舖兵戶 dispatch-bearer household, a category of Ming population registration used in part to determine labor service

puchen gongying yin 舖陳供應銀 bedding and entertainment funds, a division of **lijia** service system records

pudian 僕佃 servile tenants

pudong qinggeng 浦東青梗 a kind of cotton

puli 僕隸 bondservants

puyi 僕役 bondservant labor service, system whereby servile-surname households in a village were required to provide services (at marriages, funerals, etc.) for the master-surname households

qian 阡 a subdivision of a polder

qianwujingbu 錢嗚涇布 a kind of small cloth (**xiaobu**), two to four feet wide

qihuabu 碁花布 a kind of checkered **fan** cloth

qinding 親丁 male and female bondservants

qingji 輕齎 a method for equalizing taxes on government land, by commuting rice payments into cotton cloth payments

qiru 耆儒 elders (late Yuan, early

Ming)

qiudunbu 酋墩布 cotton cloth a little over 3 *chi* wide

qizhang 耆長 elders (Song dynasty)

qu 區 divisions (for tax collection purposes in Shandong); a large county had 8 *qu*, a small one, 6

quannongting 勸農廳 Department for the Promotion of Agriculture

ranghua 瓤花 ginned cotton

renli 人力 errand-runners and miscellaneous yamen menials

ruhu 儒戶 scholar household, a category of Ming population registration used in part to determining labor service

rushi 儒士 elders (late Yuan, early Ming)

saimianchou 賽綿紬 fine cotton gauze

sancong 散從 errand-runners and miscellaneous yamen clerks

sandeng jiuze 三等九則 ninefold classification system, used to divide households into nine grades, on the basis of which labor service was allocated

sanfasha 三法紗 a kind of thin silk cloth

sanlao 三老 elders in charge of education in rural districts (Han dynasty)

sansha 三紗 a kind of cotton cloth, the same as three-shuttle cloth

sansuobu 三梭布 three-shuttle cloth; see **sansha**

sefu 嗇夫 clerks who aided in tax collection (Han dynasty)

senghu 僧戶 sangha household, a category of Ming population registration used in part to determine

mine labor services

shanggong 上供 furnishing tribute (a **lijia** service)

she 社 community (system): a community consisted of 50 families, and was led by a captain (see **shezhang**) whose duties were to encourage agriculture, to provide moral instruction, and to supervise mutual aid

shengci 生祠 Living Shrine, a temple in honor of a man who is still alive

shenghuabu 勝花布 "victory flower" cloth, a kind of **fan** cloth

shenjiying 神機營 Miraculous Garrison (in Beijing)

sheyi 社邑 associational cohesive relations, which grew up among the masses after the breakdown of the equal field system; see also **yi**

shezhang 社長 a **she** captain, captain heading a community of 50 families

shiduan fa 十段法 ten-sections system, a system devised to rationalize labor service assessment: the total acreage and number of adult males in each county was divided into ten sections (**jia**), and each year one section was responsible for the services; see also **shiduan jince fa**

shiduan jince fa 十段錦冊法 ten-sectioned brocade register system, like the **shiduan fa,** designed to assess labor service as rationally and equitably as possible

shiduan wence 十段文冊 ten-section register, used to assign labor service under the **shiduan fa**

shihao 勢豪 the strong and powerful

shipai 拾排 **jia** captains

shipu 世僕 hereditary bondservants

shisan taibao 十三太保 "thirteen bullies," yamen toughs who oppressed the people

shiyin 市隱 urban recluses

shouli 手力 errand-runners and miscellaneous yamen menials

shuajing 刷經 brushed warp cloth a kind of small cloth (**xiaobu**): see also **paijiang**

shuangkou 雙扣 1) a kind of thin cloth (**xibu**) 2) a kind of wide cloth, also called **danchuan**

shuiguan yao 稅官謠 the song of the tax officials

shuijian 稅監 eunuch tax supervisors and tax collectors

shuiliang 稅糧 land tax

shushou 書手 document processors in the yamen

sibu 絲布 a blended fabric using silk thread for the warp and cotton thread for the weft; also called **jiansibu**

sichai 四差 "four duties" (equitable labor service; postal-relay service; militia service; and equitable silver levy, **junping yin** or **gangyin**)

Sinong si 司農司 Bureau of Agriculture

song jiamu 送嫁姆 accompanying matrons

suitianmi 隨田米 borrowing rice along with land, at interest

tangzhang 塘長 embankment or dike captain, a local labor service post within the **lijia** system

taoduan 套段 a kind of coarse cloth 20 *chi* long

taozhu 討主 "governing masters," the officials overseeing the watchmen of the granaries, who often supported them in embezzlement and other illegal activities

tianpu 田僕 field servants

tiansitou 田私頭 "private heads of the fields," name for landlords in the southern part of Taiping county, Zhejiang

tiaozong 條總 head of post stations

tiehu 貼戶 auxiliary households, a category in the equitable labor service system: the other type of household was the chief household, **touhu** or **zhenghu**

tiejiao guiji 鐵脚詭寄 "iron-footed registration," the practice whereby wealthy households entrusted their land to neighboring field servants in order to avoid labor service

tiesi 貼司 document processors in the yamen

tingchai 聽差 allowed assignment (system) in which the services of two or three households in the equitable labor service **lijia** fulfilled the task allocated, while the remaining households might be required to make payments in lieu of labor

tingzhang 亭長 the head of a *ting*, a ten-village unit in the Han dynasty

tong 僮 bondservants

tongnu 僮奴 bondservants

tongpu 僮僕 bondservants

tongpu qianzhi 僮僕千指 many bondservants

touhu 頭戶 chief households, a category of the equitable labor service system; they perform the labor service, while auxiliary households (see **tiehu** give assistance, with silver or labor; also called **zhenghu**

toukao 投靠 commendation, practice whereby a man submits himself as a bondservant to an official or gentry member, in order to avoid taxation or labor service; also called **toushen**

toushen 投身 another term for **toukao**, commendation

touxian 投獻 commendation, an abuse of the **lijia** system, whereby one commended one's land to a powerful person in order to avoid taxes, see also **guiji, huafen, nayi, yingshe**

tu 圖 ward of 100 households in the **lijia** system

tuanmin 團民 militiamen

tuiguan 推官 prefectural judge

weizhi lü 違制律 statutes for disobedience

Wulonghui 烏龍會 Black Dragon Association, a society of bondservants and urban hired laborers who worked as vegetable sellers

xiang 廂 suburban township; suburban **li** or 100-household unit

xianggui 鄉規 customary gifts (of firewood, rice, and barley), given to constables, village officials supposed to act in gentry interests

xianghuan 鄉宦 gentry officials (see Tanaka for contrast with **shiyin** and **xiangshen**)

xiangjing 鄉經 warping at home, system whereby a peasant would use his own raw silk, spin it, and sell it to wholesale merchants himself; in contrast to warping for wages, **liaojing**

xiangshen 鄉紳 rural gentry

xiangyi 鄉役 offices; district labor service (one division of the Song system, the other being bureaucratic labor service, **liyi**)

xiangyong 鄉勇 village braves, private gentry militia soldiers

xiangyue 鄉約 village covenant

xiangzhang 廂長 **xiang** captain, a **li** captain in the suburbs

xiangzi xiangyang 相資相養 "mutual aid and mutual fostering," an ideal description of landlord-tenant relations

xiannian 現年 name for a current-year **li** captain (see also **gainian, jiannian**)

xianwei 縣尉 assistant subprefect (Song dynasty)

xiaobu 小布 1) small cloth; 2) a common name for sheeting, (**koubu**), a kind of coarse cloth (**cubu**)

xiaojia 小甲 1) **jia** warden, a local labor service within the **lijia** system; 2) a small **jia** (10-household unit), in contrast to a comprehensive **jia** (**zongjia**)

xiaomaihuanghua 小麥黃花 a kind of cotton

xiaonu 小奴 bondservants

xiaoweihu 校尉戶 guardsman household, a category of Ming population registration used in part to determine labor service

xiawenbu 斜文布 twills, a category of **fan** cloth

xibu 稀布 1) thin cloth, a kind of coarse cloth (**cubu**); for varieties, see **dankou, shuangkou**; 2) wide cloth, also called **danchuan, shuangkou**

xibu 細布 fine cloth, a variety of **sansha** cloth, a high-quality plain white cloth

xingshihu 形勢戶 rich local families

xingtou 行頭 contractor-boss, who hired temporary laborers at labor markets

xiniang 喜娘 female serfs or bondservants who accompanied their masters' daughters away at marriage

yache 軋車 cotton gin (modern name)

yahang 牙行 silk wholesalers, sometimes called "silk devils"

yandang 閹黨 eunuch faction

yaoban 藥斑 a dyeing method which produced a patterned blue and white cloth

yaobanbu 藥斑布 patterned blue and white cloth dyed according to the **yaoban** method

Yaoli ce 徭里册 the **junyao** and **lijia** register

yaoyin 徭銀 labor silver, a commutation of labor services

yi 役 services, service levy, poll tax

yi 邑 associational cohesive relations which grew up among the masses after the disintegration of the equal field system; see also **sheyi**

yifu 義婦 "adopted daughter," a term for a bondservant

yihu 醫戶 medical household, a category of Ming population registration used in part to determine labor service

yinan 義男 "adopted son," a term for a bondservant

yinanfu 義男婦 "adopted men and women," a term for bondservants

yinan yifu 義男義婦 "adopted sons and adopted wives," a term for bondservants

yinchai 銀差 "silver assignments," commuted services in the labor service system

ying 營 military fields (a category of tax assessment)

yingshe 影射 making a false declaration of landownership, an abuse of the **lijia** system; see also **guiji, huafen, nayi, touxian**

Yingtian si 營田司 Bureau of Civilian Cultivation, in charge of water-control and irrigation facilities in Jiangnan

yinyanghu 陰陽戶 geomancer household, a category of Ming population registration, also used to determine labor services

yishen 邑紳 local gentry

yitian liangzhu 一田兩主 the dual ownership system of land tenure, whereby one man owned the surface or cultivation rights of a field, while another owned the subsoil rights (i.e., the right to collect the rent on the land)

yitiaobian fa 一條鞭法 Single Whip reform, a reform which consolidated miscellaneous levies into one tax payment, usually paid in silver

yitiaobian paifa 壹條鞭派法 a variant term for the Single Whip reform

Yiyou zhi luan 乙酉之亂 Rebellion of 1645, a bondservant rebellion which occurred in Taicang county, Jiangsu

yongbao 庸保 hired bondservants

yonggong 傭工 hired laborers

yongnu 庸奴 hired bondservants

yongnu qianzhi 傭奴千指 many hired bondservants

yongpu 庸僕 hired bondservants

yongyin fuyi 用銀夫役 "assignments met with silver," a category of labor service, distinct from labor assignments

youdunbu 尤墩布 a kind of thick and expensive cloth

youjiao 游徼 a local official in

charge of keeping the peace (Han dynasty)

youmian 優免 exemption from labor service

youtie 由貼 (tax collection) warrant

yu 隅 urban township (in the sub-county administrative system)

yuehu 樂戶 musician households, a category of Ming population registration, used in part to determine labor service

yufu 與夫 a kind of tax assessment

yuhou 虞候 errand-runners and miscellaneous yamen clerks

Yumin zhouzhi ce 與民周知冊 Register for the general information of the people

yusheng junyao 餘剩均徭 surplus **junyao**

yuzhang 圩長 polder captains

zafan chaiyi 雜泛差役 miscellaneous assignments in the labor service system

zanghuo 臧獲 slaves

zaohutian 竈戶田 fields of salt households in coastal areas (in contrast to salt-producing households, the operators of these fields do not actually make salt, but are engaged in agricultural work)

zazhi 雜職 errand-runners and miscellaneous yamen clerks

zhanyi 站役 relay station, fees which were a category of tax assessment

zhaotian paiyi 照田派役 a labor service reform which assigned labor services according to the amount of land held

zhenghu 正戶 chief households, a category within the equitable labor service system; they perform

the labor service, while the auxiliary households (see **tiehu**) give assistance, with silver or labor; also called **touhu**

zhengwenbu 整文布 cotton cloth with a square victory pattern

zhengyi 正役 regular service levy, service as a **li** or **jia** head in the **lijia** system; also called **huyi**, household labor service, **liyi**, **li** service or **lijia zhengyi**

zhenkong jiaxing, wujun wufu, wusheng fumu 真空家鄉無君無父無生父母 "the native land of true emptiness, fatherless and lordless, and the unbegotten parents," describing the White Lotus world view

zhenren 真人 a "true man"

zhi 職 official fields, a category of tax assessment

zhihuarongbu 織花絨布 a kind of cloth

zhinongguan 治農官 agricultural administrators at the sub-prefecture and county level

zhiqian 制錢 the standard cash

zhiranju 織染局 imperial silkworks

zhiyi 職役 labor service and official service, the two kinds of compulsory services; may also refer to official functionaries or petty functionaries (clerks, **li** captains, elders, household chiefs, etc.)

zhizaoguan 織造館 Silk Manufacturing Agency

zhonghu 種戶 cultivators (rent-paying peasants)

zhuangding 壯丁 stalwart men, a category of the labor service system of the Song dynasty

zhuangnu 莊奴 tenants called "manor serfs"

zhuangyuan 莊園 manors

zhujibu 諸暨布 a kind of coarse

cloth (**cubu**)

zhupu mingfen 主僕名分 having the status of a servant vis-à-vis a master

zhupu zhi fen 主僕之分 having the status of a servant vis-à-vis a master (with respect to hired laborers)

zhushou 主首 township headman, post determined by the size of a man's landholdings

zhuxiang 助餉 "supply aid," one of a series of imposts levied to provide military supplies needed for defense against the Manchus

in the late Ming (see also **chaoxiang, lianxiang**)

zihua 子花 unginned cotton

zihuabu 紫花布 a purple cotton cloth, a kind of coarse cloth (**cubu**); also called **zhujibu**

zongjia 總甲 1) a **jia** overseer, a local labor service post within the **lijia** 2) comprehensive **jia** (in contrast to a small **jia, xiaojia**)

zu-yong-diao 租庸調 land, service levy, cloth (handicraft items and tribute); the three categories of taxable items

zuzhan 租棧 rent bursaries

Japanese

doreisei keiei 奴隷制経営 slave management system

hōkenteki kyōdōtai 封建的共同体 feudal communities

kafuchōteki doreisei keiei 家父長的奴隷制経営 base of patriarchal slave management

kafuchōteki dorei shihai 家父長的奴隷支配 the master's firm patriarchal domination

kanshinteki tochi shoyū 官紳的土地所有 official-gentry landownership

kiseiteki jinushisō 寄生的地主層 parasitic landlord group

kobetsuteki jinshin shihai 個別的人身支配 individual personal subjugation

kyōdō gensōsei 共同幻想性 vision of community

kyōdōtai 共同体 community

kyōdōtai kisei 共同体規制 community regulations

kyoshin jinushi 郷紳地主 gentry landlords

seiji katei 政治過程 political process, the state and superstructure

seikatsusha 生活者 indirect producers

seisansha 生産者 direct producers

suiri kyōdōtai 水利共同体 irrigation communities

zaichi no gutaiteki na tochi yōeki 在地の具体的な土地用益 actual obligations arising from common land usufruct (all the people in a community shared the use of the natural resources of the community and were required to participate in group work ; in practice, **kyōdōtai kisei**, community relations)

BIBLIOGRAPHY

Primary sources in Chinese

Note: Entries for Ming works which are included in Wolfgang Franke's *An Introduction to the Sources of Ming History* include the catalogue number from that bibliography.

Baike ting zhaigao 百可亭摘稿 [Selected drafts from Baike Pavilion], by Pang Shangpeng 龐尚鵬 (js 1553). 1832. Held at Tōyō Bunko. Franke 5.6. 17.

Bai Luoyuan yigao 白洛原遺稿 [Surviving drafts of Bai Luoyuan], by Bai Yue 白悅. 1567. Held at Naikaku Bunko.

Banjiang Zhao xiansheng wenji 半江趙先生文集 [The works of Master Zhao of Banjiang], by Zhao Kuan 趙寬. 1561. Held at Naikaku Bunko.

Bianmin tuzuan 便民圖纂 [Illustrated guide for the people], compiled in the Ming period. Beijing: Nongye Chubanshe, 1959.

Bu nongshu 補農書 [Supplemented treatise on agriculture], edited by Zhang Lixiang 張履祥. 1658. Includes Zhang's notes on the *Shenshi nongshu* 沈氏農書 [Shen's agricultural treatise]. Reprint. Beijing: Zhonghua Shuju, 1956.

Chishan huiyue 赤山會約 [The agreement at Chishan], by Xiao Yong 蕭雍. Wanli era. In *Jingchuan congshu* 涇川叢書. Reprinted in *Congshu jicheng* 叢書集成.

Chouban yiwu shimo: Daoguang chao 籌辦夷務始末—道光朝 [A complete account of the management of foreign affairs: the Daoguang reign]. Compiled 1856. Beijing: Gugong Bowuyuan, 1929.

Chuanjia bao 傳家寶 [Family treasures], by Shi Chengjin 石成金. 1707. Held at Seikadō Bunko.

Chuogeng lu 輟耕錄 [Writing and cultivating], by Tao Zongyi 陶宗儀. 1366. Reprints. 1925; Beijing: 1959.

Congxian weisu yi 從先維俗議 [The proposals of Congxian], by Guan Zhidao 管志道. In *Taikun xianzhe yishu* 太崑先哲遺書.

Da Ming huidian 大明會典 [Collected statutes of the Ming dynasty], edited by Shen Shixing 申時行. 1587. Reprint. Shanghai: Shangwu Yinshuguan, 1936. Franke 6.1.2.

453

Da Ming lü 大明律 [The Ming code]. 1397. In *Huang Ming zhishu*. Franke 6.3.3.

Da Qing lichao shilu 大清歷朝實錄 [Veritable records of the Qing dynasty]. Tokyo: Ōkura Shuppan, 1937.

Da Qing lü jijie fuli 大清律集解附例 [The annotated Qing code with substatutes appended], by Fu Yijian 傅以漸. 1646. Revised 1725. The 1725 edition is held by Ōki Bunko, Tōyō Bunka Kenkyūjo.

Da Qing lüli anyu 大清律例按語 [A compiler's notes on the Qing code], anon. Preface by Huang Entong 黃恩彤. 1847.

Daxue yanyi bu 大學演義補 [Supplement to explications on the Great Learning], by Qiu Jun 丘濬. 1506. Franke 9.2.1.

Deyi lu 得一錄 [Record of attaining the absolute way], by Yu Zhi 余治. 1869. Held at Naikaku Bunko.

Dieshan ji 疊山集 [The works of Xie Dieshan], by Xie Fangde 謝枋得. Jiajing era. Reprint. Shanghai: Shangwu Yinshuguan, 1934.

Dongjiang jiacang ji 東江家藏集 [The writings of Gu Dongjiang held by his family], by Gu Qing 顧清. Jiajing era.

Dongshe xiansheng jiacang ji 東畬先生家藏集 [The writings of Master Qian Dongshe held by his family], by Qian Qi 錢琦. 1568.

Dusu tang wenji 篤素堂文集 [Collected works from Dusu Hall], by Zhang Ying 張英. Qing dynasty.

Fangtang Wang xiansheng wencui 方塘汪先生文粹 [The literary remnants of Master Wang of Fangtang], by Wang Si 汪思. 1575. Held at Naikaku Bunko.

Fu'an yigao 黼菴遺藁 [Surviving drafts of Chai Fu'an], by Chai Qi 柴奇. Jiajing era. Held at Beijing Library.

Fushe jilue 復社紀略 [Brief record of the Fu she], by Lu Shiyi 陸世儀. Reprinted in *Guocui congshu* 國粹叢書, no. 3, 1908.

Fuyi quanshu 賦役全書 [Complete book of land taxes and service levies]. 1694. Reprint. Tokyo: Kyūko Shoin, 1973.

Gaiyu congkao 陔餘叢考 [Notes while attending my parents], by Zhao Yi 趙翼. Reprint. Shanghai: Shangwu Yinshuguan, 1957.

Gao Taishi fuzao ji 高太史鳧藻集 [The works of Gao Taishi], by Gao Qi 高啓. Reprinted in *Sibu congkan*.

Gaozong chunhuangdi shilu 高宗純皇帝實錄 [Veritable records of Emperor Gaozong (Qianlong)]. Reprint. Taibei: Huawen Shuju, 1964.

Ge Duansu gong ji 葛端肅公集 [Collected works of Ge Duansu], by Ge Shouli 葛守禮 (1505–78). Reprint. 1802. Franke 5.6.15.

Gujin tushu jicheng 古今圖書集成 [Compendium of texts ancient and modern], by Chen Menglei 陳夢雷. Completed 1722. Reprint. Shanghai, 1898.

Gu Wenkang gong wencao 顧文康公文草 [The writings of Gu Wenkang], by Gu Dingchen 顧鼎臣 (1473–1540). 1640. Franke 5.5.16.

Haiguo tuzhi 海國圖志 [An illustrated gazetteer of the maritime countries], by Wei Yuan 魏源. 1847.

Han shu 漢書 (Han dynastic history], by Ban Gu 班固. Reprint. Beijing: Zhonghua Shuju, 1962.

Henan fuyi zongkuai wence 河南賦役總會文冊 [Statistical register of the land tax and service levy of Henan]. Jiajing era. Held at Beijing Library.

Houhu zhi 後湖志 [Back Lake records], edited by Gao Jie 高傑. 1611.

Huangchao jingshi wenbian 皇朝經世文編 [Collected writings on statecraft of the Qing dynasty], by He Changling 賀長齡. 1827.

Huangchao wenxian tongkao 皇朝文獻通考 [A compendium of documents concerning the Qing dynasty]. 1747. *Tushu jicheng* reprint. Shanghai, 1901.

Huang Ming jingshi wenbian 皇明經世文編 [Collected writings on statecraft of the Ming dynasty], by Chen Zilong 陳子龍. 1638. Reprint. Taibei: Guofeng Chubanshe, 1964. Franke 5.1.8.

Huang Ming tiaofa shilei zuan 皇明條法事類纂 [Categorized sub-statutes and regulations of the Ming dynasty], by Dai Jin 戴金. Completed 1533. Reprint. Tokyo: Koten Kenkyūkai, 1966. Franke 6.3.5.

Huang Ming wenheng 皇明文衡 [Exemplary documents of the Ming dynasty]. Reprinted in *Sibu congkan*.

Huang Ming zhishu 皇明制書 [Regulations of the Ming dynasty], by Zhang Lu 張鹵. 1579. Reprint. Tokyo: Koten Kenkyūkai, 1967. Franke 6.1.5.

Huang Qing zouyi 皇清奏議 [Memorials of the Qing dynasty], edited by Qinchuan jushi 琴川居士. Reprint. Taibei: Wenhai Chubanshe, 1967.

Huangzheng jiyao 荒政輯要 [Essentials of famine administration], by Yao Tianpu 姚天璞. 1768. Held at Naikaku Bunko.

Hunan shengli cheng'an 湖南省例成案 [The provincial regulations and leading cases of Hunan]. 1820. Held at Tōyō Bunka Kenkyūjo.

Jiangsu Shanyang shouzu quanan 江蘇山陽收租全案 [Complete documents concerning rent collection in Shanyang county, Jiangsu], edited by Li Chengru 李程儒. 1827. Held in the Niida Collection at Tōyō Bunka Kenkyūjo. Reprinted in *Qingshi ziliao* 清史資料, vol. 2: Zhonghua shuju, 1981.

Jiangsu shengli 江蘇省例 [Provincial regulations of Jiangsu]. Jiangsu Shuju, 1899–1902.

Jianwen zaji 見聞雜記 [Notes on things seen and heard], by Li Le 李樂. 1598. Held at Naikaku Bunko.

Jijiu qinxi Chen xiansheng ji 祭酒琴溪陳先生集 [The works of Master Chen], by Chen Huan 陳寰. Ming dynasty. Held at Naikaku Bunko.

Jilu huibian 紀錄彙編 [A compendium of narrative records], by Shen Jiefu 沈節甫 (1533–1601). 1617. Reprint. Shanghai: Shangwu Yinshuguan, 1938. Franke 9.4.3.

Jinghu zizuan nianpu 鏡湖自撰年譜 [Autobiography of Duan Jinghu], by Duan Guangqing 段光清. Reprint. Shanghai: Zhonghua Shuju, 1960.

Jingxin tang cao 鏡心堂草 [Collected writings from Jingxin Hall], by Tao Yunyi 陶允宜. Ming dynasty. Held at Naikaku Bunko.

Jiting waiji 幾亭外集 [The unofficial writings of Chen Jiting], by Chen Longzheng 陳龍正. 1665. Held at Naikaku Bunko.

Juyi tang ji 居易堂集 [Collected writings from Juyi Hall], by Xu Fang 徐枋. 1684. Reprinted in *Sibu congkan*.

Keyue zhi 客越志 [Notes of a traveler in the south], by Wang Zhideng 王穉登. 1567. Held at Beijing Library.

Langya daizui bian 琅邪代醉編 [Drunken meditations at Langya Mountain], by Zhang Dingsi 張鼎思. 1597. Held at Naikaku Bunko.

Li'an quanji 例案全集 [A collection of precedent cases], by Zhang Guangyue 張光月. 1722.

Lin Ciyai xiansheng wenji 林次崖先生文集 [The collected works of Lin Ciyai], by Lin Xiyuan 林希元 (1480–1560). Revised edition, 1753. Franke 5.5.20.

Lishu zhinan 吏書指南 [The clerk's handbook], anon. Yuan period. Published with *Jiaju biyong shilei* 家居必用事類 [Family encyclopedia]. Held at Jimbun Kagaku Kenkyūjo, Kyoto University.

Lu Wending gong ji 陸文定公集 [The works of Lu Wending], by Lu Shusheng 陸樹聲. 1616. Held at Sonkeikaku Bunko.

Mao shangshu zougao 毛尚書奏稿 [Draft memorials of minister Mao], by Mao Hongbin 毛鴻賓. 1910.

Meicun jiacang gao 梅村家藏稿 [Draft writings of Wu Meicun held by his family], by Wu Weiye 吳偉業. Kangxi era. Reprinted in *Sibu congkan*.

Mianhua tu 棉花圖 [Cotton manual], by Fang Guancheng 方觀承 1765. Also known as *Yuti* 御提 *mianhua tu* [Cotton manual bearing the emperor's poems].

Ming chen zouyi 明臣奏議 [Memorials by Ming ministers]. 1781. Reprinted in *Congshu jicheng*. Franke 5.1.9.

Ming dufu nianbiao 明督撫年表 [Chronological tables of Ming governors and supreme commanders], by Wu Tingxie 吳廷燮. About 1930. Franke 3.8.4.

Ming shi 明史 [Ming dynastic history], edited by Zhang Tingyu 張廷玉. 1736. Reprint. Beijing: Zhonghua Shuju, 1974. Franke 2.1.9.

Mingshi jishi benmo 明史紀事本末 [A record of specific events in Ming history], by Gu Yingtai 谷應泰. 1658. *Wanyou wenku* edition. Franke 2.2.11.

Ming shilu 明實錄 [Veritable records of the Ming]. Reprint. Taibei: Zhong-yang Yanjiuyuan Lishi Yuyan Yanjiusuo, 1962–68.

Mumian pu 木棉譜 [Treatise on cotton], by Chu Hua 褚華. Reprinted in *Shanghai zhanggu congshu* 上海掌故叢書 [Collectanea on the history of Shanghai]. Shanghai: 1935.

Nancun chuogeng lu 南村輟耕錄 [Writing and cultivating in Nancun]. See *Chuogeng lu*.

Nianer shi zhaji 廿二史劄記 [Miscellaneous notes on the twenty-two dynastic histories], by Zhao Yi 趙翼 (1727–1814). Reprint. Beijing: Shangwu Yinshuguan, 1958.

Nong shu 農書 [Treatise on agriculture], by Wang Zhen 王禎. 1313. Reprint.

Nongzheng quanshu 農政全書 [Complete treatise on agriculture], by Xu Guangqi 徐光啓. 1640. Reprinted with annotations under the title *Nong-zheng quanshu jiaozhu* 校注. Shanghai: Guji Chubanshe, 1979. Franke 9.1.3.

Paoweng jiacang ji 匏翁家藏集 [The writings of Wu Paoweng held by his family], by Wu Kuan 吳寬. 1449. Reprinted in *Sibu congkan*.

Peiyuan tang oucun gao 培遠堂偶存稿 [Occasional drafts from Peiyuan Hall], by Chen Hongmou 陳宏謀. Reprint. 1896. Qing edition held by Seikadō Bunko.

Piyu zaji 甓餘雜集 [Miscellaneous notes on minor matters], by Zhu Wan 朱

紈 (1494–1550). 1587. Franke 5.5.12. 1587 edition held at Naikaku Bunko.

Qinding xu Wenxian tongkao 欽定續文獻通考 [Imperially approved further compendium of historical documents]. 1747.

Qingbai leichao 清稗類抄 [Unofficial records of the Qing dynasty]. Reprint. Taibei: Zhongyang Yanjiuyuan Lishi Yuyan Yanjiusuo, 1966.

Qingshi liezhuan 清史列傳 [Qing biographies], compiled by Guoshi guan 國史館 [Office of national history]. 1928. Reprint. Taibei: Wenhai Chubanshe, 1974.

Qingyuan tiaofa shilei 慶元條法事類 [Compendium of legal articles of the Qingyuan era (1195–1200)]. Photolithographic edition. Tokyo: Koten Kenkyūkai, 1968. Original held at Seikadō Bunko.

Qinshan ji 芹山集 [Writings from Celery Mountain], by Chen Ru 陳儒. 1569. Held at Naikaku Bunko.

Qinyi Liangzhe junping lu 欽議兩浙均平錄 [Imperially approved record of equitable dispensation for Zhejiang], edited by Pang Shangpeng 龐尚鵬. 1566. Held at Sonkeikaku Bunko.

Renzong ruihuangdi shilu 仁宗睿皇帝實錄 [Veritable records of Emperor Renzong (Jiaqing)]. Reprint. Taibei: Huawen Shuju, 1964.

Rizhi lu 日知錄 [Record of things learned daily], by Gu Yanwu 顧炎武. 1695.

Sanchao Liaoshi shilu 三朝遼事實錄 [Veritable records of Liaodong over three reigns], by Wang Zaijin 王在晉. 1638. Reprint. 1931. Franke 7.10.9.

Sangang shilue 三岡識略 [Brief notes of Sangang], by Dong Han 董含. 1697. Franke 4.7.6.

Shandong jinghui lu 山東經會錄 [Fiscal accounting records of Shandong], edited by Zhou Yude 周于德, et al. 1571. Previously in collection of Naitō Konan, original now lost.

Shangcheng yilan 商程一覽 [Merchant routes at a glance], edited by Tao Chengqing 陶承慶. Wanli era. Held at Naikaku Bunko. Franke 8.2.7.

Shang Wenyi gong ji 商文毅公集 [The works of Master Shang Wenyi], by Shang Lu 商輅 (1414–86). 1603. Franke 5.3.3.

Shen bao 申報 [Shanghai news]. Reprint. Taibei: Xuesheng Shuju, 1964.

Shenshi nongshu. See *Bu nongshu.*

Shenzong shilu 神宗實錄 [Veritable records of Emperor Shenzong (Wanli)]. 1630. Reprint. Taibei: 1966. Franke 1.1.11.

Shifeng gao 始豐稿 [Drafts from Shifeng stream], by Xu Yikui 徐一夔. Hongwu era. Copy of original edition held at Seikadō Bunko. Reprinted in *Wulin wangzhe yizhu* 武林往哲遺箸 [Literary remnants of former Hangzhou writers], 1894.

Shijingtang ji 世經堂集 [Writings from Shijing Hall], by Xu Jie 徐階. Wanli era. Held at Naikaku Bunko.

Shizheng lu 實政錄 [Notes on effective administration], by Lü Kun 呂坤. 1598. Franke 6.2.13. 1598 edition held in Ōki Bunko at Tōyō Bunka Kenkyūjo.

Shizong xianhuangdi shilu 世宗憲皇帝實錄 [Veritable records of Emperor Shizong (Yongzheng)]. Reprint. Taibei: Huawen Shuju, 1964.

Shouhe riji 守禾日記 [A crop-watcher's diary], by Lu Chongxing 盧崇興. 1739. 1788 enlarged version.

Shuangjie tang yongxun 雙節堂庸訓 [Common admonitions from Shuangjie Hall], by Wang Huizu 汪輝祖. In *Wang Longzhuang xiansheng yishu* 汪龍莊先生遺書 [Literary remnants of Master Wang Longzhuang].

"Shuanglin ji zengzuan" 雙林記增纂 [Amended records of Shuanglin in Guian county, Huzhou prefecture]. Late Qing period. Manuscript held at Seikadō Bunko.

Shuilu lucheng 水陸路程 [Water and land routes], edited by Shang Jun 商濬. 1617. Held at Sonkeikaku Bunko.

Shuyuan zaji 菽園雜記 [Bean garden miscellany], by Lu Rong 陸容. 1494. Reprinted in *Tushu jicheng (chubian)*. Shanghai: Shangwu Yinshuguan, 1937. Franke 4.5.6.

Sichuan chongkan fuyi shuce 四川重刊賦役書册 [Reprinted register of the land tax and service levy for Sichuan]. Wanli era. Held at Beijing Library.

Siyou zhai congshuo 四友齋叢說 [Collected dissertations from Siyou Studio], by He Liangjun 何良俊 (1056–73). 1579. Reprint. Beijing: Zhonghua Shuju, 1959. Franke 4.3.5.

Songchuang kuaibi 松窗快筆 [Quick jottings at the pine window], by Gong Liben 龔立本 (js 1615). Late Ming. Abridged edition published in *Xiaoshi shanfang congshuo* 小石山房叢說, 1874. Franke 4.4.3.

Songjun Louxian junyi yaolüe 松郡婁縣均役要略 [Outline of Lou county, Songjiang prefecture], by Li Fuxing 李復興. 1675. Reprint. 1788.

Song shi 宋史 [Song dynastic history], by Ouyang Xiu 歐陽修. Reprint. Beijing: Zhonghua Shuju, 1977.

Songtian lubi 頌天臚筆 [Writings in praise of heaven], by Jin Risheng 金日升. 1633. Franke 2.8.7.

Song xueshi quanji 宋學士全集 [The complete works of scholar Song], by Song Lian 宋濂. 1552. Reprinted in *Sibu congkan*.

Su Pingzhong wenji 蘇平仲文集 [The collected works of Su Pingzhong], by Su Boheng 蘇伯衡. 1442. Reprinted in *Sibu congkan*.

Suyuan cungao 素園存稿 [Preserved drafts from the Simple Garden], by Fang Hongjing 方弘靜. 1611. Held at Naikaku Bunko.

Taizu shilu 太祖實錄 [Veritable records of Emperor Taizu (Hongwu)], edited by Hu Guang 胡廣. 1418. In *Ming shilu*. Franke 1.1.1.

Tianxia junguo libing shu 天下郡國利病書 [The strengths and weaknesses of the various regions of the empire], by Gu Yanwu 顧炎武. Preface dated 1662. Reprint. Shanghai: Shangwu Yinshuguan, 1936; Kyoto: Chūbun Shuppansha, 1975.

Tinglin yuji 亭林餘集 [Miscellaneous collection of Gu Tinglin's writings], by Gu Yanwu. Reprinted in *Sibu congkan*.

Tingyu jitan 聽雨紀談 [Conversations while listening to the rain], by Du Mu 都穆. Reprinted in *Huang Ming baijia xiaoshuo* 皇明百家小說 [Stories from the Ming dynasty].

Tu Kangxi gong wenji 屠康僖公文集 [The collected works of Master Tu Kangxi], by Tu Xun 屠勳. Zhengde era. Held at Naikaku Bunko.

Wang Wenke gong ji 王文恪公集 [The works of Master Wang Wenke], by Wang Ao 王鏊 (1450–1524). Franke 5.4.16.

Wang Zhen nong shu. See *Nong shu.*

Wanli san dazheng kao 萬曆三大征考 [An examination of the three great military expeditions during the Wanli era], by Mao Ruizheng 茅瑞徵. Preface dated 1621. Reprint. Beijing: Yanjing Daxue Tushuguan, 1930. Taibei: Wenhai Chubanshe, 1971. Franke 7.2.9.

(*Santai*) *Wanyong zhengzong* (三台) 萬用正宗 [(Yu Santai's) Multiple-use encyclopedia], edited by Yu Xiangdou 余象斗. 1599. Held in the Niida Bunko at Tōyō Bunka Kenkyūjo.

Weng Tie'an nianpu 翁鐵庵年譜 [Chronological biography of Weng Tie'an], by Weng Shuyuan 翁叔元. In *Jieyue shanfang huichao* 借月山房彙鈔 [Jieyue Lodge collectanea].

Wenxian congbian 文獻叢編 [Collected historical materials]. Beijing, 1936. Reprint. Taibei, 1964. Franke 9.3.1.

Wenxian tongkao 文獻通考 [Compendium of historical documents], by Ma Duanlin 馬端林.

Wufeng lu 吳風錄 [Record of the customs of Suzhou], by Huang Xingzeng 黃省曾 (1490–1540).

"Wushi fenshandian jingli zongbu" 吳氏墳山佃經理總簿 [Wu family general account books for grave hill tenants]. 1567. Photocopy of manuscript held at Tōyō Bunko.

Wuxi ji 梧溪集 [The works of Wang Wuxi], by Wang Feng 王逢 (1319–88). Reprinted in *Zhibuzu zhai congshu* 知不足齋叢書.

Wuxing zhanggu ji 吳興掌故集 [Historical materials on Wuxing], by Xu Xianzhong 徐獻忠. 1564.

Wuyue shanren ji 五嶽山人集 [The works of Wuyue shanren], by Huang Xingzeng 黃省曾. Held at Seikadō Bunko.

Wu zazu 五雜俎 [Five miscellanies], by Xie Zhaozhe 謝肇淛. Wanli era. Reprint. Beijing: Zhonghua Shuju, 1959. Franke 4.3.11.

Wuzong shilu 武宗實錄 [Veritable records of Emperor Wuzong (Zhengde)], edited by Fei Hong 費宏. 1525. In *Ming shilu.* Franke 1.1.8.

Xianzong shilu 憲宗實錄 [Veritable records of Emperor Xianzong (Chenghua)], edited by Liu Ji 劉吉. 1491. In *Ming shilu.* Franke 1.1.6.

Xiaoxia xianji zhaichao 消夏閑記摘鈔 [Excerpts from random notes written while whiling away the summer], by Gu Gongxie 顧公燮. 1785. Collected in *Hanfen lou miji* 涵芬樓祕笈.

Xiaozong shilu 孝宗實錄 [Veritable records of Emperor Xiaozong (Hongzhi)], edited by Li Dongyang 李東陽. In *Ming shilu.* Franke 1.1.7.

Xicun ji 西村記 [Notes from West Village], by Shi Jian 史鑑 (1434–96). Reprint, Taibei: Shangwu Yinshuguan, 1972.

Xijinzhi xiaolu 錫金識小錄 [A supplementary record to the Wuxi and Jinkui county gazetteers], edited by Huang Ang 黃卬. 1752. 1896 reprint held at Tōyō Bunko.

Xing'an huilan 刑案匯覽 [A collection of criminal cases]. 1834. Held in Ōki Bunko at Tōyō Bunka Kenkyūjo.

Xingshi hengyan 醒世恒言 [Stories to awaken the world], edited by Feng Menglong 馮夢龍. Tianqi era. Reprint. Beijing: Sanlian Shudian, 1965.

Xishan riji 西山日記 [Diary of Xishan], by Ding Yuanjian 丁元薦. Wanli era. Reprinted in *Hanfen lou miji*. Franke 4.3.10.

Xizong shilu 熹宗實錄 [Veritable records of Emperor Xizong (Tianqi)], edited by Wen Tiren 溫體仁. 1637. In *Ming shilu*. Franke 1.1.13.

Xuezhi yishuo 學治臆說 [An opinion on administering learning], by Wang Huizu 汪輝祖. In *Duhua zhai congshuo* 讀畫齋叢說.

Xu Wenchang quanji 徐文長全集 [The complete works of Xu Wenchang], by Xu Wei 徐渭 (1521–93). 1614. Reprint. 1911.

Xu Wenxian tongkao 續文獻通考 [Further compendium of historical documents], by Wang Qi 王圻. 1586. Franke 6.6.2.

Xu zhai ji 蓄齋集 [Writings from Xu Studio], by Huang Zhongjian 黃中堅. 1711. Held at Naikaku Bunko.

Xu Zizhi tongjian changbian 續資治通鑑長編 [Rough draft for a continuation of the comprehensive mirror], by Li Dao 李燾. Reprint. Taibei: Shijie Shuju, 1968.

Yangyuan xiansheng quanji 楊園先生全集 [The complete works of Master Yangyuan], by Zhang Lixiang 張履祥 (1611–74). 1872. Reprint. Taibei: Zhongguo Wenxian Chubanshe, 1968.

Yanshan waiji 儼山外集 [Private works of Lu Yanshan], by Lu Shen 陸深. 1545. Franke 9.5.1.

Yanshan wenji 儼山文集 [Collected works of Lu Yanshan], by Lu Shen 陸深. 1546.

Yantang jianwen zalu 研堂見聞雜錄 [Yantang's notes on things seen and heard], by Wang Jiazhen 王家禎. Ca. 1664. Reprinted in *Zhongguo neiluan waihuo lishi congshu* 中國內亂外禍歷史叢書 [Collectanea on the history of internal and external disorder in China], 1936.

Yanzhou shiliao 弇州史料 [Sources on the history of Yanzhou], by Wang Shizhen 王世貞. 1614. Franke 2.2.8.

Yehuo bian 野獲編 [Notes informally collected], by Shen Defu 沈德符. 1619. Reprint. Beijing: Zhonghua Shuju, 1959. Franke 4.1.5.

Yiban lu 一斑錄 [A miscellany], by Zheng Guangzu 鄭光祖. 1852. Held at Tōyō Bunka Kenkyūjo.

Yingzong shilu 英宗實錄 [Veritable records of Emperor Yingzong (Zhengtong)], edited by Li Xian 李賢. 1467. In *Ming shilu*. Franke 1.1.5.

Yongchuang xiaopin 涌幢小品 [Drifting thoughts], by Zhu Guozhen 朱國禎. 1621. Reprint. Beijing: Zhonghua Shuju, 1959. Franke 4.1.6.

Yongzheng zhupi yuzhi 雍正硃批諭旨 [Imperial rescripts and edicts of the Yongzheng emperor]. Reprint. Taibei: Wenhai Chubanshe, 1965.

Yuan shi 元史 [Yuan dynastic history], by Song Lian 宋濂. Reprint. Beijing: Zhonghua Shuju, 1976.

Yueshi bian 閱世編 [A survey of the age], by Ye Mengzhu 葉夢珠. Ca. 1690. Reprinted in *Shanghai zhanggu congshu*. Franke 4.9.9.

Yuezhong jinshi ji 越中金石記 [Epigraphic records of Yuezhong], by Du Chunsheng 杜春生. 1830.

Yulu xiansheng ji 與鹿先生集 [The works of Master Yulu], by Zhou Shi 周詩. Ming dynasty. Held at Naikaku Bunko.

Yuyang shuoyuan 虞陽說苑 [Yuyang's explications], edited by Ding Zuyin 丁祖蔭. 1917.

Zhang Taiyue xiansheng wenji 張太岳先生文集 [The collected works of Master Zhang Taiyue], by Zhang Juzheng 張居正. 1612. Franke 5.6.2.

Zhenze xiansheng ji 震澤先生集 [The works of Master Zhenze], by Wang Ao 王鏊. 1536. Held at Naikaku Bunko.

Zhifu qishu 致富奇書 [The wonderful book about achieving wealth], anon. Ming dynasty. Held at Naikaku Bunko.

Zhinang bu 智囊補 [Repository of knowledge, supplementary edition], by Feng Menglong 馮夢龍. 1634.

Zhuo zhai shiyi 拙齋十議 [Ten proposals from Zhuo Studio], by Xiao Lianggan 蕭良幹. Wanli era. Reprinted in *Jingchuan congshu*. Franke 6.5.2.

(*Xinzeng*) *Zizhi xinshu quanji* (新增) 資治新書全集 [The complete new book on government, newly enlarged]. Edited by Li Yu 李漁. 1663. Held in Ōki Bunko at Tōyō Bunka Kenkyūjo.

Zu he 租覈 [A study of rents], by Tao Xu 陶煦. Completed 1884, first published 1895. Reprint 1927. Also reprinted in *Kindai Chūgoku nōson shakaishi kenkyū* 近代中國農村社會史研究 [Studies in the history of village society in modern China]. Tōyō shigaku ronshū 東洋史學論集 [Essays on Oriental history], vol. 8. Tokyo: Daian, 1967.

Chinese local gazetteers

Baxi zhi 巴溪志. Reprint. 1924.
Changshu xianzhi 常熟縣志. 1503.
Changshu xianzhi. 1539.
Changxing xianzhi 長興縣志. 1749.
Changxing xianzhi. 1892.
Changzhou xianzhi 長洲縣志. 1684.
Changzhou xianzhi. 1766.
Chaoyi zhi 潮邑志 (Chaozhou). 1519.
Chongde xianzhi 崇德縣志. 1611.
Chongming xianzhi 崇明縣志. 1681.
Chuyang zhi 滁陽志 (Chuzhou). 1614.
Guangshan xianzhi 光山縣志. 1786.
Gusu zhi 姑蘇志 (Suzhou). 1506.
Haining xianzhi 海寧縣志. 1557.
Haiyan xian tujing 海鹽縣圖經. 1624.
Haiyan xian xutujing. 海鹽縣續圖經 1748.
Hangzhou fuzhi 杭州府志. 1579.
Huating xianzhi 華亭縣志. 1521.
Huating xianzhi. 1878.
Huizhou fuzhi 徽州府志. 1564.

Jiading xianzhi 嘉定縣志. 1605.
Jiading xianzhi. 1673.
Jiading xianzhi. 1881.
Jiading xianzhi. 1885.
Jiahe zhi 嘉禾志. 1288.
Jianchang fuzhi 建昌府志. 1618.
Jiangnan tongzhi 江南通志. 1684.
Jiangnan tongzhi. 1736.
Jiangwan lizhi 江灣里志. 1924.
Jiangxi sheng dazhi 江西省大志. 1597.
Jianning fuzhi 建寧府志. 1541.
Jinshan weizhi 金山衛志. 1517.
Jinshan xianzhi 金山縣志. 1752.
Kaihua xianzhi 開化縣志. 1631.
Kunshan xianzhi 崑山縣志. 1576.
Leqing xianzhi 樂清縣志. 1572.
Longyan xianzhi 龍巖縣志. 1557.
Macheng xianzhi 麻城縣志.
Min shu 閩書 (Fujian). 1630.
Nanhui xianzhi 南滙縣志. 1735.
Nanhui xianzhi. 1793.

Nanji zhi 南畿志 (South Zhili). 1534.
Nanxun zhenzhi 南潯鎮志. 1863.
Ningguo fuzhi 寧國府志. 1577.
Qingpu xianzhi 靑浦縣志. 1788.
Qiongzhou fuzhi 瓊州府志. 1617.
Quanzhou fuzhi 泉州府志. 1612.
Quanzhou fuzhi. 1763.
Quzhou fuzhi 衢州府志. 1622.
Shanghai xianzhi 上海縣志. 1524.
Shanghai xianzhi. 1588.
Shanghai zhi 上海志. 1504.
Shangyu xianzhi 上虞縣志. 1606.
Shangyuan xianzhi 上元縣志. 1593.
Shanxi tongzhi 山西通志. 1682.
Shimen xianzhi 石門縣志. 1683.
Shimen xianzhi. 1879.
Songjiang fuzhi 松江府志. 1512.
Songjiang fuzhi. 1631.
Songjiang fuzhi. 1663.
Suzhou fuzhi 蘇州府志. 1379.
Suzhou fuzhi. 1748.
Suzhou fuzhi. 1824.
Taiping xianzhi 太平縣志. 1811.
Tongli zhi 同里志. 1812.
Tongxiang xianzhi 桐鄉縣志. 1678.
Wenzhou fuzhi 溫州府志. 1605.
Wucheng xianzhi 烏程縣志. 1681.
Wucheng xianzhi. 1746.
Wujiang xianzhi 吳江縣志. 1561.
Wujiang xianzhi. 1684.

Wujiang xianzhi. 1747.
Wujiang zhi 吳江志. 1488.
Wujun Puli zhi 吳郡甫里志. 1765.
Wuqing zhenzhi 烏靑鎮志. 1760.
Wuxian zhi 吳縣志. 1642.
Wuxian zhi. 1933.
Wuxi jinkui xianzhi 無錫金匱縣志. 1814.
Xiangshan xianzhi 象山縣志. 1548.
Xiaogan xianzhi 孝感縣志. 1673.
Xijin zhi xiaolu 錫金識小錄 (Wuxi and Jinkui). 1752.
Xinghua fuzhi 興化府志. 1503.
Xinyu xianzhi 新喻縣志.
Xiushui xianzhi 秀水縣志. 1596.
Yi xianzhi 黟縣志. 1871.
Yixing xianzhi 宜興縣志. 1590.
Yongfu xianzhi 永福縣志. 1612.
Youxi xianzhi 尤溪縣志. 1636.
Yuanshi xianzhi 元氏縣志. 1642.
Yufeng zhi 玉峯志 (Kunshan). Chunyou era (1241–52).
Yuhang xianzhi 餘杭縣志. 1808.
Yunnan tongzhi 雲南通志. 1576.
Yuyao xianzhi 餘姚縣志. 1603.
Zhenjiang fuzhi 鎮江府志. 1597.
Zhenyang xianzhi 鎮洋縣志. 1744.
Zhenze xianzhi 震澤縣志. 1746.
Zhenze zhenzhi 震澤鎮志. 1844.

Secondary sources in Chinese

Beijing daxue wenke yanjiusuo 北京大學文科研究所 [Beijing University humanities research institute], ed. *Mingmo nongmin qiyi shiliao* 明末農民起義史料 [Historical materials on peasant uprisings in the late Ming]. Beijing: Kaiming Shudian, 1952.

Beijing tushuguan shanbenbu 北京圖書館善本部 [Beijing library rare books department]. *Beijing tushuguan shanben shumu* 北京圖書館善本書目 [Catalogue of rare books in the Beijing library]. Beijing: Zhonghua Shuju, 1959.

Chen Baichen 陳白塵. *Song Jingshi lishi diaochaji* 宋景詩歷史調查記 [Historical investigation of Song Jingshi]. Beijing: Renmin Chubanshe, 1957.

Chen Shoushi 陳守實. "Ming-Qing zhi ji shiliao: nubian" 明清之際史料一奴變 [Historical materials of the Ming-Qing transition: bondservant rebellions]. *Guoxue yuebao* 2:3 (1927), pp. 101–10.

Fu Yiling 傅衣凌. "Mingji nubian shiliao shibu" 明季奴變史料拾補 [Annotated materials on Ming bondservant rebellions]. *Xieda xuebao*, no. 1 (1949), pp. 163–68.

———. *Ming-Qing nongcun shehui jingji* 明清農村社會經濟 [Rural socioeconomy in the Ming and Qing]. Beijing: Sanlian Shudian, 1961.

———. "Ming-Qing shidai Jiangnan shizhen jingji de fenxi" 明清時代江南市鎮經濟的分析 [An analysis of the market town economy in Jiangnan in the Ming-Qing period]. *Lishi jiaoxue*, 1964, no. 5, pp. 9–13.

Gugong bowuyuan 故宮博物院 [Palace museum], ed. *Qingdai waijiao shiliao* 清代外交史料 [Materials on the diplomatic history of the Qing dynasty]. Beiping, 1932.

Han Dacheng 韓大成. "Mingdai shangpin jingji de fazhan yu zibenzhuyi de mengya" 明代商品經濟的發展與資本主義的萌芽 [Sprouts of capitalism and the development of a commercial economy during the Ming dynasty]. In *Ming-Qing shehui jingji xingtai de yanjiu* 明清社會經濟形態的研究 [Studies on socioeconomic forms in the Ming and Qing], edited by Zhongguo renmin daxue Zhongguo lishi jiaoyanshi 中國人民大學中國歷史教研室 [Chinese People's University Chinese history group], pp. 1–102. Shanghai: Renmin Chubanshe, 1957.

Jiang Ruizhen 蔣瑞珍. "Ming-Qing zhi ji Wuzhong de nubian" 明清之際吳中的奴變 [Bondservant rebellions in the Suzhou region during the Ming-Qing transition]. *Jiangsu yanjiu* 2:11 (1936), pp. 1–3.

Jiangsu sheng bowuguan 江蘇省博物館 [Jiangsu provincial museum], ed. *Jiangsu sheng Ming-Qing yilai beike ziliao xuanji* 江蘇省明清以來碑刻資料選集 [Selected Ming-Qing epigraphic materials from Jiangsu province]. Beijing: Sanlian Shuju, 1959.

Li Tianyou 李天佑. *Mingmo Jiangyin Jiading renmin de kang Qing douzheng* 明末江陰嘉定人民的抗清鬥爭 [Popular anti-Qing struggles in Jiangyin and Jiading at the end of the Ming]. Shanghai: Xuexi Shenghuo Chubanshe, 1955.

Li Wenzhi 李文治. *Wan Ming minbian* 晚明民變 [Late Ming popular uprisings]. Shanghai: Zhonghua Shuju, 1948.

Li Yan 李棪. *Donglin dang jikao* 東林黨記考 [An examination of the records of the Donglin group]. Beijing: Renmin Chubanshe, 1957.

Liang Fangzhong 梁方仲. *Mingdai liangzhang zhidu* 明代糧長制度 [The tax captain system in the Ming]. Shanghai: Renmin Chubanshe, 1957.

———. "Mingdai yitiao bianfa nianbiao" 明代一條鞭法年表 [Chronological table of the Ming Single Whip reform]. *Lingnan xuebao* 12:1 (1952), pp. 15–49.

———. "Yitiao bianfa" 一條鞭法 [The Single Whip reform]. *Zhongguo jindai jingji shi yanjiu jikan* 4:1 (1936).

Liu Yan 劉炎. "Mingmo chengshi jingji fazhan xia de chuqi shimin yundong" 明末城市經濟發展下的初期市民運動 [The early urban residents movement in the context of the development of regional market economies during the late Ming]. In *Zhongguo zibenzhuyi mengya wenti taolunji* 中國資本主義

萌芽問題討論集 [Essays on the sprouts of capitalism in China]. pp. 401–35. Beijing: Sanlian Shuju, 1957.

Nanjing daxue lishixi Zhongguo gudaishi jiaoyanjiushi 南京大學歷史系中國古代史敎硏究室 [Nanjing university history department, Chinese history teaching and research group]. *Zhongguo zibenzhuyi mengya wenti taolunji, xubian* 中國資本主義萌芽問題討論集續編 [Essays on the sprouts of capitalism in China], vol. 2. Beijing: Sanlian Shudian, 1960.

Nie Chongqi 聶崇岐. "Song yifa shu" 宋役法書 [On the service levy system of the Song]. *Yanjing xuebao*, no. 33 (1947), pp. 195–270.

Peng Zeyi 彭澤益. "Yapian zhanhou shinian jian yingui qianjian bodong xia de Zhongguo jingji yu jieji guanxi" 鴉片戰後十年間銀貴錢賤波動下的中國經濟與階級關係 [The Chinese economy and class relations under the fluctuations of the copper-silver exchange rate during the ten years after the Opium War]. *Lishi yanjiu*, 1961, no. 6, pp. 40–68.

Qi Longwei 祁龍威. "Qianren hui qiyi diaochaji" 千人會起義調查記 [Investigation of the uprising of the Society of the Thousand]. In *Xinhai geming Jiangsu diqu shiliao* 辛亥革命江蘇地區史料 [Historical materials on the 1911 revolution in the Jiangsu region], edited by the History Department of Yangzhou Shifan Daxue. Nanjing: Jiangsu Renmin Chubanshe, 1961. Reprint. Tokyo: Daian, 1963.

Qing Ruji 卿汝楫. *Meiguo qin Hua shi* 美國侵華史 [A history of American encroachment in China]. 2 vols. Beijing: Sanlian Shudian, 1952–56.

Taiping Shanren 太平山人. "Daoguang chao yinhuang wenti" 道光朝銀荒問題 [The problem of the silver shortage during the Daoguang era]. *Zhonghe yuekan* 1:8 (1940), pp. 61–75.

Tan Bi'an 譚彼岸 "Zhongguo jindai huobi de biandong" 中國近代貨幣的變動 [Changes in modern China's currency]. *Zhongshan daxue xuebao*, 1957, no. 3, pp. 184–204.

Wei Hongyun 魏宏運, *Shi Kefa* 史可法 [Shi Kefa]. Shanghai: Xinzhishi Chubanshe, 1955.

Wei Jianyou 魏建猷. *Zhongguo jindai huobi shi* 中國近代貨幣史 [A history of modern Chinese currency]. Shanghai: Chunlian Chubanshe, 1955.

Wei Qingyuan 韋慶遠. *Mingdai huangce zhidu* 明代黃冊制度 [The Yellow Register system in the Ming]. Beijing: Zhonghua Shuju, 1961.

Wu Han 吳晗. *Dushu zaji* 讀書雜記 [Miscellaneous notes from reading history]. Beijing: Sanlian Shudian, 1956.

Wu Jingxian 吳景賢. "Ming-Qing zhi ji Huizhou nubian kao" 明清之際徽州奴變考 [An examination of bondservant rebellions in Huizhou during the Ming-Qing transition]. *Xuefeng* 7:5 (1937), pp. 1–15.

Wu Tingxie 吳廷燮. *Ming du fu nianbiao* 明督撫年表 [A chronological table of Ming governors and supreme commanders].

Xie Chengren 謝承仁. *Yiliusiwunian Jiangyin renmin shoucheng de gushi* 一六四五年江陰人民守城的故事 [Anecdotes concerning the people's defense of Jiangyin in 1645). Beijing: Zhongguo Qingnian Chubanshe, 1956.

Xie Guozhen 謝國楨. "Mingji nubian kao" 明季奴變考 [An examination of bondservant rebellions in the Ming]. *Qinghua xuebao* 8:1 (1932), pp. 1–28.

———. *Nan Ming shilüe* 南明史略 [A brief history of the southern Ming]. Shanghai: Renmin Chubanshe, 1957.

———. *Qingchu nongmin qiyi ziliao jilu* 清初農民起義資料記錄 [A compilation of sources on early Qing peasant uprisings]. Shanghai: Xinzhishi Chubanshe, 1956.

Xu Daling 許大齡. "Shiliu shiji shiqi shiji chuqi Zhongguo fengjian shehui neibu zibenzhuyi de mengya" 十六世紀十七世紀初期中國封建社會內部資本主義的萌芽 [The sprouts of capitalism within Chinese feudal society during the sixteenth and early seventeenth centuries]. *Beijing daxue xuebao: renwen kexue*, 1956, no. 3, pp. 17–48.

Xu Tiantai 徐天胎. "Mingdai Fujian Deng Maoqi zhi luan" 明代福建鄧茂七之亂 [The rebellion of Deng Maoqi in Fujian during the Ming]. *Fujian wenhua*, no. 31 (1941), pp. 11–30.

Xu Weinan 徐蔚南. *Shanghai mianbu* 上海棉布 [Shanghai cotton textiles]. *Shanghai Bowuguan congshu*. Shanghai: 1936.

Yang Duanliu 楊端六. *Qingdai huobi jinrong shigao* 清代貨幣金融史稿 [A draft history of currency and finance during the Qing dynasty]. Beijing: Sanlian Shudian, 1962.

Ye Shichang 葉世昌. *Yapian zhanzheng qianhou wo guo de huobi xueshuo* 鴉片戰爭前後我國的貨幣學說 [Theories on our country's currency around the time of the Opium War]. Shanghai: Renmin Chubanshe, 1963.

Yuan Songzhou 原頌周 *Zhongguo zuowu lun* 中國作物論 [On Chinese products]. Shanghai: Shangwu yinshuguan, 1925.

Zhongguo renmin daxue Zhongguo lishi jiaoyanshi 中國人民大學中國歷史教研室 [Chinese People's University, Chinese history teaching and research group]. *Zhongguo zibenzhuyi mengya wenti taolunji* 中國資本主義萌芽問題討論集 [Essays on the sprouts of capitalism in China]. Beijing: Sanlian Shudian, 1957.

Zhongguo renmin yinhang zonghang canshishi jinrong shiliao zu 中國人民銀行總行參事室金融史料組 [Chinese people's bank, general office advisory group, sub-group for materials on financial history]. *Zhongguo jindai huobi shi ziliao* 中國近代貨幣史資料 [Materials on the history of currency in modern China]. 2 vols. Beijing: Zhonghua Shuju, 1964.

Zhu Shijia 朱士嘉, ed. *Zhongguo difangzhi zonglu* 中國地方志總錄 [Union catalogue of Chinese local gazetteers]. Shanghai: Shangwu Shudian, 1958.

Japanese-language sources

Adachi Keiji 足立啓二. "Minmatsu Shinsho no ichi nōgyō keiei—*Shinshi nō-sho* no saihyōka" 明末清初の一農業經營—沈氏農書の再評價 [Farm management in the late Ming and early Qing—a reconsideration of *Shenshi nongshu*]. *Shirin* 61:1 (1978), pp. 40–69.

———. "Min-Shin jidai no shōhin seisan to jinushisei kenkyū o megutte" 明清時代の商品生產と地主制研究をめぐって [Studies on commodity production and the landlord system in the Ming-Qing period]. *Tōyōshi kenkyū* 36:1 (1977), pp. 125–35.

————. "Shindai Kahoku no nōgyō keiei to shakai kōzō" 清代華北の農業經營 と社會構造 [Agricultural management and social structure in North China during the Qing]. *Shirin* 64:4 (1981), pp. 66–91.

Amano Motonosuke 天野元之助. "Chin Fu no *Nōsho* to suitōsaku gijitsu no tenkai" 陳旉の農書と水稻作技術の展開 [Chen Fu's *Nong shu* and the development of wet-rice farming technology]. *Tōhō gakuhō* (Kyoto), no. 21 (1952), pp. 37–133.

————. *Shina nōgyō keizairon* 支那農業經濟論 [Chinese agricultural economics]. Tokyo: Kaizōsha, 1940.

Asada Kyōji 淺田喬二. "Nihon shokuminshi kenkyū no genkyō to mondaiten" 日本植民史研究の現況と問題點 [The present situation and problems in the study of Japanese colonial history]. *Rekishi hyōron*, no. 300 (1975), pp. 178–98.

————. "Nihon shokuminshi kenkyū no kadai to hōhō" 日本植民史研究の 課題と方法 [Problems and approaches to the study of Japanese colonial history]. *Rekishi hyōron*, no. 308 (1975), pp. 63–83.

————. "Nihon teikokushugi to shokuminchi mondai" 日本帝國主義と植民 地問題 [Japanese imperialism and the problem of colonies]. *Rekishi hyōron*, no. 309 (1976), pp. 42–59.

Banno Ryōkichi 坂野良吉. "Shanhai Shōtōkai no hanran" 上海小刀會の叛亂 [The rebellion of the Shanghai Small Sword Society]. *Rekishigaku kenkyū*, no. 353 (1969), pp. 1–13.

Bekkuya Hideo 鼈宮谷英夫. "Kinsei Chūgoku ni okeru fueki kaikaku" 近世 中國に於ける賦役改革 [Fiscal reform in early modern China]. Pt. 2. *Rekishi hyōron* 1:3 (1946), pp. 48–64.

"Chūgoku no kindaika" 中國の近代化 [China's modernization]. In *Sekai no rekishi* 世界の歴史 [History of the world], vol. 11, pp. 300–20. Tokyo: Chikuma Shobō, 1961.

Fei Xiaotong 費孝通. *Shina no nōmin seikatsu* 支那の農民生活 [Peasant life in China], translated from English by Senba Yasuo 仙波泰雄 and Shioya Yasuo 鹽谷安夫. 1939.

Fujii Hiroshi 藤井宏. "Chūgoku ni okeru shin to kyū" 中國に於ける新と舊 [Old and new in China]. *Tōyō bunka*, no. 9 (1952), pp. 21–40.

————. "Ichijō benpō no ichi sokumen" 一條鞭法の一側面 [An aspect of the Single Whip reform]. In *Wada hakushi kanreki kinen Tōyōshi ronsō* 和田博 士還暦記念東洋史論叢 [Essays on Oriental history in honor of Dr. Wada's sixtieth birthday], pp. 571–90. Tokyo: Kōdansha, 1951.

————. "Kyōshin" 鄉紳 [The gentry]. In *Ajia rekishi jiten* アジア歴史事典 [Encyclopedia of Asian history], pp. 406–7. Tokyo: Heibonsha, 1959.

————. "Mindai enjō no kenkyū" 明代鹽場の研究 [A study of salt fields during the Ming]. *Hokkaidō daigaku bungakubu kiyō*, no. 3 (1954), pp. 89–132.

————. "Mindai no dendo tōkei ni kansuru ichi kōsatsu" 明代の田土統計に 關する一考察 [An investigation of Ming land statistics]. Pt. 3. *Tōyō gakuhō*

31:1 (1947), pp. 97–134.

————. "Min: shakai keizai" 明：社會・經濟 [The Ming: society and economy]. In *Ajia rekishi jiten* アジア歴史事典 [Encyclopedia of Asian history], vol. 8, pp. 418–22. Tokyo: Heibonsha, 1961.

————. "Minsho ni okeru kinkōfu to zeiryō to no kankei" 明初に於ける均工夫と税糧との關係 [The relationship between the equalized labor levy and taxation in the early Ming]. *Tōyō gakuhō* 44:4 (1962), pp. 1–30.

————. "Shin'an shōnin no kenkyū" 新安商人の研究 [A study of the Xin'an merchants]. 4 pts. *Tōyō gakuhō* 36: 1–4 (1953–54), pp. 1–45, pp. 180–208, pp. 335–88, pp. 533–63.

————. "Sōkōki no ichijō benpō: Fu Kanshin no jōgen o meguru sho mondai" 創行期の一條鞭法—傅漢臣の上言をめぐる諸問題 [The Single Whip reform in its initial stages: problems concerning the memorial of Fu Hanchen]. *Hokkaido daigaku bungakubu kiyō*, no. 9 (1961), pp. 21–52.

Fujioka Jiro 藤岡次郎. "Senhappyakugojūsan-nen 'Katei nōmin kigi' to sono rekishiteki haikei" 一八五三年嘉定農民起義とその歴史的背景 [The "Jiading peasant uprising" of 1853 and its historical background]. *Hokkaido gakugei daigaku kiyō* 10:2 (1960), pp. 158–69.

Fujita Masanori 藤田正典. "Jūshichi-hachi seiki ni okeru Ei-Shi tsūshō kankei" 十七八世紀に於ける英支通商關係 [Anglo-Chinese trade relations in the seventeenth and eighteenth centuries]. *Tōa ronsō*, no. 1 (1939), pp. 19–122.

Fujita Toyohachi 藤田豊八. "Sō-Gen jidai kaikō to shite no Kōshū" 宋元時代海港としての杭州 [Hangzhou as a seaport during the Song and Yuan periods], 2 pts. *Shigaku zasshi* 27: 9 (1916), pp.54–72; 10 (1916), pp. 63–80.

————. *Tōzai kōshōshi no kenkyū* 東西交渉史の研究 [Studies in the history of East-West exchange]. 2 vols. Tokyo: Oka shoin, 1932–33.

Fukutake Tadashi 福武直. *Chūgoku nōson shakai no kōzō* 中國農村社會の構造 [The structure of Chinese rural society]. Tokyo: Yūhikaku, 1951.

Fuma Susumu 夫馬進. "Minmatsu no toshi kaikaku to Kōshū minpen" 明末の都市改革と杭州民變 [Late Ming urban reform and the popular uprising in Hangzhou]. *Tōhō gakuhō* (Kyoto), no. 49 (1977), pp. 215–612.

Funabashi Sadao 船橋貞男, Hoshi Ayao 星斌夫. "Mindai no tōchō ni tsuite" 明代の塘長について [Embankment captains in the Ming]. *Rekishi no kenkyū*, no. 6 (1958), pp. 58–70.

Furushima Kazuo 古島和雄. "*Ho nōsho* no seiritsu to sono jiban" 補農書の成立とその地盤 [The compilation of the *Bu nongshu* and its social background]. *Tōyō Bunka Kenkyūjo kiyō*, no. 3 (1952), pp. 81–117.

————. "Minmatsu Chōkō deruta ni okeru jinushi keiei" 明末長江デルタに於ける地主經營 [Landlord management in the Yangzi delta during the late Ming]. *Rekishigaku kenkyū*, no. 148 (1950), pp. 11–23.

Goi Naohiro 五井直弘. *Kindai Nihon to Tōyō shigaku* 近代日本と東洋史學 [Modern Japan and the study of Oriental history]. Tokyo: Aoki Shoten, 1976.

Hamada Yoshimichi 濱田好通. "Sangyō shihon dankai ni okeru Amerika no gaikoku bōeki" 產業資本段階に於けるアメリカの外國貿易 [American foreign trade at the stage of industrial capitalism]. Pt. 4. *Ryūtsū keizai ronshū* 6:1 (1971), pp. 33–38.

Hamashima Atsutoshi 濱島敦俊. *Mindai Kōnan nōson shakai no kenkyū* 明代江南農村社會の研究 [Rural society in Jiangnan during the Ming dynasty]. Tokyo: Tokyo Daigaku Shuppankai, 1982.

―――. "Mindai Kōnan no suiri no ichi kōsatsu" 明代江南の水利の一考察 [An examination of water control in Ming-dynasty Jiangnan]. *Tōyō bunka kenkyūjo kiyō*, no. 47 (1969), pp. 1–62.

―――. "Minmatsu Sekkō no KaKo ryōfu ni okeru kinden kin'eki hō" 明末 浙江の嘉湖兩府に於ける均田均役法 [The land tax and service levy equalization system in Jiaxing and Huzhou prefectures, Zhejiang, during the late Ming]. *Tōyō bunka kenkyūjo kiyō*, no. 52 (1970), pp. 139–88.

Hamashita Takeshi 濱下武志. "Jūkyū seiki kōhan Chūgoku ni okeru gaikoku ginkō no kin'yū shijō shihai no rekishiteki tokushitsu—Shanhai ni okeru kin'yū kyōkō to no kanren ni oite" 十九世紀後半中國に於ける外國銀行 の金融市場支配の歴史的特質―上海に於ける金融恐慌との關連に於いて [Historical characteristics of foreign banks' control over the Chinese financial market in the latter half of the nineteenth century, in relation to the financial panic in Shanghai]. *Shakai keizai shigaku* 40: 3 (1974), pp. 26–43.

―――. "Shihonshugi-shokuminchi taisei no keisei to Ajia" 資本主義―植民 地体制の形成とアジア [Asia and the formation of the capitalist-colonial structure]. In *Kōza Chūgoku kingendaishi* 講座中國近現代史 [Lectures on China's modern and contemporary history], vol. 1, pp. 13–44. Tokyo: Tokyo Daigaku Shuppankai, 1978.

Hatada Takashi 旗田巍. *Chūgoku sonraku to kyōdōtai riron* 中國村落と共同 體理論 [Theory of community in Chinese villages]. Tokyo: Iwanami Shoten, 1972.

Hoshi Ayao 星斌夫. See Funabashi Sadao.

Hosoi Masaharu 細井昌治. "Shinsho no shori" 清初の胥吏 [Yamen clerks in the early Qing]. *Shakai keizai shigaku* 14:6 (1944), pp. 1–23.

Hosono Kōji 細野浩二. "Rirōjin to shūrōjin" 里老人と衆老人 [Lijia elders and popular elders]. *Shigaku zasshi* 78: 7 (1969), pp. 51–68.

Ichiko Chūzō 市古宙三. *Kindai Chūgoku no seiji to shakai* 近代中國の政治と 社會 [Modern Chinese politics and society]. Tokyo: Tokyo Daigaku Shuppankai, 1971.

―――. "Kyōshin to Shingai kakumei" 鄉紳と辛亥革命 [The gentry and the 1911 revolution], in *Sekai no rekishi*, vol. 15. Tokyo: Chikuma Shobō, 1962, pp. 93–118. Later included in Ichiko, *Kindai Chūgoku no seiji to shakai*, pp. 331–60.

Imahori Seiji 今堀誠二. *Chūgoku kindaishi kenkyū josetsu* 中國近代史研究 序説 [Introduction to the study of modern Chinese history]. Tokyo: Keisō Shobō, 1968.

―――. "Shindai no kōso ni tsuite" 清代の抗租につい [Rent resistance during the Qing period], *Shigaku zasshi* 76: 9 (1967), pp. 37–61. Revised and included in Imahori, *Chūgoku kindaishi kenkyū josetsu*, pp. 92–132.

Ishida Yoneko 石田米子. "Daikanryō to kyōshin" 大官僚と郷紳 [High officials and the gentry]. *Chūgoku bunka sōsho* 中國文化叢書 [Chinese culture series], vol. 8, pp. 246–66. Tokyo: Taishūkan Shoten, 1968.

Iwami Hiroshi 岩見宏. "Mindai chihō zaisei no ichi kōsatsu: Kanton no kinpeigin ni tsuite" 明代地方財政の一考察—廣東の均平銀について [An inquiry into local finance in the Ming: the equitable silver levy in Guangdong]. *Kenkyū*, no. 3 (1953), pp. 72–82.

——. "Mindai no minso to hokuhen bōei" 明代の民壯と北邊防衛 [The Ming militia and northern frontier defense]. *Tōyōshi kenkyū* 19: 2 (1960), pp. 156–74.

——. "Min no Kasei zengo ni okeru fueki kaikaku ni tsuite" 明の嘉靖前後に於ける賦役改革について [On fiscal reforms around the Jiajing era of the Ming]. *Tōyōshi kenkyū* 10:5 (1949), pp. 1–25.

Kataoka Shibako 片岡芝子. "Kahoku no tochi shoyū to ichijō benpō" 華北の土地所有と一條鞭法 [Landownership and the Single Whip reform in north China]. In *Shimizu hakushi tsuitō kinen Mindaishi ronsō* 清水博士追悼記念明代史論叢 [Essays on Ming history in memory of Dr. Shimizu], pp. 139–63. Tokyo: Daian, 1962.

——. "Minmatsu Shinsho no Kahoku ni okeru nōka keiei" 明末清初の華北に於ける農家經營 [North China peasant enterprise in the late Ming and early Qing]. *Shakai keizai shigaku* 25: 2–3 (1959), pp. 77–100.

Katayama Seijirō 片山誠二郎. "Mindai kaijō mitsubōeki to enkai chihō kyōshinsō" 明代海上密貿易と沿海地方郷紳層 [Ming maritime smuggling and the gentry in coastal areas]. *Rekishigaku kenkyū*, no. 164 (1953), pp. 23–32.

Katō Shigeru 加藤繁. *Shina keizaishi gaisetsu* 支那經濟史概說 [An outline of Chinese economic history]. Tokyo: Kōbundō Shobō, 1944.

Kawakatsu Mamoru 川勝守. *Chūgoku hōken kokka no shihai kōzō* 中國封建國家の支配構造 [The structure of control of the Chinese feudal state]. Tokyo: Tokyo Daigaku Shuppankai, 1980.

Kikuchi Hideo 菊池英夫. "Tō-Sō jidai o chūshin to suru iwayuru 'koyō rōdō' ni kansuru shokenkyū" 唐宋時代を中心とするいわゆる雇用勞働に關する諸研究 [A review of studies on "contract labor" during the Tang and Song periods]. *Tōyō gakuhō* 43: 3 (1960), pp. 49–66.

Kitamura Hironao 北村敬直. "Chūgoku no jinushi to Nihon no jinushi," 中國の地主と日本の地主 [Chinese and Japanese landlords], *Rekishi hyōron*, no. 2 (1960), pp. 19–25.

——. "Minmatsu Shinsho ni okeru jinushi ni tsuite" 明末清初に於ける地主について [On landlords in the late Ming-early Qing]. *Rekishigaku kenkyū*, no. 140 (1949), pp. 13–25.

——. "Shindai no jidaiteki ichi" 清代の時代的位置 [The place of the Qing in Chinese history]. *Shisō*, no. 292 (1948), pp. 47–57.

——. *Shindai shakai keizaishi kenkyū* 清代社會經濟史研究 [Studies in Qing socioeconomic history]. Osaka: Osaka Shiritsu Daigaku Keizai Gakkai, 1972.

Kobayashi Kazumi 小林一美. "Kyōdōtai no rekishiteki igi o megutte" 共同體

の歴史的意義をめぐって [On the historical significance of community].
Shichō, no. 2 (1977), pp. 87–94.

Kojima Shinji 小島晉治. "Taihei Tengoku" 太平天國 [The Taiping Heavenly Kingdom]. In *Sekai no rekishi* 世界の歴史 [History of the world], vol. 11, pp. 111–53. Tokyo: Chikuma Shobō, 1961. Reprint. 1979.

————. "Taihei Tengoku kakumei" 太平天國革命 [The revolution of the Taiping Heavenly Kingdom]. In *Sekai rekishi* 世界歴史 [World history], vol. 21, pp. 281–334. Tokyo: Iwanami Shoten, 1971. Reprint. 1979.

————. "Taihei Tengoku to nōmin" 太平天國と農民 [The Taiping Heavenly Kingdom and the peasants]. 3 pts. *Shichō*, nos. 93 (1965) pp. 44–77; 96 (1966) pp. 1–30, 97 (1966) pp. 85–102.

Kojima Yoshio 小嶋淑男, "Shinmatsu Minkoku-shoki Kōnan no nōmin, undō" 清末民國初期江南の農民運動 [Jiangnan peasant movements in the late Qing and early Republic]. *Rekishi kyōiku* 16:1–2 (1968), pp. 116–24.

Kuribayashi Norio 栗林宣夫. "Mindai kōki no nōson to rikōsei" 明代後期の農村と里甲制 [Villages and the *lijia* system in the latter part of the Ming]. In *Tōyō shigaku ronshū* 東洋史學論集 [Essays on Oriental history], vol. 4, pp. 365–400. Tokyo: Fumaidō, 1955.

————. "Mindai rōjin kō" 明代老人考 [An examination of elders in the Ming]. In Yamazaki Hiroshi, ed., *Tōyō shigaku ronshū*, vol. 3, pp. 129–40. Tokyo: Fumaidō, 1954.

————. "Rikōgin ni kansuru kōsatsu" 里甲銀に關する考察 [An investigation of *lijia* silver]. In *Tōyō shigaku ronshū*, vol. 2, pp. 329–54. Tokyo: Fumaidō, 1954.

————. "Sekkō no teiden ni tsuite" 浙江の丁田について [Poll- and land-tax assessment in Zhejiang]. In *Yamazaki sensei taikan kinen Tōyō shigaku ronshū* 山崎先生退官記念東洋史學論集 [Essays on Oriental history in honor of Professor Yamazaki's retirement], pp. 175–84. Tokyo: Daian, 1967.

Liao Baoxian 廖寶賢. *Shina heisei no seikakuteki kenkyū* 支那幣制の性格的研究 [Studies in the characteristics of China's currency system], translated from German by Katsutani Arito 勝谷在登. Tokyo: Hakuyōsha, 1940.

Mainichi shimbunsha tosho henshūbu. 毎日新聞社圖書編集部 [Book editing department of Mainichi Shimbun]. *Sekai no rekishi* 世界の歴史 [World history], vol. 3. Tokyo: Mainichi Shimbunsha, 1949. Reprint. 1952. Contributing authors: Matsumoto Yoshimi, Niida Noboru.

Mantetsu chōsabu 滿鐵調查部 [Research department of the South Manchurian Railway Co.]. *Hoku Shina menka sōran* 北支那棉花總覧 [A survey of North China cotton]. Tokyo: Nihon Hyōronsha, 1940.

Matsumoto Yoshimi 松本善海. "Kyū Chūgoku shakai no tokushitsuron e no hansei" 舊中國社會の特質論への反省 [A reconsideration of the theory of the special characteristics of pre-revolutionary Chinese society]. *Tōyō bunka kenkyū*, no. 9 (1948), pp. 20–35; no. 10 (1949), pp. 37–51.

————. "Mindai" 明代 [The Ming dynasty]. In *Shina chihō jichi hattatsushi* 支那地方自治發達史 [History of the development of local self-government in China], edited by Wada Sei 和田清. Tokyo: Chūka Minkoku Hōsei

Kenkyūkai, 1939.

Miyazaki Ichisada 宮崎市定. *Ajiashi kenkyū* アジア史研究 [Studies in Asian history]. Kyoto: Tōyōshi Kenkyūkai, 1957.

——. "Chūgoku kinsei no nōmin bōdō" 中國近世の農民暴動 [Peasant uprisings in early modern China]. *Tōyōshi kenkyū* 10: 1 (1947), pp. 1–13. Included in *Ajiashi Kenkyū*, vol. 3 pp. 213–26.

——. "Mindai So-Shō chihō no shidaifu to minshū" 明代蘇松地方の士大夫と民衆 [The literati and the masses in the Suzhou-Songjiang region during the Ming]. *Shirin* 37:3 (1954), pp. 1–33.

Momose Hiromu 百瀬弘. "Shindai ni okeru Supein doru no ryūtsū" 清代に於けるスペインドルの流通 [Circulation of Spanish dollars during the Qing]. 3 pts. *Shakai keizai shigaku,* vol. 6 (1936); no. 2, pp. 1–25; no. 3, pp. 38–60; no. 4, pp. 43–65.

Mōri Kenzō 毛利健三. *Jiyū bōeki teikokushugi: Igirusu sangyō shihon no sekai tenkai* 自由貿易帝國主義―イギリス産業資本の世界展開 [The imperialism of free trade: the global spread of British industrial capital]. Tokyo: Tokyo Daigaku Shuppankai, 1978.

Mori Masao 森正夫. "Jūnana seiki no Fukken Neika-ken ni okeru Kō Tsū no kōso hanran" 十七世紀の福建寧化縣に於ける黄通の抗租反亂 [The anti-rent rebellion of Huang Tong in Ninghua county, Fujian, during the seventeenth century]. 3 pts. *Nagoya daigaku bungakubu kenkyū ronshū,* no. 59 (1973), pp. 1–31; no. 62 (1974), pp. 1–35; no. 74 (1978), pp. 25–65.

——. "Jūnana seiki shotō no shokuyō no hen o meguru ni-san no shiryō ni tsuite," 17 世紀初頭の「織傭の變」をめぐる二三の資料について [Materials concerning the "rebellion of the hired silk workers" at the beginning of the seventeenth century], *Nagoya daigaku bungakubu kenkyū ronshū,* 80 (1981), pp. 1–22.

——. "Jūroku-jūhachi seiki ni okeru kōsei to jinushi denko kankei" 十六―十八世紀に於ける荒政と地主佃戸關係 [Famine relief and landlord-tenant relations from the sixteenth to eighteenth centuries]. *Tōyōshi kenkyū* 27:4 (1969), pp. 69–111.

——. "Jūyon seiki kōhan Sekisai chihō no jinushisei ni kansuru oboegaki" 十四世紀後半浙西地方の地主制に關する覺書 [Note on landlordism in western Zhejiang in the latter half of the fourteenth century]. *Nagoya daigaku bungakubu kenkyū ronshū,* no. 44 (1967), pp. 67–88.

——. "Min-Shin jidai no tochi seido" 明清時代の土地制度 [The land system of the Ming and Qing periods]. In *Sekai rekishi* 世界歴史 [World history], vol. 12, pp. 229–74. Tokyo: Iwanami Shoten, 1971. Reprint. 1979.

——. "Minsho Kōnan no kanden ni tsuite" 明初江南の官田について [State land in Jiangnan during the early Ming], pt. 2. *Tōyōshi kenkyū* 19: 4 (1961), pp. 1–18.

——. "Nihon no Min-Shin jidaishi kenkyū ni okeru kyōshinron ni tsuite" 日本の明清時代史研究に於ける郷紳論について [Theories of the gentry in Japanese studies of Ming-Qing history]. 3 pts. *Rekishi hyōron,* no. 308 (1975), pp. 40–60; no. 312 (1976), pp. 74–84; no. 314 (1976), pp. 113–280.

——. *Nuhen to kōso: Minmatsu Shinsho o chūshin to suru Kachū-Kanan on*

chiiki shakai ni okeru minshū no teikō undō 奴變と抗租—明末清初を中心と
する華中華南の地域社會に於ける民衆の抵抗運動　[Bondservant revolts
and anti-rent struggles—local society and popular protest movements in
central and south China in the late Ming and early Qing]. Nagoya: by the
author, 1980.

―――. "Senroppyakuyonjūgo nen Taisōshū Sakeichin ni okeru uryūkai no
hanran ni tsuite" 一六四五年太倉州沙溪鎮に於ける烏龍會の叛亂について
[The Black Dragon Society rebellion in Shaxi town, Taicang subprefecture,
in 1645]. In *Nakayama Hachirō kyōju shōju kinen Min-Shin shi ronso* 中山
八郎教授頌壽記念明清史論叢 [Articles on Ming-Qing history in honor
of Professor Nakayama Hachirō], pp. 195–232. Tokyo: Ryōgen Shoten,
1977.

Morita Akira 森田明. "Minmatsu ni okeru tōchōsei no henshitsu ni tsuite"
明末に於ける塘長制の變質について [The deterioration of the embank-
ment captain system at the end of the Ming]. *Tōhōgaku*, no. 26 (1963), pp.
85–94.

―――. "Shindai no tōchōsei ni tsuite" 清代の塘長制について [The embankment captain system in the Qing]. *Chūgoku suirishi kenkyū*, no. 1 (1965),
pp. 49–62.

Moriya Mitsuo 守屋美都雄. "Furō" 父老 [Elders]. *Tōyōshi kenkyū* 14: 1–2
(1955), pp. 43–60.

Motoyama Yoshihiko 本山美彦. "Igirisu shihonshugi no sekaika to Ajia:
ahen o meguru Higashi Indo Gaisha to Kanton shōsha no kakuchiku"
イギリス資本主義の世界化とアジア—阿片をめぐる東インド會社と廣東
商社の角逐 [Asia and the global spread of English capitalism: the contest
over opium between the East India Company and the Canton trading
houses]. In *Sekai keizai to teikoku shugi* 世界經濟と帝國主義 [Imperialism
and the world economy]. Edited by Ono Kazuichirō 小野一一郎 et al.
Tokyo: Yūhikaku, 1973. pp 273–313.

Muramatsu Yūji 村松祐次. *Kindai Kōnan no sosan* 近代江南の租棧 [Rent
bursaries in modern Jiangnan]. Tokyo: Tokyo Daigaku Shuppankai, 1970.

Nakayama Hachirō 中山八郎. "Banmin no nuka nuhen: 晚明の奴禍奴變
[Bondservant disasters and rebellions in the late Ming]. *Rekishi kyōiku*
10: 11 (1936), pp. 53–58.

―――. "Mindai no shokusenkyoku" 明代の織染局 [The Ming imperial
textile workshops]. *Hitotsubashi ronsō* 9: 5 (1942), pp. 479–502.

Negishi Tadashi 根岸佶. *Chūgoku shakai ni okeru shidōsō: kirō shinshi no
kenkyū* 中國社會に於ける指導層—耆老紳士の研究 [The ruling strata in
Chinese society: studies in elders and the gentry]. Tokyo: Heiwa Shobō,
1947.

"Nihon ni okeru Chūgoku kenkyū no kadai II: shimpojiumu" 日本に於ける
中國研究の課題 II：シンポジウム [Themes in Japanese studies of China],
pt. 2. *Ajia keizai* 11: 7 (1970), pp. 48–71.

Niida Noboru 仁井田陞. *Chūgoku hōseishi kenkyū: dorei nōdo hō, kazoku
sonraku hō* 中國法制史研究—奴隷農奴法家族村落法 [Studies in the his-
tory of the Chinese legal system: slave and serf law, family and village law].

Tokyo: Tokyo Daigaku Shuppankai, 1962. Reprint. 1981.

———. *Chūgoku hōseishi kenkyū: keihō* 中國法制史研究—刑法 [Studies in the history of the Chinese legal system: criminal law]. Tokyo: Tokyo Daigaku Shuppankai, 1962. Reprint. 1981.

———. "Chūgoku kyūshakai no kōzō to keibatsuken" 中國舊社會の構造と刑罰權 [Penal authority and the structure of China's pre-revolutionary society], *Chūgoku hōseishi kenkyū: keihō*, pp. 3–33.

———. "Chūgoku shakai no 'hōken' to 'fyūdarizumu'" 中國社會の「封建」とフューダリズム ['Feudalism' and *'fengjian'* in Chinese society] *Tōyō bunka*, no 5. (1951) pp. 1–39. Included in *Chūgoku hōseishi* 中國法制史 [Chinese legal history]. Tokyo: Iwanami Shoten, 1963, pp. 135–59.

———. "Chūgoku no nōdo koyōjin no hōteki mibun no keisei to henshitsu—shuboku no bun ni tsuite 中國の農奴・雇傭人の法的身分の形成と變質—主僕の分について [The formation and transformation of the legal status of serfs and hired labor in China—the legal status of master and servant], in *Chūgoku hōseishi kenkyū: dorei, nōdo hō, kazoku sonraku hō*, pp. 147–93.

Nishijima Sadao 西嶋定生. *Chūgoku keizaishi kenkyū* 中國經濟史研究 [Studies in Chinese economic history]. Tokyo: Tokyo Daigaku Shuppankai, 1966.

———. "Chūgoku shoki mengyō shijō no kōsatsu" 中國初期棉業市場の考察 [An examination of the market in the early Chinese cotton industry], in *Chūgoku keizaishi kenkyū*, pp. 873–903.

———. "Jūroku-jūnana seiki o chūshin to suru Chūgoku nōson kōgyō no kōsatsu" 十六十七世紀を中心とする中國農村工業の考察 [An examination of Chinese rural industry in the sixteenth and seventeenth centuries], in *Chūgoku keizaishi kenkyū*, pp. 729–52.

———. "Mindai ni okeru momen no fukyu ni tsuite" 明代において木棉の普及について [The spread of cotton cultivation during the Ming dynasty], in *Chūgoku keizaishi no kenkyū*, pp. 753–804.

———. "Shōkōfu ni okeru mengyō keisei no katei ni tsuite" 松江府に於ける棉業形成の過程について [The formation of the cotton industry in Song-jiang prefecture]. *Shakai keizai shigaku* 13: 11–12 (1944), pp. 107–114.

———. See also Suzuki Shun.

Nomura Kōichi 野村浩一. "Kindai kokkakan e no chōsen" 近代國家觀への挑戰 [A challenge to the concept of the modern state]. *Asahi Ajia rebyū*, no. 1 (1971), pp. 16–23.

Numata Tomoo 沼田鈑雄. "Ichijō benpō josetsu" 一條鞭法の序節 [Introduction to the Single Whip reform]. *Rekishi to chiri* (Fuzanbō) 10 (1934).

Obata Tatsuo 小畑龍雄. "Mindai kyōson no kyōka to saiban" 明代鄉村の敎化と裁判 [Moral instruction and adjudication in Ming villages]. *Toyōshi kenkyū* 11: 5–6 (1952), pp. 23–43.

———. "Mindai kyokusho no rōjinsei" 明代極初の老人制 [The elders system at the beginning of the Ming]. *Yamaguchi daigaku bungakukaishi*, no. 1 (1950), pp. 61–70.

———. "Minsho no chihō seidoto rikōsei" 明初の地方制度と里甲制 [Local

institutions and the lijia system in the early Ming]. *Jimbun kagaku* 1:4 (1947), pp. 25–57.

Okuzaki Hiroshi 奥崎裕司. *Chūgoku kyōshin jinushi no kenkyū* 中国郷紳地主 の研究 [Studies in Chinese gentry landlords]. Tokyo: Kyūko Shoin, 1978.

———. "Mindai ni okeru jinushi no shisō no ichi kōsatsu" 明代に於ける地主 の思想の一考察 [An inquiry into landlord thought in the Ming]. *Tōyō gakuhō* 51:2 (1968), pp. 28–67.

Ono Kazuko 小野和子. "Tōrinha to sono seiji shisō" 東林派とその政治思想 [The political thought of the Donglin party]. *Tōhō gakuhō* (Kyoto), no. 28 (1958), pp. 249–82.

Orihara Hiroshi 折原浩. *Kiki ni okeru ningen to gakumon* 危機に於ける人間 と學文 [Scholarship concerning people in crisis]. Tokyo: Miraisha, 1969.

Otake Fumio 小竹文夫. "Min-Shin jidai ni okeru gaikoku gin no ryūnyū" 明清時代に於ける外國銀の流入 [Inflow of foreign silver during the Ming-Qing periods]. In *Kinsei Shina keizaishi kenkyū* 近世支那經濟史研究 [Studies in the history of modern China's economy]. Tokyo: Kōbundō Shobō, 1942.

Ōtsuka Hisao 大塚久雄. *Kindai Ōshū keizaishi josetsu* 近代歐洲經濟史序節 [An introduction to the economic history of modern Europe]. Reprinted as vol. 2 of *Ōtsuka Hisao chosakushū* 大塚久雄著作集 [Collected works of Ōtsuka Hisao]. Tokyo: Iwanami Shoten, 1980.

———. *Kindai shihonshugi no keifu* 近代資本主義の系譜 [The development of modern capitalism]. Reprinted as vol. 3 of *Ōtsuka Hisao chosakushū*. Tokyo: Iwanami Shoten, 1980.

Oyama Masaaki 小山正明. "Chūgoku shakai no hen'yō to sono tenkai" 中国社會の變樣とその展開 [The transformation and development of Chinese society]. In *Tōyōshi nyūmon* 東洋史入門 [An introduction to Oriental history], edited by Nishijima Sadao. pp. 33–58, Tokyo: Yūhikaku, 1967.

———. "Fueki seido no henkaku" 賦役制度の變革 [Reforms in the tax and labor service system]. In *Sekai rekishi* 世界歴史 [World history], vol. 12, pp. 313–45. Tokyo: Iwanami Shoten, 1971.

———. "Mindai Kahoku fueki seido kaikakushi kenkyū no ichi kentō" 明代華北賦役制度改革史研究の一檢討 [An examination of studies on the history of fiscal reform in north China during the Ming]. *Tōyō bunka*, no. 37 (1964), pp. 99–113.

———. "Mindai no jūdanhō ni tsuite" 明代の十段法について [The Ming ten-section system], 2 pts. Pt. 1: in *Zenkindai Ajia no hō to shakai: Niida Noboru hakushi tsuitō ronbunshū* 前近代アジアの法と社會―仁井田陞博士追悼 論文集 [Law and society in premodern Asia: essays in memory of Dr. Niida Noboru], vol. 1, pp. 365–86. Tokyo: Keisō Shobō, 1967. Pt. 2: *Chiba daigaku bunrigakubu bunka kagaku kiyō*, no. 10 (1968), pp. 1–40.

———. "Mindai no ryōchō ni tsuite" 明代の糧長について [Tax captains in the Ming]. *Tōyōshi kenkyū* 27: 4 (1969), pp. 24–68.

———. "Minmatsu Shinsho no dai tochi shoyū: toku ni Kōnan deruta chitai o chūshin ni shite," 明末清初の大土地所有―とくに江南デルタ地 帶を中心にして [Large landownership in the Jiangnan delta region during the late Ming-early Qing period]. *Shigaku zasshi* 66: 12 (1957), pp. 1–30; 67:1 (1958), pp. 50–72.

———. "Rikōsei setchi no nendai ni tsuite" 里甲制設置の年代について [Dating the establishment of the *lijia* system]. Paper presented at the Jisseiroku kenkyūkai, Tōyō Bunko, March 1962.

Rekishigaku kenkyūkai 歴史學研究會 [Historical Science Society]. *Kokka kenryoku no shodankai* 国家權力の諸段階 [The stages of state power]. Tokyo: Iwanami Shoten, 1950.

Rinji Taiwan kyūkan chōsakai 臨時臺灣舊慣調査會 [Provisional investigation committee of laws and customs in Taiwan]. *Shinkoku gyōseihō* 清國行政法 [Administrative laws of the Qing state]. Tokyo: 1910.

Saeki Tomi 佐伯富. "Shindai no kyōyaku chiho ni tsuite" 清代の鄉約地保について [Village covenants and constables in the Qing]. *Tōhōgaku*, no. 28 (1964), pp. 91–100.

Saeki Yūichi 佐伯有一. "Mindai zenpanki no kiko" 明代前半期の機戶 [Weaving households in the first half of the Ming dynasty]. *Tōyō bunka kenkyūjo kiyō*, no. 8 (1956), pp. 167–210.

———. "Minmatsu no Tō-shi no hen: iwayuru 'nuhen' no seikaku ni kanrenshite" 明末の董氏の變—いわゆる「奴變」の性格に關聯して [The Dong family rebellion in the late Ming: the nature of so-called bondservant rebellions]. *Tōyōshi kenkyū* 16:1 (1957), pp. 26–57.

———. "Nihon no Min-Shin jidai kenkyū ni okeru shōhin seisan hyōka o megutte" 日本の明清時代研究に於ける商品生產評價をめぐって [Japanese evaluations of commodity production in the Ming-Qing period]. In *Chūgokushi no jidai kubun*, edited by Suzuki Shun and Nishijima Sadao, pp. 253–321.

Saeki Yūichi, Tanaka Masatoshi 田中正俊. "Jūgo seiki ni okeru Fukken no nōmin hanran" 十五世紀に於ける福建の農民叛亂 [Peasant rebellion in fifteenth-century Fujian]. *Rekishigaku kenkyū*, no. 167 (1954), pp. 1–11.

———, ———. "Jūroku jūnana seiki no Chūgoku nōson seishi kinuorigyō" 十六十七世紀の中国農村製糸絹織業 [Chinese rural silk-spinning and weaving industry in the sixteenth and seventeenth centuries]. In *Sekaishi kōza* 世界史講座 [Lectures on world history], vol. 1, pp. 240–53. Tokyo: Tōyō Keizai Shinpōsha, 1955.

———, ———. "Kinuorimono-gyō: sōsetsu, Chūgoku" 絹織物業: 總說, 中国 [The silk weaving industry: general discussion, China]. In *Sekai rekishi jiten* 世界歷史辭典 [Encyclopedia of world history], vol. 5, pp. 66–74. Tokyo: Heibonsha, 1951.

Sakai Tadao 酒井忠夫. *Chūgoku zensho no kenkyū* 中国善書の研究 [Studies on Chinese morality books]. Tokyo: Kōbundō, 1960.

———. "Mindai zenchūki no hokōsei ni tsuite" 明代前中期の保甲制について [The *baojia* system in the early and mid-Ming]. In *Shimizu hakushi tsuitō kinen Mindaishi ronsō* 清水博士追悼記念明代史論叢 [Essays on Ming history in memory of Dr. Shimizu], pp. 577–610. Tokyo: Daian, 1962.

Sano Manabu 佐野學. *Shinchō shakaishi* 清朝社會史 [A social history of the Qing dynasty]. 3 vols. Tokyo: Bunkyūdō, 1947–48.

Sanshigyō dōgyō kumiai chūōkai 蠶絲業同業組合中央會 [Central committee of the silk industry union]. *Shina sanshigyō taikan* 支那蠶絲業大觀 [Overview of the silk industry in China]. Tokyo: Okada Nichieidō, 1929.

Sasaki Masaya 佐々木正哉. "Kanpō ni-nen Gin-ken no kōryō bōdō" 咸豐二年鄞縣の抗糧暴動 [The tax resistance uprising in Yin county in 1852]. In *Kindai Chūgoku kenkyū* 近代中国研究 [Studies on modern China], vol. 5, pp. 185–299. Tokyo: Tokyo Daigaku Shuppankai, 1963.

———. *Shinmatsu no himitsu kessha* 清末の秘密結社 [Secret societies at the end of the Qing], vol. 1. Tokyo: Gannandō, 1970.

Shigeta Atsushi 重田德. "Chūgoku hōkensei kenkyū to hōhō: rikuchō hōkenseiron no ichi kentō," 中國封建制研究と方法─六朝封建制論の一檢討 [Methodology and the direction for research on Chinese feudalism in the six dynasties], *Rekishi kagaku*, no. 33 (1970), later included in Shigeta, *Shindai shakai keizaishi kenkyū*, pp. 378–98.

———. "Hōkensei no shiten to Min-Shin shakai," 封建制の視點と明清社會 [The feudal perspective and Ming-Qing society], *Tōyōshi kenkyū*, 27: 4 (1969), pp. 164–81, later included in Shigeta, *Shindai shakai keizaishi kenkyū*, pp. 350–78.

———. "Shincho nōmin shihai no rekishiteki tokushitsu: chiteigin seiritsu no imi suru mono," 清朝農民支配の歷史的特質─地丁銀成立のいみする もの [The historical characteristics of Qing dynasty peasant rule: the significance of the introduction of *didingyin*], in *Nihonhō to Ajia: Niida Noboru hakushi tsuitō ronbunshu* 日本法とアジア─仁井田陞博士追悼論文集 [A commemorative collection of essays for Dr. Niida Noboru: Japanese law and Asia]. Tokyo: Keisō Shobō, 1967, pp. 387–412; later included in Shigeta, *Shindai shakai keizaishi kenkyū*, pp. 98–122.

———. "Shindai Kishū shōnin no ichimen," 清代徽州商人の一面 [One aspect of Huizhou merchants during the Qing dynasty]. *Jinbun kenkyū* (Osaka Shiritsu Daigaku) 19: 8 (1968), pp. 1–40, later included in Shigeta, *Shindai shakai keizaishi kenkyū*, pp. 294–349.

———. *Shindai shakai keizaishi kenkyū* 清代社會經濟史研究 [Studies on Qing socioeconomic history]. Tokyo: Iwanami Shoten, 1975.

———. "Shinsho ni okeru Kōnan kome shijō no ichi kōsatsu" 清初に於ける 湖南米市場の一考察 [An investigation of the Hunan rice market in the early Qing]. *Tōyō bunka kenkyūjo kiyō*, no. 10 (1956), pp. 427–98, included in *Shindai shakai keizaishi kenkyū*, pp. 1–66.

Shimizu Morimitsu 清水盛光. *Chūgoku kyōson shakairon* 中國鄉村社會論 [Chinese rural society]. Tokyo: Iwanami Shoten, 1951.

Shimizu Taiji 清水泰次. *Chūgoku kinsei shakai keizaishi* 中國近世社會經濟史 [Socioeconomic history of early modern China]. Tokyo, 1950.

———. "Ichijō benpō" 一條鞭法 [The Single Whip reform]. In *Kuwabara hakushi kanreki kinen Tōyōshi ronsō* 桑原博士還曆記念東洋史論叢 [Essays on Oriental history in honor of Dr. Kuwabara's sixtieth birthday], pp. 191–211. Kyoto: Kōbundō shobō, 1931.

———. "Mindai hanseki no kenkyū" 明代版籍の研究 [A study of Ming census registers]. *Kōa keizai kenkyūjo kiyō*, no. 1 (1943), pp. 25–74.

———. "Mindai ni okeru ekihō no hensen" 明代に於ける役法の變遷 [Changes in the service levy during the Ming]. *Shikan*, no. 8 (1935), pp. 64–81.

———. "Mindai no kokōsatsu (kōsatsu) no kenkyū" 明代の戶口册(黄册) の研究 [A study of Ming population registers (Yellow Registers)]. *Shakai keizai shigaku* 5: 1 (1935), pp. 1–33.

———. "Mindai no zeieki to kiki" 明代の稅役と詭寄 [Taxation and land registration transfer in the Ming]. *Tōyō gakuhō* 17: 3–4 (1929), pp. 72–84.

———. "Min no Seisōchō ni okeru Soshū chihō no jōryō" 明の世宗朝に 於ける蘇州地方の丈量 [The land survey of the Suzhou region in Ming Shizong's reign]. *Tōa keizai kenkyū* 26: 1 (1942), pp. 1–22.

———. "Min no Taiso no sengo tochi keiei" 明の太祖の戰後土地經營 [The founding of the first Ming emperor's postwar land management]. *Tōa keizai kenkyū* 24: 3 (1940), pp. 302–324.

———. "Minsho ni okeru gunton no hatten to sono soshiki" 明初に於ける軍 屯の發展とその組織 [The development and organization of military colonies in the early Ming], pt. 2. *Shigaku zasshi* 44: 6 (1933), pp. 29–72.

Shiozawa Kimio 鹽澤君夫. *Ajiateki seisan yōshikiron* アジア的生産樣式論 [The Asiatic mode of production]. Tokyo: Ochanomizu Shobō, 1970.

Soda Hiroshi 相田洋. "Byakuren-kyō no seiritsu to sono tenkai" 白蓮敎の 成立とその展開 [The formation and evolution of the White Lotus sect]. In *Chūgoku minshu hanran no sekai* 中國民衆反亂の世界 [The world of Chinese popular rebellion], pp. 147–217. Tokyo: Kyūko Shoin, 1974.

———. "Genmatsu no hanran to sono haikei" 元末の叛亂とその背景 [Rebellion in the late Yuan and its background]. *Rekishigaku kenkyū*, no. 361 (1970), pp. 1–17.

Sogabe Shizuo 曾我部靜雄. *Sōdai zaiseishi* 宋代財政史 [History of fiscal administration in the Song dynasty]. Tokyo, 1941.

Sutō Yoshiyuki 周藤吉之. *Chūgoku tochi seidoshi kenkyū* 中國土地制度史 研究 [Studies in the history of Chinese land systems]. Tokyo: Tokyo Daigaku Shuppankai, 1954. Reprint. 1971.

———. "Sōdai no denkosei: dorei kōsaku to no kanren ni tsuite," 宋代の佃 戶制—奴隸耕作との關聯に於いて [Tenancy in the Song period—in relation to cultivation by slaves], in *Chūgoku tochi seidoshi kenkyū*, pp. 107–177.

Suzuki Chūsei 鈴木中正. *Shinchō chūkishi kenkyū* 清朝中期史研究 [Studies in mid-Qing history]. Toyohashi: Aichi Daigaku Kokusai Mondai Kenkyūjo, 1952.

———. "Shinmatsu jōgai undō no kigen" 清末攘外運動の起源 [The origins of the anti-foreign movement in the late Qing]. *Shigaku zasshi* 62: 10 (1953), pp. 1–28.

Suzuki Shigetaka 鈴木成高. *Hōken shakai no kenkyū* 封建社會の研究 [A study of feudal society]. Tokyo: Kōbundō shobō, 1948.

Suzuki Shun 鈴木淳, Nishijima Sadao 西嶋定生, ed. *Chūgokushi no jidai kubun* 中國史の時代區分 [Periodization in Chinese history]. Tokyo: Tokyo Daigaku Shuppankai, 1957. Reprint. 1979.

Suzuki Tomoo 鈴木智夫. *Kindai Chūgoku no jinushisei* 近代中國の地主制 [The landlord system in modern China]. Tokyo: Kyūko Shoin, 1977.

Tachibana Shiraki 橘樸. *Shina shakai kenkyū* 支那社會研究 [Studies of Chinese society]. Tokyo: Nihon Hyōronsha, 1936.

Takimura Ryūichi 瀧村龍一. *Marukusushugi kokkaron* マルクス主義國家論 [The Marxist theory of the state]. Tokyo: San'ichi Shobō, 1971.

Tanaka Masatoshi 田中正俊. "Ajia shakai teitairon hihan no hōhōronteki hansei," アジア社會停滯論批判の方法論的反省 [Reflections on methodological approaches in the critique of Asian stagnation], in *Chūgoku kindai keizaishi kenkyū josetsu*, pp. 3–23.

———. Bibliography in *Hatten tojōkoku kenkyū* 發展途上國研究 [Research on the developing countries]. Tokyo: Ajia Keizai Kenkyūjo, 1978, pp. 41–51.

———. *Chūgoku kindai keizaishi kenkyū josetsu* 中國近代經濟史研究序說 [Introduction to the study of modern Chinese economic history]. Tokyo: Tokyo Daigaku Shuppankai, 1973. Reprint. 1981.

———. "Chūgoku rekishi gakkai ni okeru 'shihonshugi no hōga' kenkyū" 中國歷史學界に於ける〈資本主義の萌芽〉研究 [The study of the "sprouts of capitalism" in Chinese historical circles]. In *Chūgokushi no jidai kubun*, edited by Nishijima Sadao and Suzuki Shun, pp. 219–52.

———. "Chūgoku shakai no kaitai to Ahen sensō," 中国社會の解體とアヘン戰爭 [The disintegration of Chinese society and the Opium war], in *Chūgoku kindai keizaishi kenkyū josetsu*, pp. 101–158.

———. "Chūsei Chūgoku ni okeru kokka kenryoku to tochi shoyū kankei," 中世中國における國家權力と土地所有關係 [State power and landownership relations in medieval China]. Paper presented at the Rekishigaku kenkyūkai, Tokyo, February 1961.

———. "Ichiden-ryōshu-sei to ganden kōsō," 一田兩主制と頑佃抗租 [The multiple landownership system and rent resistance by refractory tenants]. Paper presented at the annual meeting of the Shakai Keizaishi Gakkai, Tokyo, Chūo University, May 1960.

———. "Minmatsu Shinsho no dai tochi shoyū ni tsuite—gakusetsushiteki tenbō," 明末清初の大土地所有について一學說史的展望 [Large-scale landownership in the late Ming and early Qing: from the perspective of the history of interpretations]. Paper presented at the Hikaku Tochi Seidoshi Kenkyūkai, University of Tokyo, Shakai Kagaku Kenkyūjo, July 1958.

———. "Minpen, kōso, nuhen," 民變抗租奴變 [Popular revolts, rent resistance and bondservant rebellions], in *Sekai no rekishi*, vol. 11, Tokyo: Chikuma Shobō, 1961, pp. 41–80.

———. "Minsho tochi mondai no ichi kōsatsu," 明初土地問題の一考察 [An investigation of the land question in the early Ming]. Paper presented at the annual meeting of the Tōyōshi danwakai, University of Tokyo, July 1963.

———. "Seiō shihonshugi to kyū Chūgoku shakai no kaitai—Mitcheru hōkokusho o megutte," 西歐資本主義と舊中國社會の解體「ミッチュル報告書」をめぐって [Western imperialism and the disintegration of Chinese society—on the Mitchell Report]. In *Chūgoku kindai keizaishi kenkyū josetsu*, pp. 159–202.

———. "Tachiagaru nōmintachi: jūgo seiki ni okeru Chūgoku no nōmin hanran" 起ちあがる農民達―十五世紀に於ける中國の農民叛亂 [Peasants in revolt: Chinese peasant rebellion in the fifteenth century]. In *Sekai rekishi kōza* 世界歴史講座 [Lectures on world history], vol. 2, pp. 191–228. Tokyo: San'ichi Shobō, 1954.

———. "Tō Moshichi no ran no shoden ni tsuite" 鄧茂七の亂の所傳について [Source materials on the Deng Maoqi rebellion]. In *Shimizu hakushi tsuitō kinen Mindaishi ronsō* 清水博士追悼記念明代史論叢 [Essays on Ming history in memory of Dr. Shimizu], pp. 637–72. Tokyo: Daian, 1962.

———. See also Saeki Yūichi.

Tanaka Masatoshi, et al. "Chūgoku no kindaika" 中國の近代化 [Modernization in China], in *Sekai no rekishi*, vol. 11, pp. 300–320.

Tanaka Tadao 田中忠夫. *Shina keizai no hōkai katei to hōhōron* 支那經濟の崩壞過程と方法論 [The process of economic decline in China and the methodology of its study]. Tokyo: Gakugeisha, 1936.

Tanigawa Michio 谷川道雄. *Chūgoku chūsei shakai to kyōdōtai* 中國中世社會と共同體 [Medieval Chinese society and community]. Tokyo: Kokushi Kankōkai, 1976.

Terada Takanobu 寺田隆信. *Sansei shōnin no kenkyū* 山西商人の研究 [Studies on the Shanxi merchants]. Kyoto: The Society of Oriental Research, 1972.

Thorp, James. *Shina dojō chirigaku* 支那土壤地理學 [The geography of the soils of China]. Translated from English by Itō Takakichi 伊藤隆吉. Tokyo: Iwanami Shoten, 1941.

Tokyo kyōiku daigaku Chūgoku shakai keizaishi kenkyūkai 東京教育大學中國社會經濟史研究會 [Chinese socioeconomic history research group of Tokyo University of Education]. "Chūgokushi no sekaishiteki haaku wa dō susunda ka: chūseishi kenkyū no kadai" 中國史の世界史的把握はどう進んだか―中世史研究の課題 [How has the global understanding of Chinese history advanced: themes in medieval studies], pt. 2. *Rekishi hyōron*, no. 186 (1966), pp. 31–40.

Toyohara Jiro 豐原次郎. *Amerika shōhin ryūtsū shiron* アメリカ商品流通史論 [History of the distribution of American commodities]. Tokyo: Miraisha 1971.

Toyoshima Shizuhide 豊島靜英. "Chūgoku saihokubu ni okeru suiri kyōdōtai ni tsuite" 中國西北部に於ける水利共同體について [Water-control communities in northwest China]. *Rekishigaku kenkyū*, no. 201 (1956), pp. 24–35.

Tsurumi Naohiro 鶴見尚弘. "Mindai ni okeru kyōson shihai" 明代における郷村支配 [Rural control in the Ming dynasty], in *Sekai rekishi* 世界歴史 [World history], vol. 12, Tokyo: Iwanami Shoten, 1971, pp. 57–92.

———. "Mindai no kireiko ni tsuite" 明代の畸零戸について [Supernumerary households in the Ming]. *Tōyō gakuhō* 47: 3 (1964), pp. 35–64.

————. "Shoki Min-ōchō no nōmin shihai" 初期明王朝の農民支配 [Control of peasants in the early Ming]. *Shichō*, no. 75 (1961), pp. 73–74.

Ubukata Naokichi 幼方直吉. "Nankin momen kōbōshi" ナンキン木棉興亡史 [History of the rise and fall of 'Nankeen' cotton]. *Tōa ronsō*, no. 1 (1939), pp. 257–85.

Umehara Kaoru 梅原郁. "Gendai saekihō shōron" 元代差役法小論 [Comment on service levy labor in the Yuan dynasty]. *Tōyōshi kenkyū* 23: 4 (1965), pp. 39–67.

Usui Sachiko 臼井佐知子. "Taihei Tengoku zen, Soshū-fu Shōkō-fu ni okeru fuzei mondai" 太平天國前蘇州府松江府に於ける賦税問題 [Tax problems in Suzhou and Songjiang prefectures in the period before the Taiping rebellion]. *Shakai keizai shigaku* 47: 2 (1981), pp. 59–82.

Wada Sei 和田清, ed. *Shina chihō jichi hattatsushi* 支那地方自治發達史 [History of the development of local self-government in China]. Tokyo: Chūka Minkoku Hōsei Kenkyūkai, 1939.

Watanabe Kin'ichi 渡邊金一. *Bizantsu shakai keizaishi kenkyū* ビザンツ社會經濟史研究 [Studies in Byzantine socioeconomic history]. Tokyo: Iwanami Shoten, 1968.

————. "Bizantsu teikoku ni okeru hōkensei no mondai: hitotsu no shiron," ビザンツ帝國における封建制の問題——一つの試論 [Problems of feudalism in the Byzantine Empire]. *Rekishigaku kenkyū*, no. 242 (1960), pp. 26–35. Included in *Bizantsu shakai keizaishi kenkyū*, pp. 51–78.

Yamane Yukio 山根幸夫. *Chūgoku nōmin kigi bunken mokuroku* 中國農民起義文獻目錄 [A bibliography of Chinese peasant uprisings]. Tokyo: Tokyo Joshi Daigaku Tōyōshi Kenkyūshitsu, 1976.

————. "Jūroku seiki Chūgoku ni okeru aru kokō tōkei ni tsuite: Fukken Keianken no baai" 十六世紀中國に於けるある戶口統計について—福建惠安縣の場合 [Some population figures for sixteenth-century China: the case of Huian county, Fujian]. *Tōyō daigaku kiyō*, no. 6 (1954), pp. 161–72.

————. "Kananshō Shōjōken no shinshisō no sonzai keitai" 河南省商城縣の紳士層の存在形體 [The composition of the gentry stratum in Shangcheng county, Henan]. *Tōyōshi kenkyū* 40: 2 (1981), pp. 59–84.

————. "Mindai richō no shokuseki ni kansuru ichi kōsatsu" 明代里長の職責に關する一考察 [An investigation of the duties of *li* captains in the Ming]. *Tōhōgaku*, no. 3 (1952), pp. 1–9.

————. *Mindai yōeki seido no tenkai* 明代徭役制度の展開 [The development of the Ming labor service system]. Tokyo: Tokyo Joshi Daigaku, 1966.

————. "Minsho no kinkōfu ni tsuite" 明初の均工夫について [On the equalized labor levy in the early Ming]. *Tōyō gakuhō* 39: 3 (1956), pp. 99–103.

————. "Teiryō to kōgin" 丁糧と剛銀 ['Adult male labor fees' and 'summarized payments']. In *Wada hakushi koki kinen Tōyōshi ronsō* 和田博士古稀記念東洋史論叢 [Essays on Oriental history in honor of Dr. Wada's seventieth birthday], pp. 1027–38. Tokyo: Kōdansha, 1961.

Yamazaki Takeji 山崎武治. "Ichijō benpō no sōkō ni tsuite" 一條鞭法の創行について [On the introduction of the Single Whip reform]. *Ritsumeikan bungaku*, no. 152 (1958), pp. 38–56.

Yasuno Shōzō 安野省三. "Minmatsu Shinsho Yōsukō chūryūiki no dai to-chi shoyū ni kansuru ichi kōsatsu" 明末清初楊子江中流域の大土地所有に關する一考察 [An investigation of large scale landowning in the central Yangzi region during the late Ming and early Qing]. *Tōyō gakuhō* 44: 3 (1961), pp. 61–88.

————. "Shindai no nōmin hanran" 清代の農民叛亂 [Peasant rebellion in the Qing]. In *Sekai rekishi* 世界歴史 [World history], vol. 12, pp. 197–228. Tokyo: Iwanami Shoten, 1971. Reprint. 1979.

Yokoyama Suguru 横山英. *Chūgoku kindaika no keizai kōzō* 中國近代化の經濟構造 [The economic structure of China's modernization]. Tokyo: Aki Shobō, 1972.

————. "Chūgoku ni okeru shōkōgyō rōdōsha no hatten to yakuwari: Min-matsu ni okeru Soshū o chūshin to shite," 中國における商工業勞働者の發展と役割一明末における蘇州を中心として [The development and role of Chinese commercial and handicraft workers in Suzhou in the late Ming], *Rekishigaku kenkyū*, 160 (November 1952), pp. 1–13.

————. "Jūkyū seiki chūyō no kōryō fūchō " 十九世紀中葉の抗糧風潮 [The tide of tax resistance in the mid-nineteenth century], in *Chūgoku kindaika no keizai kōzō*, pp. 227–49.

Yoneda Haruyasu 米田治泰. "Bizantsu hōkensei kenkyū no dōkō" ビザンツ封建制研究の動向 [Trends in studies of Byzantine feudalism]. *Seiyō shigaku*, no. 66 (1965), pp. 44–54.

Yoshimoto Takaaki 吉本隆明. "Kotai, kazoku, kyōdōsei to shite no ningen" 個休, 家族, 共同性としての人間 [People as individuals, families, and communities]. In his *Yoshimoto Takaaki zen chosakushū* 吉本隆明全著作集 [The complete works of Yoshimoto Takaaki], vol. 14. Tokyo: Keisō Shobō, 1972.

————. *Kyōdō gensō ron* 共同幻想論 [The vision of community]. Tokyo: Kawade Shobō, 1968.

Western-language sources

Beattie, Hilary. *Land and Lineage: a Study of T'ung-ch'eng County, Anhui, in the Ming and Ch'ing dynasties*. Cambridge: Cambridge University Press, 1979.

British Parliamentary Papers, China. Area Studies Series, vols. 6, 38, 39, 40. Shannon: Irish University Press, 1971–72.

Bruchey, Stuart. *Cotton and the Growth of the American Economy: 1790–1860, Sources and Readings*. Ann Arbor: Michigan State University Press, 1967.

Chaudhuri K.N. *The Economic Development of India under the East India Company, 1814-58, A Selection of Contemporary Writers*. Cambridge: Cambridge University Press, 1971.

Chang, Chung-li [Zhang Zhongli]. *The Chinese Gentry*. Seattle: University of Washington Press, 1955.

Cordier, Henri. *Bibliotheca Sinica*. Vols. 1–4. Paris: E. Guilmoto, 1904–8. Vol. 5. Paris: Paul Geuthner, 1922–24.

Couling, Samuel. *The History of Shanghai* Shanghai 1921.

Elvin, Mark. *The Pattern of the Chinese Past*. Stanford: Stanford University Press, 1973.

Fei, Hsiao-Tung [Fei Xiaotong]. *Peasant Life in China*. London: Routledge and Kegan Paul, 1939.

Fogel, Joshua. "Prewar Japanese Studies of Republican China." *Chinese Republican Studies Newsletter* 4:2 (1979), pp. 13–20.

Fong, H.D. [Fang Xianting]. *Cotton Industry and Trade in China*. 2 vols. Tianjin: Chihli Press, 1932. Reprint. Washington: Center for Chinese Research Materials, 1972.

Franke, Wolfgang. *An Introduction to the Sources of Ming History*. Kuala Lumpur: University of Malaya Press, 1968.

Greenberg, Michael. *British Trade and the Opening of China, 1800–42*. Cambridge, 1951. Reprint. New York: Monthly Review Press, 1979.

Grove, Linda, and Joseph Esherick. "From Feudalism to Capitalism: Japanese Scholarship on the Transformation of Chinese Rural Society." *Modern China* 6: 4 (1980), pp. 397–438.

Hamashima, Atsutoshi. "The Organization of Water Control in the Kiangnan Delta in the Ming Period." *Acta Asiatica*, no. 38 (1980), pp. 69–92.

Hamashita Takeshi. "A History of the Japanese Silver Yen and The Hongkong and Shanghai Banking Corporation, 1871–1913." In *Eastern Banking: essays in the history of the Hongkong and Shanghai Banking Corporation*, edited by Frank H. H. King. London: Athlone Press, 1983, pp. 321–49.

————. "The role of intermediaries in local and national Chinese finance, 1898–1916." A paper presented at the Eighth International Economic History Congress, Budapest, August 1982.

Hao, Yen-P'ing [Hao Yanping]. *The Comprador in Nineteenth Century China: Bridge between East and West*. Cambridge: Harvard University Press, 1970.

Hirth, F., and Rockhill, W.W. *Chau Ju-kua*. St. Petersburg: Printing Office of the Imperial Academy of Sciences, 1911.

Hommel, Rudolf P. *China at Work*. New York: John Day, 1937. Reprint. Cambridge: The M.I.T. Press, 1969.

Huang, Ray [Huang Renyu]. *Taxation and Government Finance in Sixteenth Century Ming China*. Cambridge: Cambridge University Press, 1974.

Hucker, Charles O. "Su-chou and the Agents of Wei Chung-hsien, a Translation of K'ai-tu ch'uan-hsin." *Silver Jubilee Volume of the Zinbun-Kagaku-Kenkyusyo, Kyoto University*. Kyoto, 1954.

Jenks, H.L. *The Migration of British Capital to 1875*. London, 1963.

Kann, Edward. *The Currencies of China*. 2nd ed. Shanghai: Kelly and Walsh, 1927. Reprint. New York: AMS Press, 1972.

King. W.T.C. *History of the London Discount Market*. London, 1936.

Littrup, Leif. *Subbureaucratic Government in China in Ming Times: a Study of Shandong Province in the Sixteenth Century*. Oslo: Universitetsforlaget, 1982.

Liao, Bao-Seing [Liao Baoxian]. *Die Bedeutung des Silberproblems für die Entwicklung der chinesischen Währungsverhältnisse* [The significance of the silver problem for the development of the Chinese currency situation]. Berlin, 1939.

Lubbock, B. *The China Clippers*. Glasgow, 1914.

Marriner, Shelia. *Rathbones of Liverpool, 1845-73*. Liverpool, 1961.

Martin, R. Montgomery. *China, Political, Commercial and Social: In an Official Report to Her Majesty's Government*. 2 vols. London: Madden, 1847.

Marx, Karl, and Engels, Fredrick. *The Collected Works of Karl Marx and Frederick Engels*. Moscow: Progress Publishers, 1975.

"Mitchell Report." In *British Parliamentary Papers*.

Mori, Masao. "The Gentry in the Ming Period: An Outline of the Relations between the *Shih-ta-fu* and Local Society." *Acta Asiatica*, no. 38 (1980), pp. 31-53.

Morse, H.B. The *Chronicles of the East India Company Trading to China, 1635-1834*. 5 vols. Oxford, 1926-29.

———. *The Period of Conflict, 1834-60*. The International Relations of the Chinese Empire, vol. 1. London, 1910.

Muramatsu, Yūji. "A Documentary Study of Chinese Landlordism in the Late Ch'ing and Early Republican Kiangnan." *Bulletin of the School of Oriental and African Studies* 29: 3 (1970), pp. 566-99.

North China Herald, The

Pritchard, E.H. "The Crucial Years of Early Anglo-Chinese Relations, 1750-1800." *Research Studies of the State College of Washington*, 4:3-4 (1936).

Quesnay, François. "Despotisme de la Chine." 1767. In *Oeuvres Economiques et Philosophiques de F. Quesnay*. Paris, 1888, 563-660.

Semedo, Alvaro. *The History of the Great and Renowned Monarchy of China*. Translation. London: John Crook, 1655.

Sumiya, Mikio, and Koji Taira. *An Outline of Japanese Economic History, 1603-1940*. Tokyo: University of Tokyo Press, 1979.

Sun, E-tu Zen, and Sun, Shiou-chuan. *T'ien-kung K'ai-wu: Chinese Technology in the Seventeenth Century*. University Park: Pennsylvania State University Press, 1966.

Thorp, James. *The Geography of the Soils of China*. Nanjing, 1936.

Tilly, Charles. *The Formation of National States in Western Europe*. Princeton: Princeton University Press, 1975.

Tooke, Thomas. *A History of Prices, and of the State of the Circulation, during the Nine Years, 1845-56*. Vol. 6. London, 1857.

Twitchett, Denis. "A Critique of Some Recent Studies of Modern Chinese Social-Economic History." *Transactions of the Conference of Orientalists in Japan*, no. 10 (1965), pp. 28-41.

Watson, Ernest. *The Principle Articles of Chinese Commerce*. 2nd ed. Shanghai, 1930.

Yamane, Yukio. "Trends in Postwar Japanese Studies in Ming History: A Bibliographical Introduction." *Acta Asiatica*, no. 38 (1980), pp. 93-123.

INDEX

Adachi Keiji, 9
agricultural implements, 46
agricultural manuals, 39
agriculture
  cash crops, 207
  character of, 38
  integration with handicrafts, 84–85
  promotion of, 378, 385n147
  reproduction, defined, 245–46
  reproduction, and state, 273
Alcock, Rutherford, 393, 417,423,
  424–25
Allum (Alum), 419
Amano Motonosuke, 123, 270
ancestor worship, 107
ancestral sacrifices, 22
Anhui, 116–19, 124, 194, 232
Anqing prefecture, 120
Antingzhen, 52, 53
anti-rent movement. *See* rent resistance
  struggles
anti-tax movement. *See* tax resistance
  struggles
Araki Moriaki, 101–2
autocracy, 352

Bailian jiao. *See* White Lotus Sect
Bai Shangdihui, 222. *See also* Taiping
Baitian, 107
Baitian gangshe ji, 107
Bai Yue, 108
baku-han system (Japan), 101–2
bandang, 119, 154n61. *See also* tenants,
  servile
bandits, 131
  mines, 201–2
banks
  Bank of England, 400
  Chinese, 425, 426n4, 431–32n92
  in English-Chinese trade, 423
  foreign, 389
baolan, 384n140
Baring, Francis, 409
Baring & Co., 400, 402, 409
barley, 38, 140
barter

British capital, 387,424
  as credit, 422–23
  defined, 408
  effects of, 387
  excessive trade, 417
  items, 410–13, 415, 417, 419–20
  mechanism, 410
  in Ningbo, 431n75
  origins, 417–19
  parliamentary testimony on, 410–411
  and surplus goods, 415
batou, 170, 174
Bell & Company, 395, 414, 422
Bianmin tuzuan, 270
Binshan county, 142
bipu, 108
Black Banner, 229, 239
Black Dragon Association, 197
Board of Revenue, 28
boche, 47
Bohai, 170
bondservant. *See also* bondservant rebellions
  abuses by, 131, 152n22, 368, 370, 371
  adopted daughter, 192
  adopted men and women, 113–114,
  125, 126
  adopted sons, 133, 153n22, 154n35,
  156n72, 192
  area cultivated by, 127
  arrogant behavior of, 193, 194, 377
  causes for becoming, 192–93
  class differentiation, 369
  class interests of, 193
  control of, 129
  in cotton industry, 62, 67
  emergence of, 271
  as family servant, 105–6, 135,152n22,
  157n72, 192, 369
  and fictive family relationship, 135, 147
  gentry, relations with, 134, 364, 368
  as gentry force, 371
  hereditary status of, 119, 120, 121, 124,
  154nn26, 51, 61, 193, 198, 370
  with independent budget, 121, 122, 123
  independent reproduction by, 129

485

bondservant (*continued*)
labor by, 104, 106–12, 121, 124, 125, 126, 128, 147, 152–53n22, 155n71, 157n75, 192, 196, 198, 354, 369, 384n133
land granted, 122, 123, 125–26, 128
manager, 125, 128, 193, 362, 369–71
manumission, 121, 126, 147, 196, 197
ownership, 124
personal bonded servant, 152n22
rent payment by, 128
rights, 193
sale of, 121
as slaves, 122–23, 129
status of, 124, 126, 151n8, 155n61, 156n72, 192, 199
as tenant, 122, 135
terms for, 102, 158n84
theories on, 193, 368
as yamen clerk, 148
bondservant rebellions, 192, 194–200, 371
by arrogant bondservants, 194, 195, 196, 198, 199
causes of, 196
as class struggle, 194, 195, 200
effect of on wealthy, 197–98
in Guangshan county, 196
in Gushi county, 196
locations of, 194
motivation to participate, 195, 196, 198
participants in, 115, 135, 196, 198
rebellion of 1645, 197, 198
in Runing prefecture, 196
in Shangcheng county, 196
in Taicang, 197
types of, 194
in Xiuming counry, 194–95
in Yi county, 194–95
books, didactic, 382n72
border regions, rebellions in, 232
Bowring, John, 395–98
Bozhou, 170
Braine, G.T., 416
bribery, 131, 172, 359, 363
British East India Company, 389, 394, 398, 400, 415
brokerage house, 169
bullies
appointed tax collectors, 172
and eunuch extortion, 171
Bu nongshu, 127
bureaucracy
factions in, 181
non-hereditary nature of, 357
bureaucrats

authority of, 349
and central rule, 351
as class, 340, 341
as gentry, 351, 381n40
Bureau of Agriculture, 248
Bureau of Civilian Cultivation, 248
burgher oppositon, 190–91

Canton, trade volume, 418
Cao Shipin, 173, 175
Cao Shizhong, 111
Cao Wengui, 113
capital
British, 424
commercial, and handicraft industry, 142
foreign, Japanese scholarship on, 387–88
capitalism, 13–14, 18, 70, 79–81, 85, 87, 93, 189–90, 350
castration, eunuchs, 212n11
Chai Qi, 108
chaiyi, 131
Chang Chung-li, 13
Chang Gate, 170, 188
Changqing county, 318
Changshu county, 107, 148, 149, 229
Changxing, 91–92
Changxing county gazetteer, 91–92, 93
Changzhou city, 27
Changzhou county, 33, 81, 107, 108, 109, 173, 307n17
Changzhou county gazetteer, 109
Changzhou prefecture, 108, 194, 302, 329, 332n19
chanping wang, 203
chaoxiang, 171
Chaoyi county, 284
Chaoyi county gazetteer, 284, 292
Cha Xian, 205
chebutou, 145
Chedun, 49
Chen Dashou, 137
Chen Feng, 181
Chen Ganchu, 113
Cheng Chang, 294
Chenghua emperor (Xiantong), 50
chengtou, 137
Chen Hongmou, 136
Chen Huan, 107
Chen Jinting, 367, 378
Chen Jiru, 53, 176
Chen Lake, 108
Chen Longzheng, 158n83
Chen Mei, 107
Chen Wenrui, 185

Chen Yu, 107
Chen Zhengjie, 228
children, sale of, 131
Chiliad Commanders, 107
Chizhou county, 121
Chong'an county, 202
Chongde county, 81–83, 110, 140,
    161n119, 194, 207, 210
Chongde county gazetteer, 83, 86, 94
Chongming county, 39, 52, 133, 158n94,
    160n108
Chongqing prefecture, 290
Chongyang county, 229
Chongzhen emperor (Yizong), 167
Christianity, 33
    Jesuits, 63–64
Chu, court faction, 182
Chu Fangqing, 359
Chu Hua, 38–39
Chun'an, 111
chushi, 355
Chuzhou subprefecture, 255
citian, 358
cities
    commercial, growth in, 169
    migration to, 178
    uprisings in, 192
class
    alienation, 341
    anti-aristocratic, 190
    conflict, 94, 166, 167, 175, 190, 191,
        272, 361, 363
    conflict, bondservant rebellion as, 194,
        195, 198
    consciousness, peasant, 190
    differentiation, 130, 132–33, 135, 147,
        346, 369
    divisions, 340
    relations, after Song, 349
clipper ships, 403–4
commendation
    and bondservitude, 192–93, 196,
        199–200, 368, 369
    of households, 134
    of land, 158n100, 299–300, 359, 360,
        361, 374, 382n83
commodity
    circulation, 346
    economy and silver, 201
commodity production
    agrarian, 38–39, 202
    of cotton, 31–32, 37, 39, 56, 66, 68–69
    development of, and agricultural in-
        dependence, 347
    development of, and class conflict,
        271–72, 362

development of, relation to resistance
    movements, 178, 181, 192, 212n15,
    271–72
in handicraft industries, 87
and merchant capital, 89–95, 364
of silk, 79–80, 84–88, 141
commoners
    status of, 155n61, 156n72
    urban, 190, 191
    victims of bondservant abuse, 371
community
    China-Europe comparison, 246
    control by landlord, 166
    control by state, 378
    feudal, 147
    integration in, 347
    Japanese scholarship on, 11, 68–69,
        166, 246, 342
    and *lijia*, 263–64
    punishment within, 145
    regulations, 105–6, 146, 147, 148, 251
    solidarity, 137, 148, 342–43, 363
    system, Yuan, 254–55
    tenant alliance, 143, 146, 160–61n112,
        206, 362–63
    work quota, 146
"Complaint of a Weaving Wife" (poem),
    59–61
concubines, 107
Confucian classics, 62
control
    dualism in, 344, 358, 359
    patriarchal, 135
    of social hierarchy, 251
    of wealthy, difficult, 355, 358
    Yuan, 354–55
coolies, 376
corruption, local government, 224, 293,
    376
"Cotton" (poem), 34–35
cotton
    cloth, calendering, 170, 211–12n8
    cloth, import volume 417
    commodity production, 31–32, 37, 39,
        56, 66, 68–69, 141
    dyed, 48, 52–53
    market, national, 44–45, 54, 67, 68
    ginning, 22, 23, 39–44, 46, 55, 59
    goods, price, 420, 421
    government, purchase by, 66
    imported, to spin, 141
    for military uniforms, 19
    "Regulations for cotton taxes," 53
    sizing, 47–48
    spinning, 19, 22–23, 46–47, 55–59, 62,
        84

cotton (*continued*)
  standard cloth, 54
  for taxation, 64–66
  twills, 23, 51–52, 54, 58
cotton cultivation, 19, 20–21, 22–23,
  33–45, 68
  management of, 36–45
  prices, 40–44
  profit rates, 44, 141
cotton gin, 39, 46
cotton industry, 8, 9, 69, 102
  and agriculture, 84
  British, 402, 410–13, 416
  division of labor in, 55–67, 69
  and foreign trade, 19, 411, 415, 434
  management of, 62–67
  raw materials for, 19, 23, 36, 44–45
  study of, 79
  technology, 20–23, 28, 39, 46–48
  wholesalers, 312n8
cotton textiles, 49–54
  marketing of, 80–81
  varieties, 36–37
county runners, 231
court, imperial, 170, 182
craftsmen, 131
credit, in barter, 423
crop rotation, 37
cubu, 53–54
Cui Gong, 289
cuilang lizheng, 286
cultivation rights. *See* landownership,
  dual, surface rights
currency
  cash coin, 389
  dollars, chopped, 394
  dollars, speculation, 395
  standard cash, 390, 427n4

dabu, 54
Dachengguo, 228
dahu, 133, 360
dahu baoyin, 153n22. *See also* landlords,
  wealthy
daiguanhu, 275n43
dami, 159n108
Da Ming Huidian, 50, 291, 304
Daming prefecture, 295
danchuang, 54
dang, 208
dankou, 54
dapengche, 145
Da Qing lü jijie fuli, 377
dasinong, 385n147
Daxue yanyi bu, 297
debts

extortion of, 130, 131
  and indenture, 213n47
  poor people and, 131, 132
degree-holders, 110–12, 348
Deng Bosun, 204
Deng Maoba, 202
Deng Maoqi, 202–4, 211
  evil eliminating king, 203
  rebellion of, 201, 270
Deng Qi, 290
Deng Yunxiao, 173
Deng Zhenglei, 228
Dengzhou prefecture, 171, 319
Dent & Co., 416
Department for the Promotion of Agriculture, 385n147
despotism, 151, 167, 179, 342
diandang jiaren, 152n22
dianding, 158–59n102
dianhu, 159n102, 200
dianpu, 115, 132, 133
dianshang, 138, 208
diaodian kangzu , 207
diding yin, 101, 335, 364
dingnan, 133, 153n22. *See also* laborer,
  male
dingnu, 108
Ding Yuanfu, 172, 173, 176
Ding Zhigong, 107
direct producers, 150, 216
doctors, 231
dongchang, 183
Dong Chang, 319
Dong Han, 112
Dong Hongdu, 59
Dong Jiaozeng, 121
Donglin Academy, 181, 375
Donglin party
  as burgher opposition, 191
  members of, 148, 182, 184, 190, 191
  in power, 181, 182–83
Dongpengkou, 57
dongsheng, 202, 270
Dong Xianliang, 55, 60
doreisei keiei, 106
double-cropping, 37–38
Doulaohui, 205
drafts
  and bullion, 405–7
  exchange rate, 406–8
  trade settlement and, 394–400, 408,
    413
drainage work, 146
Duan Guanqing, 224
dubao, 254
dumping, in trade, 415–16

Du Mu, 112
duomin, 119
Du Qi, 238
dykes, building of, 384n132, 385n148

edicts, imperial, reading of, 184
Edo period. *See* Tokugawa Japan
education, traditional, 107
eight-banner system, 378
elders
  lijia, 261
  rural, 22
  village, 204, 253
Engels, Friedrich, on urban class, 190
equal fields system, 134, 281, 342
equalized labor service
  assessment, 324
  assignment, 291, 325
  described, 282–85, 287–90, 315
  exactions, 251
  and *lijia*, 267
  regional expansion of, 289
  registers, 287–89
  and tenants, 251
Equitable Service Levy Tables, 287
Esang Company, 419
eunuchs, 51. *See also* Sun Long, Wei
    Zhongxian
  abuses, 171, 183, 189, 212n15
  literati on, 177
  power of, 182, 201, 212n11
  recruitment, 212n11
  tax collection by, 170–71, 181
Ewart, W., 412
"Examination of the equitable assign-
    ments," 293
examination system
  and class formation, 343, 357
  degree holder and, 348
  function of, 348
exchange rate, in foreign trade, 405–6,
    407
exploitation
  government, 179
  and rent resistance, 221
  and surface rights, 222
extortion, 130
  by eunuchs, 171, 183, 212n15
  of indebted poor, 131, 132
  of service levy, 202, 293

famine, 159–60n108
fanche , 144. *See also* water wheel
fan cloth, 50–52
Fang Hongjing, 122
Fang Kezhuang, 176

fangkuobu, 54
fangsha, 46
Fan Longyou, 238
fanren, 156n72. *See also* commoners
fanxian, 46
Fan Ying, 31
Feicheng county, 317
feihuabu, 49–50, 59
feixi, 301
Fei Xiaotong, 145, 161n132
Fengxian county, 20
Fengyang, 118
Fengzhou county, 228
fenqing shengbu, 53
fertilizers, 156n71
feudalism, 104, 106
  from above, 349, 357
  from below, 357
  bureaucratic, 382n69
  rise of, 101
  societies compared, 151, 357
financial and price history, 13–14
financial crisis, measures against, 179
financial network, world, 408
financial panic (England), 400, 407, 420
fiscal treatises, Japanese scholarship on,
    279
Fish-scale Registers, 327
Five Great Banners, rebellion of, 229,
    239. *See also* White Lotus
flax, 27–28, 81, 84
food supply, and pawning, 143
foreign relations, 14
fortunetellers, 231
free men, 121, 131, 197, 198
fuchai, 132
fuhao dahu, 360
Fujian province, 19–22, 36, 39, 55, 108,
    124, 194, 202, 203, 205, 209
Fuji Hiroshi, 162n137
Fujita Toyohachi, 21
fuju diantian, 121
Furushima Kazuo, 105–6, 126, 127,
    153n22, 162n139, 268, 272, 345, 346,
    358, 361, 368
Fushe movement, 360
fuyi, 157, 281, 365
fuyi ce, 284, 329
fuyi huangce, 283. *See also* Yellow Regis-
    ters
Fuyi quanshu, 330, 351
Fuzhou prefecture, 183, 293

Gan Fengchi, 238
Gansu province, 170
Gao Cai, 183

Gao Panlong, 182, 183, 184
Gao Qi, 107
Ge Cheng, 173, 176, 177, 179–80
gengnu, 110
gentry
   abuses, 172, 359, 361, 366–67, 372,
      375–76, 377
   bondservant use by, 368
   as civilian autonomous organization,
      338
   composition of, 177, 183, 198, 338,349,
      351, 354, 356, 381nn39, 40, 382n72
   defined, 13
   domination by, 336, 337, 362n84
   emergence of, 267, 337, 339, 351
   and examination system, 348
   as illegitimate offspring of bureaucrat-
      ism, 343, 349, 360
   isolation of, 362
   as intermediary group, 338–39, 344,
      352, 373
   as landlord, 12, 13, 144, 273, 336,
      345–46, 347, 348, 355, 357, 359, 360,
      364, 367, 368, 372, 379
   lifestyle, 134, 354
   in *lijia* system, 357–58
   and local officials, 213n26, 373
   and merchant capital, 363–64
   moneylending by, 172
   in 1911 revolution, 380n2
   parasitic, 346
   power of, 366, 375
   private forces, 337
   privileges, 350, 357, 358, 359, 360,
      367–68, 372, 374
   and rent resistance movements, 363
   role of, 337, 341, 364
   rule of, 336, 337, 340, 343, 344, 345,
      347, 349, 350, 351, 352, 353, 360,
      365, 367–68, 372, 373, 376–77, 378,
      379–80
   and silk workers rebellion, 176
   as socio-political category, 352–53
   and state power, 360, 361, 363, 372,
      377, 378, 379
   supportive of peasants, 367
   tax collection by, 383n105, 384n140
   tenants, relations with, 363
geomancers, 231
Ge Shouli, 322, 325
Gibb, Livingstone Company, 402, 419
gifts, customary, 363
God-worshipping Society, 222. *See also*
   Taiping
gold
   price, 405

   rush, and world market, 398
gongfei, 267
Gong Mingyang, 113
gongshi, 267
gongxing, 212n11
gonsitian, 125
government. *See* state
government, local
   agricultural administrators, 385n147
   clerks, 231
   clerks, bondservants as, 148, 149
   clerks, corruption, 130, 148–49, 224,
      293, 326, 338
   on Deng Maoqi rebellion, 203, 204
   on mines, 202
   offices occupied, 185
   official-gentry, landownership by, 345
   officials, privileges, 300–301
   officials, resident, 359, 367, 369,
      381n40
   purchase of cotton, 66
   on silk workers rebellion, 177–179
   grain, pawning of, 140
   grain measure, unification demanded,
      205
Grain Measure Society, 205, 206
grain tax, peculation of, 376
granary, management of, 208
Great State of Cheng, 228
Gregson, Samuel, 394
guaming, 135
guanbu, 29, 30, 49, 58, 64, 66–67
Guan county, 228
Guangdong, 19–22, 36, 39, 55, 194, 209
Guangdong yongping lu, 328
Guanghua Temple bridge, 170
Guangshan county, 115, 194, 196
Guangxi province, 232
Guangzhou, 194
Guan Ming, 24
Guan Zhidao, 113–14
Gu Dazhang, 183
Gu Dingchen, 108
gugong, 152n22, 156n72, 157n73. *See also*
   laborer, hired
gugongren, 153n22
Gu Gongxie, 134, 158n102
Guian county, 157n18
Gui family, 53
guiji. See commendation, of land
guituo, 129
guofei, 238
Guo prefectural gazetteer, 51
Guo Tianzu, 248
Gu Qing, 110
Gushi county, 115, 194, 196

Gusu gazetteer, 294
Gu Xiancheng, 181
Gu Yanwu, 24, 103, 191, 194, 199, 311, 359, 368
Gu Yu, 28, 55
Gu Zhenqing, 197

Haimen, 39
Hainan island, 22–23
Hai Rui, 374–75
Haiyan county, 20, 57–59, 114, 157n81
Haiyan county gazetteer, 57, 296
Hakka, 231, 232
Hamashima Atsutoshi, 12, 378
Hamashita Takeshi, 114
Han, emergence of, 337
handicraft, rural, 7–9, 27, 63, 68, 79–95
   and agriculture, 86, 141–42
   industry, commercialization of, 142, 146, 147
   industry, development of, 88–89, 143
   landlord-tenant relations, 101
   theory of, 165
Han Foshou, 205
Hangzhou city, 27
Hangzhou prefectural gazetteer, 299
Hangzhou prefecture, 33, 111, 168, 172
Hanyang, 181
haomin, 130. See also landlords, wealthy
haonu, 193, 368, 370
haopu, 377
haoshen, 340, 343
haoyu, 355
haozu, 342, 352
harvest, yields, 128, 140, 156n71
head presser, 137
Heavenly Principle sect, rebellion of, 232
Hebei province, 232
He Liangjun, 111, 156n71, 199, 359, 363, 368, 372, 375
hemp, 81, 84
Henan fuyi zhonghui wence, 330
Henan province, 19, 115–16, 119, 124, 194, 196, 205, 232
Hengchun county, 228
He Qiaoyuan, 282
He Rushang, 114
He Shangyin, 114
Hirth, F., 21
hōkenteki kyōdōtai, 147
hongfang, 48
hongsha guanbu, 49
Hongwu emperor (Taizu), 25, 247–49, 250, 252–54
Hongzhi emperor (Xiaotong), 51
Hosono Kōji, 261

household
   attached, 258–59, 275n43
   auxiliary, 292–93
   civilian, 284
   and labor service system, 292–93
   official, 359
   poor, tax exemption, 360
household registration system, 344
   abuses of, 299, 301
   categories in, 258, 322–23, 284, 307n14
   saltern, 300, 301
   service, 283
   status, and commendation, 299–301
   supernumerary, 258–59, 283
   and Yellow Registers, 255–56
huafen, 201, 360
Huaian, 238
Huai River, 19
Huang, Taoist nun, 21–23, 28, 50
huangcao, 27, 81, 84
Huang Jianjie, 172
Huang Juezi, 390
Huang Ming tiaofu shilei zuan, 130
Huang Run, 322n19
Huangtin yi, 359
Huang Tong, 206
Huang Xingzeng, 123, 363
Huang Zhonggui, 123
Huang Zhongjian, 137
Huang Zongxi, 191
Huang Zunsu, 182, 184, 187, 188, 191
huatian, 35
Huating county, 20, 21, 24–25, 31–32, 51, 53, 60, 64–65, 112, 356, 359
Huating county gazetteer, 27, 32, 111–12
huayi, 39
huazu, 45
Hubei province, 124, 232
hufang, 148. See also revenue department
Huguang province, 19, 205, 232
Huizhou county, 121
Huizhou prefectural gazetteer, 294
Huizhou prefecture, 119–20, 122, 123, 124, 194, 256, 382n66
Hunyuan, 233
Hu Shangbin, 117
hushu, 103
huyi, 283
Huzhou city, 27
Huzhou prefecture, 33, 81, 91, 174, 206, 254, 255, 256, 273

imperial industries, 69
imperialism, Japanese scholarship on, 14, 17, 88
Imperial Rescript, 120

Imperial Secret Service, 183, 184
Imperial Silkworks, 212n15
Imperial Textile Workshops, 51
indigo, 48
indirect producers, 215–16
institutional history, 279–80
interplanting, 38
Iron Ruler Society, 238
irrigation, 34–35, 144–45
    collective pumping, 145, 161–62n132, 206
    by family, 145
    by government, 37
    property, 385n148
    water wheels, 26, 34, 144–45, 146
Iwami Hiroshi, 12

Japan, invasion of Korea, 170
Jardine, Matheson & Co., 409, 428n25, 429n44
ji, 374
jiading, 102, 106, 135
Jiading county, 20, 30, 34–36, 38, 52–53, 62–63, 136, 191, 194
Jiading county gazetteer, 30, 38, 51–52
jiagong, 375
jianbu, 52
Jianchang prefectual gazetteer, 294
Jiang Mengquan (Jiang Tingyi), 322
Jiangnan gazetteer, 116–17
Jiangning prefecture, 116, 118, 178, 194
jiangsha, 48
Jiangsu province, 107–8, 112, 191, 205, 209, 232
Jiangsu Shanyang Shouzu quanan, 363, 379
Jiang Tingyi (Jiang Mengquan), 322
Jiangwan village, 142
Jiangxi province, 19, 47, 287, 299
Jiangxi sheng dazhi, 304
Jiangyin county, 191, 229, 233
Jianning prefecture, 202
jianpu, 114
jiansheng, 376
jiansibu, 52
jianu, 105, 157n72, 192. See also bondservant, as family servant
Jianyang county, 202
jiaohuabu, 53
Jiaoshan ji, 176
Jiaozhou, 321
jiapu, 106, 192, 368
jiaren, 105, 107, 111, 112, 152n22, 192, 369. See also bondservant, as family servant
Jia Sidao, 24

Jiashan county, 57, 157n81, 158n83, 224
jia system
    composotion of, 258
    heads, 259–61, 283
    and self-police groups, 202, 203
jiatong, 105, 106, 110, 192
Jiaxing city, 27
Jiaxing prefecture, 20, 33, 57, 81, 113, 148, 158n102, 174, 194, 206, 208, 296
jibei, 21. See also cotton textiles
Jie Ji, 287
jigang zhi pu, 125, 193, 362, 369. See also bondservant, manager
jilinghu, 275n45, 283
Jinan prefecture, 318
Jin Changzhen, 196
Jin Da, 288
jingbu, 52, 62
jingche, 47
Jingfu ce, 330, 332n16
jinghua, 42
Jingmen subprefecture, 237
Jing Song, 315
Jinhua county, 255
Jinhua prefecture, 111, 255, 285, 295
jinhua yin, 201, 290
Jinkui county, 136, 141, 375, 376, 377
Jinling county, 194
Jin Luqing, 225
Jin Mengtiao, 197
Jinshan cloth, 27
Jinshan county gazetteer, 54, 58
Jinshan wei, 57, 59
jinshen, 381n40
jinshi, 364
Jintan county, 135
Jin Yipai, 81–86, 91, 93
Jinzezhen, 25
Jin Zhangzhen, 115
jisakunō, 104
Jishan district, 108
jizhuang, 301, 320
Jizhuang yi, 374
jungongfu system, 251, 282, 291. See also equalized labor service
junping yin, 316
juntian, 342
juntian fa, 281
juntian junyi, 268
junyao, 267, 291, 315. See also equalized labor service
Juzhou, 321

kafuchōteki doreisei keiei, 368
kafuchōteki dorei shihai, 123
kaidu, 184

Kaidu incident, 168, 179, 184–88, 191
  mass action in, 184–87, 188, 189
  sources on, 213n40
Kaixiangong village, 145, 161n132
kanshinteki tochi shoyū, 345
Kataoka Shibako, 9
Katayama Seijirō, 380n20
Katō Shigeru, 279
Kawakatsu Mamoru, 12
kiseiteki jinushisō, 126
Kitamura Hironao, 104–6, 127, 153n122,
  269, 345, 361, 368
Kobayashi Kazumi, 10, 12
kobetsuteki jinshin shihai, 344
Kojima Shinji, 229
kongyinji, 23
Korean cloth, 51–52
kosakuin, 200
koubu, 54
Kuang shui zhi hai, 171
kuangzei , 201
Kunshan county, 20, 30, 108, 149, 173,
  176, 177, 194
Kunshan county gazetteer, 53
kyōdōtai, 206, 246, 263, 378. *See also*
  community
kyōkyo jinushi, 104

labor
  cultivation, by poor, 384n132
  force, bondservants as, 152n22
  exchange, 264
  power, 133
  pump work allocation, 161n132
laborer
  hired, 152n22, 156n72, 231, 384n133
  hired, and bondservant labor, 198
  hired, and bondservant rebellion, 195,
    198
  hired, and bondservitude, 196
  hired, as criminals, 153n22
  hired, defined, 213n47
  hired, status of, 194
  hired, unemployment of, 172
  indentured, 195
  male, 153n22, 249
  slave, 153n22
labor market
  contractor boss, 170
  textile industry, 64
labor service levy, 42, 65, 83, 88. *See also*
  equalized labor service
  abolition demanded , 205
  assessment, 374
  assignment, inequalities in, 298–99
  assignments, labor, 296, 315, 325

assignments, labor/silver, 294
assignments, silver, 315, 316, 374
  by bondservants, 128
  bureaucratic, 282
  commutation of, 291–92, 293–97, 325
  ding charge, 326
  district, in Song, 282
  duty categories, 267, 281–82, 283
  equalization, 268
  European corvée compared, 281
  evasion, 129, 292, 299–302, 358, 359.
    See also commendation, of land
  excessive, 134, 203
  exemption, 297, 300, 360, 366, 374
  extortion, 202, 293
  gate charge, 326
  in Han, 281
  household categories, 292
  and land tax, 298
  lijia system and, 103
  and landlords, 105, 161n125
  mending charge, 326
  Ming, 283–84
  miscellaneous, 130, 283–86, 297, 326,
    331n10
  in Northern and Southern dynasties,
    281
  payment methods, 294
  pre-Single Whip, 384n132
  reforms, 104, 365
  register, 284, 329
  regular, 283
  in Song, 281–82
Laiwu county, 318
Lake Tai, 141, 143, 145, 161n132, 205
land
  accumulation, 132–33, 345, 359, 364
  allotments, 249–50
  annexation, 163n150, 359
  common, 105
  concentration, 286, 359
  entrusted, 129, 374
  managerial, 128
  registration, 66–69, 129, 384n132
  registration, fraudulent, 359–60, 361.
    See also commendation, of land
  relations, 8–9, 80, 95, 102
  rent, 9, 25, 39, 45
  state, 24–25, 29–30, 35, 253–54, 259
  system, 9, 66–69, 103–4
landlordification, defined, 209
landlords
  absentee, 103, 104, 106, 202, 203, 204,
    354, 361, 364
  abuses by, 130, 133, 355
  and agricultural technology, 269

landlord (*continued*)
  alienation from reproduction process,
    362, 364, 371
  alliance with officials, 206–7
  armed force, 159n102, 204
  and bondservant managers, 193
  as bondservant master, 106–12, 124,
    129, 147
  control by, 150, 166, 207, 371
  and Donglin party, 182
  as economic organization, 365
  as extra-economic force, 150
  as gentry, 347, 359, 364, 367, 368, 372,
    379
  landholdings, 144, 163n150
  landholdings, fragmented, 206
  lifestyle, 354
  and *lijia* system, 358
  local, 358, 359
  loss of local character, 361–62
  managerial, 124, 126, 128, 129, 130,
    147–48, 198, 271–73, 355
  as merchant, 346
  parasitic, 126
  relations with gentry, 382n84
  rent collection, 136, 162n141
  and rent resistance, 148, 205, 365
  and reproduction conditions, 385n148
  resident, 104, 106, 345, 346
  and rice speculation, 364
  as ruling class, 344, 360, 365
  in South China, 147
  and state, 252–54, 365
  structural changes in system, 364
  tax evasion by, 326
  and tax payments, 225
  tenants, relations with, 91, 142–43,
    144, 150, 196, 198, 200, 206–7, 210,
    214n82, 225, 251, 270, 346, 349, 350,
    353, 354, 361, 362, 363, 368, 379,
    385n151
  urban, 103, 104, 106, 148, 161n125,
    346, 354, 364
  wealthy, 124, 131, 132, 133, 134,
    153n22, 342, 384n132
landownership
  burden of, 384n132
  breakdown of system, 347
  cotton industry and, 45
  dual, 209, 221
    cultivation rights, 201, 209
    defined, 214n82
    subsoil rights, 162n139, 210, 214n82
    surface rights, 162n139, 209, 214n82,
      220, 221, 222
  estate size, 82

feudal, 150, 335, 347, 361
and gentry, 13, 345–46, 348, 360
income from, 63
large scale of, 9, 345, 347, 359
parasitic, 269–70
quota, 259
and rent resistance, 94
and slave system, 135
small scale, 103–4
land tax
  assessment, 322–23
  assessment, "gate silver," 323
  combined with poll tax, 101, 171, 335,
    336, 364, 365, 376, 383n107
  commutation of, 290–91, 294
  constituent parts, 322
  increase, 171
  liability, 289
  lijia system and, 103
  reform, 104
  register, 329
  and rent, 226
  and rural landlords, 105
  tenant responsibility, 83
  transformation, 377
  wastage rates, 322
laonong, 104
lanna, 163n149
"Leading the bondservants out to the
    fields" (poem), 110
Le'an, 47
Leizhou prefecture, 294
Leqing county gazetteer, 305
li
  captains, 258, 259–61, 283, 346
  composition of, 258
  responsibilities, 260, 286
  and service levy, 281, 283
Lian Fangcheng, 236
Liangguang, 21
Liang Menglong, 323–24
liangren, 197
liangya, 148
liangzhang, 31. *See also* tax captains
Liangzhe circuit, 21
Lianjitang, 34
Li'an quanji, 116
lianxiang, 171
Lianxi ward, 170
lianyu jiejia, 143, 146, 206, 362
Lian Zaiyou, 236
Liaodong border, 171
liaoxiang levy, 171
liaoyin, 331n10
licentiates, Confucian, 231
lichai, 291, 315. *See also* labor service

levy, assignments, labor
Licheng county, 318, 320
Li Chun, 51
Liduo shigua, 109
Li Guozhu, 187
Li Hongbin, 427n9
lijia system, 11–12
    and community functions, 263, 264
    decline of, 104, 106, 150, 163n149,
        268–73, 346, 347, 365
    elders, 261
    established, 254–56
    and gentry, 357–58
    Japanese scholarship on, 245
    and landlords, 268–69
    landownership quotas, 259
    and local control, 246–47, 262–66
    Ming, 345
    and natural village, 256, 258
    posts, 259–62
    registers, 255
    service, 103, 283
    service categories, 316
    silver levy, 267, 316
    state exaction, 346
    and tax reform, 266–68
    and tax transmission, 64–65
    units in, 256, 257
lijia yin, 316
lijia zhengyi, 283
Li Lai, 332n16
lilaoren, 204
limian, 374
Li Nanzhou, 205
Lin Duanqi, 108
lineage, and bondservants, 112–13
Lingnan province, 19
Linjiang prefecture, 287
Linqing prefecture, 181
Lin Xiyuan, 354, 355, 356, 359, 362,
    366–67, 370, 372, 375, 384n141
lipai, 64
lishen changsui, 152n22
Li Shi, 184
Li Taiping, 239
literati, 368, 372, 375
    described, 176–77
    discontent, 177
    honor Wei Zhongxian, 188
    and Kaidu incident, 189
    land, 379
    masses, relations with, 189
    recruit army, 204
    and silk workers rebellion, 177
    support Zhou Shunchang, 184
    in Suzhou, 175–76

in trade, 182
urban, 177, 190–91
Liu Cai, 320
Liu Nan, 120
Liu Que, 238
Liu Song, 233
Liu Wencheng, 232
Liu Yingchen, 294
Liu Zhaokui, 233
Liu Zhixie, 233
Li Yan, 211
Liyang county, 194
liyi, 282, 283
Li Yingsheng, 184, 188
Li Yuanyang, 304
lizhang, 65, 288. *See also li*, captains
Li Zicheng, 167, 210, 211
loan
    contracts, 140, 207
    usurious, 208, 209
longguche, 144. *See also* water wheel
Longxi county, 123, 155n66
looms
    drawloom, 23, 48
    waist loom, 48
Loutangzhen, 52
Lu Chong, 306n3
Lu Chongxing, 113, 148, 149
Lü Kun, 366
Lü Liuliang, 191
Lu Shen, 110
Lu Shusheng, 356, 357–58, 370, 373
Lu Zhaocheng, 236
Lu Zhenfei, 360
Lu Zongbo, 108

MacGregor, Francis, 423
Macheng county, 123, 124
Ma Duanlin, 281, 306n3
maidian zuopu, 117
Maitreya, 222, 226, 227
Ma Jie, 188
Manchu
    invasion, 167, 171, 210
    rebellion against, 191
manor
    development of, 342, 343
    serfs, 118–19
    in Tang-Song, 151
Mao Hongbin, 160n112
Mao Yilu, 185, 186, 187, 188
marginal people
    displaced, 197
    propertyless, 197
    and rebellions, 232
    unemployed, 149

Maritime Trade Office, 21
market. *See also* labor market
  limited scope of, 91
  national, 80
  for silk exchange, 86–87
marketing
  of cotton, 60–61
  distribution system, 90
  of silk, 82
market towns, 25, 52, 58, 103, 169
martial arts
  and counterrevolutionaries, 238–39
  masters, 132, 231
  and religious rebellions, 239
  training, 238
Ma Ruzhang, 303
Marxism
  Asiatic mode of production, 8
  historiography, 3, 4, 5, 6
masses, role in Kaidu incident, 189
master
  governing, 149–50
  patriarchal domination by, 123
  servant, relations with, 147, 153n22,
    155n61
  surname conferred, 123, 133, 152n22
Masubuchi Tatsuo, 342
Matheson, Alexander, 408, 413–14
Matheson, James, 409
Matsumoto Yoshimi, 103–5, 269, 335,
  339, 341–42, 343–44, 345
meizhibu, 50, 59
merchant capital
  and agriculture, 89–92
  control of marketing, 92–95
  and gentry, 363–64
  and land control, 361
  in silk industry, 83, 87, 91
merchants
  Cantonese, 142
  cotton, 38, 45, 55, 57, 61, 63, 142
  handbook for, 57
  in Huizhou, 382n66
  influence of capital on agriculture,
    65–66, 68–69
  itinerant, 108, 231
  landlord, 346
  mortgaging, 138, 208
  silk, 81–95
  and tax collection, 31
  as urban class, 190
  usurious loans, 209–10
  wholesale, 172, 175
Mianhua tu, 41–42, 46
miansha, 46
miansui, 46

miantian, 35
Miao Chengqi, 182, 184
michian, 138, 208
middle loom, 54, 58
migration
  to cities, 178
  migrants, 202
  and rebellions, 231–32
military
  campaign expenses, 170
  colony land, 35, 250
  conscription, 131, 134
  deserters, 231
  field fees, 24
  salary in cloth, 50
militia, private, 160n108, 337, 367, 371
mines
  bandits, 201–2
  closed, 181
  exploitation of, 202
  government expenditure on, 171
  opening of, 170
  production, levies on, 171
Ming, fall of, 167
Ming shi, 25, 282, 287
Ming shilu, 287
minhu, 284
Ministry of Revenue, 116
Ministry of War, 110
minority groups, 211
Min shu, 282, 292, 302, 303
Minsu, 123
mobu, 53
modernization, 70
monastery fields, 24
monetary
  market, Chinese, 389
  market, London, 399, 402, 416
  standards, 426n1
  system, bimetallic, 426n1
  theory, Qing, 390–91, 395
money economy, 31–32, 87–88, 104
  development, 347, 362
  in Ming, 141
moneylending, 364
moral instruction, 261
morality, social, decline of, 94
moral leaders, 359
Mori Masao, 13, 251
Mōri Kenzō, 388
morongbu, 52
mortgage, 138, 139
mulberry, 21, 27, 81, 84, 110, 114
Mumian pu, 38–39, 46–48, 51–52
Muramatsu Yūji, 9, 383n105, 384n140
Murky Origin sect, 233

Muslims, 211

Naitō Konan, 8, 311, 312
names, posting of, 135
Nancun chuogenglu, 201
Nanhai county, 154n41
Nanhui county, 20, 47, 54
Nanhui county gazetteer, 46, 52, 53–54, 58
Nanjing, Treaty of, 400
Nanxiang, 194
Nanxun township, 144
nayi, 301
Negishi Tadashi, 337–39, 341, 345
Nian Army, 223, 229
Nicol, William, 410–11, 413
Niida Noboru, 270, 343–45, 361
ninefold classification system, 318
defined, 284
in Shandong, 322
and Single Whip reform, 319–20
1911 Revolution, 229
Ningguo county, 121
Ningguo prefecture, 119–20, 178, 298
Ninghua county, 206
Ningxia prefecture, 170
Nishijima Sadao, 8, 12, 79, 89, 102, 165, 335, 342
Niu Jinxing, 211
Niu Ruoyu, 315
Ni Yue, 293
nongshu, 39
North-China Herald, 425
North Zhili province, 19, 42
nu, 108, 112, 113, 116, 152n22
nubi, 102, 112, 113, 152n12, 152–153n22, 156n72, 192
nuli, 102, 116, 133, 134
nupu, 102, 112, 152n22, 192

Obata Tatsuo, 261
official fields fees, 24
One Stick of Incense Sect, 232
opium
as barter item, 414, 415
and British East India Company, 400
and Chinese banks, 425
trade, 400, 402, 417
trade, and drafts, 408
trade, and silver oulflow, 390–91
oppression, official, 224
Oriental Bank , 423
Oriental Banking Corporation, 423
Ōtsuka Hisao, 18
An Outline of Japanese Economic History 1603–1940, 102

Ouyand Duo, 329, 332n19
owner-cultivators, 104–5
fostering policy, 249–50
holdings, 249
small peasant, 353
Oyama Masaaki, 9, 10, 271, 347, 348, 361, 363, 368

paijiang, 54
palace building, reconstruction of, 170
Pang Shangpen, 328, 360
Pan Jixun, 328
Panlongtang, 27
Parliament, British, Select Committee on Commercial Relations with China, 409–10
pawning, rice for silver, 87, 94, 138, 140
pawnshops, and sericulture, 82–83, 89–91
peasant rebellions, 9–11, 80, 93–94, 103, 204
analyzed, 217–19
against government extortion, 171–72
Japanese scholarship on, 215–17
Li Zicheng, 210–11
Shi Kefa, 191
sources on, 10–11
types of, 192
peasants
alliance with other classes, 191
area cultivated by, 127
army, 203, 210–11
in bondservant rebellions, 198
as class, 340
class consciousness of, 190
differentiation, 358
conscript evasion by, 131
control of, 256
as cultivators, 102, 254
debt bondage, 193
desire for tenancy, 220, 221
dislocation of, 132–33
economy, 27, 39, 63, 67, 68, 88
exploitation of, 171
farming, 87–95
feudalistic, 361
fugitive, 132, 133
in Fujian, 202
harassment of, 133, 134, 371
and hired workers, relations with, 178
in Kaidu incident, 191
labor services by, 132
landed property of, 131
landless, 379
and *lijia* system, 358–59
migration, 178
nature of, 336

peasants (*continued*)
  oaths, against landlord, 137, 138
  pawning by, 140
  vs. slaves, 101
  tax arrears, 153n149
  as tenants, 135
  and usurious loans, 202
  world view of, 230–31
Peasant War in Germany, 190
penal authority, 344, 366, 372, 383n125
Peng Zengke, 228
periodization, in Chinese history, 7
petition leader, 137
piaofang, 48
pingfen baiduo, 377
Pinghu county, 157n81
pingmi, 29
pingshe, 366
pingxiao, 54
plays, for solidarity, 137, 160–61n112,
  206, 362–63
polder
  divisions, 145, 146
  tenant alliances, 206
political process, defined, 380n2
poll tax
  abolished, 365
  combined with land tax, 101, 335, 336,
    364, 365, 376, 383n107
pollution, from mines, 202
pongee, 81, 82, 93
postal-relay service, 316
poverty, caused by taxes, 26
power, dual, 358, 359
Prideaux, F.W., 394
"Proclamation on Instructing the People," 261, 263, 264
producers, direct, 190
production
  Asiatic mode of, 8
  forces, development of, 165, 169, 171,
    207, 208, 209, 210, 346
property rights, split. *See* landownership,
  dual
"Prose Poem on Cotton Cloth," 60–61
pu, 102, 115, 120, 157n75
pudian, 122
Pudong, 46
puli, 114, 125, 126, 133, 153n22
Puli township gazetteer, 103
pump, 144, 145. *See also* irrigation
punishment
  within comminuty, 145
  capital, 179
  Palace Punishment, 212n11
  power of, 344

statutes for disobedience, 377
Pure Water sect, 239
Pu Shanlin, 354
putting-out system
  in cotton industry, 62, 63, 66, 69
  in silk industry, 87, 90, 93–94
puyi, 119
Pu Zonghui, 110

Qi, court faction, 182
qian, 389–90
Qian Laichen, 149
qianpiao, 427n4
Qian Pu, 315
Qian Qi, 131
Qian Qianyi, 148, 149, 191, 194
Qian Qingyu, 27
Qianrenhui, 229
qianwujing, 54
Qian Yuanpu, 51
Qian Zhen, 110
qianzhuang, 425
qihuabu, 51
qingbai leichao, 112
qingding, 111
qingji, 29
Qinglong, 52
Qing lu, 377
Qingpu county, 20, 62, 67, 229
Qingshuijiao, 239
Qingyan zhupu, 115
Qin Huitian, 136, 159n108
Qin Shan, 61
Qin Shuyang, 176
Qinyi Liangzhe junping lu, 328
qiudun cloth, 50
Qiu Hong, 289, 291
Qiu Jun, 133, 291–92, 297–98
qu, 261–62
Quanzhou prefecture, 194, 304, 355
Qu Shisi, 148, 149, 194

ramie, 27–28, 52, 53, 81, 84
ranghua, 42
rape, 130, 131, 211
Rawson, Christopher, 411, 413
rebellions. *See also* bondservant rebellions; Deng Maoqi; Five Great Banners, rebellion of; Kaidu incident;
  Murky Origin sect; peasant rebellions; rent resistance struggles; tax resistance struggles; White Lotus, rebellion
  anti-Machu, 191
  banana-leaf fan, 172, 173
  in border regions, 232

in Bozhou, 170
in Hanyang, 181
of hired silk workers, 168, 172–73, 191
for interest reduction, 228
listed, 181
and marginal people, 232
and martial training, 237
in Ningxia prefecture, 170
in North China, 210
of 1645, 202
public indignation, 178, 179
religious, 222, 227, 231, 233, 234–35, 240
rural, types of, 192
in Shandong, 237
significance of, 211
slave, 371
urban, 168, 190, 191–92
in Wucheng, 181
reclamation
land, 248–49, 250
sandy, fields, 24
Rekishigaku kenkyūkai, 4, 5, 10
relay station fees, 24
religious sects, 234–35
leaders, 233, 236
Renhe, 111
rent
arrears, 136
bursaries, 383n105, 384n140
collection, and bribery, 363
collection by bondservants, 193
inequities, 219
in kind, 270, 364
livelihood by, dangerous, 210
on managerial land, 128, 129
payment by bondservants, 128, 129
payment by tenants, 138
payment refused, 205
reduction demanded, 205
supplementary, 202, 205
and tax, 365
winter gift, 202, 270
rent resistance struggles, 10, 80, 94, 101, 136–37, 143, 144, 192, 200–206, 219, 228, 347, 379. See also tenants, resistance by
and bondservant rebellions, 200
causes of, 209–10
change in nature of, 200
in Chongshu county, 229
and class alliances, 227
demands in, 205–6, 219
and exploitation, 221
in Fengzhou county, 228
form of, 138

and gentry, 365
in Guan county, 228
as habit, 137
in Hengchun county, 228
ideology of, 219, 227
in Jiangyin county, 229
and landlord-tenant relations, 368
location, 200, 205
motivation, 207
in Shanyang county, 363
in Shimen county, 228, 229
significance, 211
Society of the Thousand, 229
in Sonzi county, 228
in Suzhou, 271
and tax resistance, 223, 226–27
tenant violence, 159–60n108
in Tonglizhen, 229
in Wu county, 205
in Wuxi county, 229
in Xunzhou prefecture, 228
reparations, 394
resettlement, 248–49, 250
resist dyeing, 48, 52–53
revenue department, 148, 150
rice, 34–35, 37–38, 68, 84
cultivation of, 83, 141, 144
market exchange, 87
mortgaging, 208
pawnshops, 209
prices, 40–44
profitability, 86–87
speculation, 364
Rizhi lu, 194, 199
ruling class
components of, 337, 340–41
by dynasty, 352
gentry as, 343, 344–45, 347, 360
intermediary, 351–52
landlords as, 344
Runan, 116
Runing prefecture, 194, 195
rural industry
premodern, 67
sideline, 58–63, 68–69
Ruyi Temple, 117

Saeki Yūichi, 10, 269, 345
saimian chou, 50
Sakai Tadao, 381nn43, 63
sale contract, 132
salt, distrubution system, 316
salt household land, 35
salt-maker, 131
sandeng jiuze, 318. See also ninefold classification system

sanfasha, 81
Sanlintang, 52
Sano Manabu, 339–41, 343
sansha cloth, 49–50
sansuobu, 50
Sasaki Masaya, 224
scholars. *See also* literati
  and gentry, 381n43
  as gentry, 338
  metropolitan graduates, 364
  as officials, 363–64, 381n39
Secret Service Office, 186–87
secret societies, 197, 228
seiji katei, 380n2
seikatsusha, 215–16
seisansha, 216
self-defense corps, 261
Semedo, Alvaro, 63–64
serfs. *See also* bondervants; servants;
  slaves
  as direct producers, 150
  residence of, 123
sericulture, 21, 27, 81–95
  commodity production of, 141
  equipment for, 82–83, 89–90
  and merchant capital, 89–92
  profits from, 86–87, 140, 208
  in Suzhou, 168
servants. *See also* bondservants; serfs;
  slaves
  extortion of, 171
  indentured, 193
  peasants turned, 132
service levy. *See* labor service levy
Shaanxi province, 19, 20, 232
Sha county, 203
Sha county gazetteer, 304
Shagang, 49
Shan county, 236
Shandong jinghui lu
  compilation of, 315
  description of, 312–17
  extant editions, 327
Shandong province, 19, 36, 42, 232
  rebellions in, 237
  tax resistance in, 229
Shangcheng county, 115, 194, 196
shanggong, 267
Shanghai, 63–64
  trade volume, 418
  as treaty port, 417–19
Shanghai county, 20, 34–35, 41, 47, 52,
  66–67, 110, 144, 194
Shanghai county gazetteer, 27, 51, 63
Shang Lu, 111
Shangyan county, 363, 378–79

Shangyuan county, 301
Shangyuan county gazetteer, 329
Shangyu county gazetteer, 293
Shanxi province, 19
Shaowu county, 238
Shaoxing prefecture, 293
she, 254
She county, 122
Shen bao, 221, 226
shenghuabu, 51
Sheng Yong, 304
shengyuan, 376, 378
Shengze village, 169
Shen Yang, 188
sheyi, 342, 343
Shi Chengjin, 373
shidafu, 368
shiduan fa, 302
shiduan wence, 302
Shigakkai, 4
Shigaku zasshi, 6
Shigeta Atsushi, 13
Shihou zhi, 329
Shi Kefa, 191
Shimen county, 136, 140, 210, 228, 229
Shimen county gazetteer, 83, 94, 207
shimin, 190
Shimizu Taiji, 279, 325
Shinchō shakaishi, 339
ship building, 367
shipu, 119, 124, 154n61. *See also* bondservants, hired
Shisan taibao, 376
Shi Tianji, 112, 152n22
shiyao, 382n83
shiyin, 177, 347
Shizheng lu, 374
Shouchang county, 130, 131
"The Shrine to the Taoist Nun Huang"
  (poem), 22
shuangkou, 54
shua sha, 47
shu huayi, 46
shuiguan yao, 176
shuiliang, 322
Shuyuan zaji, 50
sibu, 52
Sichuan chongkan fuyi shuce, 330
Sichuan province, 19, 170, 232
silk
  bartered, 417
  market, 88, 91–92
  price, 435
  raw, 27, 84–87, 93
  for taxation, 82, 88
silk industry

and agriculture, 84
artisans, 64, 67
and bondservant labor, 108
in Chongde, 81–83
commodity production, 84–87, 93, 141
cotton industry and, 23
damask, 168, 169
division of labor in, 68, 86, 212n15
floss, 169
gauze, 141, 170
in Huzhou and Jiaxing, 81
in Jiangnan, 79–95
pongee, 169
private, 212n15
satin, 170
Shengze damask, 169
in Suzhou, 64, 168, 169
Silk Manufacturing Agency, 385n147
silk textiles, 27, 40
blends with cotton, 52
brocade, 23, 52, 53, 81
cloud pattern, 23
damask, 50–52, 57
regulations for, 61
weaving techniques, 52
silk workers
overseer boss, 174
rebellion, 172–73
solidarity of, 175
strike by, 172
wages, 174
silkworms, income from, 140
silver, 104. *See also* sycee
bullion, 394, 405–7
circulation, 32, 201, 291, 389–90, 391
debased with tin, 82–83, 91
exchange, 31
gold floral silver, 290
inflation, 390
outflow, 389–95, 396–97, 428n19,
428n19, 429n44
for palace reconstruction, 170
shortage of, 395, 407–9, 426n4
speculation, 170, 395, 426n4
for tax payment, 29–30, 58, 65, 66–67,
87, 138, 140, 174, 294, 315, 316
in trade, 404–5
Single Whip reform, 11–12, 31, 201, 304,
305, 306, 326
equitable, 325
land sales following, 384n132
and *lijia* system, 267–68
and ninefold classification system,
319–20
in Shandong, 317–21, 324–25
Sinology, Japanese, 3–15, 81, 101

Sinong si, 359
Siyouzhai congshuo, 359
Siyouzhai conshuo zhaichao, 111
slave relations, Japan, 101–2
slavery
banned, 249, 250
failure of ban, 251
slaves, 122–23. *See also* bondservants;
serfs; servants
commendation and, 133
defined, 192
hired, 153n22
male and female, 152n12
management system, 106, 130, 147, 368
reliance on gentry, 134
society, 9, 101–2
Small Sword Society, 229
small yellow registers, 255
society, and state, separation of, 339–40,
344
Society of the Thousand, 229
Sogabe Shizuo, 281
soldiers, 131
Song Duan, 51
song jiamu, 123
Songjiang city, 49, 59, 66
Songjiang prefectural gazetteer, 29–30,
49–50, 53–54, 55–58, 65, 294
Songjiang prefecture, 20, 21, 23–33, 57,
80–81, 108, 141, 174, 194, 264, 286,
329, 332n19, 356, 371
Song Jingshi, 229, 239
Song Qi, 194–95
Song River, 110
Song Xin, 249
Song Yingxing, 23
Songzi county, 228
South Zhili gazetteer, 20
South Zhili province, 19, 30
speculation
in silver, 170, 395, 426n4
in *sycee*, 390
in tea, 421
by tenants, 208
spinning wheel, 46–47
stagnation theory, Asian, 8, 17, 68–69, 81
state
despotic, 377, 378
exploitation by, 179
finances, 170
gentry, relations with, 336, 361,
377–78, 379
land, 24–25, 29–30, 35, 253–54, 259
maintenance of social order, 339, 340
power, theories on, 341–42
predominance of, 83, 87–89, 343, 344,

state (*continued*)
 345, 348
 profiteering by, 170
 rule, 352
 and society, separation of, 339–40, 344
 tax collection, 339, 340
 and tax resistance, 226
 and village administration, 342
Staunton, George, 409
Straits produce, & Co., 425
strongmen, 132, 137, 159n102, 196, 355.
 See also bullies
students
 county school, 231
 in Kaidu incident, 185, 186, 189
 sympathy for silk workers, 176–77
subsoil rights. *See* landownership, dual,
 subsoil rights
sugar candy, 39
suiri kyōdōtai, 378
Sumiya Mikio, 102
Sun Dafeng, 232
Sun Dayou, 237
Sun Gongying, 34
Sun Long, 172, 173, 178
surface rights. *See* landownership, dual,
 surface rights
surplus goods
 in barter trade, 408, 415
 of tenants, 207
Sutō Yoshiyuki, 151
Suyuan cungao, 122
Suzhou city, 27, 64, 103, 168, 177
Suzhou prefectural gazetteer, 52, 53
Suzhou prefecture, 20, 23–24, 33, 34–36,
 46–47, 53, 80–81, 107, 112, 169, 170,
 172, 173, 174, 175, 177, 191, 194,
 205, 249, 264, 271, 286, 290, 294,
 301, 329
Suzuki Chūsei, 232, 238
sycee. See also silver
 defind, 390
 demand for, 407–8
 exchange rate, 428n21
 outflow, 394, 429n44
 in remittance, 413–14

Tachibana Shiraki, 340, 341, 343, 345
Taicang county, 20, 30, 34–35, 149
Taicang subprefecture, 194, 249
Taihe county, 154n41, 233
Taiping
 Heavenly Kingdom, 228
 period, 228
 rebellion, 229, 241
 vision of, 226, 227

Taiping county, 147
Taiping prefecture, 178
Taira, Koji, 102
Taiwan, 238
Taizhou, 194
Taizu shili, 129
Takimura Ryūichi, 216
Tanaka Masatoshi, 8, 10, 269, 346–47,
 381n43
Tanaka Tadao, 123
Tang Shen, 172, 173, 176, 179
Tang Zuogeng, 205
Tanigawa Michio, 12, 342
taoduan, 54
Taoism, 21–23
Tao Xu, 220
Tao Yunyi, 111
taozhu, 149
Tao Zongyi, 21–22, 201
taxation system,
 assessment, 24
 and bondservant labor, 118
 and class struggles, 95
 collection, 130, 139, 149, 150, 163n149,
 170–71, 172, 181, 260
 combined system 225, 366
 commercial, 170
 for cotton, 19, 28, 30, 53, 58, 64–66
 and cotton industry, 18, 30, 60, 68–69,
 79
 of domestic industry, 88–89
 dual, 281
 evasion, 266–67, 326
 exemption for poor, 360
 funds, expropriation, 148–49
 gold floral silver, 201, 290
 heavy, 82–83
 increases, 170, 172, 174
 Japanese scholarship on, 281
 landed interest, outside, 301, 320
 land tax, 42, 134, 136
 and *lijia* system, 11–12, 64–65
 "materials" silver, 331n10
 Ming-Qing, 12
 miscellaneous, 323, 324
 national standards, 25
 objects of, 87–88
 office, 148
 payment
 arrears, 134, 136, 163n149
 defaults, 378
 proxy remittance, 384n140
 and landlord-tenant relation, 225
 reforms, 11–13, 29–33, 58, 66, 101,
 266–68, 364–65. *See also* Single Whip
 reforms

registers, types of, 327–31
and rent, 365
for silk, 89, 172
in Songjiang, 24–33
stations, 171
supervisor, 181
tax-remitting housholds, 66–67, 268
transport expenses, 29
tax captains, 31, 261–62
abuses, 131
in Ming, 255
replaced by gentry, 347
responsibilities, 262
as ruling strata, 265
tax resistance struggles
in Chongyang county, 229
and class alliances, 227
and Donglin party, 181
ideology of, 223
limitations of, 226–27
and local elite, 226–27
in Qingpu county, 229
and rent resistance, 223, 226–27
in Shandong, 229
and state power, 226
in Tiantai county, 223
in Yin county, 224
tea
as barter item, 411, 415
bonding system, 430n57
Chinese merchants and, 422–25
demand for, 421
price of, 420–21, 22
speculation, 421
tax reduction demanded, 413
trade, 401–2, 411–13
as unprofitable, 409–24
Tecan shihao lezha shu, 117
technology, in cotton industry, 20–23, 28, 46–48
tenancy
banned, 249, 250
peasant desire for, 220, 221
post-Taiping, 220
rights, 209
tenants
autarky, 142
blood oaths, 137
in bondservant rebellions, 195, 198
as bondservants, 116–18, 122, 134, 196
bribery by, 363
cash from surplus sales, 208
control of, 135, 150, 193, 226, 355, 365, 377
cultivation rights, 201
deception by, 207

defined, 200
and equalized labor levy, 251
exploitation of, 210
and handicraft industry, 143, 146, 147
independence of, 146, 147, 361
labor by, 141
as landlord force, 158–59n102
male, 158n102
under managerial landlords, 103, 129, 142
rent payment by, 138, 139
sale of, 122
servile, 119–20, 124, 132, 133, 154n61
social relations, 200
solidarity, 143, 144, 146, 147, 148, 160–61n112, 206, 362–63
and spare land, 124
resistance by, 136–37, 144, 200, 203, 205, 206, 363, 365, 368, 379. *See also* rent resistance struggles
as serfs, 147, 162n139
as slaves, 101–2, 144
soldiers in Deng Maoqi rebellion, 203–4
speculation, 208
status of, 121, 122, 135, 201
and surplus goods, 207, 208
tax payments by, 283, 225
violence by, 159–60n108
Tengxian, 321
ten-section method, 267, 276n74
in Fujian, 304
in Jiangnan, 304–5
and labor service evasion, 302
operation of, 303–5
register, 302, 305
Single Whip, 305
in Wujin, 303
textile. *See also* cotton; cotton industry; cotton textiles; silk; silk industry; silk textiles
cotton, management, 54–67
production, rural, 58–63
production, urban, 58–59, 63–67
technology, 19, 21–23
urban industry, 56, 58–59, 63–67
textual criticism, 311
three shuttle cloth, 29, 50, 53, 58–59
Thunder Trigram, 223
Tianfu zhi, 330
Tiangong kaiwu, 23
Tianli, 232
tianmianquan, 219
tianpu, 129
Tianqi emperor (Xizong), 180, 213n35
tiansitou, 147

Tiantai county, 223
Tianxia junguo libing shu, 202, 285, 289, 295
Tiechihui, 238
tiehu, 292
tiejiao guiji, 129
tingchai, 293
Tokugawa Japan, 101–2, 104
tong, 111
tongnu, 107, 108, 158n84, 192
tongpu, 102, 109, 110, 192, 364
Tongxiang county, 124, 126, 127, 128, 157n81
Tonglizhen, 229
touhu, 292
toukao, 199, 368, 369
toushen, 369
touxian, 131
town, and village distinguished, 178
township-ward system, 254
trade
    balance of, 393–95
    bilateral (U.S.-England), 399
    clipper ships, 403–4
    England-China, 409–10, 416–17
    linkage structure, 399, 402
    mechanism, 414–15, 419–20
    settlement, multilateral pattern, 394
    shipping volume, 404
    Southern Seas, 23
    triangular (England-India-China), 402, 419
    trilateral (England-U.S.-China), 398, 401–2
    U.S.-China, 433, 400–404
trading firms, British, 402
transportation, by water, 57
transport fees, 29, 33
treadle wheel, 23, 46–47
true men, 219, 231
Truly Mandated Son of Heaven, 222
Tsurumi Naohiro, 11–12
tuanmin, 160n108
tuhao, 196
Tumi incident, 285
Tu Xun, 111
Twitchett, Dennis, 13

uklad, 151

vagrancy, 202
Veritable Records, 50–51, 237, 284, 288, 291, 304
village
    as autonomous organization, 342, 343
    elders, 204, 253

and town distinguished, 178
    unity in, 347. *See also* tenants, solidarity
vision of community, 216–17, 230

Wada Sei, 279
wages, silk worker, 170, 174
Wallerstein, Immanuel, 14
Wang Ao, 107, 290, 307n17
Wang Chen, 186, 212n11
Wang Fashen, 233
Wang Feng, 22
Wang Fuzhi, 191
Wang Guotai, 117
Wang Huilong, 237
Wang Huizu, 124, 338, 388n128
Wang Jing, 186
Wang Lesha, 109
Wang Lun, 237, 239
Wang Shiduo, 228–29
Wang Si, 121–22, 205
Wang Sishan, 109
Wang Wenyan, 183
Wang Yi, 329, 332n16
Wang Yijue, 37
Wang Zhihe, 27
Wang Zitong, 233
Wang Zongji, 108
Wan Pengcheng, 317
warp, 47–48
water control, 12, 101, 261, 264, 273, *See also* irrigation
water wheels, 26, 34, 144–45, 146
weavers
    anti-tax struggle, 175
    independent, 142
    in Suzhou, 168
    wages, 170
weaving
    cotton, 22–23, 57–67, 84
    households, 174, 175
    professional 58–59, 63–67
    rural, 58–63, 67
    silk, 84–87
    technology, 19
    urban, 58–59, 63–67
"Weaving Song," 55, 60
Weber, Max, 6
Wei Dazhong, 182, 183
Wei Tingzhen, 120
Wei Yuan, 427n8
Wei Zhenyuan, 116, 118
Weizhi lü, 377
Wei Zhongxian, 182, 183, 184, 185, 188
well-field system, 125, 126, 127
Weng Shuyuan, 134
Wen Ruzhang, 304

Wenxian tongkao, 281, 306n3
Wen Zhenheng, 186
Wen Zhenmeng, 188
Wenzhou prefectural gazetteer, 305
Western Rice sect, 233
wheat, 38
White Lotus, 22
  confession of member, 239
  leadership, 228, 229, 233
  Qingshuijiao, 239
  Qingzhou branch, 239
  rebellion, 228, 229
  "unbegotten parents," 237
  world view, 231, 236–37
Wilkinson, Alfred, 414, 422–23
Wittfogel, Karl A., 8
women
  serfs, 123
  servants, as brides, 123
  in textile industry, 33, 56 59–64
woodblock cloth print, 48
wool, 52
workers
  handicraft, in rebellions, 191–92, 198
  hired, 151n73
world view, 231. *See also* vision of com-
  munity
Wuchang, 181
Wucheng county, 110, 136, 157n81
Wu county, 103, 137, 143, 185, 205,
  307n17, 374
Wu county gazetteer, 301
Wu dialect, 47
Wufeng lu, 363
Wujiang county, 108, 109, 169, 229, 255,
  329
Wujiang county gazetteer, 292
Wujin county, 108, 303
Wujin county gazetteer, 302
Wu Kuan, 107–8
wulai, 159n102
Wulonghui, 197
Wu Mo, 188
Wunijing, 21–23, 28, 50
Wuqing township, 143, 206, 362
Wu Sangui, 210, 211
Wu Shiwang, 303
Wusong county, 194
Wusong River, 107, 110
Wu Weiye, 34–55
Wuxi and Jinkui counties supplementary
  gazetteer, 371
Wuxiang, 110
Wuxi county, 136, 141, 181, 229, 375,
  376, 377
Wuxili, 62

Wu Yu, 108
Wuyuan county, 116–19
wuzou, 184

xiangguan, 369, 376, 381n40
xianggui, 363
xianghuan, 176
Xianghua prefecture, 355
xiangmin, 83
Xiangshan, 301
xiangshen, 13, 176, 213n26, 337, 339, 351,
  377, 378. *See also* gentry
Xiangshen yue, 372–73
Xiang Shouli, 318, 320
xiangyi, 282
xiangyong, 337
xiangzi xiangyang, 362
Xianlong village district, 123
Xi'an prefecture, 284
xianwei, 162
xiaobu, 54
Xiaodaohui, 229
xiaojia, 202
xiaomin, 83, 134, 140
xiaomu, 196
Xia Shi, 287–89, 308n29
Xiasha, 58
Xiashazhen, 52
Xia Tianyou, 233
xiawenbu, 51
Xiayi county, 237
xibu, 49, 54
Xie (Tingjie), 305
Xie Fangde, 21
Xie Qing, 107
Ximi, 233
Xinchang, 58
Xin'gan county, 132
Xinghuan prefecture, 294
xingshi hu, 347
xingtou, 170
xiniang, 123
Xintai county, 318
Xiuning county, 194
Xiushui county, 138, 139, 208
Xiushui county gazetteer, 94–95
Xiuzhou, 21
Xuanmiaoguan, 172, 173
Xu Cheng, 172, 173, 176
Xu Danfu, 144, 145
Xue Dan, 355
Xu Fang, 109
Xu Feng, 111
Xuguan Gate, 187
Xu Guangqi, 33–39, 42, 46–47, 56
Xu Guoxiang, 116–19

Xu Jie, 25
Xu Liangfu, 303–4
Xu Minwei, 110
Xu Nauxi, 107
Xunzhou prefecture, 228
Xu Qianxue, 149
Xu Xianzhong, 60–61, 62
Xu Xuanhu, 27
Xu Yikui, 110, 199
Xu Yuanwen, 149
Xu Zhenfu, 149

yache, 46
Yamane Yukio, 10, 12, 13
yamen toughs, 376, 377, 385n146
yandang, 182
Yang family, 62
Yanggu county, 238
Yang Jiang, 184
Yang Lian, 182, 183, 188
Yang Nianru, 188
Yang Shi, 181
Yang Xuan, 289
Yang Yingling, 170
Yangyuan xiansheng quanji, 127
Yangzhou prefecture, 112, 191, 194
Yangzi delta region, 19, 20, 111, 115
Yan Peiwei, 179, 180, 186, 187, 188
Yanping prefecture, 304
Yanzhou, 319
Yanzhou shiliao, 369
yaobanbu, 48, 52–53
Yao Ruxun, 302, 374, 384n132
Yao Ximeng, 188
Yaoyi yi, 103
Yasuno Shōsō, 345, 346
Yazhou, 22–23
yellow grass, 27, 81, 84
Yellow Registers, 289, 290, 292, 327
    compilation, 258, 260–61
    and household registration, 255–56
    and li captains, 260
    and lijia system, 283
Ye Mengzhu, 41, 357, 371
Ye Shichang, 426n1
Ye Xianggao, 183
Ye Zongliu, 202
yi, 342, 343, 365
Yi county, 194
yifu, 192
Yihuang county, 163n150, 355
yinan, 133, 153n22, 154n35, 156n72, 192
yinanfu, 125
yinan yifu, 113
yinchai, 291, 294–95, 315. See also labor
    service labor, assignments, silver

Yin county, 224
ying, 24
Ying Jia, 332n19
Yingtian prefecture, 329, 331, 332n19
Yingtian si, 248
Ying Xia, 332n16
Yingzhou, 118
Yin Tang, 291
yishen, 381n40
yitian liangzhu, 209, 221. See also land-
    ownership, dual
yitiaobian fa, 317
Yiwu county, 255
Yixing county, 30, 194
Yiyang county, 160–61n112
Yiyou zhi luan, 196
Yi Zheng, 325
Yizhou, 321
Yizhuxiang, 232
yongbao, 109
Yongchuan county, 290
Yongfu county gazetteer, 293
yonggong, 115, 153n22
Yongjia county, 160n108, 305
Yongkang county, 295
Yongkang county gazetteer, 285, 289
yongli fuyi, 294
yongnu, 152n12, 153n22, 158n84
yongnu qianzhi, 108, 154n26, 154n51
yongpu, 111
yongyin fuyi, 294
Yongzheng emperor (Shizong), 119–20
Yongzheng zhupi yuzhi, 120, 121
Yoshimoto Takaaki, 216
youdun cloth, 50, 59
youmian, 360
youmin, 149
Youxi county, 203
Yuanhe county, 220
Yuan Huazhong, 182, 183
Yuan Liaofan, 382n72
Yuanshi county gazetteer, 292
Yu Boxiang, 196, 197
Yucheng county, 236
Yue, court faction, 182
Yuehu ji, 109
Yueshi bian, 40–44, 58–59, 378
yufu, 24
Yu Kuang, 117–18
Yu Lian, 238
Yunnan province, 232
Yuyao county, 42
Yu Zi, 117–18

Zafan chaiyi, 130
zanghuo, 152n15

Zhang Baotai, 233
Zhang Bi, 30
Zhang Chang, 109
Zhang Congzheng, 233
Zhang Feng, 42
Zhang Guangyue, 116
Zhang Hanru sugao, 148
Zhang Huan, 24
Zhang Juzheng, 163n150, 181
Zhang Lixiang, 113–14, 124, 126, 127, 137, 199, 359, 362, 370
Zhang Mao, 111
Zhangqiu, 318
Zhang Quan, 233
Zhang Shicheng, 24, 252
Zhang Shiyi, 356
Zhang Shouzhong, 22
Zhang Wanxuan, 233
Zhang Xianyi, 176
Zhang Xiaoyuan, 233
Zhang Xuyue, 62
Zhang Yanzhan, 139
Zhang Yingfu, 109
Zhang Yinglong, 184, 186
Zhang Youxuan, 64–65
Zhang Yunru, 238
zhanyi, 24
Zhao Kuan, 109
Zhao Nanxiang, 181
Zhao Nanxing, 183
Zhao prefecture, 294
Zhao Rugui, 22
zhaotian paiyi, 374
Zhaowen county, 221
Zhao Xixiao, 103, 134, 144
Zhao Yi, 21
Zhao Yuxuan, 22
zhehua, 42
Zhejiang province, 20, 42, 46, 58, 108, 110, 111, 202, 205, 209, 329
Zhending prefecture, 292
Zheng Bi, 30
zhenghu, 292
Zhengua, 233
zhengwen cloth, 52
zhengyi, 283
Zhenjiang city, 27, 33, 81, 332n19
zhenkong jiaxiang, wujun wufu, wusheng fumu, 231
Zhenming tianzi, 222
zhenren, 219. *See also* true men
Zhenyang county gazetteer, 38, 54
Zhenze county, 168
Zhenze market town, 169
Zhexi province, 24–28

zhi, 24
zhigongdui, 199
zhihuarong, 50
Zhili, 36
zhinongguan, 385n147
zhiqian, 390, 427n4
zhiranju, 172
zhiyi, 281
zhizaoguan, 385n147
Zhonggu, 52
zhonghu, 254
Zhongmou county, 237
Zhou Bowen, 27
Zhou Chen, 29–32, 49, 53, 58, 133, 153n22, 183, 286–87, 298, 307n24
Zhou Kunlai, 238
Zhoupu, 58
Zhou Qiyuan, 182, 184
Zhou Shi, 111
Zhou Shunchang, 184–89
Zhou Wenyuan, 188
Zhou Xiangqian, 224
Zhou Yude, 315
Zhou Zongjian, 182, 184
zhuangnu, 118
zhuangyuan, 151
Zhu De, 287, 288, 291
Zhuo Guozhen, 24, 183
Zhu Heling, 110
zhujibu, 54
Zhu Li'an, 107
zhupu mingfen, 147, 153n22, 155n61
zhupu zhifen, 153n22
Zhu Qing, 24
Zhu Tingyi, 35
Zhu Wan, 366
Zhu Wenxiang, 237
zhuxiang, 171
Zhu Xiang, 379
Zhu Xiaohe, 237
Zhu Xiaomeng, 237
Zhu Xieyuan, 173
Zhu Ying, 289
Zhu Yuangzhang, 247, 248. *See also* Hongwu emperor
zihua, 42
zihuabu, 54
zisun, 156n72
zongjia, 202
Zou Yuanbiao, 181
Zu he, 220
Zuo Guangdou, 182, 183, 188
zu-yong-diao taxation system, 281
zuzhan, 383n105